# FOUNDATIONS OF MODERN SOCIOLOGY

With contributions
from books in the
*Foundations of
Modern Sociology
Series* by:

**Joseph Ben-David
Albert K. Cohen
Amitai Etzioni
David M. Heer
Alex Inkeles
Theodore M. Mills
Wilbert E. Moore
Thomas F. O'Dea
Talcott Parsons
Patricia Sexton
Neil J. Smelser
Melvin M. Tumin**

# SECOND EDITION

# FOUNDATIONS OF MODERN
# sociology

METTA SPENCER

University of Toronto

With the editorial collaboration of
## Alex Inkeles

Stanford University

**Prentice-Hall, Inc.**
**Englewood Cliffs, New Jersey**
07632

# In memory of ARCHIE HANLAN

*Library of Congress Cataloging in Publication Data*

SPENCER, METTA (date)
Foundations of modern sociology.

(Prentice-Hall foundations of modern sociology series)
"With contributions from books in the Foundations of modern
sociology series by Joseph Ben-David . . . [et al.]."
Includes bibliographies and indexes.
1. Sociology.   2. Social history—20th century.
I. Title.
HM51.S86   1979      301      78–10373
ISBN   0–13–330308–X

PRENTICE-HALL
FOUNDATIONS OF MODERN SOCIOLOGY SERIES
Alex Inkeles, Editor

10   9   8   7   6   5   4   3   2   1

PRENTICE-HALL INTERNATIONAL, INC., *London*
PRENTICE-HALL OF AUSTRALIA PTY. LIMITED, *Sydney*
PRENTICE-HALL OF CANADA, LTD., *Toronto*
PRENTICE-HALL OF INDIA PRIVATE LIMITED, *New Delhi*
PRENTICE-HALL OF JAPAN, INC., *Tokyo*
PRENTICE-HALL OF SOUTHEAST ASIA PTE. LTD., *Singapore*
WHITEHALL BOOKS LIMITED, *Wellington, New Zealand*

Editorial production supervision
by Tom Pendleton, Serena Hoffman
Interior design by Walter Behnke
Cover design by Walter Behnke
Manufacturing buyer: Nancy J. Myers

## PHOTO CREDITS

Chapter 1 (pages 2, 3) Photo Trends
Chapter 2 (pages 22, 23) Culver Pictures
Chapter 3 (pages 52, 53) United Press International
Chapter 4 (pages 82, 83) Kenn Goldblatt/DPI
Chapter 5 (pages 108, 109) Grete Mannheim/DPI
Chapter 6 (pages 138, 139) APF, Photo Trends
Chapter 7 (pages 172, 173) Mimi Forsyth/Monkmeyer
Chapter 8 (pages 208, 209) Bill Owens/Magnum
Chapter 9 (pages 234, 235) Jim Jowers/Nancy Palmer
Chapter 10 (pages 268, 269) John Running/Stock, Boston
Chapter 11 (pages 306, 307) Jeff Albertson/Stock, Boston
Chapter 12 (pages 336, 337) Frederick D. Bodin/Stock, Boston
Chapter 13 (pages 366, 367) Cary Wolinsky/Stock, Boston
Chapter 14 (pages 402, 403) Ellis Herwig/Stock, Boston
Chapter 15 (pages 428, 429) Christopher S. Johnson/Stock, Boston
Chapter 16 (pages 462, 463) Jerry Frank/DPI
Chapter 17 (pages 494, 495) Algimantas Kezys/DPI
Chapter 18 (pages 524, 525) United Press International
Chapter 19 (pages 556, 557) Thomas Hopker/Woodfin Camp

# CONTENTS

## OUTLINE

## chapter 4
## SOCIALIZATION
*page 83*

## chapter 5
## SEX ROLES
*page 109*

## chapter 6
## SOCIAL GROUPS
*page 139*

**chapter 7**
## DEVIANCE AND CONTROL

*page 173*

*PART TWO*
# Social Interaction   207

**chapter 8**
## ORGANIZATIONS

*page 209*

# chapter 9
## SOCIAL STRATIFICATION

*page 235*

# chapter 10
## RACIAL AND ETHNIC GROUPS

*page 269*

**chapter 11**
## COLLECTIVE BEHAVIOR AND SOCIAL MOVEMENTS
*page 307*

# PART THREE
## Social Institutions  335

**chapter 12**
## THE FAMILY
*page 337*

**chapter 13**
RELIGION

page 367

**chapter 14**
EDUCATION

page 403

## PART FOUR
## Changing Society  493

# FOREWORD, PREFACE, AND ACKNOWLEDGEMENTS

## FOREWORD

For some years now Prentice-Hall and I have been working to bring the best of sociological thought and writing to a wide audience through the medium of our series on the FOUNDATIONS OF MODERN SOCIOLOGY. The series is now planned to include more than two dozen volumes covering all major areas in the field of sociology. Each book, written by an outstanding specialist, introduces a particular subfield within the discipline. The books in the series have become quite popular with both teachers and students and have enjoyed persistent and enduring support.

Over many years of teaching large lecture sections for introductory sociology, however, I was always struck by the difficulty of finding suitable introductory books—books of high quality yet effectively adapted to the needs of beginning students. So we resolved to develop, as part of the Foundations

Series, a new introductory textbook. Professor Metta Spencer, who undertook the work, brought to the task excellent advanced training, extensive research experience, and equally important, many years of teaching the introductory course.

This new text, which takes its title from the series, has more than fulfilled the goals that were set for it. The book deals with the systematic study of groups and societies. The major aspects of social life are analyzed, with special reference to the role of each aspect in the development, functioning, and change of large social systems. No other introductory text contains such a richness of material in its exposition of theoretical perspectives, in its elaboration of sociological knowledge and basic concepts, and in its description of empirical research. These qualities, linked to clear, interesting writing and strong organization, have resulted in an introductory sociology text of the highest quality.

*Alex Inkeles*

# PREFACE

One of my friends who has taught introductory sociology for many years keeps all her letters from former students, who are now doing things like selling insurance, editing newspapers, guiding tour groups through Asia, and administering foreign aid programs. These people often make the same remark in their letters: as students they hadn't realized how much they were gaining from their sociology course, but those earlier studies now come up repeatedly in their personal life and in their work. Years later they are writing thank-you notes for the most useful course they ever took.

Sociology does not *necessarily* connect with people's lives. Indeed, it is hard work to show students how to use sociology to understand their social experiences. People talk about sociological problems every day of their lives—on subways, in court, in the dentist's waiting room, everywhere. I hope that the information in this book and the kind of perspective it provides will add value to such conversations.

It is probably impossible for an introductory course to teach students to think like sociologists. It takes a lot of courses to accomplish that. But the introductory course can give students a good start in that direction. It can at least present some basic facts about the social structure of our society. More important, a good sociology course can help students begin to develop critical independent thinking by pointing out vital issues and controversies. Facts never speak for themselves. They only speak for people who know how to assess their significance. And sociology as a discipline can provide its students with both factual information and a heightened ability to judge the *significance* of those facts.

To that end, this book focuses not only on the facts that sociologists know (and we do know a lot), but also on the arguments and debates that underlie those facts. It does no good to give students answers until they first understand the questions. Indeed, I am just as pleased when a student discovers a new problem to be puzzled over, as I am when a student provides a satisfying answer to that problem. After all, that is what sociology consists of—identifying questions, suggesting answers to those questions, and identifying new questions and problems in the suggested answers. Introductory students can begin to participate in that ongoing process of discovery too. When they do, they find that their sociological skill enhances what they have to say during the coffee break, or on the job, or almost anywhere else. Because then (and only then) does sociology truly connect with their lives.

## ORGANIZATION

Each chapter is divided into three major sections: (1) a basic core section; (2) a Social Research section; and (3) a Social Policy section.

The *basic core section* of each chapter contains an orderly presentation of the major concepts and theories of the topic area of that chapter. Important sociologists past and present and the exciting controversies that sometimes swirl around them are discussed. The core section emphasizes the lasting aspects of sociology—the basic concepts and significant issues that sociologists think about.

The *Social Research: Sociologists at Work* section always appears on an orange background to set it off from the rest of the chapter. It focuses on recent empirical research in the topic area of the chapter and discusses one or more landmark studies. It emphasizes the way sociologists come to know what they know and the people and events that contributed to that store of sociological knowledge.

The *Social Policy: Issues and Viewpoints* section always appears on a gray background. This section talks about political, economic, or ethical issues about which people have to make decisions. By discussing roles that sociologists can play in shaping the world of the future, this section serves to answer questions that are sometimes raised about the "relevance" of sociology.

## FEATURES

Other elements of the book have been designed to make learning more effective for students:

GLOSSARIES    A glossary containing several hundred careful definitions of all important concepts is found at the end of the book for easy reference. In addition, key terms within the body of the text are printed in color, defined when they are used for the first time, and reviewed in lists of key terms at the end of each chapter. This reinforces the learning of the most important terms found in this book as well as in advanced books and courses on particular areas of sociology.

SUMMARIES    Each chapter is followed by a summary that reviews the most important ideas presented in the chapter. Basic concepts are again stressed.

READING LISTS    Extensive reading lists appear at the end of each chapter, with descriptive annotations to suggest potential uses of the books.

GRAPHS, CHARTS, AND TABLES    Because much empirical research in the field of sociology is reported in tabular form, a selection of this type of material is included. Students are given a thorough introduction on how to read and construct tables in Chapter 2.

PHOTOGRAPHS    A lively array of pictures has been chosen to provoke thought and to make points visually that could not be expressed in words.

THE REFERENCE PAPER    An appendix at the end of the book is addressed to students. Its purpose is to show how to use the library and how to write a term paper.

## SUPPLEMENTS

Three supplementary aids have been designed to accompany the book:

THE STUDY GUIDE AND WORKBOOK    reviews the material in the textbook through presentation of chapter objectives, basic sociological concepts, and various self-administered tests. Three testing formats are used—multiple-choice, fill-in, and matching—with answers supplied for immediate feedback. Questions cover the basic core material, as well as the Social Research and Social Policy sections, and are cross-referenced to the appropriate pages of this text.

A TEST ITEM FILE    includes a thousand items selected to test the student's understanding of introductory sociology. The questions, primarily multiple-choice, are referenced to the appropriate text page. Essay questions are also included.

THE INSTRUCTOR'S MANUAL    outlines the basic structure of each chapter, facilitating additional lecture materials and discussion questions. Class projects and research topics are included for each chapter, as are audiovisual aids.

# ACKNOWLEDGMENTS

Any textbook owes a great debt to the vast literature on which it draws, and I have drawn on the work of many outstanding sociologists. This particular text owes a special debt to the individual books in the Prentice-Hall FOUNDATIONS OF MODERN SOCIOLOGY series. In preparing a new but different book in that series, I was able to draw directly from the material in the other volumes and, equally important, upon the editorial skill and sociological expertise of Alex Inkeles. His good judgment has played a vital part in the development of this book. While I want to acknowledge my debt to others and to the series authors in particular, final responsibility for errors or misinterpretation must rest with me.

One of the high points of writing a book comes in thanking the people who have contributed by sharing their knowledge and parts of their lives with the author. For me to do so fully would be to double the length of this book; so many magnificent colleagues and friends have helped me, and I cannot say all that I feel about their generosity, nor can I name them all.

This book has benefited greatly from the comments of Ralph Beals, Lawrence Felt, Paula Felt, Diane Horowitz, Leslie Howard, Nancy Howell, Brian Hull, John Kervin, Pierre Lorion, Stanford Lyman, Ted Mann, Richard Ofshe, Alice Propper, Rheta Rosen, Diana Russell, Edward Shorter, Edward Silva, John Simpson, Kenneth Walker, and Jennifer Welsh. Other people provided critical reviews of various drafts of the manuscript: Mark Abrahamson, Patricia Allen, J. Cameron Coleman, Spencer Condie, Joseph E. Faulkner, Lee Frank, Richard Hall, Mark Hutter, John Klein, Thomas Koebernick, R. L. Liverman, Betty Metz, Dennis Morton, Anthony Orum, David Payne, Daisy Quarm, Elaine Smith, Ann Sundgren, and Ernest Works. Their comments were most useful.

Students also played a major part in helping me develop the book. I distributed drafts of various chapters to several classes in both large public universities and small private colleges. The final result is much better because I have had the benefit of their responses to these drafts, and I thank my students for their helpful suggestions.

Madeline Richard and Susan Robbins contributed excellent research assistance. Mary Paul and Beverley Thomas were helpful in secretarial capacities. Ann Finlayson contributed editorial suggestions.

The Prentice-Hall staff has been terrific. I am grateful to Irene Fraga for her administrative help, and to David Stirling for his coordination in marketing. The production has been handled admirably and pleasantly by Ann Torbert, Tom Pendleton, Walter Behnke, Serena Hoffman, and Nancy Myers.

Two editors have at different times and in different ways made an exceptional contribution to the style and organization of the manuscript — Ray Mullaney and Carolyn Smith. Their contributions appear on almost every page, and I am deeply grateful to both of them.

Edward Stanford, Prentice-Hall's good-natured and unflappable executive, was involved in every important decision that arose in developing this book. Every time I work with him I gain more appreciation for his excellent judgment. And I want to thank Alex Inkeles for his good advice and the friendly association I have enjoyed with him.

Our lives expand by recognizing magnificence in others, quite beyond the limiting circumstances of our relationships. And here I want to honor all that I have recognized in Ross Johnson, Jim Fisk, Susan Ingram, and my son Jonathan Spencer, the liveliest companion of my life.

*Metta Spencer*

# introduction

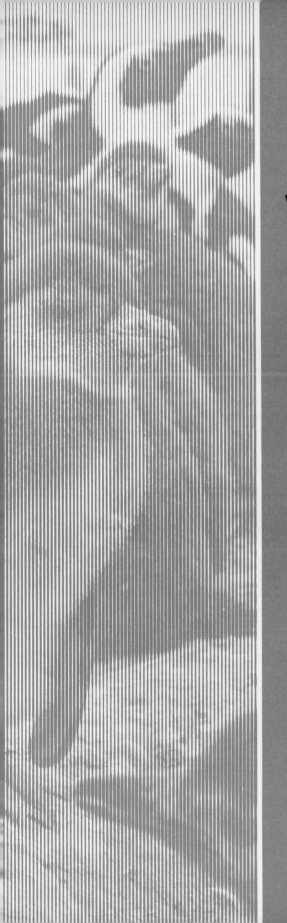

# WHAT IS SOCIOLOGY?

A delightful scene in an old French play features a character who becomes very pleased with himself when he finds out that he has been speaking prose all his life. You may be just as surprised to learn that you have been "speaking sociology" all your life. For example, you may have had conversations on the subject of why some youngsters become delinquent and others do not, or why there is less birth control in poor countries than in rich ones, or whether it is lonelier to live in a city than in a small town, or whether the portrayal of violence on television leads to violent actions by members of the TV audience. If so, you have discussed sociological issues. But just as some people speak prose better than others, so also some people talk about sociological issues with more knowledge than others. In this book I want to acquaint you with some of the most important contributions of people who study social relationships, that is, *sociologists*. Their field—the study of human group life—is called sociology. Its basic goal is to understand how human beings fit their activities together into a system of stable social arrangements. But this is only the beginning of a definition. We will devote this whole chapter to explaining more fully what sociology is, but first we need to know what is meant by the terms *society* and *social system*.

A society is a large, permanent, self-sufficient, self-perpetuating group of interacting people who share certain common values and beliefs. Japan is a society, and so is Canada, for example. Collectively, the members of a society perform billions of social acts during a single day. Yet the usual outcome is not total confusion but enough order to permit each person to do his or her own thing while others do theirs. Indeed, our actions generally help other people attain their goals and vice versa. The primary purpose of sociology is to explain how this happens, how the activities of individuals fit together to produce orderly collective life.

Society was here before we were born;

we did not invent it. We enter social systems that are already working, and we learn how they work by participating in them. A social system is made up of the interactions among of two or more people. Each person is both an actor and an object of the other's actions. Each person's actions are guided by the expected response of the other, that is, by how the other person is likely to react. Social systems may be small, such as a mother and her baby, a rapist and his victim, or two snowmobilers passing on a narrow trail. Or they may be large, such as the Royal Canadian Mounted Police, the Shell Oil Company, or the passengers and crew of a ship crossing the Atlantic—or an entire society.

Sociology is one of the broadest fields imaginable. Sociologists can study almost anything human beings do. What is special about sociologists is the *way* they study any given topic—the kind of questions they ask and the methods they use in trying to answer those questions. Of course sociologists experience social life personally just as other people do —they fall in love, they go to war, they work and play, and so on. But *as sociologists* they do not think of love the way a bride does, nor of war the way an admiral does, nor of work and play the way grocers and children do. In their work they think of these topics as social patterns to be explained in a scientific way, for sociology is a social science.

## The social sciences

A *science* is a branch of study that is concerned with discovering and organizing facts, principles, and methods. The *natural sciences* (e.g., physics, biology, astronomy) study physical phenomena; the *social sciences* deal in a scientific way with relationships among human beings. There are several different social sciences, but the boundaries between them are very hazy. Many of the articles and books that we will discuss were written by social scientists who are not sociologists but might just as well have been written by sociologists. Yet since the different social sciences tend to cover different aspects of human relationships, a description of some of the other social sciences may help you understand what sociology is.

## ECONOMICS

Economics is concerned with the production and distribution of goods and services. It deals with such factors as the flow of money and the relationship of prices to supply and demand. Few economists pay much attention to an individual's actual behavior or attitudes. Neither do they study business enterprises as social organizations. They leave such matters to the psychologist or the sociologist. Moreover, sociologists often study topics that are related to economics — for example, the social backgrounds of businessmen and managers and the contributions of education to productivity.

Although economists have limited their horizons, they have developed a highly focused, coherent field of study. Other social scientists envy them for the precision of their terminology, the extent to which they agree on certain basic principles, and their ability to make practical suggestions for public policy.

## POLITICAL SCIENCE

Traditionally, political science could be broken down into two branches — political the-

*Sociologists can study almost anything that human beings do. Someone may be studying you right now.*

Frank Siteman/Stock, Boston

ory and government administration. Until 30 or 40 years ago it paid little attention to political behavior but was concerned chiefly with how to make government organizations efficient. Topics such as the workings of bureaucracy, the social backgrounds of political activists, and the way people acquire their political beliefs were studied by political sociologists, not political scientists.[1] However, political scientists have been turning more and more toward behavioral concerns. Today political scientists are concerned with subjects such as popular attitudes and values, the membership of radical movements, and how decisions are made in cities and bureaucracies. There is no longer any distinction between the sociologists and political scientists who study behavior.

## HISTORY

Historians, as everyone knows, study the past. Sociologists are usually more interested in the present or the recent past. Historians takes pride in telling us in great detail how a past event actually happened. Sociologists like to compare a set of similar events in order to find out why some of them turned out one way and some another way. A historian might study the Russian Revolution, while a sociologist might compare several different revolutions and come up with statements about which revolutionary situations lead to war and which do not, about the stages that all revolutions go through, about the outcomes of various types of revolutions, and so on. After studying fourteen revolutions, the sociologist may conclude that the rebels never win unless the government's army defects. This is a causal statement about a general class of events—the sort of statement that traditional historians avoid. To the historian each event is unique; to classify it or generalize about it is to risk distorting it. This argument is fast losing supporters, however—in fact one traditional historian whom I met recently remarked glumly

that "all the historians are turning into sociologists." No doubt he exaggerated, but it is true that there are many similarities between historians and sociologists.

Some of the greatest historians have written *social* history, dealing not with kings and wars but with the less glamorous events that interest sociologists, such as changes in landowning patterns or in the relations between men and women in the family.

## GEOGRAPHY

Geography is concerned with the relationship between human beings and their natural environment. Geographers usually study particular areas or particular *kinds* of areas, such as irrigated river basins or tropical forests. They may be interested in ecological problems or in the way economic systems develop in different environmental settings. Thus they may try to find out why trade routes, harbors, or markets are established in some areas and not in others, as well as their effects on the environment. Hence, geography is partly a natural science and partly a social science. While physical geographers are often interested in climate, agriculture, oceanography, soil composition, and other natural phenomena, social or cultural geographers may share many interests with sociologists. For example, they may study the logging industry or the use of milk products around the world. Urban geographers and urban sociologists sometimes work together; for example, they may team up to study the impact of various kinds of housing on family life. In such cases social scientists work in very similar ways regardless of whether they were trained as economists, political scientists, geographers, or any other kind of social scientist.

## PSYCHOLOGY

Psychology is often called the science of mind. It deals with mental processes such as

*Geographers are social scientists who study the relationship between human society and the natural environment. They may specialize in certain kinds of environments, such as settlements around harbors. You may recognize this harbor as Hong Kong.*

thinking, learning, remembering, and decision making. Modern psychologists also study feelings, emotions, motives, and personality.

Some experimental psychologists do biological or physiological research, but it is in the area of social psychology that psychology comes closest to sociology.

Some social psychologists are interested in how personality and behavior are influenced by a person's social background or by the social setting in which that person finds himself or herself. For example, Solomon Asch's studies showed that people will frequently describe a line as shorter or longer than it actually is, even while looking at it themselves, if a majority of the other people around them say that the line is shorter or longer than it actually is. Thus Asch showed that even what one sees is influenced by a *social* situation—majority pressure on a minority.[2]

Other social psychologists are especially interested in how a person's *personality* influences his or her social behavior. Thus studies of voting patterns have shown that Americans with rigid and intolerant personalities are more likely than other Americans to favor an isolationist foreign policy.[3]

It is often hard to see any difference between the work of researchers who were trained in sociology and that of researchers who were trained in psychology. Many people argue that social psychology should be considered a distinct field rather than a branch of sociology or psychology. Both the

University of Michigan and Columbia University have set up separate programs offering degrees in social psychology.

### ANTHROPOLOGY

Anthropology is as varied as sociology. It includes archaeology, physical anthropology, cultural history, many branches of linguistics, and the study of all aspects of primitive humanity everywhere. Like psychology, it has strong ties with the natural sciences, especially biology.

Anthropology overlaps sociology as a science of culture. *Culture*—by which we mean the system of symbols, including language and beliefs, that is shared by a particular group—is the subject matter of anthropology in the same sense that power and authority are the subject matter of political science and the distribution and production of goods is the subject matter of economics.

Anthropologists study primarily primitive or nonliterate humanity, whereas sociologists study more advanced civilizations. One result of this difference is that anthropologists tend to study societies as *wholes*. If they specialize, it is usually in a particular *culture area* (e.g., Melanesia or the Arctic). Sociologists, by contrast, usually study *parts* of a society. They generally specialize in some institution, such as the family, or in some process, such as the spread of rumor. Anthropologists often live in the community they are studying, directly observing the behavior of its members or recording its customs. Sociologists, on the other hand, tend to rely on statistics and questionnaires. Finally, anthropologists study small, self-contained groups or communities, whereas sociologists study large, impersonal organizations and processes.

### SOCIAL WORK

Social work is not actually a social science. It is a profession that trains its own members. However, it is often confused with sociology.

When someone asks me what I do for a living, I usually reply, "Sociology." About one time in three the other person says something like, "Oh, my cousin is a social worker too."

Social work is to sociology what engineering is to physics. It is an applied field that draws upon the principles of sociology, psychology, psychoanalysis, and other social sciences, but it also uses its own set of techniques in helping people solve personal and group problems. Sociologists do research, but they almost never try to influence people directly through personal contact, as social workers do. Professors of social work also conduct research, however, and such research often overlaps that of sociologists.

## A brief historical survey

Philosophers have been writing about human relationships for thousands of years. Some of them, notably Aristotle, made contributions that present-day sociologists sometimes draw upon. However, sociology as such did not exist until the late nineteenth century and was not generally included among the social sciences until 30 or 40 years ago. Most of its growth and development has occurred in the past 20 years. In fact you are about to study a very new science.

### THE EARLY SOCIOLOGISTS

We usually say that Auguste Comte (1798–1857) was the first real sociologist. Comte, who coined the word *sociology*, believed that society is governed by certain "social laws" just as the physical universe is governed by certain physical laws. He wanted other scholars to join him in discovering and describing these social laws. For example, he believed that all societies passed through the same series of stages. All of the early sociologists believed this notion, and as we will see later, they tried to identify the principles of "social evolution." Concern with social evolution was abandoned early in this century, but today there is renewed interest in this notion. Today nobody talks about social laws the way Comte did, but we continue the search for regular relationships among social patterns.

Herbert Spencer (1820–1903), like Comte, was more influential in his time than he is today. His three-volume *Principles of* *Sociology*, published in 1877, was the first full-scale, systematic description of sociology as a science. In it he defined sociology as the study of the family, politics, religion, social control, and industry or work. These topics are still among the primary concerns of sociologists. We will meet Spencer several times in this and later chapters.

The writer who probably had the greatest impact on sociology was Karl Marx (1818–1883), a cranky genius whose revo-

## Karl Marx

In 1818, near the border between Germany and France, a son was born to a Jewish lawyer who had officially converted to Christianity to avoid religious persecution. This boy was Karl Marx, whose political ideas later shaped history and still affect our lives. Marx hoped in his youth to become a professor. He studied philosophy at the University of Berlin, but he quickly chose the losing side in a conflict with authorities—a pattern of behavior that persisted throughout his life. By the age of 24 he was blacklisted from an academic career and had lost his first job (as newspaper editor) so he went to Paris where he studied radical politics and British economic theory. There he met his lifelong co-worker, Friedrich Engels.

In 1848 most of Europe was upset by left-wing revolts against many governments. Marx and Engels had already begun supporting radical causes; they had written the *Communist Manifesto* a short time before the revolts began. Marx was expelled from France and Germany because of radical activities and he spent most of his life in London, where he sometimes wrote for the New York *Tribune*. Engels helped support Marx's family but they were always desperately poor. In fact, at least one of his children starved and others died of diseases related to poverty. Marx was outraged by the workers' living conditions and he sought both to explain capitalism theoretically and to fight it politically. His book, *Capital*, was his most successful work, published in 1867. He died in 1883, but his works became official doctrine shaping the policies of many nations throughout the following century.

lutionary activities got him thrown out of several European countries. Along with Friedrich Engels (1820–1895), Marx helped shape not only modern intellectual life but also modern history. Today many governments and political groups admire him and try to make their policies consistent with his writings.

Marx was a man of many interests and a strong sense of justice. He was upset by the misery of the working classes. He was very good at seeing connections between ideas in different fields and pulling them together. Having studied the ideas of English economic theorists, philosophers, and socialist political thinkers, he ripped them apart with savage criticism and then used the remaining shreds as the foundation of Marxism. Throughout this book you will run into various aspects of Marxism, yet they represent only a tiny fraction of Marx's writing. Marx wrote mountains of material, much of which has never been translated into English. Many sociologists disagree with him for all sorts of reasons, but most sociologists see in Marx's work both profound intelligence and deep concern for the human condition.

Two later writers share with Marx the honor of being the most influential of sociologists. They are the Frenchman Emile Durkheim (1858–1917) and the German Max Weber (1864–1920). Although they studied many of the same problems and each had many followers, neither seems to have been familiar with the other's work. They both compared different types of societies. Indeed, Durkheim, who called sociology "the science of societies," believed that only through such systematic comparisons can we explain complex social relationships.[4] By observing a social pattern in many different groups and circumstances, he said, we come to understand its causes and its results.

While Durkheim is best known for his comparative work on suicide, religion, and education, Weber wrote extensively on religion, various aspects of economic life (including money and the division of labor), political organization and authority, bureaucracy, class and caste, the city, and music. We will have more to say about Weber in the pages ahead.

## SOCIOLOGY IN THE UNITED STATES

The real growth of sociology as a science took place in the United States. A few years ago a weekly news magazine reported that 70 percent of the world's sociologists were American. I'm not sure where it got that figure, but it was probably fairly accurate, at least until the past decade. The rest of the world is catching up, but American publications are still being used for teaching purposes. All of the writers to be mentioned later are often referred to in sociology courses around the world.

The first department of sociology was established in 1893 at the University of Chicago. The American Sociological Association was formed by a group that split off from the American Economic Association in 1905. There was quite a bit of resistance to this strange new science among the more conservative private colleges in the East. Harvard did not establish a department of sociology until 1930; and as late as 1960, 5 of the nation's 20 leading liberal-arts colleges still did not offer any courses in sociology.

Members of the older and wealthier families of the East Coast cities tended to study the classics, literature, or history and to avoid sociology. As a result most of the early American sociologists came from rural rather than urban areas. Almost all of the first two dozen presidents of the American Sociological Association were from rural backgrounds. A surprisingly high number were descended from ministers or were themselves trained in the ministry. They included

Lester Ward, who is often called the father of American sociology.

The early European sociologists dealt mainly with theories of history or used the lives of primitive people to illustrate their ideas about evolution, religion, and society. Although similar themes and sources may be seen in the work of Ward and a few other early American sociologists, these scholars paid

more attention to the severe social problems that seemed to spring up everywhere in American society. This was especially true at the University of Chicago, which for more than two decades (1915–1940) was almost unchallenged as the center of sociological training in America. In the living laboratory provided by the city of Chicago they studied the slum and the ghetto, the prostitute and

## Max Weber

Max Weber was born in 1864, the son of a wealthy German politician, one of the leading figures of Berlin society. Weber (pronounced Vayber) was emotionally torn by his parents' unhappy marriage. His father was heavy-handed and bullied his mother, a gentle and sensitive woman. Max went away to university, where for a while he lived up to the blustering male sex role common to Germans of his day. However, he soon moved beyond that lifestyle, possibly influenced by his mother's idealism. He was impressive to everyone who met him—handsome, independent in spirit and mind. He began by studying law but soon read widely in many other fields as well. Perhaps no one anywhere has read or remembered as much as Max Weber in the fields of economics, philosophy, linguistics—and especially world history.

By his early thirties, however, Weber quarreled with his father and threatened never to speak to him again unless he treated his mother better. Shortly after their quarrel, the father fell dead and Max suffered an emotional breakdown (perhaps from guilt) that lasted about 7 years. Unable to work, he traveled occasionally, but mostly just stared out the window, depressed. By 1904 he resumed work and over the remaining 16 years of his life he wrote astonishing amounts of important works in many fields. He is known today for works on bureaucracy, stratification, economic history, religion, and even the sociology of music. Late in his life he turned to practical politics, serving as a diplomat at the close of World War I. But in 1920, at the age of 56, he died of pneumonia, deeply respected by his many students for his personal integrity and the brilliance of his mind.

the juvenile delinquent, the professional criminal and the drug addict.[5]

One University of Chicago professor, Robert E. Park, had studied in Germany with a sociologist named Georg Simmel, had served as a secretary to Booker T. Washington, and had worked as a journalist. These factors all influenced his view of sociology. In his writing and teaching he imported Simmel's thought to North America. One result was increased emphasis on the study of conflict and personal relationships in urban settings. To Park, a community was an area of both cooperation and competition, much as in nature an ecological habitat is an area of cooperation and competition for the species within it. His approach became known as social ecology.

After World War I several other scholars—Charles Horton Cooley, George Herbert Mead, John Dewey, W. I. Thomas—developed an approach that came to be called the "Chicago school" of social psychology. Until that time psychologists had explained human behavior largely in terms of inborn instincts. By contrast, the Chicago school stressed the importance of social interactions in the shaping of human behavior.

During the 1930s Harvard University also became an important center of sociological thinking. The work done there was rather different from the work done in Chicago; it was more similar to European sociology. Pitirim Sorokin, a Russian refugee, influenced a number of students at Harvard, but he was outclassed in fame by a younger, rival professor named Talcott Parsons. Parsons, who had studied sociology in Germany, introduced to American scholars the ideas of Durkheim and Weber. He has written a number of complex theoretical books that are often very difficult for undergraduates to understand. Many of his former students, however, were so stimulated by Parsons' work that they went on to make major theoretical contributions of their own. Among them are Wilbert Moore, Robert Merton,

Kingsley Davis, and Neil Smelser—names that will become familiar as you read this book. They share an approach called *structural functionalism*, about which we will have much more to say.

Especially since World War II, American sociologists have tended to use mathematical tools in their research and to obtain much of the data from questionnaires, census information, and the like. For about 20 years the best place to learn these techniques was Columbia University. However, during the past 10 or 15 years the University of Michigan has been the leading center for researchers who use mathematics and computers.

## Dominant perspectives in sociology

Sociology is a science. Its task is to describe how social systems work. Every scientist carries in his or her head a model of the subject on which he or she is working—a sort of mental map of how it is put together. Shakespeare's metaphor, "All the world's a stage," is a model suggesting that people play their roles according to scripts they have memorized. A sociological model, thus, is a description in general terms of the way a particular social system works. A sociologist's theories will always be based on the model that he or she believes is more accurate than any other. A theory is an explanation offered to account for a group of facts or phenomena. A model is much broader than the theories that it generates. A theory is more limited and precise, and often it can be proved wrong. A model can be called incomplete, misleading, or unproductive, but it can't be proved wrong.

The belief that diseases are caused by germs is a model on which theories about the causes of particular diseases (e.g., diphtheria or smallpox) are based. The model encourages the scientist to search for specific germs and to control particular diseases by killing the germs that cause them. The germ model has been useful in stimulating scientific discoveries, but it is not helpful to the scientist who is trying to explain illnesses that are caused by poor diet or by chemical or radiation poisoning. Therefore, while models are important, we pay a price if we hold to only one model and ignore all other possible models.

Ideally, scientists should not hold too closely to any one model and should be ready to abandon their particular picture of the world as soon as a better one comes along. In practice, however, scientists' models often become rigid and important new facts and ideas are brushed aside. A scientist will often resist any effort to replace his or her favorite model. Such resistance is especially dangerous in sociology because of the moral and political implications of sociological models. In the following pages I will describe some of the dominant points of view within sociology and the models on which they are based.

Since different schools of sociology generally fight about the merits of the models they favor, a brief introduction to these models will also serve as an introduction to the main schools of sociological thought and the controversies that have arisen within the science of sociology over the years.

The four most important models and the perspectives based on them are *evolutionism*, *structural functionalism*, the *conflict model*, and *symbolic interactionism*. For a long time the field was dominated by evolutionism. Structural functionalism developed later and was the leading model for many years, but during the past decade it has lost support as the conflict model has become more popular, especially among radical sociologists and others who focus on political processes and social upheavals. Finally, the symbolic-interactionist perspective has long held a very influential position among certain groups of sociologists but not all.

These models are not necessarily incompatible. Marx, for example, held to both an evolutionary model and a conflict model. And Durkheim was both an evolutionist and a structural functionalist. Nevertheless when sociologists get into an argument at a party or in a professional journal the debate often hinges on the differences between the models they favor. Therefore I want to sketch for you the four basic models. Each will be discussed more fully in later chapters.

## EVOLUTIONISM

Beginning with Comte, all the early sociologists held to an evolutionary model of society — the belief in a law of historical progress. Comte believed that all societies go through stages of increasing complexity. This perspective, evolutionism, was generally supported by the founders of sociology — Spencer, Marx, Engels, and Durkheim. It was equally adaptable to the politics of the left and those of the right.

### Social Darwinism

Spencer used the idea of evolution to block social reform and change, arguing that social evolution must follow its own slow course. This conservative outlook has been called *Social Darwinism,* and it became popular shortly after Charles Darwin had published his explanation of the evolution of biological species (1859). Darwin noted that there are variations among the members of any given species of plants or animals and that every species tends to produce more offspring than the environment can support. Thus there is a struggle for existence, and within any species the individuals that are better able to cope with their environment will survive. The weaker individuals will be weeded out. This is why species change over time: The survivors in the struggle for existence pass on their superior genes to their offspring. The Social Darwinists applied this idea to human populations and came to the conclusion that competition resulted in progress because it eliminated the weaker individuals.

### Marxism

At the opposite political extreme the communists Marx and Engels, who were also influenced by the evolutionary model, argued that each stage of civilization prepared the ground for the next. Each stage (or *era*) contained within itself "the seeds of its own destruction" and would be followed by a higher stage of development. Thus, according to Marx, socialism was bound to come after capitalism, but only after a violent revolution.

### Durkheim

In each generation the leading sociologist used to come forward with a new way of classifying societies into different levels on the basis of the stage of development each society had reached. Durkheim produced a model that is still quite influential, though it is a much less sweeping version of evolutionism than those proposed by earlier sociologists. Durkheim's model should cause he was not convinced that any social changes amounted to progress toward perfection.

## Emile Durkheim

Emile Durkheim was born in 1858 in eastern France, the son of a rabbi. He became a serious young scholar who turned his talents toward the scientific study of social order, soon using empirical methods and statistics to explain the forces that he believed made social events regular and predictable.

By middle age, Durkheim was in Paris, the first full-fledged professor of sociology in any French university. He was a liberal in political matters, yet also a strong nationalistic Frenchman. His work throughout his life explored the moral basis underlying society that makes order possible. His last great book, *The Elementary Forms of Religious Life*, was his most successful effort to explore this theme. In it he pointed out that religious ritual symbolizes human society and strengthens group spirit. He was not a religious person himself, but he appreciated very well the contribution that religion makes to social cohesion.

Durkheim was never a colorful personality and at the end of his life he was a deeply saddened man. His son Andre was killed as a soldier in fighting the Germans in World War I, and Durkheim never recovered from his grief. He died in 1917, but his fame has continued to grow as university students throughout the world study sociology and always learn to recognize the name of Emile Durkheim.

Durkheim did, however, believe that there was a steady historical trend toward greater specialization, that is, toward increasing division of labor.[6] He divided societies into two types on the basis of how far division of labor had progressed in the society. The first type was the small primitive or peasant community in which specialization is limited. In such a society people are bound together in close, isolated groups. Durkheim called this sort of closeness *mechanical solidarity*. Population increases are the force behind social evolution, because they cause people to specialize in different activities. As a result a new type of society is created, based on what Durkheim called *organic solidarity*. In such societies relations are less intimate and personal, and people are linked mainly by common material interests, by contract, and by more abstract symbols.

### Contemporary evolutionism

After Durkheim the evolutionary model became quite unpopular and remained so for about fifty years. However, within the past few decades a new version of this model has gained some support.[7] Contemporary evolutionists believe that the human species as a whole has gone through a number of evolutionary stages, but they do not claim that each society must go through all or most of those stages.[7]

The new version of evolutionism suggests that the spread of industrialization is resulting in the development of similar institutions and social patterns throughout the world. This process of modernization will be discussed further in various parts of this book.

### STRUCTURAL FUNCTIONALISM

Human society has often been compared to a giant organism made up of many structures, all functioning together to maintain the whole system just as our liver, lungs, kidneys, and other organs function to maintain the human body. According to this model, if you want to understand any given structure (and any regular social pattern can be seen as a structure) you must discover its function in society. These two related concepts, *structure* and *function*, were used by Spencer and Durkheim and became important in American sociology through the influence of Talcott Parsons. They gave rise to what is now known as the *structural-functional* school of sociology—or, more briefly, functionalism, that is, the belief that a social pattern is best understood in terms of its functions in a given society.

Functionalism is not incompatible with evolutionism, but most structural functionalists have studied somewhat different problems than evolutionists have. Instead of tracing the history of social patterns, they tend to look at one social pattern at one point in time in order to see how it helps maintain the society as a system. Instead of looking for the origins of a particular custom, they tend to look for its results—its functions, its contribution to the flow of social life. For example, what is the use of the painful rites in which adolescents become fullfledged members of some primitive societies? These ceremonies do nothing pleasant or helpful for the adolescent boy who must suffer through them. However, from the functionalist's point of view they are useful training in bravery and endurance, qualities that men must have in societies that rely on hunting scarce or dangerous game for food.

Here is another example. The function of our own society's pattern (or "structure") of romantic love and courtship may be to "push" young people to become independent of their families, to take the first step toward moving away and forming their own families.

Functionalism has many critics. It is accused of trying to discover a function for every existing structure. Since it is usually possible to imagine such functions, it is easy to assume that everything that exists in a society at any given time is there because it is "functional." As a result some functionalists have opposed any experimentation and social reform on the basis of the illogical claim that whatever exists is functional and therefore must be kept the way it is.

### Functional requisites

We will save our main discussion of both evolutionism and functionalism for Chapter 19, when you will have read several examples of theories based on the two models. However, I should mention here the question that most concerns functionalists: If social life is to continue, what conditions must be met by the group? Several of Parsons' students have listed what they call the *functional requisites* of any social system.[8] I will simplify their list by grouping all the requisites under three headings: (1) the external environment, (2) the biosocial nature of humanity, and (3) the condition of collective living.

THE EXTERNAL ENVIRONMENT  For a group to survive, it must be able to provide its members with food, shelter, and clothing. It must also provide care for the helpless young and protection against animal and human enemies. Many of the structures of any society are designed to serve these basic functions.

HUMANITY'S BIOSOCIAL NATURE  A human group cannot survive if it fails to meet the deep inner needs of its members. The emotional, spiritual, and cultural needs of human beings are complex. All societies provide activities that allow a person to express his or her inner feelings (e.g., dance, and the arts). All societies provide special arrangements for differences in sex and age and for important events such as birth and death. Thus we have christenings, weddings, birthday parties, farewell banquets, funerals, and many other occasions to celebrate human life. Wherever there is social life there are structures or patterns of art, recreation, and religion.

COLLECTIVE LIVING  Because they live in groups, men and women must consider the needs of the group as well as their own needs. Hence, they make rules and provide orderly procedures for deciding who will occupy a given site, controlling the use of force, coordinating traffic, regulating sexual behavior, governing the exchange of goods, and so on. The invention of social organization was even more important in setting

*Every society must arrange to deal with the external environment by providing food, shelter, and protection for its members: This is one functional requisite. At some periods in our lives we can give help—at other times we must receive help. No one ever gets through life entirely on his or her own.*

Eric Kroll/Taurus Photos

humanity apart from the animal world than the invention of tools.

### The equilibrium model

A special version of the functionalist approach is the equilibrium model of society, developed most fully by Parsons. It is based on the notion of *feedback,* a term that refers to the processes by which a system regulates itself automatically. For example, a thermostat keeps the air in a house at a particular temperature. It turns the furnace on when the air becomes cooler than that temperature and turns it off when the air warms up to that temperature. The thermostat does this automatically by "feeding back" to the furnace information about the temperature in the house.

Living organisms have similar self-regulating mechanisms. For example, when you cut your finger the blood vessels leading to the injured area immediately contract; clotting mechanisms go into action; the production of red blood cells increases; and so forth. In this way the body prevents the blood loss from the cut from upsetting its balance. The system then gradually returns to its former state.

Following this model, Parsons and others argue that society is a system with similar mechanisms for automatically regulating itself. For example, suppose that some group within a society abandons its children and fails to bring them up properly. The result might be an increase in the number of juvenile delinquents—a social nuisance. The equilibrium model suggests that the society would take corrective action —perhaps increasing its social-work services, developing community youth centers, and so on. With enough social adjustment the "wounded social organism" would "heal" itself and restore its own balance.

### THE CONFLICT MODEL

The strongest criticism of the equilibrium model comes from those who favor what they call the conflict model of society. It is an illusion, they say, to believe that society, especially modern society, is in a balanced state. On the contrary, societies are usually in a state of conflict. The basic condition of life is not harmony but competition among different groups for power and status. The dominant social process, therefore, is not a steady effort to restore harmony or equilibrium but an endless struggle for advantage. The equilibrium model, according to those who support the conflict approach, favors the status quo. It is a pair of rose-colored glasses that distorts reality by screening out conflict.

Marx is the best known of the conflict theorists. Scholars who have been influenced by Marx ask such questions as, What group stands to gain from this social arrangement and what group stands to lose? How does this group maintain enough power to exploit that group? Conflict theorists assume that very few social patterns exist because they are in *everybody's* interest. Instead, they assume that whenever one group gains, a different group is likely to lose.

### SYMBOLIC INTERACTIONISM

Also strongly opposed to the structural-functional model (especially its equilibrium version) are those who argue for symbolic interactionism, the view that social relationships are built up through social interactions on a symbolic level, that is, through language and gestures. It is unrealistic, they claim, to picture society as an organism. Society does not contain organs; it does not feel needs, nor does it have purposes. Symbolic interactionists accuse structural functionalists of believing that individuals do not exist at all in their own right but are only parts of a large social system. According to the symbolic interactionists, only people have needs and purposes; only people act. Society is not an organism with a fixed arrangement of parts. It is not born, and it does not have a life cycle. It is not at all real the way people are

*Is this a scene of conflict or harmony? The answer you give may depend on which sociological model you prefer—the conflict model or the functional model.*

real. Forget the mythical "social system," they say, and look at real people, at individuals acting in relation to each other. Each person tries to figure out what others are doing and adjusts his or her own behavior accordingly. People communicate about what they are planning to do, and often, though not always, they are able to make plans that fit together to make an orderly collective activity, such as playing golf or launching a rocket. They are constantly cooperating in new ways, not merely playing the fixed roles of an unchanging social system. Instead, they are always adjusting to changing conditions. Symbolic interactionism, more than most other models, tends to explain the actions of a group in terms of its members' *definition of the situation.* Its explanation of the orderliness of social rela-

tionships centers on the communication that takes place between people as they fit their actions together.

### WHICH MODEL TO CHOOSE?

Which model is the "right" one? I can't answer this question. Societies show both conflict and harmony—some relatively more conflict, some more harmony. Some institutions within a society may depend on harmony more than others. Thus in our chapter on family life we will find that most of the main theories are based on structural functionalism, whereas in our chapter on politics the Marxist theory derived from the conflict model will be more important. No single model is likely to be able to answer all our questions. Holding too firmly to evolutionism, structural functionalism, the conflict model, or symbolic interactionism will lead us off the track. We need to maintain a healthy skepticism toward each of these models, keeping in mind that any model will lead us to emphasize some facts and ignore others.

## Values, research, and policy

Sociologists often study the values and norms of a society. But it is easy to look at a society's values in a biased way because one's own values conflict with them. We may hate a given nation's political system so much that we can't appreciate its contributions to preschool education or business management. Our patriotism may lead us to claim that marriages are happier in our country than they are in other countries, and so on.

Many sociologists admire the cool, unemotional approach of the physical scientists and worry about their own tendency to turn research reports into religious or political propaganda. They argue that sociological studies should take a naturalistic approach, explaining the causes and effects of social events as natural phenomena without ever revealing the attitudes of the person conducting the study. Thus one is supposed to write only about *what is* (and how it came to be the way it is) and never about *what should be*. Personal values must to be expressed only outside of one's professional work.

There is a lot of truth in this argument. Many beginning sociology students fail to understand that analysis and propaganda do not mix well. These students' papers often serve as platforms for some cause to which they are morally or politically committed. Professors, who have to guard against the tendency to sermonize in their own writing and teaching, are likely to be critical of such papers. You and I have personal prejudices that distort our vision of reality; to struggle against them is to strive for honesty. We also have personal political commitments that we have a right to express, but sociologists have long believed that it is improper to express them in the role of social scientist. This ideal of unbiased, value-free, pure social science may be impossible to achieve. "The only answer," writes Morris Cohen, "is that this is true also of the ideal of beauty, of holiness, and of everything else that is ultimately worthwhile and humanly ennobling."[9]

In recent years many social scientists have become concerned about the negative effects of this ideal. They believe that research projects should be chosen for their relevance to society's current problems. They argue that if social scientists, who specialize in the study of human interaction, are not willing to make suggestions on the basis of what they know about human society, then who is going to make those suggestions? Refusing to contribute one's knowledge to solving society's problems is irresponsible behavior.

We cannot pursue this debate here. As in all significant debates, a case can be made for both sides. Our own goal is to reach, if possible, a balance between the two opposing values of objectivity and social concern. Such a balance, we know, will be delicate at best.

## SUMMARY

**1.** *Sociology* seeks to explain the nature of social order and disorder. A *social system* is a set of relationships among one or more people who interact.

**2.** A science is concerned with discovering and organizing facts, principles, and methods. Sociology is a social science dealing with human relationships. It overlaps to some degree with economics, political science, history, geography, psychology, anthropology, and social work.

**3.** Auguste Comte is called the "father of sociology." He and Herbert Spencer were among the early sociologists who developed the evolutionary perspective. Other influential sociologists were Karl Marx, Emile Durkheim, and Max Weber.

**4.** In America the center of sociological research for many years was the University of Chicago. Robert E. Park, George Herbert Mead, Charles H. Cooley, and W. I. Thomas worked there and social psychology and social ecology were developed there.

**5.** During the 1930s Harvard also became an important center of sociological thinking. Pitirim Sorokin and Talcott Parsons taught there and introduced from Europe an approach called *structural functionalism.*

**6.** The four major models or perspectives in sociology are evolutionism, structural functionalism, the conflict model, and symbolic interactionism. Social Darwinism was one variant of evolutionism, but Marx and Durkheim were also evolutionists, at least in some ways. For a while structural functionalism, based on an image of society as an organism with interdependent parts, replaced evolutionism as a dominant perspective in sociology. The notion of functional requisites still remains important, but functionalism is otherwise declining in importance.

**7.** Sociologists do not all agree about whether it is possible or desirable for scholars to keep their values and personal opinions distinct from their professional writing and research. We will attempt to balance objectivity and social concern.

## KEY TERMS

**conflict model**   the belief that societies are usually in a state of conflict and that the basic condition of life is competition for power and status.

**evolutionism**   the belief in a law of historical progress; in sociology, that all societies go through stages of increasing complexity.

**functionalism**   the belief that a social pattern is best understood in terms of its functions in a given society.

**model**   a mental map of a subject that may be incomplete or misleading but cannot be proved wrong.

**social system**   the stable pattern of the interactions among two or more people.

**society**   a large, permanent, self-sufficient, self-perpetuating group of interacting people.

**sociology**   the study of human group life.

**symbolic interactionism**   the belief that social relationships are built up through social interactions on a symbolic level.

**theory**   an explanation offered to account for a group of facts or phenomena; can be proved wrong.

# FOR FURTHER READING

BERGER, PETER. *Invitation to Sociology.* New York: Doubleday, 1967. This small paperback is often used in introductory sociology courses because its style is charming and readable. It is a good introduction to the sociologists' distinctive assumptions.

COLLINS, RANDALL, and MICHAEL MAKOWSKY. *The Discovery of Society, 2nd Edition.* New York: Random House, 1978. This is a moderate-sized paperback treatment of the history of several aspects of social theory, with a light, entertaining touch. It's almost bedside reading.

COSER, LEWIS A. *The Functions of Social Conflict.* New York: Free Press, 1956. Coser gives us a modern-dress staging of Georg Simmel's thinking on the good consequences of conflict for social relationships. I have not presented enough about Simmel in this book, so you may want to turn to Coser for more.

FRIEDRICHS, ROBERT W. *A Sociology of Sociology.* New York: The Free Press, 1972. If you are interested in a career in sociology, have a look at this book, which describes how professional sociology is set up as a field of work.

GOFFMAN, ERVING. *The Presentation of Self in Everyday Life.* New York: Doubleday Anchor, 1959. Goffman is probably the most interesting sociologist now writing, but he has an approach unlike anything you will learn in this book. When I read *Presentation of Self,* I lay awake all night, mentally arguing against Goffman. I lost the argument. Besides, he writes with a marvelous style.

INKELES, ALEX. *What is Sociology: An Introduction to the Discipline and Profession.* Englewood Cliffs, N. J.: Prentice-Hall, 1964. If Inkeles' book seems vaguely familiar to you, it is because part of my first chapter is drawn from it. However, there is plenty left in his book that I have not used up.

MacRAE, JR., DUNCAN. *The Social Function of Social Science.* New Haven: Yale University Press, 1976. This book discusses some of the problems involved in using social research to answer questions about social policy. There are many practical problems that sociologists can help solve in that way, along with the other social sciences.

MERTON, ROBERT K. *Social Theory and Social Structure.* New York: Free Press, 1968. This is one of the most important collections of theoretical essays by any contemporary sociologist. Merton is a functionalist. He also presents some of his work on the sociology of knowledge herein.

MILLS, C. WRIGHT. *The Sociological Imagination.* New York: Oxford University Press, 1959. Mills was a critical sociologist who wanted his colleagues to join him in attacking social injustice and inequality. He died in the early 1960s but is still the hero of many young radical sociologists, who look to this book for inspiration.

SILLS, DAVID, ed. *The International Encyclopedia of the Social Sciences.* New York: Macmillan, 1968. This multivolume encyclopedia covers just about all the topics in the social sciences. Each entry is written by an eminent specialist on the subject. Remember it when you have term papers to write or examinations to prepare for.

SIMMEL, GEORG. *Conflict.* Translated by Kurt H. Wolff. New York: Free Press, 1955. Instead of reading Coser, as shown above, you may want to read the book that inspired it. Simmel was a great sociologist whose approach influenced the Chicago school.

ZEITLIN, IRVING. *Rethinking Sociology.* Englewood Cliffs, N. J.: Prentice-Hall, 1973. This book is an effort to integrate several different sociological traditions, including some that do not fit together in any obvious way, such as G. H. Mead and Karl Marx. It should not be the second sociology book you read but, say, the twentieth or thirtieth one. By then you will have something to rethink.

# METHODS OF SOCIAL RESEARCH

Research is detective work. There's always a mystery, a puzzling problem to be solved. There's often a sense of adventure, of "aha!" There's the thrill of closing in on the solution, of getting the last piece of evidence needed to make an airtight case. Sociologists occasionally become addicted to their work the way some people become addicted to murder mysteries.

There are differences, of course. For one thing, in a mystery there is usually a dead body. This means that the problem is obvious: whodunit? The researcher, by contrast, has to look for a problem; it may not be obvious at all. Indeed, the most sophisticated, exciting scholars are the ones who are able to persuade other people that a given problem really is a problem when they may never have recognized it as a puzzle before. Half the skill of scholarly detective work consists of finding a good mystery that is worth working on.

There's another difference too. When a detective is successful, the murderer is led away in handcuffs and convicted in a courtroom. Sociologists rarely have the satisfaction of knowing that they have proved a case so conclusively. Instead, they must be satisfied by the fact that people who read the results of their research agree, on the whole, that it has been done carefully and that the results are convincing. But it is very likely that someone else will take up the puzzle in another research project and make a fairly good case for a very different theory. Sometimes only after many such studies have been done is it possible to determine whose answer is the true solution to the mystery.

Still, sociology is a living, moving process made up of men and women working on real problems. In this chapter I want to give you a feel for the challenge and excitement of research. I will begin by telling you about a simple research project done by a sociology class I taught over a decade ago, when the Beatles were on an American tour.

# A research project: explaining Beatlemania

The course was on research methods, and the plan was to do a study as a whole team. But for several weeks we could not find a puzzle that was challenging enough to whet our enthusiasm. Then one day some of my students came to class talking excitedly about three women from their dormitory who had gone to a Beatles concert. At the concert they had lost all self-control and had begun screaming and crying. My students were bewildered by their friends' public display of hysteria. This, then, became our puzzle: how to explain Beatlemania.

### THE THEORY

It was almost as hard to make up a theory to explain Beatlemania as it had been to find the problem in the first place. Nobody had any idea why three ordinary freshman women in a respectable Catholic women's college would give way to such silly behavior. Finally one student gave us a clue. Her roommate, she said, was one of the Beatlemaniacs. Whenever she listened to Beatles records she would get excited and start bopping around in rhythm to the music—*but only if another person was present.* When she thought she was alone she seemed to be unaffected by the sound.

It appeared, then, that Beatlemania was a performance put on for other people. But why? What was to be gained from this display? Another student had an idea. At the time the Beatles were popular with teenagers all over the world. (Later members of other age groups began to like them too, but without the same degree of passion.) Beatlemania was a symbol of being a teenager. Perhaps, the student suggested, adolescents who have doubts about whether they are adequate teenagers adopt the symbols of teenage culture in order to proclaim to the world that they are full-fledged, genuine teenagers. Those who do not have such doubts do not need to worry so much about their public image and will not get so worked up over the symbols. This, then, became our theory: Beatlemania is a way of loudly claiming to be a normal adolescent. It is inspired by self-doubt.

### TESTING THE THEORY

Any causal theory is a statement that two or more different elements are regularly linked together. Our theory stated that within a teenage population self-doubt (the cause) was regularly linked with Beatlemania (the effect). This theory suggested the following hypothesis: *The greater the self-doubt, the greater the Beatlemania.* To find out whether this was actually the case, we needed additional data about teenagers so that we could estimate the strength of both self-doubt and Beatlemania. But how do you "measure" such attributes as self-doubt or Beatlemania? These are not physical objects but mental attitudes. To obtain such data we simply question people about themselves and give their answer sheets a score, much as a teacher gives each pupil a mark on a spelling test by adding up the number of correct answers.

Because Beatlemania was found primarily among high-school youth, the class asked the principals of two local high schools for permission to present a questionnaire to some of their female pupils. Both principals gave their permission, and four students visited the schools and obtained answers from more than 400 students.

Figure 2.1 is the questionnaire that we presented to the students. It consists of two series of questions. The first series measures Beatlemania by asking such questions as

"Would you borrow money, if necessary, to buy a new Beatles record?" Each person's Beatlemania score was calculated by adding up the points for each question. A respondent (the person filling out the questionnaire) with no Beatlemania whatever would score 0, while the most fanatic Beatlemaniac might earn as many as 8 points by answering yes to all of the first four questions. The particular teenager whose answers are shown in Figure 2.1 scored 1 on Beatlemania, which we decided was a low score. Scores between 2 and 4 we called medium, and any score of 5 or higher we called extreme Beatlemania.

The other series of questions was meant to measure the teenager's self-doubt. It consisted of six adjectives to be used by each respondent in describing both her ideal teenager and herself. We assigned one point for each adjective on which the ideal and the real differed. For example, Figure 2.1 shows that respondent number 004 said that her ideal teenager would be sexually attractive but that she herself was not. We gave her one point on the self-doubt index for this difference. She also said that the ideal teenager would not be very quiet but that she was quiet. This earned her another point, for a total score of 2 on the self-doubt index. The lowest possible score was 0 and the highest score 6. We defined scores of 0, 1, or 2 as low, 3 and 4 as medium, and 5 and 6 as high. Anyone with a score of 6 would probably feel very inadequate, because her ideal teenager would be the opposite of her own self-image.

If our questionnaire had been a long one given to a very large sample, punched cards and a computer would have been needed to analyze the replies. In our case, however, six students were able to add up the Beatlemania and self-doubt scores, and they simply marked them on the edge of the questionnaire sheet. We drew a grid on the blackboard and tallied the questionnaires according to whether they were high, medium, or

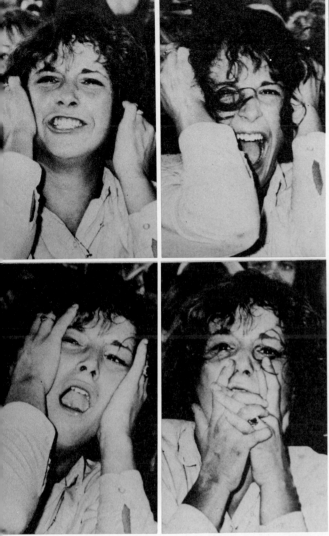

*Can you explain the wild enthusiasm teen-agers sometimes display for their favorite performers? These were the Beatles. Earlier teen-agers swooned over Frank Sinatra, just as later ones fainted over the Bay City Rollers.*

low on self-doubt and on Beatlemania, as shown in Figure 2.2. Thus a questionnaire that scored high on Beatlemania would be placed in the first, second, or third column of the top row, depending on whether it was low, medium, or high in self-doubt. The numbers in Figure 2.2 are called frequencies because they show the number of questionnaires in each category.

What we want to know is whether teen-agers who score high on Beatlemania are evenly distributed across all three categories of self-doubt. Reading across the top row of Figure 2.2, we see that they are not. The highly self-doubting group contains far more Beatlemaniacs than the group with lower self-doubt. However, the total number of high self-doubters is smaller (139) than the number of low self-doubters (153), so Figure 2.2 is not conclusive. We need to find out whether the *proportions* of Beatlemaniacs are the same in all three categories of self-doubt. To do so we calculate the *percentages* of high, medium, and low Beatlemaniacs in all three categories of self-doubt, as shown in Figure 2.3. In other words, we find out what percentage of high self-doubters are high Beatlemaniacs, and so on. This is done by dividing the number in each cell of Figure 2.2 by the total number of cases in the column in which it appears. For example, the 83 in the top right-hand cell of Figure 2.2 is divided by 139 to get the 60 percent shown in the top right-hand cell of Figure 2.3. Continuing in this way for all the cells, we arrive at the percentages shown in Figure 2.3.

Figure 2.3 gave the class the results it was looking for—the test of our hypothesis. We compared all the figures across a single row of the table. We saw that the proportion of high Beatlemaniacs increases from 7 percent among the low self-doubters to 31 percent among the medium self-doubters and to 60 percent among the high self-doubters. Beatlemania *was* related to self-doubt! The empirical findings supported our theory. To celebrate, we all went out for pizza together.

**FIGURE 2.1**
*Beatlemania questionnaire*

Case Number ___004___

Please circle the correct response to the following questions:

1. Would you borrow money, if necessary, to buy a new Beatles record?

    (0 = No)
    1 = Maybe
    2 = Yes

    0

2. Would you hitchhike 50 miles, if necessary, to go to a Beatles concert?

    (0 = No)
    1 = Maybe
    2 = Yes

    0

3. Would you skip writing a required term paper, if necessary, to go to a Beatles concert?

    0 = No
    (1 = Maybe)
    2 = Yes

    1

4. Do you become emotionally excited when you hear the Beatles play?

    (0 = Not at all)
    1 = Somewhat
    2 = Yes, very excited

    Beatlemania    0
    Score = 1

Please place an X in the column beside each adjective that describes your ideal teenager.

Please place an X in the column beside each adjective that describes your own personality.

| 5. Interesting | X | | Interesting | X | | 0 |
| 6. Sloppy | | | Sloppy | | | 0 |
| 7. Popular | X | | Popular | X | | 0 |
| 8. Hard working | | | Hard working | | | 0 |
| 9. Sexually attractive | X | | Sexually attractive | X | | 1 |
| 10. Quiet | | | Quiet | X | | 1 |

Self-doubt
Score = 2

Thank you very much for your cooperation!

**FIGURE 2.2**

*Beatlemania by self-doubt (frequencies)*

Self-doubt

| Beatlemania | | Low | Medium | High |
|---|---|---|---|---|
| | High | 11 | 46 | 83 |
| | Medium | 52 | 55 | 47 |
| | Low | 90 | 48 | 9 |
| | Total | 153 | 149 | 139 |

The class research project was fun to do. It was also, believe it or not, pure scientific research. To be sure, it was a simple inquiry conducted with rough-and-ready methods, but this is true of many important studies,

**FIGURE 2.3**

*Beatlemania by self-doubt (percentages)*

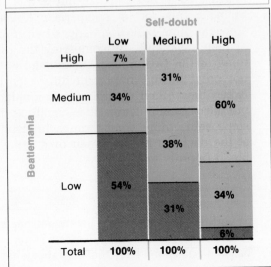

such as Galileo's legendary experiment in which he dropped things from the top of the leaning tower of Pisa in order to study gravity. Of course modern professional researchers use a variety of methods that are too complex to be discussed in detail here. However, it will be useful to mention a few of the concepts and methods that social scientists use.

## Sociology as a science

In what sense are the social sciences "scientific"? Researchers in these fields do not peer through microscopes, dissect animals, or calculate the distances between stars, but they are nonetheless scientists. They share with physical scientists the purpose of discovering and explaining regular relationships among phenomena. Science is a search for knowledge about such relationships, and scientists all try to make generalizations, or statements that apply to whole classes of similar events. Newton was not interested in explaining why one particular apple fell to the ground; rather, he wanted to come up with a theory that would account for the tendency of all sorts of objects to fall toward the earth. So it is with the social sciences. The goal of our Beatlemania study was not to find out why three particular college freshmen sobbed and yelled at one particular concert. Instead, we wanted to explain a widespread social phenomenon. Of course explaining a phenomenon in general terms also usually allows us to explain particular cases as well.

### CASE STUDIES

A case study is an in-depth investigation of a single case of a given phenomenon for the purpose of understanding it as fully as possible. Case studies are designed to produce clues to the explanation of a whole category of similar phenomena. Thus we might have approached the phenomenon of Beatlemania by setting up a case study in which our three college Beatlemaniacs were observed and interviewed in great detail. Though this might have given us some strong clues, it would not have been conclusive until further research was done to see how widely the explanations apply to other cases. Thus a case study is often a first step toward solving a puzzle, but it is always necessary to go beyond the single case study and compare many different cases. Only in this way can we arrive at a general theory that covers all the particular cases.

Let's look at an example of a case study. Rex Lucas studied the feelings and behavior of two groups of men who had been trapped for a week in different areas of a coal mine.[1]

*Sometimes sociologists study one event in great detail, as for example a particular mine disaster. This is called a case study. Eventually another researcher may compare several such studies and discover a generalization that fits all of them.*

United Press International

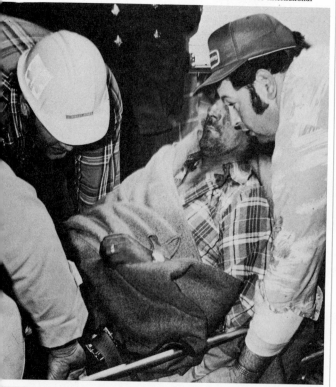

He wanted to find out how the men had reacted during their ordeal. Although he was reporting only a single incident, Lucas did not look for the aspects that made it unusual, the way a reporter might have. Instead, he looked for patterns of reaction that might be generally true of human beings in similar disasters. For instance, he found that one of the two groups had been trapped in a small space where they had to interact almost constantly and maintain group morale. They banned any crying or any loss of emotional control in the presence of the group. Some of the men retreated from group pressure by sleeping or crawling away into the dark, where they could weep or talk to themselves. The other group, which was trapped in a larger area, was able to tolerate emotionalism. Notice that Lucas' study suggests that emotional control may *generally* be more necessary for groups in small spaces than for groups that have much more room. Because it goes beyond plain description and suggests generalizations, Lucas' account is scientific research, not just good news reporting. Science is cumulative. Other researchers may try to see whether Lucas has hit upon a real generalization that explains group behavior in other, similar situations, such as a stalled elevator or a disabled submarine. To a certain extent Lucas was able to make this sort of comparison himself, since the mine explosion trapped two groups of men separately. By comparing the reactions of the two groups Lucas determined not only the one important difference between them (their control of emotionalism) but also certain similarities — such as the steps both groups went through in arriving at the decision to drink their own urine or blood in order to stay alive.

## MAKING UP THEORIES AND TESTING THEM

Scientific inquiry always has two aspects — theory and research. A theory is a statement based on observed facts that explains what is supposed to be a causal relationship between those facts. For example, in a murder mystery the detective's theory is supposed to show how all the facts consistently point to a single conclusion. A good theory will make sense of the scientific facts, show how they fit together as a pattern, and allow us to predict future findings. In the Beatlemania study, for example, our theory explained the teenagers' hysteria in terms of their anxiety about being adequate teenagers. This theory led us to predict that, *in general*, teenagers with high self-doubt are more likely to be Beatlemaniacs than teenagers with low self-doubt. On the same grounds we might expect Beatlemaniacs to be likely to pick up other symbols of teenage culture—up-to-date slang, new fads in clothes and dancing, and the like. Thus a theory generates hypotheses, or specific predictions that may be verified by empirical findings.

The empirical aspect of research consists of the practical activities involved in finding out how events turn out. This is necessary if scientists are to get closer to the truth. Theory alone can go only so far. For example, Aristotle was probably the greatest scholar who ever lived, but all he knew about physics was what he arrived at by pure reasoning, not experimentation. He declared that the speed of a falling object was determined by its weight divided by the resistance of the air through which it fell. Heavy objects would therefore fall faster than light ones. More than 1900 years passed before anyone bothered to test the theory empirically. When Galileo dropped light and heavy objects from the top of the tower of Pisa at the same moment, he found that they landed at almost the same time, contrary to Aristotle's prediction. Experience made it necessary to change the theory. Empirical research is the practical work of collecting facts, however they may be obtained.

There is a constant interplay between theory and empirical observation. We develop a theory to make sense of the events that we have observed empirically. The theory is a generalization expressing some supposed causal relationship between two or more phenomena (such as weight and speed of fall or self-doubt and Beatlemania). From this theory, in turn, we derive new hypotheses that we go on to test empirically.

If our empirical findings do not turn out as our hypotheses predicted, we may either (1) check our procedures to make sure our empirical findings amount to a fair, accurate test of the theory or (2) try to develop a new theory and then test it. We keep a theory only as long as it *works*—as long as it makes sense of known facts. Whenever new facts will not fit the theory, we must change it. This constant checking and rechecking forces us to improve our theories, and the theories, in turn, suggest what procedures we must set up to gather the facts and test them. Without a theory, we would not know what to look for when making our empirical observations.

Of course not all sociologists do empirical research themselves. Some stick to the work of improving theories and leave all the practical observations and calculations to others. *Theorists* are concerned mostly with making sure that the terms in a theory are used in a consistent way and that the meanings are clear and not self-contradictory. They may worry about whether Mr. Smith's theory about a given phenomenon is compatible with Ms. Brown's theory about a related phenomenon. They may be able to propose a new theory to explain a number of different studies that have not previously been seen as similar. This sort of work involves specializing in logical reasoning. On the other hand, some sociologists specialize in the technical problems of empirical study and can tell others how to test their hypotheses by careful observation and by the use of statistical calculations. These specialists are called *methodologists*. In the rest of this chapter we will deal mainly with the concerns of this latter group.

## Variables

A variable is a characteristic that differs among situations, individuals or groups and can be measured. Length, color, population size, temperature, income, wisdom, and race are examples of characteristics which may differ. Theories consist of general statements that explain one variable in terms of one or more other variables. A theory may be a very simple idea linking two factors that can vary. (e.g. "Wealth makes for happiness," "Watching violence on TV stimulates kids to fight," or "High rates of unemployment produce high rates of divorce.") Whatever is assumed to be the cause is called the independent variable. Whatever is assumed to be the effect is called the dependent variable, because the value it takes depends on the value of the independent variable. In our example Beatlemania is the dependent variable and self-doubt is the independent variable. Both are "variable" in the sense that in our study they took on different values. Some teenagers rated high on self-doubt, some medium, and some very low. Some teenagers rated high on Beatlemania while others rated low. If everyone had been a Beatle fan to the same degree or had not differed in degree of self-doubt, these two factors would have been *constants*, not variables. In such a case we could not have made any causal statement about the relationship between them.

If one variable causes another, its value determines the value of the other. Thus the higher the value of the self-doubt score, the higher the value of the Beatlemania score.

## Indicators

Physical scientists can actually affect the physical phenomena they study by, say, freezing things or increasing the pressure on them. Social scientists, on the other hand, deal with more abstract variables that they cannot put their hands on to measure directly. How do you measure something like self-doubt, which has no weight or length? The social scientists must use indicators, or concrete representations of abstract variables. We used the teenagers' answers to a series of questions as an indicator of self-doubt. We might have used other indicators of the same variable. For example, we might have asked each pupil's teacher to estimate the pupil's degree of self-doubt. Or we might have asked the teenagers to volunteer for a difficult leadership job and classified those who volunteered as self-confident and those who did not as self-doubting. A wide variety of indicators are possible, but some would be better than others.

The sociologist always has to choose what sort of *data* to use as indicators of the variables in his or her theory. These data result from the objective observations that are systematically carried out in the course of empirical research. In our Beatle study the data consisted of completed questionnaires, but this would not be the case in all studies. For example, consider a theory that upper-class people are more likely to commit suicide than lower-class people.[2] A questionnaire would not be a good source of data for testing this theory (you can't very well ask people whether or not they have committed suicide), but other indicators are available. All governments keep records showing the number of deaths that occurred during a given period. These records usually give the cause of death and contain certain facts about the deceased person, such as sex, marital status, and occupation. It is possible to use these statistics as indicators of both the independent variable (social status) and the dependent variable (suicide rates). By studying the record of everyone who died during a given year in a particular place, one can determine whether suicides are more likely among people with high-status jobs than among those with low-status jobs. (Usually they are.)

## Validity

This raises another problem, however. How do we know that the government's records are accurate? Suicide, for example, puts such a great strain on the dead person's relatives and friends that they often try to hide the true cause of death. Some physicians are willing to sign a certificate showing a false cause of death. Hence, we know that these documents are not always *valid* indicators of whether or not a person's death was due to suicide. Validity refers to the ability of an indicator to genuinely and accurately represent the variable that it is meant to represent. Researchers often have to give some thought to the possibility that their indicators may not be valid. Do our Beatlemania and self-doubt scores validly represent teenagers' self-confidence and fanaticism about the Beatles? If we had any reason to believe that these indicators are invalid, we would not have much faith in our findings. Most questionnaires that ask simple, factual questions are answered truthfully and can be assumed to represent real facts validly. For example, when we ask a person his or her sex the answer will almost certainly be valid. On the other hand, we know that crime statistics are very far from accurate indicators of the true amount of crime committed. Their validity cannot be taken for granted at all.

## Representativeness

Social scientists collect data in order to identify causal relationships between variables. Always, however, they want to be able to generalize. For example, in our Beatlemania study we wanted to be able to say that self-doubt is a cause of Beatlemania not only for this *particular* group of teenagers but for a whole population of teenagers. However, to make such a generalization with any confidence we need to be fairly sure that the high school students who filled out our questionnaire were a typical group of teenag-

ers, that is, that they were *representative of the population* of teenagers—the whole group of adolescents in Western society. (A population is the whole number of units from which one draws a limited sample about which to collect data.)

In many studies it would not be good enough to assume, as we did with the high school students, that one's data are typical, or representative, of the population. One would try to make sure that is is so by selecting data by means of systematic *sampling* procedures. This is particularly true of public-opinion surveys, such as the Roper or Gallup polls, that try to estimate very precisely the amount of support for a given candidate or political issue among all the voters in the nation. Pollsters can make very accurate estimates on the basis of a sample of only about 2000 respondents. This is possible only because of the great care they take in choosing a set of respondents who are representative of all the voters. To do so they may use quota sampling, or sampling in which the percentage of people with a given characteristic is equal to the percentage of such people in the whole population. First they find out a great many facts about the population they wish to study—in this case the voters of a given country. Having determined the percentages of voters in different age categories, cities of various sizes, different jobs, different regions, and so on, they set *quotas* in which the percentage of people in a particular age category, city size, occupation, and region is equal to their percentage in the whole population. Their quotas define exactly what sort of person the interviewer must locate, so that the choice is taken out of the interviewer's hands. If interviewers were allowed to pick the respondents, they would probably pick mostly well-dressed, handsome people of about their own age. Such a sample would be unrepresentative. It would yield wrong estimates about voters as a whole group.

Even when they are using great care to

select a representative sample, most sociologists (and today, many polling firms) do not use quota sampling; instead, they use simple *random sampling,* or sampling in which every member of the population has an equal chance of being chosen as part of the sample. An example of a simple random sample might be the selection of every fifth name on a voter registration list. A population may be *stratified* (divided into groups) before the random sampling is carried out, as when the voter registration list is separated into Democrats, Republicans, and independents. Random sampling is then used to draw a given number of respondents from each subgroup.

### Prediction

When social scientists have arrived at a valid generalization showing the relationship among two or more variables, they can make predictions. Now I am not trying to say that sociologists are fortunetellers. They make statements of *probability,* not certainty, and their predictions are always conditional. The sociologists may say, "If X happens, then there is a high probability that Y will happen," where X and Y refer to two variables that are known to vary together. Knowing something about the relationship between X and Y may enable the sociologist to improve his or her predictions.

Again using our class project as an example, suppose you are given only one fact: In the high school sample 32 percent scored high on the Beatlemania variable, 35 percent in the medium range, and 33 percent in the low range. Now if you were asked to guess (or predict) the Beatlemania score of some

*"And what brand of iced tea mix do you use?" Consumer polls in shopping centers don't pay as much attention to selecting representative samples as do most sociological polls.*

Sybil Shelton/Monkmeyer

unidentified person in the sample, what would you predict? The best guess would be that her score is in the medium range, though this is not a very much safer guess than the other two possibilities. If you guessed medium, you would be right 35 percent of the time.

But now let's assume that you are given two new facts: (1) the results of Figure 2.3 and (2) the information that the person whose rating you are to guess scores low on self-doubt. Now what Beatlemania rating should you guess? Look at Figure 2.3 and decide. You will conclude that you should predict her Beatlemania score to be low and that 54 percent of the time you will be right. Your predictions are greatly improved by knowing about the relationship between the independent and dependent variables. Of course if the two had not varied together you would not have improved your predictions on either variable by knowing how a person scored on the other.

## Sources of sociological data

### DOCUMENTS

Sociologists use many different sources of data in their search for meaningful facts. One of those sources consists of various types of documents.

*Written documents* include public records such as job and school records, books, newspapers, legal codes, the minutes of committee meetings, court records, voter registration lists, corporations' annual reports to their stockholders, and the like. Historians regularly use such documents in their work, and so do many sociologists. Historians often need old documents that may have been lost or destroyed or are in fragile condition because of their age, while sociologists are more likely to use recent records that are more readily available.

In addition to these public records, private, personal documents are sometimes useful sources of data. Letters, diaries, household budgets, wills, and the records in old family Bibles are documents of this sort. One imaginative researcher used his friends' Christmas card lists as data. He found that people tend to send cards to people whose social status is higher than their own and to receive cards from people whose social status is lower than their own.

In a classic study early in this century W. I. Thomas and Florian Znaniecki studied the adjustment of Polish immigrants to North America by analyzing personal documents—especially the letters they exchanged with relatives in Poland.[3]

*Graphic documents* include other records that are not written but contain information in a usable form—maps, films, revolutionary posters, art objects, and the like. The range of such documents is limited only by the researcher's imagination. For example, David McClelland wanted to find out when the ancient Greek trading empire covered its widest area. To do so he referred to a map that showed the sites where ancient Greek jars that once held wine and olive oil had been discovered. Because olive oil and wine were major trade products, McClelland was able to use the ages of the jars and their distribution to estimate when Greek merchants must have been traveling the greatest distances and in the greatest numbers.[4]

Philippe Ariès wrote a brilliant historical study describing the changes that took place in Europe over many centuries in the people's views of childhood and in the way children were treated.[5] Besides using public documents, such as published autobiographies, and private documents, such as diaries and letters, Ariès used the art of each period, observing the way painters had depicted children in portraits of families—how they were dressed, how adults were interacting with them, and so on.

Some types of documents do not fit neatly into the written or graphic category, and others—such as sound recordings—belong to a special group of audiovisual documents. In fact the variety of documents available to the imaginative researcher is endless. One researcher used charts of Chicago's water pressure as data. He found that during a break between popular television programs people all over town are busy flushing toilets and drawing tap water to brew coffee, and so the water pressure drops. The amount of decrease in water pressure indicates how many viewers were deeply involved in the television program that just ended. The greatest drop in pressure occurred at the end of the season's most important football game.[6]

Tombstones are a splendid source of data. One scholar estimated the average life span of the ancient Romans from the dates on their tombstones.[7] As a careful researcher should, he thought about the problem of representative sampling and warned his readers that the stones do not lend themselves to perfect estimates. The poorest Romans probably died younger than wealthy Romans and couldn't afford engraved tombstones. Therefore the average life span of the whole population must have been shorter than that of the sample.

Another tombstone specialist showed how a town's cemeteries give us important clues to its patterns of social stratification. For example, in "Yankee City" a father was usually buried in the center of the family plot and the tombstones of males were usually larger than those of females. Sometimes when a family achieved prosperity and prestige its dead members shared in its upward social mobility by being moved to better graves in more prestigious cemeteries.[8]

The tape recorder is a very useful tool for collecting data. For example, I once wanted to find out whether the content of women's conversations was different from that of men's conversations, so I collected a lot of taped conversations—some between two females and some between two males. The typed transcripts of these tapes, in which the speakers were identified only by initials, were given to several judges, who tried to guess the sex of each person in each conversation. They might as well have flipped a coin to arrive at a guess—the two sexes could not be identified by what they talked about. However, because of the limitations of the sample I am cautious about generalizing from these findings.

Here's a source of data that you may have on your own bookshelf—a high school yearbook. I was recently trying to find out whether blacks had become better integrated into two American high schools during the past ten years. Besides interviewing teachers, I asked to see the current yearbook and the one from ten years ago. Then I counted the number of white and black faces in pictures of various clubs, class officers, and sports teams. It was clear from the number of leadership roles occupied by black students that major changes had occurred.

## OFFICIAL STATISTICS

Governments collect a wide variety of data and publish them in statistical bulletins that are available in any good library. One of the most important sources of data for sociologists is the national census, which is taken every ten years. In the United States it is done in years ending in 0; in Canada, in years ending in 1. An effort is made to contact every adult who is living in the country at the time and to ask a certain number of questions. At the same time, various samples of the population are asked additional questions. Researchers use the facts collected in this way to calculate tables, and those tables are printed in a number of government bulletins and other publications.

The *Monthly Catalog of U.S. Government Publications* is a complete index of all documents published by the U.S. government (except secret ones), as well as a list of important publications soon to be released. Canada publishes a similar index of its public documents.

Another important source of data is the

*Statistical Abstract of the United States,* which is published each year. It includes summaries of facts about income, education, birth and death rates, immigration, and dozens of other topics—mostly in the form of tables.

For international statistics sociologists often refer to publications of the United Nations and its agencies, such as UNESCO (the United Nations Education, Scientific, and Cultural Organization) and the ILO (International Labor Organization), which publish information in both French and English.

### INTERVIEWS

Sometimes social scientists conduct interviews instead of going to the library for data. Whenever possible, they select certain highly informed individuals for especially detailed interviewing. Structured interviews use a standard list of questions. In unstructured interviews the respondent is asked open-ended questions that lead to an open discussion of the topic. The interviewer may probe ("Could you tell me a little more about that, please?") or go off into new, unplanned topics, even though he or she usually begins with a list of topics to be covered. It doesn't matter whether they come up in order as long as they are eventually mentioned.

The unstructured interview is more flexible and allows the interviewer to clear up misunderstandings by changing the wording of questions. It allows for a complex discussion. However, the disadvantage of unstructured interviews is that they make it hard to compare the answers of many different respondents. The questions may have been worded in such different ways that each respondent understood them in a different way; as a result the answers have different meanings and may be less precise. In a structured interview each respondent is asked the same questions in the same words.

Whether the approach is structured, unstructured, or some combination of the two, the interviewer who listens to the respondent in a friendly, curious way will get the best results. The interviewer must be careful not to influence or bias the respondent by looking *too* pleased or displeased with a given response, and should never express opinions that might influence the respondent's later answers.

### QUESTIONNAIRES

The structured interview depends on the use of a prepared set of questions that are read to the respondent exactly as they were written. A questionnaire is a printed list of questions given to respondents, who fill in the answers themselves, without an interviewer. You may have received questionnaires through the mail with return-addressed envelopes. This method is far cheaper for researchers than the use of interviewers. One advantage of the questionnaire is that the respondents can be anonymous. They sometimes feel more free to express unpopular opinions or reveal embarrassing facts about themselves than they would in an interview. However, about 10 percent of the population of North America cannot fill out even a simple questionnaire.[9] Thus it is not always an appropriate way of collecting data. Also, most of the time only about half of the potential respondents return their completed questionnaires, so that the resulting sample may be quite unrepresentative. The type of questionnaire that is most likely to be returned is one that is short, interesting, and easy to fill out and return; it also helps if the questionnaire is under the letterhead of a prestigious organization.

### OBSERVATION

Many studies of ongoing events can best be understood at first hand. Sometimes the researcher simply watches what is going on without getting involved in the action. This is called detached observation. For example, sociologists sometimes watch groups through one-way mirrors. In order to observe events even more closely, a researcher often finds it useful to take some role within the group. This is called participant observation. Because this technique is so subjective, observers must continually take notes for future use and be on guard against allowing their opinions and beliefs to bias their observations. There is no such thing as pure objectivity, but some observers are more objective than others.

Scholars who use observation to get information have another problem: Their presence may influence the outcome of the events they are observing. Anthropologists have always been aware that by visiting a primitive society and talking with its members they may raise questions about things that the members had always taken for granted. This may lead to social change. Also, there may be ethical problems in either participating fully in the group's activities or refusing to participate. One cannot claim to be an impartial observer if one tries to break up the event that one went to observe. One anthropologist whom I know had been staying with a primitive tribe at a time when it felt sure that another tribe was about to attack it with bows and arrows. Members of the anthropologist's group pleaded with him to let them use his rifle to defend themselves. He refused, but he never felt quite sure that he had done the right thing. When sociologists study criminal gangs they may have to decide whether or not to tell the police when an illegal act is being planned. Whatever decision observers make in cases like these, they can never be sure whether the events they observed would have turned out the same way if they had not been there. There are no formulas for solving these problems. They are built into the situation itself.

In the study I am about to describe, the researcher did not face any serious ethical problems. However, we may wonder whether by being a sociable and supportive participant observer this sociologist helped create the very sense of community that was, to her, "unexpected."

Arlie Hochschild's book *The Unexpected Community*[10] is a case study of Merrill Court, a housing project for senior citizens. Hochschild began her research in 1966 by taking a job there as a "reporter" for the project's monthly newsletter. She stayed there for almost three years, gradually becoming acquainted with the residents. She describes this process as follows:

Initially, my watching went on in the Recreation Room, where I sat and did handiwork at a table with five or six others. As I drove residents to the doctor, to the housing office, to church, and occasionally to funerals, joined them on visits to relatives, shopped with them, kept bowling scores, visited their apartments and took them to mine, I gradually came to know and like them. Through sharing their lives I came to see how others treated them and how their own behavior changed as their audience did. Finally, I lived at Merrill Court for two weeks, sleeping in a sleeping bag under a bird cage as a guest of one of the widows.

Most of my goals concerning Merrill Court coincided with most of theirs. However, as a person of a different age and social class, and as a sociologist, my perspective differed from theirs. I thought the widows were old and they did not think they were. I thought that, as welfare recipients, they were poor; they thought they were "average." I initially felt that there was something sad about old people living together as old people, and although they felt that they had problems, they did not think that they *were* one.[11]

The purpose of Hochschild's observations was to determine whether or not, as some theorists had suggested, people "disengage" from life as they grow old and approach death by gradually reducing their interactions with other people until they "die" socially before they die biologically. Some old people do go through this process, but not the Merrill Court residents, for they were not socially isolated. Hochschild found during her visits in residents' apartments that they received about one phone call an hour. One widow's monthly telephone bill recorded 413 message units for outgoing calls, in addition to the calls received. While surveys that study old people by means of questionnaires report that the elderly working-class population is poorly informed (they do not know the names of school board candidates or the Secretary of State), Hochschild's participant observation tells quite a different story. The elderly do know a lot about things that *they* think are important — such as the name of the store where they bought a school ring for a grandchild, the price of yarn at all the nearby stores, and the birthdays of 20 or 30 grandchildren and great-grandchildren. The surveys simply don't ask questions about such matters.

Far from being lonely, these widows played in a washtub band, met for potluck suppers, made rugs together from plastic bread wrappers, and took chartered bus trips to the Ice Follies, singing all the way home.

On the basis of observations at Merrill Court Hochschild developed a theory to explain why these elderly people were so much more alive than other old people: They had each other, and most of them also had children living nearby. Both kinds of relationships were important, and neither could entirely replace the other. An old woman can share in the pleasures of life by identifying with her daughter and grandchildren. If her daughter buys a new house, she can take part in all the adventures, such as planning the garden or buying an eye-level avocado oven, as happily as if the house were her own.

But old people also need someone their own age. Instead of living only through their children, elderly people can live life fully when they have each other. Only through participant observation could a researcher come to know the widows at Merrill Court well enough to see how their relationships with one another complement their relationships with their families.

### LABORATORY EXPERIMENTS

One form of social research that is quite important for social psychologists, though not so important for other sociologists, is the laboratory experiment, in which a study of groups or individuals is carried out in an environment controlled by the researcher. Although we cannot study large groups, such as labor unions, kinship systems, or political parties, in private rooms with one-way mirrors, many small-group processes can be studied in such a setting. Also, personality patterns that have important implications for larger groups can be studied in a laboratory. For example, much of what we know about authoritarianism has been discovered through experimental procedures.

In 1950 an important book, *The Authoritarian Personality*, was published by several social psychologists.[12] It showed that several personality traits and "packages" of attitudes tended to occur together in the same people. These traits included political and economic conservatism, anti-Semitism and prejudice against other minorities, a tendency toward fascism, and a belief that one's own way of life is the best way, if not the only proper way, to do things. This group of traits has come to be called *authoritarianism*. It is shared by people who are greatly concerned with toughness, strength, dominance, and power, are uncritical of people in positions of authority, and react strongly to any violation of rules. Authoritarians also dislike ambivalence (i.e., having mixed feelings on any subject) and therefore repress negative feelings about themselves or anyone they love.

One of the authors of *The Authoritarian Personality*, Else Frenkel-Brunswik, studied ambivalence in young children.[13] Among other things, she showed that authoritarian children avoid feelings of ambivalence toward their parents and even avoid any other ambiguity.

Authoritarians usually have firm opinions, make judgments without allowing for the possibility of error, and stick to them. The world is not always that simple, however. Situations may be fluid, unclear, and unstable. People who are wonderful in one respect may be less wonderful in other re-

**FIGURE 2.4**

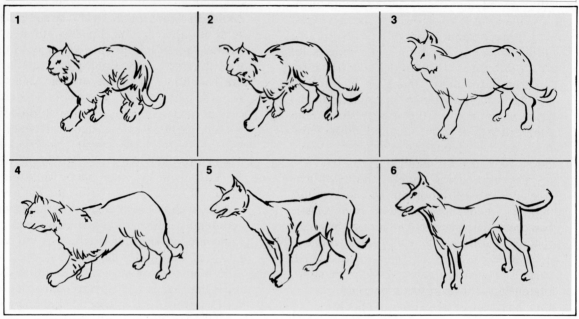

*Source:* Institute of Human Development. Berkeley, California.

spects. One needs to recognize subtle changes and avoid making hasty judgments when dealing with complex situations. Frenkel-Brunswik showed that authoritarian children find ambiguity hard to tolerate. She brought a number of children into her laboratory. Some of the children were prejudiced and some unprejudiced. (Prejudice is characteristic of authoritarian children and adults alike.) She showed each child a series of pictures, one after the other, in which a cat is shown changing gradually into a dog (see Figure 2.4). The child was asked to identify each picture when it was displayed. The prejudiced children continued to call the ambiguous animal a cat well after the other children had mentioned its dog-like characteristics.

## CONTENT ANALYSIS

Magazines, books, newspapers, and television programs are an important source of data about the ideas to which the public is exposed during a given period. Also, diaries and letters can be used to find out about the thoughts and experiences of individuals. With materials of this sort sociologists use a procedure called content analysis, in which they study representative samples of writing from a given period or by particular individuals in order to discover common or repeated themes.

In recent years, for example, many scholars studied the way sex roles are portrayed in children's stories. One such study, done by Lenore Weitzman and her associates, chose as its sample 18 books that had been winners or runners-up for the highest award in children's books during the preceding 5 years.[14] A total of 261 pictures of males appeared in those books, but only 23 pictures of females. In close to one-third of the books no women were mentioned at all. The few female characters who did appear in stories usually were unimportant, and all they were allowed to do was watch and help. Little boys were constantly doing things, but little girls wore frilly pink dresses and smiled a lot but could not cope very well. One little girl was pictured with a small dog that she could not control, while a little boy did not even need a leash to control his much bigger dog.

The portrayal of adults in the books studied showed the same pattern. Not a single woman in any of the books had a job. The researchers then compared two nonfiction books, called *What Boys Can Be* and *What Girls Can Be,* for a list of suggested jobs. Of the jobs for women, 11 are performed indoors and only 3 outdoors. Of the jobs for men, only 3 are done indoors while 11 are done outdoors. Several glamourous jobs are suggested for girls (e.g., movie star or model), but these are open only to pretty girls. A plain girl learns from these books that her role must be that of nurse, housewife, secretary, or the like.

This study did not try to show a causal relationship between what a child reads and what he or she becomes but was limited to a careful description of the content of children's books. The researchers simply assumed that books do influence children's views of themselves. However, other studies have shown that children's books have lasting psychological effects on their readers.

## Organizing the data and preparing a report

### PREPARING DATA FOR ANALYSIS

*Qualitative* research, whether the sociologist is reading historical documents or living with a group of people as a participant observer, consists of a set of personal impressions. The conclusions of qualitative research are not reached by counting events or comparing percentages in a table. Instead, they are based on the intuition of the scholar, who tries to be sensitive to the subject he or she is studying.

However, many of the research methods that we have discussed in this chapter are *quantitative.* That is, they are procedures by which the researcher either collects statistics calculated by governments or other agencies or gathers data that can be classified and counted. Whether data are obtained from questionnaires, laboratory experiments, content analysis of magazine articles, or even the birth and death dates shown on tombstones, the researcher has to sort the data into categories and compare the number of cases in various categories in order to reach conclusions.

Thus in quantitative research there is often a period after data have been collected during which the data are prepared for numerical analysis. This preparation may involve the following: coding the data into categories; transforming the coded data into a medium that can be read by a computer (keypunching); and preparing numerical indexes to use as indicators of independent or dependent variables.

Coding is the process by which raw answers are sorted into categories that can be tallied and counted. The most common form of coding is performed in survey analysis, in which large batches of questionnaires or interview sheets are obtained from samples that may number in the thousands. A coder will look at each questionnaire and, using a codebook, write a number representing each answer in a particular space on a sheet of paper. For example, in the space reserved for the respondent's sex the coder will probably mark a 1 if the respondent is male and a 2 if the respondent is female.

These papers (*coding sheets*) will then go to a keypunch operator, who makes a punched card for each case. In a survey a *case* is an individual respondent, but in other types of research each case may be a business firm, a city, a war, a magazine, and so on. A punched card has eighty columns, of which a few are reserved for the number of the case and the rest are used for the codes assigned by the coders. For example, column five may be designated as the space where each respondent's sex is recorded. The operator will punch either the 1 space (male) or the 2 space (female) of that column.

After one or more cards have been punched for each case, it will be the computer programer's turn to work on the research project. The programer will prepare a series of cards to precede and follow the data cards. These will tell the computer how to calculate the tables and statistics that the researcher needs.

Finally, before the theory can be tested the researcher may have to construct several indexes or scales for measuring variables. In our study of Beatlemania, for example, we made up two simple scales, one representing Beatlemania and the other representing self-doubt. These were ways of giving each respondent a score on both variables. Many research projects use scales that are far more complicated than the two in our example.

### CONSTRUCTING AND READING TABLES

Quantitative research depends largely on tables, which computers can produce in a fraction of a second. What takes time and attention is interpreting the tables once the computer has spewed them forth. The ability to read tables does not come automatically. Tables are compact ways of organizing information, and sometimes they are so complex that even experts must spend hours puzzling over them to grasp their implications. Here, however, we will stick to simple tables. Even if you never read another sociology book you will come across tables in magazines and books on many subjects, so it is worth your while to learn how to interpret them. I hope you will follow my reasoning closely throughout this section, even though it will not be the liveliest part of the book by any means.

Look again at Figures 2.2 and 2.3. For each variable, a given respondent will be assigned to one of three *values*—high, me-

## Punching Cards for the Computer

Although the Beatlemania study did not do so, many research projects use punched cards and electronic computers that produce tables and statistics very fast. The following illustration demonstrates how data can be prepared for computer processing. A questionnaire is coded according to the system that the research sets up. Each respondent (or case) will be assigned at least one computer card, and an identification number that is punched on the card. After the identification number, each item on the questionnaire is assigned to one or more columns, and the particular answer given by an individual will be shown by having a hole punched in a particular space within that column, according to the code that is established. Later, when these cards are put through the card reading machine, they all pass over tiny wire brushes that have electrical currents passing through them. When a hole is punched in a particular spot, the current can pass through there, and the computer's memory records precisely where each card was punched. The information will then be combined with data from other cards to yield complex tables or calculations. These will be printed by the computer's machinery and studied by sociologists. Here you can see a brief questionnaire that has been coded and the holes that would be punched on the corresponding card.

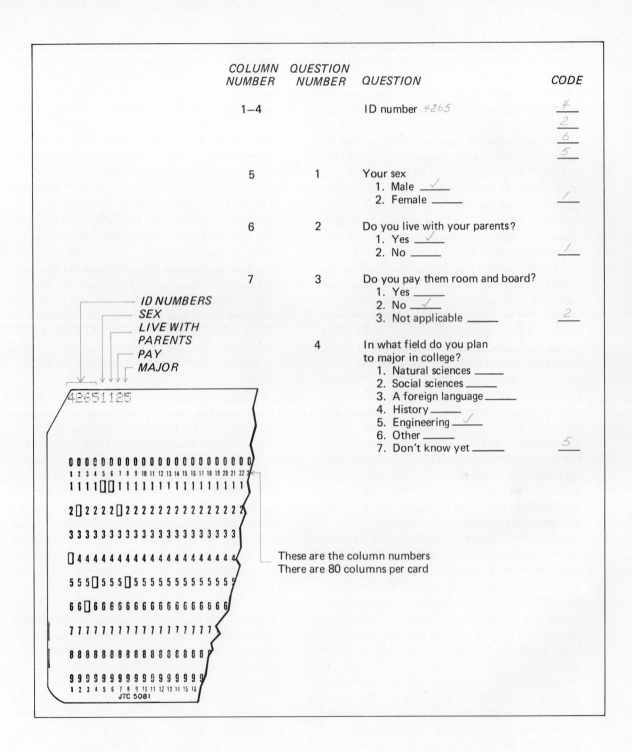

COLUMN NUMBER | QUESTION NUMBER | QUESTION | CODE

1–4 ........ ID number *4265* ........ *4* / *2* / *6* / *5*

5 ........ 1 ........ Your sex
  1. Male ✓
  2. Female ____ ........ *1*

6 ........ 2 ........ Do you live with your parents?
  1. Yes ✓
  2. No ____ ........ *1*

7 ........ 3 ........ Do you pay them room and board?
  1. Yes ____
  2. No ✓
  3. Not applicable ____ ........ *2*

........ 4 ........ In what field do you plan to major in college?
  1. Natural sciences ____
  2. Social sciences ____
  3. A foreign language ____
  4. History ____
  5. Engineering ✓
  6. Other ____
  7. Don't know yet ____ ........ *5*

ID NUMBERS
SEX
LIVE WITH PARENTS
PAY
MAJOR

42651125

These are the column numbers
There are 80 columns per card

JTC 5081

dium, or low on self-doubt and also on Beatlemania. A table shows the cross-classification of our respondents, so that each case will be counted in one of the nine possible cells, according to what value her answers take on both variables.

Most of the tables you will encounter will show either raw frequencies (numbers of cases), as in Figure 2.2, or percentages, as in Figure 2.3. Percentaged tables are always derived from frequency tables, just as we derived Figure 2.3 from Figure 2.2. Sometimes both the raw frequencies and the percentages are shown in the same table.

Notice that in Figures 2.2 and 2.3 the different values of the independent variable are found in different vertical *columns* while the values of the dependent variable are found in different horizontal *rows*. This is the most common way of displaying data, but it is not universal. Sometimes you will find the independent variable shown vertically (running from top to bottom) and the dependent variable shown horizontally (running from left to right). That does not really matter. What does matter is that whoever computes or reads the percentages must decide which variable is to be considered independent and which dependent. If one variable might have an effect on the other, assume that it is the independent variable. Sometimes this is very obvious because a cause cannot happen later in time than its effect. For example, in a table showing the relationship between sex and income, sex must be the independent variable. Sex might have an effect on income, but income could hardly have any effect on sex. Unfortunately, in some cases it is hard to figure out which variable is independent.

Remember this rule: *Always calculate percentages within categories of the independent variable and compare percentages across categories of the independent variable.* Look at Figures 2.2 and 2.3 again if you need to. Because the independent variable is in different columns, percentages are calculated *within columns.* That is, we divide each cell frequency by the total of its column to arrive at each cell percentage. In our examples, 11 divided by 153=7 percent, and so on for each of the nine cells. The percentages in all the cells of a given column should add up to 100 percent. Refer back to the description of our Beatles research if you aren't sure how the percentages are calculated.

Now let's interpret the results. Remember the rule? Because the values of our independent variable are in different columns, we compare the percentages within a given row *across columns,* horizontally. Thus reading across the top row tells us the percentages of students rating high on Beatlemania among those rating low, medium, and high on self-doubt. We see that 7 percent of those who are low, 31 percent of those who are medium, and 60 percent of those who are high on self-doubt score high on Beatlemania.

Suppose you come across a new table. How will you read it? First read the heading or title. It will usually name the variables and tell you what the numbers represent—probably numbers of cases (frequencies) or percentages. It may also reveal the source of the data and the year in which they were gathered. Next determine whether the values of the independent variable are displayed in columns and those of the dependent variable in rows, as is usually the case. Let us assume that this is true in this example. Read the headings labeling each column and each row. Then read the column totals, which will tell you the total number of cases of each value of the independent variable. In a table displaying percentages the column totals will often be presented in parentheses at either the top or the bottom of the table.

Only at this point should you proceed to read the interior cells of the table, always comparing across categories of the independent variable. In doing so you will be looking for differences by mentally subtracting one percentage or one number from another. If there is no causal relationship between the two variables, the percentages in different columns of the same row will be nearly the same — the difference between them may be about 5 percentage points but probably not much more. If the difference is very great — say, 40 or 50 percentage points — it may reveal a strong causal relationship between the two variables.

### Introducing Controls

By this time you can probably read most of the tables you will encounter. Now let's take a look at the logic behind a procedure that sociologists often use when they think they have found a causal relationship in a table. To check the relationship between the independent and dependent variables, researchers introduce a third variable and *control* it so that it cannot vary. A control, thus, is a variable that is held constant in order to check the apparent cause-and-effect relationship between two other variables. The following example, though a somewhat silly one, will help you see how controls are used.

George Bernard Shaw once made a curious observation: Men who wore top hats seemed to live longer than men who wore soft caps. Now let's pretend that we are taking this idea seriously and have made up a table that shows Shaw's observation to be correct.[15] I have made up an imaginary table to illustrate it. (See Figure 2.5).

In this example we display both the frequencies and the percentages in the same table. Remember that, because the independent variable is in columns, the percentages are obtained by dividing each cell frequency by the column total. Thus in the upper left-hand cell we divide 540 by 800 to obtain 67 percent.

Comparing percentages across the top row, we learn that 67 percent of the cap wearers die by age 60 while only 43 percent of the top-hat wearers die that young. The table seems to support Shaw's hypothesis. However, it is clear that the relationship

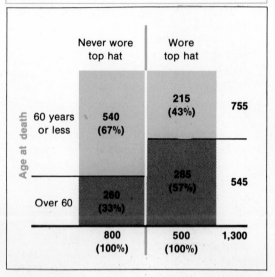

**FIGURE 2.5**

*Men's hat style by longevity: fictitious data (raw frequencies and percentages)*

between long life and hat style may be *spurious*. It is possible that the independent and dependent variables are both related to a variable that precedes both of them and is the true cause of long life. We know that in Shaw's day, at the turn of the century, the life span of poor people was much shorter than that of wealthy people, who had better food, shelter, medical care, and other comforts. Most poor men wore soft caps, and most rich men wore top hats. Maybe the true cause of long life was people's social class, not the hats they wore. Maybe the crucial factor was whether or not a person had much money.

How can we find out whether this is so? By preventing the suspected crucial variable from varying and then observing whether hat style and long life still vary together. In other words, we control *social class* so that it is *constant* and observe the relationship between the first two variables. Figure 2.6 shows what happens when we introduce social class as a control. But before you try to

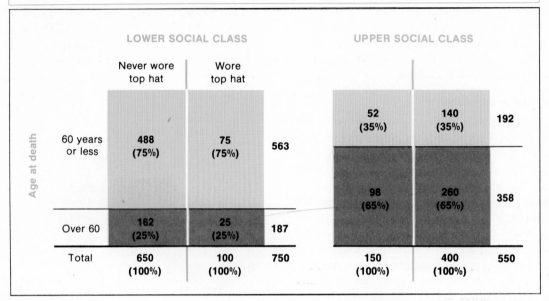

**FIGURE 2.6**

*Longevity by men's hat style and social class: fictitious data (raw frequencies and percentages*

interpret Figure 2.6 you should understand how the two new tables were derived.

The cases in Figure 2.6 are the same as the cases in Figure 2.5, except that they are sorted into more categories. For every man in our imaginary sample we know three facts—his age when he died, the type of hat he wore, and whether his social class was high or low. In Figure 2.5 we classified them only in terms of the independent variable (hat worn) and the dependent variable (age at death); now we also classify them in terms of a control (social class). We divide all cases in all cells into two new groups—those high in social class and those low in social class. Thus the 540 cases in the upper lefthand cell of Figure 2.5 are sorted into the upper left-hand cells of the two new tables: 488 of them go into the lower-social-class table and only 52 of them into the upper-social-class table. These two new tables are called *partials* because each of them is composed of only part of the original data. Notice that there are 750

cases in the lower-class partial and 550 cases in the upper-class partial. If we put them back together we would have 1300 cases as we do in Figure 2.5. The same goes for all the frequencies shown in the two partials. Both cell frequencies and marginal frequencies (i.e., totals) could be combined to obtain the numbers in Figure 2.5.

After we know the frequencies of the partials we can calculate the percentages for each one as before (e.g., 488 ÷ 650 =75%). We need the percentages in order to interpret the results.

Each partial shows the relationship between long life and hat style separately for part of the original collection of men—either the lower-class group or the upper-class group. *Within* each partial, however, social class is constant—it does not vary. One partial is lower class and the other is upper class; the classes do not mix. Among lower-class men, did those who wore top hats still live longer than those who did not? No, 75 percent of all lower-class men died by the age of 60, regardless of what they wore on their heads. Among upper-class men, did those who wore top hats live longer than those who did not? No, only 35 percent of the men died by age 60, regardless of their hat habits. That is, when we compare percentages in a given row across the columns in each partial in Figure 2.6, the percentage difference is zero in each case (75% − 75% = 0 and 35% − 35% = 0). In Figure 2.5 there was a large percentage difference (67% − 43% = 24%). We have found that the relationship between hat style and long life vanishes when we hold social class constant (or "control" for social class).

Why did our imaginary top-hat wearers live longer than other men? Not because of any special powers in the hat itself but only because they were richer than the other men. (Of the 500 top-hat wearers 400 were upper class, while of the 800 soft-cap wearers only 150 were upper class.) The few men who were rich but did not wear top hats lived just as long as the rich men who did wear top hats. On the other hand, a few lower-class men (100 of them) somehow obtained top hats and wore them, but this did not increase their life span, poor chaps. Social class made a lot of difference in life span; hat style made no difference at all. The apparent effect of hat style on life span was *spurious*; in other words, it disappears when we control for the real cause, which actually helps determine hat-wearing habits.

The tables dealing with hat styles were all made up to come out the way we wanted them to come out. The idea was to make the notion of spuriousness obvious. Most of the time the reason for controlling a third variable is that the researcher suspects that a relationship may be spurious and wants to determine whether this is the case. If the original relationship still holds within each partial (that is, if the differential between the percentages does not decrease markedly or disappear), the relationship is not spurious.

Like many students, you may find that you need to go over this section several times and practice reading other tables. You will notice that most tables are not divided into neat little cells. I have done this in order to make it easier for you to see how the rows and columns are related. You will also quickly discover that all tables are not meant to test a causal relationship between an independent variable and a dependent one. Some tables merely present statistical information in an organized form.

**THE RESEARCH REPORT**

After the researcher has analyzed the data he or she will usually write a report. A professional sociologist always hopes to have his or her report published, either as a book or as an article in a journal. Students' research reports usually take the form of term papers, presented to the instructor of a course, or theses, presented to meet degree requirements. Whatever the purpose of the report, it must be as clear as possible.

In a report the researcher should do the following things:

1 Explain the problem the study is trying to solve.
2 Discuss the research procedures, such as how the sample was selected and what sources of data were used.
3 Explain the results.
4 Suggest the conclusions that may be based on the results. Also, mention any questions that remain unanswered and that seem to call for more research in the same area.[16]

## Evaluations research

During the past ten years or so a large and increasing part of the research done by social scientists has been for the purpose of evaluating the results of various public policies. Many government agencies, as well as a few private philanthropic foundations, regularly support projects designed to find out how successful various programs have been in solving social problems. Thus whenever a new law is proposed to improve some shortcoming of group life, a study or studies may be done either before or after the law is passed. Thus in education the Head Start program has been studied by a number of researchers. The effects of busing children from one school to another for the sake of achieving racial balance is another topic that has been evaluated by social scientists. Researchers may be asked to find out whether one system of welfare or medical care is better than other possible systems. Or whether watching violence on TV makes kids more aggressive. Or whether outpatient treatment of mental patients should be preferred over hospital care. And so on.

Research of this kind goes beyond ordinary scientific puzzle solving. It involves political decision making. The researcher knows that he or she is directly involved in the policy-making process. Indeed, it is not unusual for congressional committees to use sociological research as evidence for or against a proposed law. A research report prepared for this purpose is always oriented very much toward the fourth item in the list just presented: It is designed to suggest the implications of the research and the questions that remain unanswered and call for more research.

## SUMMARY

**1.** Social researchers are scientists in that they try to arrive at generalizations. A *causal theory* is a statement that two or more different elements are regularly linked together.

**2.** A case study is an in-depth study of a single case of a particular phenomenon. A case study cannot serve as a basis for generalizations. One needs to compare more than one case (and preferably many) to find out how they are similar and how they are different.

**3.** *Theories* are generalizations that make sense of known facts. They also produce new hypotheses that, in turn, call for the collection of new evidence so that the facts can be checked empirically, that is, through experience. Thus there is a constant interplay between theory and empirical investigation.

**4.** Whatever a theory assumes to be a possible cause of a phenomenon is called the *independent variable*. Whatever is assumed to be its possible effect is called the *dependent variable*.

**5.** Social scientists do not usually observe physical phenomena; instead, they study abstract variables such as attitudes, urbanization, population size and suicide rates. They must use *indicators* to represent those variables. And they must be aware of the possibility that their indicators may not be *valid*—that they may not truly represent what they want to measure.

**6.** Another problem is that of obtaining representative data. We want to generalize about a whole population on the basis of the facts that we discover about a limited, but typical, *sample* of that population; if the sample is not typical, our generalizations will be incorrect.

**7.** Successful generalizations about regular relationships among two or more variables allow the social scientist to improve his or her *predictions*. Scientific predictions take the form, If X occurs then there is a high probability that Y will occur.

**8.** Social data come from many sources. Written and graphic *documents* and *official statistics* are often used. In addition, many researchers use *interviews* and *questionnaires,* either in small, informal studies or in large, standardized surveys that may obtain data from hundreds of thousands of respondents. Some researchers carry out *participant observation;* others do *laboratory experiments,* mostly with small groups and individuals. Another method of obtaining evidence is *content analysis,* in which documents, books, magazines, TV programs, and the like are studied in an attempt to find common or repeated themes.

**9.** After quantitative data have been collected they must be prepared for analysis. This often involves *coding* (sorting the data into categories, often giving each category a numerical value) and *keypunching* (putting the coded data on punched cards that can be read by computers). Sometimes scales or other indexes must be prepared for use as indicators of variables.

**10.** The researcher must often construct and read tables. Sometimes tables are used to determine whether there is a causal relationship between two variables. If a relationship does show up, the researcher sometimes introduces *controls* to find out whether the apparent relationship is spurious. That is, two variables may be linked not because one is the cause of the other but because both are associated with some other (antecedent) variable, which is the true cause of the dependent variable. When a relationship is spurious it will be greatly reduced or will disappear in partial tables when the antecedent variable is introduced as a control.

**11.** When you are constructing tables, always calculate percentages *within* categories of the independent variable. When you are reading tables always compare percentages *across* categories of the independent variable.

## KEY TERMS

**case study** an in-depth investigation of a single case of a given phenomenon.

**coding** the process by which raw answers are sorted into categories that can be tallied and counted.

**content analysis** the study of representative samples of writing from a given period or by particular individuals in order to discover common or repeated themes.

**control** a variable that is held constant in order to check the apparent cause-and-effect relationship between two other variables.

**dependent variable** a variable that is assumed to be the effect of an independent variable.

**detached observation** observation in which the researcher watches what is going on without getting involved.

**experiment** a study of groups or individuals carried out in an environment controlled by the researcher.

**frequency** a number that shows the total of items in a given category.

**generalization** a statement that applies to a whole class of similar events.

**hypothesis** a specific prediction that may be verified by empirical findings.

**independent variable** a variable that is assumed to be the cause of a dependent variable.

**indicator** a concrete representation of an abstract variable.

**participant observation** observation in which the researcher takes some role within the group being observed.

**population** the whole number of units from which a sample is drawn.

**questionnaire** a printed list of questions given to respondents to answer themselves.

**quota sampling** sampling in which the percentage of people with a given characteristic is equal to the percentage of such people in the whole population.

**random sampling** sampling in which every member of the population has an equal chance of being chosen as part of the sample.

structured interview  an interview that uses a standard list of questions.

theory  a statement based on observed facts that explains what is supposed to be a causal relationship between those facts.

unstructured interview  an interview in which the respondent is asked questions that lead to an open and spontaneous discussion of the topic.

validity  the ability of an indicator to genuinely and accurately represent the variable that it is meant to represent.

variable  a characteristic that changes among situations, individuals, or groups and can be measured.

# FOR FURTHER READING

DAVIS, JAMES A. *Elementary Survey Analysis.* Englewood Cliffs, N.J.: Prentice-Hall, 1971. This little paperback does a fine job in a very readable way. It is the most painless way I know for learning to understand tables and why particular variables should or should not be introduced as controls.

DENZIN, NORMAN K. *Sociological Methods: a Sourcebook.* New York: McGraw-Hill, 1978 (2nd ed.) This set of essays has been collected by a sociologist who prefers participant observation over techniques that emphasize counting and making tables. It is therefore very different from the book by Davis.

HAMMOND, PHILLIP E., ed. *Sociologists at Work: Essays on the Craft of Social Research.* New York: Basic Books, 1964. This will not teach you how to do research in any systematic way, but it does give you a chance to attend dress-rehearsals and hang around backstage. Several different sociologists present accounts of the problems they ran into and how they reformulated their problems along the way in the course of the research. It even gives an account of a research project that turned out to be a flop, producing hardly anything publishable.

LABOVITZ, STANFORD, and ROBERT HAGEDORN. *Introduction to Social Research.* New York: McGraw-Hill, 1971. This is another slim paperback that gently inducts you into the matters discussed in this chapter. It would be a good thing to pick up and read on your own because it is simple enough to get through without a teacher's help. You can do it in an evening.

MADGE, JOHN. *The Origins of Scientific Sociology.* New York: Free Press, 1962. Madge summarizes the logic underlying several landmark studies. Along the way, you will pick up a certain sophistication that will help you plan research of your own, if that is what you are after. This reads easily, too, though I don't think you can do it in one evening.

MICHELSON, WILLIAM, ed. *Behavioral Research Methods in Environmental Design.* Stroudsburg, Pa.: Dowden, Hutchinson & Ross, 1975. This book encourages practical, useful research projects.

SELLTIZ, CLAIRE; MARIE JAHODA; MORTON DEUTSCH; and STUART W. COOK. *Research Methods in Social Relations.* New York: Holt, Rinehart & Winston, 1959. This is the text I was "brought up on" as an undergraduate, and it is still good, meaty reading. Because it is so thorough, you would do well to head for it when you need a reference book for some particular methodological problem—how to do interviews, say, or how to plan an experiment with a control group.

WEBB, EUGENE J., ET AL. *Unobtrusive Measures: Nonactive Research in the Social Sciences.* Chicago: Rand McNally, 1966. This paperback gives lots of examples of offbeat research that use strange and imaginative sources of data. It is a delight to read, whether you plan to do research or not.

# ONE
# the individual in society

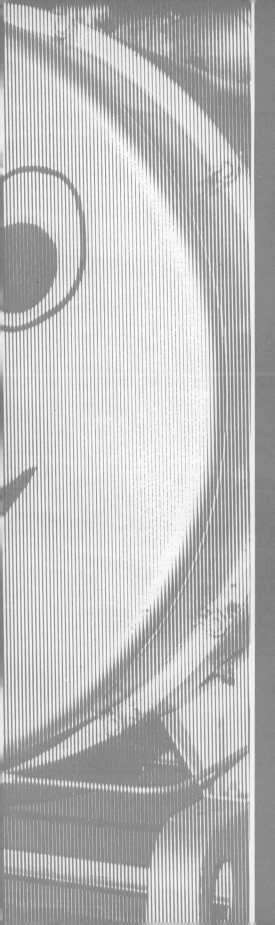

# CULTURE

One evening not long ago I had three conversations in which the world *culture* was used, and each of the people I was talking to seemed to mean something slightly different from the others. In the first conversation I was listening to Ada, a rather round blonde woman who had recently become engaged to a Muslim engineer and seemed anxious about living in the Middle East. But at one point her mood brightened and she said, "Anyway, I won't have to be constantly on a diet anymore. In Arab culture men prefer women to be fleshy. And I certainly am that!" Ada was referring to Arab culture as a *normative system*—a set of expectations about how people should look and act.

My second conversation was with Sam, a young man who had recently spent a year abroad. He was describing the Italian family with whom he had lived in Florence. "They were so cultured!" he exclaimed. "Every dinner conversation was about Donatello or Dante or some string quartet. I wasn't used to such highbrow discussions, and I learned a lot from them." By *cultured* Sam meant what we might call "Culture with a capital C," that is, the finest arts and traditions of a high civilization. In this sense culture is primarily an *expressive system*.

The third conversation was with two sociologists who were arguing loudly about the Hindu taboo against eating beef. Zoltan claimed that religion was preventing India from modernizing. In India he has seen lots of scrawny cows that no longer gave milk but would provide protein if people would eat them. Karen, on the other hand, argued that a taboo against eating beef makes sense in India, where wood is so scarce that cow dung is an essential source of fuel for fires. She pointed out that even old cows sometimes have calves, and this makes them valuable because their male calves become oxen, which are essential for ploughing the fields. Furthermore, she denied that religion is the real reason why Hindus refuse to eat beef. "For one thing, there is evidence that no matter what they claim to do, lots of Hindu farmers manage to get rid of their old cows when it is really advantageous for them to do so. Besides, religion is a cultural explanation, and I'm always suspicious of cultural explanations," she added. "I believe there is generally a good practical reason, in material terms, for a society's traditions. Many of the people may not *know* the reason, and they may tell you they are simply observing their religious customs, so you have to look at the social structure to find out the real explanation."

In making this distinction between culture and social structure, Karen meant something by the word *culture* that neither Sam nor Ada had meant. She was thinking of culture as a *system of ideas*, as a set of values that people claim to believe in but that may be quite different from what they actually do.

Thus the world *culture* has at least three somewhat different meanings. Most people use it in all three ways from time to time, but it is probably fair to say that in the humanities it is usually used to refer to an expressive system. In anthropology it often is used to refer to a normative system, but in sociology it commonly (but not always) is used to refer to a system of ideas. These meanings differ from each other only slightly, of course, but let's define **culture** as a system of ideas, values, beliefs, knowledge, and customs transmitted from generation to generation within a social group.

## Elements of culture

As a biological organism, the human being compares rather poorly to a number of other beasts. We can neither swim as well as fish nor run as fast as horses nor kill as efficiently as tigers nor swing through the trees as gracefully as monkeys. Trait by trait, we are inferior to some other animal. However, we are more flexible mentally and

Robert W. Young/DPI

*Japanese culture has traditionally emphasized the value of visual beauty. Their codes of artistic expression have encouraged simplicity and naturalness. You may know people who would prefer a dozen plastic daisies because they last longer. (Western values emphasize the practical side of things.)*

physically than other animals. A human being can perform more different kinds of physical activities than other animals and can take advantage of a wider range of opportunities in the natural environment. Our species has been able to master the many environments of the earth better than any other species, and we pass along this mastery from one generation to the next by means of culture.

Probably the best-known definition of culture was proposed by an early British anthropologist, Sir Edward Tylor, who called it "that complex whole which includes knowledge, belief, art, morals, law, custom, and any other capabilities and habits acquired by man as a member of society."[1] A culture is a growing, living tradition. We each contribute a small part to the historical tradition on which our daily life is based. Over time a society develops values, symbols, folklore, myths, laws, religions, and ideals that may differ greatly from those of the people who live across the river or beyond the mountains.

## SYMBOLS

Culture is made up of ideas. These ideas exist in symbolic form. A symbol is anything that represents something else, anything that has meaning. Language is a system of symbols. Through language human beings are able to share their experiences and fantasies with others and even to describe their thoughts about possible future experiences. For this to happen the words and other symbols used by the speaker must mean the same thing to the listener that they do to the speaker. Symbols must be shared for the members of a group to share a culture.

## VALUES

A cultural value is something that is widely believed within a given collectivity to be desirable for its own sake. Values are the standards used to judge behavior and to choose among various possible goals. They are ideas that are shared by the group. When as a child you complained about having to make your bed, your parents probably justified their demand in the name of neatness, a value they taught you to take for granted.

Of course some societies value neatness more than others. Cultures differ a great deal in their emphasis on honesty, politeness, equality, self-reliance, reverence for God, democracy, and other values. Beauty is an important value to the Japanese. Masculine bravery is emphasized in Spanish culture. Politeness is stressed in Java more than in Europe or North America. Javanese personal relationships tend to be more formal than would seem "natural" to Westerners.

### NORMS

Norms are rules that tell people how to behave in particular situations. They are more specific than values and must be justified in terms of one or more values. For example, the norm against cheating on examinations is justified by a cultural value, fairness. Values are abstract ideals. But it is not enough to tell people to be guided by their love of beauty, truth, fairness, and the like. We need concrete norms as well—norms that tell us what behavior to consider fair and what unfair, what to consider beautiful and what ugly, and so on. We learn these standards of behavior as parts of our culture.

### FOLKLORE

All societies, from the most primitive to the most advanced, have an oral tradition or folklore, a collection of jokes, superstitions, lullabies, old wives' tales, slang words, ghost stories, and the like. Folklore is often very old. Some children's jump-rope rhymes date

back to medieval England (e.g., "I saw Esau sawing wood, And Esau saw I saw him; Though Esau saw I saw him saw, still Esau went on sawing"). You know far more folklore than you may think. How often do you break a wishbone with a friend or recite under your breath, "Thirty days hath September . . ."? Myths, too, are part of folklore. What Western child does not know Santa's reindeer by name or has not received a coin from the tooth fairy? (In France a mouse performs the tooth fairy's duties.) All of these traditions are part of culture.

### LAW

Primitive societies maintain order by means of informal procedures and customs. Modern societies, however, more often do this by means of law. But laws, if they are to be obeyed, must be justified by cultural values. Speed limits, for example, are justified in the name of safety, a shared value. Thus the laws and customs of a society are part of its culture.

### IDEOLOGY

An ideology is a doctrine that is used to justify a group's actions in pursuing its own interests. For example, in Chapter 1 we mentioned Social Darwinism, a theory of social evolution suggesting that the protection of weak individuals from economic competition would weaken the human population as a whole. Today most of us would call this belief an ideology. That is, it helped the rich capitalists feel less guilty about exploiting the workers for profit. (It is likely that very few Social Darwinists were poor.) Not all ideologies are complex systems of philosophy, however; they may be short phrases such as "Finders keepers, losers weepers" or "The Lord helps those who help themselves."

# Three views of culture

Let's return now to the three conversations mentioned earlier and the three ways of looking at culture that they illustrate. Probably what comes to mind most often when social scientists think about culture is that people are expected to conform to it. This is what Ada had in mind when she happily anticipated being freed from the North American requirement that women stay slim. Every cultural system is *normative;* that is, it contains strong requirements as to what one must and must not do. The American sociologist William Graham Sumner introduced two important terms to the study of culture as a normative system. The fairly trivial norms or conventions shared by members of a society he termed folkways; the really important ethical rules he termed mores.[2]

Folkways are conventions such as style of clothing, dietary habits, and manners. If, for example, you went to school wearing the grass skirt and shark-tooth necklace of a New Guinean tribesman, you would have violated a folkway. You might have to take a lot of teasing, but you probably wouldn't be punished. One should not talk or fidget during a church service. One should not comb one's hair at the dinner table. One should not rip coupons out of magazines in a public library. These norms are all folkways, and a person who fails to conform to them may be thought of as thoughtless or crude, but not as a criminal or a sinner.

Mores, by contrast, are moral rules such as the prohibition of murder, theft, rape, incest, and the like. These are rules about which all the members of a society share

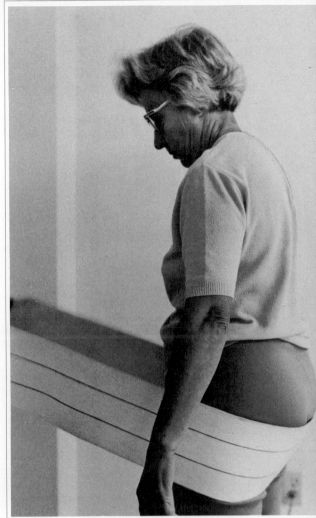

Burk Uzzle/Magnum Photos

*Still trying. Western culture demands that women keep slim.*

strong feelings. Those who violate them must pay a heavy penalty. However, even mores may differ greatly from one society to another. For example, in some early societies adultery was a crime that was punishable by death, whereas in others, such as the Eskimo, a host must offer his guest the opportunity to have sexual relations with his wife. Failure to make such an offer would be an insult to the guest.

### Social control

What happens when someone violates a norm? Some other member of the group will punish the offender. The punishment helps persuade others to follow the norm that was violated. This process is called social control. The members of a group support desired forms of behavior and discourage undesired forms. They do this by means of sanctions—actions that reward conformity to norms or punish nonconformity. An icy stare and a firing squad are both social sanctions. Both are tools of social control in that people try to behave in such a way that they will not have to face either stares or a firing squad.

Most of us do not conform to cultural norms simply because they are backed up by sanctions. We usually live up to them even when nobody would know if we had violated them. We do not sense norms as burdensome rules that we would like to resist. Instead, we usually want to conform to them. We make them part of our personality; we feel responsible for them, as if we had invented them ourselves. There could never be enough police officers to enforce the laws if everyone wanted to break them. Law and order are possible in a society only because most of the time people police themselves.

### Cultural relativism

We have already mentioned that the norms that apply in one society may not apply in another. This is easy to grasp when reading a textbook, but it is not always so easy to accept in real life, as many anthropologists can tell you from personal experience. It's all in a day's work for field researchers to visit a headhunter or a voodoo priestess, and these researchers use the term culture shock to describe the anxiety they feel while they are adjusting to the norms of other cultures. We learn in our own society not only how things are done but also how they should be done. If we learn the lesson well, we believe in it. Belief in the superiority of one's own traditions is normal.

We tend to judge other ways of life by the standards of our own group—a habit that is called ethnocentrism. For example, an ethnocentric person may believe that Muslim men who marry several wives are "weird," "sick," "sinful," or at best "ill advised." An ethnocentric Westerner may laugh at the Hindu taboo against eating beef, and the ethnocentric Chinese may laugh at the Westerner's unwillingness to eat dogs. The ethnocentric European may be amused by the Indian custom of eating with the fingers, while the ethnocentric Indian may be embarrassed for a European who is so ill mannered as to touch food with his or her left hand. The ethnocentric person is showing a prejudice that comes from believing too much in the norms of his or her own group.

Although such prejudice is normal for people whose social world is isolated from other cultures, those who overcome it develop a broader outlook on life. Many studies have shown that highly ethnocentric people tend to be harsh, rigid, and unable to deal with ambiguity or complexity. Fortunately, education tends to reduce ethnocentrism, and the social sciences play an important role in this process because they compare different cultures as objectively as possible.

Social scientists usually avoid saying that a given tradition is "good" or "bad." Instead, they say that it is "well adapted" or "poorly adapted" to the habits and needs of a particular society. In ancient China the feet of high-status females were kept tightly bound from early childhood. This resulted in small, deformed feet that the Chinese saw as beautiful. This practice fit in with the restrained life style idealized by many Chinese, to whom tiny feet were a status symbol, living proof that the family could afford idleness and leisure, for clearly no woman with such feet could be very active. In modern China such a practice would be unthinkable because the cultural values of the Chinese

Revolution stress equality and productivity, not leisure and social status. Thus to understand a custom such as foot binding we must understand other aspects of the culture in which it is found.

The folkways and mores of various parts of the world are so different that it would be easy to conclude that there is no rule that is universally recognized by all societies. This is not the case, however. All societies frown on incest, lying, stealing, and violence within the in-group and on failure to maintain some control over one's impulses. These standards of behavior are universal.

An anthropologist who goes to live with a remote tribe usually decides to leave his or her own morality at home as much as possible and to live by the code of the tribe. This does not mean that he or she will approve of any act performed by a member of the tribe, for there will be deviant acts there too. It does mean that the anthropologist will judge tribal behavior in terms of the tribe's normative system, not his or her own. This policy is called cultural relativism. It is based on the assumption that all cultures are equally valid and that any culture deserves respect. An act that is immoral in one culture may be moral in another. But it is meaningless to ask which culture is "right," for all are equally "right." The only way of judging a particular culture is by using standards that are themselves part of *some* culture. According to cultural relativists, any attempt to judge one culture by the standards of another is sheer ethnocentrism. This is an important issue, and we will return to it in the section on social policy at the end of this chapter.

### CULTURE AS AN EXPRESSIVE SYSTEM

When my friend Sam described his Florentine hosts as "cultured" he had in mind a particular range of activities—music, literature, dance, art, and the like—that are enjoyed for their own sake, not as a means to some other end. Every society has developed a variety of practices that break the monotony of day-to-day living, providing for pageantry, collective excitement, and other meaningful experiences. Such expressive events may be stylized rituals—for example, the Japanese tea ceremony or the changing of the guard at Buckingham Palace—or periods of excitement when self-control can be relaxed—such as a bullfight, a carnival, or a drunken orgy.

Societies differ greatly in the expressive events that they encourage. When a group of young people get together to create a cultural event, they follow the traditions of their community in planning the activity, whether it is a rodeo or a chamber music concert. One community may have only a small range of simple events to choose from; another may have a wide variety of complex activities that can be mastered only after long training.

When we speak of "culture" as an expressive system we are not usually referring to such events as drunken orgies or pie-eating contests (although these are, I will grant, expressive activities of a sort). Rather, we are thinking mainly of the arts, which require a certain amount of training of the participants.

### Artistic expression as a code

All art is a social experience. This may sound like a strange statement, because after all one can listen to records or paint a landscape when one is entirely alone. Some artists live like hermits and are uncomfortable at parties or club meetings. Nevertheless all art is made by human beings who are influenced by the art made by other human beings. Art is a symbolic activity, a way of communicating an inner experience. It is obvious that one must learn to paint and that learning is a social experience. But it may not be so obvious that one must also learn to *see* paintings and to *hear* music. Of course all of us can focus our eyes on a picture, but we may not get much out of it. As a way of communicating, an art form uses what we will call a code. Code making is a human activity that develops naturally in the context of social experience. You may have invented your first picture code when at the age of three you drew a circle around two dots and a U-shaped smiling mouth and called it "Mommy." Think of a code as a grammar or set of rules that may be passed along from one generation to the next. The rules for the game of chess are a code that dates back 1000 years or more. When you play the piano you can use 88 keys, no more, and when you play any given piece of music you use only certain combinations of those keys because the Western codes of musical composition rely on the use of scales, or sets of tones that we think sound pleasant together. When you hear Indian singing for the first time you may think it sounds like a cat in pain because you will not understand a code that permits the voice to slide around between tones.

A creative composer, painter, or poet is one who knows how to use his or her chosen code to the fullest. Of course only an audience that understands the code will be able to appreciate the artist's achievement. I have become somewhat familiar with Indian music and greatly enjoy it, but I still cannot tell whether a singer is performing well or poorly. I simply don't yet know the code that well. It is only through long training that we develop our own understanding and appreciation of the code.

Each period or style of art is, in a sense, a game. Just as you can play many different card games with the same deck of cards, depending on what set of rules (or code) you follow, so too there are many styles of art that can be played with the same brushes and tubes of paint. "Primitive" painters like Grandma Moses follow a code that pays little attention to perspective but requires the picture to represent something real—a landscape, perhaps, or animals or human figures. On the other hand, the code of cubism does not represent an object realistically but may

present it as if it were being seen from several angles at once. The late American painter Jackson Pollock used to paint by dribbling colors straight from the can onto the canvas. The game he invented was a code that we might call "Let's-see-what-kind-of-interesting-patterns-we-can-make-with-dribbles." That's ok. Any set of rules is ok. However, some codes have more possibilities than others. Pollock went about as far with dribble art as anybody is likely to go. On the other hand, the complex and difficult styles of the Renaissance required many years of training and contained possibilities that were not exhausted by any single artist.

### Publics

Every artist creates or performs for some audience. In some preindustrial societies every adult is probably able to understand and appreciate all the art that is produced in that society. Wherever culture is uniform the same artistic codes are shared by all the members of the society. However, our society is characterized by *cultural pluralism*, in which a number of very different codes are used by different artists. Consider music. We hear punk rock and Wagnerian opera, New Orleans jazz and barbershop quartets, bluegrass and concertos for oboe and kazoo. Nobody could possibly understand all those codes, so we specialize. You may say, for example, that you are "into" Led Zeppelin or (less probably) Lawrence Welk. You are then part of a particular public—a group of people who specialize in enjoying a common code of musical expression.

Some codes are harder to learn than others. *Hamlet* is harder to read than a James Bond novel. It requires more of the reader—more attention, more homework, more vocabulary, and so on. And over the years most readers who have learned to appreciate *Hamlet* have agreed that it was worth their effort.

Thus it seems fair to compare publics in terms of the complexity of the codes they understand. This is why we sometimes speak of "highbrow," "middlebrow," and "lowbrow" tastes. If you subscribe to the *New York Review of Books, Partisan Review,* or any glossy art magazine and if you often go to chamber music concerts, poetry readings, and late-night showings of film classics like *Children of Paradise,* you are a highbrow. You can make your own list of standards for middlebrows and lowbrows.

Sometimes we speak of publics as supporting either "high culture" or "popular culture." The term *popular* or *mass culture* refers to artistic codes that are not difficult to understand. Often these are products of the mass media and are enjoyed by millions of people as a form of relaxation. Magazines, TV quiz shows, and popular music are examples of popular culture.

One public may be uninterested in or even hostile to the codes understood and enjoyed by another public. Thus people who have a taste for popular culture may call the high-culture public "snobbish" or "phony." And members of the high-culture public may call popular-culture fans "uncultured"— though only behind their backs. (One does not say such things in public these days.) Yet people who like popular culture and mass media entertainment may be very critical of art that employs the codes that they understand; for example, they may recognize the difference between a good James Bond novel and a bad one. To do that is to be "cultured" according to that particular code.

Instead of calling people "uncultured," it is a little more polite to refer to them as "culturally deprived." This unfortunate term implies that the "deprived" group or person is a clod who cannot do or appreciate anything that is excellent. Of course the understanding and enjoyment of great music, literature, drama, ballet, and so on is a splendid human achievement. If you have had an opportunity to learn how to conduct symphonies, you are very lucky. Furthermore, if familiarity with the codes of high cultures is a gift that some people receive, then obviously other people are deprived of it, and I suppose it is fair to call them "culturally deprived." However, some "deprived" people are brilliantly creative in the codes with which they *are* familiar. Much primitive art, for example, is marvelous. Thus to be "deprived" of high culture is not necessarily to be uncultured. Not at all.

The culturally sophisticated person is familiar with a variety of different codes of expression. This familiarity enriches his or her experience and adds to the pleasures of daily life. We are not underplaying the importance of high culture when we add that popular culture is ok too. In short, great art is great, but lots of ordinary things are nice too.

## CULTURE AS A SYSTEM OF IDEAS

When you hear the word *culture* you will probably be correct 90 percent of the time if you interpret it as referring to normative and/or expressive traditions. However, you should be aware that sociologists sometimes use the term in a narrower sense, as Karen was using it in her argument with Zoltan about the Indian taboo against eating beef.

When we speak of the culture of a group, we have in mind both its customary *practices* and the *ideas* that guide those practices. We don't normally need to distinguish the practices from the ideas. However, some sociologists do make this distinction. Talcott Parsons, for instance, believes that a culture is a world view acquired by a person as a member of his or her society—the system of ideas, the symbols that enable him or her to interpret the world meaningfully. Culture gives us an idea of our place in history, our relationship to nature, to a God or gods, and to the universe. It stresses some values over others, thereby providing the principles on which a specific set of social patterns is based. Parsons distinguishes between the culture and the social system, or the roles and *actual practices* that exist among members of social groups. Thus he would be careful to distinguish between the *role* of a painter (which is part of the social system) and the painter's *knowledge* about art (which is part of the cultural system). The social system is what people do; the cultural system is the set of ideas that they share.

Obviously there is a close relationship between the two systems. The culture controls and shapes the social system. People form relationships and organizations that are guided by the general values and ideas that they all share.

### Culture and social structure

The process through which the culture influences the social system is called institutionalization. It translates general values into the specific norms that directly govern the actions of the members of a group. For example, one of the values or ideas shared by members of Western culture today is intellectual ability. As a result, we have institutionalized certain practices for the purpose of creating and maintaining intellectual ability as widely as possible. These practices are carried out in schools and universities. And within the university we have institutionalized a number of specific norms of behavior, such as the requirement that you do your own work without cheating. Most of our everyday activities are institutionalized aspects of our roles. These activities are part of the social system and can be distinguished from our values and ideas, which are part of the cultural system.

Many, if not most, sociologists agree with Parsons that the social system is controlled by the cultural system—that people live largely according to their ideas about what is desirable and good. Not all sociologists do agree to this, however. Some point out, quite sensibly, that we can't always live up to our ideals. The conditions in which we live do not always give us the chance to meet those standards. These sociologists therefore look for what they call "structural" explanations for social events, that is, the opportunities and limitations that people have to adjust to. When people are trying to solve a problem they ask such questions as, What materials are available? Who is around to help us? Are they willing to cooperate? If not, do we have ways of forcing them to help? What would we have to give up if we used all our time and materials to carry out this project? Will this solution create worse problems for us in the long run? And so on. To answer such questions you don't worry about the cultural system. Rather, you are concerned with the social system that *now exists*—the *social structure*—and with the opportunities for and limitations on future action contained in that structure. This is the point that Karen was insisting on when she claimed that Hindus have good practical reasons for prohibiting the slaughter of cows for beef. Zoltan, on the other hand, thought this particular norm could be explained by the cultural system of India—the Hindu religion.[3]

In that particular argument I tend to agree with Karen that Indian society might lose more than it would gain if Hindus gave up the taboo on beef. But on the broader issue I cannot agree with her. Of course the cultural system shapes the social system. And of course it does not completely determine the social system. This argument seems to me to be about the same as arguing over whether people do what they would like to do or what they have a chance to do. Obviously, they do what they would like to do. (They act on the basis of their ideas, their culture.) And obviously they cannot do everything that they would like to do. (Their opportunities are limited by reality, which includes the existing social structure.)

Institutionalization is the bridge linking the cultural system and the social system. Our beliefs and ideas shape our actions. It is by establishing regular patterned ways of doing things (i.e., institutionalizing a practice) that we turn our shared ideas into shared habits, customs, organizations, and so on. These common shared arrangements constitute the social system or the social structure (for most purposes the two terms can be used interchangeably). Through institutionalization our cultural system shapes our social system.

## Technology

Every society institutionalizes certain practical techniques for mastering its environment and controlling nature. This is technology. We can define **technology** as the institutionalized application of knowledge to control nature for human uses. It includes the skills, materials, methods, and social structures that make it possible for us to maintain a given standard of living. Primitive tribes have a very simple technology because their knowledge is limited. But modern societies, having a cultural system that includes knowledge about physics, physiology, and the like, have institutionalized a number of social structures to control nature by building dams, splitting atoms, repairing heart valves, and so forth. The worldwide telephone system is one example of modern technology. It involves the regular use of knowledge in the social relations of millions of people every day. Thus the cultural system (which includes such knowledge as the principles of electronic engineering) has been institutionalized, creating a complex social structure—the telephone system.

Technology differs from expressive systems such as the arts, religion, and sports in this way: It improves and develops. It is cumulative. This is not so with the arts. Many cave paintings would be praised as great works of art even if they were painted today. However, the technology of cave dwellers was far inferior to that of even the most backward twentieth-century nations.

The difference is that painting is primarily an expressive activity. Within any type of art some works will be better than others. When it comes to rock operas, I think *Godspell* is superior to *Tommy*. However, rock operas do not become better and better as more are written. If a good one is written, other composers will not necessarily learn from it and write better ones. Composing as a skill does not make steady progress the way technology does. Indeed, it is harder to judge expressive cultural forms than it is to judge technology. Artistic standards are more open to disagreement—for example, you may think *Tommy* is better than *Godspell*.

*It's easy to tell whether a new product works better than the old one. Technology keeps improving, but does technology improve a society? How do you suppose photography has made this African tribesman's life different from his grandfather's?*

Jerry Frank/DPI

With technology we are on firmer ground, for we judge technology in terms of *efficiency*. Technology is used to satisfy some human need, and it is usually possible to tell whether a new method is more efficient than the old one. The old method will usually be replaced by the new one. This is not necessarily true for expressive activities such as art, religion, sports, or drama. After Pablo Picasso and Henri Matisse had radically changed the style of modern painting, many painters, such as Andrew Wyeth, went right on painting realistic landscapes that were almost 100 years "out of date" but still had great artistic value. In contrast, when the Sabin polio vaccine came into use production of the older Salk vaccine almost stopped.

Although new methods replace old ones, it often happens that a method that seemed to be an improvement turns out to have harmful side effects that were not foreseen. Indeed, some people believe humankind will be destroyed by the side effects of our technological "improvements." Jacques Cousteau's divers report, for example, that marine life, poisoned by industrial waste products, is declining in all of the world's oceans. From one point of view this is because technology has developed too fast, but from another point of view it is because technology has not developed fast *enough*. We must work as fast as possible to find new methods of recycling industrial wastes, and we must create new political institutions that will force industry to use the new recycling methods. Thus technological progress creates new problems that call for new technological solutions. Some people are so upset by this fact that they have been saying, in effect, "Stop the world, I want to get off!" However, the world's population is now too large to allow us to retreat from technological problems by returning to a simpler life style, churning our own butter, grinding our own flour, traveling on horseback, and so

forth. For most of us the solution will have to involve more technology, not less.

The term cultural lag is sometimes used to explain social problems, such as pollution, that arise because there is a time lag between a technological change and the social and cultural changes that the technological change requires. This term was introduced by William F. Ogburn, who suggested that technological changes tend to occur quickly and to cause new situations that require normative changes in social relationships.[4] Because we are slow to change our norms, problems often occur during the lag time. Perhaps the best example of Ogburn's point is the current "population explosion." Technological methods of limiting (i.e., postponing) deaths are in use, but in many places old norms discourage the use of new methods of limiting births. As a result populations are growing at a disastrous rate in many areas while the culture resists normative change. Culture lag is one example of a society's failure to maintain integration among its structures.

## Cultural integration and diversity

Norms are built up by many people, usually over a long period. They have to fit together to form a workable system for all the members of a society. If we each made up our own rules, the social system would quickly break down, for we would not see all the ways in which our actions affect others. A society is a unified collectivity, and the lives of its members are interdependent. Thus its folkways, mores, and values have to be compatible. We say that the parts of a society need to be *functionally integrated*. Anthropologists who study distant cultures have gathered surprising evidence that even primitive cultures are integrated systems. These researchers have shown how the change of one minor custom can have far-reaching and unforeseen effects on the social and cultural system. Consider the following example.

The Yir Yoront tribe used to live in a barren part of Australia, using a technology as primitive as that of any society on earth.[5] They were literally a Stone Age society; in fact they treated their stone tools with great reverence. To them, a stone ax was a rare and marvelous object to be cared for by a few respected high-ranking tribesmen. The ax played a part in certain religious ceremonies, in which it was a symbol of the group's ancestry. The tool could also be used for nonreligious tasks and was one of the tribe's most valuable objects. When a man needed the ax he would ask one of the tribal leaders for permission to use it. Only if the leader thought he was worthy would he be given that permission. Thus the rarity of the valuable tool made permission to use it a privilege and a method of social control.

Then white people came, bringing with them modern technology—steel axes. Even in the middle of the desert a tribesman could easily get a steel ax from a trader or missionary. These axes were far better than the old stone ax. But the effects of this change were not all good. It undercut social control and respect for tradition. No longer could the old men keep the youth in line by refusing to let them use an ax. Those of higher rank lost their control over those of lower rank. The structure of authority within the tribe became confused and great tension resulted.

In the early days of anthropology field researchers usually described societies in terms of a list of culture traits. A culture trait is the smallest unit of culture. I have already mentioned several examples: the tooth fairy, the custom of eating with knives and forks, the use of stone axes, Santa's reindeer, the Eskimo custom of wife lending, and so on. It was assumed that these traits were independent of one another and that each could

be "grafted" onto a different culture without changing any of its other traits. The early researchers would not have foreseen any difficulty in "grafting" the use of steel axes onto tribal culture. Gradually, however, social scientists became aware that the traits of a given culture often fit together and reinforce each other. This is what we mean by *cultural integration*.

A given rule may perform a vital but unrecognized function in maintaining the whole system—so much so that unforeseen problems arise if it is changed. The norms governing the use of an ax may be, at the same time, rules by which manliness is rewarded, political authority is recognized, and loyalty to the society is expressed. Many anthropologists today are so impressed by the cultural integration of the societies they visit that they are opposed to almost any influence on those societies from the outside world.

However, it is not always true that a whole society shares the same cultural beliefs, values, and norms. Although the various cultural elements of a given society often fit together very well, the extent of cultural integration differs from one society to another. Modern societies are particularly likely to show much cultural diversity. In North America, for example, we have a great variety of groups with different cultures and life styles. There are ethnic communities in which life goes on the way it did in the "old country" and deviant communities that support theft, drug use, or sexual fetishes. There are unusual religious communities, astrological societies, nudist camps, prohibitionist groups, and so on. These groups are based on different subcultures. Their members share values and ideas that differ from those of the wider society of which they are a part.

The word counterculture has come into the language since the 1960s. It refers to a subculture (such as that of hippies or dropouts) that included a core of beliefs and traits that differed from those of the wider culture of Western society. However, it wasn't just *different* from the "straight" or mainstream culture; it was *in opposition to* that culture. Its purpose was to *counter* the "straight" culture by looking scruffy, using drugs, believing in astrology and the tarot, experimenting with unusual sexual relationships, living on yogurt and sunflower seeds, selling candles and beads on the sidewalk, and the like. The ideas that were common to the counterculture included belief in natural foods, enlightenment through drugs, and communal living. It claimed not to value achievement, commitment, materialistic success, or competition.

## What influences culture?

Many theories have been proposed to explain why cultures differ so greatly from one society to another. I will mention three types of theories: racial, geographical, and technological. They are all, at best, partial explanations of cultural variation, and they are not necessarily incompatible. It is possible that all three could play a role in the development of a given culture. Even so, however, all three theories taken together still would not explain many differences between cultures. Two societies in similar geographical settings, whose people are of the same racial stock, share the same language, and have similar technological skills, may still be very different in terms of culture. Culture seems to be free to develop in a number of different directions. Hence, the best we can hope to do is to point out some of the factors that influence the development of culture. Unfortunately, most of the theories that have been proposed throughout history cannot even do that. Racism is one such theory.

### RACE AND CULTURE

The confusion between race and culture has had a harmful influence on the history of ideas. Human beings inherit certain physical traits (e.g., skin color and facial features) that mark them as "Caucasian," "Asian," and so on. These traits are passed from parents to offspring by tiny genes that are found in all living cells. Until recently many people believed—and a few still do—that cultural traits are transmitted in the same way. On

*During the 60's many people were upset with the direction of Western culture. To show their contempt for the culture they lived in they painted their faces and wore weird clothes. This was a way of loudly saying, "I don't want to be a part of this culture!" This was a counterculture.*

Teresa Zabala/Palmer

this basis they decided that some human populations are born to greatness while others are doomed to fail. Hitler, for example, claimed that the German people were destined by their genetic superiority to rule Europe, if not the world.

The flaw in this theory is obvious. The genetic traits of breeding populations are far more stable than their cultural traits. For example, the genetic explanation cannot explain why the Italians, who built and ruled the Roman Empire, now live in one of the poorer countries of Europe and rule nobody but themselves.

I could list hundreds of similar examples. The Indian descendants of the Mayas live in poverty in Yucatan in the very shadow of the huge stone temples built by their ancestors. China had the most brilliant civilization on earth during the T'ang Dynasty (A.D. 618–907). If the Chinese people were "cultured" because of their heredity, why did that civilization flower and then wither? The racial explanation of cultural variation is clearly mistaken. Yet racism is such an important issue that we will discuss it further in Chapter 10.

### GEOGRAPHY AND CULTURE

The geographical theory, also widely held, explains cultural traits in terms of the society's physical setting. This theory is not entirely false, but it is very limited. It was popular 30 or 40 years ago, when it was widely noted that all the high cultures of the world are found in places with temperate climates.[6] Is there something stimulating about mild weather? The argument seems valid at first, but it is not supported by historical evidence. Most of today's leading industrial societies are found in the temperate zone, but the lost civilizations of ancient times were located in areas with a wide range of climates.

The physical setting does not determine what a culture *will* become, but it sets limits on what it *can* become. Thus Eskimos don't dance in grass skirts. People have to keep warm, and they have to use whatever materials are available. Still, within these limits they could develop many different ways of dancing. The environment contains both opportunities and limitations, but even a rich environment does not guarantee that a society will develop an advanced culture. Thus the California Indians lived in one of the most hospitable environments on the earth, but they were among the most primitive tribes of North America. Culture must work with Mother Nature, but she does not draw its design.

Moreover, as technology improves, the influence of nature decreases. Technology overcomes the limitations of nature so that there are more opportunities than there were before. For example, though Eskimos might never have invented hula dancing in grass skirts, they may take up such dancing when they live in well-heated brick houses.

### TECHNOLOGY AND CULTURE

Sociologists sometimes distinguish between two aspects of technology—ideas and social practices. Some writers argue that the ideas (i.e., the culture) are shaped by the technological practices (i.e., the social structure). Let's look at three writers who take this position: Karl Marx, Harold Innis, and Marshall McLuhan.

#### Marx: technology and ideology

Marx's philosophy is called *historical materialism* because it assumes that history is determined by the material circumstances that people face—especially the necessity of earning bread.[7] Marx believed that the social structure (the technological practices) of a group determines its culture. That is, people do what they have to do in order to survive. Then they think up ideals to justify what they do. These ideals are really ideologies.

The technology of producing food, clothes, shelter, and other necessities is the basic factor in any social group. This is the true basis of its social structure. People who own the means of production (land, livestock, factories, etc.) form the ruling class. Naturally, they try to justify their dominant position, and they support teachers, writers, priests, and politicians as long as these people produce ideas that support their position. These ideas are the culture of the society, but to Marx they were simply ideologies. For example, religion teaches workers to be humble. It tells them to look for their reward in the next life, not in this one. Thus religion is ideology, and so are politics, literature, philosophy, art, and all the other aspects of culture. Through ideology the ruling class hoodwinks the workers and keeps them in line.

Marx distinguished between those social institutions that handle basic economic production and those that handle cultural matters. The latter he called *superstructure*. The educational system, the religious, legal, and political institutions are all part of the superstructure. Marx believed that whatever happened in the superstructure depended entirely on what happened in the institutions that handled economic production. Historical changes were always determined by bread-and-butter issues, not by abstract ideals or noble values. And for that matter, when you look below the surface, even the abstract ideals are invented to protect some group's bread-and-butter interests—or so Marx believed. Thus the economic structure—the technology of production—determined culture. Marxists still assume that this is the case.

### Innis and McLuhan:
### communication and culture

Marx's position is not the only materialist interpretation of culture. Many non-Marxist theorists also focus on the influence of technology on culture. Let's look at two more recent materialist theorists, Harold Innis and Marshall McLuhan, who both stress the technology of communication rather than the technology of production.

Innis, an economic historian, showed that the culture of a society is greatly influenced by the nature of the media through which the culture is communicated.[8] In particular, he emphasized the differences between societies that depend on oral communication and those that use writing. The human voice has certain physical characteristics that put limits on *preliterate* (i.e., oral) societies. First, because of the voice's short range, members of a group must be close together to communicate with one another. Second, because sound is not permanent, an oral society is "time bound." A verbal event happens in a moment and is gone. It cannot be recaptured except in the memory of its hearers, and memory distorts reality. People whose culture is oral cannot keep records. In speaking of past events they are free to invent. As a result such societies do not separate history from fiction. Their stories are imaginative and illogical.

Writing changes all this. Written communications are permanent and are not distorted by memory. A *literate* group (one that uses writing) can spread out over a large area and still maintain its identity and its political coordination. Bureaucratic empires become possible. Reason replaces traditional sacred authority. Members of a literate society can check documents against other historical records. Their standards of judgment become objective and consistent. The culture of a literate society becomes critical, logical, and empirical.

The distinction between preliterate and literate societies is such an important one that many of these observations had been made by other writers. Innis, however, found that even small technological improvements in the media of communication often had great historical impact. For instance, the cost, durability, and portability of writing materials are important technological factors. Thus as papyrus replaced clay tablets

**FIGURE 3.1**

*In these drawings, from about 2800 years ago, the first line shows the inscription as originally written; it is read from right to left, as has been the custom in Semitic languages. In the second line the same message is reversed so as to read from left to right. The next line translates the Semitic letters into the modern alphabet. The fourth line includes the unwritten vowels to show pronunciation, and the final one is the English translation.*

1. ꟼꟽ.ꟼ ꟼꟽ.ꟽ ꟼꟽ.ꟼꟽ.ꟼꟽ.ꟼꟽ.ꟼꟽ.ꟼꟽ.ꟼꟽꟼ

2. ꟼꟽꟼ.ꟽꟼ WO.ꟼꟽ.ꟽꟽ ꟽꟽꟼꟼ.ꟽꟼꟼ.ꟽꟼꟼ

3. ꟾ N K · M S ᶜ · B N · K M S M L D · M L K · M ꟾ B

4. ꟾAN°Kⁱ MᵉShᵃᶜ  BᵉN  KᵃM°ShMᵃLD  MᵉL°K  M°ꟾAB

5. I    Mesha    son-of Kamoshmald    king-of Moab

*Source:* "The Evolution of a Writing System," from *The Human Adventure* by G. H. Pelto. © Copyright 1962 by Macmillan Publishing Co., Inc.

and was itself replaced by parchment and then by paper, the number and kinds of written documents multiplied and culture spread more rapidly. Without paper, the development of printing would not have been possible.

McLuhan calls one of his own books a "footnote" to some of Innis' writings.[9] His more famous work, *Understanding Media* (1964),[10] explores the cultural effects of different communications media even further. This book stimulated much debate.

McLuhan sees the media as extensions of the human body. Just as a crowbar extends the power of the human arm, so too media can extend the power of human senses. A telescope and a movie camera both extend the power of the human eye. The telescope allows it to see things that are far away, and the movie camera allows it to see things that are distant in both space and time—World War I battles or the peak of Mount Everest, for example. We can see the world and communicate with others in new ways by using technological inventions, but by doing so we change ourselves too.

Consider the members of a preliterate society. They use all their senses, but a lot of their attention is directed toward hearing, for it is almost their only means of contact with the thoughts of others. Now suppose these people learn to read. They then learn by using their eyes rather than their ears. It's as if literacy enlarges one's eyes and shrinks one's ears.

In addition, literacy takes people out of the real world and into the world of books. As McLuhan points out, these two worlds are quite different. He asks us to suppose that we are looking at a red, white, and blue flag with stars and stripes on it. Then someone takes it down and puts in its place a piece of paper on which are written the words *American flag.* The words cannot fully replace the real flag.

A nonliterate person experiences his or her culture as a large number of impressions that bombard the senses all at once in no logical order. These impressions are associated with mythical ideas, fantastic images, and magical symbols. A literate person, on the other hand, experiences culture through words read one at a time. These words must be strung together in a logical order, and they are a poor substitute for real objects.

We read a book with detachment. It does not affect us as deeply as contacts with real people. But McLuhan goes further, claiming that a literate society is *generally* more detached, critical, and rational than a nonliterate one. He believes that by reading books we develop mental habits that we carry over into the real world.

For better or worse, literate culture is about to become a thing of the past, according to McLuhan. Modern electronic media are changing the world. We are entering a "postliterate" era. Television counteracts some of the effects of literacy. It forces people to use their ears as well as their eyes. It pours out a simultaneous, nonsequential, illogical flood of impressions that demand

the active participation of the viewer. A television viewer is not detached but becomes involved with the people who appear on the screen, real people who live all over the world. People around the globe are linked together by the electronic extensions of the human nervous system — telephones, television, tape recorders, and so forth. The logical thought and careful reasoning of literate humanity decline in the culture of post-literate humanity and are replaced by a renewed tendency to use myths and symbolic imagery.

These, then, are McLuhan's main ideas. They have been criticized widely, and McLuhan does not bother to defend them very seriously. Instead, he views these ideas as something that he has been playing with, and he invites us to play with them too.

# SOCIAL RESEARCH:
## Sociologists at Work

Two cultural topics have been given a lot of attention by social scientists during the past ten years or so. One is the "culture of poverty." The other is the impact of the mass media (especially TV) on human behavior.

### THE CULTURE OF POVERTY

The anthropologist Oscar Lewis has spent many years getting to know poor people in Latin America. Several of his books tell the life stories of Mexican families living in slums. One, *La Vida*,[11] compares the lives of Puerto Rican people living in New York City with those of their relatives living near San Juan. After comparing poor people in several different societies, Lewis concluded that he had found a similar pattern in all of those societies. He called this pattern the

culture of poverty.[12] Although it is really a sub-culture rather than a culture, we will use Lewis' term.

### The structural setting

The culture of poverty is not found in poor preindustrial societies. It develops only in societies with the following characteristics:

1 The economic system is capitalist.
2 There is much unemployment among unskilled workers.
3 The low-income population is unorganized.
4 Kinship is traced through both the male and female lines, as it is in North America.
5 The dominant class values thrift and property and believes in upward mobility.

These conditions create the setting in which the culture of poverty develops. Slum dwellers, having no real chance of getting anywhere, adapt to their hopeless state. Not all poor people who live in such settings develop such an outlook, however. Lewis estimates that perhaps 20 percent of the American poor have this orientation. But once a child has been socialized to

The culture of poverty looks pretty much the same wherever it is found. One of these streets is in New York City—the other is San Juan, Puerto Rico. Can you tell which is which?

hold such values, his or her chances of success are slight. The culture of poverty is self-perpetuating. It is an adaptation to poverty that tends to perpetuate poverty. And its traits are the same all over the world. As a life style it is not limited to any region or any nation, and it is the same in the country and in the city. Lewis believes that many of the unwholesome characteristics of black American society are not the traits of an ethnic culture but those of the culture of poverty. Public welfare helps maintain it by not giving enough to any person to enable him or her to escape from poverty.

### Life style

One characteristic of the culture of poverty is a pattern of common-law marriages and households headed by women. According to Lewis, this pattern is due to the fact that poor men have no prospect of passing on any wealth to their children and poor women have little to gain by marrying such men. Hence, the typical family pattern is mother-centered, with the children competing for the mother's limited resources and affection. Living in poverty, the woman cannot much cherish or protect her children. Her relations with her husband are detached, for his main attachment is to his mother's household.

This culture is also marked by a pattern of nonintegration, nonparticipation, and apathy toward community life. Most primitive societies have a richer community life than modern slum dwellers do. Poor people feel hostile to the dominant classes and to their institutions—the government, the church, and so on. They know little about other life styles.

Personality formation in such a social environment leaves much to be desired. Very early the child develops a feeling of inferiority that lasts throughout his or her life. Along with inferiority feelings come fatalism, dependency, and a sense of helplessness. In addition, the young boy is often confused about matters of sexual identity, though his confusion is disguised by a heavy emphasis on masculinity—called *machismo* in Latin America.

Poor people live in the present, not planning for the future. They satisfy their impulses in a spontaneous, sensual way whenever they have the chance. It is a shallow culture, full of misery and mistrust.

### A further empirical test

Lewis' description of the culture of poverty is based on empirical research. There can be no doubt that the traits that he describes are indeed shared by many poor people. But there is some question as to whether this culture is created and sustained by the experience of poverty itself or whether it is simply the traditional way of life of certain ethnic groups. One effort to test Lewis' claims may be seen in a research project published in 1969 by Lola Irelan and her associates.[13] This study compared the male heads of over 1000 California families. All of these families were "poor," but only half of them were on welfare. The men were either Spanish-speaking Americans, black Americans, or Anglo-Americans.

If Lewis' observations are correct, the culture of poverty will be shared to an equal extent by poor families in all three ethnic groups. To test this prediction the research team analyzed data that had already been collected for a different research project. The authors concluded that the culture of poverty did vary by ethnic group. Table 3.1 presents a few selected items to illustrate their conclusions. One reason I have included this table is to give you some more experience in reading complex tables, so let's look at it in some detail.

The question you want to ask while looking at Table 3.1 is whether, for any given item, ethnicity or welfare (public assistance) makes more difference in the kinds of answers people give. To judge the effect of ethnicity alone, compare the percentages across a given row, first among the recipients, then among the nonrecipients. For the first item, for example, the Spanish-speaking men show the greatest dependency and the Anglo-Americans the least.

Next, judge the effect of welfare on the answers of each ethnic group separately. Again you need to compare the percentages in the top row, but in a different way. Compare the Anglo-American recipients and nonrecipients. There is a difference of 6 percentage points (26 − 20 = 6). Next, compare the Spanish-speaking recipients and nonrecipients. Their differential is 4

---

**TABLE 3.1**

*Selected attitudes among low-income Anglo-American, Spanish-speaking, and black recipients and nonrecipients of public assistance*

| | PERCENT AGREEING OR GIVING POSITIVE REPLIES AMONG: | | | | | |
| | RECIPIENTS OF PUBLIC ASSISTANCE | | | NONRECIPIENTS OF PUBLIC ASSISTANCE | | |
| | ANGLO (N = 210) | SPANISH-SPEAKING (N = 212) | BLACK (N = 165) | ANGLO (N = 189) | SPANISH-SPEAKING (N = 227) | BLACK (N = 151) |
|---|---|---|---|---|---|---|
| **DEPENDENCY BEHAVIOR** Because I want to be liked, I tend to be apologetic and won't stand up for what I know are my real feelings. | 26 | 40 | 31 | 20 | 44 | 24 |
| **DEPENDENCY FEELINGS** I feel out of sorts if I have to be by myself for any length of time. | 34 | 44 | 30 | 20 | 39 | 27 |
| **PRIMACY OF FAMILY OF ORIENTATION** The responsibilities of taking care of his wife and children should not keep a husband from spending plenty of time with his own parents. | 36 | 58 | 51 | 40 | 50 | 48 |
| **FATALISM** Planning only makes a person unhappy, since your plans hardly ever work out anyway. | 55 | 69 | 67 | 50 | 70 | 56 |
| **OCCUPATIONAL VALUES** Would you stay in a job or take one if it would mean that you'd have to take on more responsibility? | 84 | 80 | 88 | 88 | 77 | 83˙ |
| **ALIENATION** People who go out of their way to help a personal friend are usually disappointed. | 47 | 56 | 75 | 40 | 57 | 60 |

*Source:* Adapted from Lola M. Irelan, Oliver C. Moles, and Robert M. O'Shea, "Ethnicity, Poverty, and Selected Attitudes: A test of the 'Culture of Poverty' Hypothesis," *Social Forces*, 47, no. 4 (June 1969), 320, 322, 323. Reprinted by permission.

---

points (44 − 40 = 4), but not in the direction predicted by Lewis. Finally, compare the black recipients and nonrecipients. Their differential is 7 points (31 − 24 = 7). In other words, a Spanish-speaking background had more impact on dependent behavior than being on welfare.

If you go on comparing the items in Table 3.1, you will reach similar conclusions. Only in the last item are the Spanish speakers outdone by any other ethnic group. The authors conclude that Lewis may have found the culture of poverty in the groups that he studied because they are from a Spanish-speaking background, not because they are poor. However, it seems to me that this study is not a true test of the culture of poverty. We should not compare poor people who do receive welfare aid with poor people who do not. It would be better to compare poor people with rich people from the same ethnic backgrounds. The real question is, Do poor people tend to develop a culture of poverty? My guess is that they do, when compared with rich people.

Lewis stirred up a hornet's nest by writing

about the culture of poverty. Many social scientists worried that his views might lead government officials to make some bad decisions. His critics agreed that Lewis described life in the slums quite accurately, but they did not think he was correct in calling this way of life a "culture." Not *culture,* but *social structure,* is the cause of that life style. A culture is a way of life that people believe in and teach their children to prefer. But people in slums believe in the same values as other people. The reason they don't live up to them is that they are sometimes unable to do so. For example, there is an obvious reason why poor people tend to spend money as soon as they get it instead of saving it, and it is not a cultural reason: they have no other way of paying for their next meal. One critic wrote, "In my experience, people do not go to usurers because they want to, but because they must."[14]

The critics claim that the frequent absence of fathers from poor households must be due to structural factors such as low wages and unemployment rather than to cultural factors. And it's no wonder that the poor are fatalistic, hopeless, dependent, and mistrustful of government officials, employers, and priests. They are *in fact* discriminated against and exploited. Lewis has put the cart before the horse. It is not their fatalism and mistrust that keeps them poor; rather, it is their poverty that keeps them fatalistic and mistrustful, or so say Lewis's critics.

There is something to be said for both views. Certainly poverty is the chief source of hopelessness, dependency, mistrust, and all the rest. Lewis says so himself. But it seems clear too that sometimes people with these attitudes fail to take advantage of any opportunity that does occur simply because they don't believe they have any chance of succeeding. It is a vicious cycle in which poverty causes fatalism and vice versa. The question that policy makers must ask is, How can we break the vicious cycle? We will consider this question soon, but first let's take a look at recent research on another element of modern culture—the mass media.

POPULAR CULTURE
AND THE MASS MEDIA

In any heterogeneous society (i.e., one with a variety of subgroups), there is likely to be con-

flict among different cultural publics. North American society is no exception. At times such conflicts enter the political arena. One such conflict is over the question of whether the government should uphold specific cultural standards. It might do so, for example, through censorship, through power to grant or withhold broadcasting licenses, or by means of subsidies to struggling artists and cultural groups such as opera companies.

People who would like more government support for "high" culture usually give one or both of the following reasons: (1) High culture deserves special treatment simply because of its excellence, and/or (2) popular culture is often harmful to society and therefore should not be encouraged. Of course these two arguments are quite separate. You can accept one without accepting the other.

Herbert Gans has studied the evidence for the second argument and has concluded that it is largely mistaken.[15] He believes that the mass media offer many more benefits than dangers. What are those "dangers," anyway? Various critics of popular culture see different ones. Some fear that psychological disturbances and even sex crimes may be caused by pornography. Some are concerned about the wasteful, materialistic attitudes that are encouraged by advertising. Others are offended by the commercials themselves. Some are concerned about the effects of watching violence. Some are worried that people may model their lives on those of their favorite stars. Finally, many critics are particularly concerned about the power of journalists and TV newscasters to influence public opinion through biased reporting.

Gans' general conclusion—and he admits that it is a personal one—is that there is no cause for alarm. People are not helpless victims of the media who believe everything they see on the TV screen. Media audiences are usually groups—families, dating couples, and so on—who choose programs that are consistent with their own values and opinions. They have a chance to argue against the statements they hear or even to decide to turn off the TV or cancel a magazine subscription. Sensible adults learn to "discount" claims made in the media, especially when those claims are intended to persuade or influence the reader or viewer—as

Eric Kroll/Taurus Photos

*Massage parlors and pornography theaters are seen by many as a threat to the quality of Western culture.*

is obviously true of political speeches and advertising.

By and large people do not accept news reports uncritically, but TV newscasts still have a lot of influence on the political "agenda." That is, the media report certain events and not others, and what they report determines what becomes a matter of public debate. It does not, however, determine the answers that will come out of the political process.[16] Nor does political advertising have a major impact on the outcome of elections. The only reason for concern about such advertising is that all the candidates or issues do not always have equal access to the media, and media ads often make some difference when elections are close.

Gans believes that many observers have probably overestimated the influence of the media on manners and morals. He sees no reason to believe that many adults, or even teenagers, model their lives or base their choices of

dates or spouses on their favorite performers. Instead, people base their choices of TV programs and reading matter on their own values.

There is no doubt that good advertising leads to higher sales, but whether this is socially harmful or not is a question to which there is no clear answer. We will give this matter more attention later in the book, but for now we may simply note that most people in Western societies do not seem to mind advertising. I find many ads obnoxious, but sometimes I am glad to be informed about something that I would otherwise have missed.

The pornography issue is a complicated one. Erotic movies definitely arouse sexual feelings for a while. However, the Commission on Obscenity and Pornography found that the use of erotic materials cannot be shown to have long-term effects. Danish law has permitted unlimited display of pornography for several years without an increase in sex crimes.[17] On the other hand, in areas where massage parlors, "skin flicks," and other pornographic performances, are located crime, drunkenness, drug abuse and prostitution commonly increase. Often other businesses leave because the area becomes so sleazy. The legal action involved in closing massage parlors is often long and fruitless. Some cities have responded to the problem with zoning laws, which do not prohibit such places but require them to be several blocks apart so that no area decays because of their presence.

Finally, we must think about the very important issue of violence on TV and in movies. By now it is clear that at least some people are affected at least some of the time by watching violence. Laboratory evidence shows that violent films stimulate aggressive behavior by youths immediately after watching them, but there is no evidence of long-term effects. Several recent studies, including one sponsored by the Surgeon General's Advisory Committee (1972)[18] and one directed by Judy La Marsh for the Canadian government (1977), have concluded that television viewing and violent behavior are linked.

However, not all people are equally affected by TV violence. Girls do not respond with aggression. Emotionally disturbed people apparently are affected more than stable people. Gans believes that TV violence cannot be a very strong influence on the amount of violence that occurs in the general population, for the amount of violent crime has actually decreased during the years since TV came into widespread use.[19] Nor is there any theoretical reason to think that the media would be a major influence on violence. Police records show that the poor are more violent than the rich, which is what most of us would predict. Poverty is obviously a major and steady source of frustration. Moreover, studies of children indicate that parents and peers have more influence on a child's behavior than the TV set. Thus although the mass media no doubt play a very important role in influencing public life, at their worst they are probably not as harmful as some people have feared. There is some basis for concern about TV violence, however, since it does affect the behavior of males, the poor, children, and emotionally unstable people. In Chapter 10 we will discuss other issues relating to the mass media.

*The controversy continues over the way and the extent to which television influences its viewers, but there can be no doubt that it does enthrall them.*

Jean-Claude Lejeune/Stock, Boston

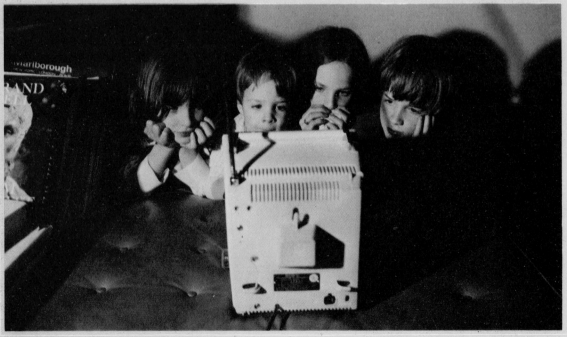

# SOCIAL POLICY:
## Issues and Viewpoints

To the extent that sociology is a science, it is interested not in what *should be* but only in what *is*. However, sociology is both a science and more than a science. Human society, the subject of sociological study, is organized through an endless series of decisions. And we, either individually or collectively, must make those decisions. Thus the social sciences contribute factual knowledge that is useful to all of us in reaching our decisions. To illustrate this point I want to return to three issues that we touched on in our discussion of culture: (1) How does cultural relativism apply to contacts between developed and underdeveloped societies? (2) How can we overcome the "culture of poverty"? (3) Should public policy favor high culture or popular culture?

### CULTURAL RELATIVISM AND ETHICS

You will recall that cultural relativism is the belief that any society's practices must be judged only in terms of its own cultural values. Many social scientists take this position at the beginning of their careers but later move away from it. It is hard to maintain. Few relativists, for example, could bring themselves to eat human flesh if it were offered to them by a cannibalistic host, even if that practice happened to be acceptable in the society they were visiting.

Today most scholars, while they admit that their judgments are imperfect and that there could be no perfection anyway, recognize that it is impossible to avoid making judgments about other cultures. We do have to decide what to support and what to oppose. Cultural relativism arose in reaction to the arrogance of Europeans who looked down on primitive societies. However praiseworthy it may have been originally, since World War II this policy has come to be recognized as socially irresponsible. As Erich Fromm has pointed out in his analysis of Nazism, it is possible for whole societies to be "sick"—to have perverted values, to carry out policies that they may later feel ashamed of. Relativism does not allow the scholar to view such societies as "sick." A relativist is bound to accept genocide as valid if it is a true cultural ideal in the society, or cannibalism, sexism, racism, or anything else.

From an aesthetic point of view, some groups offer fewer expressive forms than other groups do. A relativistic outlook would not allow us to conclude that one group is "culturally

*Cultural relativism, if held to strictly, leaves no room for considering one society healthier than another. But what are we to think about these Hitler Youth? They may have started out like well-scrubbed boy scouts, but that's not how they ended up.*

Wide World Photos

impoverished" compared to another. But in some cases that is a reasonable conclusion.

Moreover, from a technological point of view it is obvious that not all cultures are equally advanced. Although all societies value life and health and comfort, they are not equally able to attain these benefits. Therefore many social scientists have abandoned the effort to remain neutral toward foreign cultures. They now work actively to modernize underdeveloped countries. Modernization requires changes in values and life styles. Some researchers in poor societies try to persuade people to boil their drinking water and to plant new strains of rice seed. A few relativists still view such activities as a form of "cultural imperialism" that threatens the society's cultural integrity. They point to the Yir Yoront as an example of what happens when a society imports a foreign technology.

This is a valid objection. Truly, bringing in a new technology will change a society in many ways. Yet it is no longer possible for many of us to maintain a totally relativistic viewpoint—especially when the native peoples themselves are eager to import modern technology. We could not keep people from getting steel axes even if we wanted to . The world *will* change, and problems will result. To make responsible decisions we have to judge cultures normatively, that is, by some set of standards. Nevertheless the relativists are correct on one point: We can't be entirely sure that our judgments will hold up or that our policies will be helpful. Therefore it is important to show the highest possible respect for the values of other societies in all our dealings with them.

### POVERTY: CULTURAL OR STRUCTURAL?

In some circles you are using fighting words if you talk about the "culture of poverty." There are many conflicting views about how to fight poverty. Some lawmakers may have been misled by the view of poverty as a "culture" into developing an outlook similar to Social Darwinism. Lewis' critics have therefore opposed the notion of the "culture of poverty" on political grounds, not just for theoretical reasons.

The issue is this: If poverty is *structural* in origin, then laws that provide new opportunities and more income will solve the basic problem.

On the other hand, if poverty is primarily *cultural,* resulting from the unfortunate attitudes and habits of the poor themselves, then providing new opportunities will *not* solve the problem. Instead, those who have learned the culture of poverty will continue to live the way they always have because they prefer that life style. No wonder people often resent the idea of a culture of poverty! It seems to blame poverty on the poor themselves, rather than on the very real problems they face every day. And it seems to suggest no way of overcoming poverty. The "structural" interpretation, on the other hand, tells us exactly what the poor need: more. Just *more.* A bigger share of everything.

To be fair to Lewis, he never suggested that more than 20 percent of the American poor had adopted the "culture" of poverty. And he and his critics agreed about how to break the vicious cycle of poverty, whether it is cultural or structural. He, too, thought the poor should have more. The critics' objections were not to *his* policies but to the policies that they thought politicians would develop on the basis of his theory. Social scientists generally agree that the only real way to fight poverty is to distribute the society's wealth more equally.

### HIGH VERSUS POPULAR CULTURE

Which public should control the mass media? At present the government does not involve itself much in this issue but simply lets the law of supply and demand determine the outcome. This means, in practice, that popular culture is well served while high culture, which appeals to smaller audiences, is not well served. Commercial success requires large audiences.

I would prefer greater diversity. I'd like to see every public enjoy its own television programs, records, plays, books, movies, and newspapers. I certainly don't think high culture should dominate the media. In general, the public does not need to be protected from its own popular taste. The problem is that sometimes the TV channels are all showing soap operas or quiz shows and there is no choice between popular culture and high culture.

Smaller publics with special interests (e.g., ethnic groups) deserve access to their own cultural products, and we would all be enriched if this were made possible. Herbert Gans, among other writers, supports a policy of cultural pluralism instead of uniformity. All groups—intellectuals, workers, minorities, and so on—should be able to find cultural products that suit their needs and tastes. For every culture is a living human tradition that deserves the respect of others.

# SUMMARY

**1.** A *culture* consists of a system of ideas, values, beliefs, and knowledge that is passed from one generation to the next within a social group. The term is sometimes applied to a system of norms or obligations. Sometimes it refers to an expressive system, especially the arts. And sometimes sociologists think of "culture" as distinct from the social system or structure. In that sense the culture is a set of ideas that the social system tries to live up to by institutionalizing specific practices.

**2.** Culture is communicated largely through symbols. A *symbol* is anything that stands for something else. A culture includes values, norms, folklore, law, and ideology. A *value* is something that is widely believed to be desirable or worthwhile for its own sake. A *norm* is a rule prescribing how to behave in particular situations. Primitive societies have informal ways of enforcing their norms, but modern societies use written laws. *Folklore* consists of myths, jokes, superstitions, songs, stories, and the like. An *ideology* is a set of beliefs that enable a group to justify (at least to its own members) what it is doing.

**3.** *Technology* consists of the use of knowledge in an institutionalized way to control nature for practical purposes. It differs from expressive forms of symbolic activity in that it normally improves and develops over time. Technology is judged on the basis of efficiency, while expressive forms are judged by aesthetic standards, which are more subjective than the standard of efficiency.

**4.** There is a tendency for cultures to be *functionally integrated*; that is, the parts of any given cultural system tend to fit together. However, in modern societies there is much cultural diversity, and many different subcultures may be found within the same society.

**5.** Several different theories have been proposed to explain, in part, why cultures differ so greatly from one society to another. The racial theory is based on the mistaken notion that some cultures are more advanced than others because their members inherit a high level of ability in their genes. Another theory holds that cultural differences are due to differences in geographical factors, including climate. This theory has also been shown to have little validity. Technological factors are the basis for certain other theories, especially those of Marx, Innis, and McLuhan. Marx thought technology produced changes in the basic structure of society. Culture, on the other hand, was part of the "superstructure." That is, it depended on the basic structure—the economic arrangements. McLuhan and Innis pointed out how technology of communication influences the culture of a given society and even the personality traits of people who belong to it.

The Innis–McLuhan version of the technology theory simply points out that the kind of media used to communicate messages (e.g., clay tablets or television) determines how a person will experience the act of communicating. Reading is a very different experience from watching television, and so people who mostly read probably differ psychologically and culturally from people who mostly watch television. The read-

ing culture is very logical and critical; the television culture is more likely to participate actively in the communication process.

# KEY TERMS

**code**   a grammar or set of rules that may be passed along from one generation to the next.

**counterculture**   a subculture (such as that of hippies and dropouts) that is opposed to the conventional culture of the wider society.

**cultural relativism**   the assumption that all cultures are equally valid and that any culture deserves respect.

**cultural lag**   a term used to explain social problems that arise because there is a time lag between a technological change and the social and cultural changes required by that change.

**culture**   a system of ideas, values, beliefs, knowledge, and customs transmitted from generation to generation within a social group.

**culture trait**   the smallest unit of culture.

**ethnocentrism**   the tendency to judge other ways of life by the standards of one's own group.

**folklore**   a society's oral tradition (its collection of jokes, superstitions, lullabies, old wives' tales, slang words, ghost stories, etc.)

**folkway**   the trivial norms or conventions shared by members of a society.

**ideology**   a doctrine used to justify a group's actions in pursuing its own interests.

**institutionalization**   the process through which culture influences the social system; the development of structures to carry out the shared values of the society.

**mores**   a society's important ethical rules.

**norm**   a rule that tells members of a society how to behave in particular situations.

**public**   a group of people who share a particular code and an interest in a given issue or tradition.

**sanction**   an action that rewards conformity to norms or punishes nonconformity.

**social control**   the process by which members of a group support desired forms of behavior and discourage undesired forms.

**social system**   the roles and actual practices that exist among members of a social group.

**subculture**   a group whose members share values and ideas that differ from those of the wider society.

**symbol**   anything that represents something else, i.e., anything that has meaning.

**technology**   the institutionalized application of knowledge to control nature for human uses.

**value**   a standard used by members of a society to judge behavior and to choose among various possible goals.

# FOR FURTHER READING

BENEDICT, RUTH. *Patterns of Culture*. Baltimore: Penguin, 1946. A classic in anthropology, this is pleasant to read as well. It pursues the relationship between character-type (personality) and culture configurations, drawing largely upon American Indian tribes to illustrate the great diversity of cultural patterns among the societies of humankind. Small and delightful.

HALL, EDWARD T. *Beyond Culture*. New York: Doubleday, 1978. Hall deals here with the latest findings by psychologists and experts on communication. He is describing the way human beings, as biological organisms, learn and pass along ideas.

HARRIS, MARVIN. *Cannibals and Kings: The Origins of Cultures*. New York: Random House, 1977. Harris is the most stimulating writer in anthropology I have read in a long time. Everything he writes is exciting. This book is about cultural evolution. As usual, he has a strong point of view, and backs it up with evidence from the strangest sources.

MANNHEIM, KARL. *Ideology and Utopia.* Translated by Louis Wirth and Edward Shils. New York: Harcourt, Brace & Jovanovich, 1936. Mannheim was an innovator in what has come to be called the sociology of knowledge. This is one of his most important books on the subject. It is a serious theoretical book, but not very hard to get through.

READ, WILLIAM H. *America's Mass Media Merchants.* Baltimore: Johns Hopkins University Press, 1977. This treats the political and economic factors that have allowed American magazines, movies, and TV to spread around the world.

ROSZAK, THEODORE. *The Making of a Counter Culture.* New York: Doubleday, 1969. This is the best treatment I know on the counter-culture of the 1960s. Besides, it gives a fine treatment of Norman O. Brown and Herbert Marcuse, plus several other influential contemporary thinkers.

SELZNICK, GERTRUDE JAEGER, and PHILIP SELZNICK. *"A Normative Theory of Culture."* *American Sociological Review* 29 (October 1964), 653–669. This is an article, not a book. It tries (I think successfully) to reconcile various definitions of culture as used by humanists, anthropologists, and other scholars. If you feel unsatisfied with cultural relativism, have a look at this paper. It will give you some good ammunition against relativism.

SUMNER, WILLIAM GRAHAM. *Folkways.* New York: New American Library, 1960. First published, 1907. This is Sumner's most famous book, and it still is popular in the little paperback edition. I have never read it straight through, but I like to dip in here and there for a chapter or two. It lends itself to that sort of reading.

# SOCIALIZATION

What was the last beverage you drank? Milk? Coffee? Beer? Why did you choose that beverage? Because you need it? Where did that "need" come from? Is it a basic part of your makeup? Clearly the need for *some* sort of liquid is a basic need of all human beings. But the preference for one particular beverage is shaped by experience. Your "need" for coffee or beer has been learned through your relationships with coffee drinkers and beer drinkers. If you had grown up in a different society you might dislike both.

What about milk? Milk drinking must be basic to human nature, for we are all mammals. That is true, but in many societies adults never drink milk. What happens to their "need" for milk as they grow up? Do they substitute an artificial need for a natural need when they begin choosing tea instead of milk? Are some needs natural and others artificial? What about blood? Members of some African tribes drink cow's blood with great pleasure. If you had grown up in such a tribe you would too.

You are born with a few basic, unspecific needs, but as you grow to adulthood in a particular society you develop a great many specific needs. We say that general needs are *channeled* by social experience. Your need for liquid may be channeled away from milk toward tea. It may even be channeled toward more and more specific preferences—away from oolong tea and toward Darjeeling tea, for example.

The Karimojong tribe of Uganda rarely slaughter their cattle for meat, but they obtain protein from them anyway—by drinking blood and milk. A thong is tightened around the cow's neck to make its jugular vein stand out a little, then an arrow is shot into the vein. When 4 to 8 pints of blood have been taken, the thong is released and the blood stops flowing.

Africapix

Adult needs and motives develop largely out of the individual's experience of social interaction. However, it does not make sense to ask an adult which of his or her preferences are basic and which have been channeled by his or her social experience. People feel as strongly about their acquired needs as they do about the basic ones out of which the acquired ones develop.

The channeling process begins in early infancy and continues throughout life, even when one is not aware that it is taking place. For example, one study observed the development of infants' preferences for different kinds of juice. Nurses offered the babies both orange and tomato juice several times, always allowing the children to choose between the two drinks. Fairly soon it became clear that each child was beginning to choose the juice that the nurse herself preferred.[1] The nurses had no intention of influencing the children, but social interaction always has an effect on the participants whether it is intended or not. The channeling process ordinarily prepares a person to fit comfortably into the community and take part in its affairs. Through socialization we learn to need the things that our community can provide for us and not to need other things. This is usually a good thing; a North American child who developed a strong need to drink cow's blood, for example, would be quite a misfit.

"All the world's a stage" wrote Shakespeare, "and all the men and women merely players." This is pure sociology. A social system is organized according to a script that all of its members have learned. For example, we know roughly how people have to behave in order to create the collective activity that we call a bank. We do not spread a picnic lunch on the floor of the bank lobby or hunt Easter eggs behind the tellers' windows because those actions would not follow the script; in fact they would disrupt the performance.

All the participants in a collective activity have particular roles to play. These roles form a system. The teller's role and the customer's role are interdependent aspects of a collective activity. Each requires something from the other.

Role performances are guided by norms. Thus if a bank teller ignores a customer and spends ten minutes gossiping with a friend, he or she is violating a norm. The teller is supposed to wait on the customer, not chat with a friend, so the customer has a right to get huffy. The term *norm* usually means "average," as when we say that a girl is shorter than the norm for her age. In sociology, however, norms do not simply define behavior that is "typical" of people who play a given role; rather, they refer to behavior that is obligatory. Norms define how roles *ought* to be performed.

Role conflict (or role strain) is the awkward situation in which a person occupies two roles governed by conflicting norms. It may be impossible, or possible only at great cost, to conform to all of those norms. Generally, social groups try to prevent role conflict by keeping people from occupying positions in which there is an obvious "conflict of interests." For example, universities discourage professors from dating their students because the role of lover conflicts with the role of grader of term papers.

An institution is a complex system of roles organized around some central activity or social need. Institutions are the main building blocks of a society. Examples include courts, schools, churches, hospitals, prisons, and the like. The number of institutions and their degree of specialization vary from one society to another. Highly developed societies have many specialized institutions characterized by extreme division of labor with each part performing a narrow range of tasks.

Socialization is the process of learning the rules of behavior for a given social group as well as acquiring the motivation to perform properly. But through socialization people acquire not only culturally prescribed needs and motivations but also many other aspects of personality. They acquire language, knowledge and skills, commitment to particular norms and values, and the ability to perform in many role relationships.

Socialization is the process through which people come to *want* to do what they *must* do. That is, a society has patterns and traditions that can survive only if its new

*"All the world's a stage." Which of these acts have you played?*

UPI

members learn them and accept them. Thus the social system is the context within which the personality system must take shape. I want to discuss three important aspects of socialization: (1) the biological factors that human beings inherit and that affect their ability to learn and perform, (2) the family setting and its part in early learning, and (3) the continuing importance of socialization throughout the life cycle.

## Biological factors in socialization

We often wonder whether a particular behavior pattern was acquired through socialization or whether it is dictated by the body's basic needs. This sort of question arises when we study universal human traits. For example, is every human being *born* with a natural tendency to fight? Or do we *learn* to fight through socialization? (If fighting is social in origin, perhaps a different way of socializing children might eliminate war.) We may also ask how many of the traits that distinguish males from females are *biological* in origin and how many result from the different *social* experiences of males and females. Do human females *inherit* the tendency to protect their infants, or is this tendency *learned*? Few such questions have been answered satisfactorily, but a new field, called *sociobiology*, specializes in research on such topics. Seldom has any new field of study made so many enemies so quickly! A great many people, including some social scientists, are unwilling to believe that *any* behavior pattern is determined by biological factors. One reason is that this would imply that human beings have no more freedom of choice than other animals. Moreover, some feminists object to the idea that biological factors are responsible for, say, the attachment between mothers and their babies, for the quality of a person's sexual experience, or for the tendency of males to dominate females.

The social scientists who mistrust the biological explanation of behavior are often scholars who recall similar research that proved to be fruitless in the past. Two generations or so ago many psychologists were interested in listing the "instincts" of human beings. This turned out to be useless because we now know that human behavior is not predetermined the way animal behavior seems to be; therefore the notion of "instinct" can hardly apply to human beings the way it applies to lower animals. Birds have an instinct to fly south, but we have to learn to read road maps when we want to take a trip. This is one reason that the human infant is dependent on its family for so long. It takes 15 or 20 years for a child to become socialized because so much more than instinct is involved in human behavior. In any case a new interest in these issues has emerged during the past five or ten years, and sociobiologists are studying them.

Besides looking for species-wide (universal) biologically based patterns of behav-

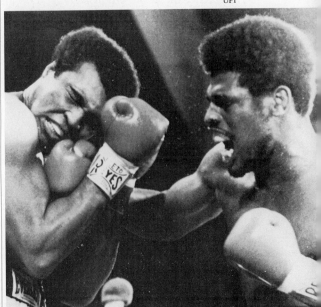

*Are people born with a natural tendency to fight or do they learn fighting? Sometimes people can't distinguish between their own "natural impulses" and their learned patterns of behavior.*

UPI

ior, we sometimes wonder whether biology is responsible for the differences between individuals or between groups. When we talk of "biologically" determined traits we usually mean genetic traits—traits that are determined by the genes that are contained in the cells of the body. These traits are obviously permanent. No scientist has yet been able to change your genes. But of course not all "biological" influences are genetic. The environment has important influences on the biological organism, and these influences may or may not be permanent. For example, we may ask questions about an individual's prenatal environment. Did the mother eat a balanced diet when she was pregnant? What medicines did she take? Was her hormone system balanced? Many other biological factors are not genetic but environmental. Some children may be unusually sensitive to certain chemicals that are commonly added to food, and become jumpy and distracted when they eat them. Some people's moods may be influenced by the balance of positive and negative ions in the air. However, here we are concerned only with *genetic* factors that may influence behavior.

Which is the more important influence on behavior: heredity or the social environment? This is a very tricky question, and I want to point out why. Let me give you an analogy: Is skin color determined more by heredity or by the environment? The answer has to be that it depends on whom you are comparing. If you are trying to explain the variations in skin color among, say, the white children in an average classroom, you will probably conclude that heredity is mostly responsible for whatever differences you find. Some kids have olive skin and some are pale—they are born that way. Now suppose that half of the children in the class are black and half are white. Then most of the variation in skin color is clearly due to heredity. But suppose we are considering a class in which there are no black children but in which half of the children have been to the

beach and are deeply tanned while half have stayed indoors and are pale. Obviously most of the variation among the members of that class would be caused by environmental, not genetic, differences.

By the same token, since personality traits are influenced both by heredity and by the environment, in a particular group hereditary factors may explain most of the variations in a given trait. But if we look at a different group we may find that environmental factors explain most of the variations among its members. A careful scientist would not say, for example, that "intelligence is mostly hereditary," but might say that "within a great many groups, though not all groups, most of the variation in intelligence is due to heredity." There is no doubt that genetic factors are important influences on intelligence as well as on other aspects of personality.

We have other evidence of this. For example, identical twins have identical genes, and indeed, their intelligence scores are usually almost identical. Fraternal twins (not identical) have genes that are no more similar than those of any pair of nontwin siblings, and their scores on IQ tests are usually about as far apart as those of any other pair of nontwin siblings. Similar genes make for similar intelligence—usually—unless something quite unusual has happened in the social or physical environment that had a strong impact on one twin but not on the other. For example, if one twin has experienced a serious vitamin deficiency or brain injury or has been greatly disadvantaged in his or her social relationships, these environmental differences will make for a big IQ difference between the twins.

Heredity may explain many other differences in the abilities and personality traits of individuals. Even mental illness seems to be influenced by hereditary factors. That is, some people seem to inherit a tendency toward schizophrenia. Whether they actually become schizophrenic or not probably depends on other factors as well, but those factors are not yet understood by scientists. The social situation is certainly among those factors, but no one knows just how important it is. Its importance may differ for different people. For example, one person's genes may create such a strong tendency toward schizophrenia that she will have a breakdown in a situation of very mild stress. Another person's genes may create only a slight tendency toward schizophrenia, but a situation of stress may become so severe that he breaks down anyway. But this is only speculation. Scientists don't really understand these processes yet. The point I want to make is that behavioral variations among individuals may be due to genetic factors in many cases.

Finally, let us ask whether behavior differences between groups may be due to genetic differences. The answer depends on what kinds of groups you are comparing. Males and females? No doubt many behavioral differences are influenced by hormones, which we know men and women produce in different amounts. We will return to this issue later. How about social classes: Are the differences between the life styles of the upper class and the lower class caused by genetic factors? No—or maybe to a tiny extent. Perhaps the upper class includes a slightly higher percentage of individuals who have inherited a gift for, say sports, singing, or mechanical tinkering that has enabled them to get rich. And perhaps the lower class includes a slightly higher percentage of individuals with a genetic handicap that keeps them from winning out in the competition for jobs. But these genetic differences between social classes cannot explain the differences between their life styles.[2] To account for these differences we have to understand that different classes have different subcultures. And we have to understand much more about the structural factors involved—such as job discrimination and unequal opportunities of all kinds.

What about differences in behavior be-

tween, say, Christians and Jews? Or between Asians, blacks, and whites? Or between English Canadians and French Canadians? Can we explain any difference between their patterns of behavior in terms of genetic differences? No. Any genetic difference would certainly be minor compared to the strength of cultural tradition. And culture is passed from one generation to the next through the socialization process, not through genes. I mentioned this issue in Chapter 3 and must return to it again in Chapter 14. But the basic answer to the question of whether differences in groups' behavior are due to genetic differences is very simple: No.

## The family and early socialization

Because it is so obvious that the quality of a young child's experience is a crucial factor in his or her later development, most research on socialization has focused on the impact of different family arrangements on child development. Psychologists have discovered in the laboratory what everybody knew already—that "tender loving care," or good parenting, is the most important element in an infant's experience. A baby becomes attached to someone (usually its mother) by about the sixth month of life and goes into deep mourning if it is separated from her even for a few days. There is evidence that the lack of such a close relationship for a long period leaves permanent scars on the personality. At first children who are deprived of their mothers cry a lot; then they gradually withdraw from any human relationship. Often they seem unaffected by close contact with human beings. When they becomes adults their inability to care deeply about others may take the form of superficial, exploitive attitudes toward other people. Of course it is not just the mother who is important to the child. The entire family serves as the context in which

*Moments like this give babies a fund of inner good feelings to draw on throughout life. They are able to love themselves inwardly, like Mommy loved them.*

abilities and values are learned. And the structure of the family is an important factor in the child's development.

### FAMILY STRUCTURE AND CHILD DEVELOPMENT

Although North Americans are generally aware of the population explosion as a world problem and are willing to limit the size of their families, sometimes this willingness is mixed with regret. You may share the feelings of a young woman I know who said, a little sadly, "It's too bad my kids won't have the warmth and fun of growing up in a big, rollicking family."

Don't worry. Research suggests that big families offer less, in general, to children than small families do. Children from smaller families tend to do better in school, show greater motivation to achieve, and score higher on intelligence tests, even with-

in the same social class.[3] And the fun and warmth? Well, children from small families are at least as well adjusted, if not better adjusted, than those from larger families.[4] Possibly this is because they get less physical punishment.[5] And probably it is also because their parents can give them more attention than they would if they had more children.[6]

Besides, when most families are small, a higher percentage of children have the chance to be the first child in the family. And firstborn children are lucky. They are usually bigger than later-born children of the same age and adults are more likely to talk with them. They receive more warmth from their parents in the early years than their younger brothers and sisters do. Firstborns are usually models for their siblings and sometimes dominate them. However, parents dislike such domination and are likely to punish the firstborn for it.[7] In any case firstborns are far more likely to be successful in later life than their siblings. This is not because they are more intelligent but because they are more likely to be oriented toward adults and adult-approved activities such as schoolwork.[8]

### LEARNING LANGUAGE AND IDEALS

One of the family's most vital contributions to the child is help in learning to use language. The child who has more chances to talk with adults gets more intellectual stimulation than a child who spends more time talking with peers. Children brought up in orphanages and other institutions are more backward in their speech than in any other area.[9] It seems that even infants need the stimulation of adult speech. It is probably because they are around adults more often that firstborns and children from small families do better than other children, by and large.

*Lucky kids. Children in small families have advantages over children in large families.*

Not only must the child learn speech in the family; he or she must also internalize the values of the wider group. Internalization means making those values part of one's personality so that they become one's own rules, not rules imposed by others. For example, a child who has internalized the norm forbidding theft will not ordinarily *consider* stealing. Internalization does not require any special attention by adults—it happens as a matter of course in the normal family setting. Many parents used to think they needed to provide moral teaching for their children, say, in Boy Scout meetings, Sunday school, or the like. However, research has shown that children who have been trained in such programs are no more honest than those who

have not received this kind of training.[10] Parents who start teaching morality early and are strict with their children do not have greater success than other parents in teaching their children moral standards.

What does count then? Not moral lectures but close relationships. You and I learned our values by interacting with the people who were important to us. We noticed not just what they said but what they *did* in situations involving choices between different values. And our relatives, because they were dearer to us, probably had a greater influence on our lives than strangers and authorities such as clergyman and teachers.

Most of us have internalized our parents' values. They have become part of our personalities. Later in life we may react against them, try to overcome them, or even organize our life style around the goal of opposing them. Yet even then those parental values will always be there inside us, always significant, because of those early bonds of affection.

Urie Bronfenbrenner believes that American children simply do not get enough attention from adults. His conclusions are based on a comparison of American and Soviet child-rearing practices.[11] Over 10 percent of Soviet children under age 2 and about 20 percent of those between the ages of 3 and 6 are in public nurseries. About 5 percent of all school-age children are in boarding schools and "schools of the prolonged day" (which care for children all day but not overnight). The children are protected but are taught obedience, self-discipline, or commitment to the group to which they belong. Collective play is emphasized, and the children are taught that "mine is ours; ours is mine." This preschool training fits in with a school system that emphasizes the group rather than the individual. Competition is encouraged, but always between groups, not between individuals. On the first day of school the teacher will say, "Let's see which row can sit up tallest" but not "Let's see which pupil can sit up tallest."

The teacher sets the standards, but she teaches the peer group to enforce those standards, so that gradually authority passes from the teacher to the peer group. The peer group learns to encourage each member, helping children who are in trouble and scolding those who do not perform well. Each pupil has responsibilities to carry out in the classroom and must also take a younger child to school, help that child with his

or her homework, and act as an older sibling.

This peer group method of socialization is effective. Russian children are less willing to engage in antisocial behavior than their age mates in other Western countries, and boarding-school students are even more resistant to antisocial behavior than their age mates in regular schools. The children are obedient and hardworking.

In principle, Bronfenbrenner believes that socialization in a family is better than peer group socialization. Adults are better role models than children, and two adults can be twice as effective. One parent can act as a role model while the other praises the modeled behavior for the child's benefit. (Daddy might say, for example, "My goodness, what a good girl mommy is, eating so much spinach!" And Mommy might exclaim "Yum! Yum!")

However, most American children do not spend much time with their parents, and for this reason Bronfenbrenner believes they are more deprived than Soviet children. He points out that in North America social life is segregated by age. Adults do not take children with them to parties or to work. Children spend most of their free time in front of the TV set or in unsupervised, aimless activities. Millions of American kids ride around on bicycles for hours every day after school, going nowhere.

The young Soviet peer group is trained to socialize children according to adult values; the American child's peer group is expected somehow to arrive at an understanding of social norms without being taught them by adults. This doesn't work. The Soviet peer group discourages antisocial behavior, but American children who spend most of their time with other children engage in more antisocial behavior than other children. They also have negative views of themselves, of the peer group, and of their own future.

If American parents neglect their chil-

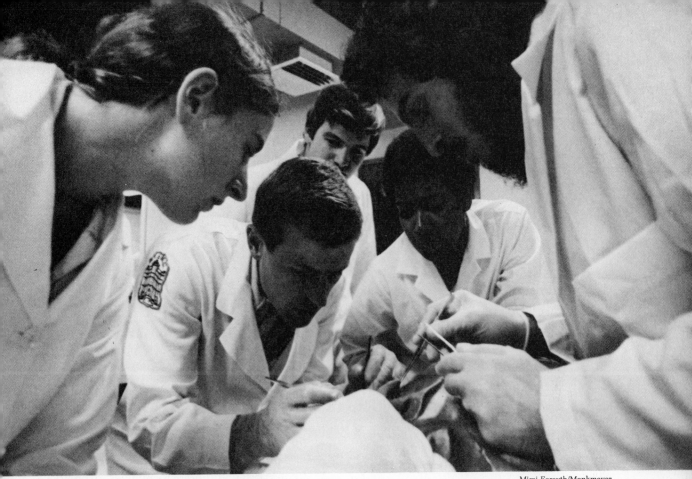

*Career training is a form of socialization which may extend for many years.*

dren by allowing them to drift without guidance, it is only because they value independence very highly. Russians value conformity more highly than independence, and their method of socialization reflects this value. It is protective and close. Bronfenbrenner believes that the Russian practice is better for the children. Americans carry independence too far, so that the effects on youth are harmful. Bronfenbrenner suggests that parents pay closer attention to their children and share more experiences with them. He does not think child care centers can really substitute for good family socialization, but he prefers them to the present pattern of relative neglect.

## Socialization through the life cycle

Childhood is only the first stage of our socialization. Each new stage of life puts us into new situations, and at each new stage we take on new roles. And to perform any new role we must understand the skills it requires, as well as what others will expect of us when we play that role and what we can expect from them in return. Educational institutions have been set up to provide the background knowledge that we need when we play our various roles. But

93

important though they are, schools can do only so much to prepare us. We must learn the roles themselves through experience and by watching role models. Some of this learning we must do as we go along, but we try to do some of it in advance.

We must have at least some understanding of a wide variety of roles, if only because we must interact with the butcher, the baker, the candlestick maker, and all the rest. But when there is a chance that we may play a particular role ourselves at some future time we usually try to learn a lot about it. This is called anticipatory socialization. We try out various roles in our imagination to see how they feel. And we look for role models— people who are already playing the roles that we expect to play, or people whom we admire. Role models are particularly important to young people, who often develop an intense curiosity about some famous person whom they would like to resemble. (For me it was Ingrid Bergman; I used to practice a Swedish accent in private.) Adults are not as given to hero worship as youths, but they too sometimes feel a need for anticipatory socialization. Thus a woman who is planning her first Caribbean cruise may read etiquette books and travel magazines so that she can appear sophisticated while playing her new role.

One obvious difference between childhood and adulthood is the fact that adults usually have more chances to choose what roles they will play and to arrange for their own socialization. This can be a heavy responsibility when one is preparing for a difficult role, such as that of physician. In their study of medical students Blanche Geer and Howard Becker found that the students took their own training very seriously and were upset when they found that no matter how hard or how long they studied they couldn't possibly learn everything that they might someday need to know. And nobody could possibly tell them with any certainty what they should study thoroughly and what they could skip or go over lightly. Their uncertainty made for painful anxiety, and one way in which they coped with this anxiety was by forming close relationships with their classmates. By checking their guesses against those of other students, they collectively developed some idea of the subjects they should study most thoroughly. Sometimes their standards conflicted with those of their professors, but they protected themselves from feeling guilty or inadequate by developing these informal standards and trying to live up to them.[12]

A lot of adult socialization cannot be done in advance but has to be done on the job. You simply feel your way through new situations, paying attention to how other people react, and hope for the best. Consider parenthood, for example. No matter how well you try to prepare for it, you still have to improvise to meet unexpected situations. Indeed, it makes almost as much sense to say that the baby socializes the father into his role as a parent as it does to say that the father socializes the baby. Certainly infants keep their parents informed about how they are feeling and parents take that information seriously.

At each stage of the life cycle we look ahead and vaguely plan for the next stage. We can hardly imagine the stages that are far in the future, and sometimes we even forget how far we have already come. Most societies have ceremonies that mark the transition from one stage to another. These are called *rites of passage.* They include such events as christenings, confirmations, Bar Mitzvahs, weddings, retirement banquets, farewell parties, and funerals. In many primitive societies young boys have to undergo painful initiation rites similar to (or worse than) the "hazings" that new fraternity members sometimes have to go through in North American colleges. These rites remind us of the passing of time so that we will update our self-image to match the society's views about what we can appropriately do or expect others to do. We may forget to update our self-image unless we are prodded by others, for we do not feel any different than we did thirty years before. Only our bodies seem to keep changing. In her study of aging,

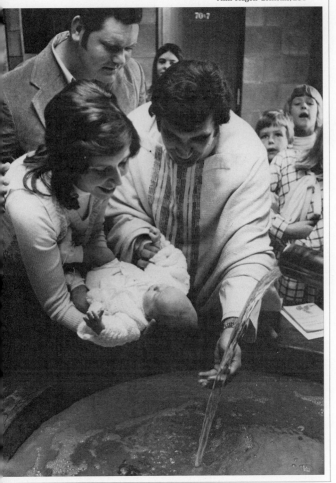

*Your first ceremonial celebration may have been a christening or a brith. Every community has some way of symbolically welcoming newborn members.*

Ann Hagen Griffiths/DPI

Simone de Beauvoir mentions what any middle-aged person has experienced—the shock one feels when one passes a mirror unexpectedly, the surprise or even denial that one's body actually is the way it appears to be. One might say, "Oh well, it's only a bad day. Tomorrow I will look like myself again." But not so. And eventually, at some point during middle age, we stop measuring our lives in terms of how many years have gone by since we were born and begin counting the years we probably have left.

Thus people must be socialized, whether they are willing or not, for the roles that they must play in the middle and later stages of their lives. Women shopping together may ask each other, "Do you think I'm too old to wear a two-piece swimsuit?" Men playing golf may compare notes on buying a retirement condominium in Florida. This is socialization too, no less so than the doll play of little girls.

## RESOCIALIZATION

Not all adult socialization experiences are pleasant. Certain organizations exist for the purpose of **resocializing** an adult whose previous socialization was inadequate. Prisons are the best example of such organizations. They are not very successful, however, in that many of their "graduates" continue to behave in ways that the society disapproves of.

Erving Goffman has studied organizations whose purpose is resocialization. He calls these places total institutions because the person who is being resocialized must spend almost all of his or her time in them. They include the army, prisons, mental hospitals, convents, and boarding schools—all places where batches of recruits are herded from one activity to another according to a fixed schedule. The whole institution is designed to teach a person new roles, skills, or values. The resocialization process aims for uniformity, not individuality: new recruits often are not allowed to see their friends or relatives for several weeks after entering the institution. Their heads may be shaved; they may be dressed in ugly uniforms and made to do degrading jobs such as cleaning toilets. Only after they have shown that they are ready to conform to the demands of the organization are they gradually given full status as members. As a reward they receive an "identity kit"—the clothing, cosmetics, equipment, and services that one needs if one is going to put together the kind of personal identity and appearance that one wants to show to others.[13]

## Three views of socialization

In our study of socialization theories we will discuss three writers who studied human nature and the process of becoming civilized. They are Emile Durkheim, Jean Piaget, and Sigmund Freud.

### DURKHEIM ON MORAL AUTHORITY

Durkheim's view is the one that has most influenced sociologists' ideas about socialization. Unfortunately, however, Durkheim's understanding of psychological processes was probably his weakest point. As we will see, his discussion of social learning leaves much to be desired.

For many years Durkheim was a professor of both sociology and education, but today the teaching methods he recommended are seen as old-fashioned, rigid, and repressive. He believed that moral education was the teacher's main responsibility, and moral education (or socialization) meant impressing society's norms upon the young person in such a way that they became part of his or her personality. The educator's dominant characteristic is moral authority.

Just as the priest is the interpreter of his god, the teacher is the interpreter of the great moral

ideas of his time and of his country. Let him be attached to these ideas, let him feel all their grandeur, and the authority which is in them, and of which he is aware, cannot fail to be communicated to his person and to everything that emanates from him. . . . It is this respect which, through word and gesture, passes from him to the child.[14]

Durkheim viewed the child as a blank sheet of paper on which society writes. His advice to the teacher seems a bit heavy-handed to present-day educators. He compared the process of education to hypnosis, in that

(1) The child is naturally in a state of passivity quite comparable to that in which the hypnotic subject is found artificially placed. His mind yet contains only a small number of conceptions able to fight against those which are suggested to him; his will is still rudimentary. Therefore he is very suggestible. For the same reason, he is very susceptible to the force of example, very much inclined to imitation. (2) The ascendancy that the teacher naturally has over his pupil, because of the superiority of his experience and of his culture, will naturally give to his influence the efficacious force that he needs.[15]

For the sake of this high goal, Durkheim believed, the teacher must have a compelling will and must be consistent. "For authority implies confidence, and the child cannot have confidence in anyone whom he sees hesitating, shifting, going back on his decisions."[16]

### PIAGET ON MORAL REASONING

The Swiss psychologist Jean Piaget has contributed more than any other social scientist to our understanding of the development of children's thinking. Piaget opposed Durkheim's view of socialization in his best-known book, *The Moral Judgment of the Child.*[17] He agreed with Durkheim that morality is a product of social experience, but he disagreed with Durkheim's view of how it all comes about. To demonstrate his own point of view, Piaget conducted research that consisted mostly of asking Swiss children to teach him how to play marbles. The goal was to get the children to explain the rules of the game to him so that he could find out how they reasoned about such matters as fair play. He found that younger and older children usually have quite different ideas about rules.

The young children had a viewpoint that Piaget called **moral realism.** They believed that rules either had existed forever or had been laid down by God or some other authority figure. When Piaget asked the children whether it would still be a fair game of marbles if they agreed to change one of the rules, the child of 5 or 6 would usually say no. The authority of the rules was never questioned. Even so, the young child did not fully understand the rules and broke them all the time.

Young children also insisted on obeying the letter of the law, not the spirit of the law. Good behavior consisted of following rules exactly, whatever the situation. For example, Piaget asked children to judge which child was more naughty, a child who stole a ribbon to wear or a child who stole a roll worth twice as much to give to a hungry friend. Young children were far more likely than older ones to say that the theft of the roll was more serious because it cost more. Young moral realists have many of the attitudes that Durkheim believed were desirable. In particular, they have boundless respect for the authority of adults. In fact the child assumes that whatever decision an adult makes must be just and proper. This attitude Piaget called *unilateral respect* because the child does not expect the adult to have equal respect for him or her. The judgments of adults are not questioned.

Jim Jowers/Palmer Photo

By the age of 8 or 9 a child is usually beginning to develop a more sophisticated
form of reasoning about rules and obligations, an attitude that Piaget called the **morality of cooperation.** By perhaps 10 or 12
most children are able to reason in this way.
A child develops this ability through experiences such as the settling of disputes in
games of marbles to the satisfaction of all
players. Rules at this stage are rational, produced by argument, rather than fixed, absolute principles. In their games children at
this age are, indeed, more interested in disputes and complicated rule changes than in
the physical skills needed to play the game.
They actually follow the rules more closely
than ever now that they see them as agreements among themselves. Moreover, they
tend to be milder in punishing those who
break the rules. They choose forms of punishment that are designed to show offenders
how they have hurt others or caused them to
withdraw their trust. Their responses, then,
are designed to restore unity to the group,
not just to punish for its own sake. This is
concern for the spirit of law, for reciprocity
and equality. Piaget believes that it develops
out of *mutual* as opposed to *unilateral* respect.

It is on this point that he specifically
disagrees with Durkheim. Durkheim's advice smacks of moral realism. The child is
expected to be hypnotically compelled by
the strong will of the teacher, who is to show
in word and deed such a firm commitment to
the society's rules that the child could not
think of disobeying them. Piaget says that
this situation is, unfortunately, rather common. Young children are overwhelmingly
impressed by their teachers and would never
learn to reason on their own about moral
matters through this unilateral relationship.
It is on the playground or in other dealings
with their peers, who respect one another as
equals, that children learn to arrive at satisfactory rules on their own.

Free schools, in which children learn
mostly by reasoning together, respect Piaget
highly. Nevertheless more recent evidence
does not entirely support Piaget's claim that
peer group socialization produces more ethical children than authoritative teaching by
adults. Not all peer groups are alike, and the
ones that are most effective are probably indirectly guided by adults. As we have already seen, this is what Urie Bronfenbrenner
supports. He does not think peer group socialization is very effective unless the group
is taught to support the values adults want to
teach.

## FREUD ON REPRESSION

Though they favor very different ways of
teaching children moral values, Piaget and
Durkheim agree on one important point: Neither views the socialization process as stressful. Neither sees the child's nature as resisting society's demands. Piaget describes the
child's mental skills as developing smoothly
and naturally as the child is socialized
through a process that can be more play than
work. Durkheim believes that adult authority is necessary, but not necessarily unpleasant or coercive. After all, a blank piece of
paper does not resist the pencil.

But to Freud the child was not a blank
page at all. And Freud, the father of psychoanalysis, has left his mark on modern
sociology as well as all the other social sciences. It is to him that we owe the idea of
**repression**—the view that certain impulses
within the personality can be restrained (repressed) only with great effort.

The psychoanalyst's view of personality
has sometimes been jokingly called a "hy-
draulic model" in that it sees each person as
containing a fixed quantity of emotional energy. This energy can be channeled from one
aspect of the personality to another, but
when one tries to suppress it, it is only displaced, like water in a closed system of
pipes. Such repression causes harmful
changes in other aspects of the personality.

Freud was interested in the origins of this supply of energy and in how it is channeled. He concluded that its sources are the impulse to love, and the impulse to be aggressive and destructive. As he saw it, civilization opposes direct expression of both of these impulses. In *Civilization and Its Discontents*[18] he wrote that people cannot ever expect to attain happiness. Civilization brings material well-being, security, justice, and social order, but only at the cost of requiring us to restrain our impulses at every turn. Beauty, cleanliness, and order all require self-restraint.

It is easy to understand why civilization requires the repression of aggressive impulses, but it may not be so obvious that the love impulse and civilization are in conflict. Freud pointed out, however, that two lovers feel wholly fulfilled when they are able to express their love to one another directly. They do not need the rest of society. But civilization requires that the lovers give other people some of their attention and affection. Thus society makes claims on one's emotional energy that interfere with the expression of love. The individual is asked to inhibit love by channeling some of his or her feelings into "brotherly love," or friendliness and good will toward other members of the society.

## Sublimation

Society also requires creative, expressive work—art, gardening, scientific research, and the like. Such work uses energy that is channeled away from sexual concerns and into more refined, civilized concerns through a process that Freud called sublimation. Freud believed that sublimation was the most desirable response to society's claims on the individual. Still, he recognized that the pleasure of creating art, solving scientific problems, or gardening is mild "as compared with that derived from the sating of crude and primary instinctual impulses; it does not convulse our physical being."[19] Not

everybody could get through life comfortably by sublimating basic impulses. Each person must develop his or her own way of coping, depending on the strength of his or her particular set of needs. Some people will cope by emphasizing emotional relationships with others. Some will get their satisfaction mainly from their own mental processes. Others, needing action, will continue to challenge society by sublimating as little as possible.[20]

Freud was the most pessimistic of the writers we have discussed. To him socialization was a process by which people are taught to give up their greatest pleasures for the sake of the group. Freud did not expect this situation to improve. On the contrary, civilization can progress only through ever greater repression and sublimation. It is ironic that Freud is so often misunderstood on this point. It is commonly believed that psychoanalysis offers happiness by encouraging people to act impulsively, to follow their feelings. Actually, Freud never expected much happiness either for himself or for his patients, for the requirements of society would not be changed by psychoanalysis. All the psychoanalyst can do is help the patient use rational judgments about reality in trying to achieve happiness. Freud thought that most of his patients were unnecessarily miserable because they were *overly* repressed. Their guilt feelings overwhelmed them and kept them from seeking even pleasures that might have been perfectly all right.

### Surplus repression

Though Freud was by no means opposed to socialism, he did not believe it would increase human happiness. In *Civilization and Its Discontents* he presented his opinion of Marxism. Marx had claimed that most human misery was caused by the fact that there are not enough material goods to go around, so that people need to work. This situation is made worse by exploitation of the working classes by the idle ruling classes. Marx be-

*Freud believed that rich people are more repressed and unhappy than working-class people. (He was wrong.)*

lieved that over time the workers would unite and rebel against the ruling class, and that this would make it possible for all to share equally in a life of abundance, leisure, and pleasure.

Freud believed that such a revolution would not really make much difference. He claimed that human unhappiness is caused not by the lack of material goods but by the requirement that people repress their basic impulses. It seemed to Freud that upper-class people, who have more material goods, are more repressed and unhappy than working-class people. (We now know that he was wrong on this point. People with money generally say they are happier than poor people.)

A modern writer, Herbert Marcuse, has entered this dispute. Marcuse, who is both a Freudian and a Marxist, simply takes a middle position. He agrees with Freud that a lot of repression will always be necessary even in a classless society. However, he agrees with Marx that exploitation is the cause of a great deal of repression.[21] Some repression is the price that people must pay if they are going to live together in a civilized way, he argues. But we repress more than we need to, and it makes us unhappier than we need to be. This situation Marcuse calls surplus repression, and he thinks that it results from the domination of one class by another. We work harder than we need to work in order to produce more than we need, and we wastefully consume things that we don't need and that don't make us happy. We suppress joy and sexual pleasure. Surplus repression can be overcome by political and social liberation, but basic repression cannot be overcome entirely.

Marcuse's main point seems reasonable: Probably some repression is avoidable (at least in principle) and some is unavoidable. But I question whether his political proposals are the best way to eliminate surplus repression. He would like to have a communist revolution. Personally, however, I doubt that people experience less surplus repression in socialist societies than in capitalist societies. In actual practice, the socialist state can be as coercive as a group of stockholders, if not more so.

I have mentioned several points of view concerning the way in which an individual becomes a part of civilized society. All of these views are familiar to large numbers of people in Western society. Durkheim's position probably comes closest to that of most sociologists, for it assumes that society's goals are stamped on the child's character without any resistance by the child. Piaget's view is a more developmental one. He sees commitment to society's values as a mental skill that develops much like any other mental ability. Neither Piaget or Durkheim view socialization as stressful, however, for they do not believe that the individual has any desire to resist social influence. Freud, by contrast, views socialization as highly stressful, for each individual is forced to act contrary to his or her biological needs.

# SOCIAL RESEARCH:
## *Sociologists at Work*

### ACHIEVEMENT MOTIVATION

One topic that interests researchers is the question of how human beings come to differ so much in their desire to excel; that is, *achievement motivation.*

Every society must manage to instill in its new members a desire to accomplish great things, to master difficult challenges. However, some societies are more successful than others in doing this, just as some families are more successful than others. Max Weber suggested that the success of Protestantism in creating a motivation for hard work and ascetic living was a chief cause of the rise of capitalism.[22] (See Chapter 13 for further discussion of this point.) Perhaps the rate of economic growth in contemporary societies is determined partly by their members' motivation to achieve.

In 1948 J. W. Atkinson and David McClelland opened up a whole area of investigation into human motivations, their social causes, and their social and economic results.[23] Their method was based on the discovery that if hungry people were asked to make up stories about a series of pictures, they would mention food in their stories more often than other people would. Thus researchers could use content analysis to study the stories and obtain a measure of the strength of the storyteller's need for food. The same methods could be used to measure the strength of other needs. Indeed, one might even measure the motives of a dead writer by counting the images in a story he or she had written. McClelland began to measure the *need for achievement (n-ach)* by counting the number of times a storyteller referred to such ideas as doing well in some kind of performance, trying to achieve, and reacting emotionally to the results of one's efforts. This method enabled McClelland to score all sorts of literary documents for achievement motivation themes—even the folktales of American Indian tribes. One could then compare high scorers with low scorers to see how they differed.

This approach was used to test an extension

of Weber's theory about the relationship between motivation and success in business. McClelland established that high *n-ach* scorers usually enjoy tackling hard challenges and undertaking somewhat risky ventures that offer the possibility of real accomplishment if they are managed well. Weber had suggested that the need to achieve had been especially common among Puritans, who thought of themselves as God's stewards on earth but could never be sure that they been chosen for salvation.

Extending this reasoning, McClelland decided that a similar need for achievement may be responsible for economic growth in many countries today and that achievement motivation is probably learned through direct training in the school and at home. In looking for literary documents for a content analysis of achievement themes he hit upon children's first-grade reading books. He reasoned that such books probably reflect the degree to which a society emphasizes achievement motivation in training the young. Furthermore, if the children are exposed to large doses of achievement training, they may learn their lesson well and go on to work very hard in order to excell in later life. This high *n-ach* should be reflected in the economic growth of their countries.

This theory was supported by the evidence. McClelland found that periods when the young were socialized for achievement were followed by periods of economic expansion about thirty years later. The children had carried their high *n-ach* into adulthood. The Protestant ethic was just a special case of achievement motivation, that of the Calvinists during the Protestant Reformation. Protestants no longer have a monopoly on high *n-ach.* American Protestants do not differ greatly from Catholics when measured for *n-ach,* and many non-Christian countries have high levels of achievement content in their children's books. If McClelland is right, their economic growth will be especially rapid during the next 20 to 50 years, when the children become businesspeople. There is some evidence that it is possible to help adult businesspeople become more effective through direct training for achievement orientation. Such programs may prove helpful in fostering business skills among groups that lack a strong tradition of business management, for example, black Americans.

## CHILDHOOD SOCIALIZATION FOR ACHIEVEMENT

Despite the prospect of changing the motivations of adults, socialization for achievement is most successful with children. Many scholars have tried to pinpoint the social background that produces high *n-ach* among boys. To rear a son with high *n-ach,* parents should be affectionate, should show pleasure when their son explores and takes moderate risks, and should hug and kiss him when he excels at different tasks. A domineering, interfering father impairs his son's achievement orientation. Parents of boys with high *n-ach* usually encourage independence at a young age. They allow the child to cross town on a bus alone earlier than other parents do, expect him to make his own friends, and the like. Excessive fear of failure blocks achievement motivation: Boys with high *n-ach* prefer to take enough risks to give them a challenge, though not such great risks as to be foolhardy. For example, if children are invited to play ringtoss or horseshoes, those with low *n-ach* scores will usually set a low goal for themselves or will stand so close to the post that most of their tosses will be successful. When asked how many of his tosses will be good, the high-*n-ach* child announces the highest realistic goal and stands back far enough to make the game a real challenge; easy goals are no fun for him. It is not surprising that achievement motivation is associated with actual ability: A highly motivated person will develop skills because he or she wants to.

## ACHIEVEMENT AND FEMININITY

From the very beginning, researchers in achievement motivation have been puzzled by the responses of female subjects. The *n-ach* scores of females were not correlated with the factors to which males' achievement motivation was correlated.

In recent years, however, many new studies of female achievement have been done. Traditionally, women have been discouraged from undertaking ambitious projects; no doubt their low *n-ach* has been a way of adjusting to this situation. In the past this adjustment may have been fairly satisfying for most women, but the declining birthrate has caused many women to find their traditional role unfulfilling. However, their low *n-ach* often prevents them from pursuing important careers. Most current research is aimed toward discovering the factors that make girls less interested in achievement.

Childhood socialization experiences clearly form the basis of girls' motivations. It is also clear that expectations learned in childhood reduce women's levels of performance and ambition. Matina Horner, a Harvard psychologist, has demonstrated this fact. She claims that most women *fear* success.

The assumption underlying Horner's research was that most women have powerful affiliative motivations that conflict with their achievement motivations.[24] According to Horner, because women learn throughout life that they may be considered "unfeminine" if they perform well (especially in competition against males), they acquire a need to avoid achievement. Horner assumed that talented women who have high *n-ach* are the very ones who are most troubled by this problem, so they experience internal conflict and ambivalence. Her reasoning makes sense: Almost every woman deeply desires a close relationship with a man, but some men feel uncomfortable with ambitious women. Women who are not highly talented will probably be accepted the way they are. However, a woman who has a realistic chance of success may think twice before starting out toward her goal—especially if it means competing against men.

Horner's experiment showed that this is actually the case. She gave tests similar to those used by McClelland to test for *n-ach,* but she scored them for avoidance of success. For example, she asked female subjects to complete a story that began, "After first-term finals, Anne finds herself at the top of her medical-school class." For male subjects the lead was, "After first-term finals, John finds himself at the top of his medical-school class." At first the subjects were mostly undergraduate students at a large midwestern university. The motive to avoid success was considered to be present if the subject made up a story showing conflict about success,

anticipation of negative results of success, denial of responsibility for attaining success, denial of the lead statement itself, or some other inappropriate or bizarre response.

Of the 88 male subjects, fewer than 10 percent responded negatively to the cue in any way. Most of them showed confidence in John's future and a belief that this success would lead to other important goals, such a providing a good home for a wife and family.

On the other hand, of the 90 female subjects 65 percent were troubled by the lead statement. Most showed that they regarded Anne's success as bad news showing loss of femininity, social rejection, or some other problem:

There was a typical story, for example, in which Anne deliberately lowers her academic standing in the next terms and does all she subtly can to help Carl, whose grades come up. She soon drops out of med school, they marry, and Carl goes on in school while she raises their family.

Some girls stressed that Anne is unhappy, aggressive, unmarried, or that she is so ambitious that she uses her family, husband, and friends as tools in the advancement of her career. Others argued that Anne is a code name for a non-existent person created by a group of med students who take turns taking exams and writing papers for Anne.[25]

Horner found that people who have a high fear of success learn how to disguise their ability and drop out of the competition. To illustrate this pattern, she cites a Peanuts cartoon in which Sally says, "I never said I wanted to *be* someone. All I want to do when I grow up is to be a good wife and mother. So . . . why should I have to go to kindergarten?"[26]

Repression of ambition is costly in psychological terms. It leads to feelings of frustration, hostility, aggression, and bitterness. For example, when asked to complete a story beginning, "Anne is sitting in a chair with a smile on her face," more than 90 percent of the women who had little fear of success produced happy stories, usually about pleasant social relationships such as dates and forthcoming marriages. Those who scored high on fear of success responded quite differently, however. Fewer than 20 percent of them completed stories in this way. Here are some of their responses:

"She is sitting in a chair smiling smugly because she has just achieved great satisfaction from the fact that she hurt somebody's feelings."

"Gun in hand she is waiting for her stepmother to return home."

"Anne is at her father's funeral. There are over 200 people there. She knows it is unseemly to smile but cannot help it. . . . Her brother Ralph pokes her in fury but she is uncontrollable. . . . Anne rises dramatically and leaves the room, stopping first to pluck a carnation from the blanket of flowers on the coffin.[27]

Not all women suffer from fear of success. Some override this feeling and continue their careers. Most of the fortunate female subjects have ongoing relationships with boys who have encouraged them, usually because they both recognize that the boy is the more intelligent of the two: "He's so much smarter . . . competition with him would be hopeless." The greatest tension occurs between couples in which the girl is more intelligent.

During their later college years girls often find that their parents' attitudes suddenly reverse. Formerly they delighted in their daughters' achievements; now they become concerned about the girls' femininity and marriageability. They begin to suggest that the daughter stop studying so hard and find a husband instead. Is this a major cause of women's fear of failure? Apparently not. Research to date suggests that on this matter women are influenced less by their parents' attitudes than by the attitudes of their male peers.

In Chapter 2, I pointed out that after a sociological study has been completed and reported other scholars may conduct additional research that produces contrary evidence. This is one of those cases. A great many studies have followed Horner's and seem to be as likely to contradict her findings as to support them.[28] We are not yet able to conclude that women either do or do not have a tendency to avoid success. I find this issue very interesting, however, and am eager for someone to resolve what seem to be contradictory results.

# SOCIAL POLICY:
## Issues and Viewpoints

We cannot talk about socialization today without mentioning the women's movement's demand for changes in sex roles. These topics are linked in several important ways. First, if we are interested in public policy we must ask how children are affected by the increasing tendency of mothers to work outside the home. And if we are interested in the socialization of young children we must recognize that a new pattern of sex roles is developing that may be quite different from the traditional one. We must then ask ourselves what expectations are appropriate and fair in view of both our biological needs as males and females, and the challenges of our new social structure. What

expectations lead to unnecessary tension and unhappiness? Here we can touch only briefly on a few of the issues that are getting a lot of attention today.

### CHILD CARE
### FOR WORKING MOTHERS

Imagine that you are a well-educated North American woman living in a suburban home with your husband and a 6-month-old baby. You have an important decision to make: Will you take a job?

It is nothing new for women to work. Even in primitive societies women contribute as much to the household economy as men do, on the average. But they usually work in special settings with other women and with their children. They garden together, clean fish together, beat their laundry on the rocks together, and look after the children at the same time. Cross-cultural studies of mothers around the world point out how much more isolated North American women are than women in other societies. Your household is private, with its own kitchen, laundry room, car, TV, and so on. You don't even go to the village well, where you might talk with other women. You feel bored, lonely, and dependent on your husband. If you need money, you will go to work. If you don't, you may not. But the choice will not be easy, for there are costs to pay in either case. You will not want your baby to be the one who must pay those costs. Thus your personal decision, as well as the public decision on whether to provide day care services, should take into consideration the normal feelings of infants. And babies definitely tell you how they feel. John Bowlby, who has studied the mother—infant bond more than any other scholar, comments: "No form of behaviour is accompanied by stronger feeling than is attachment behaviour. The figures toward whom it is directed are loved and their advent is greated with great joy. . . . A threat of loss creates anxiety and actual loss sorrow; both, moreover, are likely to arouse anger."[29]

By about the sixth month of life the baby ordinarily becomes strongly attached to his or her mother and shows signs of distress when left with a stranger. Throughout the early years children are concerned mainly with their relations with members of their family; only later do they become interested in other children. Researchers who study young children are trying to find out whether various child care arrangements have any permanent effects on children's emotional development. Some psychologists[30] who believed five years ago that day care hurts children's development no longer believe this. Current research by Jerome Kagan suggests that the behavior of children who experience first-rate day care over a long period is no different from that of children brought up at home by their mothers. But "first-rate" day care is unusual. Kagan chose warm caregivers, trained them himself, and made sure that they each looked after only a few babies. Most day care institutions expect each caregiver to look after a number of children. This, plus the fact that the child may have a series of caregivers, means that day care may not usually provide the sort of social environment in which a child's attach-

ments are respected. As some researchers have noted,

The great tragedy of hastily conceived and inadequately funded all-day programs may well be in the creation of deficiencies that might not normally occur.
Our concern for the immediate welfare of the child leads us to believe that his distress signals are important messages to which environments must respond, whether in the form of policy decisions, planning concerns, or caregiving behaviors. Although we do not know the long term consequences of separation or deprivation we do know that they can produce acute immediate distress. We maintain that these grounds alone are sufficient for the serious attention of researchers and practitioners alike.[31]

About half of all working mothers in North America leave their children in the care of relatives. This is, in fact, the most commonly preferred arrangement for very young children, probably because the children have more secure, permanent, and loving relationships with these caregivers and show less separation distress with them than they show when they are left in day nurseries. Parents of somewhat older children prefer day care arrangements to home care.[32]

My own view is that the best policy would be the one that gives mothers the greatest opportunity to make their own choices. After all, mothers know their infants' needs better than anybody else and usually care more about them than anybody else. Unfortunately, public policies do not always allow much room for choice. For example, day care institutions are sometimes set up on the basis of the belief that all welfare mothers should go to work whether or not they think their children would be happy in the day nursery. I think poor mothers should have the same right to respect their children's feelings that other parents have.

I believe women should be able to choose among several alternatives. Without implying that mothers should or should not take jobs, we might find other ways of decreasing the isolation and economic dependency of mothers who choose to stay home. Some people are saying, for example, that homemaking should be a paid job. I don't know whether this idea is practical or not, but I suggest that in judging this and other ideas the welfare of children should always be a major factor.

# SUMMARY

**1.** *Socialization* is the process by which people acquire the motivation, knowledge, language, skills, roles, values, and norms that enable them to function as members of a particular group. This process works by channeling biological needs into more specific patterns of behavior that fit together with the behavior patterns of other members of the social system.

**2.** Early socialization usually takes place in the family, and researchers have found that the structure of the family has an important influence on the results. For example, children in large families and later-born children get less attention from their parents than children in small families and firstborn children. As a result the achievement, language development, and general adjustment are less satisfactory in the latter than in the former. Children form close ties with their parents, and their emotional well-being depends on this closeness. But this does not mean that children cannot be separated from their mothers for certain periods.

**3.** Bronfenbrenner's comparison of child rearing practices in the U.S. and the Soviet Union concludes that peer groups can be taught to socialize children into adult values. But to do this requires much contact with adults. Americans encourage early independence and segregate social activities by age a lot.

**4.** The controversy about the effects of day care centers should be viewed in the light of the evidence suggesting that collective child care can be more beneficial than unsupervised peer group experiences. However, separation from parents is known to be traumatic for a child who is not ready for it.

**5.** Learning to live in society is largely a matter of learning at least a little about a number of different roles. Often this involves *anticipatory socialization* — learning possible roles in advance.

**6.** Unlike children, adults can choose the kinds of socialization to which they are exposed. Sometimes, however, they may be forced into experiences that are designed to *resocialize* them. *Total institutions* have this as their main purpose.

**7.** Durkheim viewed socialization as a situation in which society teaches its ideas to the child through the authority of adults — for example, teachers. He did not see the child's readiness to learn as an issue requiring any attention. On the other hand, Piaget views socialization primarily as a process in which the child learns through exploration and interaction, especially with peers. Normal cooperative play, not heavy-handed instruction by adults, provides the setting in which moral values are acquired.

**8.** Freud's view of socialization, unlike that of Durkheim or Piaget, assumed that there are forces within each person that resist the socialization process. Love impulses and aggressive impulses are both strong, but both must be *repressed* for the sake of social order and the benefits of civilization. *Sublimation* is the process of channeling these impulses into creative activities. Marcuse, influenced both by Marx and by Freud, concluded that some repression is necessary but that some is not. This *surplus repression* could be decreased by eliminating economic exploitation.

# KEY TERMS

**anticipatory socialization** trying out a role in advance because one may play that role at some time in the future.

**institution** a complex structure of roles organized around a central activity or social need.

**internalization** the process by which one makes the society's values part of one's personality.

**moral realism** the view that rules were laid

down by God or some other authority figure and cannot be changed.

**morality of cooperation**   the view that rules and obligations are rational agreements rather than fixed principles.

**repression**   the effort to restrain certain impulses within the personality.

**resocialization**   the process by which an adult whose previous socialization was inadequate is made to behave in ways that the society approves of.

**role**   the part each person must play to create a collective activity.

**role conflict**   the situation in which a person occupies two roles that are regulated by incompatible norms.

**socialization**   the process of learning the rules of behavior for a given social group.

**sublimation**   the process by which energy is channeled away from sexual or aggressive concerns and into more refined concerns.

**surplus repression**   repression in excess of what is necessary for people to live together in a civilized way.

## FOR FURTHER READING

ARIÈS, PHILIPPE. *Centuries of Childhood.* New York: Knopf, 1962. Aries is a Frenchman, an amateur historian, whose research into the way children were treated throughout European history utilized some imaginative research techniques. He presents a stimulating theory.

ARONSON, ELLIOT. *The Social Animal,* 2nd edition. San Francisco: Jossey-Bass, 1976. This is a highly readable textbook on social psychology that explains a lot about how people influence each other through personal relationships.

BRIM, ORVILLE G., and STANTON WHEELER. *Socialization After Childhood.* New York: John Wiley, 1966. Most of the research done on socialization concentrates on childhood. This book is an exception. In fact, Brim's special field is adult socialization and whatever you see his name on probably deals with that subject.

BRONFENBRENNER, URIE. *Two Worlds of Childhood: U.S. and USSR.* New York: Russell Sage, 1970. I am not sure whether Bronfenbrenner is right or not, but I guarantee his book will "grab" you. It is highly provocative for anybody who ever plans to become a parent.

GOFFMAN, ERVING. *Asylums: Essays on the Situation of Mental Patients and Other Inmates.* New York: Doubleday Anchor, 1961. This is the book in which Goffman develops his concept of the total institution. He worked in a mental hospital and watched the way patients coped with the situation of being confined. Practically everything Goffman writes is exciting to read and this is a good one to start with.

MAAS, HENRY, and JOSEPH KUYPERS. *From Thirty to Seventy.* San Francisco: Jossey-Bass, 1975. This is about socialization for old age. The authors conclude that whatever happens in the first part of our life influences the way we experience the last part. (Which means that it's not a bit too early to begin getting ready.)

NORTON, G. RON. *Parenting.* Englewood Cliffs, N.J.: Prentice-Hall, 1977. This how-to-do-it manual reads like the instruction booklet from a child-raising kit, but you have to supply your own child. It sounds easy but I suggest you practice on other people's children before starting on your own.

SPIRO, MELFORD, and AUDREY G. SPIRO. *Children of the Kibbutz.* (revised ed.) Cambridge, Mass.: Harvard University Press, 1975. The Spiros studied the children brought up in agricultural communes in Israel, where child-rearing techniques are very different from those most of us have experienced. The first batch of kibbutz children are now grown up, and many of them have played leading roles in Israeli society.

WRONG, DENNIS. "The Oversocialized Conception of Man in Modern Sociology." *American Sociological Review,* 26, (April 1961), 183–193. This is one of the best known articles attacking sociologists' common assumptions about socialization. Wrong cautions us not to assume that all kinds of socialization are equally possible. He follows Freud's views—that we have biological tendencies that make some outcomes more attainable than other outcomes.

# SEX ROLES

Imagine that this morning when you awoke you made an amazing discovery: During the night you changed your sex! You became, in every physical way, a member of the opposite sex—your genitals, your muscles, your whiskers, everything! Nothing else changed. If you were twenty pounds overweight yesterday, you still are. If you knew how to play the saxophone yesterday, you still do. You are the same old self, only now your sex is different. Naturally you phone your doctor, who is surprised enough to make a house call and who confirms what you have discovered.

Now, pull yourself together and decide what to do about this situation. How do you feel about it? Is it your childhood dream come true or your worst nightmare? Will you have surgery to change back to your old sex or will you accept yourself as you are? In any case you will have to act differently in public, whether temporarily or permanently. Suppose you throw yourself into the experience and imagine what it would be like.

How will you dress, walk, and move? Will your gestures be expansive and energetic? Will you do many things that require strength and endurance? Will you change your own flat tires? Will being twenty pounds overweight handicap you socially and in finding jobs? Will you knit in public? Will you play your saxophone or switch to a violin?

How about showing your feelings? Will you express anger more readily? Will you cry easily? Will it be easy to say no to other people's requests in a straightforward way? Will you hint a lot or will you say what you want outright? If you have always been a bit of a clown will you have to change your act? How important will it be for you to be warm, sympathetic, and sensitive to other people? How competitive will you be in games, in work, and in bargaining for a used car? How will you behave when you are hurt? When you meet a person who attracts you sexually, will you feel free to express this fact? If so, how?

How about your interests? Will you read the sports and business pages? Will you form strong opinions about public affairs? Will you try hard to gain recognition for your work? Will you change your major in college? Will jobs open up or close for you? Will you take a job as a nursery school teacher? As an engineer? When you are on a committee, will you offer to take the minutes and brew the coffee or will you expect to chair the meeting?

Now compare the person you have just created—the self you would be if you were of the opposite sex—with the "ideal mate" whom you have always hoped to find. How do these two personalities differ? You may find that they are very far apart. Do you expect your ideal guy or girlfriend to live up to standards that you would hate to live up to yourself? Perhaps you have always wanted a gentle, quiet girlfriend who likes to cook and has no particular desire for career achievement—and perhaps you find that you would hate to be such a person yourself. Or maybe you have always wanted a competitive, responsible, assertive leader for a boyfriend, but you see that you wouldn't like the pressure of keeping up such an act yourself.

The point of this exercise is that both men and women are people—that they are all partly soft and partly hard, partly ambitious and partly dependent, partly competitive and partly sympathetic and tender. Sex roles are the source of much pleasure, for through them we find our place in the world. But sex roles can also be too harsh and rigid, limiting people in the expression of many human traits and needs. It is unkind to expect any person to be ambitious and strong all the time. It is unkind to expect any person to be tender and compliant all the time. Today we seem to be taking a new look at the claims we make on each other—at what we demand of a "real man" or a "real woman." Perhaps out of this effort will come the chance for people of both sexes to be, above all, "real human beings." Having a male or female body does not automatically make one masculine or feminine in one's social relationships.

**Sex** is the biological fact of being male or female. The first words you heard after coming into this world may have been those that announced your sex: "It's a girl!" or "It's a boy!"

**Gender,** on the other hand, is a social-psychological fact—the *awareness* of being a member of one sex or the other. Gender has two aspects, gender identity and gender role. **Gender identity** (often used interchangeably with *sexual identity*) refers to whether one considers oneself a male or a female. Ordinarily, of course, if your sex is male your gender identity will also be male. However, this is not always true, for it takes a child a couple of years to learn his or her gender identity. Moreover, there are certain unusual cases in which a male has a female gender identity or vice versa. We'll discuss these situations later.

**Gender role** (which for our purposes can be used interchangeably with *sex role*) consists of the culturally defined set of behaviors that are considered sex-appropriate within a given society. Gender roles, like all other roles, are specific to particular social groups. Thus in North America it is considered appropriate for men to carry heavy loads, while in most societies gender roles specify that women should do so. A man may ride along on a donkey, followed by his wife on foot carrying a load of firewood.

The culture defines what things are appropriate for a male or a female to do, based on the assumption that some behaviors fit better than others with certain biological facts about the two sexes. In reality, those biological "facts" may only be generally accepted beliefs. For example, our idea that it is more appropriate for males than for females to carry heavy loads is part of our definition of the male gender role, based on the "fact" that men are naturally stronger than women. This fact seems obvious to us, but it is not so obvious to all social groups everywhere.

Vivienne/DPI

*She certainly seems to know her gender identity.*

It is true, of course, that there are certain natural, biological differences between males and females, but this does not mean that one particular division of labor between males and females is more natural than all other possible divisions of labor. Thus, though gender roles in North America say that it is appropriate for women to knit and for men to change flat tires, this is not because men and women are "naturally" good at these activities. Gender roles are not natural—they are cultural. That is, they are determined not by biology but by social agreement. *Sex* is natural; *gender* is social. This does not mean, of course, that gender roles can defy the laws of nature. We cannot have norms that require human beings to flap their arms and fly, nor can we have gender roles that require males to give birth. But Mother (or Father?) Nature has nothing conclusive to say about who should knit and who should change tires or carry heavy loads. Because people are often ethnocentric, they may think their customs are natural

111

and appropriate when in fact they are simply social agreements that could easily be changed.

What, then, are the biological facts that cannot be changed?

# Sex: the biological facts

We can usually tell men from women at a glance : They differ in their typical patterns of size, body weight, and hairiness, as well as in ways that are usually covered up by clothing—the genitals and breasts. (Of course there is much overlap in these traits. Many normal women have flatter chests than many normal men. Many normal men have less body hair than many normal women, and so on.) Men can usually defeat women in a physical fight, which may be one reason why males have almost always dominated women socially. In other ways, especially physical endurance, women's strength compares favorably with men's —which may be why women often carry heavy loads in other societies.

Gender roles cannot violate these physical facts. This is why, for example, the division of labor in almost all societies has assigned child care to women. Their biological traits are thought to be very suitable for this activity. We will come back to this point later. Now, however, let's consider two biological facts about the sexes—prenatal and hormonal differences.

### PRENATAL FACTORS

Each of us began when a sperm crashed into an ovum, adding its 23 chromosomes to the ovum's 23 and thus creating a new cell with 46 chromosomes, or 23 pairs. Each chromosome is a long string with hundreds of genes strung along it like beads. The genes carry a precise pattern of the physical traits of the person who will be born.

One pair of chromosomes determines the baby's sex. The ovum always contributes an X chromosome, but the sperm may contribute an X or a Y. If it is an X, the baby will be female; if it is a Y, the baby will be male. Most conceptions are XY combinations— possibly as many as 140 for every 100 XX conceptions. However, miscarriages are more numerous for XY conceptions, so that by birth the ratio is about 105 males to every 100 females. After birth as well as before, males are more likely to be affected by disease and pain than females. As a result, by the time they reach old age women almost everywhere outnumber men by a wide margin.

During the first six weeks after conception male and female embryos form the tiny beginnings of identical sex organs. After the sixth week, however, the Y chromosome somehow signals these organs to develop testicles and start producing various (mostly male) hormones. If they don't receive this message, the organs will become ovaries. The amounts of various hormones in the embryo's system determine how the genitals develop from this point on. Inside the womb are female hormones from the mother, which will produce a female infant unless they are counteracted at critical times by the addition of male hormones produced by the embryo's testicles. If those male hormones are added to the mix, however, male genitals will develop, as shown in Figure 5.1. (If such hormones are artificially injected into a female embryo, it will develop male sex organs.)

Every embryo has a small organ that will enlarge to become the penis or will remain a small but highly sensitive female organ, the clitoris. In later years the woman's orgasms will depend on the stimulation of her clitoris either through manual stroking or through friction by a penis during intercourse. Likewise, every adult male has an organ that would have become the female womb if the testicles had not produced male hormones at the right moment in his prenatal life. However, most men do not notice this organ until

**FIGURE 5.1**
*External genital differentiation in the human fetus*

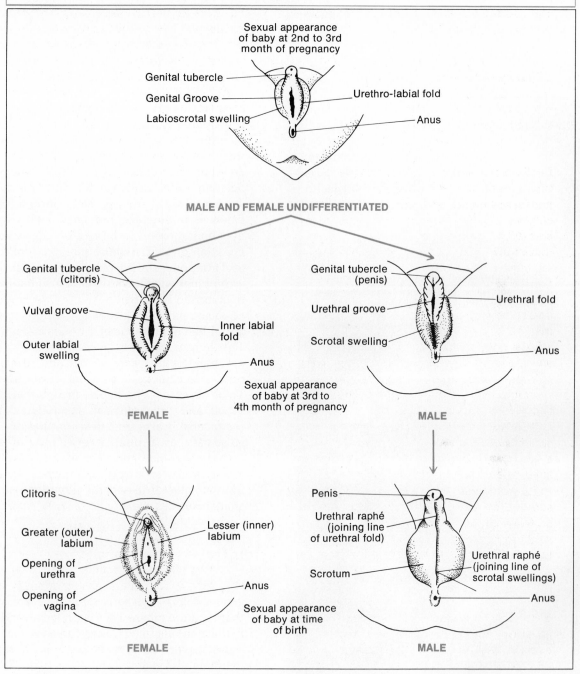

*Source:* Money, Hampson, and Hampson. *Bulletin of The Johns Hopkins Hospital,* 1955.

old age, when it may cause prostate enlargement.

HORMONES

Hormones are "chemical messengers" produced by various glands. They circulate in the bloodstream and regulate many bodily processes. We have already mentioned the importance of female and male hormones in the prenatal molding of sex organs. Scientists have begun to discover how our feelings and behavior are influenced by these substances.

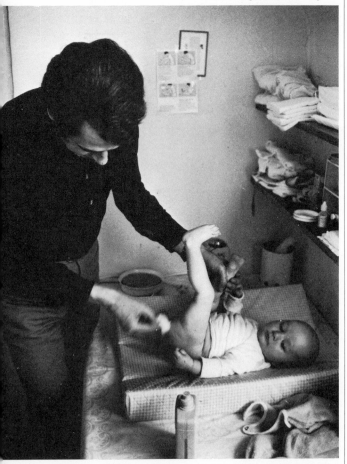

*Do infants sense in the way they are handled whether their fathers and mothers are glad or disappointed in the sex of their child?*

Thomas Hopker/Woodfin Camp

It is somewhat misleading to refer to "male" and "female" hormones, although these are common terms. In reality there are a great many different hormones that regulate all sorts of bodily processes, not just sexual ones. Moreover, both sexes produce both male and female hormones, though in different proportions. It has been found that an animal of either sex that is injected with male hormones will be sexier and more aggressive than usual. Many other abnormal behavior and growth patterns have been shown to result from prenatal hormone imbalances in animals, and some such effects may be important in human beings as well. For example, girls whose mothers took certain hormones during pregnancy may have a greater tendency toward tomboyish behavior than most other girls.[1]

The relationship between hormones and social behavior is one of mutual interaction. The hormones affect feelings and experiences, but social experiences and ideas, in turn, affect the body's output of hormones. To be sure, these biological factors do cause social and psychological experiences—but the reverse is also true. Research has not yet gone very far in linking personality to hormonal imbalance, and although this is a field that is well worth exploring further, we can hardly expect it to explain very much about gender roles.

## Gender

Both gender identity and gender role are socially learned. I feel sure that I am a woman. That is my gender identity. I may also cook, care for children, arrange flowers, be devoted to a man, be sentimental and sensitive, and so on. That is the gender role of women in my society. The two things are not the same. Today many women refuse to perform many parts of the female role, though they have no doubt about their identity as women. Once acquired, gender identity almost never changes. But gender roles may change, since they are nothing more than social agreements.

## SEX AND GENDER IDENTITY

Sex is a fact. Gender identity is a belief. People usually learn their gender identities at about the age of 2. But it is possible for them to learn the wrong gender identity, and once it has been learned it cannot be changed. Hence, there are certain unusual cases in which sex and gender identity do not match. For example, transvestites' gender identity differs from their sex. They feel that they were accidentally born into the wrong kind of body and that they should dress and behave according to their identity, not their sex. They may expect their friends to pretend that they are the sex they feel they should be. Transsexuals have gone even further: Their sex has been changed through surgery and hormone treatment. Such medical procedures are uncommon, of course, but they are becoming less so. Doctors insist that a patient undergo a psychiatric examination before they will consent to do such an operation, and very few transsexuals regret the operation.

Once in a while a baby is born with genitals that are not quite normal, so that it is assigned to the wrong sex. Looking at the child's chromosome pattern under a microscope will reveal its true sex, but this may not be done until he or she is older. Then the doctor and parents have to decide what to do about the mistake. This decision depends mostly on whether the child is old enough to have learned the wrong gender identity. Children under 2 may not have learned their identity yet, so the parents can simply "reannounce" the child's sex by telling friends that they were mistaken, and the child will grow up with the right gender identity. Children who are 3 or 4 have probably learned their gender identity. If a child has learned the wrong one, the doctor may change his or

her sex through surgery because it is easier to do this than to change gender identity, even if the identity is mistaken. In some cases children of 5 or 6 have not learned a clear gender identity because their sex was uncertain and their parents have not known what to tell them. Such children are miserably unhappy until the confusion is cleared up. The doctor may ask them to decide which sex they want to be, and this can sometimes be arranged with medical treatment.

## GENDER ROLES

Culturally shared understandings about what forms of behavior suit members of the two sexes differ widely. Margaret Mead's study of sex roles in New Guinea, done between 1931 and 1933, shows how great these differences can be.[2] Within a radius of 100 miles Mead found three tribes that had very different definitions of gender roles. The first tribe, the Arapesh, were a gentle people who believed that males and females are much alike. Members of both sexes were passive, warm, and noncompetitive. They were equally likely to initiate sexual relations and equally responsible for the care of children. The Arapesh verb meaning "to bear a child" was applied as much to fathers as to mothers, for the parental role was as important to men as women.

Not far away lived the second tribe, the Mundugumor, whose standards emphasized competitiveness and independence for both sexes. They were a violent, cannibalistic people. Members of both sexes were expected to be aggressive in their sexual encounters and equally jealous and vengeful. The women lacked any of the traits that we consider feminine. They disliked pregnancy and breast feeding and were not tender toward children, particularly their daughters.

The third tribe, the Tchambuli, defined male and female roles very differently, but their definitions were exactly opposite from ours. Tchambuli men were given the job of shopping and trading. They were nurturant toward children; they liked to gossip, play the flute, and spend a lot of time each day choosing clothes and jewelry to wear. Their wives, on the other hand, were domineering, practical, and uninterested in clothes or jewelry. They were the main economic providers for the family.

Mead concluded from her study that culture can define gender roles in endless ways. Other scholars agree, but we know today that not all possibilities are equally likely. When we compare gender roles around the world we find that the tribes Mead studied were all somewhat unusual. The most common pattern among known societies is one of **patriarchy**—male dominance over women and children. Indeed, equality between the sexes is unusual. Even when it exists, it is limited to certain areas of life, such as the running of the household or (sometimes) work situations. Although the Tchambuli women were strong and assertive, they were not matriarchs. In fact no true matriarchy has ever been found—that is, no society in which the women hold political power and dominate the men. Many societies have existed in which kinship is traced through the female line rather than the male line, but even in those societies men usually dominate.

Some of the most important parts of gender roles are the norms for the division of labor between the sexes. There is no worldwide agreement as to which jobs are best for males and which are best for females; each society has its own rules. The most common pattern is for women to be assigned tasks that they can do near home or while caring for children. However, women do some sort of work in every society and often contribute as much to the family's economic needs as the men do. (See Table 5.1 for a summary of the division of labor by gender in various societies.)

Scholars do not agree on the reasons for the prevalence of patriarchy in human societies. Some believe that it is so common be-

cause women must, for at least part of their lives, depend on men for economic support. Karl Marx and Friedrich Engels believed that the sexes would become socially equal as soon as women became economically self-sufficient and no longer had to care for children at home.

Not everyone agrees with this view, however. Another important explanation is based on the fact that men and women are not equally able to coerce each other when sexuality becomes a contest. We like to think of sexual intercourse as "lovemaking," but it is sometimes more a matter of physical combat than love. And in such a combat women are the losers. Men can rape women, but women cannot rape men. Moreover, men can forcibly impregnate women, thereby making them vulnerable and dependent for a longer time. Therefore the unique advantage that enables men to dominate is not their greater economic productivity so much as their power to make women into "sexual property." Knowing their own weakness, women rarely challenge men in physical confrontations but make use of psychological manipulation instead.[3]

It is not necessary to choose between these two explanations of patriarchy. Probably both are true. Thus people who are trying to create equality between the sexes usually work on both factors. They try to gain economic independence for women by opening up more jobs for them. And they also try to protect women against sexual exploitation by providing child care services, birth control information, abortion referral, and self-defense training (e.g., karate courses).

Some societies have gone further than others in creating such conditions, but in no society has patriarchy been entirely overcome. The Scandinavian nations, expecially Sweden, have equalized social opportunities for the sexes to a great extent by providing many more social services at public expense than formerly. The Soviet Union has been officially committed to equalizing sex roles

**TABLE 5.1**

*The division of labor by sex: a cross-cultural comparison*

| | NUMBER OF SOCIETIES IN WHICH ACTIVITY IS PERFORMED BY: | | | | |
|---|---|---|---|---|---|
| ACTIVITY | MEN ALWAYS | MEN USUALLY | EITHER SEX EQUALLY | WOMEN USUALLY | WOMEN ALWAYS |
| Pursuing sea mammals | 34 | 1 | 0 | 0 | 0 |
| Hunting | 166 | 13 | 0 | 0 | 0 |
| Trapping small animals | 128 | 13 | 4 | 1 | 2 |
| Herding | 38 | 4 | 4 | 0 | 5 |
| Fishing | 98 | 34 | 19 | 3 | 4 |
| Clearing land for agriculture | 73 | 22 | 17 | 5 | 13 |
| Dairy operations | 17 | 4 | 3 | 1 | 13 |
| Preparing and planting soil | 31 | 23 | 33 | 20 | 37 |
| Erecting and dismantling shelter | 14 | 2 | 5 | 6 | 22 |
| Tending fowl and small animals | 21 | 4 | 8 | 1 | 39 |
| Tending and harvesting crops | 10 | 15 | 35 | 39 | 44 |
| Gathering shellfish | 9 | 4 | 8 | 7 | 35 |
| Making and tending fires | 18 | 6 | 25 | 22 | 62 |
| Bearing burdens | 12 | 6 | 35 | 20 | 57 |
| Preparing drinks and narcotics | 20 | 1 | 13 | 8 | 57 |
| Gathering fruits, berries, nuts | 12 | 3 | 15 | 13 | 63 |
| Gathering fuel | 22 | 1 | 10 | 19 | 89 |
| Preserving meat and fish | 8 | 2 | 10 | 14 | 74 |
| Gathering herbs, roots, seeds | 8 | 1 | 11 | 7 | 74 |
| Cooking | 5 | 1 | 9 | 28 | 158 |
| Carry water | 7 | 0 | 5 | 7 | 119 |
| Grinding grain | 2 | 4 | 5 | 13 | 114 |

*Source:* Adapted from George P. Murdock, "Comparative Data on the Division of Labor by Sex," *Social Forces* 15 (May, 1935), pp. 551–553.

since the revolution. Partly because of the heavy loss of soldiers in World War II, Russian women have been employed in a variety of jobs—ranging from construction worker to cosmonaut—that are usually held by men in the West. However, women's employment has not always brought equality; often it has simply added to their household work, which men are unwilling to share. Furthermore, it has not led to female dominance. For example, although most Russian physicians are women, their status is lower than that of doctors in the West. Physicians who

are in higher positions—specialists, researchers, and the like—are usually men. Thus patriarchy is perhaps weaker in the USSR than in the West, but it is not absent.

One of the goals of the *kibbutzim*, or agricultural communes, of Israel was to create equality between the sexes. Men and women were expected to work together at similar tasks, and many management positions rotate so that everyone has a turn. By minimizing specialization, the communes have produced more equality than is common elsewhere. However, in recent years sex role differentiation has increased on the *kib-butzim*. Women do most of the kitchen jobs and schoolteaching, for example, while men drive the tractors and pick the oranges, just as in other societies. Still, gender roles are more equal on the *kibbutzim* than almost anywhere else.

In the light of all the evidence, we must conclude that gender roles are remarkably persistent social agreements. The societies that have tried hardest to erase the distinctions between masculine and feminine behavior patterns seem to have failed, or at least not to have succeeded. I am not proposing that we give up trying. I am suggesting, however, that the processes through which gender roles are passed from one generation to another have yet to be fully explained. We are not yet sure just how little girls learn to be feminine and little boys learn to be masculine. Even less do we know why adults hold so strongly to their ideas about what is appropriate for men and women to do or not do. Gender roles are behavior patterns about which people have very strong feelings. What is the basis for such feelings? What are the psychological components of sex role differentiation?

## Sources of sex role differentiation

In recent years social scientists have increased their efforts to find out how and why gender roles are so sharply defined. Some researchers have concentrated on explaining early-childhood socialization for masculinity. Others have concentrated on finding out whether certain biological factors make male gender roles more natural to the male sex and female gender roles more natural to the female sex. I want to describe some of the explanations that have been proposed in both areas. First we'll discuss the work of Eleanor Maccoby and Carol Nagy Jacklin[4] on sex role socialization. Then I will point out some of the biological facts that have been emphasized by Alice Rossi.

### SEX ROLES AND SOCIALIZATION

Maccoby and Jacklin have undertaken the most complete review to date of all known research on early-childhood socialization for gender. In their survey of research on behavioral differences between the sexes, they began by making three lists: (1) unsupported beliefs about sex differences, (2) sex differences that are supported by evidence, and (3) "open questions"—differences for which there is not yet conclusive evidence. I will present the first two lists but not the final one.

Let's begin with the unsupported beliefs. The first was most surprising to me, for I had always assumed that it was true: Girls are more "social" than boys. Research has shown that this is not the case. Boys like the company of others as much as girls do, are as motivated as girls to gain social rewards, and appear to be as sensitive to the emotional reactions of others as girls are. They are more oriented toward peer groups and tend to form large groups. Girls, on the other hand, "associate in pairs or small groups of age mates, and may be somewhat more oriented toward adults, although the evidence for this is weak."

Other beliefs that are not supported by evidence include the notion that girls are more "suggestible" than boys and are less "analytic" in their thinking than boys. Both of these assumptions have been disproved. Also, there is a false belief that girls are better at simple, repetitive tasks while boys are better when the task involves more complex reasoning. Actually, neither sex is superior at either type of task.

Maccoby and Jacklin argue against the idea that girls are more affected by heredity and boys are more affected by environment. In reality, boys and girls are equally likely to

*Are males more aggressive than females, or are males taught to be more aggressive? Some adult gave these children their guns. Who? And Why?*

resemble their parents and equally able to learn in a wide variety of situations. Nor are girls more sensitive to auditory stimuli and boys more sensitive to visual ones, as some people once believed. The fact is that they are equally sensitive to both kinds of stimuli.

Here is another mistaken notion: Girls have lower self-esteem than boys. Actually, males and females are equally self-confident and self-satisfied throughout childhood, adolescence, and (as far as we know) adulthood. However, girls tend to pride themselves more on their social poise while boys more often value their strength and dominance. During the college years women do have a greater tendency than men to see themselves as victims of fate rather than as able to control their own lives and to perform well. This may be because females are not expected to take the initiative in courtship while males are, so that women actually have less control over their fate in that period. After the courtship years women regain confidence in their ability to control their own lives.

Finally, there is a mistaken notion that

119

little girls are not motivated to achieve. In fact, during childhood girls' desire to achieve is generally at least as high or possibly higher than boys'. The difference is that boys are more influenced by competitive situations than girls are. When boys are stimulated to compete their interest in achievement shows a marked increase and surpasses that of girls. Girls' achievement needs are not as strongly affected by competitive situations. This research on early-childhood achievement motivation should be compared with Matina Horner's research on college-age women, discussed in Chapter 4.

Let's take a look at the sex differences that Maccoby and Jacklin believe are fairly well supported by evidence. Surprisingly, they list only four:

1 True: *Girls have greater verbal ability than boys.* Verbal skills are about equal until age 11, when girls begin to surpass boys. Female superiority in this area increases throughout high school and possibly later.
2 True: *Boys have greater visual-spatial ability.* Males' superiority in these tasks begins in adolescence and continues throughout adulthood.
3 True: *Boys have superior mathematical ability.* This superiority also begins to appear in adolescence and cannot be explained by the number of math courses taken.
4 True: *Males are more aggressive.* This has been found to be true in all societies that have been studied so far. Even at age 2 boys' play is noticeably rougher and more aggressive than that of girls, and this continues to be the case at least through the college years, if not beyond. Males usually choose other males, not females, as their victims.

*Changing expectations of parents and community for their children may expose the extent to which socialization rather than biology has dictated sex roles.*

S. M. Wakefield

## ORIGINS OF SEX ROLE DIFFERENCES

Having determined the basic facts about differences between the sexes, Maccoby and Jacklin turned to the more complex problem of finding out where those differences come from. They paid close attention to the many studies that compared the ways parents treat males and females in the very early years of childhood. We know the differences in degree of aggressiveness show up in the first two years of life, and shortly thereafter other differences, such as the preference of boys for trucks and of girls for dolls, may be seen. Children identify themselves as male or female quite early—even before they know that sex is permanent—and they have definite ideas about what males and females do. Maccoby and Jacklin conclude that these differences in identity and behavior cannot be due to the way children are treated. What they find surprising is that most mothers really do not treat little girls and little boys very differently. Certainly the greater aggressiveness of boys cannot be explained by parental encouragement. Parents dislike aggressiveness in both sexes; if anything, they discourage it in their sons more than in their daughters. They worry that boys may carry it too far.

Do biological factors account for some of the differences between the sexes? Maccoby and Jacklin point out that a sex-linked recessive gene has been shown to be at least part of the basis for the ability to do visual-spatial work. About 50 percent of all males have this gene and about 25 percent of all females have it. Other abilities may be genetically linked to sex, but this has not yet been determined. Maccoby and Jacklin conclude that it is probably easier for members of one sex to learn some things and easier for members of the other sex to learn other things. This suggests that special help is needed to make males and females equally able to perform in most areas of work—if society decides to pursue this goal.

Maccoby and Jacklin do not mean to imply that all sex role differences are biologically determined. They simply point out the drawbacks of two of the theories that have been proposed to explain the process of learning sex roles: reinforcement theory and modeling theory. The idea behind reinforcement theory is that sex role differences are caused by adults' rewarding small children for behavior that they feel is appropriate for their sex and discouraging them from "inappropriate" behavior. But most parents don't seem to do this to any great extent—at least not enough to explain the early and definite sex differences that normally appear.

The role model theory is not satisfactory either. According to this theory, boys imitate their fathers' behavior and girls imitate that of their mothers. But they don't actually do this. They seem to choose role models more at random. Their behavior is clearly sex-typed *before* they choose same-sex role models. Besides, boys still prefer to play with toy trucks rather than dolls even when they see their mothers driving the family car more often than they see their fathers driving.

A better explanation of sex role differences goes like this: Society vaguely realizes that there are biological differences between males and females that make certain activities easier for members of one sex and other activities easier for members of the other sex. We develop a division of responsibilities that fits our ideas about these biological differences. These expectations then become stereotypes—exaggerated images that children learn and try to live up to. Thus a learning situation is built onto a biological tendency. The learned roles exaggerate whatever small differences may have been inherited. Children develop their own ideas of what they are supposed to do, ideas that are based on evidence from many sources. Thus one little girl insisted that men could be doctors and women could only be nurses, even though her own mother was a doctor!

Some social scientists and a great many biologists have become more interested lately in finding out just how important biological differences are in leading people toward distinctly different sex roles. The feminist sociologist Alice Rossi has made an effort to tell sociologists about biological findings that we have tended to overlook because of our strong interest in social variables.[5] Thus Rossi believes that many more of the differences between males and females can be traced to biology than we realized in the past. Not all the differences between sex roles result from socialization experiences. She points out many universal tendencies of women around the world, traits that seem not to be learned but to be more or less instinctive.

In particular, Rossi claims that the norm that assigns child rearing to the mother is based on the recognition in all societies that there is a special bond between a mother and her child. While the male has a biologically based attraction only to the female, the female is attached *both* to the male and to her offspring. In no society (nor in any primate species) do males specialize in child rearing. Indeed, females often seem unwilling to leave their babies in the care of males.

Rossi points to the existence of certain unlearned responses in mother–infant interaction. Thus infant crying stimulates secretion of the hormone oxytocin in the mother so that milk is "let down" for the baby before and during nursing. Mothers, whether they are left- or right-handed, almost always cradle their babies in their left arm, where the baby can hear the mother's familiar, soothing heartbeat. Mothers approach their newborn infants for the first time with a common set of gestures and expressions. Mothers of pre-

mature babies who are allowed to handle their babies briefly show more interest in them months later than mothers who are not allowed to touch them. Some researchers report that the amount of early mother–child contact is directly related to the closeness of the bond between mother and baby throughout the baby's first year. Separating the mother from the child at birth, even for part of the day, is dangerous both to their relationship and to the health and development of the baby.

Moreover, there is a biological link between the mother's experience with her baby and her sexual experience. Oxytocin, the hormone that lets down milk for the baby, is also related to sexual pleasure. Whether the nipples are sucked by a baby or by a lover, oxytocin is secreted, causing the uterus to contract. After lovemaking these contractions may help move the sperm up the uterus to the ovum. During labor they move the baby down the birth canal. During nursing they help restore the uterus to its prepregnancy condition. And each pregnancy and childbirth contributes to the woman's later sexual pleasure by increasing her ability to experience intense orgasms. Thus the various parts of a woman's biological system are interrelated so that her sexual attachment to the male and her nurturant attachment to her baby reinforce each other.

The child too is strongly attached to his or her mother. Jerome Kagan notes that the biological parent has a

mysterious ability to remain the preferred target of attachment, even for young children who spend a considerable amount of time with substitute caretakers outside the home. . . . There is something special about the mother-infant relationship. The parent appears to be more salient than the substitute caretakers to the child. It is not clear why this is so.[6]

These recent studies, then, strongly suggest that the activities that are typical of male and female roles are related to biological tendencies that we inherit as members of our species. Many of these tendencies may have had important functions in prehistoric times—they may have been necessary for the survival of the species. This does not prove that they are still necessary now. But it does suggest that it may not be possible to achieve a dramatically different pattern of sex roles by shifting our methods of socialization.

# Gender roles in North America

Many women in our society have been entering the labor force who in earlier times might have been full-time homemakers. By 1975 almost half of all North American women of working age were holding jobs.[7] Those women find themselves at a disadvantage compared to male workers and have called public attention to the inequalities between existing gender roles. Let's look at some of the differences between the typical life situations of men and women.

### GENDER AND STATUS

Traditionally, the social ranking of females depended on their ties to men. In childhood a girl's status was determined by her father's position in society, as indeed a boy's status was also determined in this way. But a boy was expected to begin finding his own level in society as soon as he grew up and became independent. This was not so for women. Adulthood for a woman did not mean independence or the chance to achieve her position in society through her own efforts. Instead, it generally meant marriage, which made her dependent on her husband instead of her father. From that point on she would hold the same position on the social ladder

Sybil Shelton Monkmeyer

*Will women become less feminine by taking "masculine" jobs? Or will society stop considering these jobs as masculine?*

as he did. Much of this system remains. A married woman's own achievements may be recognized and admired, but these may still carry less weight than those of her husband.

### GENDER AND HOUSEWORK

Most women work because they need the money. However, married women who have careers have a double burden. A study of Vancouver couples analyzed the time budgets of various kinds of families.[8] It was found that women spent about 34 hours per week doing housework (including shopping and repairs) while men spent about 8 hours. Naturally, families with small children had much more housework than those with no children. However, the amount of time that men spent doing household tasks did not increase: The women did almost all of the additional work themselves. Furthermore, wives who had paid jobs continued to spend about as much time on housework as other women who had no paid jobs, mostly by catching up on weekends. Their husbands, on the other hand, did not spend more time on household jobs if their wives worked. Thus the extra burdens of a two-career family are borne more by women than by men.

### GENDER AND JOBS

In the work setting women are also disadvantaged. Certain jobs are thought to be appropriate for women and others are not. Women are still segregated into a narrow range of jobs. Indeed, a Canadian study done in 1975 showed that there has been no decrease in the sex-typing of jobs during the past thirty years.[9] Women are still found in large numbers in such jobs as nursing, typing, and teaching. Moreover, they still get lower pay than men, even when they do the same jobs. Moreover, they earn less social prestige than men do for exactly the same jobs.

### GENDER AND HIGHER EDUCATION

Women are less successful than men in climbing the occupational ladder. But another study in 1975 pointed out that when they do succeed in their jobs it is generally because they have been outstanding in their academic performance.[10] They must prove their ability in visible ways more than men must, even when there is a high demand for qualified workers. And when demand is lower, as it has been recently, higher education—and especially graduate education—is even more important to women who want successful careers. However, higher education is less common among women than among men. Since 1900, American women have been less likely than men to enter college, even though they have been more likely to finish high school.

Saul Feldman's book *Escape from the Doll's House*[11] is a report on a nationwide study of graduate students of both sexes. He was particularly interested in women's education, which, as the title of his book suggests, he sees as a way for women to escape from a life of dependency and triviality. His findings do not prove that women are discriminated against but they do point out ways in which women are handicapped in their professional education.

For one thing, Feldman establishes quantitatively what we already knew through personal experience—that some fields are considered "feminine" and some "masculine." Both sexes know which fields are which. Engineering is the most "masculine" field. Nursing and home economics are the most "feminine." And indeed, the percentage of women enrolled in a graduate program is almost perfectly correlated with the judgments people make about how feminine the field is. The fields in which exciting discoveries are being made, those that are thought to attract the best students, are the very ones in which few women enroll. Women tend to have a low opinion of their potential. They are more likely than men to say that they hope to teach rather than to do research. And they are also more likely to choose teaching positions below the university level. Many say they expect to teach in junior colleges, for example, even though they could expect more for themselves. And more women than men leave graduate school without completing their degrees. Women, more than men, believe that faculty members and other (male) students do not take them seriously.

How much of this problem can be blamed on the graduate schools? The answer is not clear. It is possible that a lot of discrimination exists—or *did* exist when the study was conducted. But what is easier to prove is that women's roles in the family get in the way of their professional education and careers. Women, more than men, say that their family obligations have to take priority over their intellectual work. They almost always put their husbands' careers ahead of their own. In some ways it is an advantage to be married—female graduate students are supported by their husbands, just as male graduate students are often supported by their wives. But for women there are also marked disadvantages in marriage.

The male graduate students in Feldman's study did better in school if they were married than if they were not. The female graduate students did *worse* if they were married. The most successful women were divorced. In addition, women's career prospects are limited by family obligations. While male graduate students generally said that they were free to take jobs in other states after completing their degrees, women much more often felt tied to the local area because of family obligations. In an academic career geographic mobility is almost always necessary if one is to get ahead.

## The women's movement

Many of the facts that I have mentioned in this chapter are well known by now. However, ten or fifteen years ago they would not have been noticed. It is the women's movement that has drawn the

Gender roles are simply social agreements. You can disagree with them, as this woman does.

B. Schlossberg/Monkmeyer

Janet Guthrie
68

public's attention to the sexism—extreme sex role discrimination—that still exists in industrial society. Hence, it may be useful to mention the situations that gave rise to the new feminist movement we see around us.

## HISTORY

Jo Freeman[12] points out that the movement is supported almost entirely by white middle-class women—people who, on the basis of their background and education, might reasonably expect to hold jobs at a professional or executive level. Black women, working-

class women, and women of various minority groups have not, on the whole, been active in the feminism that has emerged since the mid-1960s. Why only middle-class women? To answer this question we must recall a few facts about the history of female emancipation and female participation in the work force.

The early feminists were the "suffragettes"—the women who devoted their energies to gaining the right of women to vote and take part in political affairs. They believed that as soon as women could vote they would become influential in national politics. But not so. After winning the right to

*People who live in coeducational dorms may come to know each other well and work out new agreements about sex roles.*

Susan Meiselas/Magnum

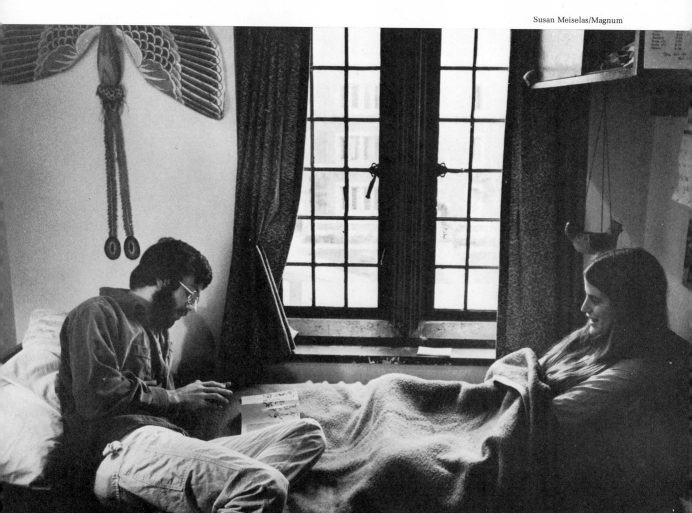

*Take a guess about the people in this picture. How do they like what they are doing? How do they like what the others are doing? The answer you give shows the ideas and attitudes you have yourself.*

vote the women's organizations fragmented, having no single agreed-upon goal. Most of the reform-minded women of the 1920s did not challenge the role assigned to women by society but worked on other issues such as prohibition, eliminating child labor, and cleaning up the sweatshops. Thus in 1920 one Ph.D. in seven went to a woman, but the figure had dropped to one in ten by 1960.[13] Women had not, by and large, succeeded in pursuing careers in a serious way.

With the Depression of the 1930s came high unemployment levels and a widespread attitude that the few jobs that existed ought to go to men (since the man was supposed to be the main breadwinner of the family) and not to women. The magazines portrayed working women in an unfavorable light, suggesting that only a callous, uncaring mother would willingly choose a job over the role of full-time homemaker. Not until World War II was this trend reversed. When the men went to war it suddenly became acceptable for married women to work. Indeed, "Rosie the Riveter" was the mythical heroine of posters and songs throughout the war years. Even middle-aged women were hired. Many of them liked working and wanted to go on working after the war ended. But they were disappointed. With peace came the closing of child care centers and training programs. Still, many women continued to work in low-level, low-paid jobs, seeking a little extra income to supplement their husbands' pay checks, usually because they wanted to buy cars, appliances, and other expensive consumer items. The number of working women did not return to pre-war levels, but their pay scales lagged badly. At the same time, the media campaigned to undermine women's aspirations outside the home. Ads featured gentle ladies in frilly aprons baking cakes. The traditional homemaker was again the only *real* woman, and working women were portrayed as tough, unfeminine, selfish, and unconcerned with their children's welfare. Ironically, just when child rearing began to take up a shorter portion of a woman's lifetime than ever before, women were told, for the first time in history, that motherhood should be their full-time occupation.[14]

Yet many women found it financially necessary to work. The outcome was that they took jobs but claimed that they didn't really *want* to work—they'd much rather be at home. Call it role conflict. Women were damned-if-they-did-work and damned-if-they-didn't. Feeling guilty about working, they didn't protest about their low pay, their inferior jobs, or their lack of promotions. It was a no-win situation.

Well-educated women were the most likely to work. And as Freeman points out,

"the median income of full-time working women with college degrees is still lower than that of male high school dropouts, and this relationship has shown little indication of changing over time."[15] Thus these working middle-class women are especially subject to *relative deprivation*. It's not that their incomes or living conditions are worse than those of working-class women. It is that they are in work situations in which they can reasonably compare themselves to the men they know whose education is no better than their own. Relative to *these men* they certainly are deprived. When they compare their own salaries and opportunities to those of their husbands and the men they knew in college, the difference seems extremely unfair. No wonder it is these women who have become the new feminists of our day.

But why now? This situation is not new. Women have been underpaid since World War II. Yet throughout the 1950s they supported the traditional homemaker ideal instead of protesting about their frustrating

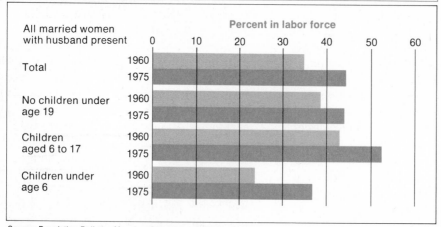

**FIGURE 5.2**

*Percent of married women with children who work in 1960 compared to 1975. Note that the percentage of women in the labor force is increasing, particularily for women who are raising children at the same time.*

*Source:* Population Bulletin, *Marrying, Divorcing, and Living Together in the U.S. Today.* Population Reference Bureau Inc., Vol. 32, No. 5, October 1977. Adapted from Table #2, p. 11.

situation. Freeman argues that the grounds for protest existed for about twenty years before the women's movement began. What explains the delay?

You can't have a social movement without a communication network that will mobilize people who feel that they have a complaint. And no such network existed for women for many years. True, there were women's organizations such as the Business and Professional Women's Club. But they had decided not to become a vehicle for protest and women who were frustrated in their careers could not "co-opt" them—that is, they could not take them over for their own purposes.

Knowingly or not, President Kennedy created the first organization that enabled angry women to get in touch with each other and plan action. In 1961 he set up the President's Commission on the Status of Women. This organization, which was chaired by Eleanor Roosevelt, not only collected a great deal of evidence showing how women were denied important rights but also led to the establishment of fifty commissions to do similar work at the state level. Most of those commissions were made up of politically active women who were dedicated to improving the condition of women. Thus a nationwide network devoted to the concerns of women came into existence.

Another major event happened in 1963. Betty Friedan published a highly readable best-seller, *The Feminine Mystique*, that led many women to see their own upbringing and acceptance of the traditional female role as ideological brainwashing. Some women who had previously blamed themselves for feeling unhappy with their situation now blamed the social system. The lady in the frilly apron became no longer the model woman but a chump.

The 1964 Civil Rights Act provided legislation to guarantee equal employment opportunities not only to blacks but also to women. But the commission set up to administer the act—the Equal Employment Opportunity Commission (EEOC)—considered this aspect of the law a joke and made no serious effort to enforce it. Still, some members of the commission wanted to see it enforced, and this group argued that if there were some sort of "NAACP for women" that would pressure the government the act might be enforced.

In 1966 the third National Conference of Commissions on the Status of Women was held. It became clear that the government

*Many women who had marched in civil rights or anti-war demonstrations eventually marched to support their "sisters."*

Jim Anderson/Woodfin Camp

would go no further without a lot of pressure. And so the National Organization of Women (NOW) was formed. A great many of its members had experience in the communications industry, and they created the impression that NOW was a large organization. Actually, by 1973 it had only 8000 members.

### THE MOVEMENT TODAY

Freeman describes the women's movement as having two wings. The older group of professional feminists had already become established when a number of younger, more radical women, known as the movement's "left wing" became active. This element is not well organized. Its activities consist mostly of rap groups (consciousness-raising, or CR, groups). Many of these younger women had worked in civil-rights groups and other New Left organizations during the 1960s. In many cases they moved toward feminism only after having been humiliated or treated with disrespect in the radical groups. For example, the young black leader Stokely Carmichael stated that in his organization, the Student Nonviolent Coordinating Committee (SNCC), "the only position for women is prone." At the 1967 National Conference for New Politics, a women's caucus attempted to introduce a resolution for discussion. The chairman claimed that their resolution was not worth consideration and ignored them when they raised their hands for attention. Eventually five women rushed the podium to demand recognition. The chairman actually patted one of them on the head and told her, "Cool down, little girl. We have more important things to talk about than women's problems."

Incidents like this infuriated radical women, and their anger drew them together into a number of local discussion groups, some of which became lasting and effective protest groups. On the whole, these early women's groups, representing enraged and militant women, were not taken very seriously by the general public. Several of their demonstrations were laughed at. Such was the case, for example, when women got back at men by mimicking their reactions to women at events such as beauty contests.

Radical feminists oppose any form of leadership, viewing it as a play for personal power. As a result their meetings are often disorderly, with participants interrupting each other and expressing their feelings whenever they want to. It also means that any woman who claims to express the views of these women runs a risk of being rejected by other radical feminists. Still, many women say that belonging to CR groups has improved their lives, giving them new energy and independence. Hence, whether or not they have had any major impact on national policies, the small groups have been important in women's personal lives.

Freeman observes that although ideas may become widespread through these groups, this does not lead to social change because these groups lack organization. She has this to say about new ideas: "Insofar as they can be applied individually, they may be acted on; insofar as they require coordinated political power to be implemented, they will not be. This is why the younger branch of the movement can at one and the same time be so innovative ideologically, and so conservative in practice. . . . It is good for personal change; it is bad for institutional change."[16]

The older, more organized wing of the movement has been more effective in promoting institutional change, primarily the Equal Rights Amendment (ERA) to the U.S. Constitution. As I write this, it is unclear whether or not the ERA will pass. It has been approved by 35 of the 38 states that must ratify it for it to go into effect, but the momentum toward ratification seems to have slowed. Still, the first National Women's

Conference in the United States, meeting in Houston in November 1977, showed that women are now being taken seriously in the political arena. Rosalynn Carter, Betty Ford, and Lady Bird Johnson all attended the convention. The most controversial issues discussed were abortion and lesbian rights. Yet President Carter's top woman assistant, Midge Costanza, included lesbian rights on her list of feminist demands. Among the other resolutions passed at the conference were the following:

1 Battered women: The government is asked to make available shelters for women who have been beaten by their husbands.
2 Employment: The government can increase women's access to jobs, training programs, and managerial positions by enforcing the laws against discrimination.
3 Health: There should be a national health program. The government should also look into the use of questionable medical and surgical procedures on women.
4 Media: Women should be portrayed in a realistic way and should be able to work in every area of the media.
5 Rape: The laws should provide for graduated penalties, depending on the amount of force used in the rape.

On the basis of present evidence, thus, it is safe to say that the women's movement is not a short-term social movement but is still expanding.

# SOCIAL RESEARCH:
## Sociologists at Work

### SECRETARIES AND BOSSES

Rosabeth Moss Kanter's book *Men and Women of the Corporation*[17] describes the office life of one of America's largest companies, which she calls by the fictitious name Indsco. I think her best chapter is about secretaries and their bosses. Almost all secretaries are women, and their bosses are almost all men. Kanter has served as a consultant to businesses that are trying to create new, high-ranking job opportunities for women. She is able to tell us from first-hand experience why this is harder to do than she would like.

The most obvious fact about the relationship between an executive and his secretary is that it is personal, even within a huge bureaucratic organization. Secretarial work is not a set routine that follows an orderly plan. The boss may buzz his secretary every few minutes and ask for some personal service. There is no clear line between an official, legitimate request and an unofficial or even illegitimate one. Hence, a secretary may wind up (either resentfully or willingly) mailing back her employer's wife's mail order shoes or dog sitting while he is on vacation. Bosses are free to set their own standards for judging their secretaries' performance.

The executives' behavior and office decoration is neutral and bland. The secretaries, by contrast, go in for big, funny posters and cartoons, celebrate birthdays, show concern for the comfort and welfare of guests. A secretary becomes devoted to a particular boss, and when he rises in status he takes her with him and provides her with an office with drapes, a fancy ashtray, and steel file trays—though he doesn't necessarily give her a much better salary or more challenging work. She can stop worrying about improving her skills and concentrate on her relationship with the boss—for his status will determine hers. A secretary may be liked if her boss is liked and disliked if he is disliked. Much as a sultan used to "own" his personal servants, the boss sees his secretary as "my girl."

The secretary is expected to get her main symbolic and emotional rewards from this relationship, not from other business contacts. Indeed, she is expected to identify with his interests rather than resent his power or (perish the thought!) compete with him for promotion. After all, by working closely with him she learns his secrets and might use them as deadly weapons if they were to compete. Hence, bosses tend to insist that the career ladder of secretaries should be entirely separate from theirs. They usually choose as their secretaries women who have been socialized in ways that are thought appropriate—parochial or secretarial schooling that trains them not to see themselves as potential bosses and not to resent their low position in the company hierarchy. The boss can judge the secretary, but her opinion of him has no impact on his fate. If she showed any threat of being able to retaliate in the future, he would be uncomfortable about giving orders. Nowadays some companies are trying to reform by promoting secretaries to managerial jobs, but on the rare occasions when this happens the switch may be pure hell for the woman involved.

In short, tradition has idealized the secre-

tary who is loyal and devoted to her boss and prefers symbolic rewards over career opportunities. The woman's "attitude" is considered more important than her ability, since most secretarial tasks are not difficult. Moreover, white-collar workers, especially women, can often be manipulated by means of prestige symbols.[18] Secretaries get praise, and they tend to become addicted to it. The constant flow of compliments and thanks is considered more important than money. Kanter even mentions cases in which a boss did not name his secretary for a higher-level job opening because he thought she might feel "rejected" at the suggestion that she move on. One secretary who was offered a promotion in another department reports that her boss said, "We love you. We want you to stay," but didn't offer more pay. This woman seems to be an exception to the rule, for her thought was, "I get the love from my husband. I work for other reasons."

Most secretaries actually depend on the appreciation and warmth they receive. Kanter found the Indsco secretaries much more reluc-

*Not typical. Most secretaries would not carry this poster.*

Elizabeth Hamlin/Stock, Boston

tant than other employees to enter jobs that would involve "both praise and criticism" or "having to show confidence." The secretaries, who were used to being praised for taking orders, did not want to stick their necks out or risk criticism.

Because their job security depends on their personal relationships, secretaries neither have nor want much power. Hence, to protect themselves they are likely to resort to gossip and emotional manipulation. This, in turn, reinforces the stereotype of women as unsuitable for executive positions that require an unsentimental, businesslike attitude.

Thus the qualities for which a secretary is rewarded are the very ones that make her unsuitable for promotion in a bureaucratic organization. She becomes timid, addicted to praise, dependent on her personal relationship with her boss, and unable to take initiative or risk criticism.

Do you find this situation discouraging? Kanter obviously does. She wanted to find out how organizations could help women in their careers, and she watched closely when Indsco undertook some major reforms to enable secretaries to move into managerial positions. The company set up a task force to work on the issue. It suggested an important change: Separate a secretary's status from that of her boss. If he moves ahead, he can't take her along. Every secretary will have the opportunity to change jobs inside the organization. As soon as secretaries see that their personal ties are less vital than before, they will begin to look for different ways of getting ahead. Maybe they'll stop being so timid and allow themselves to develop some ambition and take some risks for the sake of their careers. That was the plan.

No such luck. The company was unable to put its plan into effect because some people benefited from the old system—or thought they did. The bosses and the executive secretaries simply refused to cooperate. Worse yet, even members of the task force itself did not support the proposed reforms. The change threatened certain values—warmth and personal relationships—that many people consider important sources of relief in the impersonal and rational setting of a modern corporation.

Kanter concludes that it may be hard to open up new careers for women, but not because corporations are staffed by men who hate women and want to oppress them. The reason is more complex—it is a conflict in the hearts of good people, including women themselves. The view that personal warmth and loyalty are important values, however praiseworthy it may be, is the very attitude that helps keep women in secretarial jobs instead of executive jobs.

## SOCIAL POLICY:
## Issues and Viewpoints

One of the high political dramas of our day is the battle for equal rights for men and women. Most people, male or female, have strong feelings about this matter, usually involving a certain amount of resentment. It is easy for a discussion of this kind to focus exclusively on the issues of fairness and unfairness, which have to be settled by confrontation and struggle. I don't think conflict can be avoided altogether, for it is part of every relationship. However, it would be just as mistaken to treat sex role relationships as if they amounted to nothing more than conflicting claims and duties. Mutual enjoyment and caring also exist—and indeed are quite common within contexts of inequality and unfairness. For all I know, the peasant riding his donkey cares deeply about the wife who is walking behind him and carrying the firewood. To ask him to consider helping her is not to deny that their relationship may be richly rewarding in other ways.

Still, at this moment in history the claims

and demands of women are more noticeable than before. Middle-class women tend to want a different life style, and at the same time many men are glad to change their own roles as well. The outcome of these changes cannot be predicted, but we can see how women's demands are linked to other changes going on in Western culture. The main change is in the importance of achievement as a value. For a few hundred years it was valued very highly—at least for men. Now our attitude toward achievement is less clear. We are faced with high unemployment in an affluent society. This new situation tends to favor a value system that emphasizes consumption, leisure, recreation, and pleasure instead of hard work and achievement. On the other hand, at the same time that many men are getting out of the "rat race" and seeking a less competitive life style, many women are moving *toward* achievement and competition. The life of the passive consumer no longer satisfies them, and they find the kitchen boring. In the workplace, then, male and female roles are becoming more similar and more equal in terms of both opportunities and rewards—though these changes are certainly not happening as fast as they could.

However, even if opportunities do become equal, women may not take advantage of them. I have mentioned several reasons why sex role differences may not be eliminated, though they may be reduced. The main reason is that women will not change greatly if men do not want them

to. Unless men approve of their wives' and lovers' achievements, women may continue to avoid success. Unless men encourage their secretaries to move into executive roles, they may stay on, typing and serving coffee, simply out of personal friendship and loyalty.

A different issue is the question of whether male and female behaviors are shaped at all by biological factors. This is a matter for further research. Certainly men and women do have different tendencies and abilities, in limited areas at least. It is unlikely that these inborn differences account for many of the social roles that they specialize in as adults. We have to go ahead and make personal and public decisions even though our knowledge is limited on this subject. And the decisions we make depend on how highly we value equality. For example, even if gender role differences were strongly shaped by biological sex differences (which is highly unlikely), they could perhaps be offset by special socialization programs. For example, though boys are relatively better at mathematics and girls are relatively better at verbal skills, if we thought equality was important we could set up special language and math programs to equalize the performance of boys and girls in those areas. Thus public policy is based on opinions about what is worthwhile. Whether we create more equality in our society depends on how much we want it relative to other goals. This is a judgment in which you too will take part.

## SUMMARY

**1.** Sex is the biological fact of being male or female; gender is a social-psychological fact. *Gender identity* is the experience of considering oneself male or female. Once it has been learned, an individual's gender identity rarely changes. *Gender roles* are the

culturally defined sets of behaviors that are considered sex-appropriate in a given society. They are established by social agreement, though these agreements may be related to natural differences between the sexes.

**2.** The natural differences between the sexes are biological traits, many of which are now being investigated. The sperm that brings a Y chromosome instead of an X chromosome to the ovum stimulates the embryo to produce testicles, which produce male hormones and offset the uterine environment of female hormones. This leads to the development of male genitals and other traits that would otherwise stay female during later phases of prenatal development.

**3.** Hormones affect people's feelings and behavior throughout life. It is possible that some sex-typed behavior patterns are shaped by the secretions of glands as well as by social agreements.

**4.** Sex and gender identity sometimes don't match. Children below the age of 2 may not have developed a gender identity, so that if their sex is changed they can acquire either gender identity that is suggested to them. A few adults are troubled by mismatched sex and gender identity. This is true of transsexuals and transvestites.

**5.** Margaret Mead's study of three New Guinea tribes shows that gender roles can be defined in very different ways by different cultures. Most societies, however, specify that women's work should involve child care and house work and that women should work near home if possible, while men may go farther away (e.g., to hunt or fish). *Patriarchy* is male dominance of women and children. It is a common pattern in many societies. *Matriarchy*, or female dominance, has not been found in any known society. Even equality between the sexes is fairly rare.

**6.** Scholars disagree about the sources of patriarchy. Some think it is a result of differences in the ability to produce economic goods and the dependence of women on male providers, at least for part of their lives. Others believe it is a result of the ability of the male to dominate the female through sexual coercion. Perhaps both factors are important causes.

**7.** Some societies are more patriarchal than others, but none of the societies that have tried to eliminate patriarchy (such as the USSR, Sweden, and the Israeli *kibbutzim*) have succeeded fully.

**8.** Research suggests that, in general, (a) girls have greater verbal ability than boys; (b) boys have greater visual-spatial ability; (c) boys have superior mathematical ability; and (d) males are more aggressive than females. Some of these differences may be influenced by biological factors.

**9.** Maccoby and Jacklin argue that adults' treatment of little girls and little boys is generally fairly similar and that it cannot explain the differences in behavior patterns between the two sexes. Probably society develops certain expectations about sex role differences and children learn these expectations and try to live up to them. The learned roles exaggerate whatever small differences may be inherited as tendencies.

**10.** Maternal behavior and attachment to infants seem to be influenced by hormonal factors. However, behavior and hormones influence each other. It is no more true that biological factors determine social ones than that social factors determine biological ones.

**11.** Gender roles in North America are still marked by inequality: Working women are disadvantaged, both in career opportunities and pay and also in having to do a greater share of the housework than men. Higher education is also affected by sex roles. Married women do less well in graduate school than divorced women.

**12.** The feminist gains of the 1920s were not maintained because the Depression took job opportunities away from women. The present women's movement is a middle-class concern because middle-class women feel deprived relative to the men they know. It was Kennedy's Commission on the Status of Women that enabled feminists to form a network with political power. The New Left women gained political experience but were not recognized as equals by New Left men. Their humiliating experiences angered them and led to the formation of radical feminist groups.

# KEY TERMS

**gender**   the awareness of being a member of one sex or the other.

**gender identity**   (sexual identity)   the sex of which one considers oneself to be a member.

**gender role** (sex role)   the culturally defined set of behaviors that are considered sex-appropriate within a given society.

**matriarchy**   a system in which women are dominant over men.

**patriarchy**   a system in which men are dominant over women.

**sex**   the biological fact of being male or female.

**sexism**   an ideology that justifies a rigid assignment of roles on the basis of sex.

**transsexual**   a person whose sex has been changed through surgery and hormone treatment.

**transvestite**   a person whose gender identity differs from his or her sex and who may dress according to the gender identity.

# FOR FURTHER READING

GRIFFITHS, N. E. S. *Penelope's Web: Some Perceptions of Women in European and Canadian Society.* Toronto: Oxford University Press, 1976. This is history, of interest chiefly to people focusing on a special topic. It begins with the seventeenth century and has a moderate viewpoint.

KANDO, THOMAS. *Sex Change: The Achievement of Gender Identity among Feminized Transsexuals.* Springfield: Charles C Thomas, 1973. This is one of the very few sociological studies of transsexuals, since there are not very many of them. Kando found seventeen subjects who had become women. He says they behave in accordance with a more conventional feminine role than most woman who were born female. Not surprising. They have a point to prove.

KOMAROVSKY, MIRRA. *Dilemmas of Masculinity: A Study of College Youth.* New York: Norton, 1976. This study involves both a survey and some in depth interviews with young men in a prestigious college. It investigates their problems, their goals, and especially their attitudes toward sex roles and family life. They sounded stuffier and more traditional than the men I teach. I kept wondering whether Komarovsky liked them or not. (She doesn't say.)

LEVINSON, DANIEL J. *The Seasons of a Man's Life.* New York: Knopf, 1978. Levinson describes how young men have big dreams and what they go through in turning their dreams into reality, if they do. He looks at the vital relationships that emerge along the way—with women, and with older men who are mentors.

LOPATA, HELENA ZNANIECKI. *Occupation: Housewife.* New York: Oxford University Press, 1971. This is probably the best description of the life situations facing the majority of women at some point in their lives, if not indeed for the longest period in their lives.

MITCHELL, JULIET. *Psychoanalysis and Feminism.* London: Allen Lane, 1974. Most feminists today think Freud was a male chauvinist. (He was.) Mitchell defends him and the psychoanalytic movement against that charge, and a lot of her argument is right.

PLECK, JOSEPH H., and JACK SAWYER, eds. *Men and Masculinity.* Englewood Cliffs, N.J.: Prentice-Hall, 1974. There aren't many rigorous books on male sex roles. This is not rigorous, but it is interesting. It is a collection of essays of a highly personal nature, mostly by men who want a more flexible lifestyle than gender norms have usually outlined for them in the past.

VAILLANT, GEORGE E. *Adaptation to Life.* Boston: Little, Brown, 1977. This study has more in common with Levinson's book, discussed above, than any other here. Vaillant concentrates on the 1942, 1943, and 1944 classes of college men from what must have been Harvard. Most of these men have made brilliant careers, but Vaillant suggests that the happiest of them are the ones who settled for less.

WALUM, LAURA RICHARDSON. *The Dynamics of Sex and Gender: A Sociological Perspective.* Chicago: Rand McNally, 1977. This is a textbook that treats a lot of fascinating ideas—such as what might happen if the sexes formed different political parties, and how orgasm is similar to childbirth.

WISEMAN, JACQUELINE P. *The Social Psychology of Sex.* New York: Harper and Row, 1976. A symbolic interactionist book dealing with sexual interaction. This is Wiseman's own work, plus readings from other writers.

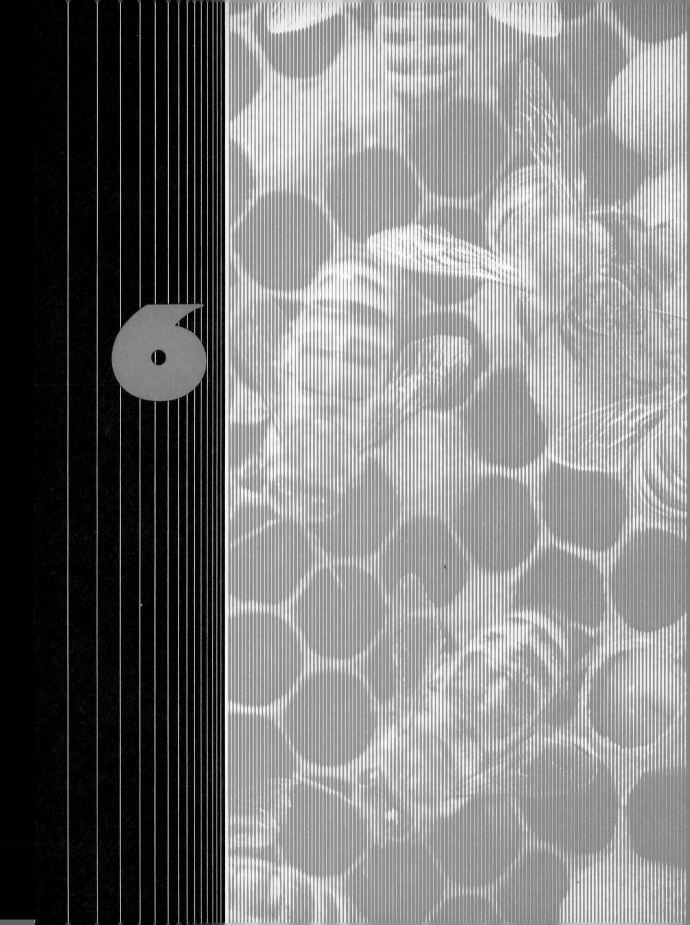

# SOCIAL GROUPS

Let me give you a koan. Perhaps you know that in Zen Buddhism a *koan* is a puzzle that has no logical answer. It's meant to boggle your mind until something inside sort of snaps. Zen Buddhists sit for hours concentrating on the koan that their teacher has given them. One favorite koan for beginners is this: What was your face before your mother and father were born?

That particular koan doesn't hold my attention very well, but over the years I have found myself wondering about a question that is very much like a koan. There is no logical answer to my koan and I can't promise you any enlightenment if you concentrate on it, but I am happy to share it with you. It goes like this: What would you be like if you hadn't ever been part of a social group? I've never solved this one, but I want to discuss in this chapter how it is that social experience is necessary for us to become fully human. You need a group in order to become yourself, just as you need parents before you can have your own face.

## The need for togetherness

### SOCIAL DEPRIVATION

Imagine a person who had never been influenced by a social group in any way — a person who had been completely free to act on impulse throughout his or her life, a person who had never known another human being. It is unlikely that such a person could survive to adulthood, but if this were possible, that person's behavior would be more animal-like than human.

The human infant, who depends on adults for a longer part of his or her life than the infant of any other species, needs many years of care. In a few cases, however, children have had no contact with other humans throughout most of their childhood. The personality development of such children gives us an idea of what human nature is like without social interaction.

Unlike Romulus and Remus, the legendary founders of Rome who were supposedly reared by wolves, children who have been isolated from other human beings *(feral children)* behave in a subhuman way. They are unable to learn to relate to human beings.[1] In some cases wild children about 8 or 10 years old have been found in the woods, where they seem to have survived alone for several years. It is rarely possible to find out whether such children were normal at birth or whether they were abandoned *because* they seemed abnormal. In any case they have become more animal-like than human — they bite and howl, for example, as if they had been reared by a mother wolf. Even after much patient mothering they never become entirely normal.

*The Wild Child*, a French film made in the late 1960s, is a true story based on a journal kept by Dr. Jean Marc Itard, who tried to educate a feral child who had been found by peasants near Aveyron in 1799.[2] The boy, who was about 10 years old when he was found, had evidently lived since early childhood by scrounging for food in the woods. He walked on all fours. When he met human beings he fled from them in terror, and he fought fiercely when they captured him. It was even necessary to teach the boy, whom Dr. Itard named Victor, how to walk in a human fashion. Although Dr. Itard taught Victor a few words, the boy's education was unsuccessful. The film ends on a hopeful note, but according to Itard's actual record, Victor never became a normal human being.

Like feral children, many mentally disturbed children may have become abnormal because of inadequate mothering.[3] Research has shown that experiences such as crooning, cuddling, pat-a-cake, and peekaboo are very important to children's development. Those who are deprived of such interaction are backward in their physical and verbal development.[4]

## PRIMATES AND PEOPLE

The need of infants for physical contact is not found only in human beings. Biologists have raised monkeys in isolation in order to see how isolation affects their behavior as adults. These experiments show the infant's need for loving contact. In one widely known experiment baby monkeys were taken from their mothers and placed alone in a cage with two "surrogate mothers"—one of them a wire frame and the other a soft cloth dummy. The babies could nurse from bottles attached to one of the "mothers." None of the monkeys became attached to the wire mother, but all of them clung to the cloth mother most of the time, whether it was equipped with a milk bottle or not. This clinging was especially likely to occur when the baby monkeys were frightened by new experiences.

No infant monkey reared in this isolated way became a normal adult. These monkeys seemed not to understand how to mate. The few females who did mate were likely to mistreat or neglect their babies.

Researchers have found that it is possible to rear infant monkeys without their mothers and still produce normal adults if the infants are allowed to play together in a group. They cuddle together in close physical contact and through their interactions make up for their lack of mothering.[5]

These monkey experiments show that the human need for social contact is shared by other species. Still, there is a wide difference between the social life of humankind and that of other primates. Some years ago a family tried to raise two infants as if they were twins. One of the infants was a female chimpanzee, the other their own son.[6] At first their son's development was slower than that of his "sister." The chimp could walk right away and quickly learned to use complicated toys. But by the age of 2 the boy began to catch up with the chimp, and soon

there was no longer a contest. The chimp couldn't begin to master language, and for this reason she could never participate in complex human activities.

Later experiments have been somewhat more successful in teaching chimpanzees to communicate in symbol systems. Some researchers have taught a chimp to make simple sentences using hand signals,[7] and another researcher has used colored plastic shapes to communicate with his chimp.[8] At the Yerkes Primate Research Center a chimpanzee named Lana has been taught to communicate using an electric keyboard. Each key is marked with a symbol that represents an English word. As Lana presses the keys the symbols appear on a display panel and a teletypewriter prints the message in English. If Lana types "?Please, machine, give milk," a vending machine attached to the keyboard pours out a cup of milk. Lana's teacher, Timothy V. Gill, reports that she now uses the names of unfamiliar objects and invents plausible new names as well. For example, one day Gill entered Lana's room holding an orange. She had eaten an orange before, but she did not know its name. However, she did know the names of six colors and several objects, including apples. She therefore asked for the fruit in Gill's hand by typing, "?Tim give apple which-is orange"[9] Although scientists are pleased with the ability of chimps to learn to communicate, they agree that trained primates cannot match the problem-solving ability of normal human beings who have been brought up with other human beings.

## PERSONAL SPACE AND EXPRESSIVE BEHAVIOR

All social scientists agree that most human behavior is *learned* and that it varies from one group to another. But they disagree over details. Clearly *some* behaviors are genetic characteristics of the human species. For example, breathing, sneezing, and muscle reflexes are certainly inborn tendencies, while harpsichord playing certainly is not. However, we cannot be so sure about all behavior patterns, and some scholars have suggested that we have failed to recognize a number of human tendencies as biologically based. They point out how our behavior resembles that of apes.

Some of these theories cannot be proved or disproved by research, but they are fascinating nonetheless. Desmond Morris' *The Naked Ape*,[10] for example, describes the human being as an odd, almost hairless primate that was forced by environmental conditions to give up bananas and berries for a carnivorous diet. This new diet required long hunting expeditions, and so the human species developed sexual bonding as a way of making sure the females would still be around when the males came home. Out of this came a number of other important social developments that gave our species a dominant place in the animal kingdom. Another book on this subject is Lionel Tiger's *Men in Groups*,[11] which suggests that males of our species have an inborn tendency to form special bonds that cannot include females.

Both of these books argue that human social patterns are at least comparable to animal traits, but neither can actually prove that there is *more* than an analogy involved. In other words, neither book proves that the human pattern of behavior is based on the fact that *Homo sapiens* is a primate species. Their arguments have stimulated interest and sometimes anger, but not much empirical research. The argument about *territoriality*, however, may turn out to be fruitful in helping us understand human social patterns.

### Territoriality

It is well known that many animal species distribute their populations over a region by limiting the number of animals that may live in any given territory or zone. In some cases these zones are assigned by contests. The winner keeps the territory

while the losers slink away to find another piece of land that they can call their own. The dominant animals chase away any animal that invades their territory. *Territoriality* is the establishment of a certain zone or space that may not be occupied by any other person or animal. In applying the idea of territoriality to human society, we should ask the following questions:

1 Do dominant people claim more space than their subordinates?
2 Do human beings, as a species, have any orderly way of assigning space to individuals?
3 Do human beings need to have a private space for themselves?

The answer to all three questions is yes.

Dominant people spread out more. This can be seen in the way people seat themselves at a crowded seminar table. The instructor will usually take a chair at the head of the table and spread out her belongings — an open briefcase on one side, perhaps a handbag on the other side, and lecture notes fanned out in front. During the lecture she may use expansive gestures while the students are squeezed together around the table, some with no room to write, all keeping their elbows out of other students' space.

Meekness can always be spotted in public by the conspicuous effort the meek person makes to fold himself or herself up into a tiny, inoffensive space. But even the meekest person maintains a claim to a certain amount of personal space surrounding his or her body. This invisible shell varies in size for different people and in different societies, but its existence can be tested by a simple experiment. Strike up a conversation with a stranger and station yourself about a foot away from him. He will probably feel that you are too close and will back away. Whenever he moves away, follow him. But be careful. Social experimentation can be just as explosive as chemical experimentation, and you may end up with a black eye.

Personal space has been described by

Erving Goffman, a daring modern sociologist. Many of Goffman's brilliant insights developed out of experiments like the one just mentioned.[12] Goffman tells us that personal space is an elongated sphere that extends outward in front of the body and not as far out on either side or in back. People who interact usually stay outside of each other's sphere, though intimates may be welcomed within it. On a crowded subway more general intrusion may be permitted, but only temporarily. The size of the average sphere differs from one culture to another. Latin Americans feel a certain coldness in North Americans, who require a greater distance between bodies in ordinary conversation. North Americans back away whenever their Latin American companions move close enough to feel comfortable. In pedestrian traffic a person becomes a sort of vehicle, shuttling between the other bodies and avoiding collisions by signaling intended movements by means of glances and gestures.[13]

The human species has developed a system of etiquette for assigning space to individuals. By settling yourself in a particular spot you can stake out a claim to a large or small space, and that claim will usually be recognized by others. Robert Sommer has studied the process by which people claim space. He asked the following question: suppose you enter a library and choose a seat at an empty table. If you want to remain alone at this table as long as possible, which chair will you choose? Sommer found that people who want to discourage others from taking a seat at that table will choose a seat in the middle.[14]

It is possible to maintain a claim to a particular space without being present in person. This is done by leaving *markers*, or personal belongings, to signal that one intends to return to the vacant space. Thus at a racetrack a folded strip of newspaper is woven between the slats of a bench to show that a seat is taken. Sommer has studied the limits on the use of markers. He found, for example, that you can hold a seat in a crowded study hall for over two hours by using a textbook and a sport jacket as markers, while a heap of magazines will work for about 30 minutes.[15]

Neither Sommer nor Goffman claim that the use of markers is a biological instinct; indeed, they would probably agree that it is not. But they both study the use of personal space in an ethological way, much as an ethologist would study the territoriality of apes or antelopes. It is likely that territoriality serves many of the same functions for all species, including our own.[16] One of those functions may be to reduce conflict. It has been noted that the street gangs of large cities have a strong claim on their "turf," often a particular street that members of other gangs dare not enter. Some people see this as an example of territoriality, evidence that the

*Personal space.*

Joanne Leonard/Woodfin Camp

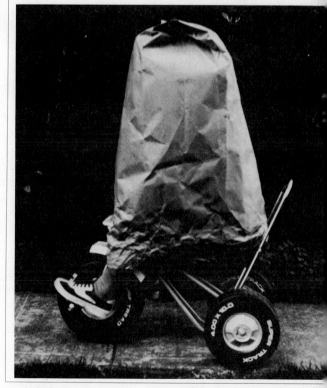

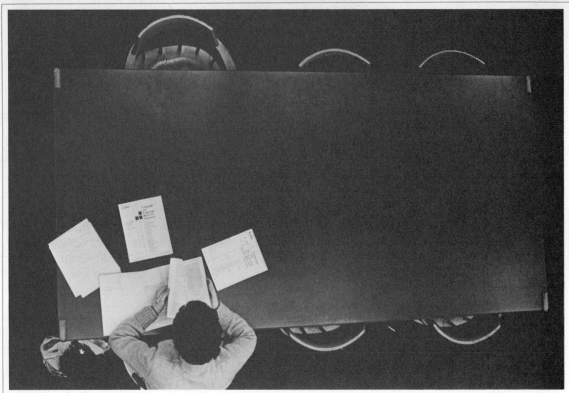

Peter Vandermark/Stock, Boston

*Does he want the entire table for himself? Why don't you think so?*

human social system faces many of the same problems that animal societies face.

### Interaction rituals

Sociologists and ethologists share an interest in another important aspect of animal behavior—interaction rituals. Most, if not all, primates have regular ways of signaling their relationships to one another through gesture, touch, and voice, especially when they meet or part. Some greeting and leave-taking rituals are similar across species. The following is Jane van Lawick-Goodall's description of the wild chimpanzees that she has studied:

Chimpanzees, like people, exchange greetings when they meet after being apart for any length of time. When this occurs, an observer can usually determine the relationship of one chimp to the other. They may meet as two friends and show

pleasure in their reunion, or one may make submissive gestures, acknowledging the other's higher rank.

When Mike arrives in any group the other chimps invariably hurry to pay their respects, touching him with outstretched hands or bowing, just as courtiers once bowed before their king. And, just as the king chose either to acknowledge a courtier or to ignore him, so Mike may take notice of his inferiors, touching them briefly, or he may do nothing. Depending on his mood, he may even threaten or strike those who hasten to greet him.

Many of the apes' forms of greeting startlingly resemble our own. They often kiss. Rodolf in particular frequently touches the face of a subordinate with his lips, or presses his open mouth onto the neck or shoulder of another adult male. Pepe and Figan, to mention but two, often press their mouths to the lips of other individuals. Hand-holding, as a gesture of greeting, is not common in the chimpanzee community at the reserve, but it does occur. Melissa for one, when first arriving in a group, occasionally holds her hand toward a dominant male until he reaches out and reassures her with a touch.

One of the most memorable reunions took place between old Mr. Worzle and timid Olly. As she approached him, panting nervously, he raised both arms as though pronouncing a blessing. Encouraged, Olly crept closer, crouching and holding her hand toward him. Mr. Worzle took her hand in his and drew her close, placing his other hand gently on her head. Then each flung both arms around the other and exchanged kisses on the neck. Finally, to complete the picture, Olly's daughter Gilka ran up, and Mr. Worzle reached out and drew her into his embrace.[17]

Goffman calls greetings and farewells *access rituals*. He has analyzed the rules governing such rituals among human beings. Most human greetings are less expansive than those of Olly and Mr. Worzle, though a good deal depends on how long the people involved have been separated. Moreover, humans follow an "attenuation rule":

Nowhere can this be seen more prettily than in the conduct of long-separated, closely related friends who newly come together during a social occasion. On first contact, an expansive greeting will occur. A moment later when the next proximity occurs, a reduced version of the initial display will be provided. Each succeeding contact will be managed with an increasingly attenuated greeting until after a time the two will exhibit the standard minimal middle-class social recognition—only a rapid grimace involving little change in eye expression, the two ends of the mouth stretching a little in a cheek flick. (After this point has been reached, the two may cooperate, of course, in seeing to it that one of them can act as though his eyes have not fallen on the other, thereby obviating all display, even the most attenuated.)[18]

### Facial expressions and emotion

Facial expressions are somewhat different from interpersonal rituals. Some scholars argue that facial expressions are learned through social interaction and that different societies have different conventions for expressing various emotions. Ray Birdwhistell, a specialist in nonverbal communication (*kinesics*), claims that humans have no uni-

versal gestures or expressions. He believes that all gestures and expressions are specific to particular cultures.[19] This is still a subject of much debate, but the research seems to be going against Birdwhistell's position. For one thing, it is clear that people who are born blind express emotions with the same facial movements that sighted people do, yet they can hardly have learned those gestures by imitation.

Probably the most important research on facial expressions has been done by Paul Ekman and his associates. These researchers believe that although a smile or a frown may provide evidence of pleasure or displeasure, it is not necessarily *intended* to show one's feelings. In fact facial expressions may even show feelings that a person does not want to show. Grief, anger, disgust, fear, and happiness seem to produce the same muscular reactions in all normal people, but these reactions may be held back when one does not want one's feelings to be known. To use Mead's terms (see page 160), the "I" may feel like weeping, but the "me" may force a smile for the sake of appearances. Moreover, each society may specify the emotions that may be shown in particular social situations, and those expressions may "overlay" the natural feelings of the people involved. For example, in some parts of Indonesia funerals are supposed to be occasions of joy and merrymaking, but anthropologists report that the laughter at these ceremonies has a tense quality that betrays the underlying presence of darker feelings.

In order to find out whether facial expressions of emotion are universal, Ekman photographed members of a variety of cultures. He was especially interested in photographing people who had never seen a white person and could never have learned to "read" a white person's face.[20] Their expressions of sadness, anger, or disgust looked just like the white person's expressions of the same emotions. Moreover, people in one society are also quite accurate in

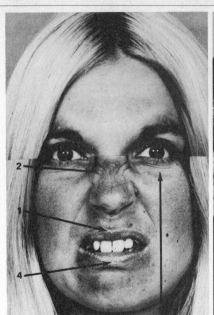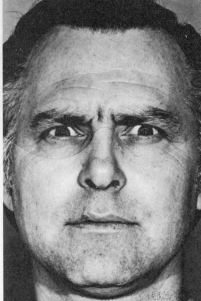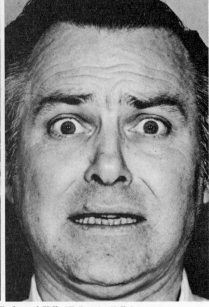

Courtesy of Paul Ekman and Wallace V. Friesen. *Unmasking the Face.* Englewood Cliffs, NJ: Prentice-Hall, Inc., 1975.

*Look at the three faces. The arrows on the face to the left indicate elements of the expression which reveal disgust. (1) The raised upper lip caused a change in the appearance of the tip of the nose. (2) Wrinkling along the sides and bridge of the nose. (4) The lower lip is lowered and slightly forward. (5) The cheeks are raised, and this produces a change in the appearance of the lower eyelid, narrowing the opening of the eye and producing many lines and folds below the eye. Now look at the other two faces. Can you tell which elements of the expression convey the particular emotion expressed? What emotions do we see in the middle and righthand faces?*

identifying the emotions of members of other societies as recorded in photographs. Apparently emotions are hard to hide. One of Ekman's most important discoveries is what he calls "leakage"—momentary lapses when one's face reveals an underlying mood.[21] Movies capture such fleeting lapses very clearly, but in ordinary interaction people don't notice them, probably because we are all taught to be tactful toward one another. When a person fails to control her face properly, her companions will normally glance away until she has recovered, though they may not even be aware of the lapse. (The same courtesy applies in other, similar lapses, as when one is caught scratching or picking one's nose.) Interaction can continue smoothly because everyone is careful to ignore such behavior. However, in some situations it is useful to be able to recognize emo-

tional "leakage." For example, a clinician may need to decide whether a depressed mental patient is really feeling well enough to be released or whether the patient is faking happiness in order to get out.

## Types of groups

Human behavior is far more varied than that of other species. These variations are caused largely by the fact that human social interactions vary so greatly. Sometimes insects are described as "social" because they live together in large colonies and interact in complex ways. However, the social activities of insects are fixed by instinct, while those of human beings are much more flexible. This is because the patterns of human behavior are passed from one generation to the next through culture, not through genes. Among animals, similar situations lead to similar responses. A swarm of bees will build a hive that looks much like all the other hives bees have been building for millions of years. A human city, however, is never like any other human city. Smash a beehive and it will be replaced by a duplicate of the old one. Destroy a human city and it will be rebuilt on a new design. The social activity of human beings is invented, not determined by biological factors. The activities of humans depend on the past experience built up by the group. Therefore it is necessary to discuss the various types of groups that are important to human beings and to study their effects on human life.

Two of the most important words used in sociology books cannot be defined precisely because they are not really technical terms. These words are *group* and *collectivity*, and sociologists use them as loosely as anyone else does. Often they are used interchangeably. One can usually tell from the context which of several possible definitions the writer has in mind. The first meaning is simply *any collection of people who are together in the same place.* (We could also call this a *physical aggregation.*) Thus the words *group* and *collectivity* might be used to refer to all the people in an elevator or all the window shoppers walking past a department store.

The second meaning is *any number of people who have some characteristic in common.* (We could also call this a *category.*) Thus the words *group* and *collectivity* might be used to refer to all the people whose names in the Chicago phone directory begin with the letter D. Or they might be used to refer to all the black shopowners in Vancouver. Or to all left-handed optometrists over the age of 90. The people in a category may not think of themselves as belonging together. The category is simply a pigeonhole into which people may be classified.

Joe Gordon/DPI

*A peer group.*

Finally, a third definition of group and, less often, of collectivity is *a social system with a name and an identity to which people are seen as belonging.* Examples are the nation of China, the National Geographic Society, and the Chicago White Sox. This definition implies that the people involved have some form of ongoing interaction among themselves. All the readers of this book do not qualify as a group in this narrow sense. You cannot all meet one another, nor do you feel even the slightest bond with one another.

Sometimes *group* is used in contrast to *collectivity.* For example, we may say that the passengers of a jet plane were merely a collectivity until the plane crashed in a jungle, and then the survivors became a true

147

group. In this narrow sense all groups are collectivities but not all collectivities are groups. They become groups if they interact and if they think of themselves as groups.

The largest collectivity with which sociology is concerned is the *society*. To be termed a society a group must meet the following standards:

1. It must be able to exist longer than the life span of the individuals in it.
2. It must gain new members at least partly by means of sexual reproduction.
3. It must share certain values and standards.
4. It must be self-sufficient.

According to this definition, the ordinary North American township, despite its high standard of living and complex organization, is not a society. It is not self-sufficient because it can't supply all its own needs and must rely on others for such things as food, water, power, medical services, and defense. A monastery is not a society because it does not gain new members through sexual reproduction. One way to decide whether a collectivity is a society is to imagine what would happen if all other groups suddenly disappeared. If there is a good chance that the remaining group could survive, then it is a society. Most primitive tribes and almost all nation-states meet this standard.

## PRIMARY GROUPS AND SECONDARY GROUPS

In this chapter we will discuss not only the *structure* of various sorts of groups but, even more important, the *quality* of those groups. In terms of quality sociologists distinguish between two types of groups: (1) **primary groups,** whose members interact in a personal, intimate, and emotional way, and (2) **secondary groups,** whose members interact in a more impersonal, unsentimental, and businesslike way.

A primary group is an intimate group whose members have a sense of "we-ness"—a family, for example, or a group of close friends. Members of such groups respond to each other as whole, unique personalities, not merely on the basis of the particular role that each performs. Primary groups are always small and usually involve face-to-face interaction. The members mean a lot to one another—so much so that a major change in their relationship requires an emotional readjustment. The members of such a group are not interchangeable. If your brother leaves home, for example, you can't rent his room to a boarder and expect him to play the role of your brother. Families are primary groups, though sometimes members of the same family become so estranged from each other that their relationship is no longer altogether "primary."

Sometimes even actual primary groups are not characterized by happy feelings. Two bitter enemies who have agreed that neither will speak to the other have, in that understanding, an intensely intimate personal relationship. To hate someone is, after all, to care about that person in a special way, and this makes it a primary relationship. This is not true of people who are indifferent to one another. The primary group is often a scene of mixed feelings, for the people we hate the most are often the people we also love the most.

There are many different kinds of primary groups, and each person needs to participate in several kinds. We need our original family in a unique way: It is the place where socialization begins and where we first experience deep emotions and serious personal commitments. Shallow primary relationships among family members make it harder for a person to develop warm relationships later on.

Friendship groups are, to varying degrees, primary groups. They differ from one another, of course, and are not the same as families. Suppose you play basketball with the same friends every Saturday for years and always have a beer together afterwards, along with a lot of horseplay and joking. This may be a rewarding primary group, but it will mean something different from the other primary experiences in your life — such as your summer love affair or your heart-to-heart conversations with your best friend.

We can understand the primary group best by comparing it with the secondary group, which is more impersonal. The relations between, say, a hotel guest and the porter are usually secondary, not primary. Guests do not care which porter takes them to their rooms and do not expect to participate in long discussions of either the porter's or their own private affairs. Each member of a secondary group is involved with only a part of the others' lives — and sometimes that part is very small. Thus to the motorist the toll booth attendant is hardly more than a hand that reaches out to take a coin. Any

hand will do, for the members of a secondary group are interchangeable. Their relations are unsentimental and limited.

I do not want to imply that primary groups are good and secondary groups are bad. Actually, we need many different kinds of relationships, and not all of them can be intimate and personal. Businesslike relationships have their place, and very little business would get done without them. Indeed, primary groups that form within business organizations sometimes reduce the effectiveness of the larger group. For instance, some offices get little work done because all the employees are great friends and talk all the time. Moreover, loyalty to a primary group can conflict with a loyalty to a larger group. For example, a small group of friends may promote one another to high positions in a business organization even though bet-

*Another peer group.*

Joan Liftin/Woodfin Camp

ter-qualified people are available. Attachment to a primary group is particularistic and may be contrary to the interests of the larger group.

Many city dwellers complain that too many of their relationships are secondary. Whether or not this is really true, it shows that many people believe that traditional village life was full of intimacy and emotional interaction. They believe that modern life is made up mostly of impersonal meetings between strangers who use each other only as a means to an end, not as individuals to be appreciated for their own sake. This complaint, which reflects a sense of isolation and estrangement, has become widespread and has given rise to a number of new social groups designed to counteract this situation.

**ENCOUNTER GROUPS
AND COMMUNES**

The workaday world of Europe and North America calls for a universalistic, emotionally neutral attitude toward others that leaves little room for mutual caring. Without quite knowing how it happened, some people find that their sensitivity even to other members of their family has become blunted. If you want to overcome this lack of closeness and reach out to others, it is not clear how you can do so safely. There are norms that limit how much you can reveal about yourself or find out about your coworkers. Not everyone has a family, and not all families want to encourage closeness. Sometimes they function only by "agreeing to disagree" and not discussing controversial topics. As a result many people have turned to strangers to share their emotions.

The *encounter group*, an idea not much more than ten years old, is a type of group that is formed with the goal of acting as an "instant" primary group. It may be set up in a church, a YMCA, or some other private organization. The members may agree to meet every week for several months with a leader who may have had some training in psychotherapy. Other groups may go away together for "marathon" weekend sessions. The members are usually strangers when the group forms, but they agree to listen to each other, to speak honestly about things they feel deeply about, and to show their emotional reactions to each other. And those reactions are often intense. Encounter groups encourage a kind of closeness that would rarely develop in an office or factory. This experience is often exciting and can lead to personal growth and change. On the other hand, it is also a risky adventure. Direct emotional interactions can shatter a personality that is going through a period of crisis. To be sure, even skilled psychotherapists sometimes make mistakes and hurt their patients, but they are less likely to do so than a group of strangers. Still, the popularity of encounter groups indicates that they may be filling a need for intimacy that is not being filled in any other way. Critics rightly point out the dangers of encounter groups, but they do not suggest other places where people might find primary groups that encourage the sharing of personal feelings.

*Communes*, like encounter groups, are set up for people who are looking for genuine caring relationships. Encounter groups are brief, isolated experiences. In contrast, the member of communes live and often work together. They may pool their income and share their expenses. Often, but not always, they live in a rural area and try to simplify their life style, avoiding waste and frills. They are trying to develop a permanent, stable primary group that is more natural than the encounter group. However, communes have problems and disadvantages too. For one thing, they often attract people who dislike rules of any kind and want to work in an environment that is free of planning or coercion. This hope rarely comes true, and many communes have been forced to make strict demands on their members to avoid falling apart.

Bob Nadler/DPI

*Encounter groups offer instant intimacy.*

## PEER GROUPS

Groups of people of similar status are called peer groups. Examples are classmates or teammates. Most close friendships are formed between members of peer groups because they have much in common and can share experiences as equals. Think about the last five people you invited to your home for dinner. What was your relationship with them? In most cases you will notice that most of those five people have a social status that is not too different from your own and that they are about your age. This is because we usually find dinner conversations easier, more enjoyable, and more relaxed when we are with peers. For the same reason, friendships most often develop between children

in the same class at school or between workers of the same rank at the office or factory. Not all peer groups are primary groups, of course, but many of our most important primary groups are made up of our peers. This is because groups often form on the basis of similarities between people and also because they come together by participating in similar activities. Often peers meet and see each other regularly because they are in the same class at school or the same scouting group, or because they live on the same block, or because they work side by side on the assembly line.

## REFERENCE GROUPS

A group to which we compare ourselves when we judge our own status is called a reference group. Often, but not necessarily, the reference group is our peer group. A parent may ask a teacher whether little Freddy is doing as well as the other kids in his class. In this case the class is both a peer group and a reference group. When someone is undergoing anticipatory socialization the reference group may be a group to which he or she wants to belong. For example, a high school girl may have friends who go to an expensive boarding school. She may follow their styles of clothing and speech instead of those of her own school. She may think of herself as poor compared to members of her reference group, though her classmates do not think of her as poor.

The people we envy usually belong to a reference group that is just a little ahead of us. We do not envy people who are much richer or more successful than we are, but we tend to envy those who might be in our position if things had worked out a little differently. A young sociologist does not envy the president of the American Sociological Association, but he may envy a classmate who finished his Ph.D. very quickly, has published several articles in the *American Sociological Review*, and is under contract for a book or two. You probably do not envy Prince Charles, but you may envy your brother-in-law, who at age 28 owns a speed-boat and a ski chalet.

### LARGE, COMPLEX GROUPS

Every person belongs not only to some small groups that may be either primary or second-ary but also to large groups that are almost always secondary. If a group is made up of hundreds, or even millions, of members, those members cannot all know one another on a personal, intimate basis. In order for large groups to function well there must be some specialization of roles and responsibil-ities. Members of such groups may form small primary groups with those whom they get to know within their special roles, but the organization as a whole is likely to be impersonal in nature. Also, for the decisions and actions of the large group to fit together there must be a system of authority and rank, with each member having authority over a particular area of responsibility.

Large groups of many kinds play a part in all our lives. Even primitive societies form large groups, which we call *tribes* or *clans*. Clans are kinship groupings—people who are related to one another—and several clans together make up a tribe. In later chapters we will deal with many different kinds of large, complex social groups. Chapter 8 deals with formal organizations. Chapter 9 focuses on *social classes*, large categories of people in similar economic positions who may or may not think of themselves as a group. In Chap-ter 10 we will discuss *ethnic groups*, loose categories of people who share cultural pat-terns and (usually) some physical traits. In Chapter 11 we will study *crowds*, large groups of people who gather in one place without any organized system of roles or authority. A crowd may become excited and act in a spontaneous way. It may hang some-one in effigy or carry a football hero on their shoulders. In other chapters we will discuss large groups such as churches, universities, multinational corporations, cities, and the nation-state. All of these groups are impor-tant, but in this chapter we will deal mostly with the small, primary group.

## Social groups and the social self

Interpersonal relation-ships within primary groups have been the main focus of an important school of sociolo-gists—the *symbolic interactionists*. These scholars have written a great deal about the process of socialization. They are interested in showing how an individual's personality and thinking habits develop through social interaction. The originator of this line of inquiry was the American sociologist Charles Horton Cooley (1864–1929). One of his most fruitful contributions to sociology is his description of the development of the social self within the primary group.[22] Fur-ther work on this topic was done by George Herbert Mead and his followers, as we will see later in the chapter.

### THE INDIVIDUAL AND THE GROUP

It seemed clear to Cooley that the distinction between the person and the group is often overstated. He argued that it is a mistake to see the individual as limited by the demands and rules of his or her social community, as if a person could be entirely free if it were not for the "oppressive" force of society. His own view of the person and the group em-phasized their interdependence: Each is an aspect of the other. Cooley believed that so-ciety is a whole made up of many individual parts. A group may be said to have a "mind" in a sense. Individuals contribute to this public mind by communicating their own ideas. Moreover, individuals gain from this process, for it is through communication that they build up their own minds. Even when there is conflict between individuals, the conflict arises only because they share a particular concern. By dealing with others each member of society both expands his or her inner experience and contributes to the whole. For example, a novelist cannot create a novel alone, uninfluenced by other literature. Novels are shaped by, and become part of, a literary tradition. Similarly, each person's mind is shaped by, and becomes part of, the intellectual tradition of his or her community.

Cooley saw each human being as a product of two distinct historical streams: (1) his or her unique biological inheritance, which is passed on to his or her offspring, and (2) his or her cultural inheritance, which is also passed to future generations. Each person is, in a sense, a fresh organization of life in which these two streams meet.

### THE LOOKING-GLASS SELF

Though Cooley describes the person as a channel through which life passes, he was quite aware that each person feels unique. In fact Cooley was very interested in the phenomenon of *self-regard*—how it develops and its effects on group life. Many of his theories were stimulated by watching the psychological and linguistic growth of his own children. It seemed to him that a sense of self is first experienced in pride of ownership. A little girl feels a special regard for the things that she can call her own and control—the things that she calls "mine." Her blanket is not interchangeable with any other blanket, for example, and her toys, her shoes, and her spoon may be loved for the same reason.

From this sense of ownership other important attitudes arise. Thus the child can take possession of the *reactions of others* just

as she takes possession of a blanket or a toy, and she can feel pride in those reactions, a sense that they are "hers." If a babysitter shows delight at the little girl's mastery of the tricycle, the youngster may feel proud of herself. In effect, the child sees herself through the eyes of people whose opinions are important to her (i.e., **significant others** such as family members) and whose approval she desires. She takes pride in the image of herself that she sees through their eyes. This self-image is "hers," something that she "owns" and seeks to control. If the babysitter tells her she is naughty, she feels shame—a stinging loss of pride in her "self." The self-image that you acquire in this way remains the core of your personal identity throughout life. Your body may change, but the sense of being "you" will remain stable and continuous even in old age. Cooley called this identity the **looking-glass self**, the self-image that a person acquires as if reflected from the eyes of others. You acquire your social self by seeing yourself as others see you. This capacity to take the perspective of others is the phenomenon that Mead later recognized as the process that makes human society possible. He called it "taking the role of the other."

### ETHICS, THE SELF, AND THE PRIMARY GROUP

Pride in oneself is often discouraged, as if love of self made it impossible to love others. Cooley realized that some forms of pride could be selfish, but he did not think this was true all the time. Pride in itself is not evil; rather, it is necessary. It does not stop you from wanting to help others; in fact it is necessary if you are going to serve others. For example, the idea of "my duty" may be full of self-importance, although it clearly involves helping others. One can take pride in one's duties and responsibilities. Moreover, we make moral commitments on the basis of self-pride. For example, Cooley suggested that maternal commitment grows largely out of a proud sense of ownership: The baby is special to the mother because it is her own.

Pride in oneself (or self-feeling) may extend to include other people or groups. It then becomes "we-feeling." Each of us, especially in childhood, needs to spend a lot of time in intimate groups whose members have a strong sense of "we-ness"—in other words, primary groups.

Rich emotional experiences occur in primary groups, and Cooley claimed that a person's highest moral capacities are always developed through primary interactions. He emphasized the importance of the play group as a context for learning to care for others and to follow rules of fair play. This view was expanded by Mead and Piaget (see Chapter 4). But Cooley first convinced social scientists that moral behavior is learned mainly through mutual relations with peers, not as a result of moral instruction by adults.

According to Cooley, there is no sharp difference between thinking about moral problems and thinking about other problems. Cooley held that being moral is being rational. Moral behavior develops out of the capacity for *sympathetic imagination*. This is the ability to create images that are inspiring. To pray, for example, is to confront our moral problems and questions with the highest "personal ideal we can form."[23] To develop this ability we need privacy from influences that are not morally instructive, Cooley suggested, and communion with those that are. Our active imagination "enables us to live with the best our lives have afforded and maintain higher suggestions to compete with the baser ones that assail us."[24]

Cooley's writings show a generosity and humanity of spirit that strike today's reader as refreshing, if somewhat quaint. His influence on American sociology is still felt, expecially within the tradition of *symbolic interactionism*.

*A primary group*

Tatarsky/DPI

## COMMUNICATION
## AND THE SELF

At the turn of the century the University of Chicago was an important center of sociological study. A number of creative social theorists, including George Herbert Mead, taught and wrote there. John Dewey was there too, directing his Laboratory School and writing about education.[25] The two men shared many ideas, and both made important contributions to sociology. Mead was known more for his teaching than for his writing. After his death, however, his students published the notes they had taken in his lectures.[26] One of those students, Herbert Blumer, conveyed his teacher's ideas to a whole generation of sociologists and coined the term *symbolic interactionism* to refer to Mead's theories and to the theories of like-minded sociologists.[27] Symbolic interactionists believe that social relationships and personality develop out of social interaction at the *symbolic* level of language and gestures.

Mead suggested that people do not respond directly and instinctively to events themselves but respond in terms of their *interpretation* of events. Among lower animals specific behavior is an automatic response to specific stimuli and is guided entirely by instincts. Human beings, however, can perform much more complex acts, and their behavior is guided by their mental images of the world. These images include abstract ideas and can extend forward and backward in time and space. Each of us carries with us a mental map of the universe, and we orient ourselves by that map. For example, we may imagine that we are sitting on a speck of dust and circling around a dot of light on the edge of a galaxy that hovers in a black and sparkling cosmos. We can imagine our planet as it may have appeared a billion years ago or as it may be a billion years in the future. Moreover, we can conjure up images that we will never experience directly—the beauty of Cleopatra, Snow White's trance, the X-ray vision of Superman, the madness of Nero, or the rage of Thor as he throws his hammer across the sky, splitting the clouds with lightning.

We act according to our imaginative interpretation of events. Columbus' crew came close to mutiny because they believed that they were sailing toward the edge of a flat world and were in danger of falling off. Their interpretation of the situation differed from Columbus'. But the fish swimming around their ships had no interpretation of the situation at all; fish have no ideas, no symbols. They simply react to internal and external stimuli. Fish do not pray to gods, nor do they make political commitments or discover mathematical laws or scold themselves for having eaten a fellow creature or wonder where the ocean came from. Adult human beings may do all of these things, however, for our world is not only a world of objective stimuli but also a subjective world of meaningful objects. For us, the nature of the objects that surround us depends on the conceptual framework within which we perceive them. Even our perceptions are based on social experience. What a North American would perceive as a baseball bat might not be perceived in the same way by other people: Australian aborigines might perceive it as a valuable piece of firewood; New Guinean tribesmen might perceive it as an excellent weapon. A baseball bat is simply not among the objects that exist for these tribesmen. Here we must emphasize Mead's distinction between mere "stimuli" and what he called "objects." The nature of an "object" is determined subjectively according to the *concept* that one applies to it, and that concept is based on social experience.

Humans begin life as empty of concepts as animals do. The newborn child has no concept of baseball bats or firewood or weapons or worlds, whether flat or round. Mead was interested in describing how a child acquires the set of *meaningful objects* that make up his or her world as an adult. Objects are perceived in terms of their meanings, and those meanings are acquired through social relationships. The baseball bat is not a meaningful concept to an infant because the infant does not know how to act toward it and has no idea what kind of experiences he or she could have with it. Other people have to define it by acting toward it in a characteristic way. The infant sees people swing bats at balls a few times, and then he or she knows a little about the meaning of bats. Much of the work involved in caring for children takes the form of defining objects for the child. ("A chair is to sit in, not to scoot around the floor, Jimmy." "We don't chew on tea bags, Lynn, we soak them in hot water.") The "meaning" of chairs and tea bags is found in the experiences one can have with them, and this is learned by seeing how other people act toward them.

Our perceptions are guided by our concepts. We don't just "see" things at random; we organize our perceptions of them as they occur. We "carve out of experience" the objects that we perceive. The objects that exist for us are organized as such by the future experiences that we could have with them. Thus the future is telescoped into the present in our perceptions. For example, if we "see" a baseball bat as smooth and hard, what we are "seeing" is really our expectation that if, in the future, we run our hands over it we will not get splinters in our fingers, and if we poke it or hit it, it will not crumble into tiny fragments or bend like a garden hose. Our perception of it as smooth and hard is really an expectation of future experience based on past experience. Likewise, our recognition of the bat as equipment for a baseball game is an expectation of future possibilities based on past experience. The bat *could* be used in the kitchen (e.g., as a rolling pin), but we do not recognize this possibility in it when we see it as a baseball bat.

Now that you understand something about Mead's basic ideas, we can take a closer look at the nature of the interaction through which we acquire a set of concepts. In doing so we will see why Blumer called Mead's theories *symbolic* interactionism. Social interaction may be symbolic or nonsymbolic. A dog fight, for example, is nonsymbolic interaction that occurs when one dog threatens another, the other responds by growling, and so on. No complex interpretation goes on; it is simply a matter of direct stimulus and response. Human beings can also interact on a nonsymbolic level, automatically, without thinking. For example, ballroom dancing is largely nonsymbolic — the dancers coordinate their movements through muscular cues. Reflex action is certainly nonsymbolic. Screams of pain are nonsymbolic communications. Boxers and wrestlers maul each other in rounds of nonsymbolic interaction. Two people who pass each other on a sidewalk avoid a collision by interacting in primarily nonsymbolic ways, that is, by automatically moving out of each other's path. Nonsymbolic communication is the simplest sort of communication; action and reaction take place at almost the same time, and there is no need to interpret the other person's behavior.

Symbolic interaction is far more complex, but Mead wanted to show how it develops out of nonsymbolic interaction. He suggested that the beginning of an act could come to be understood as a symbol standing for the whole act. Suppose a foreigner who does not know your language feels angry and wants to warn you that he is thinking of punching you. He may make a jabbing gesture but not complete the punch. This movement is symbolic. It is meant to represent a future event that both you and he can interpret in the same way. If you do not recognize what future event the jabbing gesture stands for, you do not share the symbol. You may fail to understand the warning and change your behavior accordingly.

Mead argued that the lower species are

able to understand symbols only in the simplest sense, if at all. My dog becomes very excited when he hears the words *outside* or *leash*, for they come at the beginning of a trip outside. But the dog's vocabulary of symbols is tiny compared to that of human beings. The human infant quickly learns that the word *hot* can be the first phase of an impending burn, that the word *car* can be the first phase of an impending trip, and so forth. The symbols (words) stand for the events that will occur in the future; when we learn the symbols we acquire some control over our future experience. Thus a person who understands the word *hot* can be warned in time to avoid being burned. A child who can use the word *car* can wheedle her parents into

taking her for a ride. The meaning of an action, a gesture, or a word is what it stands for in terms of future action. When two people recognize it as standing for the same future, they share a significant symbol. By sharing significant symbols, human beings can communicate in ways that would otherwise be impossible.

### Role taking

Perhaps the most remarkable contribution of the symbolic interactionists to our understanding of human nature is their analysis of **role taking,** the ability of a person to imagine the role of another person with whom he or she interacts. In order to interact with another person one must be able to an-

People learn to guide their own acts according to the anticipated reactions of others. In a tennis game the player must know how an opponent will respond.

UPI

ticipate the other's future actions. When one person starts to do anything, the other must imagine the rest of the act, anticipate future phases, and shape his or her own acts accordingly. If the two participants do not anticipate later phases of acts in the same way, one does not understand what the other is doing, and the two may fail to fit their actions together.

People guide their own acts according to the anticipated reactions of others. Take two tennis players, for example. Each player decides where to place a shot by deciding whether or not the other player can reach it. Or take the shopper buying meat in a supermarket. He may pick up a package of liver but, anticipating the groans of his children at the dinner table, may put it down and choose hamburger instead. In both of these examples the present action is guided by the expected future actions of others.

When you want to understand another person you take that person's role. Social life depends on role taking—each person must try to see the world through the other fellow's eyes. A person who is unable to do this cannot be a full member of human society.

Through role taking the individual acquires a set of meaningful concepts. We learn that a flag is not an ordinary piece of colored cloth, for instance, by watching how others act toward flags. We learn that the school principal has more authority than the teachers by watching how the teachers act toward the principal. In this way the child learns the meanings of the concepts shared by his or her social group—be they flags, principals, or baseball bats.

Among the many concepts that the child acquires through social interaction the most important of all is the *self*. Mead took Cooley's notion of the looking-glass self further by suggesting that just as other people define for you such concepts as flags, principals, and baseball bats by the way they act toward them, so also they define your *self* as a particular kind of person by the way they act

toward you. As a child you were limited to the perspectives of the people you knew. You learned the concepts that made up their world, however limited that set of concepts may have been. You were also limited to the self that you saw through the eyes of others. Thus if the group had viewed you as a slave you would have grown up viewing yourself as a slave. If your group had viewed you as a prince, you would have grown up viewing yourself as a prince. In both cases you would have behaved according to your view of yourself. The self is a social product, defined at the beginning by the actions of others.

### Self-reflexive behavior

The possession of a self as an object makes it possible for a human being to interact with himself or herself much as he or she interacts with other human beings. This interaction with the self is called self-reflexive behavior. You can look at yourself from the viewpoint of another person. For example, a child may see herself from the viewpoint of a parent. She may warn or scold herself in a gruff voice for doing something that her father disapproves of, or she may praise herself for building a fine castle in the sandbox. This sort of interaction does not end in adulthood. On the contrary, each of us continues to be an *object of our own activity*. Your self is an object in the world just as much as your car or house is an object in the world—and it needs as much attention as a car or a house. You may stand in front of a mirror and admire yourself. You may become angry with yourself and pound on your own head. The self is an object of great concern in your world, and as Mead showed, it is an image that you acquire through role taking.

### The play and game stages

Mead was curious about the process through which a child develops the ability to step outside of himself or herself and into other points of view. All children go through a stage of make-believe play during which they step outside of their own roles and become someone else. The **play stage** is a stage when a child is learning to take the roles of people he or she knows. They play cowboy and Indian, nurse and doctor, Martian and astronaut. Mead believed that this sort of play is an important aspect of normal growth, for through it the child gains skill in role taking, in taking other viewpoints besides his or her own. A little boy steps inside an imaginary phone booth, strips off his imaginary Clark Kent clothing, and creates an adventure in the role of Superman, using all the powers available to that talented gentleman. He thus extends his knowledge of role behavior by acting out roles that he may never perform in real life. But if the opportunity did arise he would have practiced; he would be ready.

The activities of children who play together in this way are not usually very well organized. The *play stage* occurs while children are fairly young, perhaps 5 or 6. There is some interaction between the players—the young nurse will hand a spoon to the young surgeon when a scalpel is needed, and the patient (often a younger brother or sister) will amiably expose his or her navel to the spoon. But the players do not fit their activities together in any very complex way. For the most part they play their separate roles side by side, not yet being skilled enough to perform actions that are truly interdependent.

However, by the **game stage,** the stage at which a child can understand a set of roles as a system, new kinds of behavior become possible and the interaction of children takes new forms. It is not possible to teach most 5-year-olds how to play baseball. They can learn to pitch, to bat, to catch, and to run, but they can't understand the game as a system. Baseball players must constantly inter-

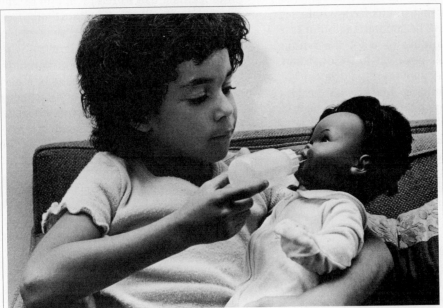

F. Leinwand/Monkmeyer

*Role playing is a major activity during the "play stage."*

act with one another in terms of a whole set of roles that all of the players understand. For example, all the players know that a runner will try to steal a base if he can. Therefore all the basemen must be ready to catch a fast ball if he tries to do this, and all the players know what all the other players will do when this happens. Thus each player must take the roles of all the other players at the same time. Young children cannot take so many roles at a time, and therefore they cannot understand the game, but a 10-year-old is in the game stage of development and is likely to be very interested in it.

The roles of baseball players can be described in terms of rules that are agreed upon by everyone who knows baseball. A little leaguer who plays first base does not have to pretend to be a particular famous ballplayer. "Playing" baseball is not like "playing" Superman; it is not make-believe. The point of the game is to follow the rules as closely as possible. In a game a participant does not take the role of *one* person, as in play, but takes the role of the generalized other. This is an abstract role that stands for a whole set of particular roles. The generalized other is a person's understanding of what the whole group has agreed upon. An individual can therefore take the viewpoint of the whole community in judging his or her performance and guiding his or her behavior. It is a sort of reference group built up by the individual through his or her relationships with people who share certain views. Thus the whole community of baseball players and fans agree about the rules and share expectations about performance. A player will take the views of this community and be guided by them.

Games are ways in which the 10- or 11-year-old practices taking the role of the generalized other, judging his or her own behavior in terms of the understandings of a large group of people. No longer guiding himself or herself from the viewpoint of one particular person at a time, the child takes the role

of a whole group and guides his or her behavior by their anticipated reactions.

When the child is able to take the role of the generalized other, he or she is mature enough to go beyond the particular situation and behave in a stable way in a variety of different situations. In early childhood he or she saw the world first through one role and then through another and was unable to cope with contradictions between those roles. After the game stage, however, the child may become interested in reconciling different interpretations of reality. He or she will try to arrive at the most general interpretation— that which best explains the views of all the individuals he or she knows. The child is now able to decide that so-and-so's reaction to his or her actions is odd and need not be taken seriously. He or she is able to form a stable self-image and maintain it in the face of contradictory reactions.

Among the highest forms of human activity, according to Mead, is the work of building a generalized other. For example, intellectuals use different points of view as material for their work—different views of society, politics, poetry, or even God. A physicist may spend a lifetime trying to reconcile two contradictory interpretations— such as whether light is a wave or a particle. This abstract work with symbols can be done only by people who have experienced all the earlier stages of role taking.

All normal adults have within them a miniature society. Each person continually makes indications to himself or herself about the immediate situation. He or she may have long internal conversations in which conflicting interpretations are discussed and perhaps reconciled. Mental activity is *internal symbolic interaction*.

### I and me

Mead distinguishes between two aspects of the self, which he terms the *I* and the *me*. The "I" consists of the impulses and feelings of the present moment—it is the spontaneous aspect of the person. But normal people do not act on all their impulses; they control themselves. One behaves in a consistent way in terms of a stable self-image. The "me," the ability to control one's impulses so as to organize one's behavior rationally, is developed through social experience. The "me" brings past experience to bear on the present. Still, in the next moment new impulses arise in the "I" phase, for both "I" and "me" are endless.

### THE ACT

Symbolic interactionists claim that human conduct is purposeful, goal-directed, problem-solving, adjustive activity and not simply a collection of responses "released" by stimuli. The basic unit of human conduct is the act, which the person develops in the course of interacting with self and others. Almost everything important that one does is part of an act, whether it takes a split second or fifty years to complete. Acts nestle inside acts, like the little sets of wooden dolls you buy in Chinatown. Picking up a pencil is an act. It may also be part of a larger act, such as writing a term paper, which, in turn, may be part of the larger act of earning a college degree, and so forth.

The act begins with a feeling of restlessness in the person, which is based on an impulse or desire. This is the "I." You may feel thirsty, for example. In order to organize an act, however, you must first identify the impulse by making an indication to yourself that you are thirsty. If you don't, you will feel restless but will be unable to carry out any complex adjustive behavior. Suppose that you do say to yourself that you are thirsty and need a drink. The act that may follow has two phases — covert and overt. During the covert phase you are preparing to act but have not yet begun to do so. Many acts never move beyond the covert stage, for the "me" aspect of the self may simply decide not to act on the desire. For example, if

you are thirsty and find yourself in a lifeboat with twenty other people and only a quart of drinking water, you may decide to limit the amount you drink or even offer your share to someone else. The feeling of thirst does not automatically lead to the act of drinking. During the covert phase one interacts with oneself and organizes future phases of the act. You may tell yourself which beverages are available, warn yourself to avoid caffeine or high-calorie drinks, or remind yourself that your companion is a teetotaler. Having taken such factors into account, you may think of a way to satisfy your desire and then take action (the overt phase) to reach your goal. This may require a series of subordinate acts such as finding a glass and turning on the faucet. Throughout all the phases of the act you will continue to adjust your plans by making indications to yourself about your situation — your glass is cracked, perhaps, and must be thrown out; the water is too warm; and so on.

Thus it is that human acts are built up. A person may undertake a very complex act that may take many years to perform and involve interactions with thousands of other people in highly changeable situations. Human beings are able to fit their acts together only because (1) they can define for themselves the nature of their situation and (2) they can build up shared ways of interpreting reality through symbolic communication. Mental activity is primarily linguistic — we are constantly talking either to ourselves or to others.

### HOW SYMBOLIC INTERACTIONISTS WORK

Mead died in 1931, but his influence on sociology has never faded. Symbolic interactionism is not the dominant approach to the study of society, but it is an important approach. Most sociologists, including most of those whose work is described in this book, like to show causal relationships — patterns of association between independent and dependent variables. To explain a given behavior pattern they look for social experiences that happened to the actor before the act was performed and therefore "caused" him or her to behave in that way. Symbolic interactionists do not attempt to answer questions about the "cause" of behavior; rather, they try to find the "meaning" of behavior. That is, they want to know how the actor interprets the situation and what he or she has in mind when responding to the situation. One comparison will illustrate this approach. Sheldon and Eleanor Glueck, two Harvard researchers, looked for the causes of juvenile delinquency by comparing 500 delinquents with 500 nondelinquents living in the same district. Both groups were of comparable age, intelligence, and ethnic origin. They found that delinquent boys were much more likely to come from families that often moved or in which there was only one parent, the father had bad work habits, alcoholism was present, and so on through a host of disadvantages. In other words, they isolated a number of important independent variables that were related to delinquency.[28]

Contrast this to the symbolic interactionist approach taken by Gresham M. Sykes and David Matza in a similar study. They did not ask what *made* a boy delinquent; rather, they asked how such boys managed to offset their own guilt by rationalizing their actions. They show that much delinquency is based on various reasons for deviance that "are seen as valid by the delinquent but not by the legal system or society at large." For example, a young mugger may deny that his victim is a victim by asserting that the victim "started it" or "asked for it." The mugger makes himself into a Robin Hood. Notice that Sykes and Matza's approach does not "explain behavior but only outlines the meaning that it has for the actor.[29]

Symbolic interactionists claim that the only way to determine how people interpret situations is to get inside their world by communicating with them directly. Thus they prefer to collect evidence by means of participant observation instead of using such methods as questionnaires. They argue that a questionnaire presents the respondent with a fixed set of answers to choose from, while none of the answers may fit his or her own interpretation. The researcher should listen to explanations instead of trying to get them to fit a predetermined list of replies.

## Group interaction

Having discussed the importance of social groups in the formation of personality and the self, let's look at some of the processes that go on within groups. We want to focus on the boundedness of groups, the interaction across group boundaries, and the sense of "we-ness" that draws members of some, but not all, groups together.

### GROUP BOUNDARIES

The University of California at Berkeley is a very informal place. I never realized this until, having done my graduate work there, I went to work at Harvard for two years. At about the same time a friend of mine moved from Harvard to Berkeley and found it almost as hard to adjust to Berkeley as I found it to adjust to Harvard. We used to phone each other and complain. Her complaint was that Berkeley people were "rude." When she joined a group, most people would stay sprawled on the floor; nobody shook hands with her or welcomed her. They treated her as if she had been part of the group all along. She could talk or not talk, whichever she preferred, and when she left nobody seemed to notice. She could drift in, talk, and drift out again without forming any relationships at all. Everyone seemed to have the same

*These kibbutz children, unlike the adult members of their community, have very strong group boundaries.*

informal relationships with everyone else. Whatever happened, happened in public; anybody could take part.

My problem was the opposite. I was shocked to find that Harvard was a set of tight, private cliques. When I sat down at a cafeteria table and overheard an interesting conversation I joined in, the way I would have in Berkeley, but people often reacted as if I was being "rude." We had not been introduced; we had not shaken hands! What became clear to both my friend and me was that Harvard groups had boundaries while Berkeley groups did not. When a group is described as cold and formal by outsiders and as warm and cohesive by insiders, it probably has a strong *group boundary*—a

clearly defined standard for distinguishing between members and nonmembers. Such a standard allows members of the group to develop closer relationships than they could maintain otherwise, but it keeps out outsiders so that they see it as cold and unfriendly. Both facts may be true. By the same token, you may find it easier to enter a group with weak boundaries, but once inside it you may not have as strong a sense of belonging.

For some purposes clear boundaries are important. Friends of mine who belong to an Israeli *kibbutz* say that their group's worst problem is its guests. *Kibbutzim* are communes that are devoted to building up cohesiveness (we-feeling) and mutual concern among members. However, each kibbutz accepts a number of outsiders who come to work there for several months, living much the way members do. The *kibbutzim* benefit financially from the presence of these visitors, but so many guests (sometimes one guest for every four members) tend to decrease the cohesiveness of the permanent community. The boundaries are weak, with strangers entering and leaving all the time. Some members try to ignore the guests, but they feel bad about doing so. No one has found a solution to this problem.

One way to maintain boundaries is to have a sense of territoriality. This is the idea that all the people who live in a given area are an in-group while others are an out-group, to be excluded from full participation and perhaps even chased away. As mentioned earlier, street gangs often show a sense of territoriality, and it may also be seen in nationalism and other forms of regional loyalty. It has both advantages and disadvantages: It allows the in-group to build up a strong "we-feeling," but at the same time it fosters unfriendly behavior toward members of the out-group.

### INTERACTION ACROSS GROUP BOUNDARIES

The "network" approach to sociology is a new way of looking at social groups. This approach, stimulated primarily by the work of Harrison White at Harvard, describes the structure of groups as a series of ties linking different individuals. These networks can be "loose-knit" or "close-knit," depending on whether the people in them all know one another. If you and I know each other and both of us know Tom, Dick, and Harry, and if Tom knows Dick and Harry and Dick knows Harry, our five-person network is completely closed. (See Figure 6.1.) But if I know you, Tom, Dick, and Harry but none of you knows each other, my five-person network is completely open. (See Figure 6.2.) However, this is not likely to happen unless I have a

strange sort of secret life. If you and I have a close personal relationship (a strong tie), you are likely to meet my other close friends (Tom, Dick, and Harry) sometime when we are together, and you will probably form at least a weak tie with them. That is, you may not become close friends but you will probably become acquaintances. Your relationship with them may not be primary, but it will be at least secondary. Thus Figure 6.1 is a more common pattern than Figure 6.2.

A person can maintain only a limited number of strong ties; we have only so much time and energy. My network could hardly include more than 20 or 30 strong ties at any given time. Again, that network could be relatively close-knit or relatively loose-knit, depending on how my friends feel about each other.

Mark Granovetter has suggested that we could diagram a large group (such as a city) as a number of clusters of networks, either close-knit or loose-knit and either separate or linked together.[30] If the city were made up mostly of separate, close-knit networks with

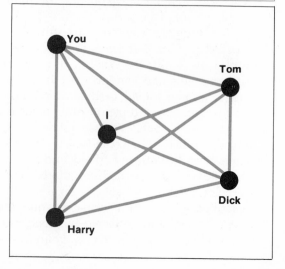

**FIGURE 6.1**
*Close-knit network*

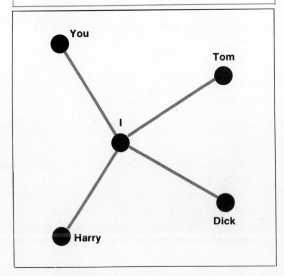

**FIGURE 6.2**
*Loose-knit network*

You

Tom

I

Harry

Dick

few ties linking them together, it could be described as cohesive from one point of view but as fragmented from another point of view. Such a city is cohesive because any person who lives there would have a close, cohesive network of friends who spend all their free time together; they would rarely spend time with outsiders. However, as a whole the city would be fragmented because each network would have strong boundaries and nobody in one network would know anybody in other networks. Granovetter claims that the ties linking separate networks together and permitting information to flow from one to another are almost always weak ties—acquaintanceships rather than friendships. He also believes that these weak ties are more important than sociologists used to think. They give members of a network access to information that they would otherwise miss. For example, if you are looking for a job you usually ask people for leads. However, if you are in a very closed network your information will be limited. Among members of your closed network one

person is unlikely to know anything the others don't know. Information travels around inside that network, but no new information comes in from a different network. You have to branch out and talk to acquaintances who have "connections" that you don't have. In doing so you use your weak ties, your bridges or links to other social networks. Indeed, most people find jobs through their acquaintances, not through close friends.

Another reason weak ties are important is that they tie the networks together so that they are not a set of separate islands but form a large, integrated system. In doing so these "bridge" relationships build a larger sense of community. Indeed, Granovetter suggests, though he admits he cannot prove, that some communities are able to muster resistance to a threat (such as a plan for urban renewal) only because their networks are tied together by a large number of weak relationships. Without those links, members of different networks would not trust each other enough to organize on a community-wide basis.

## THE SENSE OF COMMUNITY

In the early days of sociology the favorite indoor sport of evolutionary theorists was comparing traditional societies to modern ones. In general, they believed that although modern societies had advanced in many ways they had gone downhill in other ways. One such theorist was Ferdinand Tönnies (1855–1936), who was concerned about the breakdown of primary social relationships. In the old days, he said, society had been held together by a set of inflexible bonds that created stability and security. Such a social environment was a real community, and sociologists still use Tönnies' German term for community— **gemeinschaft.** With the modernization of many societies, however, relationships have become more impersonal as a result of the greater division of labor into different roles and a decline in the importance of kinship and of tradition as a way of life. This pattern of social life may be called *associational* or, to use Tönnies' term, gesellschaft. This view was shared by Durkheim, among others, who believed that the changes were caused by the spread of new technologies that called for increasing divi- sion of labor and a kind of solidarity based on the differences between people rather than on their similarities. Many present-day sociologists agree that modernization brings with it a loss of community. We will discuss this question again in Chapter 18, which deals with urban life.

# SOCIAL RESEARCH:
## Sociologists at Work

### OBEDIENCE TO AUTHORITY

Society is a collaborative system that would not function if many of its members were balky. We routinely place our lives in the control of strangers, trusting in their good will and their ability, as when we cross a street on a green light in the path of a dump truck. We follow instructions that make no sense at all to us, as long as they are issued by an expert. Compliance is necessary, and yet it can also be the source of irresponsible acts, as the social psychologist Stanley Milgram has shown in a grim experiment.[31]

### COMPLIANCE WITH
### EXPERT AUTHORITY

Milgram investigated the assumption that societies differ in the degree of compliance expected of their members. In some countries repression is extreme and subordinates obey without question, while other societies are characterized by a generally critical population. Milgram hoped to study the sources of submissiveness in authoritarian societies, but first he needed a way to test its limits, to see how far people would go in obeying an authoritative command. He and an accomplice arranged a way to test large numbers of subjects in the United States so that this sample could be used as a baseline against which to compare levels of compliance in more authoritarian societies.

The test is simple. A subject presents himself to Milgram's laboratory for a memory experiment, with the accomplice posing as another subject. Both subjects are shown the equipment, and the accomplice, seemingly by chance, draws the assignment of memorizing a list of word pairs and undergoing a "slight punishment" whenever his memory fails. He is then hooked up to a machine in another room while the subject is taught his part in the experiment. The subject is told to give electric shocks to the other "subject" whenever the latter cannot recall the right words, according to the list. The subject is shown an impressive electrical device that can be adjusted for voltages ranging from 15 to 450 volts. The device bears labels describing the severity of the shock, ranging from "Slight shock" to "Danger: severe shock." The subject is given a sample of the "slight" shock, which in fact hurts quite a lot and convinces him that the severe shocks must be terrible. (Actually, the accomplice gets no shock at all.) Then the experiment begins. The accomplice fails more and more often as time goes by, and the subject is told to increase the voltage. The subject thinks he is giving real shocks and the accomplice acts his part well. He complains, pleads, shouts, bangs on the walls seeking release, and finally falls silent when the voltage is supposedly very high. If the subject protests against his cruel task, the experimenter merely tells him that the test must continue and that he, the experimenter, will be responsible for whatever happens.

What percentage of ordinary American citizens are willing to increase the voltage to the most severe level? Milgram expected that perhaps 1 or 2 percent would do so, but he was amazed to find that *over half* of his subjects gave what they thought were the most severe electric shocks. However, most of the subjects did not enjoy the task and became more anxious and unhappy as they gave greater shocks. They would beg to be freed from role of torturer (nothing kept them from quitting if they decided to), but most of them went on as long as the experimenter told them to continue.

This experiment has been repeated in various forms many times since Milgram's first attempt. It is true that authoritarian compliance varies somewhat in different countries and in different settings. For example, an experimenter who wears dirty overalls and conducts his research in an abandoned warehouse will gain compliance from fewer subjects than a professor in a university laboratory. Well-educated subjects are somewhat less compliant than less well-educated ones. Still, the important discovery is that even among a sophisticated and humane sample, about 40 percent will give the most extreme shock. People will do almost anything when they are told that it is an experiment, presumably because of their willingness to comply with expert authority.

An important aspect of the experiment is the willingness of the experimenter to take responsibility for the outcome. Other research has shown the same effect: When people can assure themselves that they are following orders and therefore are not responsible for their actions, they may do great evil.

### GROUP PRESSURE

A person tends to lose his or her sense of personal responsibility in situations that call for compliance with authority. The same thing seems to happen in situations that call for conformity to a group. Many people will agree with almost any ridiculous claim if they have heard a number of other people in the group agree with it. This was shown in some famous experiments conducted by Solomon Asch.

In 1951 Asch arranged for groups of five people to take part in a study of "visual perception."[32] Each subject was given two cards. On the first card a single line had been drawn; the other card contained three parallel lines of different lengths, one of which was exactly as long as the line on the first card. The subject was asked to decide which of the three parallel lines was most similar in length to the one on the first card. These three lines differed so much in length that it was perfectly obvious which one matched the line on the other card. However, of the five people in each group only one was a true subject; all four of the other "judges" were trained stooges. The participants announced their judgments aloud, one after another, with the true subject's turn coming last. Asch had instructed the stooges to give a wrong answer, and they did so in a matter-of-fact way. Asch found that in about 35 percent of the tests the subjects' answers conformed to those of the group instead of to their own perceptions. Later they said that they had not *believed* that the group was correct but had given the wrong answer anyway for the sake of conforming. The results of this experiment have been confirmed in repeated tests by other researchers under varying conditions.

It has been shown that the group must be *unanimous* to have such power over the individual. Hans Christian Anderson was correct: If a single little boy announces that the Emperor has no clothes (or that a 6-inch line is obviously shorter than an 8-inch line), others will regain confidence in their own perceptions and will no longer be swayed by the rest of the group. The fact that disagreement is possible leaves room for the individual to doubt the majority and resist its pressure.

It seems that group influence is effective mainly because most people don't want to be considered deviant.[33] Individuals are highly affected by group pressure if they have doubts about being accepted by a group to which they very much wish to belong. They are also more affected if they have to respond publicly to the other group members than if they can respond in private or anonymously.

I have described group pressure in a negative light, and it is true that many studies show that such pressure decreases personal responsibility and causes people to deny both their perceptions and their moral judgment. We must not forget, however, that group pressure can be useful to society. Such pressure helps establish and maintain social norms and makes group cohesiveness possible. When we see a group doing or saying something we don't understand, most of us assume that the group members know something we don't, so we tend to follow along. Individuals could not participate in group life if they believed most of the other members were stooges who were purposely misleading them. It is normal to trust one's fellow group members and to be impressed by their opinions. It is unfortunate that this normal trust can sometimes lead to personal irresponsibility.

# SOCIAL POLICY:
## Issues and Viewpoints

Satisfying, emotionally enriching personal relationships are the most important aspect of human experience, yet they are the hardest to control by means of social policy. The quality of our relationships with others depends on two factors—our personalities and the structural opportunities we have for spending time together and getting closer. Neither factor is open to much control at the level of public policy. Our personalities are a result of our personal histories. Whether we are warm or cold, kind or suspicious, talkative or secretive depends on old emotions left over from earlier relationships that went well or badly. These color our present and future relationships, and nothing short of intense psychotherapy is likely to change these attitudes in any deep sense. As for our opportunities for getting close to others, the kind of society we live in requires many of us to give most of our attention to a large number of secondary relationships. Moreover, our networks tend to be increasingly open rather than closed. Your fellow workers will not know your fellow squash club members or your school friends, and even within those separate settings most of the participants you meet probably don't know each other. There are too many people—and besides, few middle-class people stay in the same neighborhood for long. A few years ago, for example, I realized that although for the past eight years I had given a Thanksgiving dinner party for six or eight of my close friends, none of those friends had come twice. Each had left town by the following year. Primary groups are almost impossible to maintain in such a situation.

The growth of encounter groups is probably due to the desire to fill a need for intimate relationships. Many people today feel the lack of such relationships, and there aren't many institutions that meet their needs in a satisfactory way. Every modern trend seems to break up neighborhoods, scatter individuals over wide areas, move people from one job to another, and so on. These trends are hard on primary group relationships. On the other hand, a stable, closed society with permanent primary relationships provides only the *opportunity* to develop intimacy and emotional warmth. If the personalities are not able to interact in a fulfilling way, a primary group may become not warm and satisfying but vicious and spiteful. In that case, moving away becomes, like some divorces, a move toward liberation.

I want to mention again a topic that is related both to social science and to ethics. This is the issue of group pressure and personal responsibility. Social science is discovering how human beings manipulate each other. Already we can give practical advice to advertisers, political campaign managers, brainwashers, army generals, and directors of concentration camps. But we can also advise those who want to do positive work with groups—camp counselors, group therapists in prisons, planners of library reading rooms and rock festivals, and so on. What are the ethical limits of studying such manipulation? Should social scientists refuse to do research that may be used to manipulate human beings? This is not as simple a question as it may seem. In principle we oppose any policy that would deprive individuals of free choice. But we all try to "manipulate" others at times, though we call it "influence." Parents try to influence their children to behave properly. Psychiatrists try to influence their patients to behave sanely. These efforts, like all efforts at social control, are, in a sense, manipulative.

We know from Stanley Milgram's work that it is possible to get at least half of the people in the world to torture other people. Milgram's subjects believed that they were torturing their partners, yet they followed orders without punishment or reward.

Should Milgram have done this experiment? Is it good for people to know how to manipulate others? What effect did Milgram's experiment have on the subjects who agreed to give the maximum shock? Milgram reports that many of them broke down emotionally but thanked him afterwards for showing them their own weaknesses. Often they claimed to have learned from the experience and vowed never to follow orders blindly again. Milgram's experiment is so upsetting that few social scientists could have done it, yet if it had not been done we would never have found out how many people are ready to obey like robots.

Personal irresponsibility is a major social problem. However, it is rarely called a *social* problem because we do not know what to do about it collectively. Public policy cannot easily change human character, for character is formed in private socialization through loving relatedness and through the experience of compassion.

Still, social science has a message to tell: Most of the evil in this world is done not by brutes and madmen but by Everyman. Adolf Eichmann was not mentally ill; he was an ordinary Nazi bureaucrat who followed orders to the letter.[34] The New Yorkers who watched Kitty Genovese being stabbed on the street and waited an hour before calling the police were not mad brutes but ordinary citizens who were afraid to take responsibility. This atitude is a serious social problem—one that social scientists hope to understand better in the future in order to "manipulate" the situations that give rise to it. Social phenomena that are understood may perhaps be controlled.

Irresponsibility is not a new problem. In Shakespeare's *Henry V* two soldiers discuss the morality of doing battle. One of them says, "We know enough if we know we are the king's subjects: If his cause be wrong, our obedience to the king wipes the crime of it out of us."[35] The reasoning is always the same: Evil is no evil if it is conformity.

## SUMMARY

1. A human being's need for social interaction has biological bases that are also found in other species. Territoriality is one trait that is shared by humans and nonhumans. Interaction rituals are also found in primates as well as human beings.

2. Human behavior is variable because it is guided not by instincts but by group relationships. A *primary group* is an intimate group bound together by a sense of "weness." The members of such a group relate to each other as individuals. Families and close friendship groups are primary groups. Impersonal ties based on role relationships characterize *secondary groups*.

3. *Peer groups* are made up of people of similar status. A *reference group* is the group to which we compare ourselves. Large, complex groups include tribes and clans, social classes, ethnic groups, crowds, churches, universities, and nation-states.

4. *Symbolic interactionists* such as Cooley and Mead emphasize the importance of the group for the development of our perceptions of ourselves and the world. Cooley's major contributions were the notions of the primary group and the looking-glass self.

Mead distinguished between symbolic and nonsymbolic interaction, though he recognized that they are related in complex ways. People communicate mostly by sharing significant symbols and through the process of *role taking.*

**5.** Through role taking we learn the meaning of the objects, including our selves, that exist for the other person. With a self-concept one can interact with oneself. This is mental activity. It involves taking the role of the *generalized other,* an abstract role that stands for a set of particular roles with which we have become familiar. The generalized other is not formed until the *game stage* of childhood.

**6.** The "I" is the spontaneous aspect of the self, while the "me" is the aspect that limits the impulses of the "I."

**7.** Human behavior is goal directed. It involves building up *acts,* each of which has a *covert* (internal) *phase* and an *overt* (external) *phase.*

**8.** The strength of the boundaries around groups varies. One way in which such boundaries are maintained is *territoriality,* which distinguishes in-group members from out-group members on the basis of where they live.

**9.** Networks can be close-knit or loose-knit. They can also be separate or linked together by a number of weak ties. A large group made up of a series of close-knit networks is cohesive from the individual's point of view but is fragmented as a larger community. Weak ties are important because they act as bridges between networks.

*Gemeinschaft* refers to a sense of community that is believed to characterize traditional, stable, preindustrial life. *Gesellschaft* refers to the associational type of life that is characteristic of modern societies.

## KEY TERMS

**act**   the basic unit of human conduct.

**covert phase**   the phase during which one is preparing to act but has not yet begun to do so.

**game stage**   the stage at which a child can understand a set of roles as a system.

**gemeinschaft**   a society held together by a set of stable, secure bonds; a community.

**generalized other**   an abstract role that stands for a set of particular roles.

**gesellschaft**   a social system in which relationships are impersonal or associational.

**looking-glass self**   the self-image that a person acquires from the opinions of others.

**overt phase**   the phase during which an act is actually performed.

**peer group**   a group of people of similar status.

**play stage**   the stage at which a child is learning to take the roles of people he or she knows.

**primary group**   a group whose members interact in a personal, intimate, and emotional way.

**reference group**   the group to which one compares oneself when judging one's own status.

**role taking**   the ability of a person to imagine the role of another person with whom he or she interacts.

**secondary group**   a group whose members interact in an impersonal, unsentimental, and businesslike way.

**self-reflexive behavior**   interaction with self.

**significant other**   a person whose opinions are important to one; often a family member.

**territoriality**   the establishment of a certain zone or space that may not be occupied by any other person or animal.

# FOR FURTHER READING

BLUMER, HERBERT. *Symbolic Interactionism.* Englewood Cliffs, N.J.: Prentice-Hall, 1969. Blumer was one of my favorite teachers and everything I know about symbolic interactionism and George Herbert Mead I learned from him. Several thousand other former students can say the same thing. This is his own collection of essays — mostly theoretical, but clear, plain writing.

BROWN, ROGER. *Social Psychology.* New York: Free Press, 1965. This textbook is sophisticated, but the style is marvelously personal. Brown takes various topics in social psychology and tells the history of each idea as it was developed by one researcher after another. He even manages to inject a little suspense as you wait to see how each new study turns out. Sometimes he makes little side comments, such as "Whoops! It works out wrong!"

DIMOND, STUART J. *The Social Behavior of Animals.* New York: Harper & Row, 1970. Those of you who are interested in species other than your own may find this a rewarding source of material.

EKMAN, PAUL, and WALLACE V. FRIESEN. *Unmasking the Face.* Englewood Cliffs, N.J.: Prentice-Hall, 1975. These are the results of their work on the expressions that reveal human emotions. I find this research intriguing.

HARE, A. PAUL; EDGAR F. BORGATTA; and ROBERT FREED BALES, eds. *Small Groups: Studies in Social Interaction.* 3rd ed. New York: Knopf, 1962. For years this has been one of the basic texts on small group research.

LOFLAND, LYN H. *A World of Strangers: Order and Action in Urban Public Space.* New York: Basic Books, 1973. This is a book on social interactions in public.

MEAD, GEORGE HERBERT. *On Social Psychology: Selected Papers.* Rev. ed. Edited by Anselm Strauss. Chicago: University of Chicago Press, 1964. I have never found Mead's writing easy to follow, and I never managed to get through *Mind, Self, and Society,* which was compiled posthumously by his students from his lecture notes. This collection of his papers is somewhat easier to read.

SCHOECK, HELMUT. *Envy.* London: Secker and Warburg, 1969. Some contemporary sociologists do research on human emotions and sentiments as they relate to social interaction. This is the only such book I have seen that deals with envy, an emotion that is particularly important in understanding social stratification.

SOMMER, ROBERT. *Personal Space.* Englewood Cliffs, N.J.: Prentice-Hall, 1969. A treat to read, Sommer's book is the definitive work on such topics as how people arrange their chairs when they want to talk or when they want to maintain privacy, and so on.

# DEVIANCE AND CONTROL

The subject of this chapter is knavery, skulduggery, cheating, unfairness, crime, sneakiness, malingering, cutting corners, immorality, dishonesty, betrayal, graft, corruption, wickedness, and sin — in short, deviance. When we say that someone is deviant we do not simply mean that he or she is "odd" or "different." We mean that he or she is *guilty of violating a norm*. Deviance is everywhere, for all societies (large ones like the Republic of France or small ones like your family) have rules, and where there are rules there is deviance. It may be a matter of cheating on your income tax or on your wife, of disrespect to the flag, or of not taking out the trash when it's your turn.

Why do so many people insist on violating rules? Or, to turn the question around, why, despite the obvious convenience of violating rules, do so many people insist on complying with them? Most of us do not just "go along with morality" but, as Durkheim pointed out, "find charm in the accomplishment of a moral act prescribed by a rule that has no other justification than that it is a rule. We feel a . . . pleasure in performing our duty simply because it is our duty."[1]

The satisfaction of doing right has something to do with the fact that it *is* right, even if it is difficult, dangerous, or costly. Sometimes we seek out, so to speak, moral mountains to climb and exult in the strenuous task. It makes as much sense to ask, "Why should we do wrong, despite our sense of duty?" as to ask, "Why should we do right?" These are two ways of asking the same question, because if we can explain why human beings behave properly we will at the same time explain why human beings sometimes misbehave. Thus a theory of deviant behavior is also a theory of conformity.

Whatever people want — food, shelter, sex, or contract bridge — they must get through organized social patterns in which the actions of many people fit together. There must be some understandings about who is supposed to do what and in what sit-uations. Though we can debate whether any *particular* rule is necessary or useful, we must agree on the need for *some* rules, however arbitrary they may be. For example, if traffic is to move along the highways it is less important whether the rule says that people must drive on the right or the left than that there be a rule.

However, you can't take it for granted that if you play by the rules things will go your way. You may get bored. The costs may not be worth the possible rewards. You may find that you can get what you want more quickly and easily by not following the rules. There are always temptations to cut corners or otherwise violate the norm. Every rule, then, creates the possibility of deviance.

Let's define **deviance** as any form of behavior that violates the norms of a social group or of society. You will remember that norms cover a wide range — from, say, the norm requiring us to eat fried chicken with a knife and fork in a fancy restaurant to the rule forbidding murder. Not all deviance consists of breaking laws. If you spend every dollar you own and every minute of your time playing pinball machines, you will not be a criminal but you will be deviant. If you are drunk by ten o'clock every morning, you may not be violating a law but you will be violating a strong social norm (and you won't feel very good either!). As long as any rule (or norm) is recognized as valid, however informally, then breaking that rule is an act of deviance. However, the norms that people believe in most firmly are usually backed up by laws. For this reason the study of deviance is largely a study of serious social problems, especially crime.

## Types of deviance

It is convenient to classify deviant behavior into four main categories: (1) deviant behavior, (2) deviant habits, (3) deviant psychologies, and (4) deviant cultures. In the rest of the chapter we will deal primarily with the first two categories.

## DEVIANT BEHAVIOR

The deviant acts about which you and I are, quite reasonably, most concerned are aggressive crimes such as murder, rape, and robbery. The frequency of such acts seems to be increasing throughout North America, though not at the same rate in every state or city. However, it is very hard to estimate how much crime actually occurs in society. Official police statistics may record as few as one out of every twenty-three crimes.[2] A police officer who catches a teenage boy committing a crime may decide to simply warn him and let him go without recording the crime. Throughout North America the police can use wide discretion in deciding what is to be considered a crime. Moreover, a vast number of crimes are not reported, either because the victims think it is useless to call the police or because there is no victim.

Some crimes are more likely to be detected than others: Public outrage over armed robbery or sexual assaults on children pressures the police to be especially active in trying to catch those who commit such crimes,[3] but the public is less concerned about illegal gambling or false advertising. Crimes without victims are generally not detected because they are "invisible." For example, the people involved in crimes such as drug use, homosexuality, and illegal abortion are willing participants and therefore do not report the crime.[4] Women often do not report rape because they may be questioned about their personal lives if they do. It is obvious, thus, that police records do not reflect the true patterns of deviance in a population. We can correct for the bias in such statistics to some extent, but we are always left with some doubt about the actual rate and pattern of crime in a given population.

The best estimates of crime rates are based on three kinds of information: (1) police statistics, (2) surveys asking people how many crimes they have experienced as victims, and (3) surveys asking people how many criminal acts they have participated in. According to both the FBI's index of crimes and the survey of victims, burglary and larceny are the most common crimes.

### Who commits deviant acts?

People who commit deviant acts—let's call them *offenders* to distinguish them from deviant characters—are not a sinister minority. Even if we limit our discussion to people who, at one time or another, violate criminal law, most of us are offenders. One of the first studies to prove this point was conducted by James Wallerstein and Clement Wyle.[5] They collected 1698 questionnaires listing 49 offenses that were serious enough to draw a maximum jail sentence of not less than one year. Although their sampling of men and women was not fully scientific and the results therefore do not accurately represent the larger population (i.e., that of the New York City area), they do show that the violator of the law is Everyman. The respondents were asked to check each offense that they had committed and to indicate whether they had committed it before the age of 16. Ninety-nine percent of the respondents admitted to one or more offenses, as shown in Table 7.1. (Be careful in interpreting the table. Some of the acts listed are only technically criminal. For example, fistfights might be included under "assault.") The mean number of offenses committed in adult life was 18 for men and 11 for women. The men reported a mean of 3.2 juvenile offenses; the women, 1.6. It is likely that very few of them ever came to the attention of the police.

Edmund Vaz interviewed middle-class Canadian high school boys about their delinquent acts. (See Table 7.2.) About two-thirds of the boys aged 15 to 19 admitted that they had taken little things that did not belong to them, gambled for money, driven without a license, or drunk alcoholic beverages with

**TABLE 7.1**

*Criminal offenses committed by a percent of sample of New York City metropolitan area residents*

| | PERCENT OF RESPONDENTS ADMITTING TO OFFENSE | |
|---|---|---|
| OFFENSE | MEN (N=1,020) | WOMEN (N=678) |
| Malicious mischief | 84 | 81 |
| Disorderly conduct | 85 | 76 |
| Assault | 49 | 5 |
| Auto misdemeanors | 61 | 39 |
| Indecency | 77 | 74 |
| Gambling | 74 | 54 |
| Larceny | 89 | 83 |
| Grand larceny (except auto) | 13 | 11 |
| Auto theft | 26 | 8 |
| Burglary | 17 | 4 |
| Robbery | 11 | 1 |
| Concealed weapons | 35 | 3 |
| Perjury | 23 | 17 |
| Falsification and fraud | 46 | 34 |
| Election frauds | 7 | 4 |
| Tax evasion | 57 | 40 |
| Coercion | 16 | 6 |
| Conspiracy | 23 | 7 |
| Criminal libel | 36 | 29 |

*Source:* James S. Wallerstein and Clement J. Wyle, "Our Law-Abiding Law Breakers," *Probation*, vol. 25 (March–April 1947), 110.

friends. Over half of the boys admitted that they had driven faster than the speed limit, gotten into fistfights, or destroyed property. These boys were rarely labeled delinquent, however. These kinds of misbehavior usually causes little damage to property or harm to other people, so police overlook them and concentrate on the more aggressive acts of lower-class boys.[6]

Many similar studies have focused on "hidden offenses."[7] It does not follow that there are no differences between "hidden" and "official" offenders. On the contrary, those who find their way into court are, *on the average*, likely to have committed a greater variety of offenses, more serious offenses, and the same offenses more often.[8] We are all offenders, but we differ in our patterns of offending.

**Organized crime**

There is a large and rich organization that supplies a variety of illegal goods and services—especially gambling, narcotics, and loan sharking. It is also involved in legitimate businesses, in labor unions, and even in the corruption of public officials. This enormous secret organization or "mob" is so powerful that its victims do not dare complain about its activities or testify against its

**TABLE 7.2**

*Self-reported delinquent behavior of middle-class adolescents by age group*

| TYPE OF OFFENSE[a] | PERCENT ADMITTING OFFENSE | | PERCENT ADMITTING OFFENSE MORE THAN ONCE OR TWICE | |
|---|---|---|---|---|
| | AGE 13–14 | AGE 15–19 | AGE 13–14 | AGE 15–19 |
| Driven a car without a driver's license | 28.6 | 62.3 | 9.1 | 27.9 |
| Taken little things that did not belong to you | 61.0 | 67.2 | 10.4 | 16.7 |
| Skipped school without a legitimate excuse | 13.6 | 40.8 | 3.9 | 13.6 |
| Driven beyond the speed limit | 5.8 | 51.2 | 1.3 | 39.7 |
| Participated in drag-races along the highway with your friends | 6.5 | 31.1 | 2.0 | 16.3 |
| Engaged in a fist fight with another boy | 45.8 | 56.0 | 7.1 | 8.7 |
| Been feeling "high" from drinking beer, wine, or liquor | 11.7 | 39.0 | 2.6 | 17.9 |
| Gambled for money at cards, dice, or some other game | 42.2 | 66.0 | 16.9 | 37.4 |
| Remained out all night without parents' permission | 19.5 | 25.8 | 5.2 | 9.5 |
| Taken a car without owner's knowledge | 5.2 | 12.5 | 0.7 | 3.1 |
| Been placed on school probation or expelled from school | 0.7 | 5.6 | 0.0 | 1.2 |
| Destroyed or damaged public or private property of any kind | 44.8 | 52.0 | 11.7 | 14.8 |
| Taken little things of value (between $2 and $50) which did not belong to you | 9.7 | 16.0 | 0.7 | 3.5 |
| Tried to be intimate with a member of the opposite sex | 18.2 | 37.8 | 7.8 | 17.6 |
| Broken into or tried to break and enter a building with the intention of stealing | 5.2 | 7.5 | 0.7 | 1.0 |
| Sold, used, or tried to use drugs of some kind | 1.3 | 1.0 | 0.0 | 0.3 |
| Bought or tried to buy beer, wine, or liquor from a store or adult | 3.3 | 24.8 | 0.7 | 11.7 |
| Taken money of any amount which did not belong to you from someone or someplace | 30.5 | 32.7 | 7.1 | 6.9 |
| Taken a glass of beer, wine, or liquor at a party or elsewhere with your friends | 32.5 | 64.8 | 8.4 | 35.2 |

[a]Two items are omitted because they were used solely to check reliability.

*Source:* Edmund W. Vaz, "Delinquency among Middle-class Boys," *Canadian Review of Sociology and Anthropology,* 2 (1965), 514–515.

members. Robert F. Kennedy, then U.S. Attorney General, once told a Senate subcommittee that witnesses who helped his office often had to change their names and their appearance and even leave the country for their own safety. Police officers in some cities have been corrupted by the mob, so that anyone who reports misconduct may be telling his or her story to a corrupt official who has no intention of doing anything about it.[9]

The major illegal business of the mob is gambling—numbers lotteries, sports and off-track betting, dice and hidden casinos. It is estimated that the *profits* from such business may be more than $6 or $7 billion a year, a figure higher than the *total* amount spent on legal racetrack betting. Americans bet about four times as much illegally as they do legally each year, and possibly one-third of their illegally bet dollars wind up in the hands of organized crime.

Loan-sharking operations are another profitable business. Gamblers borrow to pay for their losses; heroin addicts borrow to pay for their habit; and some businessmen borrow if they are desperate and cannot get loans through legitimate channels. Interest rates on such loans range from 1 percent to 150 percent a week, and loan sharks use violence to collect payments or to prevent borrowers from reporting them to the authorities.

Narcotics is perhaps the third-largest mob operation. Profits from this business probably exceed $20 million per year—not exactly peanuts, but small compared to the take from gambling. Organized crime seems to stick to the import and wholesale distribution of narcotics, leaving small independent pushers to do the actual selling of the drugs to users. The punishments for dealing in heroin are so severe that big-time criminals are unwilling to risk dealing at the retail level.

Prostitution and bootlegging are not important activities of organized crime. Instead, it is turning increasingly to legitimate business. For example, one syndicate owns $300 million in real estate. The mob has also begun to influence labor unions and can sometimes involve union pension funds in its business investments.

The most profitable rackets in many large cities are believed to be controlled by La Cosa Nostra, an organization formerly known as the Mafia. The code of La Cosa Nostra requires loyalty and absolute obedience by its members. If necessary, lower-level members are expected to go to prison quietly in order to protect their bosses. The boss may order the killing of any member for any reason. Because the code is so effective, it is very hard for law enforcement officials to penetrate the organization with spies, and so it operates largely beyond the control of the law.

### Other deviant behaviors

SEXUAL DEVIANCE Several forms of sexual behavior are considered deviant. Among them are homosexuality, prostitution, and incest. Laws on these matters vary from place to place, but sexual relations between siblings and between parent and child are forbidden everywhere. Prostitution, even where it is illegal, is not usually considered a very serious offense. For example, *McCall's Magazine* has reported that only 7 percent of a sample of citizens of New York City and Newark, New Jersey would clear the streets of prostitutes if they had the power to do so.[10] The Kinsey Reports on the sexual behavior of white American males (published over twenty-five years ago) suggest that about 30 percent never have any contact with prostitutes, while perhaps 15 to 20 percent have such contacts several times a year over several years of their lives.[11]

Studies suggest that about 37 percent of white American males and 13 percent of white females have engaged in a homosexual act at one time or other, and that 4 percent of the males and 1 percent of the females are exclusively homosexual.[12]

SUICIDE   Some societies have viewed suicide as noble, but our own society defines it as a sign of moral failure. Still, it is a major cause of death among white American males (about 12,000 per year) and is often studied by sociologists. Emile Durkheim's book *Suicide* is an early and important work on this subject.[13]

### DEVIANT HABITS

Not all forms of deviance are rare events like most of the ones discussed so far. Sometimes deviance becomes a way of life. Examples are alcoholism, drug addiction, and compulsive gambling. Acts that are acceptable when they are done only occasionally may become social problems when they dominate a person's life. Thus a minister may sponsor bingo games to raise money for the church yet become very concerned about a church member who cashes his or her insurance policies to raise money to bet on horses.

The most familiar example of a deviant habit is problem drinking, which the National Institute of Mental Health has called America's largest public-health problem. The average American adult consumes the equivalent of five gallons of 100-proof gin per year.[14] The results of this high rate of alcohol intake are far more serious than the health problems caused by other drugs, such as narcotics. In addition, alcohol use endangers social relationships. A study of 621 killers and 588 murder victims showed that in two-thirds of the cases either the killer or the victim or both had been drinking just before the killing. Alcohol use is a factor in about 70 percent of the divorces granted in the United States.[15] About 25,000 U.S. highway deaths per year—half the total—are caused by drunkenness. A national survey of U.S. households reported that 15 percent of the men and 4 percent of the women have severe drinking problems. An additional 9 percent say that they have had such problems in the past.[16]

Who are the heavy drinkers and why do they drink? Heavy drinking is most common among middle-aged people. Younger people tend to drink large amounts now and then, while older people drink smaller amounts more often. Single, divorced, or separated people are more likely to drink heavily than married or widowed people. Males drink more heavily than females. People of higher socioeconomic status are more likely to drink but less likely to be heavy drinkers than people of lower socioeconomic status. City dwellers are more likely to drink than country people. Whites and nonwhites drink about the same amount, except that black women are especially likely to either not drink at all or drink heavily. Catholics have the highest percentage of heavy drinkers of any religious group in the United States.[17]

There are a great many theories and a lot of empirical evidence on the causes of problem drinking. Most studies of this problem have focused on personality as the cause. A popular theory claims that alcoholism is an attempt to make up for the lack of oral satisfactions, such as sucking, biting, and kissing, during infancy. Unfortunately for this theory, empirical results do not support these claims. For one thing, drinking does not relieve the alcoholic from anxiety or depression. Indeed, these negative feelings seem to be greater during a drinking spree, and more so for problem drinkers than for others. Moreover, although a few studies have found problem drinkers to be especially dependent, most have not. On the contrary, what is more striking is that—at least for males—people who drink too much have tended since childhood to be aggressive, masculine, hyperactive, and seemingly self-confident.[18] Some researchers have assumed that this is only a mask covering feelings of anxiety and insecurity, but more recently the explanation has turned in another direction.

David McClelland and his associates have studied males who drink too much and have concluded that they drink primarily in order to feel stronger.[19] Heavy drinkers are especially concerned about personal power and for various reasons choose drinking as an outlet rather than, say, wearing flashy clothes, gambling, or showing off in aggressive ways. Of course drinking can bring on other attempts to show personal power, such as fights, car accidents, and sexual exploitation. But some men who can afford to do so may do things like collecting motorcycles instead of going on a drinking spree. It is a question of channeling the need for personal power in one direction or another. Men who turn to drinking tend to spend all their money this way, so it becomes even harder for them to express their need for power in other ways.

Personality is not the whole explanation

Not all alcoholics are labeled as such. Some drink only when they are alone.

Arthur Tress/Woodfin Camp

for problem drinking, of course. There is plenty of evidence that both biological and cultural factors play a part in this behavior—possibly even a larger part than personality. The biological aspect is supported by the fact that identical twins have the same degree of addiction to alcohol more often than fraternal twins (whose genes are as different as those of nontwin siblings).[20] Also, animal researchers have produced a strain of inbred mice that prefer alcohol.[21]

The importance of the cultural factor was shown by Don Cahalan's national survey, which tried to find out which of several factors most influences drinking habits. Cahalan concluded that personality tests were much less effective than cultural attitudes in identifying heavy drinkers. That is, problem drinkers are not noticeably maladjusted, but they are located in groups that have a very permissive attitude toward heavy drinking. They began drinking at an earlier age than other people and seem to have learned to expect at that age that alcohol would do great things for them—that it would make them feel good, improve their social life, and so on. Groups that encourage such ideas encourage problem drinking.

## OTHER TYPES OF DEVIANCE

### Deviant psychologies

About one out of twelve North Americans will spend some part of his or her life in a mental hospital.[22] A far greater percentage will become so upset by an emotional crisis that they must take time out from their usual roles, whether they admit to being "neurotic" or not. Mental and emotional disorders are forms of deviance when they interrupt routine social life. Sociologists are reluctant to use terms such as *psychosis* and *neurosis* the way doctors use the terms *pneumonia* or *appendicitis*. Even well-trained psychiatric workers do not always agree in their diagnoses of mental illnesses, which are actually matters of degree and do not fall into clear-

cut categories. Indeed, a few researchers believe that being classified as mentally ill often gives a person a "role" to live up to. For this reason a person who is thought to be mentally ill is more likely to act in odd ways than he or she would be if earlier odd behaviors had been overlooked or defined as ordinary quirks.[23] We will discuss this issue further in the Social Research section.

### Deviant cultures

Many groups within a society develop patterns of thought and behavior that set them apart from the larger group. These groups are to varying degrees deviant in the eyes of the members of "straight" society. The most obvious examples of "deviant" cultures are *countercultures*. Kenneth Westhues, who has studied countercultures ranging from the early Christian gnostics to the flower children of the 1960s, believes that countercultures are characterized by rejection of rationality and pursuit of "transcendence," or heightened consciousness. Westhues lists seven behavioral characteristics of countercultures:

1 Relationships among members of the counterculture tend to be communistic in that they share the ownership of property.
2 Sexual relationships among members of the counterculture deviate from the nuclear family and monogamous marriage. They may practice group marriage, complete abstinence from sex, or anything in between these extremes.
3 The counterculture claims superiority over the dominant society, but it does not try to impose its way of life on others. It sees itself primarily as a spiritual elite.
4 Members look to spiritual leaders who claim to have had transcendental experiences.
5 The counterculture is not political in its orientation, except when the parent culture opposes it. When this happens, the counterculture must fight for survival as a group.
6 The members reject many of the status symbols of the larger society. They are rarely concerned about the beauty of their material possessions.
7 Because of the preceding factors, the counter-

culture exists in social isolation from the main culture and builds up a system of norms all its own.[24]

Besides countercultures, there are a number of other types of subcultures that are deviant to varying degrees. Street gangs, organized crime, and certain religious sects have norms and beliefs that are quite different from those of the larger community.

# The social construction of deviance

Deviance results not only from the actions of the offender but also from the actions of conforming members of society. It is the conformers who (1) make the rules, (2) enforce them, and (3) call the offenders deviants.

## MAKING THE RULES

Deviance is possible only because there are rules to break. But rules do not just come into existence whenever they are "needed" or "wanted." This is particularly true of laws, opposed to informal social norms. Howard Becker has shown that someone must have a strong enough interest in getting a law on the books to push for its passage. He calls such people "moral entrepreneurs." They make it their business to sew another patch onto the moral fabric of society.

One kind of work that the moral entrepreneur does is to persuade others that the proposed law will protect a recognized social value. Values are general statements about what is good or desirable, but their implications for conduct in specific situations are not always obvious. Someone must search for a general value that will justify the new rule. In addition, the moral enterpreneur must defend the new rule against its opponents, who may invoke a different val-

ue in support of their position. The work includes publicity—the arousal of a sense of urgency about the proposed law. It also includes neutralization of the objections of others whose interests will be adversely affected by the law.

Becker illustrates this process by showing how the Marijuana Tax Act of 1937 was enacted. The U.S. Bureau of Narcotics was the moral entrepreneur in this case. Before 1937 marijuana was not regarded as a serious social problem, and state laws banning it were not enforced. Then the Bureau of Narcotics began to promote the idea that marijuana was a major threat to the general welfare. As a result a federal law outlawing the use of marijuana was quickly passed. The Bureau's motivation for this action was obscure, though it was probably linked to the fact that the bureau had acquired a lot of prestige as a bulwark against the evils of opiate drugs, which, unlike marijuana, are addictive. Enlargement of the Bureau's operations and enhancement of its reputation required the identification of new public enemies.[25]

## ENFORCING THE RULES

Deviance exists partly because laws exist, and the laws may or may not be of great social value. Deviance also exists partly because laws are *enforced*, and likewise, the enforcement may or may not be of great social value. Indeed, a few sociologists argue that the police actually *cause* crime. They may mean this in two different senses.

First, one tends to find crime where one looks for it. According to Aaron Cicourel, the very high crime rate in the urban ghetto can be explained largely by the fact that police expect crime to occur there and concentrate on looking for it there, thus creating a "self-fulfilling prophecy."[26] It is well known that crime is detected when and where the police are trying to detect it. Thus during a riot the crime rate in other parts of the city usually drops. This is because the police are so busy at the riot that they cannot detect the usual number of crimes elsewhere.

Second, the use of power by the police may itself lead to crime. Police work involves a certain amount of strain. The combination of personal danger and authority creates a temptation for police officers to use their authority in ways that are contrary to the rule of law. The fact that police can be dangerous was recognized far back in history. The Romans asked themselves, *Quis custodiet ipsos custodes*? ("Who will guard the guardians?"), but they do not seem to have found a satisfactory answer to their question. North Americans have become more aware of this problem in recent years after watching incidents of police violence in civil-rights and antiwar demonstrations on TV newscasts. However, after reviewing the records of such tragic incidents in American history, Gary T. Marx has concluded that the police have become more restrained over time rather than less so.[27]

### LABELING THE DEVIANT

It is one thing to commit a deviant act — lying, stealing, homosexual intercourse, or heavy drinking — but it is quite another thing to be labeled deviant, to be socially defined as a liar, a thief, a homosexual, or a drunk. Such labels suggest that one is habitually given to a particular kind of deviance and that he may be *expected* to behave in a deviant way. Fortunately, however, most people who commit deviant acts do not have the unpleasant experience of being labeled deviant. Indeed, we are all "hidden offenders," having at least technically violated some law or other, but few of us are labeled deviant. Our chance of being defined as deviant depends largely on whether we are caught performing deviant acts. Crimes without victims — drug abuse, homosexual-

ity, and abortion, for example — are not likely to come to the attention of the police or the newspapers. Therefore people who commit such acts are less likely to be labeled deviant than someone who makes a habit of stealing a police car and tearing through town with the siren on. Millions of respected homemakers secretly drink all afternoon while watching television. They may be alcoholics for several years before their neighbors find out and begin to refer to them as "that lush."

### White-collar crime

Even crimes that get onto the public record do not necessarily result in the offenders' being labeled as deviant. In 1949 Edwin Sutherland published a study of what he called "white-collar crime."[28] This was an analysis of crimes committed by 70 large manufacturing, mining, and other corporations and their subsidiaries over an average of 45 years. The offenses studied included false advertising, violations of patent, trademark, and copyright laws, financial fraud, and other offenses committed by businessmen in the course of their work. Most of these offenses had been detected by independent government commissions, and the decisions Sutherland recorded were all on acts that are defined as criminal by law. A total of 980 decisions were made against the corporations studied, an average of 4 convictions each. What these offenses cost their victims in terms of money cannot be estimated, but only a handful of cases of fraud and false advertising can cost consumers many millions of dollars. However, in most of these cases the public image of the corporation involved was not damaged and its officers continued to be respected citizens of their communities, with their good names undamaged by deviant reputations.

### Stigma

Not all offenders are as lucky as the well-to-do corporation executives Sutherland

Jim Anderson/Woodfin Camp

*Not everybody minds being labeled as deviant.*

perience **stigma,** the mark of disgrace that is attached to those in disvalued roles.

Erving Goffman has analyzed the effects of stigma on self-image and the often vain struggle of the stigmatized person to maintain self-respect and a reputable image.[29]

### Redefining deviance

Certain kinds of acts may "migrate" from one deviant category to another. What was once a "sin" or a "vice," for example, may be elevated to the gravity of a "crime" or be reduced to mere "bad taste." Similarly, the sinner may be redefined either as a "criminal" or as a "boor." Social structure and the cultural context determine the direction in which a given act will migrate. A major cultural trend of the past fifty years or so has been to reclassify as "sick" certain forms of behavior that were once viewed as vicious, depraved, or criminal; homosexuality and drug use are among those behaviors.[30] (Of course many people would rather be regarded as "bad" or "immoral" than as "mentally ill.") Homosexuals have a good chance of being redefined as neither vicious nor "sick" but simply "different," especially since 1973, when the American Psychiatric Association moved in that direction.

studied. Many have to live with ruined reputations that are in keeping with their disvalued roles. Of course not all disvalued roles are viewed as deviant. The roles of slave, hunchback, moron, and blind person are disvalued, but they are viewed differently than the roles of coward, thief, scab, or adulterer. It is assumed that no one *chooses* the former class of roles and that people who are forced to play such roles are "unfortunate" but not "reprehensible." However, the unfortunate and the reprehensible both ex-

## Controlling deviance

**Social control** consists of the various ways in which members of a group punish deviance and try to get others to live up to society's norms. The example that comes to mind most readily is the system of laws, police, courts, and prisons, but there are other sources of social control as well. The control of deviance is a matter of continual public concern, and we will return to this topic in the section on social policy. For now it is enough to mention three of the main sources of social control: socialization, group pressure, and social sanctions.

## SOCIALIZATION

Most social control is *self*-control. As we saw in Chapter 4, we usually behave properly even if no one is looking because we have *internalized* the norms of our group. This is why many patterns of deviance—especially delinquency and other antisocial acts—result from inadequate socialization. Poor interpersonal relations in the home during childhood may have long-term effects on personality and increase the likelihood that a person will perform deviant acts. Thus Travis Hirschi's 1969 study of 4000 teenage boys in the San Francisco Bay area found some correlates of delinquency that have been reported in many other such studies: (1) the boys' fathers had often been on welfare or unemployed; (2) their school performance and aspirations were low; and (3) their respect for and attachment to parents were low.[31] Hirschi claims that item (3) is one of the most important and common findings in delinquency research. Children who are close to their parents are unlikely to misbehave, whether the parent is of high or low status. Almost all delinquents say that their upbringing was unpleasant, that their parents never understood them, and that their parents were too strict.

Inadequate socialization in childhood may be the cause of many other patterns of deviance, such as homosexuality and emotional illness. However, sociologists are still trying to find out exactly what aspect or aspects of socialization must be lacking for these tendencies to arise. Some researchers suggest that some mental illnesses may be due to peculiar patterns of communication within the family, patterns that involve contradictory messages expressed in different ways. For example, a little boy's mother may

talk a lot about how much she loves him, but whenever he touches her she may stiffen, move away, or look annoyed. Which "message" should he believe—the verbal one or the nonverbal one? If he calls attention to the discrepancy, his mother may get angry. This situation has been called a "double bind" and is said to be common in the families of mental patients.[32]

## INFORMAL GROUP PRESSURE

For adolescents, perhaps even more than for adults, peer group approval is extremely important. This is why so many delinquent acts are committed by gangs rather than by individuals acting alone. By the same token, peer group pressure to conform can be an important means of social control. James Coleman, who compared the adolescent cultures of different high schools, argues that peer group pressure is far more influential than parents' opinions. He claims that each high school builds up a unified teenage culture that may differ greatly from that found in other high schools, even though the schools are similar in socioeconomic makeup. For example, one school may be sports oriented and another intellectually oriented. A teenager who goes to the sports-minded school is far less likely to be interested in schoolwork than one who goes to the other school, regardless of his or her parents' attitudes.[33]

## SOCIAL SANCTIONS

We do not depend only on socialization and peer group pressure to maintain social order. Society also uses many different **sanctions**—rewards for desirable behavior and punishments for undesirable behavior. One can be sent to jail, for instance, or fined. Even

*This could be you or me if we slip up, and we know it. That's one reason we are careful not to violate important norms.*

though this does not happen to many people, the fact that it *can* happen encourages law-abiding behavior. Thus we know that by giving tickets to speeders police officers actually save lives. The more speeding tickets are written, the fewer accidents there are. The reverse is also true. The more "lenient" a state is with speeders, the more accidents occur in that state.

Even so, punishment is not a very effective way of preventing serious offenses. There is little evidence, for example, that spending time in prison makes criminals less likely to commit new crimes than if they had not been sent to prison. The sad fact is that social scientists have no reliable suggestions as to how to induce criminals to reform.[34]

## The consequences of deviance

Almost any group can tolerate quite a bit of deviance, and in fact most groups expect it. They make plans to cope with it and to limit its disorganizing effects. Department stores, for example, allow for a certain amount of merchandise to be lost through theft, just as they allow for breakage.

They may even "insure against" theft by bonding their employees.[35]

## DEVIANCE AND DISORGANIZATION

A group can manage to survive despite considerable deviance. However, certain actions are more vital than others, and failure to carry out essential functions brings disaster to the organization. This is so, for example, if the commanding officer of a military unit deserts in the midst of a battle or if a contractor fails to honor a contract and refuses to deliver essential building materials.

Idlers, fakers, chiselers, and the like undermine an organization by making other members of the group unwilling to play their parts. If the deviant shares in the rewards without sharing in the work, the virtuous members become resentful and may withdraw from the organization.

The worst effect of deviance on organizations is the erosion of *trust*—the confidence that others will play by the rules. After all, each member has made an investment in the future of the collective activity on the assumption that if he or she plays by the rules others will too. The individual's contribution, whether it is chasing a ball in a baseball game or doing a homework assignment, makes sense only if others do their part. To distrust others is to see one's own effort as pointless and the future as hazardous and uncertain. One then feels like "pulling out of the game" and investing one's efforts elsewhere.

All organized social activity requires a certain amount of trust among the participants. This is true even of activities that are themselves deviant, such as illegal betting. A bookie, for example, cannot enforce his claims in court because his business is illegal. He must therefore be able to trust the handicappers, the wire services, and the "layoff bettors" who take large bets from minor bookies. He must also trust the honesty of the sporting events on which he is taking bets.

A study conducted several years ago showed that in New York State less than 1 percent of the money spent on illegal betting on sporting events went for boxing bets. Why? According to the report, this is a "sorry indication of the low state to which that so-called sport has fallen. Even the bookmakers avoid it because of the characters who control it, to whom a fix is normal procedure."[36] Here we see one line of business that has suffered as a result of widespread lack of trust.

## POSITIVE FUNCTIONS OF DEVIANCE

We must not assume that deviance is only harmful. There are times when it can be useful. For one thing, to deviate from the rules of a destructive organization can be to do a service to society. This is because there is a difference between what the rules *are* and what they *should be*. We may disagree on the desirability of a rule but agree on its *validity*. I may think that the speed laws in my city are silly, but I recognize that they are valid rules and that the authorities have a right to enforce them. Even so, deviance from valid but undesirable rules can be a valuable act of courage. Thus American draft dodgers and deserters protesting the Vietnam War may be considered moral heroes because they violated valid draft laws that had harmful results.

Occasionally there are other ways in which deviance may be useful. Deviance can cut red tape, act as a safety valve, clarify rules, unite the group, reinforce conformity, and act as a warning signal.

### Cutting red tape

An organization's rules may usually make sense. However, in some situations conformity to the rules will defeat rather than support the organization's goals. If those goals are to be achieved, someone must break the rules. For example, an organization may have a sensible way of distributing supplies—certain forms must be filled out, certain people must sign the forms, and so on. This system permits budgeting and planning. However, if the authorized person is not around to sign the forms, someone will usually be willing to forge his or her signature. Such deviance may actually be in the interest of the organization whose rules are being broken.

### Acting as a safety valve

Some people have wants that the rules of society do not recognize as legitimate, or they may lack access to the legitimate means of satisfying their wants. If enough people are frustrated, they may attack the rules themselves and the social institutions that they support. Therefore a certain amount of deviance, condemned but not firmly repressed, may take some of the strain off the legitimate order. For example, consider the rule that legitimates sexual relations within marriage; this norm is socially useful because it motivates people to have families. However, if a man's sexual desires are not satisfied within marriage he may turn elsewhere. If his extramarital relationship is kept impersonal, it will threaten his family much less than if they had to compete for his emotional attachment. The prostitute does not share the social status of her sexual partner the way a wife does, nor is she socially acceptable as his companion in public. It can be argued, therefore, that prostitution, a severely limited and disvalued kind of relationship, is the form of extramarital sexual behavior that is least likely to keep men from marrying, to threaten the status or security of the wife, or to create emotional ties that will compete seriously with the obligations of marriage.[37] Thus the results of this form of deviance are not wholly *dysfunctional* (against the interests of the whole social system), and laws against prostitution are not strictly enforced in most societies.

### Clarifying rules

The precise meaning of a rule is not always obvious, but when you have overstepped the bounds you will discover your mistake in the raised eyebrows, chilly looks, or amused smiles of the people around you. When one is learning the rules of a new role one may experiment a bit with borderline behavior. In a way, the person who is daring enough to confront his or her group with borderline behavior does the group a service by forcing it to "make up its mind" about a fuzzy rule. Appellate courts provide the same service by reducing the ambiguity of laws. Deviance forces the clarification or reaffirmation of a rule, thus enabling other members to understand better what other people think they should or should not do.[38]

### Uniting the group

Sometimes a deviant does a service to his group by pulling it together. This can happen in two different ways: The group can either oppose the deviant or try to convert him or her.

It is well known that nothing unites the members of a group like a common enemy, but this is also true of enemies within the group. Although it is not pleasant for him or her personally, the deviant may serve as a "built-in out-group," a scapegoat who contributes to the unity of the group in much the same way that witches, devils, and hostile foreign powers do.[39]

On the other hand, the deviant may unite the group through his or her very need to be "converted." Unity increases when members of a group subordinate their personal interests to some common goal. The goal could be to protect or reclaim a deviant or to show the group's patience and kindness in the face of repeated provocation by the deviant member.[40] Some groups seem to thrive on taking care of erring members.

## Highlighting conformity

The good deed, said Shakespeare, shines brightest in a naughty world. Most of us can remember feeling exhilaration in talking to members of a group about the blemishes and failings of some third party. In the process of criticizing another person's deviance we reward one another for our superior merit and enhance the sense of community among the conforming members of the group.[41]

## Acting as a warning signal

Truants from school, deserters from the army, runaways from prisons, and the like may force people to take a closer look at how they are running such institutions and lead to greater efficiency and morale. Thus the deviant, by sticking his or her neck out, is acting to the benefit of conformers who suffer in law-abiding silence. Acts of civil disobedience may, in fact, be organized and planned with the goal of using deviance as a warning signal. Here is an example:

Several years ago the Indiana University faculty had a high rate of violation of campus parking regulations, in part because of the disjunction between the demand for parking spaces and the supply. The virtuous left early for work and hunted wearily for legitimate parking spaces. The contemptuous parked anywhere and sneered at tickets. One response to this situation was to create new parking lots and to expand old ones. Since the new parking spaces were available to all, and not only to the former violators, this provides a clear instance where the virtuous—or perhaps the timid—as well as the deviants themselves are the beneficiaries of deviance.[42]

### THE NORMALITY OF DEVIANCE

For all of the reasons I have listed, some sociologists have concluded that, even though conformity is the usual response of human beings, a certain amount of deviance is useful in any social system. Therefore deviance is tolerated, and even encouraged, within limits. Durkheim claimed that deviance is normal and that if a society runs short of it, it will always create more by making major issues out of minor offenses. He wrote,

Imagine a society of saints, a perfect cloister of exemplary individuals. Crimes, properly so called, will there be unknown; but faults which appear venial to the layman will create there the same scandal that the ordinary offense does in ordinary consciousness. If then this society has the power to judge and punish, it will define these acts as criminal and will treat them as such.[43]

Kai Erikson has taken Durkheim's theory seriously and has attempted to test it. He

*To be or not to be? That is a social question. One's life belongs to oneself, but also to other people.*

Allen Green/Palmer Photo

searched history for a "society of saints" to find out whether deviance occurred at a relatively constant rate in that society, as Durkheim suggested. He chose the New England Puritans, who at least called themselves a community of saints, and he found that to the Puritans minor acts of religious nonconformity were crimes punishable by death. The number of deviants who were alive and active in this society remained about the same over several decades, as measured by the number of offenders brought to trial. When the supply of "real" deviants began to run low, the New Englanders discovered witches in their midst. Erikson concludes that "deviance is not a property *inherent in* any particular kind of behavior; it is a property *conferred upon* that behavior by the people who come into contact with it."[44]

# The relativity of deviance

The study of deviance, then, is not simply the study of drunkenness, drug use, extramarital sexual relations, prostitution, and so forth *as such*, for each of these behaviors is socially acceptable in some society and in some situations. What makes an act deviant?

### NORMS GOVERN ROLES

Behavior is deviant only *if the person who performs the act is subject to the norms that his or her behavior violates.* A person is deviant only in terms of his or her role as a member of a particular collectivity. Part of the meaning of a role in a collectivity is to be subject to the norms of that collectivity. Even people who do not belong to the collectivity and do not approve of its rules may still take its norms into account when judging its members. Thus, for example, non-Catholics may recognize the difference between a "good" Catholic and a "bad" Catholic. They may even admire the "good" Catholic for his or her faithful adherence to patterns of con-

duct for which they would criticize members of their own religious collectivity.

There are interesting borderline positions, such as that of the "guest," whether in a household or in a foreign country. Only in a limited sense are guests "members" of the collectivity they are visiting. Their roles are governed by a special set of understandings that may include special duties and special privileges. Guests may be deviant, but only in terms of this special set of rules. For example, it would ordinarily be deviant for a guest to reorganize your kitchen cabinets or to join in a squabble over the family budget.

### ROLE CONFLICT

Sometimes a person may have two different roles with contradictory norms so that it may be difficult or impossible to conform to them all. Conformity to one role may require deviance from another. This situation is called role conflict. For example, the role of examination proctor and the role of friend may make quite different demands on a person; however, the system may be organized in such a way that no individual is likely to play those two roles at the same time.[45] Role conflict is a source of deviance that is built into the structure and rules of the system itself; it is a *structural* source of deviance.

We have said that deviance is specific to the norms of a collectivity. Sometimes, however, people may not know exactly what those norms are. As agreement on the rules declines, the idea of deviance becomes less meaningful and less useful, and we may have to figure out *whose* version of the rules matters at any given moment. Deviance may be created or ended by changes in the rules themselves or by changes in the interpretation of the rules.

# Theories of deviance

The theories that we will mention here all seek to answer the question, How do people happen to violate norms?

Two approaches can be taken in answering this question. The first assumes that offenders are different from nonoffenders and tries to show in what way they are different and how they become different. We call this the *kinds-of-people* approach because it accounts for deviance by explaining "what kind of person" would do a particular thing. Psychologists often take this approach.

The second approach assumes that a deviant may be just like anyone else and not a different "kind of person." We call this approach *situational* because it tries to explain deviance in terms of situations that lead ordinary people to violate norms. Most sociologists take a situational approach to the question of deviance.

### KINDS-OF-PEOPLE THEORIES

Theories that attribute deviant behaviors to particular kinds of people may account for the behavior in terms of either biological characteristics or psychological characteristics. Here we will discuss both biological and psychodynamic theories of criminal or delinquent behavior.

#### Biological theories

LOMBROSIAN POSITIVISM   In the 1870s an Italian physician, Cesare Lombroso, founded the "positive school of criminology"—a theory that explained criminal behavior as caused by a genetic defect. According to this theory, a deviant person inherited a body structure and personality that were characteristic of a more primitive stage of evolution.[46] Lombroso's followers believed that they could identify "born criminals" with calipers, scales, and cameras, for all such deviants were supposed to be marked by the physical "stigmata of degeneracy." Early in this century this theory was destroyed by the research of Charles Goring, an English prison officer who compared his prisoners to a control group of noncriminals and found no

evidence of a distinct physical type among criminals.[47]

SHELDON'S CONSTITUTIONAL TYPOLOGY   Another effort to link physiology and criminology was made by William H. Sheldon, an American psychologist and physician.[48] After examining 200 wayward boys Sheldon concluded that boys with hard, rectangular ("mesomorphic") body structures were more likely to become delinquent than boys whose physiques were either soft and round or lean and fragile. Later research by Sheldon Glueck and Eleanor Glueck supported William Sheldon's findings, though 40 percent of the Gluecks' delinquent subjects were *not* primarily mesomorphic.[49] We still don't know why mesomorphs are any more likely to become delinquent than skinny boys or roly-poly ones. Perhaps the most satisfactory explanation is that people have a tendency to do the things for which they are best equipped. Delinquent street life rewards strength and physical toughness, which are characteristic of the athletic mesomorph.

XYY CHROMOSOMES   Some researchers are exploring the question of whether criminality is connected with abnormal chromosome patterns. Chromosomes are threads of living matter that contain the genes that determine our inherited characteristics—eye color, hair color, and so on. There are normally 23 pairs of chromosomes in every human cell (46 chromosomes in all). The twenty-third pair is the one that determines sex. In females, the last pair consists of two identical chromosomes called $X$ chromosomes. In males this pair consists of two different chromosomes, an $X$ chromosome and a $Y$ chromosome. But some males have an extra $Y$ chromosome, and some researchers think that criminality occurs more often in such men than in men whose chromosomes are normal. This condition seems to be present at birth but not inherited. But even if there is a connection between $XYY$ chromosomes and criminality, only a small percentage of crimes can possibly be due to this physical anomaly.[50] As of now, therefore, all biological theories of deviance are inconclusive, though there is good reason for continued research.

### Psychodynamic theories

Most kinds-of-people theories stress, not biological, but psychological characteristics. These theories try to account for deviance in terms of events in the life history of the deviant. Perhaps the deviant acquired weird motives at some point or else failed to learn the internal controls that conformists learn. Such theories are usually based on Freudian psychoanalysis, which points to defects in the superego and the ego as well as to the frustration of needs as a source of deviant conduct.

SUPEREGO STRENGTH   A person's conscience is supposed to develop out of early loving relationships with moral adults. According to Freudians, failure to develop a strong conscience, or *superego*, results in a *psychopathic personality*—a character with no guilt feelings, pity, or respect for others.[51] It is sometimes claimed that most of the prisoners in penitentiaries are psychopaths. However, some psychologists believe that the psychopathic personality is a rare condition, and still others deny that it exists at all.

EGO STRENGTH   In recent years psychoanalysts have paid increasing attention to ego defects. A weak ego is not lack of conscience but inability to organize one's activities in the real world. It can involve, for example, inability to control impulses, to postpone pleasure, and to follow plans.

FRUSTRATION–AGGRESSION   A theory based on Freud's thought but best explained by John Dollard is called the *frustration–aggression* theory.[52] It holds that frustration produces aggression, which, in turn, produces deviant behavior. If the aggression is

directed outward, the person may attack the source of his or her frustration or some substitute target. If the person's controls are very strong, the aggressive energy may be made harmless by sublimation. In this case the energy is used up in some socially acceptable or constructive way—by smashing a squash ball around, perhaps, or by writing a critical letter to the editor of a local newspaper.

This theory has been used by Andrew F. Henry and James F. Short to account for variations in suicide rates (aggression against the self) and homicide rates (aggression against another).[53] They suggest that low-status people can easily blame others, rather than themselves, for their frustration and that they will feel justified in turning their aggression outward, commiting homicide rather than suicide. Higher-status people, on the other hand, will be more likely to commit suicide under stress. Available data are consistent with this theory, though there are other theories supported by equally strong evidence.[54]

DEFENSE MECHANISMS   Psychoanalysis is the source of yet another theory. Unlike the others, which suggest that the offender loses control of his or her deviant impulse, this theory suggests that the deviant act is a device contrived by the personality to *protect itself against anxiety or guilt*. It works by concealing from the actor his or her unacceptable impulse, and only skilled analysis will bring its "true meaning" to light. Theories of this sort interpret deviant acts as *mechanisms of defense*.

In *Delinquent Boys*[55] Albert Cohen tries to use such a theory to explain why lower-class youth tend to be delinquent in ways that have no utility but show a spirit of pure meanness and negativism. Cohen argued that American children of all social classes and ethnic origins must compete against one another for approval and status under the same standards. They are rewarded for verbal ability, polished manners, achievement, and sustained effort toward long-term goals. Lower-class children are the losers in this competition because their socialization experiences in childhood differ from those of middle-class children. To cope with the feeling of being a loser, lower-class children withdraw from the game, reject the middle-class rules, and set up a new game using rules under which they can perform satisfactorily.

But the dominant value system is also in some sense *their* value system. They have, to a certain extent, internalized its rules as well as their own. They can tell themselves that they don't really care what people think of them, but their internalized values, though repressed, threaten to break through and reduce their satisfaction with the path they have chosen. To protect this choice from "the enemy within, as well as the enemy without," they fall back on reaction formation, which is, in Freudian theory, a mechanism for denying an unacceptable element of the personality through behavior that seems to *overprotest*, *overdeny*. They not only reject the dominant value system but do so with a vengeance. They engage in malicious, spiteful, ornery behavior of all sorts to show, not only to others but to themselves as well, their contempt for the game they have rejected. For example, a teenager may "prove" that he does not like or want a sports car by slashing the tires of all the sports cars he sees.

### Problems with kinds-of-people theories

All kinds-of-people theories claim that the deviant act is caused by a weakness in the character of the individual. However, this model suggests that such weak people would be *consistently* deviant, that is, that they would always commit the same deviant act in a given situation. But this is not the case. Most people who commit deviant acts are not consistently deviant. Most students

who cheat do so only sometimes and behave "normally" most of the time. To explain why *this* person commits *this* deviant act at *this* time, it is necessary to borrow explanations from other theories. Besides, most deviant acts are committed by people who are basically normal and do not have marked psychological disorders. Recall Sutherland's work on white-collar crime, for example. These acts were carried out by pillars of society, people with well-organized personalities who do not have obvious psychological problems.

### SITUATION THEORIES

In this section I will describe several theories that explain deviant behavior as arising out of the properties of social systems. The first is anomie theory as developed first by Durkheim and later by Merton. The second is cultural-transmission theory, especially as developed by Sutherland. The third is role-self theory, or symbolic interactionism.

### Anomie theory

DURKHEIM Durkheim believed that new problems—mainly class conflict and the decline in social solidarity—had resulted from increasing division of labor. The jobs of individual workers had become so specialized that the workers could no longer operate according to shared rules and understandings.[56] Therefore people doing different jobs worked at cross-purposes, and this led to confusion, inefficiency, and even social disintegration. There were no common rules for regulating the social system. Durkheim called this situation anomie, meaning normlessness or deregulation. Any period of upheaval or economic uncertainty, such as a depression, is a period of high anomie.

In his book *Suicide* he suggested that periods of rapid change—especially economic booms and depressions—make it impossible for people to expect specific rewards for conforming to society's norms.

When society and the economy are unstable, the benefits of conforming or deviating are not predictable enough to count on. People may work hard and save money for their old age, only to have their savings wiped out in a stock market crash or bankruptcy. A telephone quiz or jingle contest may, by a fluke, turn a drifter into a rich man without his making any contribution to his society. If such events occur often, they weaken a social group's ability to back up its norms with systematic rewards and punishments.

In his discussion of "anomic suicide" Durkheim notes that suicides increase both in times of depression and in times of rapidly increasing prosperity. He believed that this is due to changing ideas about how rewards should be distributed among the members of a society. It is understandable that hard times might make life seem no longer worth living. But why should prosperity produce similar results?

According to Durkheim, human wants are endlessly expandable. There is no "natural" limit to what people might crave and, therefore, to what might satisfy them. What, then, keeps us from being constantly dissatisfied? The norms that tell us how high to aim. Social rules, not biology, define what each social class is entitled to. People regulate their wants accordingly, and this creates the possibility of feeling satisfied. But a period of fast-growing prosperity upsets the usual definitions of the goals that a person may have. There is no limit on aspirations, and thus nothing produces satisfaction. Durkheim felt that the desire to live is weakened under such conditions. Suicide is caused by this state of anomie.

MERTON  Four decades after the publication of Durkheim's *Suicide*, Robert Merton published a short paper entitled "Social Structure and Anomie," that developed Durkheim's theory further.[57]

Merton described anomie as a gap between effort and reward that makes it impossible for people to have realistic goals or to plan legitimate ways of achieving their goals. He listed three different factors: (1) culture goals, the wants and ambitions that people are taught by their society; (2) norms, which prescribe legitimate means of pursuing these goals; and (3) institutionalized means, the actual resources available to the individual.

Merton claimed that North American society expects all of its members to have the same *goal* (success and high income) and the same *norms* (hard work, thrift, and the like). However, society offers different social groups quite different *institutionalized means*—unequal opportunities for education, challenging jobs, business loans, and so forth. This situation puts a strain on the lower-status groups because the means available to them don't help them achieve prescribed goals.

Frustration, hopelessness, and anger result, not from any single one of these factors—goals, norms, or means—but from the relationship among them. If a group has modest goals, follows the society's norms, and has the means to achieve its goals legitimately, there is no problem. Strain results when there is a gap between goals and institutionalized means. A person's response may be to weaken his or her commitment either to the prescribed goals, to the prescribed means of achieving the goals, or both. Merton believed that there are five possible responses to this gap. (See Figure 7.1.)

The first of these responses is *conformity;* the others are all varieties of deviant behavior. *Innovators* (e.g., professional thieves, white-collar criminals, cheaters) believe in the goals but reject the prescribed means. *Ritualists* (e.g., bureaucrats who rigidly follow the rules without thinking about why the rules are there) make a virtue of overconformity to the prescribed means at the price of underconformity to the prescribed goals. *Retreatists* (e.g., tramps, drunkards, hippies, drug addicts) withdraw from the "rat race" by abandoning both the

### FIGURE 7.1

*A typology of modes of individual adaptation illustrating Merton's theory of anomie*

| | Commitment to prescribed means | No commitment to prescribed means |
|---|---|---|
| Commitment to prescribed goals | **Conformity** | **Innovation** |
| No commitment to prescribed goals | **Ritualism** | **Retreatism** |

goals and the means. *Rebels* (e.g., members of revolutionary movements) respond in a fifth way—like retreatists, they reject both the prescribed goals and the prescribed means, but they put other goals and means in their place. They withdraw their support from a social system that they believe is unjust and seek to rebuild the society with new goals and new means of achieving them.

Notice that this approach to deviance focuses not on the characteristics of individuals but on the positions that individuals occupy within the social system. It is therefore a sociological, not a psychological, theory, but it is a limited one. Merton did not try to explain why some people choose one response while others choose another. Nor did he face the question of why some people who are under great strain continue to conform, as many do.

### Cultural-transmission theory

We turn now to a different kind of theory, sometimes called *subculture* theory and sometimes *cultural-transmission* theory. This approach comes from the Chicago

school of sociology and has been used most fully by Edwin H. Sutherland.

All of the cultural-transmission theories should be distinguished from anomie theory, which views deviance primarily as the individual's way of adapting to a situation in which no means are available for achieving the prescribed goals. Therefore he or she must innovate by inventing illegitimate means instead. Cultural-transmission theory does not picture deviant *individuals* as innovating at all. They don't think up their crimes independently. Rather, they are simply following norms that are prescribed by a limited subculture—a social group that exists within the larger society but has beliefs and norms that deviate from the point of view of the larger society. The deviant is seen as *conforming to a deviant subculture*. For example, a child brought up by thieves is not deviant, in their opinion, for stealing. He or she is simply living up to different standards from yours or mine.

Cultural-transmission theory should also be distinguished from most kinds-of-people theories, which see the deviant as abnormal and warped. According to cultural-transmission theory, deviants learn their behavior patterns the same way anyone else does—their personalities are shaped by the knowledge, attitudes, and beliefs of the people with whom they interact. They may wind up as different "kinds of people" (e.g., pickpockets or prostitutes), but they acquire such habits in the same way that we become pinball wizards or sociologists—usually by spending a lot of time with people who play pinball machines, pick pockets, study sociology, or hustle, as the case may be.

SHAW AND MCKAY  In a series of important books[58] based mostly on research done in the city of Chicago, Clifford Shaw and Henry McKay tried to explain the delinquency rates in American cities. They noted that the high-rate areas in 1900–1906 were also the high-rate areas in 1917–1923, though the ethnic

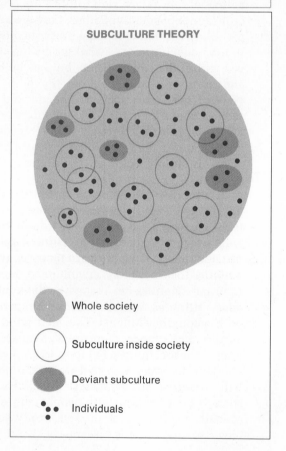

**FIGURE 7.2**

*In any modern society, such as the one represented below, there are many subcultures. Some of them are not deviant (e.g., antique collectors and rock music fans), while other subcultures are deviant (e.g., pot smokers and prostitutes). Any person's likelihood of becoming deviant is explained (in subculture theory) in terms of whether he or she is in contact with members of a deviant subculture.*

**SUBCULTURE THEORY**

Whole society

Subculture inside society

Deviant subculture

Individuals

this tradition was passed along through personal and group contacts.[59] A deviant tradition is sometimes called a *delinquent subculture*. It is passed along mainly by the play group and the gang. An individual becomes deviant not by planning to commit a deviant act on his or her own but by behaving the way the group behaves. Such a person is not an innovator but a special kind of conformist.

SUTHERLAND  Sutherland tried to develop a general theory of criminal behavior based on cultural transmission. He called it the theory of *differential association*. According to this theory, criminal behavior is learned; it is not inherited or invented by the criminal. It is learned through communication with other people, mostly in small, intimate groups. Our companions define the law favorably or unfavorably, and we take over those definitions. A person becomes criminal or delinquent because the definitions to which he or she is exposed favor violation of the law. Everyone has some contact with both kinds of definitions; what is important is the ratio of one to the other. Note that Sutherland does not emphasize contact with criminals or noncriminals; rather, he focuses on exposure to *definitions* that are favorable or unfavorable to crime. A person may have very few contacts with criminals but may have a great deal of exposure to procriminal attitudes. By the same token, however, many kinds of criminal behavior may be defined unfavorably even by criminals. The professional pickpocket may be as unfavorable toward rape, drug addiction, or murder as any conforming citizen. On the other hand, procriminal attitudes toward matters such as tax evasion may be learned from people who are basically conforming and respectable. Contacts with people are not all of equal weight; some have more impact than others. This impact varies with *frequency, duration, priority, and intensity*. If we could measure these factors, we would have a formula that

makeup of these areas had changed. As an ethnic group moved into these areas, the group's delinquency rate rose; as it moved out, its delinquency rate fell. Shaw and McKay concluded that crime had become a traditional way of life in these areas and that would allow us to make precise predictions in any particular case.[60]

Sutherland's theory implies that the larger culture is not homogeneous but contains contradictory definitions of the same behavior, one of which is backed by the people who make the laws. Rates and prevalence of each kind of criminal behavior depend on the extent to which social arrangements foster or prevent exposure to procriminal and anticriminal attitudes. For example, the mobility, diversity, and anonymity of urban life create more opportunities for procriminal contacts than the more controlled interaction patterns of rural society. Likewise, people who live in one part of town may be exposed to more criminal definitions than people who live in another area, and so the crime rates will differ between the two areas.

### Role-self theory

Role-self theory is the view that deviant behavior sometimes results when a person tries to justify his or her claims to a particular role. This theory is based on the symbolic interactionist view described in Chapter 6. You will recall that George Herbert Mead and his students emphasized the fact that we have to identify, define, and classify the objects we encounter, for we live in a world of socially meaningful objects. We have to decide what sort of objects we are dealing with. Once we identify them—an "antique," a "Picasso," a "mongrel," a "poker game"—some set of attitudes and expectations is called to mind, and this largely determines what we will do with the object. These socially defined objects include people. By living in a social group we learn the categories into which we classify people. We learn the system of roles; we have ideas about what different people are like, expectations about how they should behave, and standards for judging their behavior.

As we learn roles we acquire our own identity, for the self is also a social object. It

Jean Boughton/Stock, Boston

*Cultural transmission theories explain deviance in terms of "hanging out with the wrong crowd."*

is the actor as seen, labeled, classified, and judged by the actor himself or herself, and we have to *learn* how to do these things. Until we do so we have no "self-consciousness," and indeed, no "self." President and bartender, citizen and alien, old person and teenager, hip and square are part of the culturally defined set of roles in North American society. Some of these roles are assigned to us whether we like them or not; others are matters of choice.

The self, then, is developed in the process of interacting with others. We discover the categories to which we have been assigned and to some extent we decide what we will be. We claim to be a certain sort of person, and we must make the claim stick. To do so we must meet the cultural standards of the role. We know that we have done this when others show that they accept us as valid examples of that role. To lay a claim is to say, in effect, "I am a such-and-such sort of person. I invite you to deal with me on this basis. You may expect certain things of me." If we are accepted, we thereby confirm our view of ourselves. We cannot really tell whether we are "leaders," "glamour girls," "pool sharks," or "brains" without venturing into the icy waters of social interaction, trying out the role and seeing how others respond.

Not all of our roles are actively sought and cultivated. Some, like those of alcoholic and ex-convict, we may actively resist and deny. Some, like that of mental patient, we may accept but not enjoy. Some, like that of prostitute, we may accept for practical reasons, looking forward to a time when we may exchange it for some other, less stigmatized but equally profitable occupation. When we cannot escape being assigned to deviant roles we still try to avoid identifying with the role and claim that it does not express our "real selves."[61]

Our behavior may be designed to confirm our role claims. Thus to justify one's claim to being a philanthropist one must sooner or later "put up or shut up." We take on some roles not because they are directly important to the self but because they make it easier to perform other roles. For example, although both boys and girls steal, boys steal all sorts of things, often things that are of no earthly use to them. Girls tend to steal only things that they can use—clothing, cosmetics, jewelry, and the like. Stealing *as such* may be *role expressive*—a way of showing that one is "all boy." Girls' stealing, on the other hand, is *role supportive*; stealing as such does not express the feminine role, but the objects that girls steal help them be pretty and charming. Thus stealing *supports* the feminine role while it *expresses* the masculine role.[62] In our study of Beatlemania, discussed in Chapter 2, we concluded that screaming fits were designed to confirm or express the role of teenager.

A great deal of deviance that seems irrational makes some sense when it is seen as an effort to proclaim or test a certain kind of self. Much sexual activity, for example, is motivated less by glandular secretions than by role anxiety.[63] The novice smoking his or her first marijuana cigarette before an audience of peers is not necessarily looking for "kicks." The teenager tearing down the highway at ninety miles an hour is not necessarily going anywhere. It is clear that such behavior does not fit Merton's anomie theory because it is not a *means* to a goal. It is better understood as *evidence* that is being produced to support a claimed role.

Role-self theory is the basis of another explanation of deviance. According to this explanation, called *labeling theory*, a deviant identity may be *forced upon* a person through the very process of law enforcement. The person is "labeled" a deviant. A youth who is caught in a delinquent activity may not have seen himself as a "delinquent." However, the process of being arrested, brought to trial, and put in jail is an official "degradation ceremony" by which the deviant role is forced upon him. It is sometimes argued that this experience may be the turning point when a youth begins to see himself as a criminal and to organize his future behavior around that interpretation of himself. This means that the act of labeling someone as deviant may be the most important cause of later deviance.

### Problems with situation theories

We have already mentioned the limitations of cultural-transmission theory and anomie theory. Cultural-transmission theory does not explain how or why deviant subcultures come into existence. To do that, we must use some other approach.

Anomie theory, on the other hand, does not try to explain why some people endure strain without turning toward deviance, nor why others turn toward one deviant response rather than another. This theory is admirable for its logical simplicity but is still far from adequate.

Besides, as pointed out in the discussion of role-self theory, much deviant behavior cannot reasonably be interpreted as means (legitimate or illegitimate) of achieving any goal but only as role-expressive behavior. Tire slashing is not a way of getting something—it is merely a defiant gesture.

Role theory contributes most in combination with anomie theory because cultural goals and normative rules are closely connected to roles and to the self. Businessmen are *supposed* to make money, professors are *supposed* to write books, and ballplayers are *supposed* to win games. By pursuing those goals we try to express and justify ourselves as genuine businessmen, professors, or ballplayers. When the means and goals do not fit together nicely, businessmen may gyp their customers, professors may plagiarize, and ballplayers may cheat. However, they may also respond to the strain by *abandoning the role for another role* that they can play without violating the rules. I once chided a used-car salesman for selling me a bad car; the conscience-stricken man changed jobs as a result, explaining that business was so bad that he could no longer be a good Mormon and still make a living selling cars. Abandoning roles is one of the most common ways of avoiding the strain that Merton talked about, but it does not seem to fit into any of Merton's categories of responses.

I am not suggesting that role-self theory can replace cultural-transmission and anomie theory. Each seems to shed light on some aspect of deviant behavior. But deviance theorists still face the job of fitting the contributions of each of these theories into a single, more powerful theory, without giving up the logical unity that is characteristic of the work of Sutherland and Merton.[64]

## SOCIAL RESEARCH:
## Sociologists at Work

### MENTAL ILLNESS

Although all deviance consists of violations of norms, not all deviants are held accountable in the same way for their violations. Indeed, in the case of those who are considered mentally ill, moral responsibility is usually waived and the deviant is more pitied than blamed. But of course almost everyone has periods (or at least moments) when he or she cannot cope with the demands of ordinary role obligations because of emotional distress, mental distraction, worry, confusion, or anxiety. Hence, we all know from personal experience what might be (under some circumstances) labeled "madness."

For a great many people, however, such periods are serious enough to be brought to the attention of authorities, and many require hospitalization. Some people seek professional help in times of emotional distress. Others are committed to professional treatment against their will. A person who has been declared mentally incompetent cannot be found guilty of a crime, because the concepts of guilt and moral responsibility are applied to a person who *can* live up to ordinary obligations but voluntarily fails to do so. Such an assumption seems not to apply to a mentally disturbed person, and for this reason courts sometimes find defendants "not guilty by reason of insanity."

However, it is obvious that "mental illness" is not a single disease, and indeed it may be misleading to consider it as a medical problem anyway. In some cases, of course, when the patient's body chemistry is out of balance or when the brain is damaged by alcohol, syphilis, or other physical disorders, behavioral problems clearly do have a medical origin. However, a number of researchers consider these diseases to account for a small fraction of all the conditions that are generally labeled "mental illness." They argue that the great majority of all psychiatric patients should be considered not "ill" but suffering from problems in living. Probably the best-known spokesman for this point of view is

## FIGURE 7.3

*Over the past twenty years more mental illness has been treated outside mental hospitals than before. This has partly been the result of increasing use of tranquilizers and other medications. Moreover, mental patients are less often hospitalized because it is regarded as a bad idea to isolate them from ordinary social life for any extended period of time.*

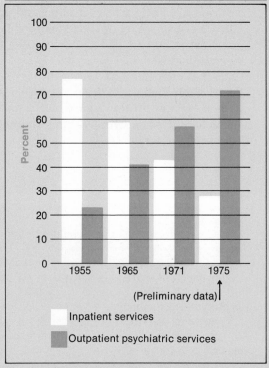

(Preliminary data)

Inpatient services

Outpatient psychiatric services

*Source:* U.S. Bureau of Census. (Washington, D.C.) *Census of Population 1970.* Vol. I, Characteristics of the Population, Part I, Table 167.

we should not assume that there is a precise, scientific diagnosis behind this label. For one thing, the other members of the patient's family may be quite disturbed themselves and may be "scapegoating" the weakest member of the family, whose madness can be best understood as a response to a crazy situation. This does happen. Most psychiatric examinations are brief. Researchers who take the time to interview disturbed people at length, especially in the home or other familiar surroundings, often find that statements that sound odd or meaningless at first can be understood when the context is taken into account.

It is often more valid to regard a given case of mental disorder as a result of a disturbed family situation than to pin it on an individual's own failings. This is not to suggest, of course, that families hospitalize their mentally ill members on flimsy or trumped-up grounds. Most families are unwilling to even consider hospitalization until they have tried every other way they know of coping with the disturbed person.[66] Still, the other family members may have problems of their own, and the troubled relationships that result make for confusion and stress all around. No doubt "craziness" is often a result of being involved in "crazy" relationships. Moreover, the experience of being judged insane, hospitalized, and treated as irresponsible undoubtedly undermines one's self-confidence and creates mistrust of those who arranged for the hospitalization. Some sociologists are convinced that labeling theory applies more clearly to mental illness than to any other form of deviance: The treatment may cause more trouble than the problem it is designed to cure. It may sometimes be more useful to overlook symptoms of mental illness than to treat them. But researchers are by no means in agreement about how often this is the case.

But if sociologists do not agree about how to treat mental illness, they do agree on one point—that problems usually originate in the social structure rather than in the failings of individual personalities. Thus social scientists have shown that mental illness is closely related to different roles and social statuses. Migration, for example, clearly leads to mental disorders.[67] Immigrants leave their social supports behind when they move to a new country, and it takes a

Thomas Szasz, who wrote a book entitled *The Myth of Mental Illness.* Szasz agrees, of course, that many people do behave in odd ways, but he would have them put in jail, rather than in mental hospitals, if they break the law.

Not many sociologists would take such an extreme position.[65] Many would agree, however, that most forms of mental illness should be examined with more skepticism. Just because someone is judged insane and kept in a hospital,

*It is hard to diagnose many cases of mental illness—but not catatonia. If someone raises the patient's arm, she will leave it up for a long time.*

long time for them to make up for what they have lost. In times of stress, the lack of such supports may leave a person unable to cope.

Sex roles are also related to mental illness. Since World War II more women than men have been mental patients—at least they have received more treatment for disorders that involve anxiety, unhappiness, and a sense of inadequacy. However, they are not more likely than men to experience disorders caused by organic conditions or personality disorders, such as addictions and violent or antisocial behavior.[68]

The most important factor related to mental illness seems to be social class. A number of studies have reported that lower-class people are much more likely to be psychotic than middle- or upper-class people.[69] They are found in large numbers in mental hospitals with symptoms that are especially serious and difficult to treat. They are more often treated with drugs, electroshock therapy, and simple custodial care than middle-class patients, who are more commonly "neurotic" and, hence, are treated with psychotherapy as private out-patients than as inmates of hospitals. The lower-class patient is likely to remain longer in the mental hospital

*201*

once admitted, and is also more likely to return to the hospital than the middle- or upper-class patient.

Any mental patient who returns to the community faces many problems. People often are embarrassed and shun such people, and employers are unwilling to hire them. But these problems seem to be more serious for lower-class than for upper-class ex-patients.

A great deal depends on the economy. Indeed, for more than a century there has been a clear relationship between upturns and downturns in the general economy and rates of mental illness.[70] People who cannot earn the income that they feel they should earn tend to break down emotionally.

The exact sequence of events is not so sim-

ple, however. Social scientists have been trying to clarify it for a whole generation and are still dissatisfied. The issue is this: Low social status and mental disorder go together. We know that. But which causes which? You can make a good case for either argument. That is, because lower-class people are under a great deal of stress, are they more likely to become mentally ill than other people? Or, conversely, because mentally ill people cannot function very well at work and in social events, do they lose their jobs and "skid" down to the lower class? Does poverty cause mental illness, or does mental illness cause poverty? We know that these two variables are strongly linked, but it is unclear which is more often the cause and which the effect.[71]

# SOCIAL POLICY:
## Issues and Viewpoints

In this section we will discuss the problem of how to turn bad guys into good guys. And we must hurry—there is not a moment to lose! Let's look at the major theoretical approaches already mentioned and see if they can offer any specific recommendations for public policy.

### POLICY AND KINDS-OF-PEOPLE THEORIES

Psychodynamic approaches to deviance recommend that *all children should experience stable affection, consistent discipline, and security,* especially in their early relationships with their parents. Thousands of studies show the effects of unhappy family life on subsequent behavior.

However, the family is the most private area of social interaction. Only in totalitarian societies does the public have the authority to tell people how to bring up their children. If North American children are abused, they may be pro-

tected from their parents; in other family matters the state is not allowed to interfere. Hence, public policy in matters of socialization is almost useless. Therapy and support should be available to anyone who needs help in family matters, but it does not look as if this will greatly reduce adult alcoholism or other forms of deviance. Fortunately, however, there are other approaches.

### POLICY AND SITUATION THEORIES

All three forms of situation theory—anomie, cultural-transmission, and role-self—make important recommendations. As with all important policy issues, these recommendations are subjects of much debate, and we expect many readers to disagree with them.

#### Policies derived from anomie theory

Merton's basic idea is that when people do not have a chance to pursue culturally approved goals through legitimate activities they are likely to turn to illegitimate activities. There are two ways of avoiding this problem. One is to persuade people to be satisfied with less. In earlier times this approach actually worked; peasants never hoped to wear velvet and eat roasted peacock, as the lord of the manor did, because they were taught to be content with their "station in life." However, those days are over. It is useless to tell working-class North Americans to be content with poverty.

The alternative, then, is to provide more *legitimate opportunities.* People often turn to crime when they cannot get what they want in any other way. This is why crime rates are often higher among underprivileged groups. Opening up new legitimate opportunities would fight crime more successfully than punishment does.

### Policies based on cultural transmission theory

Cultural-transmission theory holds that individuals learn deviant behavior by participating in deviant subcultures. Therefore we should get the individual out of a procriminal subculture if possible. The state should carry out any policy that will undercut the procriminal subcultures and turn their members toward other social groups. This, paradoxically, may be done by legalizing certain activities that are now illegal. Deviant subcultures often attract members by offering things that people want but cannot get legally—homosexual contacts, crap games, abortions, marijuana, or pornographic movies, for example. The reasons for participating in an underground community disappear if the illegal things are made legal. Thus during Prohibition people who wanted liquor had to deal with the underworld. Their contacts with this subculture led to greater tolerance for other kinds of illegal activity, and the gangsters got richer. Ending Prohibition automatically removed the ordinary wine drinker from a deviant subculture and put most bootleggers out of business.

Making an undesirable activity illegal often leads to more serious problems. Outlawing abortion does not prevent abortions; instead, it creates abortion rackets and causes many women to go through unnecessarily dangerous operations. Outlawing homosexuality does not change people into heterosexuals; instead, it makes it impossible for them to lead normal lives and enables blackmailers to exploit them. Outlawing drug use does not prevent pot smokers from turning on or junkies from shooting heroin, but it does pull them into the underworld subculture, where they learn positive attitudes toward the violation of laws. This is where marijuana users learn to become heroin users. It also enables organized crime to profit from illegal drugs and forces the addict to turn to crime to pay for drugs that would be cheaper if they were sold legally. Legalizing the use of these drugs under certain conditions would take business away from criminal outfits and, by making it unnecessary for users to have contacts with other users, eliminate the deviant subculture.

### Policies based on role-self theory

Role-self theory has attracted a lot of attention recently, especially because of its emphasis on labeling—the view that a deviant career generally begins when the offender is officially labeled "deviant." Who is a "juvenile delinquent"? It is a youth who has been caught violating a law. Many of us are *qualified* for the same role, since we have broken many laws, but we have not acquired that identity because we were not caught. Who is a "skid row alcoholic"? It is the drunk who is taken to jail instead of home. Only the official action thrusts the stigmatized role upon the offender. Once the label has been assigned, however, the offender continues to play the part of the delinquent or the drunk, as the case may be. Role-self theory suggests that we avoid stigmatizing people or labeling them as deviant. Do not make them into outsiders or endanger their relationships in normal society; instead, protect the dignity of their self-image and preserve their roles as normal, reputable human beings.

Sometimes efforts to help people backfire because this point is ignored. For example, the government has provided aid to the poor through food stamps and housing projects. But the poor can claim these benefits only by playing a stigmatized role—that of "welfare recipient." Likewise, probation officers want to identify delinquents as early as possible so that they can be "treated" before their character is firmly established. In many cases this may be the wrong approach: The "treatment" itself gives the child a delinquent identity. When in doubt, it might be better to treat children as if they were expected to behave normally rather than as if they were expected to get into trouble.

It usually causes fewer problems to let people have what they want legally (even if it is not good for them) than to try to stop them from getting what they want illegally. Thus the best way to stop organized crime might be to legalize gambling and provide free medical maintenance for narcotics addicts. The best way to keep marijuana users from switching to harder drugs might be to legalize pot. And so on.

Unfortunately, this policy is not a cure-all. Legalizing people's vices may not get rid of them, and in some cases it may even encourage them. Ending Prohibition did not end alcoholism. Thus we have not solved the problem of evil in this chapter, but we have used up our space and must leave the remaining problems for you to work on.

## SUMMARY

**1.** *Deviance* is any form of behavior that violates the norms of a social group or of society. It includes deviant behavior (e.g., crimes, sexual deviance, and suicide), deviant habits (e.g., alcoholism, drug addiction, and compulsive gambling), deviant psychologies (mental and emotional disorders), and deviant cultures (e.g., the counterculture). Deviant behavior is not uncommon. A number of studies have shown that most people have violated the law. Deviant habits are a major problem too. Heavy drinking, for example, not only has a harmful chemical effect on the body but also tends to damage social relationships.

**2.** Deviance is an interactional process that is created as much by conformist behavior as by deviant behavior. The conformers make the rules, enforce them, and label those who break them "deviant."

**3.** *Social control* consists of the methods by which members of a group try to get others to follow the prescribed norms. Among these methods are socialization, informal group pressure, and the use of social sanctions — rewards and punishments.

**4.** The worst effect of deviance on social organizations is its erosion of members' trust in the organization. However, deviance may also have effects that support social organization. These effects include (1) cutting red tape, (2) acting as a safety valve, (3) clarifying rules, (4) uniting the group, (5) highlighting conformity, and (6) acting as a warning signal.

**5.** Durkheim believed that a certain amount of deviance is tolerated by society, and in testing this theory Kai Erikson found that deviance occurred among the New England Puritans at a fairly constant rate.

**6.** Behavior is deviant only if the actor has to answer to the group whose rules his or her behavior violates. *Role conflict* happens when one has two or more different roles that make contradictory demands.

**7.** Theories of deviance may be classified into two basic types — *kinds-of-people* theories and *situation* theories. Kinds-of-people theories can, in turn, be classified as biological or psychological. The biological explanations include Lombroso's positivism, Sheldon's constitutional typology of body forms, and the chromosomal explanation. The psychodynamic explanations are based on Freudian psychoanalysis. They claim that deviance is caused by a weak superego, a weak ego, aggression caused by frustration, or defense mechanisms such as reaction formation. All of the kinds-of-people theories have one weakness: They don't explain why a certain "kind of person" commits a deviant act once in a while but not always. To explain that, one must turn to situation theories, (e.g., anomie theory).

**8.** According to Durkheim, *anomie* is a condition of social instability in which people cannot organize their behavior rationally in relation to a predictable system of rewards and punishments. This is especially true in periods of prosperity or depression, and suicides increase at such times. Durkheim believed that this happens because people's goals can't remain stable under such conditions.

**9.** Merton extended the idea of anomie as a gap between culturally approved goals and institutionalized means. He listed five types of responses to this situation—conformity, retreatism, ritualism, innovation, and rebellion. This theory does not explain why some people choose one type of deviant response and others choose another type, nor does it tell us why some people continue to conform even when they are suffering from anomie.

**10.** Cultural-transmission theory is another situation theory. It holds that the deviant is merely conforming to a subculture that is, from the point of view of the larger society, deviant. Sutherland's version of this approach (called *differential association theory*) holds that a person becomes criminal because he or she is exposed to a larger number of definitions that are favorable to violation of the law than definitions that are unfavorable to violation of the law.

**11.** Role-self theory, a symbolic-interactionist approach, is based on the assumption that a person's identity is built up and maintained by social interaction. An individual claims to be a certain kind of person and must behave in ways that support that claim. However, a deviant identity is sometimes forced on people against their will. *Labeling theory*, a version of role-self theory, holds that being arrested or committed to a mental hospital are events that label a person as delinquent or criminal or mentally ill. Cultural-transmission theories do not explain how or why deviant subcultures come into existence. Role-self theory contributes most in combination with anomie theory.

# KEY TERMS

**anomie**  normlessness or deregulation; confusion about what one may hope for or expect to accomplish.

**culture goals**  the wants and ambitions that people are taught by their society.

**deviance**  any form of behavior that violates the norms of a social group.

**institutionalized means**  the resources available to the individual and considered appropriate to use in pursuing his or her goals.

**labeling**  the social definition of a person as deviant.

**norms**  rules that prescribe the legitimate means of pursuing one's goals.

**reaction formation**  a mechanism for denying an unacceptable element of the personality.

**role conflict**  the situation in which conformity to one role requires deviance from another.

**sanction**  a reward for desirable behavior or a punishment for undesirable behavior.

**social control**  the ways in which members of a group punish deviance and try to get others to live up to society's norms.

**stigma**  the mark of disgrace that is attached to people in disvalued roles.

# FOR FURTHER READING

BECKER, HOWARD S. *Outsiders: Studies in the Sociology of Deviance.* New York: Free Press, 1963. The field of deviance is a good topic to specialize in if you are a little kinky yourself or if you like to read about odd people. There are hundreds of books on deviance that are really intriguing. Becker is one of the best writers in the field, and this book is a nice one of his to begin with.

CLINARD, MARSHALL B. *Anomie and Deviant Behavior.* New York: Free Press, 1964. Not at all kinky, but straight scholarly analysis, this is an important theoretical discussion of the implications of the anomie approach.

COHEN, ALBERT K. *Deviance and Control.* Englewood Cliffs, N.J.: Prentice-Hall, 1966. This chapter on deviance is largely drawn from Cohen's book. I suggest you go to the original to find out how much you have missed in the version presented here.

COOPERSTOCK, RUTH, ed. *Social Aspects of the Medical Use of Psychotropic Drugs.* Toronto: Addiction Research Foundation, 1974. For a good discussion of drugs, this collection of sociological papers is a sound choice.

DURKHEIM, EMILE. *Suicide.* Translated by George Simpson. New York: Free Press, 1951. First published in French by Alcan, 1897. One of the classic books in sociology, this is nevertheless not very hard to read. I assign it every year to students in Introductory Sociology, firmly believing it will do them good. Some of them agree.

HAGAN, JOHN. *The Disreputable Pleasures.* Toronto: McGraw-Hill Ryerson, 1976. For a well-written text that focuses on the relation between social control and naughty behavior, see this medium-sized book.

RADINOWICZ, SIR LEON, and JOAN KING. *The Growth of Crime: The International Experience.* New York: Basic Books, 1977. Radinowicz is an outstanding historian of criminal law and this fine book gives an excellent treatment of crime rates and theories that have been proposed to explain and control them. Very solid.

SHORT, JAMES F., JR., ed. *Delinquency, Crime and Society.* Chicago: University of Chicago Press, 1976. A fine collection of essays written from the perspective of the Chicago School. It is not an introductory treatment of issues, so I suggest that you read one or two other deviance books (e.g. Hagan's) before choosing this one.

SIMON, RITA JAMES. *Women and Crime.* Lexington, Mass.: D.C. Heath, 1978. I have my own sexist stereotypes: when I refer to a criminal, I automatically say "he," not "she." This book, however, shows how male and female offenders are punished for similar crimes. It also discusses the future of women in crime.

TURK, AUSTIN T. *Criminality and Legal Order.* Chicago: Rand McNally, 1969. Future criminologists or lawyers would do well to begin with this book—future policepersons, too.

# TWO
## social
## interaction

8

# ORGANIZATIONS

How many organizations have you had dealings with today? The phone company? The post office? The subway system? Your college? Your church? The public library? That's only a beginning. Think of the products you have used that are made by corporations — Ford, IBM, Esso, Borden's, and so on. Go on. There's more. The Weather Bureau? NBC television? The garbage collectors? Termite control? The fact is, you're in it. You're part of the system. There is no way you can avoid it!

Organizations are not modern inventions. Through organizations the pharaohs built pyramids, the emperors of China built irrigation systems, and the first popes built a universal church. But it is fair to say that modern society is *organizational society.*[1] Not only are there more organizations now than ever before, but modern life depends on them.

By fitting together a large number of human activities, the organization becomes a powerful social tool. It combines its members and its resources, bringing together leaders, experts, workers, machines, and raw materials. At the same time, it is constantly judging how well it is performing and trying to adjust itself in order to achieve its goals. As we will see, this allows the organization to serve the various needs of society and its citizens more efficiently than they could be served by smaller and more natural human groupings, such as families, friendship groups, and communities.

In this chapter we will discuss all sorts of organizations, ranging from voluntary associations, such as the sisterhood of a synagogue or the Metropolitan Opera Guild, to huge multinational corporations, such as ITT or General Motors. Most of our attention will center on complex, formal organizations called bureaucracies. These organizations greatly increase the effectiveness of human labor, but at the same time they demand obedience from members and ignore their unique personal needs.

# Characteristics of organizations

Organizations are social units (or human groups) that are deliberately constructed and reconstructed to pursue specific goals.[2] Corporations, armies, schools, hospitals, churches, public utilities, and prisons are examples of organizations, while tribes, classes, ethnic groups, friendship groups, and families are not. Three characteristics of organizations set them apart from other types of social groups: (1) division of labor, power, and communication; (2) power centers; and (3) substitution of personnel.

## DIVISION OF LABOR, POWER, AND COMMUNICATION

The organization plans how to divide up the responsibilities of its members in order to achieve its goals most efficiently. Not only is the work divided into different jobs for different people, but the division of power is carefully planned. In addition, a system is set up for providing particular kinds of information to appropriate members of the organization. None of these matters is determined by tradition or chance, as they might be in a family or a friendship group. Instead, organizations make these arrangements quite deliberately.

## POWER CENTERS

Organizations have one or more power centers that control the workings of the organization and direct it toward its goals. These power centers review the organization's performance and adjust it, where necessary, in order to increase its efficiency.

An organization can assign its members to particular roles and jobs as needed to achieve its purposes. It can remove unsatisfactory people or demote them. It can transfer members or promote them.

Other groups have some of these characteristics too, of course. Organizations are not the only groups that plan. (For example, your family may keep a budget.) Nor are organizations the only groups that have power centers (tribes have chiefs) or replaceable membership (married people can divorce and remarry). However, organizations do much more purposeful planning and have more frequent member turnover than other social groups. They are more in control of their characteristics and goals than any other social group.

## Kinds of organizations

Organizations differ in the types of goals they pursue and in the complexity of their roles. Almost all organizations have a recognized system for setting goals and changing them. Stockholders or trustees may do this by voting, for example. Organizations differ in their degree of formality — they range from the local Boy Scout troop to a complex modern hospital with research, therapy, and teaching responsibilities. Thus voluntary organizations are the least formal and bureaucracies the most formal. Let's start with voluntary groups.

### VOLUNTARY ASSOCIATIONS

You may have mixed feelings about large organizations such as insurance companies, the army, or the tax bureau. I do. We are

*Many voluntary organizations are organized simply for the pleasure and relaxation of the members.*

Peter Menzel/Stock, Boston

forced to deal with such organizations in order to get along in our society. However, you are probably more favorable toward certain other organizations. I am thinking, for example, of such groups as the YMCA, the Lions Club, the League of Women Voters, fan clubs, and amateur symphony orchestras. These are **voluntary associations** — groups that people join because they support the organization's goals and values. You join such groups knowing that you will probably participate in them only in your spare time and that you can quit whenever you choose. As a result the members are usually committed to the group and feel that it is responsive to them.

Sociologists have made many studies of voluntary organizations, and we know a lot about the people who join them. Middle-aged people are more likely to join than younger or older people. The higher your social class, your education, and your income, the more likely you are to join. Married people join more than single people. English Canadians (especially women) are more likely to join than French Canadians. Finally, men are generally more likely to join

than women. However, this factor differs quite a bit from one country to another.[3]

Do citizens of different countries differ much? Yes. James Curtis compared patterns of joining in the United States, Canada, Great Britain, Germany, Italy, and Mexico.[4] I'll present his results, leaving out the figures on people who belong to labor unions. After all, it's not clear whether a union is a "voluntary association" or a kind of bureaucracy. Curtis finds that Canada and the United States are about equally "nations of joiners." The other four countries are less so. In every country education is the most powerful factor in the rate of joining (See Table 8.1.) In most countries men are far more likely to join groups than women — but this is not so in Canada and the United States. Here the sexes are about equal in this respect. (See Table 8.2.)

If you haven't already looked at these tables, try to guess what percentage of North Americans are members of some group (other than a union). The answer: about half. Among the Italians and Mexicans only about one-quarter are members of groups. Males don't differ much when compared cross-nationally. It's the women who differ. Much

**TABLE 8.1**
*Voluntary association membership (nonunion) by education, six countries*

| COUNTRY (YEAR OF SURVEY) | PERCENTAGE OF RESPONDENTS BELONGING TO ASSOCIATIONS | | |
| --- | --- | --- | --- |
| | ELEMENTARY EDUCATION | SECONDARY EDUCATION | POSTSECONDARY EDUCATION |
| Canada (1968) | 42 | 60 | 79 |
| United States (1960) | 36 | 48 | 79 |
| West Germany (1959) | 29 | 61 | 53 |
| Great Britain (1959) | 26 | 43 | 70 |
| Italy (1959) | 22 | 31 | 46 |
| Mexico (1959) | 12 | 29 | 67 |

*Source:* James Curtis, "Voluntary Associations Joining: A Cross-National Comparative Note," *American Sociological Review*, 36 (October 1971), p. 874.

**TABLE 8.2**

*Voluntary association membership (nonunion) by sex, six countries*

| COUNTRY (YEAR OF SURVEY) | PERCENTAGE OF RESPONDENTS BELONGING TO ASSOCIATIONS | | |
| --- | --- | --- | --- |
| | MALE | FEMALE | TOTAL |
| Canada (1968) | 51 | 51 | 51 |
| United States (1960) | 55 | 46 | 50 |
| West Germany (1959) | 47 | 22 | 34 |
| Great Britain (1959) | 41 | 27 | 33 |
| Italy (1959) | 36 | 17 | 25 |
| Mexico (1959) | 21 | 12 | 15 |

*Source:* James Curtis, "Voluntary Associations Joining: A Cross-National Comparative Note," *American Sociological Review*, 36 (October 1971), p. 874.

of the strength of voluntary associations in North America is due to the exceptionally active participation of women. This is an important contribution to the integration of democratic society—one that has not been fully recognized. Let's hear it for the altar guild and the PTA!

### BUREAUCRACIES

**Bureaucracies** are organizations with a hierarchy of offices set up to do work; the army and the government are examples. Generally, bureaucracies are much more formal than voluntary associations; they have detailed rules and norms. A **hierarchy** is a chain of command in which each person has authority over several other people, who may in turn have authority over lower-ranking members, and so on. You might call it a pecking order. The hierarchy of ranks in the army is a familiar example.

I always think of a tangle of red tape when I think of a bureaucracy. In fact, however, bureaucracies are very efficient in their handling of routine matters. They may not always be personal, but they *are* rational. Unfortunately, efficiency and human happi-

ness do not always support each other. Instead of being society's obedient servant, the organization sometimes becomes its master. Not all work can be profitable and satisfying, and not all regulations are acceptable to everyone. Thus the problem of modern organizations is how to build efficient human groups that offer the maximum satisfaction to all of their members.

### The organizational revolution

An important aspect of modernization is the development of many large organizations. Nearly half of the corporate wealth in the United States, for example, is held by 200 large corporations. Modernization means building factories, schools, universities, political parties, and of course, the modern state, itself a huge bureaucracy. It is true that some forms of bureaucracy existed in preindustrial society (e.g., medieval universities, commercial organizations in the Italian city-states, and state bureaucracies in ancient Egypt, China, and Byzantium). However, these groups were few in number, had relatively few members, and differed in a number of ways from modern bureaucracies. It is only in industrial societies that organizations have become important. For example, today about half of the American labor force works for giant organizations.[5]

### Max Weber on bureaucracy

Most of our understanding of bureaucracy is based on a model that was first proposed by Max Weber. Let us begin by sketching his model of bureaucracy.[6] This is an imaginary bureaucracy that represents the principles and tendencies of real bureaucracies with which Weber was familiar. No single business or government office would show all these traits all the time. Weber's model simply outlines the traits of a perfectly rational social machine. He personally had mixed feelings about bureaucracy, for he saw that all organizations have to limit human freedom in order to be efficient. The organization has to get all its members to obey it, and this results in the loss of individual freedom to make decisions. A person becomes a "cog" in the machine. Thus an organization has two somewhat contradictory requirements: (1) to make people do what it wants them to do and (2) to make them happy with this arrangement.

As Weber saw, an organization has power — the ability to get its way despite opposition. It can use punishments and rewards to get people to meet its demands. But this may be a self-defeating process. People who are *forced* to obey tend to become alienated. They show no initiative, and in periods of crisis they may successfully disobey the rules.

Weber showed, however, that there is another way of getting people to obey. If a person sees the rules as conforming to his or her own values, he or she will consider them legitimate and find it much less uncomfortable to obey them. This is called legitimation. It does not necessarily make the rule pleasant for the person to obey, but it fulfills the person's need to follow rules that match rather than conflict with his or her own values.

Weber emphasized that there is a big difference between the need served by legitimation and other human needs. Legitimation does not change anyone's material interests. It does not make taking orders either more or less satisfying. An order may be recognized as legitimate and still be quite unpleasant, but this is not always the case.

Thus Weber used power to refer to the ability to get people to take orders and the term legitimation to refer to people's acceptance of the use of power because it is in line with their values. He used a third term, authority, to refer to the combination of the first two. A leader is said to have authority if he or she has power that is regarded as legitimate. As you will see in our discussion of politics in Chapter 15, these terms apply equally well to leadership in private organizations and in public office. A corporation president and a prime minister have much in common, and so did medieval popes and kings. All of them have the authority to make and issue binding orders.

### Weber's typology of authority

Weber described three different types of authority with three different bases of legitimation. In traditional authority the orders of superiors are seen as legitimate because that it is how things are "always done." Tradition itself justifies the existing use of power. The authority of parents over their children is traditional, even if the parents have radical values. Another example of traditional authority was that of the lord of the manor during the Middle Ages.

The second type of authority is charismatic authority. The orders of a charismatic leader are viewed as legitimate because the leader has a magnetic, compelling personal style. This type of authority is often seen in periods of social change, when old rules are pushed aside by the force of a social movement, as when a revolution or a new religion arises to challenge established authority. Russia after 1917 and Nazi Germany after

*Charismatic leaders are followed because of their magnetic, compelling personal style.*

1933 are examples of societies with charismatic leaders.

But it is the third type of authority — **bureaucratic authority** — that interests us most. The members of an organization see a ruling as legitimate if it is consistent with a set of abstract rules with which they all agree and from which the ruling is derived. In this sense it is "rational," and Weber sometimes called bureaucratic authority "rational-legal authority." The Roman courts had developed this type of authority: They gave legitimacy to specific rules derived from more general principles.

Weber suggested that modern organizations require a bureaucratic pattern of authority. Neither traditional nor charismatic authority is as effective as rational-legal authority in keeping a production line or a subway system running smoothly. But bureaucratic authority is hard to maintain; it requires impersonality, self-denial, and narrowness — traits that people may find oppressive. Thus bureaucratic organizations often break down and are replaced by either traditional or charismatic relations.

### Characteristics of bureaucracies

Weber described bureaucracies as having seven typical characteristics:

1 A bureaucracy is a "continuous organization of official functions *bound by* rules." Rules save effort by eliminating the need to derive new solutions for each case as it comes up.

215

They standardize the treatment of many cases. These advantages are impossible if each person is treated as a unique case, that is, as an individual.

2 Each member of bureaucracy has a specific *scope of competence*. Division of labor, rights, and power is necessary in a rational organization. Each member must know his or her job and have a set of duties. Each person must have the resources needed to do the job, including the authority to command others, and each position must have defined limits, rights, and power.

3 "The organization of offices follows the principle of *hierarchy*; that is, each lower office is under the control and supervision of a higher one."

4 "The rules which regulate the conduct of an office may be *technical* rules or norms. In both cases, if their application is to be fully rational, specialized training is necessary." The bureaucrat's knowledge and technical skill is the basis of his or her claim to legitimacy.

5 Organizational affairs are kept separate. The property of the organization is completely separate from the private property of its members. The bureaucrat's personal residence is separate from the organization. This keeps the person's status as a bureaucrat from becoming tangled with his or her status in other groups.

6 The official does not "own" his or her office. On the contrary, a bureaucracy's resources have to be *free to be redistributed* according to the needs of the organization.

7 Administrative acts, decisions, and rules are *recorded in writing*. When carried to an ex-

**Figure 8.1**

*Typical organization chart of a small corporation*

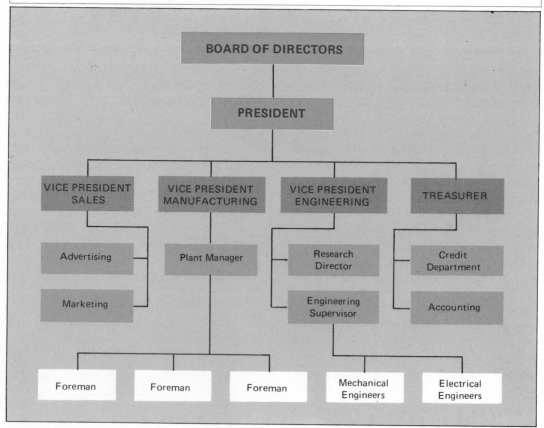

treme this procedure is often referred to as "red tape," but Weber considered it important. He argued that it is impossible to interpret norms and enforce rules in a consistent way without written records.

Weber pointed out that bureaucracies have nonbureaucratic leaders. Bureaucrats follow rules, but the person at the top decides the goals that the rules are designed to serve. Although bureaucrats are appointed, their leader is often elected or inherits his or her position. It is helpful if the leader provides a warm, visible image with which the members can identify. Historically, some bureaucracies have developed out of charismatic movements—for example, the organized church out of the early Christian movement and the Soviet Union out of the communist movement. The successors of charismatic leaders may have little charisma of their own, but keep the support of the lower-level members by using the charisma of the position they occupy. Thus the pope is viewed as representing Jesus and for this reason has inherited some of his charisma. These secondary leaders, according to Weber, never have as much charisma as the founder of the movement. On the contrary, they gradually use up the charisma of their position, until finally it is gone and they lose their legitimacy. Weber's theory of history thus suggests that an organization falls apart when a new charismatic leader overthrows the old regime and replaces it with a new one.

Because low-ranking bureaucrats have to obey orders from those above them, it does not much matter who occupies these lower positions. When a lower officer is replaced, obedience continues without interruption. This is true all the way up through the hierarchy, except at the very top. The nonbureaucratic leader of the organization is the one person to whom commitment is personal rather than bureaucratic. His or her departure or death may bring on a major organizational crisis—the crisis of succession.

Actually, needed changes are often made during this period. It may or may not be a dangerous moment in the life of an organization. For example, often a university suffers a decline after the death of its founder, only to recover when another charismatic leader takes office. Thus Weber's description of bureaucracies should not be viewed as valid in every case, even though it is the working model used by almost all later analysts.

# The structure of organizations

### FORMAL STRUCTURE

All organizations are planned. This planning involves setting up a formal structure of definite rights, duties, privileges, hierarchies of authority and power, and routines that the group is supposed to follow in carrying out its collective work. This *formal* structure can be called the "blueprint" for the organization. In the case of a large, complex organization it can be illustrated by an organization chart, a pyramid of little squares that each represent an agency or position. (See Figure 8.1.) A written constitution may also set forth rules about authority and its limits, who is to perform what jobs, what sanctions will be used to reward or punish good and bad performance, and so on. A small voluntary organization, such as a babysitting pool, may not need to write down all of its rules, but all members must understand them. For example, decisions must be made on questions such as who will keep records, how many points should be given per hour of nighttime sitting and how many per hour of daytime sitting, and the like.

### INFORMAL STRUCTURE

The formal structure is vital and cannot be ignored, but everybody who participates in a large organization soon realizes that it does not fully describe the way that organization really works. Many informal structures de-

*A prison is one example of the coercive power used by governmental organizations to see that the members of a society follow the rules.*

velop in addition to the formal ones. These are the unwritten rules and other understandings that members must keep in mind in order to get through the day. Thus on paper the vice president in charge of marketing may be responsible for contract negotiations. However, her subordinates may realize that she is absentminded and that they can get a contract approved more quickly if they go to her secretary, who knows everything and influences everything she does. Formally, the vice president has the power; informally, the secretary does. The informal structure that develops in an organization depends largely on the personal relationships among the various members. Thus, if the vice president's secretary resigns and is replaced by a

dimwit, the informal system cannot work the way it did before and some new system will develop. As we will see shortly, the human-relations approach to the study of organizations is especially concerned with informal structures.

## Organizational control and leadership

Here's the part we don't like: Every organization has to control the actions of its members. Not every action, of course, but some of them. Little control is necessary when the needs of the members fit the needs of the organization. In this happy situation people will do what is best for the organization because it also satisfies their own needs. And the organization, by serving its own needs, will serve theirs. Unfortunately, such a delightful fit between individual and organizational needs is rare. Usually organizations have to reward those who conform to its rules and punish those who do not. Organizations are artificial, planned social groups. Unlike natural social groups such as the family and the ethnic group, they cannot rely on informal social control to get their members to do their jobs. They require additional incentives. An organization gets its members to do what it wants in several ways. Let's look at some of those ways.

Organizations may use three types of social control: physical, material, and symbolic.[7] Physical means of control include devices such as guns, whips, or locks. This is coercive power. Material means of control consist of rewards such as goods, services, or money. If you use material means of control, you are using what we will call utilitarian power. Finally, symbolic means of control are such rewards as respect, prestige, love, and acceptance. When you use symbolic means, we will say that you are using normative power. For example, a successful pep talk requires normative power.

Different kinds of organizations use different kinds of power. For example, prisons are basically coercive, factories basically utilitarian, and churches basically normative. Prisoners are locked up; factory workers are paid; and church members are thanked and prayed for. We may thus classify organizations as coercive, normative, or utilitarian.

The more commitment a kind of power stimulates, the less alienating its effect is on the members of the group. Normative power stimulates more commitment than utilitarian power, and utilitarian power more than coercive power. Alienation follows the opposite pattern. Prisoners will be most alienated and least committed, factory workers

somewhere in between, and church members least alienated and most committed.

The more coercive an organization is, the less its officials can rely on *personal* power to control its members. Thus prison wardens are obeyed not because of their personal qualities but because of their coercive resources. The informal inmate leaders are the true leaders in a prison, and this is due to their personal qualities. At the other extreme, officials of normative organizations such as churches use personal power as a major resource. Parish priests may be chosen on the basis of their persuasiveness and may get further training in persuasiveness. Priests without personal power may be transfered to positions that exercise little control—to scholarly work, for example.

Hospitals are also normative organizations. Doctors must persuade patients to follow orders voluntarily. A doctor's bedside manner, or persuasive power, is extremely important because he or she has no coercive power and because patients have no way of determining whether doctors are competent or not. The instructions of the most intelligent physician may not be followed if they are given in a wavering voice.

Organizations that are basically normative are usually successful in maintaining the authority of their formal leaders. In contrast, coercive organizations often find social control slipping into the hands of informal leaders, with whom the officials have to make some accommodation. Utilitarian organizations often distribute control among organizational officials and informal leaders of employees. In industries where workers are alienated and feel coerced, informal leaders usually control all of the expressive activities and many of the instrumental ones. (Expressive activities are those that involve emotional and interpersonal relationships, such as a party or a bowling team. Instrumental activities are those done for some practical purpose, such as the work done on the job.)

In factories where workers are less alienated, formal leaders have more control, particularly over instrumental activities but even over some expressive activities. For example, the Christmas party is typical, not of the alienated factory but of the less alienated business office, where white-collar workers feel at ease socializing with one another and with their bosses under the influence of company liquor. Factory workers probably would not enjoy such a party.

### Alternatives to control

We can think of these three forms of control—coercive, utilitarian, and normative—as ways of coordinating the activities of members of an organization so that the organization can achieve its goals. However, none of these forms of control is indispensable. There are other ways of making sure that members cooperate according to plan. One alternative to control is *selectivity*; another is *socialization*.

An organization that can be selective in choosing members can spend less time and effort on control. Coercive organizations usually cannot reject anyone who is sent to them, and they therefore have to pay a lot of attention to the problem of control. However, some coercive institutions operate selectively and can use less control. Open wards in mental hospitals and unguarded prison farms are more effective than locked wards and fenced-in prisons, but this is probably because the inmates are chosen because they show promise of responding well to such programs.[8]

Utilitarian and normative organizations differ in how selective they are. For example, most democratic political parties in the West are highly unselective; the Soviet Communist party, by contrast, is highly selective. Private schools are far more selective than public schools. Highly selective organizations usually are more effective and get more commitment from their members than un-

*Japanese society is highly organized.*

Wide World

selective organizations. However, this is only partly because of their selectivity; for the most part it is because such organizations are generally richer and have more resources available to them.

The second alternative to control is socialization. The more effective the socialization, the less the need for control.[9] However, socialization is itself affected by the means of control used. For example, coercive organizations cannot effectively socialize their members, simply because they *are* coercive. (Remember, in Chapter 4 I said that socialization consists largely of learning to *want* to do what you *must* do—learning to want to play the roles that will be available for you to play, for example. Socialization works best when it works *with* your will instead of against it. If you force people to do something it is likely that they will hate doing it.)

Utilitarian organizations expect other organizations, such as schools and universities, to do their socialization for them. They can then select as their members people who are already socialized. Medical schools, for example, tend to choose students who are relatives of physicians. Why? Because they are already partially socialized, and this makes the medical school's job easier. Such students have already been exposed to professional attitudes and norms. Finally, organizations that rely heavily on normative power are the most successful in their socialization of members.

## Theoretical approaches to organizations

In sociology, as in all other fields, a point of view becomes fashionable, attracts criticism, and finally is replaced by other points of view. I want to tell you about three approaches to organizations that have had their day. The first of these goes by several names. I will call it the *classical approach*, but it is also known as the *formal* or *scientific-management* approach. The second approach is called the *human-relations* approach, and the third may be called the *structuralist* approach. It is the dominant view today, so we'll pay more attention to it than to the others. But let's discuss these three points of view in the order in which they developed.

### THE CLASSICAL APPROACH

This approach was especially concerned with establishing principles that might help a manager run a productive enterprise such as a factory. Hence the term *scientific management*. The main idea was that if a job was broken up into smaller, more specialized activities workers would become more efficient and output would increase. Those who favored this idea supposed that workers were motivated only by material rewards.

The classical school always thought of an organization in terms of its formal structure. This was the "blueprint" that defined responsibilities and authority in a rational way. The organization was supposed to be very specific about its division of labor and to have highly specialized members and a clear hierarchy of authority. A forerunner of the classical school was Adam Smith, an economist who, in *The Wealth of Nations* (1776), described how a rational division of labor increased pin production in a factory several hundred times over.

There is no question that the classical approach has influenced the way organizations function in modern society. Ordinary people think of an organization in terms of a pyramid of little boxes. I imagine you sitting in yours and me sitting in mine, with arrows connecting us. We also think in terms of incentives to get the work done better and ways of dividing up a job to get it done faster. The person who first dreamed up such plans was Frederick W. Taylor, the father of the time-and-motion study.[10] Taylor seems to have seen human beings as the parts of a machine. Many factory managers took to "Taylorism" with great enthusiasm. Charlie Chaplin made fun of Taylor's approach in a 1936 movie called *Modern Times*. See it if you ever have a chance. Chaplin plays a little man on the assembly line trying to keep up with his machine under pressure from exploitive managers. They speed up the conveyor belt, feed him on the job with an automatic feeding machine that misfires its spoon, and so on.

Taylor suggested that if material rewards are closely linked to work output the worker will respond with maximum performance. Taylor's students, the "human engineers,"

wanted to determine which physical motions were the least tiring so that the human body could do more work with less fatigue in a given amount of time. Taylor believed that workers should be paid piecework wages, for in that way their pay would be directly determined by the amount of actual work they did. Although some engineers still do time-and-motion studies, few social scientists today accept Taylor's idea that people are driven by economic motives—the fear of hunger and the search for profit. There's more to it than that.

The classical theorists tried to improve the division of labor in organizations.[11] They

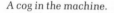
*A cog in the machine.*

assumed that the more a particular job can be divided up, the more specialized and skilled a worker can become at his or her part of the job. And the more skilled each worker becomes, the more efficient the whole system will be. As the division of labor increases, the whole system has to be coordinated and supervised according to a central plan of action. Workers need supervisors, who in turn must be supervised by someone else. Nobody should control more than five to ten subordinates. Hence the pyramid of control, with the executive leader at the top.

So far, so good. What the classical writers disagreed about, however, was the way in which the labor shoud be divided. There were four different principles of specialization, and no one knew for sure which one was most efficient:

1 Specialization by *goal*. For example, the army specializes in land defense, the navy in sea defense, and the air force in air defense.
2 Specialization by *process*, so that workers whose work is similar work together. For example, everyone who gathers military information has similar procedures to follow, whether the information is to be used by the air force, the navy, or the army. Accordingly, they all work together as a single unit.
3 Specialization by *type of clientele*. For example, teachers of the very young work in different schools from teachers of adolescents.
4 Specialization by *geographical area*. This principle proposes that jobs be grouped together if they are in the same geographical area. For example, all American military units in Southeast Asia—whether army, navy, or air force—are under one command.

Although many classical writers have tried to apply these four principles of organization, the results have not been very useful either for analyzing existing organizations or for planning new ones. It is hard to test these principles to find out which is the most efficient. Besides, managers rarely have to decide what sort of structure to set up. Most organizations simply grow up like a jungle, as a result of many separate decisions, instead of like a building, which is planned at one time.

So the classical approach has changed over time. Nowadays people aren't trying so hard to find the "right" organizational structure. But there is more interest in comparing certain *types* of structure. For example, classical writers today are discussing whether centralized or decentralized decision making is more efficient. There is no "right" answer; there are advantages and disadvantages to both approaches. It seems that centralized organizations can often provide facilities more easily than independent local organizations. However, this advantage may be offset by the fact that they may become too rigid to meet special local needs.

## THE HUMAN-RELATIONS APPROACH

The human-relations school began when various researchers made several discoveries that contradicted the assumptions of the classical approach:

1 They noticed that the amount of work done is not determined by a worker's physical capacity (as Taylor has suggested) but by his or her "social capacity," that is, relations with co-workers.
2 They saw that noneconomic rewards play a central role in the motivation and happiness of the worker.
3 They found that specialization is not always the most efficient form of division of labor.
4 Finally, they found that workers react to the norms and rewards of management not as individuals but as members of groups.

On the basis of these observations, the human-relations school focused on the role of communication, participation, and leadership.

### The Hawthorne studies

Many of these conclusions were reached as a result of research done by Elton Mayo and a group of researchers at the Western

Electric Company's Hawthorne plant in Chicago between 1927 and 1932. The results of these Hawthorne studies were so surprising that they seemed to call for a closer look at the assumptions behind the classical approach.[12]

The Hawthorne studies began as an effort to test the claim of the classical school that there is a simple, direct relationship between physical working conditions and rate of production. In their experiments they set out to vary "physical" factors such as the amount of lighting and the length of the workers' rest periods, but it soon became apparent that whether they increased these factors or decreased them the production rates rose and continued to rise! The researchers discontinued the rest breaks altogether and dimmed the lights, and still the production rate was high. The puzzled researchers were forced to conclude that the increasing production rate resulted from a "social" factor—the satisfaction the workers felt because they were put into the experimental room and given attention. This was to become the major finding of the Hawthorne studies.

The breakthrough in the Hawthorne research came with the famous bank-wiring-room experiment involving a group of fourteen workers whose job was to wire sets of switchboards (called "banks"). This experiment called into question almost all the assumptions of the classical approach. Many additional, more complicated studies have verified the findings of the bank-wiring-room study. When this experiment was set up the researchers already knew that the workers were producing far less than they could if they worked at full capacity. The investigators were simply interested in observing the workers and finding out what factors influenced their rate of production. They found the workers were following a social norm, enforced by their coworkers, that defined the proper amount of production. They did so despite the fact that they were paid the way Taylor had suggested:

individual hourly rates based on individual average output, plus a bonus determined by average group output.

The workers in the wiring room set a norm for a "day's work." This norm called for each man to wire two complete sets of switchboards each day. Workers who produced more than two sets were ridiculed as "speed kings" or "rate busters." Those who produced less than two sets were called "chiselers." The actual production averages were, day in and day out, surprisingly close to the group's norms. The workers believed that if they produced a great deal more their pay rate would be reduced or some of them would lose their jobs (the study took place during the Great Depression). They also felt that if they produced much less it would be unfair to management and they would get into trouble. Neither belief had any basis in reality.

The Hawthorne experiments concluded that the level of production is set by social norms, not by the physical abilities of the workers. Noneconomic rewards and sanctions affect the behavior of the workers and limit the effectiveness of economic incentives. Members who produced more or less than the socially determined norm lost the friendship and respect of their coworkers. This affection seemed to be more important to them than money. Workers act as members of groups, not as individuals. The lesson for management was that workers should not be treated as if they were separate units because they are clearly influenced by the group. Finally, an important finding of the bank-wiring-room study was that there are two kinds of leaders in the work force—the *formal* leaders chosen by management and given authority and the *informal* leaders, who are the best-liked workers in the group. In the bank wiring room the informal leader was admired the most; his advice was sought the most; and he spoke for the group in dealings with other factory employees. The supervisor did not have much influence on the group but was himself under pressure to conform to its rules. Later studies have shown that a foreman is more likely to be accepted if he or she uses informal leadership instead of trying to use authority to control the workers.

The human-relations approach, then, developed as a reaction against the classical tendency to view the organization wholly in rational economic terms. By contrast, the human-relations school emphasized the informal, interpersonal aspect of organizations. It stressed the importance of communication between levels of authority, of explaining to lower-level workers why a particular action is necessary and involving them in decision making, especially in matters that affect them directly. In general, the human-relations approach called for democratic, noncoercive leadership that is concerned with the problems of workers. American management has been greatly influenced by the human-relations approach, and thousands of executives and supervisors have participated in human-relations workshops.

The most dramatic attack on the human-relations approach was Alex Carey's reanalysis of the original Hawthorne studies.[13] Carey, writing in 1967, argued that the original researchers distorted their evidence to support their conclusion that the informal structure explained variations in productivity better than economic factors such as wages. Indeed, much of the evidence reported in 1939 seems to have been too skimpy to support the researchers' conclusions. (For example, one study involved only 5 female workers—too small a sample even to report.) The original study may have led scholars astray for a whole generation simply because of poor research procedures.

### The concept of harmonious interests

In most ways the classical approach and the human-relations approach were exactly opposite, but they did share one assumption. Neither school saw any conflict between organizational goals and individual human needs. The classical approach assumed that the most efficient organization would also be the most satisfying one, since it would maximize both productivity and the worker's pay. It assumed that the worker wanted to maximize his or her income but was satisfied with his or her share of the organization's income. It followed from these assumptions that what is best for the organization is best for the workers, and vice versa.

The human-relations approach also concluded that the most satisfying organization would be the most efficient one. It did not suppose, however, that workers could be happy in a cold, formal, "rational" organization that satisfied only their economic needs. On the contrary, management should recognize the workers' need for communication and informal social relationships on the job. If management encourages communication and democratic leadership, then life on the job will be happy. If the workers are happy, they will be more willing to cooperate, and thus the efficiency of the organization will increase. Many writers of the human-relations school describe factories in almost lyric passages. They portray the worker as anxious not to miss a day at the factory or to be late because he wants to spend time with his friends on the job. The worker is careful not to disappoint the foreman, who is compared to a warm and understanding parent. The work team itself is often called a "family." While the classical school saw a natural balance between the organization's goals and the workers' needs, the human relations-school believed that such a balance could be achieved only after social scientists had straightened out old-fashioned managers and taught them about informal groups.

### THE STRUCTURALIST APPROACH

Although the human-relations and classical approaches are important, not all theories of organization belong to one of these schools. Marx and Weber both had important things

Cary Wolinsky/Stock, Boston

*A sociologist who specializes in understanding organizations may spend one day with the board of directors, and the next day visiting the assembly line.*

to say about organizations, but neither could be called a classical theorist or a human-relations theorist. Moreover, many important modern sociologists strongly oppose both approaches, particularly the human-relations approach, arguing that social science should not help either workers or management manipulate the other side.

A new approach to organization theory seems to be developing, one that combines the first two. The classical idea of *formal structure* has been kept. It refers to the organizational pattern designed by management, or the blueprint of how labor is to be divided, who is to have authority over whom, the rules about wages, fines, quality control, and the like. In addition, although most current writers on this subject are opposed to the manipulative aspects of the human-relations approach, they are very interested in *informal organization*, that is, the social relations that develop among workers. Thus

modern organization theorists are discussing such matters as the relationship between the formal organization and the informal organization of a work group.

### Organizational conflict

Structuralist writers generally disagree with the assumption that the interests of management and workers are harmonious. The structuralists argue that there is a built-in conflict between organizational needs and personal needs, between rationality and nonrationality, between formal and informal relations, and between management and workers. This conflict will always exist, so that management cannot get workers to work without eventually alienating them.

According to Marx, the modern factory worker sees his or her job as meaningless, monotonous, and uncreative. The worker has no control over the pace or the location of his or her work because workers own nei-

226

ther the means of production nor the product of their labor. To Marx, and also to Weber, this alienation is a major problem in the modern world. Workers, unable to control how their labor is used, are frustrated and unhappy. Such frustration can hardly be eliminated, despite beliefs of human-relations theorists. Workers spend much of their time thinking about what they are going to do after work. Human-relations writers tended too often to see workers' dissatisfaction as a result of poor communication and not as a real conflict of interests. They emphasized the effectiveness of social rewards rather than material rewards, and their ideas were sometimes put to use by management, which tried to encourage workers by giving them inexpensive symbols of prestige and friendship instead of an increase in wages (a fancy ashtray or a more impressive job title, for example.)[14] In general, these writers believed that conflict between workers and management was undesirable.

Current writers (mostly structuralists) are more likely to base their ideas on a conflict model of society. They see value in open conflict and argue that if conflict is ignored instead of being brought out into the open, it will damage both the worker and the organization.

Structuralists are well aware that human-relations techniques have been used to help higher-level employees to manipulate those at lower levels. This happens, for example, when management invites lower level employees to participate in "democratic" decision making. In fact, however, the decisions have already been made and the real purpose of the discussion is to get the employees to accept them. Another human-relations idea is to set up suggestion boxes and "gripe sessions." Sometimes management has used such techniques to reduce the workers' alienation without actually improving their situation.

Human-relations theorists defend themselves by arguing that workers and manage-

ment are always manipulating each other anyhow and that the study of manipulation did not create that situation. Besides, many organizations that have human-relations programs also have the highest pay, the best working conditions, and the most respected unions. Using the human-relations approach may improve the worker's social situation without sacrificing his or her economic interests.

### Structuralism today

The human-relations approach is not a thing of the past. And there are some writers who still take the classical approach to the study of organizations. In general, however, the structuralists have broadened and combined the other two approaches in the following ways:

1  They study both formal and informal aspects of organizations.
2  They do not make too much of informal groups, as the human-relations writers did. For example, in his study of 1200 industrial workers Robert Dubin found that only 9 percent of his sample enjoyed the informal group life on the job.[15] Another study of 179 assembly line workers showed that there were almost no social groups on the job.[16]
3  They emphasize both material and social rewards. Workers care about both. One study showed that many steelworkers were willing to exchange their relatively nonrepetitive, skilled jobs for assembly line jobs that were more repetitive but paid about 30 percent more.[17]
4  They study both work and nonwork organizations. While the classical and human-relations theorists studied factories, banks, insurance companies, and the like, the structuralist writers often study a variety of organizations—the Communist party, the Catholic Church, or even a maximum-security prison.
5  They do not try to determine the "best kind of structure," as if one single blueprint would do for all sorts of organizations, as the classical school assumed. Instead, they recognize that different kinds of organizations are required to meet the goals of different groups. Thus instead of saying that each supervisor

should have, say, five subordinates the structuralists recognize that the ideal number may be three subordinates in one organization and fifteen in another, depending on the work they do.[18]

6 Above all, they concentrate on the *structure of the situation*, confronting various organizations, focusing on such factors as the technology that must be used and the kinds of raw material to be processed.[19]

# SOCIAL RESEARCH:
## *Sociologists at Work*

### ORGANIZATION IN CHINA TODAY

Here we'll look at an extraordinary social experiment—the reorganization of life in China since the communist regime took power. Mao was very much opposed to Western-style bureaucracy, and the Chinese have worked out systems of organization that differ considerably from any patterns that you or I would recognize. Until recently, scholars in the West had little information about what was going on in China. However, Martin Whyte has written an informative study of the Maoist style of organization, which we will use as the basis of our discussion.[20]

Whyte points out that Chinese organizations, like those in the West, are characterized by hierarchy and specialization, but he notes that leaders are chosen as much for their political standing as for their technical skill. The Chinese feel that too much emphasis on skill would create an elite class of specialists and reduce the initiative of the ordinary members of organizations.

The Chinese believe that a leader has a duty to inspire enthusiasm in subordinates. The use of political standards in choosing leaders is supposed to make the organization more open to direction by political leaders outside the organization. According to Whyte, party officials are responsible for making sure that organizational decisions do not have undesirable results and that the organization functions efficiently. The organization leader's task is to make subordinates aware that all their activities have some effect on the future of communism and socialism. The Chinese Communists do not put much

stock in rational-legal justifications of authority and in the blind obedience demanded by many large, complex organizations. The rank and file are not supposed to obey simply because they have less technical knowledge than their superiors; they should obey because they understand the importance of their role.

Party officials are required to spend part of their time working with their hands alongside their subordinates. Although this may seem like a poor use of time for skilled people, the Chinese encourage it because it brings the organization's members together and gives the leaders information about problems on the job and about how subordinates are reacting to work situations. Whyte emphasizes that the leaders' participation in the work of their subordinates is only one side of the "two participations." The other side is that subordinates are supposed to be able to take an active role in decision making.

Even when decisions are made by the leaders, they are not supposed to be accepted blindly by the rank and file. After a new policy is explained, subordinates break up into small discussion groups to go over each point in detail, whether it is a technical matter or a basic political issue. It is expected that subordinates, by playing an active, though secondary, role in decisions that affect them, will identify with the organization and contribute more to it.

According to Whyte, the discussion group is the primary tool for getting subordinates involved in decision making. These groups consist of from eight to fifteen members and have their own elected officers. It is in these groups that subordinates discuss new decisions, their own performance, political issues, and the need for improvement.

The Chinese Communists want to downplay hierarchy. Since 1965 the Chinese armed forces have eliminated ranks and symbols of rank. The commanders still have more authority than the ordinary soldier, but they have fewer visible symbols of their rank. The Chinese do not reject the basic bureaucratic view that those who hold higher posts should receive higher rewards. In fact both wages and benefits such as better apartments are distributed according to rank. However, wage differences are kept within narrow limits.

Recognition and rewards do not depend entirely on rank or productivity. Piecework wages have been largely discarded in industry, and rural communes set wages in public meetings. In setting wages the group considers not only performance but also attitudes toward work and political enthusiasm. While Westerners would expect a poorer performance to result from this system, the Chinese argue that too strong an emphasis on material rewards breeds lack of initiative. They cite many examples of organizations that improved production after they reduced material incentives and increased political ones. In other words, they replace utilitarian power with normative power.

The Chinese setup does not produce a completely impersonal organization, but personal friendships and rivalries are not supposed to influence members' activities and decisions. Everyone is supposed to show concern for everyone else. Members of a small group are expected not to criticize each other all the time but instead to try to help each other.

Although members of the group are not supposed to let personal emotions interfere with their performance, they are not expected to be totally unemotional either. Whether they are in school, on a farm, or fighting a war, the Chinese are expected to act with enthusiasm. Chinese organizations make greater demands on their members than Western or Soviet ones do. No aspect of an individual's life is viewed as irrelevant to his or her performance, and leaders try to make sure that personal relationships support, rather than undermine, organizational goals.

Whyte makes the important point that the Chinese do not accept the bureaucratic notions of job security and officeholding as a career. In the ideal type of bureaucracy these are ways of making sure that people with high-level skills are put to the best use. In China many people do serve in one position for a long time and do get promoted from one rank to the next. However, skilled people are supposed to be willing to leave comfortable posts for lower-ranking positions as manual laborers.

Nor do the Chinese believe that organizations should have detailed rules and routines so that participants will have the security and predictability needed for rational action. Instead, they feel that inflexible routines would prevent change. For this reason procedures and rules are periodically evaluated in terms of their contribution to the organization's efficiency.

The Chinese, according to Whyte, also reject the idea that everyone should deal only with his or her supervisor. Instead, many kinds of decisions are passed up and down various levels of the hierarchy, often several times. In this way ideas, reactions, and approval can be gathered from all levels of the organization. This procedure obviously results in delay and makes it hard to pin responsibility on a particular individual, but the Chinese feel that this process leads to greater involvement of members in organizational goals.

Whyte emphasizes that there are many similarities between Chinese and Western organizations. Chinese organizations, like those in the West, do have specific goals and they do have a hierarchical division of labor. Authority comes from the top, and in general, leaders have more training and experience and receive greater rewards than subordinates. In addition, files, rules, and written communications are found in Chinese organizations as well as in Western ones.

Still, there is a basic difference between Chinese and Western organizations. In the Western view the organization's main job is to achieve efficiency through the use of technical knowledge. In the Chinese view it is more important to gain the involvement and commitment of the members of the organization, particularly the "masses" at the bottom of the hierarchy.

The Maoist idea often has to be reinforced by the government.[21] Without such reinforcement, a Western type of bureaucracy seems to develop. However, Chinese organizations do show the effects of a greater sense of community. The participants are willing to work longer and harder, and they identify strongly with organizational and national goals.

# SOCIAL POLICY:
## Issues and Viewpoints

How do you like the system you are part of? Would you like to change it, drop out of it, go along with it? In what ways? Let's discuss some possible ways of viewing the situation.

You may think you understand it well enough to give up. You may be a guitar-playing commune member and raise vegetables and marijuana in your back yard. If so, your view of organizational society is probably different from that of your brother, who is a stockbroker and yachtsman. During the 1960s there were plenty of young people who felt so disgusted with the impersonal rigidity of modern society that the hippie movement was born. At least, some writers think this is what it was all about. Theodore Roszak[22] and Charles Reich[23] both described the counterculture as a rebellion against the life style required by "the system." Rather than becoming managers and "paper pushers," members of corporations or government agencies, members of the counterculture chose to live a frugal life of spontaneous expressiveness. They did not want to be programed to work from nine to five.

Reich argued that to avoid wastefulness, pollution, and endless consumerism we must conquer the large corporations. It will be necessary, he says, to change a culture that prescribes impersonality and competitiveness into one that allows for affection and openness. He may be right. But the youth movement of the 1960s and early 1970s is a thing of the past, while corporations and other large organizations are still with us. They may still be wasteful, impersonal, and so on, but more people are coming to terms with them and fewer are dropping out.

Besides, who can really drop out anyway? Unless you become a living Robinson Crusoe, completely isolated from human contact, you will depend on the technology of modern organizations. It may be pleasant to drop out of the system and raise potatoes in British Columbia. But potato growers use pickup trucks, at least. And this brings them into a distant but very important relationship with Ford, Exxon, and all the other villains they want to escape from. So who is kidding whom?

So what are the problems and how serious are they? It depends on your point of view. It seems certain that complex organizations are increasing in number and also in power. What effect do they have on their members? In *The Organization Man* William H. Whyte, Jr. has suggested that the man or woman at the upper levels of an organizational hierarchy experiences an invasion of privacy. The social life of the family, for example, is affected by the organization.[24] The bureaucrat's personality is also affected, if only because he or she must be able to tolerate a lot of frustration and must be able to postpone rewards. (No impulsiveness is allowed. Look at the rule book before doing anything.) The worker must also be able to ignore his or her personal preferences and relationships, treat clients as "cases," and follow rules consistently. He or she must have the drive to get ahead.

The organization consists of a hierarchy of positions through which an employee may move, and promotion rewards both performance and conformity. Does the worker pay a high emotional price for this? Drive! Strive! Conform! Workers dress alike—neatly and conservatively. What are the personal costs of sacrificing one's individuality and impulses to the beige-carpeted world of the corporation? We have assumed that the costs are high. Robert Merton's work, for example, has suggested that bureaucracy's system of rewards (for example, the seniority basis of promotion) leads to timidity and conservatism and discourages initiative and adventurousness.[25]

But recently another view has appeared, that of Melvin Kohn. Kohn's research has shown that instead of being unusually rigid and conforming, bureaucrats tend to be more flexible, more open to new experience, and more self-directed than people who work in nonbureaucratic settings.[26] Kohn believes that this is because bureaucrats feel secure—the organization protects them from the arbitrary power of their superiors. Instead of being in an "iron cage," as Weber thought, the bureaucrat is freer than most people. The rule book is there, of course, but it can be used as protection against the whims of the bosses. There are no sultans or dictators around IBM, General Foods, or the civil service, or so Kohn seems to believe. But it seems to me that working in a big organization does lead people to forget that they are responsible for making their own decisions. There is a real danger of becoming too obedient to the rule book, even when it conflicts with one's own moral beliefs and human feelings of pity or concern.

I have to believe that it is bad for the human soul to be always following orders. It is true that people in many other social situations as well, manage to pass the buck and avoid responsibility when they want to. Bureaucrats have no monopoly on cowardice. But I wonder: Are they more *tempted* to be irresponsible than the rest of us? Is it harder for a bureaucrat to say, "No, I won't!"?

Agreed, there are cowards in every social system and every occupation. But I'll be more willing to take my chances with officials in a democracy. There's a chance to control them there. The problem is that bureaucracy is not democratic. Sometimes bureaucracy even poses a threat to a democracy. If you're in a bureaucracy, authority runs from the top downward— never upward. Democracy runs in the other direction. These two principles don't fit together very well.

Here's how it is supposed to work: Elected government officials are supposed to set policy and then pass their orders down through the civil-service bureaucracy so that the laws and decisions are put into effect. But one problem is that the civil servants and the government agencies often have enough power so that they can ignore orders that they don't like. Elected officials are dependent on their staff members, and this may make it impossible to supervise or control them. So democracy may actually be the victim, not the master, of its own bureaucracy. Suppose the top bureaucrats, who are not elected, get too much power. Suppose they are able to pass orders all the way down through the hierarchy. Suppose their orders are obeyed. This happens. (I am thinking of J. Edgar Hoover, for example, who as director of the FBI was too powerful for any elected official to challenge.)

You may be concerned about other issues that have to do with bureaucracy—such as whether you can live a fairly independent life in

*These officials have their power supported by an enormous bureaucracy.*

an organization or whether you have to become some sort of robot. If this is what troubles you, there is reason to hope. Modern society may be moving past bureaucracy as described in this chapter. It seems to be moving toward professional colleagueship. For example, I work in a university and have more freedom than you can imagine. Bureaucracy is for the typists and lab technicians, not the faculty. It's the same for physicians and lawyers and engineers. Once you are a professional, the rules of bureaucracy don't apply to you in the ordinary way. Professionals don't boss each other around. They ask each other for advice, but if they decide to ignore the advice that's their own business. They have to cooperate to some extent, but they do it as equals, not as supervisors and subordinates. The chairman of my department would never come into my class to tell me how to teach. Nor would a surgeon barge into another surgeon's operating room to criticize the performance.

In modern society, more and more work relationships are becoming "collegial"—not bureaucratic. As we move toward a highly educated, highly professional organizational structure, there is a possibility that more jobs will be done by task forces than through the bureaucratic "system." Task forces (independent units within a large organization staffed by professionals whose relations to one another are more collegial than hierarchical) encourage initiative, independence, and authority based on skill. Professional, not bureaucratic, social relationships may well become the typical pattern in the future.

## SUMMARY

**1.** *Organizations* are planned social units with specific goals. They have a planned division of labor, one or more power centers, and can substitute personnel in various roles and tasks.

**2.** *Bureaucracies* are structured hierarchies that coordinate the activities of their members through the use of *authority*. Weber suggested that authority is power plus legitimacy and that there are three types of authority—traditional, charismatic, and rational-legal.

**3.** According to Weber, bureaucracies have the following characteristics: (1) They are organized on the basis of rules; (2) each member has a specific area of activity; (3) each lower position is under the control and supervision of a higher one; (4) the bureaucrat's legitimacy is based on knowledge and technical skill; (5) organizational affairs are kept separate from the bureaucrat's personal affairs; (6) the official does not "own" his or her office; and (7) administrative acts are recorded in writing.

**4.** Organizations have both a formal structure and an informal one. The formal structure is planned, but the informal structure results from the personal relationships of individuals.

**5.** Organizations differ in the means of control they use. Some use physical (coercive) power, others utilitarian power, and still others normative power. The more coercive an organization is, the less committed, more alienated its members will be.

**6.** There are three theoretical approaches to organizations: classical, human relations, and structuralist. The classical theorists were interested in improving the division of labor in organizations. The human-relations approach grew out of the Hawthorne studies, which found that productivity was affected less by the formal structure of an organization than by the informal structure—the personal relationships and feelings of the workers. Thus the human-relations school emphasized informal matters such as communication between ranks and nonauthoritarian leadership.

Neither the classical nor the human-relations approach saw any conflict between the organization's desire for rationality and the members' human needs. The structuralists, however, see a major conflict between these goals. Structuralists look at both the formal blueprint of an organization and its informal structure. They do not overemphasize informal groups because most industrial workers do not have close personal ties to their coworkers.

# KEY TERMS

**alienation**  the frustration and unhappiness of workers who have no control over how their labor is used; the loss of commitment of members for the goals of their groups.

**authority**  power that is regarded as legitimate by the members of the group.

**bureaucracy**  an organization with a hierarchy of offices set up to do work.

**bureaucratic authority**  authority that is seen as legitimate if its rulings are consistent with a set of abstract rules with which the members of the group agree; also called rational-legal authority by Weber.

**charismatic authority**  authority that is seen as legitimate because of the leader's magnetic personality.

**coercive power**  power based on physical means of control, such as guns or locks.

**hierarchy**  a chain of command in which each person has authority over several other people.

**legitimation**  acceptance of the use of power by the leaders of a group because it is in line with the values of the members of the group.

**normative power**  power based on symbolic means of control.

**organization**  a social unit deliberately constructed and reconstructed to pursue specific goals.

**power**  the ability to get people to take orders.

**traditional authority**  authority that is seen as legitimate because it has existed for a long time.

**utilitarian power**  power based on material means of control.

**voluntary association**  a group that people join because they support its goals and values.

# FOR FURTHER READING

BLAU, PETER, and MARSHALL W. MEYER. *Bureaucracy in Modern Society.* 2nd ed. New York: Random House, 1971. One of the best textbooks in the field.

BOREN, JAMES H. *When in Doubt, Mumble.* New York: Van Nostrand Reinhold, 1972. This is the latest among many funny little books about bureaucracy. The author claims to be the president of the National Association of Bureaucrats.

ETZIONI, AMITAI. *Modern Organizations.* Englewood Cliffs, N.J.: Prentice-Hall, 1964. The greater part of this chapter was drawn from Etzioni's book. For a really thorough introduction to the field, have a look at the original book, which has enjoyed great popularity.

KANTER, ROSABETH MOSS. *Men and Women of the Corporation.* New York: Basic Books, 1977. I say a little about this study in Chapter 5. It's the best sociology book I've read all year—friendly, sensible, and wise. Kanter describes the life situations of people who work in big corporations.

PERROW, CHARLES. *Complex Organizations: A Critical Essay.* Glenview, Ill.: Scott, Foresman, 1972. To amplify your understanding of the structuralist approach, turn to this small paperback.

SELZNICK, PHILIP. *TVA and The Grass Roots.* New York: Harper & Row, 1966. The moral of this story is this: never give away a piece of your organization to your enemies to buy their cooperation. Selznick's book added a new word to the vocabulary of organizational theorists: "cooptation."

WHITE, HARRISON C. *Chains of Opportunity: System Models of Mobility in Organizations.* Cambridge, Mass.: Harvard University Press, 1970. There is a sort of cult within sociology composed of former students of Harrison White at Harvard. They find his work masterly and exciting. It does not have that effect on me, but admittedly I have not given it a fair trial. It may do wonders for you, especially if you have a flair for mathematics. Start with this book.

WHYTE, WILLIAM H., JR. *The Organization Man.* New York: Simon & Schuster, 1956. This was an immensely popular book when it first appeared. It describes humorously but pretty accurately the life style of executives in large organizations. If you are planning such a career, read this first. Then go ahead and read Kanter's book too.

# SOCIAL STRATIFICATION

Every year I begin a lecture on social stratification by asking my students this question: Why do some people have more wealth, privilege, and influence than others? I jot down their answers on the blackboard, and then we discuss them.

I find that the students tend to divide into two groups and that before the class hour is over the two groups are at war with each other. The first group (whom I call "functionalists") gives answers like these: "The rich have earned it!" "Because they contribute more to society and are rewarded more for their efforts than other people." The other group ("conflict theorists") gives answers like these: "Because the rich take advantage of the poor." "Because they have the power to take what they want, whether it is fair or not." "Because they can afford to educate their children better than poor people can."

The issue the two groups are arguing about is that of whether social stratification results from open, fair competition or whether it results from unfair use of power by the dominant groups in society. The functionalists believe that our society is open and fair and that competition is a good thing. The conflict theorists believe that our society is neither open nor fair and that the masses would be quite justified in starting a revolution.

A third point of view is possible, and if I were teaching in a different society I might hear it often, but I never hear it in North America. It consists of answers like these: "It's fate." "The rich are powerful because it is God's will." Such answers reflect a belief that social stratification is permanent, that one cannot change one's position, and that one *should not try* to do so, either through competition and hard work or through revolution. Such answers support an unchanging, castelike society in which social status is inherited.

In this chapter we will discuss these points of view and take a look at the inequality that exists in our society.

## Social class and social status

### WHAT IS A SOCIAL CLASS?

Obviously, not all people have the same amount of money, prestige, or social influence. These things are desired by almost everyone but are unequally distributed in any population. It is possible to rank the people in a society in terms of their income, prestige, education, or power. A person's rank, based on these standards, is his or her socioeconomic status. When we speak of "status" we usually mean socioeconomic status.

More often, however, we classify people much more loosely on the basis of only one or two standards—usually income alone—and usually into only a few categories such as "upper class," "middle class," and "lower class." We may define a social class as a set of people with similar socioeconomic status. Most of the time, the terms *socioeconomic status* and *social class* are interchangeable.

The most influential social classification system was proposed by Karl Marx. His system was based on only one standard: ownership of the means of production. The ruling class owned the means of production. The working class did not. Marx recognized that many different social classes had existed at different times according to the technology used in any particular period. For example, the aristocracy, who owned the land, were the ruling class in preindustrial Europe, while the peasants, who tilled it, were the workers. However, he regarded two classes alone as the forces that shaped history during the industrial period. These were (1) the *bourgeoisie* or capitalists, who owned the factories and other means of industrial production, and (2) the *proletariat*, or workers, who had to work to earn a living. The mem-

## What is your socioeconomic status?

Sociologists commonly rate respondents' socioeconomic status (SES) by means of a composite index, using data of various kinds. The following index is an example of the sort of classification scheme that is commonly used.

|  | CATEGORY | POINTS |
|---|---|---|
| EDUCATION | College graduate | 5 |
|  | Some college | 4 |
|  | High school graduate | 3 |
|  | Some high school | 2 |
|  | Grade school only (or none) | 1 |
| FAMILY INCOME (ANNUAL) | $50,000 and over | 5 |
|  | $20,000 to $49,999 | 4 |
|  | $10,000 to $19,999 | 3 |
|  | $ 5,000 to $9,999 | 2 |
|  | Under $5000 | 1 |
| OCCUPATION OF CHIEF BREADWINNER OF YOUR FAMILY | Professional or managerial in large firm, proprietors | 5 |
|  | Semi-professional or managerial in small firms | 4 |
|  | Clerical and sales | 3 |
|  | Skilled and semi-skilled labour | 2 |
|  | Agriculture and unskilled labour | 1 |

To calculate your own socioeconomic status, add the number of points you score for all three items.

| IF YOUR SCORE IS | YOUR SES LEVEL IS |
|---|---|
| 15 points | Upper |
| 12 to 14 points | Upper-middle |
| 9 to 11 points points | Middle |
| 6 to 8 points | Lower middle |
| 3 to 5 points | Lower |

bers of a class might become aware that they had common interests; Marx called this awareness "class consciousness." If they did not have this awareness, he believed that they had "false consciousness."

Most people, whether they are sociologists or not, do not refer to the ownership of the means of production when they distinguish among social classes. They may refer to income, life style, or education, occupation, or perhaps some other standard of classification. This is why Marxists and non-Marxists classify people in somewhat different ways. For example, you and I might say that a man who lives on an income of $500 per month from his part ownership of a lumberyard is lower middle class and that a surgeon who earns $100,000 a year doing face lifts is upper class. A Marxist, on the other hand, might call the lumberyard owner *bourgeois* because he does not have to work but derives his income from the profits of the work of others, while the surgeon can be seen as working class because she makes a living from her own labor. If either person loses the use of his or her hands, the surgeon might soon be poor, but the lumberyard owner's income would not be affected.

How many social classes are there? There is no single answer to this question. Sociologists usually use between three and six categories. For years many surveys referred only to "upper," "middle," and "lower" classes, and most North Americans would claim to be "middle class," even though they did manual labor and therefore should be called "lower class." However, it finally became clear that people knew when they were "lower class" but did not like to describe themselves in those words. When the term *working class* was added to the list of choices, most respondents chose it instead of middle class or lower class.

When six categories are used to describe a stratification system, the upper, middle, and lower classes are divided into upper and lower levels. Thus the upper upper class consists of "old money" — people whose families have been rich for generations. Members of the lower upper class may be just as rich, but they have become rich more recently and have not yet learned the upper-class subculture. Their clothes and cars are more likely to be flashy and their vocabulary not as plain as that of the upper upper class. In New York City, many dogs walked by lower-upper-class owners wear rhinestone collars, while those walked by upper-upper-class owners are on ropes instead of leashes.

The upper middle class consists mostly of business and professional people who live comfortably in attractive surroundings. Members of the lower middle class are not as well off; they work as shopkeepers, in clerical jobs, and the like.

An upper-lower-class person may earn as much as any middle-class worker, but he or she does manual work — as a machinist, a plumber, or an assembly line worker, for example. Finally, the lower lower class consists of welfare recipients, the unemployable, and people who do unskilled work when they do any.

## SOCIAL STATUS

### Ascribed and achieved status

Chickens in a barnyard, I understand, establish a "pecking order." The top chicken can peck all the others. The next chicken can peck all the others except the top one, and so on down the hierarchy. The bottom chicken, poor dear, can be pecked by all the others but can peck no one else at all.

People work out such arrangements too. If you are invited to dinner at an embassy, the seat you will be given at the table depends on how you rank in comparison to the other guests. You will quickly find out whether to defer to a given person or to expect that person to defer to you. Your rank is your social status.

What determines whether you will rank high or low, whether you will be seated near the host or far away, whether you will take orders or give orders more often, whether you will bow and scrape to other people or they will bow and scrape to you? What determines your social status? The answer; the roles that you occupy. Some roles rank higher than others and are assigned more privileges and assets than others. In principle, it is possible for a group to assign roles and status to its members on the basis of any agreed-upon standard — the color of their eyes, how far they can throw a javelin, whether they are left-handed or right-handed, or anything else. Sociologists are often interested in whether roles are assigned on the basis of standards over which a person has some control (achieved status) or over which he or she has no control (ascribed status). When status is ascribed, people are assigned to high or low positions on the basis of their characteristics—such as skin color or royal birth or sex. When status is achieved, people are assigned to high or low positions on the basis of how well they have shown their ability to perform various roles. The high rank of physicians is achieved status; they have to show certain abilities before they are allowed to practice medicine. The high rank of a princess is ascribed; she is assigned to that role simply by being born to her particular parents instead of to the plumber and his wife the waitress.

All societies assign status on the basis of both kinds of standards. In general, however, preindustrial societies are more likely to use ascribed status and industrial societies are more likely to use achieved status. It sometimes offends us to see people given special privileges that they have not earned. Yet our lives are influenced by ascribed status in ways that we sometimes fail to notice. Physical beauty, for example, influences life chances, especially for women. Attractive women generally marry men of somewhat higher status than less attractive women do.[1] Men are affected in similar ways: Tall men earn somewhat more money than short men and are more likely to be promoted to high rank.[2]

Age is another characteristic that is hardly "achieved," and yet it is a basis for social discrimination. A person is granted certain rights upon reaching a given age, regardless of his or her maturity and ability; the same person is stripped of certain rights upon reaching "retirement" age, again regardless of his or her ability.

A final example is sex. Males have al-

*Ascribed status. (She never had to audition for the role.)*

UPI

most always been chosen as leaders and females expected to be followers, regardless of their other characteristics. The aged, the unattractive, women, short men, and teenagers are all discriminated against in one way or another on the basis of ascribed status.

However, industrial societies tend to move away from ascribed status and toward achieved status. As mentioned in the preceding chapter, industrial work requires division of labor. We break up the work into more and more specialized jobs and assign each of these to people who are able to do those jobs. If all jobs were equally difficult and all human beings equally talented, it would not matter how we decided who should do what job. But that is not the case in today's technological society, so it really matters to us that the person who pilots the airplane we fly in or performs open-heart surgery on us is the best person for the job. This is why we insist that roles be based on *what people can do,* not on the basis of *who they are.*

In preindustrial societies, on the other hand, most status is ascribed. The division of labor is not very extensive, and most jobs are simple enough for almost anyone in the society to perform satisfactorily. No competition is necessary. In primitive societies kinship determines status. In feudal society, too, a serf's son would be a serf and a noble's son a noble, with rare exceptions. The system of stratification was ascribed and closed; no movement up or down the hierarchy was possible.

ASCRIPTION BY CASTE  Probably no society has ever been totally closed. However, the caste system of India until the past few decades was the most closed stratification system we know of. It was justified by the Hindu religion, which holds that (1) every soul is reborn over and over again into new bodies, human or nonhuman; (2) a person's sins or virtues follow him or her from life to

life and determine his or her life chances; and (3) one has a duty to perform well in the role to which one was assigned at birth. A person is born to be a potter, a prostitute, or a priest because this is the status he or she has earned in former lives. One must try to be good at potting, prostitution, or priesthood, as the case may be. It would do the potter no good to try to perform the role of the priest; it is not that person's duty. A low position or any other misfortune in this life was earned by past misdeeds. Thus striving for a higher social position is fighting against the law of the universe.

Every Hindu belongs to one and only one *jat,* or caste. There are some 3000 such groups in India, and membership in each is permanent and hereditary. Marriages are legitimate only between a man and a woman of the same *jat.* (The government recognizes intercaste marriages, but powerful traditional authorities do not.) Originally all male members of any one *jat* had the same occupation, and it was their duty to provide services for other castes. Nowadays Indians often take jobs other than those traditionally performed by members of their caste, but in the villages it is not unheard of for members of a local *jat* to be beaten by their neighbors for failing to perform their customary duties. The traditional Hindu's occupation is predetermined, and he or she is not permitted to carry out the duties of other *jats.* A high-caste Hindu may not sweep, for example, and is therefore dependent on the very low-ranking sweeper group for clean floors.

There is some upward social movement in India, but it is generally the entire *jat,* not the individual, that moves up. For example, the leaders of a *jat* may make up a story that the *jat* was originally of high rank but was not recognized as such. At the same time, the caste members may adopt upper-caste customs such as banning meat, alcohol, and the remarriage of widows. After a generation or two they may succeed in being reclassified at a higher rank.

CASTE WITHOUT HINDUISM The anthropologist Gerald Berreman holds that caste in India is not very different from the two-caste system (black and white) of the United States.[3] He defines caste as a hierarchy of social groups in which membership is hereditary and permanent and in which marriage between people who belong to different groups is forbidden. In both societies the dominant caste maintains its position by means of economic and physical sanctions and uses the lower castes as a supply of cheap labor. Men of the dominant caste have sexual access to both high- and low-caste women, while low-caste men have access only to low-caste women. Members of different castes avoid each other in both societies; members of the upper caste believe that they would be contaminated by contact with members of the lower caste.

The main difference is that in India there are many castes, and each one gets certain satisfactions from being above others and certain dissatisfactions from being below others. Most people claim that their group deserves to be ranked higher than it is, but few oppose the whole caste system the way the black American usually does.

### Status inconsistency

The various standards of social status are never perfectly correlated. Many people rank higher by one standard than by another, and this results in status inconsistency. Some people are well educated but earn very little, like the Ph.D. who drives a cab. Some earn a lot of money through activities that bring them little or no prestige, like rich gangsters or rich junk dealers. Some people have power even though they are poor, like a welfare recipient on a grand jury.

Gerhard Lenski has observed that such status inconsistencies may be a source of psychological stress.[4] His theory is based on the assumption that people try to maximize their satisfaction even at the expense of other people. This means that people with inconsistent statuses tend to think of themselves in terms of their highest status or rank and to expect others to do the same. Meanwhile, those who come into contact with them tend to treat them in terms of their lowest status or rank.

You can see how this works by imagining the interaction between a poor novelist and a rich bricklayer in a situation in which neither writing nor bricklaying is relevant. The writer will try to base their relationship on occupation, while the bricklayer will try to base it on income. Because each believes his own point of view is right and proper, and because neither is likely to view the problem objectively, one or both are likely to be frustrated, and probably angered, by the interaction.

"One-upmanship," as this pattern has been called, is so common in everyday life that most of us give it hardly any thought. One result, however, is feelings of stress for many people with inconsistent statuses. Lenski believes that the psychological stress of status inconsistency leads such people to demand social changes. If so, they would be expected to prefer left-wing political parties over right-wing parties. During the 1950s the evidence seemed to support his hypothesis. For example, data gathered in two sample surveys of Greater Detroit showed that people with inconsistent statuses were more likely to support the Democratic party and take liberal positions on issues than people with consistent status. Unfortunately, recent studies fail to support this theory. Sometimes status inconsistency seems to be related to demands for change, but the effect is too small to be important. No doubt new studies will shed light on this question.[5]

COMPONENTS OF CLASS
AND STATUS

The term social stratification refers to a hierarchy of layers, or *strata* (singular: *stratum*) that are unequal in terms of property, power, and prestige. In short, stratification means social inequality.

Property may be defined as rights or control over goods and services. It can be converted into money, and so for most purposes wealth and property are the same thing. However, as Thorstein Veblen has pointed out, one gains a certain amount of prestige by showing off one's wealth, and to do that one must display it in the form of property.[6] This was more true a generation or two ago than it is today, but even today if you have a million dollars in the bank but live like a pauper you will miss out on a lot of the social deference that comes to those who consume property wastefully and showily.

In Marx's view, on the other hand, the crucial standard determining one's social class is not rights over consumer goods or income but ownership of a special *kind* of property — the means of production.

Power refers to the ability to achieve one's goals even in the face of opposition. The amount of power we have depends mostly on the roles we occupy. Certain jobs carry with them responsibilities and the right to give orders to others. Thus a police officer must have such powers as the right to reroute traffic at the scene of an accident, the right to stop and question a stranger in a dark alley and so on. Roles that carry especially heavy responsibilities usually carry considerable power as well. Often, though not necessarily, power and property go together. He who pays the piper calls the tune. Money can buy power to a certain extent, and power can help one get the chance to accumulate money. Moreover, both high income and power usually come with the same jobs.

Some kinds of social honor are distributed unequally, so that some groups and some roles enjoy great respect and deference, while others do not. This kind of social honor is called prestige. It is usually attached to roles that also have property and power. Yet prestige and wealth are not interchangeable. For example, no matter how rich you are you cannot buy a Nobel prize or influence the judges to award it to the person of your choice. The prize is awarded in recognition of remarkable achievements, and its prestige value would be lowered if it could be won on some other basis.

Not all kinds of social honor are stratified. Thus we sometimes distinguish between prestige and esteem, the kind of appreciation we feel for each other regardless of rank. For example, in hard times my grandmother picked cotton to help support

*You can't buy a Nobel prize.*

UPI

Peter Southwick/Stock, Boston

*Not everything about people can be ranked. Bootblacks have very low prestige, but their friends and clients may admire them and hold them in great esteem for their special personal qualities.*

her family, pushing her two children along in a baby carriage between the rows of cotton plants. One feels high esteem for such a courageous approach to life. Later on, as the wife of her town's only physician, she received not only esteem but also the prestige that is generally given to doctors and their families. Esteem is the respect we hold for a person who does her best to meet a situation well, whether she is in a high position or a low one. Prestige is a different kind of respect that we have for a high position simply because it is high. Esteem is not necessarily limited, but prestige is. Thus you may have high esteem for all your classmates and

enjoy each one's company. Not all of your classmates can have high prestige, however; only those who are ranked above average can.

Fortunately, not everything that is worthwhile about human beings is either scarce or arranged in a hierarchy of values. We may esteem others because they are playful, helpful, honest, kind, or creative, for example, so that every member of a group may have some special traits that win esteem. This is not so in the case of prestige. My son claims that he enjoys prestige among his high school classmates because he uses notebooks marked with a university coat of arms. If all the students possessed such notebooks, nobody would derive prestige from them. Prestige is unequal social recognition.

The kind of prestige that is most important in society is based not on such trivial symbols as the kind of notebooks one uses but, rather, one's occupation. Your job determines not only how much property and power you have but also how much respect you are likely to get from others. Although esteem and prestige need not go together, they often do. Thus most Nobel prize winners have both prestige and esteem. (See Table 9.1 for a prestige ranking of occupations.)

If occupation largely determines one's social status, education in turn largely determines one's occupation. This is why educational achievements are so important in modern society. But education affects your social status not only by determining your occupation but also more directly in connection with prestige. People recognize each other's level of prestige right away. Go to a party and see how quickly people recognize a high-ranking guest and show their admiration. It takes only a few questions; a person's education shows up in the accent, vocabulary, and content of his or her answers. More than any other factor, one's level of education is a clue to one's life style, and prestige depends on the respect people have for one another's life style.

**TABLE 9.1**
*Prestige ranking of selected occupations*

| OCCUPATION | SCORE | OCCUPATION | SCORE |
|---|---|---|---|
| Physicians | 82 | Welders | 40 |
| College teachers | 78 | Sales representatives | 40 |
| Judges and lawyers | 76 | Wholesale trade | 40 |
| Physicists | 74 | Carpenters | 40 |
| Astronomers | 74 | Restaurant and bar | |
| Dentists | 74 | managers | 39 |
| Bank officers | 72 | Receptionists | 39 |
| Psychologists | 71 | Jewelers and | |
| Architects | 71 | watchmakers | 37 |
| Aeronautical engineers | 71 | Meter readers, | |
| Airplane pilots | 70 | utilities | 36 |
| Chemists | 69 | Brick and stone | |
| Sociologists | 66 | masons | 36 |
| Political scientists | 66 | Bakers | 34 |
| Mathematicians | 65 | Motion picture | |
| Optometrists | 62 | projectionists | 34 |
| Registered nurses | 62 | Boilermakers | 31 |
| Elementary school | | Roofers and slaters | 31 |
| teachers | 60 | Book binders | 31 |
| Accountants | 57 | Sign painters | 30 |
| Economists | 57 | Furniture finishers | 29 |
| Draftsmen | 56 | Butchers | 28 |
| Social workers | 52 | Mine operatives | 26 |
| Embalmers | 52 | Weavers | 25 |
| Computer programmers | 51 | Gas station | |
| Artists and | | attendants | 22 |
| entertainers | 51 | Taxi drivers | 22 |
| Recreation workers | 49 | Warehousemen | 20 |
| Flight engineers | 47 | Farm laborers | 19 |
| Musicians and | | Produce packers | 19 |
| composers | 46 | Garbage collectors | 17 |
| Keypunch operators | 45 | Janitors | 16 |
| Real estate agents | | Food counter and | |
| and brokers | 44 | fountain workers | 15 |
| Telegraph operators | 44 | Bell hops | 14 |
| Mail carriers, post | | Cleaners and | |
| office | 42 | charwomen | 12 |
| Typists | 41 | Bootblacks | 9 |

*Source: National Data Program for The Social Sciences: Cumulative Codebook for the 1972–1977 General Social Surveys.*
Chicago: National Opinion Research Center, University of Chicago, October 1977, pp. 224–235.

# Social inequality

## CHARACTERISTICS OF
## SOCIAL STRATIFICATION

### Stratification is social

We have said that biological, inherited characteristics such as differences in strength, intelligence, age, sex, height, and looks may be the standards for assigning status. However, what makes such traits important is the judgment of a society's members. Height would not make any difference unless people decided that it was important, and the same goes for sex, age, and many other traits. In some societies, for example, fat women are considered gorgeous; in others thin ones are; and in still others a woman's shape is not important. This example shows that stratification on the basis of physical characteristics is still determined by social judgments. No biological trait is a standard for social classification until it becomes part of the beliefs, attitudes, and values of the members of the society.

### Stratification is found everywhere

No society (not even a socialist society) can be found in which there is no stratification at all. Even among the Bushmen, hunters and gatherers who live in self-governing bands of 50 to 100 people, some stratification is found. There are socially determined inequalities between men and women and between adults and children. Thus inequality of power, property, and prestige is universal.

### Stratification varies in form and degree

Though some inequality is universal, the amount and nature of the inequality varies greatly from one society to another. Traditional India was perhaps the most highly stratified of all societies, and the *kibbutzim* of Israel approach total equality.

### Stratification is important

If you ask a number of sociologists to choose the factor that most often predicts differences in social life, almost all of them will choose social class. Different social strata have different life styles. This means that they have different patterns of eating and dressing, of cultural and recreational activities, of relationships between parents and children, and so on. We'll come back to some of these differences later.

More important, different strata also have very different life chances. That is, patterns of infant mortality, physical and mental illness, childlessness, marital conflict, separation, divorce, and the like vary from one social class to another. The chance of getting a good job varies by class. The chance of going to jail varies by class. The chance to travel abroad varies by class, and so on. Our

opportunities are opened or shut for us by the social class we belong to. We will return to this subject later, too.

### INCOME INEQUALITY

Although stratification exists everywhere, it differs in extent from one time and place to another. Those who are most seriously affected by it are the poor. Although we will be discussing poverty in North America, we must remember that the widest gaps between standards of living in the world today aren't between individuals but between whole societies. Societies such as the United States and Canada are far richer than societies such as India, Bangladesh, or Haiti, where millions of people live on the sidewalks or in cardboard packing crates, eating garbage or whatever scraps they can find, wearing rags, suffering from sores and toothaches, feeling too weak to work even if they could find jobs. Everything I say about poverty in our own society is nothing compared to the misery of people in less developed nations. Moreover, the gap between the rich nations and the poor ones is not decreasing—quite the contrary. And *within* the poor nations there is even greater inequality of income than in advanced societies.[7] That is, the gap between the income of the poor and the income of the well-to-do is bigger than in North America. We will return to these problems in a later chapter. For now, however, let's stick to the situation in North America.

In his 1972 book *Inequality* Christopher Jencks reminded us how much Americans differ in the life chances available to them. Our incomes are shockingly unequal and are staying that way. Jencks compared the 1970 incomes of the richest fifth and the poorest fifth of the U.S. population. The average American family had an income of $10,100 that year. The average income of the poorest fifth was only 28 percent of that, while the richest fifth's average income was over twice that amount.[8] This degree of inequality did not change much from 1946 to 1960, but for a

**FIGURE 9.1**

*Distribution of wealth in the United States in 1973. As this graph indicates, prosperity in the United States is very unequally distributed, with the poorest 20% of the population owning less than ½ of one per cent of the wealth.*

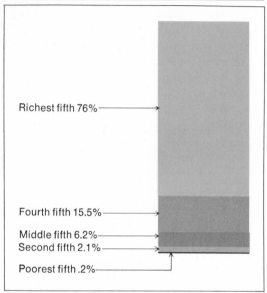

Richest fifth 76%

Fourth fifth 15.5%

Middle fifth 6.2%
Second fifth 2.1%

Poorest fifth .2%

*Source:* Data taken from the Executive Office of the President, Office of Management and the Budget, *Social Indicators, 1973.* (Washington, DC: U.S. Government Printing Office, 1973), Table 5.

while during the 1960s incomes tended to become slightly more equal. We have no evidence that this trend has continued in the 1970s.[9] Over the years the income of every group has increased, but not all to the same degree. Thus between 1946 and 1968 the average annual income of the poorest fifth rose about $1000 while that of the richest fifth rose about $4000.[10]

### WHO IS POOR?

About 12 percent of all Americans live in poverty.[11] Who are they? Poor people come in all shapes and sizes, all colors, ages, sexes, and personalities. No generalization applies to all individuals, rich or poor. It's bad enough for people to have to suffer poverty without being stigmatized as well. Many people think it's disreputable to be poor. They believe that no decent person who works hard will be poor — or at least won't stay poor very long. Of course there's an opposing view — that all poor people are helpless victims of the social system or of fate, that they are unable to escape from an impossible situation. The truth, of course, is that the poor include both drifters and hard-working people who have had bad luck — and all sorts of people between these two extremes.

### Employment

Most poor people do work. Many more would like to. Over half of the poor earn most of their income from wages.[12] But they often have trouble finding regular work, so they take temporary and part-time jobs and usually find themselves unemployed for part of the year.[13] About one-third of the working poor are under age 25.[14] Figure 9.2 shows one reason why: Unemployment rates are very high for young workers.

### Education

One factor that is closely related to poverty and unemployment is lack of education. Young people who have skills and a basic education have better luck finding good jobs than dropouts. Over a lifetime college-educated people can expect to earn between two and three times as much as people who have fewer than eight years of schooling.[15] (See Figure 9.3).

### Sex

Income is by no means equally available to the two sexes. Nowadays almost half of all women have paid jobs, but they are not paid at the same rates as men, nor do they have the same chance of getting better jobs. Although laws have been passed requiring greater equality, the results of these laws cannot be seen in the actual earnings of the two sexes. Thus in 1970 the average salary of full-time American female workers was

**FIGURE 9.2**

*Unemployment rates are highest for young workers.*

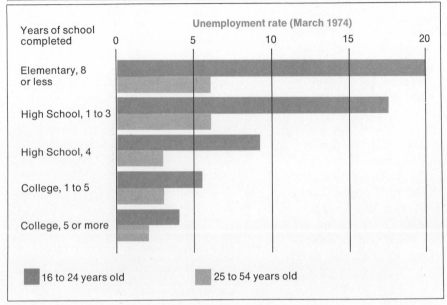

*Source:* U.S. Dept. of Labor, Bureau of Labor Statistics, 1976 Bulletin 1875: *Occupational Outlook Handbook*, p. 19.

**FIGURE 9.3**

*Estimated lifetime earnings for men tend to rise with years of school completed.*

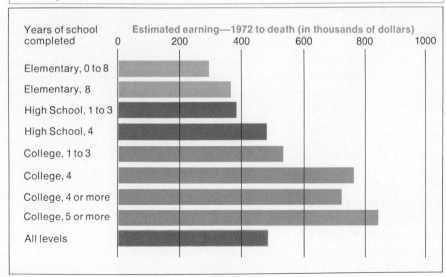

*Source:* U.S. Dept. of Labor, Bureau of Labor Statistics, 1976. Bulletin 1875: *Occupational Outlook Handbook*, p. 19.

about 59 percent of that of men working full time. How much had that gap closed by 1975? Not at all.[16]

This means that, although more and more wives are working they do not contribute much to the family income. Indeed, to be specific, for white American families in which both husband and wife were employed in 1974, only 25 percent of the family income was earned by the wife.[17]

### Race

As I'm sure you already know, poverty in the United States is lopsided: Too many nonwhite members of the population are poor. (See Figure 9.4) In 1975 only 10 percent of white Americans compared to 31 percent of black Americans were living in poverty.[18] This is an important problem, and we will come back to it in the next chapter.

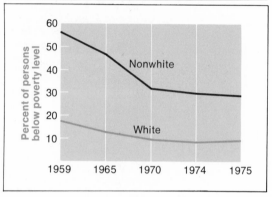

**FIGURE 9.4**
*Poverty by race in the United States, 1959 to 1975. Poverty level is based on the U.S. Social Security Administration index that adjusts income level for family size, sex of family head, number of children under 8, and farm/nonfarm residence.*

*Source:* U.S. Bureau of the Census, *Statistical Abstract of the U.S. 1976,* 97th ed. (Washington, DC, 1976).

### INEQUALITY AND UNFAIRNESS

I have mentioned the stigma on poor people—the fact that they are often blamed for their misfortune. Now I want to point out a few of the ways in which the societies we live in are unfair to poor people. You may not be aware of how middle-class Americans and Canadians get opportunities and advantages that they do not "deserve."

For example, rich people pay less for goods and services than poor people do. Why? Because poor people can't pay cash. They turn to merchants who will let them buy television sets, washing machines, and other appliances on credit. Middle-class people are in a better position to shop around and find bargains. Not only do goods cost more when they are bought from "credit" merchants, but by buying on the installment plan the poor pay far more in the long run because of the very high interest rates on what are actually loans. Sometimes the payments are not made, and then the mer-

chant repossesses the furniture or appliance, something that rarely happens to middle-class families. And it is not only expensive appliances that cost more. Poor people spend more even for groceries and clothing.[19]

You have probably heard a lot of grumbling about the welfare system and the people who benefit from it. However, there is a system of disguised welfare that you may be unaware of, and it pays out far more benefits than the one you know about. Its benefits go more to the rich than to the poor. This disguised welfare system is income tax. Its "disguise" is the odd way it operates—it "pays" without sending checks to anyone. The benefits consist of the money the government allows people to keep. Moreover, unlike welfare recipients, who are stigmatized for being on welfare, the well-to-do who receive their disguised welfare benefits are admired for their cleverness.

How does it work? Tax rates are supposedly based on the principle that those who can afford to should pay at a higher rate. Very poor people shouldn't be taxed at all, and they are not. We operate with a set of "tax brackets" that resembles a staircase. Suppose that you are climbing a stair or "bracket" each year. The first few thousand dollars you earn are all in the lowest bracket and you will be taxed at a very low rate— maybe 25 percent or so—on that income. But if you earn a few thousand more and move into the next-higher bracket, this additional amount will be taxed at a higher rate. If you are lucky enough to earn a lot more than the average person, the top few dollars you earn may be taxed at a rate of 50 percent or even more. Not your *whole* income, of course. Just the part of it that is in the topmost bracket.

This is fair enough. But the catch is in the deductions. It seems reasonable that we should be allowed to deduct whatever expenses we pay out as a necessary cost of earning our income. And we are. But the deductions are subtracted from the topmost bracket. Suppose you and I each paid $500 last year for necessary travel expenses. We each deduct it from our taxable income, as we are permitted to do. But suppose my income was so great that my top dollars are taxed at 50 percent while you earn much less, so that your top dollar is taxed at 25 percent. This means that I can subtract 50 percent of my $500, but you can subtract only 25 percent of your $500. I am richer than you are, and though our travel expenses were equal, the government in effect sends me a welfare check for $250 and sends you one for only $125.

As it happens, there are many more ways for a rich person to subtract from his or her taxable income. The effect is that well-to-do people are given subsidies that amount to far more than what the government spends annually on direct assistance to the poor. These figures are published by the U.S. government and are open to congressional control. In Canada, however, these subsidies are not matters of public record or discussion.[20]

*Life chances depend on differences in social class.*

Sepp Seitz/Woodfin Camp

Tim Carlson/Stock, Boston

# The results of stratification

It is obvious that poor people have a hard time getting ahead. We don't really have a system of equal opportunities; it is not nearly as equal as we sometimes like to think.

What are the results of stratification? So far we have limited ourselves to economic issues, and indeed these are serious problems. To be lower class means, above all, to be poor—to have to watch every penny you spend. But it also means to be uneducated. And it means to be looked down upon—not invited to certain parties, not considered a suitable date, not called "Mr. Brown" but only "Jim." Such experiences add up, especially since they happen day after day in many different sorts of situations. To be middle class is to experience the world in a very different way from upper- or lower-class people in the same society. Let's look at just a few of the effects of class—on family life, health, life style, participation in groups, religion, politics, and the problems of life.

## CLASS AND FAMILY

First of all, your class has a lot to do with the mate you choose. There is a good chance that you will marry somebody with about as much education as you have. And if you have a lot of education, your marriage is likely to be more stable than if you (and your spouse) have less education. That is, you are less likely to divorce and remarry if you are well educated. However, this stability is only partly a result of education itself. It depends partly on the age of the bride and groom. Couples who marry young have less chance of marital happiness than couples who marry when they are more mature.[21] And well-educated couples are, of course, somewhat older, on the average, than less-educated couples.

### Fertility

Fertility is the rate at which children are born into a population. Middle-class families in Western Europe and North America tend to limit the size of their families more than either working-class or upper-class families. However, birthrates are changing everywhere at a dramatic rate, and it is likely that in the future the differences in fertility between classes will disappear in Western populations.[22]

### Child rearing

Patterns of child care in the United States have changed a great deal during this century.[23] Between about 1930 and 1945 working-class mothers were more permissive than middle-class mothers. Middle-class mothers followed a rigid feeding schedule, while working-class children ate whenever they were hungry. But after World War II baby care manuals began to offer more permissive advice, and middle-class mothers have become more easygoing, allowing their children to have what they want more readily than working-class mothers do. But although they allow more impulsiveness and freedom they also expect more of their children than working-class mothers expect.

As for discipline, working-class parents are more likely to slap or spank, while middle-class parents are more likely to reason with their children, send them to their room, or try to get them to feel guilty. "Love withdrawal" techniques are also used by middle-class parents—they simply let children know how disappointing their behavior is. Here too, however, the gap between the social classes has been narrowing since 1945.

### Divorce

Since the 1920s better-educated white Americans have obtained fewer divorces than people with less education. However, among blacks the divorce rate has *increased* with education up to the college graduate level, where it declines sharply. Black college graduates obtain almost as few divorces as people with very little education.[24]

## CLASS AND MORTALITY

High-status people have a greater chance of staying alive than low-status people, though the difference in death rates has decreased sharply during this century. Mortality rates in all age groups are higher for black Americans than for whites. Infant mortality is twice as high for blacks as for whites, and maternal mortality in childbirth is four times as great among blacks as among whites. In 1974 a newborn white male could expect to live 68.9 years, compared to 62.9 years for black males. Newborn white females could expect to live 76.6 years and black females 71.2 years.[25]

## CLASS AND LIFE STYLE

Max Weber was particularly interested in the life styles—patterns of taste, speech, and manners—of different status groups, and sociologists continue to compare life styles as clues to social status. When you meet someone at a party, how long does it take you to estimate his or her social class? How long does it take in a phone conversation? The clues you use are aspects of life style.

A life style may develop as a result of other inequalities. For example, in order to enjoy literature one needs education, leisure, and the company of others who like to talk about books. But these opportunities are distributed unequally. On the other hand, a life style is sometimes used as a tool for gaining higher status: Thus a person may change his or her place of residence or join a different church to move to a new social level.

## CLASS AND VOLUNTARY-ASSOCIATION MEMBERSHIP

Several studies have shown that social class is related to participation in voluntary associations. For example, Melvin Tumin and Arnold Feldman found that education was linked with organizations membership in Puerto Rico.[26] James Curtis found the same relationship in Canada, Great Britain, Germany, Italy, Mexico, and the United States.[27]

## CLASS AND RELIGION

There are several ways in which social class and religion are connected. People of different strata tend to belong to different denominations and to show different degrees of religiousness. Church attendance also differs from one class to another. Although each Protestant church tends to get its members mostly from one class, the very rich and the very poor are not likely to be influenced by churches. Thus churches are mostly middle-class institutions.[28]

## CLASS AND POLITICS

As you might expect, social classes differ on political matters. That's understandable—people know "which side their bread is buttered on." And bread of the upper class is not buttered on the same side as the bread of the working class. Not only do their interests conflict, but their life styles, educational levels, and access to information differ, and all of these factors may lead to political differences.

In the United States (but not in Canada) members of different classes tend to vote for candidates of different parties. The working class has traditionally voted Democratic and the upper class Republican. The middle class has tended to be split between the two parties. There are so many more Democrats

**TABLE 9.2**

*Marital life style and social class*

| | HIGHBROW | UPPER MIDDLEBROW |
|---|---|---|
| How Girl Meets Boy | He was an usher at her best friend's wedding | At college, in the psychology lab |
| The Proposal | In his room during the Harvard-Princeton game | In the back seat of a Volkswagen |
| The Wedding | In her living room, by a federal judge | College chapel (nondenominational) |
| The Honeymoon | Mediterranean | Bahamas |
| Marriage Manual | *Kama Sutra* | *Sexual Efficiency in Marriage,* volumes I and II |
| Sleeping Arrangements | Double bed | King-size bed or twin beds with one headboard |
| Sleeping Attire | He: nothing. She: nothing | He: red turtleneck nightshirt. She: gown with matching peignoir |
| Background Music | Ravi Shankar or the Beatles | Wagner |
| Turn-Ons | Pot | Champagne and oysters |
| The Schedule | Spontaneously, on an average of 2.5 weekly (that means 2 times one week and 3 times another) | Twice a week and when the kids go to the Sunday matinee |
| Number of Children | 1 each by a previous marriage, or as many as God provides | 2.4 |
| Anniversary Celebrations | A weekend in Dublin | He gives her a new dishwasher. She gives him a power lawn mower |
| Quarrels | "I don't care what your analyst says" | "I don't care if he is your brother" |
| If the Marriage Needs Help | He consults her analyst. She consults his | They go (a) to a marriage counselor; (b) to the minister |
| The Affair | "But I assumed you knew" | "It was basically a problem in communication" |
| Sex Education | "Ask Doctor Grauber, dear, when you see him tomorrow" | "Well, you see, Daddy has something called a . . . etc. And Daddy and Mommy love each other very much" |
| Vacations | Europe in May. She takes the children to the Cape. He commutes | Europe in July. Family camping in Yosemite |
| Financial Arrangements | Separate trust funds | Joint checking account |
| Who Raises the Children | English nanny, boarding school, and Dr. Grauber | Mommy and Daddy, Cub Scouts, and Dr. Freud |

From William Simon and John Gagnon, "How Fashionable Is Your Sex Life?," *McCall's* (October 1969), pp. 58–59.

| LOWER MIDDLEBROW | LOWBROW |
|---|---|
| In the office, by the water cooler | On the block |
| After three drinks in an apartment he borrowed | In her home one night when Mom and Dad were at the movies |
| City Hall | Neighborhood church |
| Any Hilton hotel | Disneyland |
| Van de Velde | None |
| Twin beds with matching night tables | Double bed |
| He: pajamas. She: pajamas | He: underwear. She: nightgown |
| Sound track of *Dr. Zhivago* | Jackie Gleason and the Silver Strings |
| Manhattans and whisky sours | Beer |
| Twice a week and when the kids go to Sunday school | Twice on Saturday night |
| 3 | As many as God provides |
| Corsage and dinner out | Whitman Sampler and dinner at Howard Johnson's |
| "What do you think I'm made of?" | "Drop dead!" |
| He: to his successful brother. She: to her best friend | He: to the bartender. She: to her mother |
| "It was bigger than both of us" | "Some things no woman should have to put up with" |
| "Well, you see, Daddy puts the seed in Mommy's tummy, etc., etc." | "We got you at the hospital" |
| He hunts or fishes. She visits Mother with the children | They visit Brother Charlie in Des Moines |
| She budgets | He gets weekly allowance |
| Mom and Dad, the Little League, and Dr. Spock | Mom, the gang, Ann Landers, and good luck |

than Republicans that one would not expect Republicans to win many elections, but there is one factor that works in their favor: Members of the working classes participate less in politics and turn out for elections in smaller numbers. This means that Democrats often lose votes because they can't count on their supporters to show up at the polls. So Democrats have traditionally been concerned with "getting out the vote"—calling people up and offering to drive them to the polling place if necessary. In nice weather Democratic candidates usually do better.

These patterns are changing, however. More working-class citizens participate in politics than before. And not all U.S. elections show the familiar pattern of class-differentiated voting.

Which classes are more conservative, which more liberal? Seymour Martin Lipset has shown that it is important to distinguish between *economic* and *noneconomic* issues when discussing liberalism.[29] Working-class people take a liberal position on economic issues, as you might expect. That is, they want many social services to be supported with taxes, and they don't mind if the government regulates business and trade as long as such regulation is in the interests of ordinary people. They'll vote for the candidate who promises jobs, support for unions, unemployment insurance, and so on. Middle- and upper-class people are more wary of such matters and tend to believe that workers' economic problems should be solved by their families or by private charities such as churches. "Protect individual initiative!" is their slogan.

But on noneconomic issues things go in the other direction. These are issues such as tolerance of the rights of minorities. On issues such as abortion, homosexual's and women's rights, or legalization of marijuana we find a pattern of liberalism among the upper and middle classes and conservatism among the working classes.[30]

## CLASS AND PERSONAL ADJUSTMENT

Because classes have different subcultures, they also have somewhat different personality patterns. Families in different classes orient their members along different lines.[31] Thus the upper class works to maintain its social position; the middle class concentrates on achievement and mobility; and the lower class is concerned with problems of income, illness, and unemployment. One review of research on stratification and personal adjustment came up with the following conclusions:

1 Lower-class women show less imagination, are more impulsive, have greater fear of the unknown, and are more likely to fear that they will not succeed.
2 Lower-class women participate more in basic household decisions.
3 Lower-class families are less willing to postpone rewards than other families.
4 Lower-class men and women are more direct and unrestrained in their expression of emotions.
5 Lower-class parent–child relationships are more hierarchical and rigid.
6 Middle-class people are more strongly oriented toward achievement, and this is reflected in their personalities.
7 There is a higher percentage of authoritarians in the lower class than in either the middle class or the upper class.
8 There is a greater sense of helplessness, powerlessness, and distrust in members of the lower class, who are more likely to see the world as hostile.

Not all of these generalizations have been proved, but enough of them are supported by evidence to be consistent with the fact that there is a relationship between social class and hospitalization for mental illness. To experience life as a lower-class citizen is to undergo stress every day. This stress weakens one's trust and ability to cope. Self-esteem is the most important ingredient of emotional well-being. And it is hard to have high self-esteem as a member of the lower class in a society that expects people to compete for status and to judge their own worth in terms of their rank.

## Social mobility

Social systems differ greatly in their openness, in the degree of opportunity their members have to move from one status level to another and from one job to another. The study of such movement is the study of social mobility. Movement toward higher status is called *upward* mobility; movement toward lower status is called *downward* mobility; and movement either upward or downward is called vertical mobility. The opportunity to change jobs without gaining or losing status is called horizontal mobility. For example, if a file clerk becomes a phone operator, this is horizontal mobility. Here we will concentrate on *intergenerational* vertical mobility—that is, the occupational status of a person relative to the occupational status of his or her father. If the son of a Supreme Court justice ends up as a street sweeper, he has shown a dramatic degree of downward mobility; if a street sweeper's son becomes a Supreme Court justice, he is an example of upward mobility. Few people move so far up or down the stratification ladder, however.

In a perfectly open society one's chance to occupy a given position is limited only by one's preferences and ability. At the opposite extreme is the totally closed society, in which mobility is impossible. Once a person has been assigned to a given position it cannot be changed. Both of these types of societies are imaginary; all real societies fall somewhere between these two extremes (even traditional India was not totally closed).

Industrial societies all have higher rates of social mobility than agrarian societies, for two reasons. First, industrial societies tend to assign status on the basis of achievement rather than ascribed characteristics. Second, the percentage of upper- and middle-status jobs increases as a society industrializes. This means that upward mobility is more common than downward mobility in industrial societies, while the reverse is true of agrarian societies.

### MOBILITY IN AMERICA

Mobility rates have remained fairly stable in America for many years. Between 1962 and 1970 there has been a trend toward managerial, professional, and skilled work and away from less-skilled manual work. This change was more rapid during the 1960s than during the 1950s, but less so than during the period from 1942 to 1952.[32]

There is evidence that these rates are not, on the whole, higher in the United States than in other Western countries, contrary to popular belief. The United States is not the only land of opportunity.[33] In *Social Mobility in Industrial Society* Seymour Martin Lipset and Reinhard Bendix present evidence that the general pattern of social mobility is much the same in all the Western industrial societies.[34] Other researchers, however, have found that although the United States does not differ from other countries in *total* upward mobility, it is more open for *low-status males* than other countries. That is, while middle-class American males do not have a very high chance of moving up, lower-status males do. The percentage of working-class American men who move into high-ranking jobs is higher than in any other society.[35]

Lipset and Bendix argue that mobility patterns in Western industrial societies are determined far more by occupational opportunities than by differences in values. They believe that "the desire to rise in status is

*The people who live under systems of closed stratification have very little chance for vertical mobility. India's traditional caste system was the most closed society known.*

intrinsic in all persons of lower status. . . . Individuals and groups will attempt to improve their status (and self-evaluation) whenever they have any chance to do so."[36] Thus it is obvious that the fact that there are more computer operators and fewer blacksmiths today than fifty years ago has nothing to do with the ambitiousness of the computer people or with the open hiring policies of employers. People have been upwardly mobile simply because the jobs at the top have opened up.

### THE CAUSES OF MOBILITY

The most important study of mobility done so far in the United States is Peter M. Blau and Otis Dudley Duncan's *The American Occupational Structure.* This 1962 study was based on responses from 20,700 males between 20 and 64 years of age. It revealed class boundaries that limit mobility between three strata—white collar, blue collar, and farm. Whatever mobility one experiences is likely to take place within one of these categories, with one exception: Many farm workers have been forced to move into other lines of work because of the mechanization of agriculture over the past 50 years. Many farmers' sons have gone into blue-collar work, for few can compete for white-collar jobs.[37]

The sons of white-collar workers prefer to remain in the white-collar class, even if such jobs pay less than do manual jobs. On the other hand, blue-collar workers are not so willing to sacrifice economic advantages for white-collar status. Therefore nonmanual jobs such as that of file clerk or sales clerk are usually filled by sons of white-collar workers rather than by upwardly mobile workers from blue-collar backgrounds.

There is more upward mobility than downward mobility, and education is the most important factor in mobility. (See Figure 8.3.) Another important factor is willingness to move some distance from home for a better job. The men who lived in their home towns from childhood through adulthood were far less successful than those who moved away after age 16.[38]

It is an important advantage for a child not to have many siblings—especially younger siblings. Blau and Duncan found that the first-born sons and the youngest sons in small families were better educated and more upwardly mobile in their careers than middle children. Only children did even better in school, but their occupational success was not much greater than that of first-born or youngest sons.[39]

Contrary to popular belief, Blau and Duncan found that a man's chances of moving upward are not affected by the status of the woman he marries. The men who married high-status women were themselves unusually able and could get good jobs without depending on their wives' status.[40]

In recent years scholars have been interested in finding out how status is acquired. Here is what Jonathan Kelley has found.

Think of four or five young adult men whom you know. Now suppose you are trying to guess which of them will be most successful later in life. What fact about their present life will tell you the most about their future? Their present job? Their income? Their family background? Their education? Answer: their present job. That's the main thing you need to know to predict future status. Present income doesn't help a man get ahead. It is nice to have, of course, because he can spend it. But he can't invest it in any way that is likely to make much difference in his future status. His family background is not important after his career is under way. It

makes a difference in getting him started in his first job, but after that he's on his own. Daddy can't do much for him. What about his education? It's the same story. Education makes a big difference in the job a man gets at first, but after that he has to prove what he can do. However, education is somewhat more important than either family background or present income because it continues to be a factor in how well a man is likely to do during the middle of his career. Otherwise, what a man did or had in the past is unimportant. It's what he can do now that determines where he is going.[41]

## SOME EFFECTS OF MOBILITY

What are the effects of mobility on a person's values and attitudes? We're not sure. Early studies suggested that the political and social outlook of downwardly mobile people is similar in all countries. They appeared to vote more conservatively than the other members of the class into which they had fallen. Mostly they held to a conservative view of stratification itself—a view that would have been appropriate in their original status but not in the lower one to which they had fallen. It was as if they were trying not to identify with the working class and hoped that by thinking of themselves as middle or upper class they could regain the status they had lost. "Skidders," as they are called, continued to believe that they live in an open-class society and to hope for middle-class positions for themselves and for their children.[42]

Later studies have not always supported the findings of the earlier studies, and today some sociologists doubt that socially mobile people differ in any consistent way from other people. It is pretty clear, however, that a change in status causes psychological strain, whether the movement is upward or downward. There is some evidence that downwardly mobile people tend to hold onto their self-esteem by showing scorn for others. A study of 150 Chicago veterans found that strong negative attitudes toward blacks were most common in the downwardly mobile group, while the upwardly mobile group was least prejudiced.[43] Other researchers have also found a weak tendency for upwardly mobile people to have liberal political attitudes.[44]

Upwardly mobile people have their own problems, however. It has been shown there is a relationship between emotional tension and upward mobility.[45] Moreover, upwardly mobile people are likely to judge their own occupational group favorably if they are accepted by its members, and in this way they reduce the strain of mobility. But if they are not accepted by the members of their occupational group they are likely to react by disliking that group.[46]

## Three approaches to stratification

There are three main approaches to social stratification: (1) Marxism, (2) the ideas of Max Weber, and (3) the functionalist view, best represented by Kingsley Davis and Wilbert Moore.

### MARX

"The history of all hitherto existing societies," Marx declared in his famous *Communist Manifesto*, "is the history of class struggle." And struggle is the most important concept in Marxist sociology. Marx pointed out that classes develop on the basis of the different positions that exist in a given system of production. In an agrarian society the main classes are landowners versus tenants. In an industrial economy the main classes are the capitalist owners of the factories versus the workers.

I say *versus* because that is how Marx saw it. Different classes have opposing interests. The ruling class always keeps whatever profit it can squeeze out of the workers. And the workers cannot afford to complain much because the ruling class is in control. Besides, the workers may not understand their situation very well. They may not even know that they are a social class. Marx referred to a group that is a class but is not aware of this fact as a class "*in* itself." Its members are in the same economic boat.

Marx was confident that in time workers would develop "class consciousness" and thereby become a class "*for* itself"; that is, they would recognize that they had common interests and develop a sense of solidarity. The final stage of class consciousness would be reached when the working class came to believe that only by overthrowing the capitalist owners could they seize what was rightfully theirs. Then they would join together to take over the means of production—the factories, the tools, and all the rest.

### WEBER

Max Weber is sometimes viewed as the opposite of Marx. This is a mistake; Weber agreed with many elements of Marxist thought. In particular, he also saw the economy as the main cause of stratification. For both Marx and Weber control over property is a basic factor in the life chances of an individual or class. However, Weber added to the economic dimension of stratification two other dimensions: *power* and *prestige*. Weber saw property, power, and prestige as three separate, though interacting, factors. Property differences produce *classes*; prestige differences produce *status groupings* or *strata*; and power differences produce what he termed *parties* (meaning factions or political blocs).

So far we have used the terms *status* and *class* as if they were interchangeable. In most sociological writings they do mean about the same thing. But to Weber they did not. Classes were based on property, status groups on prestige.

While Marx assumed that the members of any economic class would develop class consciousness and recognize their common interests, Weber did not expect this to happen all the time. In fact Weber said that economic classes do not normally form communities while status groups do. Status groups are based on shared prestige or honor, and economic factors alone do not determine honor or prestige. Many people who have suddenly become rich have found that their new fortune will buy a mansion but will not get them invited into the homes of the old-rich families who live next door.

Usually, Weber says, members of a high-status group feel united in trying to "put down" people who think money entitles them to prestige. Indeed, the high-status group usually tries to make its status independent of property. Its members may lose their money, but they continue to emphasize the superiority of their life style, family connections, and so forth. This limits movement into or out of the high-status group.

According to Weber, property differences have important effects on life chances but status differences lead to differences in life style—tastes and manners. Whether you spend an evening at the opera or at the bowling alley may say nothing about your financial condition but say quite a bit about the status group to which you belong. Differences in life styles are an important element in the exclusiveness of various status groups. To feel comfortable in a high-status group one must be able to use the proper accent and the right fork; such elements of life style can be acquired only through experience, often expensive experience. Thus, along with Marx, Weber recog-

*How much can you guess about the life style of these men off the job?*

Lizabeth Corlett/DPI

nized the importance of property differences *in the long run* in forming status groups and in hardening the lines between them. Over many generations money will produce status groupings, but only if it is used to "buy" a life style. Newly rich people may not be invited to dinner, but if the children go to private schools and learn "proper" manners they will eventually gain prestige and honor.

Weber differed from Marx in that he emphasized the importance of status groups and believed that it was unlikely that the working class would develop class consciousness. Also, he was very interested in the social changes that result from the interaction between status and class. Marx's theory simply does not lead us to look at the psychological strain involved in having status inconsistency (conflicting status and class), but Weber's theory is well suited to this question.

The third type of stratification listed by Weber is the *party.* Although according to Weber the basis of classes is economic and that of status groups is honor, " 'parties' live in a house of 'power.' " Parties are possible only within communities that have rules of order and a "staff or persons who are ready to enforce [them]. For parties aim precisely at influencing this staff, and seek, if possible, to recruit it from party followers."[47] Again, we must remember that the term *party* is used here to refer to any group that is formed for the purpose of dominating an organized group. It refers as much to a group seeking power within a social club as to a political party. Weber believed that parties may form on the basis of similar "class" interests or similar "status" interests or both, "but they need be neither purely 'class' nor purely 'status' parties, and frequently they are neither."[48]

To sum up, Weber's approach suggests that society is made up of three kinds of social groups. These groups differ in unity and in the kind of social resources with which they are concerned. Classes are based on economic resources, status groups on prestige or honor, and parties on power. These groups often have overlapping memberships, and sometimes an economic class is practically identical with a status group and a political party. But this is only one of many possibilities.

Suppose a sociologist agrees with Weber on the matter of stratification. How does this approach differ from the Marxist approach in practice? The answer is that the Weberian will probably classify people into different social strata according to subjective rather than objective standards. The objective Marxist would use property ownership or levels of income. The Weberian would use more subtle indicators of social status than the Marxist. In fact most Weberians rely on techniques developed in 1930 by W. Lloyd Warner in the study of a community that he called "Yankee City."[49] Warner's approach asks how the people within a given population see themselves and one another, regardless of the objective differences in their incomes or occupations. Warner would seek information on the following questions:

1 What are the standards by which the members of a society judge each other to be equal or unequal?
2 How much importance do they give to each of these standards?
3 How many groups or strata do they see in their community?
4 How do they rate themselves?
5 How are they rated by others?
6 Who associates with whom in various social contexts?

Once a population has been divided into strata a sociologist of the Warner school studies other factors, such as patterns of career ambitions or rates of mental illness, to see the extent to which these factors (or "dependent variables") differ for members of the different social strata. The Warner approach assumes that life chances and life styles are determined not only by place of residence, occupation, and the like but also by the importance given to these various factors by the population being studied.

## THE FUNCTIONALIST VIEW

Although Marx strongly emphasized social inequality, he did not think it was a permanent condition of human society and certainly did not believe it was either useful or necessary. To Marx, stratification represented injustice and exploitation, nothing more. But many social theorists both before and since Marx's time have disagreed, and none have been as convincing as the modern functionalists. More than thirty years ago Kingsley Davis and Wilbert Moore proposed a theory that has been debated ever since.[50] Today the Davis–Moore theory is challenged by more sociologists than ever before because it is the kind of conservative, functionalist doctrine that is maddening to reformists.

Davis and Moore argued that there are limits to the possibility of creating social equality, that social stratification is not only universal but functionally necessary for any society. (By *stratification* they mean unequal distribution of prestige and material rewards.) The reason stratification is necessary is very simple: Society uses prestige and material rewards to get people to occupy positions that are socially important and difficult to perform, jobs that require special training and uncommon ability. It is a matter of getting the best-qualified people to fill the most demanding and key positions in society. They wrote:

Some positions require innate talents of such a high degree that the persons who fill them are bound to be rare. In many cases, however, talent is fairly abundant in the population but the training process is so long, costly, and elaborate that relatively few can qualify. Modern medicine, for example, is within the mental capacity of most individuals, but a medical education is so burdensome and expensive that virtually none would undertake it if the position of the M.D. did not carry a reward commensurate with the sacrifice. . . . The position, if functionally important, must have an attractive power that will draw the necessary skills in competition with other positions. This means, in effect, that the position must

be high in the social scale—must command great prestige, high salary, ample leisure, and the like.[51]

Davis and Moore saw social stratification as a sort of market system, with scarce skills selling for high prices (prestige, power, and high salaries). They claimed that every society has to be stratified in order to motivate people to take on heavy responsibilities.

But you may have already noticed some problems with this explanation. For one thing, no society shows a strict one-to-one relationship between rewards and performance in important, socially useful positions. Swindlers sometimes become rich without performing any useful service to humanity. Some people inherit property and never have to work. Movie stars are paid astonishing salaries, but are their roles more "important" or do they need more training than truck drivers? It is possible to accept the functionalist argument and still think that there is a great deal more inequality in any given social system than is needed to fill important roles. Thus even if Davis and Moore have correctly described how societies use social rewards to attract qualified people to fill important roles, it does not follow from this theory that any particular society has the best possible distribution of rewards.

Worse yet, one must assume that even if there is a good distribution at first, any system of rewards will tend to drift toward inequality because power is one of the rewards attached to key positions. Once people gain power, they are likely to use it to maintain their privileges even if they fail to perform socially useful services. They are also likely to use it for their relatives and friends. In short, power corrupts, and therefore no system of social rewards is free from the possibility of injustice. Thus even a person who accepts Davis and Moore's basic theory still has to worry about social justice.

We must go further, however, and question whether the basic theory is worth accepting at all. Davis and Moore argued that if key positions were not highly rewarded qualified people might not be attracted to them. This is not necessarily so. No one argues that varying rewards keep an *ascriptive* society going. In India, as we have seen, people traditionally performed whatever role they were assigned by birth, regardless of how unattractive it was. Only an achievement-oriented society can be said to depend on a hierarchy of rewards, and even in such a society there are many exceptions to this rule. In the family, for example, role performance does not depend on rewards for good behavior. We do not think up "incentive plans" to get women to be good mothers. If the role is not its own reward, no system of rewards will do any good.

But what makes certain jobs more attractive than others, if not the pay and prestige that go with them? Possibly the authority they carry.[52] Authority is so important that it may make other rewards unnecessary. A key position is one that is *necessarily* authoritative. In what sense does the executive play a "key" role while his or her secretary does not? The answer is this: The secretary's activities are organized around the executive, not vice versa. We can imagine a company in which a secretary's salary is higher than that of the president, but we can hardly imagine a company in which the president must dictate only the kinds of letters that the secretary enjoys typing. The role of the executive involves authority, not because it is a "reward" but because it is an essential part of the role. Because most people enjoy having authority the "key" positions in society carry with them a major reward, the pleasure of using authority, and other rewards of a material nature may be unnecessary.

## SOCIAL RESEARCH: Sociologists at Work

One of the issues Marxist and non-Marxist sociologists argue about is whether there is a "ruling class" in America. Marxists, of course, say that there is, but others disagree. They admit that there are some enormously rich people in America, many of whom head corporations, so of course they are powerful within their companies. But are they a ruling *class*? No. They don't know each other, and therefore they couldn't be called a group any more than, say, the first 500 people listed in a phone book. A "ruling" class that never gets together cannot arrive at a common policy and therefore is not in any position to "rule."

Here I want to tell you some of the points G. William Domhoff makes in his little book, *The Bohemian Grove and Other Retreats.*[53]

### RULING-CLASS COHESIVENESS IN THE UNITED STATES

Beside the Russian River in a spectacular redwood forest called Bohemian Grove about 65 miles north of San Francisco, about 1500 men meet each year for a two-week vacation. The Bohemian Club may be the largest and yet the most exclusive group of rich and powerful men in America. Since 1880 its members have met each year to enjoy activities such as skeet shooting, swimming, and hiking. The setting is rustic and the lodgings not particularly expensive or posh because the men enjoy "roughing it"—living together in tents and doing many of their own chores.

But the point is hardly to save money. The club spends about $30,000 each year for one night's entertainment—a play written for the occasion and performed by the members themselves. Famous entertainers also come to perform at the camp—free of charge. Every day at 12:30 P.M. there is a talk by a well-known person in the arts, literature, science, or (especially on weekends, when attendance is high) the government. Political comments are all "off the record." In 1971, however, President Nixon had to cancel a talk at the club because newspaper reporters objected to being excluded. Past speakers have included governors, Supreme Court justices, senators, and at least one former President of the United States.

Men (and only men) come to the Grove from all over the United States. Domhoff studied lists of members and their guests and found that they included at least one officer or director of 40 of the 50 largest industrial corporations in America and 20 of the 25 top commercial banks. In addition, officers of 12 of the top 25 life insurance companies came to the camp. Of the 797 top-level corporations listed by *Fortune* magazine for 1969, 29 percent were "represented" in the club by at least one officer or director.[54]

The Bohemian Club is not the only such meeting place for America's top elite. Domhoff mentions other men's clubs that bring together powerful people on an informal basis. One is a Southern California club called Rancheros Visitadores that takes a cross-country horseback trip each year. Over half the Rancheros are businessmen, about one-fifth of them with corporations large enough to be listed in *Poor's Register of Corporations, Executives and Directors.*

There is a similar club in Colorado—the Roundup Riders of the Rockies—which is a copy of the Rancheros Visitadores. Again, about one-fifth of the out-of-state business members are listed in *Poor's* directory. Two other clubs that imitate the Rancheros are the Desert Caballeros and the Verde Vaqueros, both based in Arizona. Not one to mince words, Domhoff names many of the most famous members of these clubs and their corporations.

Domhoff claims that cohesiveness is quite strong within these clubs. Further, he believes that they function as meeting places at which policies are worked out by members of America's ruling class. He does not suggest that they are the only organizations of this kind. Indeed, he has studied the membership of several other, more formal organizations. And he shows that the membership of these groups overlaps to a great extent. For example, of the 197 people who were members of the Business Council in 1973, 31 went to the Bohemian Grove in 1970, 49 were trustees of the Committee for Economic Development, and 42 were members of the Council on Foreign Relations. All of these groups are part of the interlocking set of private organizations that, according to Domhoff, make up America's ruling class.

# SOCIAL POLICY:
## Issues And Viewpoints

I am going to ask you some questions. Take your time to answer—they're hard. You may need the rest of your life to think about them.

1. *What kind of stratification system do you want?* You get three choices: (1) an ascribed, highly stratified society; (2) a stratified but open society in which rank is assigned on the basis of merit; and (3) an unstratified society in which rewards are distributed equally to all members who meet certain standards of behavior.

We needn't bother to talk about the first choice, because I doubt that you want such a society. Hardly anybody does, these days, since it's a caste system. Moving to the second and third choices, however, we run into some real issues. These are expressed in the following questions.

2. *To industrialize, does a poor society have to choose between inequality and totalitarianism?* Our period of history is one in which many societies are trying to make the leap from an agrarian to an industrial economy. But how can they get the cash to pay for factories, dams, schools, and the like? There is simply not enough money to build all these institutions, but somehow it has to be scraped together. Later we'll talk about how this was done in the West when our own industrialization was taking

place. But what is happening today in very poor nations?

If a country's wealth were distributed equally, and if people were allowed to spend their share, they would certainly do so. They would buy bread, shoes, refrigerators, bikes, and other things. But what a developing country has to do is get people to go barefoot and invest the money in power plants, steel mills, and so on, until these industries are established. In most underdeveloped countries land and wealth are held primarily by a small elite, a group that consumes scandalously more than its fair share. But there is *some* surplus for investment—probably a lot more than there would be if wealth were distributed equally.

It has been argued that if material inequality is to be corrected in a poor nation it must be replaced by a coercive political system that will repress the masses just as harshly as private ownership. Capital formation requires squeez-

ing the peasants. The question is, Who will do it? The rich owners or the government? Neither choice is pleasant, but poor nations have to choose one or the other if they are to catch up. Or so it is generally argued. I'm not sure. But obviously this is an important issue that must be considered before we can answer the first question. We'll discuss it again in later chapters. We can look for factors that seem to affect economic development, but the issue is too complex for this book to settle. We may not know the answer to this question for a generation or two.

3. *In an open, stratified system would the children of upper-status people still tend to win upper-status positons?* Suppose we provide all children with equal socialization experiences, equal education, the same vitamins every morning, piano lessons, trips to Europe, and equal opportuntiies to get good jobs. After that they would be promoted strictly on the basis of merit.

*Some authority seems to be necessary. I don't think it would work for people to take turns being justices of the Supreme Court.*

UPI

What would happen? Would the children of professionals and business executives continue to take the lion's share of the professional and executive jobs? Or would the children of plumbers and bus drivers move into these high positions in great numbers, with the children of the middle and upper classes having no more career success than any other group?

We don't know. A few sociologists think that ability is largely passed on through genes. I mentioned this possibility in the chapter on socialization. If children succeed or fail mostly on the basis of the genes they acquire from their parents, then more equal opportunity would not lead to more social mobility. Most working-class youth would become working-class adults, as they do now. Would that seem unfair to you? If so, the only remaining way to reduce unfairness would be to reduce stratification itself. That is, we could deliberately equalize incomes and status (e.g., by changing the tax laws). Your point of view on this issue will affect your answer to the first question.

4. *Would equal rewards undermine economic growth?* Economic conservatives think so. They think people work simply to get ahead. If it were not possible to get ahead because equality was guaranteed to all, people might stop working hard. The economy would come to a screeching halt.

There is some historical evidence to support this view. Early experiments in equalizing rewards in the Soviet Union had to be given up because the economy actually did not work very well. Yet in other places much greater equality has been achieved — communist China is one example.

Some say that people could be socialized to work regardless of whether they were rewarded with money or prestige. In the family, for example, we do our share of the work because we feel love or a sense of duty, not for rewards. Could society be organized in such a way that people would do their jobs in the same unselfish way?

5. *Could we enforce a policy of equality?* Suppose we passed a law that everyone must be paid the same wages. We know that some secretaries, for example, are better at their jobs than others. I think an employer would find a way to outbid other employers seeking to hire the best secretary. "Come to work for me, and I'll give you an office with a carpet, two afternoons a week off, and all the postage stamps you can use." How long would equality of rewards hold up?

We could probably maintain a lot more equality than we do, but never total equality.

6. *Could a society do without authority?* I think this is where equality is most likely to break down. Things don't run well if no one is in charge. Someone must make decisions. In a very simple organization we could rotate authority so that you would be chairperson this week and I'd take over next week, and Judy and Sam would have their turns too. But in a complex system specialization is necessary. I don't want flight attendants and baggage handlers to take turns piloting the airplane I fly in or running the air traffic control system. And you don't have time to learn all you would need to know to be prime minister for a week. Besides, by the time you have learned how to be a good prime minister you may want to keep the job, and you may have enough power to do so. The chance to use power appeals to many people. Those who like power often manage to keep it. Thus it is hard to equalize power or even to rotate it.

Now go back and think about our first question again. Take your time!

# SUMMARY

**1.** A *social class* is a set of people with similar socioeconomic status — similar amounts of property, prestige, and power.

**2.** *Ascribed status* is assigned on the basis of characteristics that one cannot control, such as race, sex, height, or age. *Achieved status* is assigned on the basis of performance. Both achieved status and ascribed status are found in all societies, but industrial societies use achievement as a standard more than preindustrial societies do. Caste is the most obvious example of ascribed status. Social classes are more open to mobility than castes are.

**3.** The term *social stratification* refers to a hierarchy of positions that are unequal in property, power, and prestige, the three bases of status. *Property* may be defined as rights over goods and services. *Power* refers to the ability to achieve one's goals even in the face of opposition. *Prestige* is social honor given to a person on the basis of the roles he or she occupies.

**4.** *Status inconsistency* results when a person has high status by one standard but low status by another—for example, high power and low prestige.

**5.** Life chances and life style are affected by social status. Compared with upper- and middle-class people, lower-class people have less chance of a successful marriage, have more children, are less permissive in their child rearing, and are somewhat less likely to have a long life. They are less likely to belong to a church, less likely to support conservative economic policies or liberal policies on matters of civil liberties and civil rights, and are more likely to be hospitalized for mental illness.

**6.** *Social mobility* refers to movement from one level of a social system to another or from one job to another. *Vertical mobility* refers to upward movement (gaining status) or downward movement (losing status). Changing jobs without gaining or losing status is called *horizontal mobility.*

**7.** Marx's view of social classes are based on the assumption that there is a con-flict between the owners of the means of production (e.g., factories) and the workers, who must sell their labor to survive. He assumed that the workers would develop class consciousness and would seize the means of production.

**8.** Weber's interpretation was not entirely opposed to Marx's, but he viewed status as consisting of three different, though interacting, hierarchies—classes, status groups, and parties (or factions). The three groups are based on differences in property, prestige, and power, respectively. Weber believed that class consciousness is rather uncommon but that status group consciousness is usual. A high-status group usually tries to make its status independent of property. In the long run money *does* produce status groupings, but only by "buying" a special life style for the well-to-do.

**9.** W. Lloyd Warner used a subjective method of classifying populations into strata. His approach is still used by researchers who hold to Weber's interpretation of status groups as different from social classes.

**10.** Functionalism views social stratification as necessary and universal. According to this approach, society uses prestige and material rewards to get people to perform roles that are socially important and difficult.

Critics of functionalism argue that no society has an entirely logical distribution of rewards. Besides, we have no way of finding out how much inequality is necessary. Clearly, however, authority cannot be equalized even if prestige and material rewards can.

# KEY TERMS

**achieved status** status assigned on the basis of standards over which a person has some control.

**ascribed status** status assigned on the basis of standards over which a person has no control.

**caste system** a closed stratification system.

**esteem** appreciation of a person regardless of his or her rank.

**horizontal mobility** social mobility that does not involve a gain or loss of status.

**life chances** patterns of infant mortality, physical and mental illness, childlessness, marital conflict, separation, divorce, etc; the opportunity for well being.

life style   patterns of eating and dressing, cultural and recreational activities, relationships between parents and children, etc.; the way people express their personal taste.

power   the ability to achieve one's goals even in the face of opposition.

prestige   social honor attached to particular roles.

property   rights or control over goods and services.

social class   a set of people of similar socio-economic status.

social mobility   movement from one status or occupation to another.

social stratification   a hierarchy of layers or strata that are unequal in terms of property, power, and prestige.

status   a person's rank based on income, prestige, education, or power.

status inconsistency   the situation in which a person ranks higher by one standard than by another.

vertical mobility   social mobility that involves movement toward higher or lower status.

# FOR FURTHER READING

ABRAHAMSON, MARK. *Stratification and Mobility.* New York: Macmillan, 1976. For most students, looking for a first textbook in stratification, this is a good choice. It has a number of articles on various topics, commonly with a functionalist slant. If you don't want any more functionalism, try a Tumin book instead, like the one below.

BLAU, PETER, and OTIS DUDLEY DUNCAN. *The American Occupational Structure.* New York: John Wiley, 1967. This is not meant to be light reading, but it is a truly definitive study of social mobility in the United States.

COLLINS, RANDALL. *Conflict Sociology: Toward An Explanatory Science.* New York: Academic Press, 1975. This is the most important theoretical book to appear in several years. It's not hard, but it's long, so it's not a good choice to take to the beach or on your ski trip.

CURTIS, JAMES E., and WILLIAM G. SCOTT. *Social Stratification: Canada.* Scarborough, Ont.: Prentice-Hall, 1973. A useful compilation of articles and parts of other books, all dealing with Canadian data.

DAVIS, KINGSLEY, and WILBERT MOORE. "Some Principles of Stratification." *American Sociological Review,* 10 (April 1945), 242–249. This article gives the classic formulation of the functionalist theory of social stratification. If you take a course in stratification, it is sure to be assigned reading.

GLENN, NORVALL D.; JON P. ALSTON; and DAVID WEINER. *Social Stratification: A Research Bibliography.* Berkeley: Glendessary, 1970. The field of social stratification is so wide that anybody planning research needs some help in sifting through the bibliographies to decide what is worth reading. This publication serves that purpose.

PORTER, JOHN. *The Vertical Mosaic: An Analysis of Class and Power in Canada.* Toronto: University of Toronto Press, 1968. This is probably the best sociology book ever written about Canada. Unfortunately, it is somewhat out of date by now. Keep that in mind while you read it, but do read it anyway.

RUBIN, LILLIAN B. *Worlds of Pain.* New York: Basic Books, 1977. This is a sensitive description of the personal life of lower-class Americans. The title gives away the plot.

TEPPERMAN, LORNE. *Social Mobility in Canada.* Toronto: McGraw-Hill Ryerson, 1975. Includes a lot of Canadian data on career mobility aspirations and impediments to mobility among such groups as French Canadians, women, and immigrants.

TUMIN, MELVIN M. *Social Stratification: The Forms and Functions of Inequality.* Englewood Cliffs, N.J.: Prentice-Hall, 1967. Part of this chapter was drawn from Tumin's book. Before you read the original book you should read the Davis-Moore article. Tumin gives the impression of being a sheriff on the lookout for some bad guys whose names he does not mention. (It's Davis and Moore.) If you too are opposed to functionalism, he may become your hero.

# RACIAL AND ETHNIC GROUPS

Toronto, where I live, is a city of immigrants from many nations. Every Friday at sundown one of the elevators in my apartment building observes the Sabbath. It starts going up and down, stopping at every floor automatically, so that Orthodox Jews can enter or leave their apartments without pressing the button, which is considered to be work and thus must not be done on the Sabbath. Most of the names beside the door buzzers downstairs are non-Anglo-Saxon. When I enter clothing stores nearby the salespeople speak to me in Portuguese or Italian. In one area the street signs are in Chinese as well as English. Children go to special classes after school or on Saturdays, usually in church basements, to learn how to read and write in their native language— Ukrainian, Greek, or one of the dozens of other tongues I hear spoken on the streets.

Ethnicity means different things to different people. I enjoy restaurants and movies, newspapers and grocery stores that cater to West Indians, Israelis, Poles, and so on. But a Pakistani friend is sometimes insulted by teenagers on the subway. And a student from India, who drives a cab at night to pay his way through college, says that a passenger makes a rude remark to him about once a night. Nobody calls me insulting names, but I can remember what it was like when my family moved from Oklahoma to California and, as a girl of 13, I blushed with shame and anger at being called an "Okie."

Okies were white Oklahomans who had long been American citizens, yet we were discriminated against as an ethnic group. We were recognized by our accents, but other aspects of our life style were different too. Okies came to California in search of jobs, and they had to take jobs at lower wages than local workers, who naturally hated them and wanted to keep them out.

My experience has been shared by members of many minority groups—ethnic groups that are discriminated against. I wish

discrimination and interethnic conflict were things of the past. But it's not—just look at your morning paper. You will read about Arab refugees in the Middle East or about American Indians who are jobless or about Jews in the Soviet Union or about the demands of some linguistic group for more power or for political separation from another linguistic group—the Tamils in India, the Québécois in Canada, the Basques in Spain.

Ours is an era of ethnicity. At the end of World War II we thought this would not be the case. We had seen in Nazi Germany what nationalism and racism could lead to, and we thought the world had learned its lesson. We hoped that the boundaries between nationalities, races, religious groups, and linguistic communities would soon be erased and that we would become "one world." Unfortunately, this did not happen, even in the United States. There are more new movements led by ethnic groups, nationalities, and religious groups now than there were then. Contrary to Marx's prediction, the history of our period is not one of *class* conflict but one of conflict between ethnic groups, including religious communities, linguistic groups, tribes, racial groups, nationalities, colonized native peoples—any big group that is held together by ascribed, not achieved, bonds.

Clearly there are two ways of looking at ethnicity. It produces variety, but it also produces conflict and discrimination. As you read this chapter you may find that your feelings are mixed. Pay attention to your feelings as you read about these matters. Feelings of resentment and scorn always accompany our beliefs and attitudes about justice and injustice, about dignity, equality, and our place in the ethnic hierarchy. It is likely that you will be more indignant about discrimination against "your people" than you would be about discrimination against your social class. By "your people" I mean your ascribed community. Whom do you have in mind when you say, "My people, the . . ."? Is it "We, the Arabs"? "We, the black Americans"? "We, the Quebec Anglophones"? You probably don't ever mean "We, the middle class"; rather, you mean your ethnic group.

# Ethnic groups, minorities, and racial groups

### ETHNIC GROUPS

An **ethnic group** is a large collectivity in which membership is generally inherited. Its members share a feeling of identification with the group. Examples are Polish Americans, Irish Catholics, Palestinian refugees, and the Parsis of India. The terms *ethnic group*, *ascribed community*, and a *people* are interchangeable. An ethnic group has the following characteristics:

**1** It is largely biologically self-perpetuating.
**2** It shares basic cultural values that are expressed in unified cultural forms.
**3** Its members communicate and interact with one another.
**4** Its members form a category that can be distinguished from other, similar social categories.[1]

The term *ethnic group* is sometimes used to refer to people of a particular national origin, such as Polish Americans. Our definition includes nationality, but it also includes tribes, linguistic groups (such as Anglophones and Francophones in Canada), racial groups (such as blacks and whites in the United States), and some religious groups—those that are ascribed, such as the Catholics and Protestants of Northern Ireland. Our definition is not limited to the small subgroups within a society but may include the dominant group as well, such as the WASP (White Anglo-Saxon Protestant) group in the United States. Jews are an ethnic group because they feel a strong sense

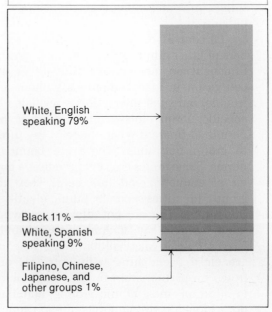

**FIGURE 10.1**

*Ethnic composition of the United States population.*

White, English speaking 79%

Black 11%
White, Spanish speaking 9%

Filipino, Chinese, Japanese, and other groups 1%

*Source:* Data taken from U.S. Dept. of Commerce, *Statistical Abstract of the U.S., 1977*

of "peoplehood" and meet the other standards of our definition, but it is not clear whether they should be understood as a nationality or as a religious community.

Ethnic groups always have **boundaries**— codes and customs that define a person as a member or nonmember. One knows whether or not one belongs to the group because belonging means accepting the group's norms. Indeed, it is highly unusual, and can even be dramatic, to cross group boundaries. It would be strange, for example, for a Mexican American to refuse to reply in Spanish to a question asked by a fellow Chicano, or for a Jew to take communion in an Anglican church.

It's hard to change ethnic groups. Membership in the group is supposed to be once and for all. To see other people as fellow members is to recognize that they are "playing the same game." They have the same social codes that you do. You know that outsiders have different ways of looking at things, and you limit your relationships with outsiders.

Of course you are bound to meet members of other ethnic groups. Indeed, interaction between members of different groups can go on in many situations without any trouble. But such interaction is regulated by specific norms. Interethnic contact is not permitted in areas where there is any threat to group traditions. These are boundary norms. Some topics are kept private as a matter of etiquette, and this helps keep the groups' identities separate. Ethnic identity is *imperative:* You are not allowed to switch around and be, say, an Arab this week and a Jew next week. Many ethnic groups discourage close friendships with outsiders and frown on participation in their ceremonies. In addition, most ethnic groups' boundary norms include strong norms of *endogamy*— the rule that members must marry within the group. Some groups disown members who violate this rule.

Strong boundaries keep ethnic groups separate, and therefore very few people are marginal. A **marginal person** is one who belongs to two or more separate groups that are supposedly mutually exclusive. An example would be a child whose mother is Christian and whose father is Muslim.

A society usually has certain rules for determining the identity of marginal people so that they can be defined as members of only one community. In societies that trace kinship through the father's side of the family, the child is usually assigned to his father's community. Children of Protestant–Catholic marriages are assigned to the Catholic community. In the case of black–white unions in the United States the child is defined as black. Other societies have different ways of defining marginal black–white people, however. In some Latin

American societies a child of a black–white marriage will be defined as black if his or her parents are poor but as white if they are rich. Indeed, if a poor black child becomes a rich adult the boundary norm will permit him or her to cross over from the black group to the white group! In South Africa the community of black Africans is defined as completely separate from the other three ascribed communities—the whites, the Asians, and the "coloreds," or mulattoes (mixed black and white). It is important to realize that these boundary norms are *social* definitions. They are not biological facts about a person but social rules that differ from one society to another. A mulatto, for example, would probably be considered black in the United States, "colored" and *not* black in South Africa, and perhaps white in Latin America.

The boundaries between some groups are much weaker than those between other groups. When boundaries are weak the number of marginal people may increase over time, people may stop paying much attention to which group they belong to, and the communities may gradually merge. Eventually the original groups no longer have separate identities. This is rare, however. Usually it is hard for a person to change his or her ethnic identity, either because the new group does not accept him or her or because changing is considered disloyal. Loyalty to an ascribed group can be a powerful social bond. One may view oneself as a traitor for "passing" as white if one was born black or becoming Christian if one was born Jewish. One does not feel guilty if one moves out of one's parents' social class, but ethnic membership is supposed to be permanent.

## MINORITY GROUPS

In some societies there are many ethnic groups that are about equal in prestige and privileges. In other times and places some groups are dominant and others subordinate. We call the subordinate ethnic groups minority groups, although in many cases their members actually outnumber those of the dominant groups. Examples are blacks and Chicanos in the United States, French speakers and Eskimos in Canada. A minority group suffers from discrimination regardless of whether it is large or small in proportion to the dominant community.

Boundaries are often used to control intergroup interactions. In certain cases, however, members of minority groups accept their low status and feel shame (stigma) because of it. In such cases boundaries still exist in that members are still able to recognize each other but may try to "pass" as members of another community. For example, the Norwegian social anthropologist Harald Eidheim reported that the Lapps of northern Norway try to conceal their ethnic identity, which they treat as a shameful secret.[2] During the early stages of his study, Eidheim was unable to determine who was and who was not Lappish, except that some people spoke a slightly broken Norwegian. He did notice, however, that many villagers made an effort to show off their Norwegianness—for instance, by pretending to know a lot about other parts of the country. He also found that many homemakers took pride in their kitchens and talked for hours about

*The worst thing about ethnicity is that members of minority groups may even feel ashamed of their identity. Many Lapps in Norway hide the fact that they are Lappish.*

Dirk Ketting/Stock, Boston

their cleanliness and good housekeeping habits. (Among Norwegians Lapps are considered dirty.) Eidheim avoided any mention of ethnic differences until he had shown that he was unbiased and that he knew a great deal about the Lappish population. Gradually the villagers told Eidheim that they spoke Lappish in private; Eidheim then told them that he could speak Lappish too. This led some villagers to admit that they had identity problems. They confessed that they were, after all, a kind of Lapp. Their parents had lived in turf huts and had worn Lappish costumes. They even revealed that they were worried that their low standard of living might be due to their being members of an inferior and stupid race.

The Lapps' poor self-image reflected the poor opinion Norwegians had of them. Eidheim noted that the Lapps were afraid to reveal their identity in relationships with Norwegians, who even consider the use of the Lappish language in their presence as highly improper. Thus two or three Lapps may speak Lappish quietly in a public hallway or staircase, but when a Norwegian approaches they shift languages temporarily. This norm, maintained by both groups, is part of the boundary governing the interaction between the two peoples. The Lapps know perfectly well who is a member of their community. However, because they want to be full members of Norwegian society they reserve their ethnic identity for life "backstage."

### RACIAL GROUPS

*Physical anthropologists* are scientists who classify the human species into various groups based on certain physical characteristics. These groups are commonly called *races*. (Not all physical characteristics are used to define races. For example, all people with red hair do not make up a race.) Some anthropologists claim that there are several hundred different races, whereas others recognize only a few. In fact, many physical anthropologists do not use the term *race* at all.

The number of categories an anthropologist uses is a matter of convenience, for races are simply pigeonholes set up by the researcher for his or her own purposes.

Everyone has a body, and everyone's body can be classified as to race, according to the breeding population to which its genes belong. However, *not everyone belongs to a racial group.* A **racial group** is an ascribed community (ethnic group) to which members are assigned on the basis of shared, inherited biological traits. The best-known example is the blacks; the American Indians and Eskimos are other examples. Not everyone is assigned to or participates in an ethnic group based on racial similarity. Consider, for example, an Eskimo girl adopted at birth by an American couple and brought up in Atlanta without every meeting any Eskimos or learning anything about Eskimo culture. A physical anthropologist might measure the little girl's body proportions, take blood samples for chemical analysis, and so on and determine that she belongs to the Eskimo *race*. However, there is no ethnic group of Eskimos living in Atlanta, so she could not belong to any such *racial group*. She may acquire an ethnic identity, however, by becoming a member of a group based on language, say, or religion. She may be brought up as a Polish American or as a Jew, for example. If she should happen to go to the Arctic and meet some Eskimos, she would have as much trouble understanding them as you or I would. She is a member of their "race," but she is not a member of their racial group—their ascribed community.

People who have certain racial traits in common may or may not constitute an ethnic group sharing a sense of "peoplehood." If they do, we define that community as a racial group. The blacks in the United States think of themselves and are thought of by others as a racial group. They communicate among themselves and share certain cultural understandings as well as physical traits. However, a Nigerian visiting the United States would be a member of the same race as American blacks but would not be a member of their racial group. The Nigerian might have as much trouble adjusting to life among American blacks as the Eskimo girl raised in Atlanta would have adjusting to life in an igloo. Belonging to a race is a matter of biological heredity, but belonging to a racial group is a matter of social experience. Thus a racial group is merely an ethnic group with a special type of boundary norm; it defines membership on the basis of biological characteristics.

Still, people may be members of a racial group without having inherited the racial traits that are supposed to define membership in the group. Many "black" people are blue-eyed blonds with hardly any Negroid traits, but if their social background is the black community they are full members of the black racial group.

## Minorities in North America

In this section I will describe the situation of several minority groups in North America—beginning, in most cases, with a quick look at their histories and then turning to the conditions they face today. In some cases the problems of minority groups are quite different in the United States and Canada.

### NATIVE MINORITIES

#### Indians in the United States

When Columbus arrived in North America there were probably between 1 and 3 million Indians living here. From that time until about 1900, the Indian population decreased steadily, partly because of diseases, such as smallpox, brought by the whites and partly as a result of slaughter by whites. Early in

this century the population began to increase, and it has now reached about 800,000 in the United States alone. Nearly one-quarter of these Indians live in Arizona and western New Mexico. The next-largest group—over 50,000—lives in Oklahoma.

The white explorers found a number of nonliterate peoples in North America—tribes that mostly hunted and gathered food. Their first contacts were often friendly. Conflict arose only when whites began taking over Indian land. In 1754 the British government forbade the buying or seizing of Indian lands, but the colonists broke this rule everywhere. After the American Revolution treaties were signed with various Indian tribes, but whenever the tribes failed to accept government terms military force was used. Moreover, treaties were often violated.

Early American settlers had tried to use

*Native peoples are the poorest minority groups in North America today.*

Karen Rosenthal/Stock, Boston

Indians as slaves, but the Indians were too successful at escaping and making their way through the woods to their own people. By 1700 black slaves were being brought in, but the whites feared that these new slaves might join forces with the Indians. Indeed, many blacks did run away, often to the Spanish colonists in Florida. The whites in the South played one group against another—tribe against tribe, village against village. They forbade any contact between Indians and blacks and tried to prevent Indians from coming into the area. They used black slaves as soldiers against the Indians and hired Indians to track down runaway slaves. The colonists also paid Indians to help put down slave revolts.

West of the Mississippi, relations between Indians and whites were affected by the gold rush and the settlement of the midwestern plains. The government took advantage of tribal rivalries to get Indians to kill Indians. In the long run, however, the tribes were not beaten by military force but by starvation caused by the whites' killing of buffalo.

In 1871 Congress decided that from then on no Indian tribes should be recognized for purposes of treaties but that they should become wards of the government instead. The purpose was to assimilate Indians into the American way of life. Indians were given portions of land and forced to become farmers. Their children were sent to boarding schools and forbidden to use Indian language or dress.

*Wounded Knee is a place with special historical meaning to American Indians. Some very angry Indians chose that spot to make a bitter demonstration against white America in 1973.*

UPI

By 1933 it was obvious that the Indians were resisting the pressure to adopt white ways. The government's policy then shifted toward one of greater respect for native traditions and self-government. The program did improve the Indians' situation. By 1948 they were able to vote in all states. However, the government again reversed its policy in the 1950s. It decided to gradually cease to recognize the Indians' special claims on it. The Bureau of Indian Affairs was to be closed. To the Indians this policy (known as *termination*) looked like another way of forcing them to give up their traditional way of life. Meanwhile Public Law 280 was passed, allowing state governments to govern Indian reservations. Until then the tribes had largely governed themselves.

The Indians were so demoralized by these changes that again the government recognized its mistake. By 1968 the Civil Rights Bill reversed Public Law 280 so that states cannot take over a reservation without tribal consent.

The Indians are the poorest group in America. Their birthrate is nearly double the national average, and their infant mortality is also far above the national average. The average life span of Indians is around 44 years. Over half of the Indians have less than an eighth-grade education, and about one-quarter of them are illiterate.[3] Unemployment, alcoholism, and disease are all everyday facts of life to Indians. Nothing in their experience prepares them to compete with white Americans on an equal basis. Yet their population is increasing very fast, partly because of their high birthrate and partly because it has become possible to control tuberculosis better than before. What will happen to these people as American society moves ahead and leaves the Indians even more disadvantaged compared to the rest of the population?

Resentment, even rage, is one thing that happens. In 1973, for example, the American Indian Movement (AIM) demonstrated its rage at Wounded Knee, South Dakota, where Indians had been massacred by whites many years ago. Today Indians demand (1) protection of treaty rights, (2) social services for Indians who are not living on reservations, (3) the right to have a voice in policies that concern them, and (4) a more responsive role for the Bureau of Indian Affairs.[4]

### Indians in Canada

From the beginning the Canadian government was generally more responsible toward its Indian population than the American government. For example, Mounted Police went west to prevent Indian wars of the kind that were so common in the American territories to the south. Only two important Indian rebellions occurred in the Canadian West, both led by Louis Riel, a Metis. [The Metis (pronounced MAY-tee) are a population of partly European, partly native Canadians who today number about 60,000.]

However, it is not clear that the Canadian policy toward Indians has been any better for the native peoples than the American policy. The Canadian government never recognized the tribes as separate nations for treaty purposes, nor did it permit tribal self-government. The effect of the dependency that resulted was a passive personality that makes it harder for many Indians to become assimilated. Yet today the government officially emphasizes a policy of assimilation.[5]

There are now almost a quarter of a million Canadian Indians, each registered as a member of one of the 557 Indian bands. They live on over 2000 different Reserves (Metis are not registered Indians and do not live on Reserves). Living conditions on the Reserves are not good. For example, about half the Reserve homes lack electricity.

### Eskimos

The Indians and Eskimos of the far north have fared no better than the natives farther south, though the situation varies from one place to another. The Alaskan Eskimos are better off than the others because they hold title to valuable land that may provide income from mineral and oil rights. The Eskimos of Labrador are under the jurisdiction of the Province of Newfoundland and do not have any special legal status. The other Canadian Eskimos are defined as a tribe of Indians and are controlled under the Indian Act. Their well-being has increased in recent years, but relative to the Kabloonas (whites) their standing is still very low. Before the fur trade period Eskimos pursued animals wherever they roamed, but after trading posts were set up they settled near them in small communities of between 300 and 500 people.[6]

The social life of the Arctic has been greatly affected by the military presence and also by the government, which has made the native people its wards. Housing standards have improved, though they are still far below those of Canada as a whole. Famine is no longer likely, and the death rate has been reduced; as a result the population of Canadian Eskimos, which numbered 8000 in 1948, has almost doubled since then. The region is overpopulated now relative to the wildlife, so it would no longer be possible for the people to return to their former way of life—today only a minority are full-time hunters and trappers. The others work for wages, sell handicrafts, or live on public support. Less than one-quarter of Canadian Eskimos are fully employed; most are government laborers.

Several organizations, such as the Canadian Welfare Council, are trying to find young Eskimos with leadership ability and to encourage political participation and autonomy. There is no tradition of strong leadership among the Eskimos, however, and this is a real problem today.

## ASIAN MINORITIES

Immigration laws prevented Asians from coming to live in North America during the period of mass immigration early in this century. Thus today the U.S. Asian population is not much more than 1 million of whom about 450,000 are of Chinese origin, about 600,000 of Japanese origin, some 100,000 from the Philippines, and a smaller number from India. In Canada there are only about 100,000 Asians, though many have arrived during the past decade or so.

### The Chinese

The ancestors of most of the Chinese people in North America were brought here to help build railroads. They stood out in the West during the Gold Rush, wearing long pigtails and felt slippers. In Canada many Chinese workers settled in scattered towns and became integrated into the society. Practically every Canadian town, no matter how small, now has a Chinese restaurant owned by the descendants of railroad workers. In the American West, those who did not return to China found their opportunities limited by discriminatory laws. Most of them lived crowded together in San Francisco, doing laundry work or selling vegetables on the street.

Unlike the scattered Chinese in Canada, who were more likely to be assimilated into the larger population, the urban California Chinese were close enough to one another to maintain their identity and traditions. They are still a distinct community today.

Legal immigration of Chinese stopped almost entirely between 1882 and 1943, though illegal immigrants continued to arrive. As a result the Chinese community has been very stable until recent years. Today, however, some new immigrants, with their revolutionary background, resent the traditional attitudes of the Chinese community. Violence has erupted within the community for the first time in decades.[7]

### The Japanese

Japanese immigration began when Chinese immigration stopped in the 1880s, and reached its peak just after 1900. The early Japanese arrivals were mostly unmarried men who worked for low wages as railroad, cannery, and logging camp laborers because they were unable to get more desirable jobs in industry. Gradually they moved into agricultural work, where they were so successful that by 1920 they farmed about one-eighth of California's irrigated land. They had taken large areas of undesirable land and made it fertile. But anti-Japanese lobbyists succeeded in limiting their access to new land in 1920, and second-generation Japanese turned to other occupations. However, as Stanford Lyman has pointed out, the Japanese had settled in rural areas where they could not always keep in touch with each other the way the Chinatown dwellers did. Therefore they were assimilated into the white communities.

The integration of the Japanese did them no good in 1942. Americans and Canadians were shocked and frightened by Pearl Harbor and expected an invasion at any time. They forced the Japanese to sell their farms quickly (usually at a loss) and spend the war years in relocation centers. There was no evidence that these citizens were any less loyal than Americans or Canadians of non-Asian origin, and after the war most of them returned to their former communities. They have become completely acculturated into those communities. Indeed, few Japanese schools or newspapers can be found today on the West Coast, where more than 300,000 Japanese now live. They are a very successful group within North American society— they actually exceed whites in occupational achievement,[8] in schooling, and even in life expectancy.[9]

### SPANISH-SPEAKING MINORITIES

The 1970 census counted more than 9 million Americans of Spanish-speaking background. This total includes the population of Puerto Rico, who are American citizens, and 5 million people of Mexican ancestry who live in the southwestern United States. Actually, most experts think there are a lot more than 9 million—the census may have undercounted by 3 million or so. This is a very rapidly growing part of the American population. In fact some people believe that by the time today's college students are senior citizens the United States will be a bilingual society—speaking Spanish as much as English!

### Puerto Ricans

Puerto Rico is a commonwealth of the United States. It may maintain its commonwealth status, become independent, or become a state. Because of a high unemployment rate on the island, as well as a high birthrate, many Puerto Ricans come to work on the American mainland—mostly in New York City, where more than 1 million Puerto Ricans now live. About one in three Puerto Ricans—usually young people—live for some time in the United States. Many return to the island, but an increasing percentage of those who stay on the mainland are gaining higher status and moving to New York's suburbs.

### Mexican Americans

Some of the Spanish villages north of Santa Fe, New Mexico were founded in 1598—long before the Mayflower's arrival. However, most of the immigration to the United States from Mexico has taken place during this century, chiefly workers in search of agricultural jobs in the Southwest. Despite the frequent movement of laborers across the border (both legally and illegally), the great majority of Mexican Americans are native-born American citizens. In New Mexico about half the population is made up of "Hispanos"—descendants of sixteenth-century Spanish explorers. In some counties the Hispanos cannot be considered a minority group, for they control the government. Anglo–Hispano relations are good in these areas.[10]

In other areas, however, though Mexican migrants ("Chicanos") are more numerous, their status is much lower than that of Hispanos. They have to compete with Anglos and use the English language. Their children have been discriminated against in the schools, and even the amount spent on their education is much lower than the amount spent to educate Anglo children. They are much less likely than Anglos to go on to college.[11] Their income is much lower than that of Anglo-Americans—though more than that of black Americans.

In the mid-1960s things began to change. The Chicano movement, a cultural and political movement that cuts across all social classes, got under way. Some Chicanos began to organize a political party and nominate candidates—in 1972 La Raza Unida's candidate for the governorship of Texas won 6 percent of the state's total vote. The best-known Chicano leader is Cesar Chavez, the man who organized the Mexican American farm workers. His support comes from many sources—from churches as well as from radicals who would like to stimulate a revolution along the lines of Castro's Cuban revolution.[12] But the Chicano movement's success has been largely cultural. It has created the feeling of pride and dignity that Mexican Americans call *chicanismo*.

### FRENCH CANADIANS

About 30 percent of all Canadians speak French as their native language. French is one of the two official languages of Canada. The settlement of New France (now mostly Quebec) began at the beginning of the seventeenth century with the fur trade. The original idea was to set up a feudal society with peasants, lords, and clergy. However, the lords gradually fell short on lordliness and generally became poor farmers themselves. The British conquered New France in 1760 and added it to their New England colonies. Soon afterwards, however, the American Revolution began and about 100,000 loyal British subjects fled to the British territories to the north. These English-speaking Canadians (Anglophones) soon dominated the Francophones in economic matters, and their descendants have continued to do so. Canadian society was isolated from the social changes brought about by both the democratic American Revolution and the antireligious French Revolution. Hence, with the approval of the British government the Canadians remained conservative for 200 years, until recently.

Although Quebec is still over 80 percent French-speaking the Anglophones have always held the most important positions in the economy. English was the language of business. Francophones had a high birthrate and might have overtaken the English-speaking population in Canada if they had been more interested in moving westward as settlers. Instead, they tended to move south into New England, where they were assimilated in the American "melting pot" within two generations. The far western Canadian provinces became mostly English speaking—so much so that the scattered French, greatly outnumbered, could not prevent their children from learning the language spoken around them. In Canada the French are far more likely than the English to become bilingual.

In recent decades Francophones had to worry about the possibility that French would cease to be spoken even in Quebec. Their birthrate has dropped greatly, so that they can no longer hope for the "revenge of the cradle." Also, Anglophones were migrating into Quebec to fill new jobs that required educated people, for the Francophones tended to be less well educated. Moreover, the Francophones were discriminated against. The difference in income between French- and English-speaking men was not due entirely to different levels of education. Statis-

*Canadians were stunned in 1976 by the victory of Quebec's separatist party, led by René Levesque, now premier of that French-speaking province.*

tics reveal that French speakers have been kept out of good jobs.[13]

The French Canadians awoke to their situation in 1959 and began their "Quiet Revolution." A Liberal government came to power in Quebec, promising educational reforms and more government jobs for Francophones. Some Québecois began to demand that Quebec become separate from Canada. The Parti Québecois gained a lot of popular support. However, in 1970 a tiny group of separatists became active terrorists and the federal government responded with repressive actions that violated the civil liberties of many Québecois. Most Anglophones outside of Quebec supported the government's reaction, and this attitude angered the Francophones even more.

French Canadians have given up hope that the French language will survive long outside of Quebec, especially in the prairie provinces. But within Quebec French still has a chance. That's where all the excitement is now. In 1974 Quebec passed the controversial Bill 22, which has had an important effect on the education of children whose native language is not English. About 90 percent of the new immigrants to Canada had chosen English, rather than French, as their new language. Their children, most of whom went to English-language schools, were suddenly forced to switch to French schools unless they could speak English well by the age of 6. Anglophones living in Montreal were outraged by this law. No doubt it will reverse the general

281

trend for Quebec to become increasingly Anglophone as a result of immigration.

The 1976 Quebec elections stunned the rest of Canada. The Parti Québécois, led by separatist René Levesque, came to power, promising a referendum. Quebec was to vote on whether to remain part of Canada or not. I am writing this in 1978, and now the polls do not suggest that the separatists will win the referendum. But by the time this book appears in print the polls may have changed, and so may Canada.

If Quebec secedes, it will not be for economic reasons. Everybody recognizes that separation would be costly. But sometimes people make decisions on the basis of factors that seem more important to them than economic matters. Ethnicity and the survival of a culture and a linguistic tradition are important emotional matters.

### Slavery in the colonies

Oppression of blacks has a long history in North America. The people of Jamestown had slaves by 1619; those of New France had them by 1629.[14] (In the French colony, most slaves were Indians.) By 1750 the southern colonies were using the plantation system, so that slavery was very good for the economy. The invention of the cotton gin in 1793 resulted in an even greater demand for cheap plantation labor. Between 1790 and 1803 another 100,000 slaves were imported, mostly to southern plantations. In the North, by contrast, slaves were not necessary to the economy. Thus by 1790 all the blacks in Massachusetts were free while in some other states there were as many slaves as there were free blacks.[15]

The situation of slaves was far better in New France than in the English-speaking areas of North America. They were protected by special laws and had many of the rights of free people. Punishment was no more severe for them than for any other person. The Cath-

olic church accepted slaves, and the French sometimes married their slaves, both Indian and black.[16] Slavery was considered to be a temporary condition, and in many cases it actually was. France itself did not permit slavery, so officers who returned to France from Canada could not take their slaves with them. The British Loyalists brought slaves with them when they fled north from the American Revolution. But they too treated their slaves less severely than other American slave owners. By 1800 slavery had been abolished in Canada.[17]

Slavery in the southern colonies was far worse. Slaves had no rights in the eyes of whites. In response, slaves sometimes resisted the system both passively and actively. Many committed suicide; others rebelled. Herbert Aptheker has counted 250 slave rebellions involving 10 or more people. Some blacks shuffled around, smiled, and worked as inefficiently as possible. Many "played sick." One study of a plantation's sick records shows that an average of one work day in seven was missed on account of "illness," though almost no one was sick on Sunday. On the other hand, a great many slaves tried to maintain their dignity by holding their heads high whenever they could, working hard, and establishing close ties within their families.[18]

During the early period of slavery there was considerable genetic intermingling between Indians and blacks. One study estimated that up to one-quarter of all black Americans have some Indian ancestry. Later on, the sexual exploitation of black women by white men resulted in some mixing of the genes of blacks and whites.[19]

### Blacks in modern society

Slavery ended in 1865, but oppression of blacks did not. For many generations whites maintained their "superiority" through Jim Crow laws and by terrorizing any black who claimed equality. Discrimination was required by law throughout the South. Lynchings and Ku Klux Klan raids were common. No black dared challenge the system. Being "uppity" could result in death.

But changes were taking place. For the past several decades blacks have been moving from the South to the North and West and from farms to cities. Today only about half of all blacks live in the South. Blacks amount to about 12 percent of the American population, and this percentage is slowly increasing because their birth rate is still fairly high.

One of the great dramas of our century was the civil-rights movement. We already look back on it with a sort of nostalgia even though many of the leaders of the movement are still alive and active. It was a stirring period. Thousands of courageous people marched and sang together, facing angry opponents who wanted to keep them in their "place." The black leaders varied in style and personality—some were radical and militant, others cool and patient but just as determined. They ranged from Whitney Young to Stokely Carmichael to James Farmer to Angela Davis. And above all, there was Martin Luther King, Jr.

The civil-rights movement is the story of the blacks' search for pride and dignity. But did it succeed? How much did the movement actually achieve? The answer is that it accomplished many things but failed in some areas. Let's look over the gains and the areas where progress has been slow or nonexistent.

One positive result is that the government passed some important legislation. The Civil Rights Act of 1964 outlawed discrimi-

*The civil rights movement was deliberately calm and steady about demanding social change. This 1962 sit-in was led by black students, who quietly sat at the Woolworth counter until they were served.*

UPI

nation in employment and public facilities, created the Equal Employment Opportunity Commission, and acted to end segregation in schools. Later in the decade additional legislation forbade discrimination in the selling or renting of housing. The "Great Society" programs of the 1960s helped the poor (of whom a large percentage were black) with urban renewal, funds for education, and job training. Real opportunities opened up for blacks in many areas as a result of these programs.[20]

Equally important, perhaps, were the changes in white attitudes. There is no doubt that the civil-rights movement shifted public opinion away from prejudice and discrimination. For example, by 1972, 84 percent of a national sample of white Americans said that they would not be disturbed if a black with the same income and education moved onto their block. Even by the mid-1960s about 80 percent of the white population believed that blacks were as intelligent as

whites and that they could benefit from education to the same degree as whites. Support for integrated schools increased to 84 percent by 1972.[21] All of these results show much greater acceptance of blacks by whites than was the case before the civil-rights movement.

The effects of these attitude shifts began to be seen in the figures on employment and education. Today many blacks work in jobs that were formerly reserved for whites. The gap between the educational levels reached by the two races has narrowed. And the average income of black families has risen slightly more rapidly since World War II than the average income of white families.[22]

This is progress. But these gains all took place during the 1960s, not later. What we must realize is that the 1960s was a decade of economic prosperity and expansion. When the economy is moving along nicely it is easier to share the benefits than it is during hard times. And the 1970s are hard times, at least

*Some blacks have gained considerably as a direct result of the civil rights movement.*

Owen Franken/Stock, Boston

compared to the 1960s. Reynolds Farley has reviewed the evidence on education, employment, prestige, income, and earnings to determine whether the gains of the 1960s have held up for blacks during the 1970s. He finds that, on balance, blacks have held onto the progress made in the past decade. While the forward movement is not as great now as it was ten years ago, the life chances of blacks have not fallen relative to those of whites. Farley summarizes his research in these words:

Blacks and whites, especially the young, are more alike in years of school completed than ever before. Racial differences in the occupations of employed workers continue to decline . . . Indexes describing the income of specific types of families or the earnings of individuals generally reveal that racial differences moderated during the early years of the 1970s.

In some areas, the gains are impressive. Black women, for instance, obtain earnings comparable to those of white women with similar characteristics. However, not all indicators show improvement. Employment opportunities are apparently severely limited for many black men. The very high rates of unemployment and nonparticipation in the labor force suggest that numerous young blacks experience great difficulty in launching careers.[23]

Now for the bad news: Farley concludes at the end of his report that

reductions in inequality are small when compared to the remaining racial differences on many indicators. A continuation of the trends of the 1960s and 1970s offers no hope that racial differences will be eliminated soon. For instance, a higher proportion of white men in 1940 than black men in 1976 held white-collar jobs. The purchasing power of the typical black family in 1974 was equivalent to that of a white family twenty years earlier, and the earnings of black men lag far behind those of white men.[24]

There you have it. There has been progress; but not enough progress, not nearly enough.

## JEWS

The Jews in North America are descended from either Sephardic Jews (who had lived in Spain and the other Mediterranean countries for hundreds of years) or the *Ashkenazim* (who had lived in northern Europe and who resembled other northern European peoples). The earliest Jewish settlers in North America were a few Sephardic groups who came to the colonies in the seventeenth century. Their families had left Spain during the Spanish Inquisition.

In the eighteenth and early nineteenth centuries most of the Jewish immigrants to North America were Western Europeans. They included prosperous merchant families from Germany, who spoke German at home, supported Reform Judaism, and did not have a strong sense of Jewish identity.

Mass immigration of Jews began in the 1870s. During that decade the Jewish population of Canada more than doubled, and similar increases occurred in the United States. In 1881 the first Russian *pogrom* took place; it was followed by many others. Thousands of Russian Jews fled to the New World, where their fellow Jews helped them as best they could. Because they had lived in isolated villages in Eastern Europe, this group had maintained a strongly orthodox culture quite different from that of the sophisticated Jews of Western Europe. This new group of poor Jews took work as unskilled tradesmen or small businessmen, threatening the status of other poor Americans.

Most of the early Jewish settlers had become successful merchants and were considered equal to their Christian neighbors. However, the Jews from Eastern Europe experienced North America's first wave of anti-Semitism, which first arose among the WASP upper class. This group felt threatened by the new class of rich industrialists and took refuge in exclusive boarding

FREE
SOVIET
JEWRY

NEVER AGAIN
JEWISH DEFENSE LEAGU

Owen Franken/Stock, Boston

*Human rights has become an international concern, particularly for groups who have members throughout the world.*

schools, resorts, and country clubs. The resulting social restrictions, which had never existed before in America, filtered down into other classes, which were more affected by competition with the new immigrants, the East European Jews. "Old Stock" associations arose, in which social status was based on the date when one's ancestors had come to North America. Not only Jews but also Catholics and other minorities became scapegoats.[25] During the 1920s and 1930s anti-Semitism was at its peak. Jews were either entirely excluded from many important public institutions, such as universities, or admitted under a quota system.

The situation of Jews in America has improved greatly since World War II. Little open discrimination, but a fair amount of prejudice, still remains. In part this is a re-sult of the traditions of Christianity, which labeled Jews "Christ killers." Partly in response to the research of sociologists who showed that Christian rhetoric has been a strong factor in anti-Semitism, the Catholic church has stated that the Jews were not to blame for the death of Christ.[26]

Recent research suggests that in some communities anti-Semitism remains alive among American youth.[27] This is partly because many non-Jewish teenagers envy the success, wealth, popularity, and leadership skills of many high-status suburban Jewish teenagers. A second reason for their resentment stems from the concern of Jewish parents with maintaining their cultural tradition. For this reason they strongly hope that their children will not marry non-Jews. During the adolescent years, when dating be-

286

gins, Jewish parents encourage their children to date only members of their own group. Apparently, on occasion, non-Jewish teenagers interpret this tendency as "exclusiveness" or "clannishness." They feel hurt by what they see as social rejection and take on anti-Semitic attitudes in reaction.

On the other hand, the concern of Jewish parents about the possibility of intermarriage is well founded. About one-third of young Jewish people in the United States do marry outside of their faith.[28] Such high rates of intermarriage seem to threaten the future of the Jewish community to some degree.

## Prejudice and ideology

### PREJUDICE

**Prejudice** means "prejudging." In interethnic relationships it means prejudging *against* individuals on the basis of characteristics believed to be shared by members of the entire ethnic group. Moreover, this prejudging tends to be intense. A prejudiced person looks upon members of the out-group (usually a minority group) with such disfavor that no amount of evidence can persuade him or her to accept them. We are all familiar with prejudice against blacks, Jews, Puerto Ricans, and so forth, but we may not realize how extensive it really is.

Every normal person acquires the basis for certain prejudices against members of other ethnic groups in the course of growing up. It is impossible *not* to pick up such notions, for they are part of the culture. One learns such ditties as "Eenie meenie minie mo, catch a nigger by the toe" the same way one learns "Thirty days hath September, April, June, and November" or "One, two, buckle my shoe, three, four, shut the door."

Through social interaction one learns the normative boundaries that define one's group and how to identify "our people" and "them." At the same time, one learns the

relative ranks of "our people" and "them." One learns not only one's group's position but also the group's views on how it *should* be ranked.[29] A person does not develop this view independently on the basis of personal experience. Instead, it is the product of the group. A person's own experiences with the out-group may have been delightful. Still, if his or her group defines the out-group as a threat, as a loyal member he or she will be expected to maintain a guarded attitude toward them. Prejudice is created and maintained by the group; it is an ideological system that looks down upon the cultural and psychological traits of a rival group.

Prejudice involves making up a **stereotype**—a sort of mental cartoon—that exaggerates the traits of the typical member of the rival group. Perceptions of real members of that group tend to be distorted by the expectation that each person will resemble the stereotype. Thus blacks used to be stereotyped as unintelligent, irresponsible, with a strong sense of rhythm. The individual may never be given a chance to show his or her unique qualities; instead, he or she is judged entirely on the basis of his or her group membership. Prejudice consists of assuming too much on the basis of too little information. It is unreasonable to assign all the statistical facts about a collectivity—even if they are accurate facts—to each individual member of that collectivity. If a man's ethnic group has a mean income of $10,000 per year, a mean of 2.3 children, and a mean IQ of 102, this hardly proves that *he* has an income of $10,000 per year, 2.3 children, and an IQ of 102. Members of all ethnic groups vary in endless ways.

Gertrude J. Selznick and Stephen Steinberg have suggested that we all learn prejudice simply because we all learn popular culture. However, they also note that some people go on to learn a more sophisticated culture, usually through advanced education.[30] This second, more sophisticated culture offers a far more complex way of viewing human beings and members of other groups. It encourages a more tolerant outlook. People who reach this level of culture set aside simplistic prejudices they learned from popular culture. These stereotypes are never really "lost," however, for even a well-educated person remembers many childish descriptions of minority groups just as he or she remembers the myths that Scots are stingy and that redheads have hot tempers. But he or she does not take such myths seriously or base his or her actions on them. The prejudiced (often uneducated) person, on the other hand, continues to believe them.

### RACISM

One of the most influential ideologies of the past few centuries is racism. It arose and was passed along through the popular culture because many people did not know the difference between "races" and "racial groups." Racism can be defined as the belief that ethnic and racial groups are based on genetic similarities rather than on social agreements between people. That is, according to this theory the members of a racial group are bound together biologically rather than by choice.

Boundaries between peoples have existed for thousand of years, but the theory of racism has existed for only about 200 years. It began in northern Europe, and some of the people who developed it were liberal, humane scholars who appreciated the variety of human communities. They never suggested that one national community was better than any other. During this period the peoples of eastern Europe, especially Germany, were entering a period of ethnic awakening. The romantic movement made much of their growing nationalism, portraying humanity as made up of a number of ethnic groups, or "folk," each of which had its own collective "Geist," or spirit. The folk dances, art, histo-

ry, mythology, and other national traditions were all expressions of this *Geist*, which should be enjoyed and preserved. Each *Geist* was spiritually attached to its soil, its homeland. Its members were bound together by common ancestry, or "blood." One could find one's own identity only by fully participating in one's ancestral community. Each folk *Geist* was a single collective mind emerging into consciousness—a real, living being.

This racist theory confused a number of different ideas. It mixed together "race," "culture," "language," "homeland," and "group spirit." The implication was that one's membership in a particular group was determined by one's genetic makeup, not by the socialization process. The theory romanticized group membership as mystical and wonderful. Still, the theory was not necessarily harmful, for it did not imply that one folk was better than another or that one group should dominate another.

The transformation of racist theory into belief in the natural superiority of the German people came later, and with it came the conflicts leading up to World War II. The anti-Semitic composer Richard Wagner glorified the folk myths of the "Nordic race" in his operas, which inspired nationalists to believe that the Germanic "folk" were genetically equipped for dominance. Writers like Houston S. Chamberlain and Madison Grant urged that the "great" race not be mixed with inferior races—people who were fit only to be slaves.[31] Such ideas were very attractive to colonialists who wanted to justify aggression against "inferior races." As Ashley Montagu has noted in the title of one of his books, racist theory may be one of man's most dangerous myths.[32]

Let us repeat: A *race* is an objective classification based on skull measurements, blood types, endocrine secretions, hair texture, and the like. A *group*, on the other hand, has boundaries. Members can identify each other and have a sense of belonging together. However, groups *may* use a variety of different standards to define their boundaries—for example, religious affiliation, native language, or even physical traits such as shape of the head, hair texture, skin color, and the like. Though a race does not always constitute a group, a group may form on the basis of easily seen racial similarities. Social boundaries may be defined on any basis people choose, and the boundaries will be as real as people decide they are. If people decide that the basis for full membership in their group should be vegetarianism or baptism or circumcision or even Nordic ancestry, then any of those standards can become the boundary norm.

However, racists held that social boundaries were natural, not merely social. Something deep in the genetic system tied people together as a "folk" and gave them a spiritual attachment to their native land and a feeling for a certain language and culture. One could not escape one's racial–social identity. Indeed, one could find personal identity only through the culture to which one was biologically tied. Perhaps some people enjoyed a warm sense of belonging when they turned this idea over in their minds. But others had reason to feel otherwise, for the theory implied that psychological qualities are *necessarily* linked with physical traits and that they can never change. The "inferior" ethnic group must remain inferior forever.

Racist theory is almost a thing of the past. However, intergroup conflicts did not begin with racism and will not end with it. Groups can hate each other for all sorts of reasons without attributing the reasons to hereditary qualities. You and I may agree that our enemies, the Xrplmrqvtsp community, have bad manners, false gods, an unpronounceable language, clumsy art, animal-like sexual behavior, and halitosis without attributing any of these qualities to their genes. We may be uncharitable, but we are not racists for feeling this way. Only if we explain their behavior in terms of *hereditary qualities common to their breeding population* are we racists.

We should distinguish between racism and institutional racism, which is not a theory but the practice of indirect discrimination against minority races caused by policies of established institutions. For example, banks' lending regulations often demand collateral and a good credit rating. These regulations keep many black people from getting loans, even though every employee of the bank may like and respect black people. Thus institutions may keep certain groups in a minority position without meaning to. Institutional racism is different from personal racism, but the effect on minorities may be just as serious.

### NATIONALISM

Social scientists agree that social boundaries are arbitrary conventions. But this does not answer the question of why group feeling runs high in some historical periods. For example nationality simply was not important in the Middle Ages or in the Roman Empire, but it became important in Europe in modern times. Will tribalism, religious conflict, and nationalism become unimportant in the near future? If so, why?

Any answer to those questions requires a theory that will account for variations in the importance of ethnic-group membership. Karl Deutsch has proposed such a theory. He argues that modernization almost always increases ethnic consciousness (nationalism) and leads to demands for national autonomy. He uses the term *mobilization* to refer to periods of rapid modernization.[33]

Mobilization consists of increased communication. In a peasant community most interaction is limited to contacts between lifelong friends. Because peasants are not mobile, their social network is small and is

*When nationalism leads to fights for control of a particular homeland, some group is usually left homeless. This camp is the only home remaining for Arab Palestinian refugees, who have still not been resettled since Israel was founded as a Jewish state in 1948.*

composed of people they know well. They may worry about drought, bugs, and disease, but they do not have to worry about their relationships with other human beings. Modernization breaks up this social network and makes it necessary to interact with strangers. They go to sell their crops in the market and must bargain with people who may be untrustworthy. They learn to read newspapers written by people with strange and perhaps dangerous ideas. They move to town and see shop windows full of objects whose value they don't know. They register to vote and must choose which stranger to vote for.

These are all aspects of modernization. They move a person into a larger social network in which he or she must make fateful decisions in a context of uncertainty. The peasant does not know whom to trust, for it is necessary to communicate with strangers, both face to face and through mass media. Gone are the days when his or her dealings were only with people he or she knew.

Deutsch suggests that it is in just this situation that people try to reconstruct their familiar world. If they do not know whom to trust, they tend to choose people who are most similar to themselves. They seek out and magnify all the things they have in common, telling themselves that they have found new people who resemble those whom they have always known. Similar dialect, similar cooking, similar religion, similar folklore become the basis for solidarity. An ersatz community is built up out of desperation in an alien world. People may seek to live and work with others of their own ethnic group; they may vote for members of their "own people"; and they may demand political autonomy for their group. This is nationalism, or ethnic-group chauvinism. The nationalistic fights of the Balkan region are the classic examples of this pattern. The separatist movements within India, Belgium, Canada, and Nigeria also fit this pattern, and so does black nationalism in the United States. Whenever a group's we-feeling is built up, as happens in nationalism, conflicts with other groups become more likely.

It is obvious that more people will be uprooted in the future and that even the most remote village will be reached by communications from the outside world. All this mobilization will be unsettling and will lead to greater emphasis on ethnicity and nationality. On the other hand, other forces will tend to *integrate* groups into their wider social environment. These forces of integration sometimes have a stronger effect than mobilization itself. People may find it possible to gain some control over their social situation through the political process and other forms of association such as trade unions and schools. Thus they may set up business and social connections beyond the limits of their ethnic community, so that any nationalistic appeal may strike them as chauvinistic. Such developments lead toward assimilation and reduce the importance of ethnic affiliations. In most countries, however, mobilization will probably occur more rapidly than integration. In the future nationalism will probably flare up more and more often, causing many nations to split into smaller regional units.

# Patterns of group interaction

In this section I am going to introduce a classification system or *typology*. My typology of ethnic relations consists of three outcomes that might result when two or more ethnic groups come into contact with each other. They are (1) ethnic stratification, in which the groups form a hierarchy of dominance, as in caste societies and colonial regimes (e.g., South Africa); (2) ethnic pluralism, in which the groups become equal and live together on good terms, neither dominating the other (e.g., Switzerland); and (3) integration, in which equality is achieved by reducing the separation between the groups and encouraging them to participate in the same activities (e.g., Mexico). Let's discuss each of these possible outcomes in turn.

## ETHNIC STRATIFICATION

Ethnic stratification exists when two or more ethnic communities in an area have regular relationships of dominance and subordination that all members understand. The groups may depend on each other in some ways. The dominant group fares better in these transactions than the subordinate group. Two familiar examples are colonialism and segregation.

### Colonialism

For several hundred years European nations have dominated the rest of the world. This began when Columbus planted the Spanish flag on the soil of the New World, claiming the land for Spain. Before long almost every patch of territory around the globe had been "claimed" by one European monarch or another. Traders, settlers, and colonial administrators went to every corner of the world to bring "civilization" to the natives. Only in recent years have native peoples begun to win back the right to manage their own affairs. But until they won their independence and founded the many new nations of the world, they were treated as subordinates by the colonizers from Europe.

Colonialism was the most widespread system of ethnic stratification. As we have seen, the Europeans justified their exploitation of nonwhite natives in terms of racism. The colonizers considered themselves superior because of their biological traits and therefore felt no guilt about controlling and oppressing countless brown or black "subjects" in Africa, Asia, or America. The effect was to destroy the way of life of the colonized groups.

Robert Blauner has pointed out that the situation of blacks in America is very similar to the situation of colonized people around the world.[34] Unlike other immigrants to America, they did not come voluntarily, were unable to move around freely, and were not allowed to maintain their African traditions. Blacks had no control over their own institutions until recently, for the ghettos were controlled by "welfare colonialism" administered by white teachers, social workers, police officers, and politicians. Blauner argues that the ghetto riots of the 1960s were just like the anticolonial wars for independence that have been fought around the world since the last world war. The purpose was to clear out the aliens and allow the ethnic community to gain control of its own institutions.

### Segregation and discrimination

Colonialism is not the only form of ethnic stratification. Far more common is a pattern in which two or more ethnic groups live in the same area but have unequal status. Certain groups have minority status while others are in dominant positions. Indeed, in heterogeneous societies this pattern is more common than equality. The dominant group maintains its advantage through segregation and discrimination.

Segregation is the practice of forcing minority group members to work or live in separate areas whenever possible and to use facilities separate from those used by the dominant group. Whites in the United States used segregation as a way of maintaining distance between themselves and blacks, though the courts have ruled it illegal. Segregation in southern states, called Jim Crow, and was used to force blacks to use separate toilets, schools, drinking fountains, and restaurants and to sit in different sections of theaters and public vehicles. Segregation in South Africa, called *apartheid*, is still an official policy.

Segregation can result from the exclusiveness of one or more ethnic groups. Usually the dominant group enforces segregation, either through laws or through informal agreements. Discrimination is the process by which the dominant group informally deprives the minority group of equal access to privileges and opportunities—good jobs, seating in restaurants, membership in clubs, and the like.

Sometimes the minority group prefers a policy of self-segregation. Its members choose to live and work in a certain area of a city simply because other members of the same ethnic community live and work there. Such areas may be considered "ghettos" if people live there involuntarily and "neighborhoods" if people live together there voluntarily.

When segregation is carried to an extreme, the result is *partition*, in which the various ethnic groups live in separate areas that are no longer parts of the same country. When intergroup tension runs high, it is not uncommon for some members of one or all of the groups involved to propose partition as a solution. This outcome does not necessarily end the conflict between the groups, however. For example, the partition of Palestine led to the creation of the state of Israel but did not end the tension between Israel and its Arab neighbors. The partition of Ireland into Protestant and Catholic regions did not end the religious conflict in Ulster. The partition of Canada into two separate states may create an independent Quebec, with results that cannot be foreseen.

When partition occurs, the ethnic-group members who are located in the area claimed by the other group find themselves in an unfavorable position. For example, the Arabs living in what became Israel do not have the same status as Jewish Israeli citizens. Similarly, Catholics living in Northern Ireland are at a disadvantage compared to Protestants. Their militant members, the Irish Republican Army, turned to terrorism in an attempt to change this situation.

### Expulsion or annihilation

Expulsion is often used by new regimes to put down dissent. The minority group members are simply sent to another country. General Idi Amin of Uganda has expelled a number of minorities from his country, notably the Asians who made up most of the Ugandan business class.

Expulsion is a severe way of treating minorities, but a far worse policy has sometimes been pursued — annihilation. That is, one ethnic community may simply attack another and destroy its whole population. Many American Indians were annihilated during the opening of the West. Over 4 million Jews were annihilated by Germany during World War II. It is sad to realize that *genocide*, or the planned annihilation of whole peoples, is not a rare outcome of ethnic stratification.

### ETHNIC PLURALISM

The second category of our typology is ethnic pluralism. This is the situation that exists when two or more ethnic groups live side by side with neither group trying to dominate the other. Each community is politically, economically, and culturally distinct from the other. The groups do not interact to any great extent. The boundary norms are well-understood and discourage inter-

group relations in most matters. Members of the different groups do not try very hard to communicate across the gap between them but are satisfied to consider each other strangers. You can think of a plural society as two or more quite separate communication networks in the same region.

Societies that are characterized by ethnic pluralism are attractive in many ways. After all, ethnic pluralism is the basis for cultural

*The pleased look suggests that their demand for ethnic pluralism is rather playful, not the serious political movement of an oppressed minority group.*

Owen Franken/Stock, Boston

**FIGURE 10.2**

*Origin of United States legal immigrants in 1976.*

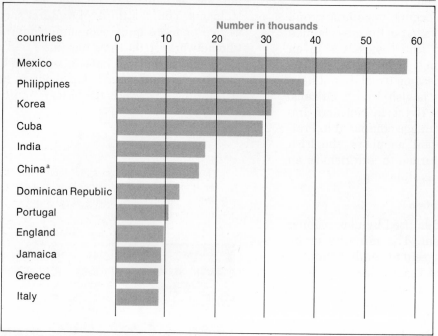

ᵃIncludes the People's Republic of China and Taiwan.
*Source:* Data supplied by Statistics Branch, U.S. Immigration and Naturalization Service.

diversity. Each ethnic community keeps its own traditions, and these special ways of life enrich the lives of their members. To belong to a community with its own folklore and graceful rituals is to have symbols that enhance experience. Who would want to blend all these traditions into a single, unified culture? Not I. Exploring a foreign country is exciting simply because it is foreign. Diversity is enriching.

You may find it hard to imagine a plural society because ethnic stratification is so familiar to you. But Switzerland and Canada are, in different ways, plural societies. Canadians often say that they want their society to be not a "melting pot" but a "salad bowl." The Canadian government supports a policy of *multiculturalism* — it encourages diversity whenever possible, helping groups maintain their own identities and traditions. The best historical examples of plural societies are

those of the Far East before colonial rule. Wolfram Eberhard has described the Orient in general, and medieval China in particular, as a series of "layers" of peoples. These groups lived in the same area but had separate communication networks and separate cultures.[35] Sometimes several groups were unable to speak to one another because of language differences, yet they lived in the same towns for generations. Each community had its own norms and its own legal system. Though all Chinese were subjects of the emperor, the only authorities that most people knew about were the leaders of their separate communities.

These communities might be spread over a large area. For example, a trading group might have members living in separate communities in every large town throughout the Far East. They would visit one another to find brides and to keep in touch, even though they were living among aliens. Another "layer" might be the community of monks who lived in monasteries throughout Asia. The groups of monks kept in touch with one another, though they remained aloof from the natives of the societies in which they lived. Every person's social world was centered in his or her "layer," which was usually an ascriptive community. The Chinese peasants did not know that they were part of the Chinese Empire; they knew only that they were part of their "people" — their "layer." These layers were not integrated into a "nation." They interacted very little, and members of one layer would be familiar with their own traditions but quite unfamiliar with those of their neighbors.

If a country is interested in pursuing a policy of ethnic pluralism, it will support the various groups in their efforts to maintain separate institutions and traditions. It will allow each child to be educated in his or her native language rather than in a single national language. It will support ethnic newspapers, churches, businesses, and festivals. It will give people time off from work to celebrate their group's special holidays, always taking care not to favor one ethnic group over any other.

### INTEGRATION

The third and final category in our typology of ethnic relations is integration. It is almost the opposite of ethnic pluralism. In an integrated society there is full, joint participation by different ethnic groups in the same

These American Indian women reflect the situation of many minority groups. They seem to be doing all they can to move into middle America, while the store behind them displays a blonde haired mannequin in "Indian" style dress.

Henri Cartier-Bresson/Magnum

activities. Instead of maintaining separate institutions, the communities take part in the same activities on an equal basis. Instead of separate rules for each community, there is a single set of rules that apply to all members of all communities. Instead of clear-cut memberships, the groups have weak boundaries, many marginal members, and many chances for individuals to associate with members of other groups. Instead of segregating itself from other groups and discriminating in favor of its own members, each group shares its culture with anyone who wants to participate and may adopt aspects of other cultural traditions.

The process by which a group integrates itself into the culture around it is called as-similation. The group gives up its distinctive life style, adopts the culture of the larger society, and eventually loses its identity as a separate community. However, it might contribute some aspects of its own culture to the larger culture. For example, Mexican Americans have made tacos and enchiladas as popular as hamburgers among Anglos who live in the Southwest.

Most immigrant groups in the United States have tended to become assimilated after about three generations. But of course the outcome is not as homogeneous as the melting-pot image would have us believe. Instead, even when ethnic groups lose some of their distinctive traits as nationalities, they tend to maintain strong religious identities—Catholic, Protestant, or Jewish.[36] America's melting pot seems to have three separate compartments for assimilating ethnic groups of these three religious traditions. The grandchildren of Catholic immigrants may not identify themselves as Polish Americans or Italian Americans, but they do think of themselves as Catholics. And they will tend to choose Catholic friends and mates. The same holds for Jews and Protestants. People maintain their religious identity, and it counts.

But let's not overstate the case. Ethnicity is still a real factor in American society.

More than any other sociologist, Andrew Greeley has collected evidence to prove that white Americans, both Protestant and (especially) Catholics, identify more with their ethnic community than is generally assumed. Greeley also shows that real differences in behavior patterns can be found even among people who have no special identification with their ethnic group. For example, Irish people tend to be heavier drinkers and more active politically than members of other ethnic groups, and these tendencies are passed on to their children even though the children think of themselves as completely assimilated Americans.[37]

In a society that has been integrated for a long time there is enough intermarriage to produce a great deal of physical similarity among members of the whole society. This blending of racial types through long interbreeding is called amalgamation. Amalgamation has taken place to some extent in Hawaii, where whites, Hawaiians, and Asians have intermarried for a long time. Many Hawaiian people have some physical traits that are characteristic of all three original populations.

## Reactions of minority groups to dominance

People who are mistreated may react in many different ways, depending on the situation and on their beliefs, values, and ideologies. In general, the reactions of minority groups can be classified into three patterns: (1) passivity and withdrawal, (2) nonviolent resistance, and (3) violent resistance.

### PASSIVITY AND WITHDRAWAL

When the dominant group is much more powerful than the minority and is oppressive toward the minority, the minority group has no choice but to hide any tendency to resist and to appear to accept whatever the oppressor says or does. This was the reaction of the Lapps mentioned earlier in this chapter. Whatever anger they may have felt toward the Norwegians could be expressed only in private. This was the typical reaction of many native peoples toward their European rulers in the early days of colonialism, before nationalistic movements arose. At such times the minority group turns to its own members in privacy for mutual support. This usually involves avoiding the dominant group whenever possible. Intergroup contacts may be governed by a complex etiquette in which the minority must appear humble. Such behavior damages the emotional well-being of the minority people, whose self-esteem and confidence are hurt by their low status and by the anger that they must turn inward.

## NONVIOLENT RESISTANCE

When a minority group resists the oppressor the resistance sometimes takes the form of a peaceful appeal to the conscience of the oppressor. Martin Luther King led blacks in nonviolent demonstrations of this sort, following the philosophy of Gandhi, who had used this method to free India from British rule. Nonviolent resistance requires self-discipline. Participants must steel themselves to accept blows without fighting back, if it comes to that. They are saying that they do not hate their oppressors and will not fight them, but that they will no longer cooperate in their own oppression. They may sit down passively and wait to be jailed. Often such

*Ireland has been the scene of an ongoing violent conflict that has proven very difficult to end because of the overlapping religious and nationalistic conflicts.*

Jim Anderson/Woodfin Camp

quiet action makes the oppressors ashamed of their violence.

### VIOLENT RESISTANCE

Finally, minority groups sometimes react to their oppressors with violence. This violence may take the form of collective riots and armed rebellion or individual antisocial behavior such as crime.

Frantz Fanon, a black psychiatrist, worked with his Algerian countrymen to win independence from France. He believed that the personalities of oppressed peoples were so damaged by the treatment they had received that only through violence could they regain any psychological strength. Psy-

chologists who are familiar with other minority groups have noted that many forms of mental illness and personality disorders are direct results of longtime discrimination. The need to cope with anger and channel it in a healthy way is one of the daily emotional problems that minority people have to face. Not all have to become aggressive, fortunately, but when aggression does occur it is usually due to the smoldering resentment created by deprivation and discrimination. The victims of this anger are not always members of the dominant group but usually whoever happens to be nearby at the moment—often other members of the minority group.

## SOCIAL RESEARCH:
## Sociologists at Work

During the past decade a lot of sociological research has focused on problems of ethnic relations. Here we will discuss two particularly important topics: the relationship between heredity and intelligence as applied to racial groups, and the social causes of hostility between groups.

### IQ AND RACE

Since World War II racism has decreased. Fewer people believe behavioral differences between racial groups are caused by biological factors, and more people believe such differences (where they exist) are due to cultural and environmental factors. However, in the late 1960s this issue flared up again when psychologist Arthur Jensen published an article suggesting that blacks inherit lower intelligence than whites, on the average.[38] As soon as the article was published angry students began to attack Jensen for reopening an issue that had such ugly implications and had led to so much persecution and discrimination in the past.

Social scientists were just as quick to attack

Jensen, but they did so for different reasons. Many pointed out that Jensen had gathered evidence that supported one conclusion but had wrongly used it to support quite a different conclusion. His evidence actually supported the conclusion that, for most ordinary populations, intelligence test scores are determined more by genes than by the social environment. He cited a number of studies showing that identical twins (who always inherit exactly the same genes) usually have IQ scores that are very similar, even if they have been separated in infancy and reared in different families. On the other hand, the IQ scores of adopted children are usually much closer to those of their natural mothers than to those of their adopted parents or siblings, in whose social environment they were brought up. If social environment determined intelligence more than genes, this could not happen. Indeed, many social scientists are prepared to agree with Jensen that the IQ scores of, say, the population of white North Americans are determined about 80 percent by genetic factors and 20 percent by environmental factors such as access to good books, hobbies, travel, stimulating dinner-table conversations, and the like.

But it does not follow that the IQ scores of all individuals or all subgroups *within* a population are determined 80 percent by genes and 20 percent by the environment. For example, suppose a normal baby was kept locked in a dark room without human contact throughout childhood. If such a baby survived, his or her IQ score at age 10 would not be much more than zero, but this would obviously result from environmental deprivation, not genes. It is likely that within any large population there are certain subgroups that have experienced such serious social deprivation that, for them, IQ scores are determined more by the environment than by genes. The only way to find out whether this is so would be to separate pairs of twin infants, rearing one of each pair in a normal way and exposing the other to poverty, humiliation, and discrimination. We would not be surprised to find that the abused youngsters scored 10 or 15 points lower on IQ tests than the well-treated youngsters, despite their identical genes. Of course no social scientist would conduct such a monstrous experiment with human lives, so we will never have a very precise answer to the question. But does it matter, anyway? No matter how people became the way they are, whether mostly through heredity or mostly through environment, they still deserve to be treated fairly, given as much education as they want, and given equal access to opportunities and benefits.

Black Americans score, on the average, about 10 or 15 points lower on IQ tests than white Americans. Most sociologists suppose, though they cannot prove—and Jensen cannot disprove—that this difference results from social factors. Other factors could also play a large part. For example, women who are poorly nourished during pregnancy give birth to babies whose intelligence tends to be permanently damaged. And far more black women than white women are poorly nourished. This may be the main reason for the black children's lower IQ scores.

Moreover, the IQ tests used to make black–white comparisons were almost all set up to measure intelligence in whites only. What bright black children learn in their cultural environment is somewhat different from what bright white children learn in theirs. Yet the tests measure only what the white child is normally expected to learn. Any comparison based on such tests should not be taken very seriously. For all of these and many other reasons, almost all sociologists are very skeptical of Jensen's conclusions.

## COMPETITION AND INTERGROUP HOSTILITY

Many people believe that hostility between ethnic groups results from the fact that the members of those groups do not know each other well. According to this theory, if two ascribed communities have hostile relationships, the solution is to bring members of both groups together and encourage them to communicate with each other. Once they know each other well, they are sure to like each other and their prejudice will decrease. Unfortunately, there is evidence that this does not always work. The question is not how *much* contact members of different groups have with each other but the *kind* of contact they have. The best illustration of this point comes from an experiment done by a social psychologist, Muzafer Sherif, in Robbers Cave, Oklahoma, once a hideout of Jesse James.[39]

As his subjects, Sherif chose a number of healthy, well-adjusted 11- or 12-year-old boys from similar favorable social backgrounds who did not know each other. No children from minority groups were included. The boys went to summer camp at Robbers Cave without realizing that they were part of an experiment. They were assigned to two different campsites some distance apart, where they spent a week getting to know their own campmates; each group was unaware of the presence of the other campers nearby. Within that week groups began to form, leaders were recognized, and friendship and solidarity began to develop within each group. One group called itself the "Rattlers" and the other the "Eagles."

Then the researcher arranged a tournament in which the two groups competed against each other as teams in games such as baseball, touch football, tug-of-war, a treasure hunt, and so on, with prizes for the winning team. As time went by, good sportsmanship was replaced by hostility, and the participants began to call their rivals "stinkers," "sneaks," and "cheats." Threatening posters appeared, green apples were gathered to be used as ammunition, and finally scuffling and raids became the order of the day. By the end of the tournament each group refused to have anything to do with the other. However, *within* each group morale improved and cooperativeness and solidarity increased greatly.

Sherif had created hostility between groups of boys who had no cultural or physical differences separating them. He did so by simply setting up a competitive situation in which for one group to win the other group had to lose. Could he reverse the process and undo the results of his experiment? Not easily. First he tried moral appeals. At the camp's Sunday worship service the minister spoke on the subject of brotherhood. The boys seemed impressed, but right after the service they fell back into their hostile behavior pattern.

Next Sherif tried to set up situations in which the two groups were brought together in enjoyable activities. They saw movies together, ate in the same dining room, set off fireworks on the Fourth of July, and so forth. This did nothing to reduce the tension. Instead, it provided opportunities for the rival groups to throw paper, food, and vile names at each other. Contact *in itself* did not seem to affect either group's attitudes.

Finally, Sherif reasoned that "*if conflict develops from mutually incompatible goals, common goals* should promote cooperation. But what kind of common goals? . . . Those that have a compelling appeal for members of each group but that neither group can achieve without the participation of the other."[40] He set up new situations that would not only bring the campers into contact with each other but require *interdependent* action by all the campers. For example, he arranged for the water supply system to break down so that all the boys had to cooperate to find the source of the trouble. He arranged for their food truck to break down so that Rattlers and Eagles had to pull it together to get it started. This strategy worked. Not immediately, but after several such events, the boys began to treat each other civilly and even to like each other.

Sherif and other social psychologists have concluded from this experiment and others like it that intergroup conflict can be created among normal people with similar cultural, religious, linguistic, or racial characteristics. Group competition increases their conflict; working together to achieve common goals decreases it. It seems, then, that ethnic conflict is caused by competition between groups. Cooperative interdependent interaction reduces hostility among groups.

Sherif's experiment shows that contact alone does not necessarily lead to harmonious intergroup relations. It is often assumed that bringing people together will automatically make them like each other more. But Sherif has shown that the outcome depends on whether their contact consists of competition or interdependent action toward some shared goal. Neutral association seems to have no effect whatever on hostile relations.

On the other hand, ethnic harmony is likely to be increased by cooperative interdependence among ethnic groups that share a common goal. However, social scientists have little control over such matters in real life. We can't go around sabotaging water supply systems in order to force people to work together.

Indeed, trends in the developing nations point in the opposite direction. Everything seems to be getting scarce as population pressure increases. This may increase competition for land, water, energy, food, and other resources, and such competition may lead to greater ethnic and national hostility.

# SOCIAL POLICY:
## Issues and Viewpoints

I pointed out earlier that one can have mixed feelings about ethnicity. I like diversity, but I hate discrimination. The trouble is, we usually don't get one without the other. I also suggested that you pay attention to your feelings as you read the chapter. Ethnic relations is an emotionally loaded topic. We have strong feelings of loyalty to "our people." And we also have strong feelings about fairness, equality, and openness. This produces a dilemma: the need to choose between two opposite principles—universalism and particularism.

First, before going on, decide which of the

three types of ethnic relations you would prefer for your own society—(1) ethnic stratification, (2) ethnic pluralism, or (3) integration. I will assume that you would not choose ethnic stratification. Unfortunately, we often get it anyway when we really want one of the other two systems. Both ethnic pluralism and integration are unstable and tend to break down, so that we end up with ethnic stratification whether we want it or not.

What would be required to maintain a strictly pluralistic system? A strictly integrated system? In the following pages we will look at the types of problems that must be expected if we try to pursue either of these two policies.

## SUSTAINING A PLURALIST SOCIETY

Ethnic pluralism allows for group traditions and supports a rich variety of cultures—folklore, languages, styles of cooking, holiday parades, and so on. But the trick is to keep these groups from becoming stratified, with one of them holding all the advantages and keeping others in subordinate positions. We don't want domination or undue competition between the ethnic groups of our pluralist society. So in order to keep it truly pluralist—characterized by both variety and equality, we'll need to encourage (1) tolerance, (2) economic autonomy, (3) legal autonomy, (4) unambiguous group membership, and (5) some discrimination.

### Tolerance

If pluralism is to succeed, people must tolerate diversity even when they find it disagreeable. Foreign travel is fun because there is charm in diversity. But diverse groups that must live together may not find each other charming. Sociology assumes that a society can hold together because it shares common values and beliefs. Agreement is the basis of harmony, but diversity is the opposite of agreement. If one group is not to impose on another, its members must ignore what it views as the errors of other groups, but this is sometimes intolerable. It is almost intolerable for Hindus to live near Moslems, who kill and eat cows. Mormon polygamy was intolerable to most Americans a century ago. It is almost intolerable for many westerners to see

Christian Scientists and Jehovah's Witnesses refuse blood transfusions for their sick children. Cultural diversity is not as easy to maintain in a real society as in the imagination.

### Economic autonomy

Each community must have control over its own resources, its own productive arrangements, and the products of its labor. Still, any integration between groups must involve cooperative activity toward some shared goal. In real life, however, most economic interaction involves competition as well, and this usually results in more advantages for one side than for the other. For example, whenever one ethnic community is the traditional landlord group and another community is traditionally the tenant group, there is usually tension between the groups. It would be better if the two communities had their own separate economies. It is not easy to apply this policy in modern societies, however. This would require that each ethnic community own and run its own businesses and maintain its own markets, factories, farms, banks, and so forth. A good deal of integration may be necessary for an industrial economy. If an ethnic community gains control over the small businesses within its area, it may achieve considerable economic autonomy (Chinatowns are an example). However, this will not make it economically equal to an ethnic group that controls large corporations and industries. Thus the requirements of a modern economy tend to shift a society away from pluralism toward either economic integration or ethnic stratification.

### Legal autonomy

For an ethnic group to maintain its own identity it must have social control over its members' lives. In addition, it must be able to make and enforce its own rules. This conflicts with the principle of having a *single* rule of law. It would severely limit the activities of the state.

In India, for example, the laws governing marriage, divorce, inheritance of family property, and the like are different for Hindus and Moslems. It is important to distinguish between universalism and particularism. Any rule that is followed in dealing with all people in the society is universalistic. The practice of making special rules to fit special people or groups is particularism. In India, instead of a single universalistic code of family laws there are particularistic legal systems that apply separately to Hindus and Moslems. This permits each group to maintain and enforce its own customs with the backing of the state. In the United States some religious and ethnic communities also have rules that they try to enforce. The Catholic Church, for example, has its own legal system. But such a group can impose its own rules only on members who obey willingly. If a Catholic rejects the authority of the church, no legal power can force him or her to obey it.

We agree that the *real* law is the set of laws passed by the government. Our law is universalistic — it applies across the board to all citizens. Ethnic communities have their own particularistic norms, but they don't have the force of law. Maybe your ethnic group forbids you to marry an outsider or to drink liquor or to get a divorce. You may think twice before doing these things, but the group cannot legally prevent you from doing them. In the end such rules fade away because members won't obey them when they don't want to. Thus a universalistic legal system gradually weakens the legal systems of the ethnic groups within the society. It strips them of the power to punish members who violate their norms.

### Unambiguous group membership

In a pluralistic society everyone must belong to some ethnic community, willingly or not. And if various ethnic groups have separate economic institutions, then everyone must belong to one of those groups in order to find a job. Group membership cannot be "voluntary." The boundaries must be firm and clear-cut. Marginal people would be rare, and a person would be unable to move from one group to another. I wouldn't like to be locked into an involuntary, ascribed system — but ethnic groups *are* involuntary and ascribed. The price of admission is lifelong loyalty.

### Discrimination

Ethnic loyalty amounts to discrimination. Boundaries are actually patterns of discrimination. You treat fellow group members in a special way. This may or may not be harmless. When it's just a matter of sharing an in-joke or singing some old songs together or borrowing a

recipe for Easter bread, then outsiders are not "excluded." No harm is done.

But all ascribed communities tend to go beyond that. Not only do they pass their folksongs, recipes, and jokes along to other members; they also pass along their material goods. You might feel safer buying a used car from a member of your own group. Some of the ethnic restaurants near me have two menus — one in English and one in the "other" language — Portuguese or Russian, say — and the English menu charges more than the other one. This is normal, but it's also discrimination. We could call it petty particularism.

On a large scale, discrimination in favor of one ethnic group means cutting other groups out of some important advantages. And when one group begins to have more than another, passing the advantage from one generation to another may increase the inequality. This takes us right back down the road to ethnic stratification.

## AN INTEGRATED SOCIETY

We have seen how hard it would be to maintain a pluralist society, but integration is probably even harder to achieve. Integration is based on a commitment to universalism. The principle is to apply general rules equally to everyone. Never discriminate in favor of your friends, your kin, or members of your own ethnic community.

Try living by that rule for one day. You will quickly find that we hold to another rule too, one that requires us to treat our "own people" in a special way. One sociologist gave his class the assignment of acting like guests in their own homes for one day.[41] For example, a male student was to rise when his mother was standing and sit only when she sat, ask permission before getting a snack from the refrigerator, shake hands with his father upon his arrival home, and the like. In almost every case students reported that their behavior caused major emotional upsets. Not knowing what was going on, their families tearfully or angrily accused them of coldness. One does not treat everyone according to the same set of rules.

Each person is subject to two different norms, the principle of universalism and the principle of particularism. There are rules to determine when each principle applies. There is tension between the two principles, but neither ever wins out entirely. An integrated society supports universalism more than a pluralistic society does, but one is still expected to treat one's "own people" in a special way. You can do things for your own child that you would not do for all the children in the neighborhood. You can send party invitations only to your friends. You can donate money to charities that only serve the poor of your own ethnic community. All of these cases of particularism can be tolerated in an integrated society that is basically universalistic. Still, it is necessary to limit particularism, for it weakens equality by allowing groups to limit certain privileges and opportunities to their "own people." It is usually considered proper to be particularistic in private activities but not in public affairs. Thus you may invite only your friends to a private party, but you may not favor them when you are hiring public employees, awarding scholarships, or seating customers in a restaurant. Controlling particularism is always difficult in a society that is committed to universalism and integration.

It seems that private discrimination is all right, while public discrimination is not. This formula appears reasonable, but it may not be enough to prevent ethnic stratification. Private social relationships include families, churches, clubs, and friendship networks. Many advantages are reserved for in-group members through participation in such private groups. These are real advantages — the kind that make a person better able to compete in public life, where universalistic rules apply.

For example, suppose private relationships are segregated and your ethnic group is the underdog. You may be shut out forever. Why? Because the skills and knowledge necessary for success are passed along through family ties and other private relationships to a much greater extent than through schools, libraries, television, and other *public* institutions.

Do you see the problem? No one wants the government to meddle in private associations. But there may be no other way to achieve real equality and ethnic integration.

I asked you to choose between ethnic pluralism and integration, and I warned you that this is a loaded and complex issue. I have never been able to choose one or the other wholeheartedly. As a result I have no general principles to use in deciding what is fair or unfair in matters of ethnic relations. Or rather, I have contradictory principles. It's easy to choose between right and wrong. What is harder is having to choose between two opposing *rights* — universalism and particularism.

## SUMMARY

**1.** *Ethnic groups* (ascribed communities) may be based on similar religion, nationality, language, culture, tribe, race, or some other standard. Such groups have *boundary norms* that define who is a member and who is not; these norms also govern relations between members and nonmembers. Relations with nonmembers are always more limited than relations with members.

**2.** Boundary norms are used to define a *marginal person* as a full member of one and only one such group. Ethnicity is supposed to be a secure, permanent aspect of one's identity.

**3.** *Minority groups* are ethnic groups that have a subordinate or oppressed status compared to one or more dominant ethnic groups. A minority group may actually have more members than the dominant group, but it is still called a minority if it is subordinate.

**4.** *Racial groups* are ethnic groups whose members share certain physical characteristics; these characteristics are inherited. People who have similar physical traits may or may not feel that they belong to a group with a shared identity. Thus while everyone can be classified into a particular "race," not everyone is a member of a racial group. Race is biologically determined; racial groups are socially determined.

**5.** *Prejudice* consists of prejudging a person by overgeneralizing. Each person in a particular group is seen as having traits that are believed (rightly or wrongly) to be typical of members of that group. Prejudice involves making up a *stereotype* that exaggerates the traits of the "typical" member of that group. Everyone acquires stereotypes and prejudices about out-group members as part of the popular culture learned during childhood. Some people, however, also acquire a more sophisticated culture that is more accurate and fair in its view of minorities.

**6.** *Racism* is a theory that has been very influential and has had disastrous results. According to racist theory, racial groups are not *socially* defined but are biologically determined. Members of such groups are supposedly held together by biological ties, some inherited tendency to behave in a particular way, to prefer a particular language, culture, and homeland, and so on. Racist theory was used by white Europeans to justify oppression of "inferior races" around the world. It was also used to justify the Nazis' annihilation of minorities, such as Gypsies, blacks, and particularly Jews, all of whom were considered genetically inferior.

**7.** *Nationalism* (or ethnic consciousness) develops, according to Deutsch, when increased communication breaks down the secure social world of traditional society and forces people into insecure relationships with strangers. In an attempt to regain their former sense of community, people emphasize their ethnic similarities. When nationalism is widely accepted there is a great danger that a group will become violently hostile toward out-groups.

**8.** Three patterns of group interaction are possible in ethnically heterogeneous societies: (1) *ethnic stratification* (in which one or more groups dominate other groups), (2) *ethnic pluralism* (in which various ascribed communities live together as equals but without much contact between them), and (3) *integration* (in which groups interact in a wide variety of settings and tend to assimilate gradually into a single group with a shared life style).

**9.** Minority group members may react to oppression in several different ways. They may avoid interacting with the dominant group whenever possible but show passive acceptance of the dominant group's actions when they do interact. They may resist nonviolently and build up self-respect within the minority group. Or they may resist violently or even turn their aggression against their own people in antisocial behavior.

## KEY TERMS

**amalgamation**  the blending of racial types through long interbreeding.

**annihilation**  destruction of the entire population of one ethnic community by another.

**assimilation**  the process by which a group integrates itself into the culture around it.

**boundaries**  the codes and customs that define a person as a member or nonmember of a particular group.

**discrimination**  the process by which a dominant group informally deprives a minority group of equal access to privileges and opportunities.

**ethnic group**  a large collectivity in which membership is generally inherited and whose members share a feeling of identification with the group.

**ethnic pluralism**  the situation in which ethnic groups are equal and live together on good terms.

**ethnic stratification**  the situation in which ethnic groups form a hierarchy of dominance.

**expulsion**  the sending of minority group members to another country.

**institutional racism** indirect discrimination against minority races caused by established policies of institutions.

**integration** the situation in which equality is achieved by reducing the separation between ethnic groups and encouraging them to participate in the same activities.

**marginal person** a person who belongs to two or more groups that are supposedly mutually exclusive.

**minority group** an ethnic group that is subordinate to another group.

**nationalism** ethnic-group chauvinism.

**particularism** bending rules or making special ones to fit special persons or groups.

**prejudice** prejudging against individuals on the basis of characteristics believed to be shared by all members of their ethnic group.

**racial group** an ethnic group to which members are assigned on the basis of inherited biological traits.

**racism** the belief that ethnic and racial groups are based on genetic similarities rather than on social agreements.

**segregation** forcing minority group members to work or live in separate areas whenever possible and to use facilities separate from those used by the dominant group.

**stereotype** a mental cartoon that exaggerates the traits of the typical member of a particular group.

**universalism** adhering to the same rules in dealing with all people.

# FOR FURTHER READING

CLAIRMONT, DONALD H., and DENNIS W. MAGILL, *Africville*. Toronto: McClelland and Stewart, 1974. It is a chatty description of a black community that was moved to Halifax, Nova Scotia and destroyed by the move. Interesting and sound.

DAVIS, MORRIS, and JOSEPH F. KRAUTER. *The Other Canadians: Profiles of Six Minorities*. Toronto: Methuen, 1971. A handy little paperback that provides a nice description of the situation of several ethnic groups in Canada.

GENOVESE, EUGENE D. *Roll, Jordan, Roll: The World the Slaves Made*. New York: Pantheon, 1974. Genovese is a Marxist historian who has written a great deal about the life of American slaves. Among other arguments, he rejects the notion that slaves were promiscuous, asserting that they had rather Victorian morals, on the whole. An important book.

GLOCK, CHARLES Y.; ROBERT WUTHNOW; JANE PILIAVIN; and METTA SPENCER. *Adolescent Prejudice*. New York: Harper & Row, 1975. A survey analysis of relations between Christian and Jewish teenagers in three towns not far from New York City. Some unexpected sources of anti-Semitism are explored.

GORDON, MILTON. *Assimilation in American Life*. New York: Oxford University Press, 1966. Gordon presents a theory about the stages ethnic groups go through in becoming assimilated to American society.

HUNT, CHESTER L., and LEWIS WALKER. *Ethnic Dynamics: Patterns of Intergroup Relations in Various Societies*. Homewood, Ill.: Dorsey, 1974. Full of interesting facts about ethnicity around the world.

ISAJIW, WSEVOLOD. *Ethnic Group Relations in Canada*. Toronto: McGraw-Hill Ryerson, 1976. A survey of literature on ethnic group relations, particularly with reference to the Canadian scene.

LIPSET, SEYMOUR MARTIN, and EARL RAAB. *The Politics of Unreason: Right-Wing Extremism in the United States, 1790–1970*. New York: Harper & Row, 1970. A historical and survey research analysis of bigotry in American politics.

WILKINSON, DORIS Y., and RONALD L. TAYLOR. *The Black Male in America: Perspectives on His Status in Contemporary Society*. Chicago: Nelson-Hall, 1977. This collection of essays covers socialization, stigma, interracial mating, and stratification factors.

# COLLECTIVE BEHAVIOR
# AND
# SOCIAL MOVEMENTS

A punk-rock guitarist, chains and safety pins dangling from his cheeks, spits on his pogoing audience. A nightclub burns to the ground, its occupants piled up just inside the exit, trapped by their own stampede. The survivors of an earthquake emerge from the wreckage and organize teams to rescue their neighbors. A million Christmas shoppers pay good money for "pet rocks." A furious mob runs through a business district, smashing store windows.

What do these scenes have in common? They are all cases of collective behavior— passing events during which groups of people improvise new ways of behaving.

While ordinary activities are organized according to fairly stable norms, in collective behavior a number of people, together, without much planning, depart from ordinary patterns of behavior. This usually occurs in situations of stress. Collective behavior such as panics, riots, political demonstrations, and protest rallies is most likely to take place under such conditions. However, in this chapter we will also be concerned with certain other forms of behavior that are not necessarily caused by stressful conditions. Emotional religious revivals, fads and fashions, and public celebrations are examples. Such behavior may occur when people are simply bored and want a change of pace.

Indeed, when we define collective behavior as spontaneous, transitory, noninstitutionalized group action, we do not intend to set it off as wholly different from all institutionalized group action. Group behaviors take a wide variety of forms. They range from extreme forms of collective behavior, such as a lynching or a rout on the battlefield, to extreme forms of institutionalized, formal behavior, such as the Japanese tea ceremony or the coronation of a king. Most forms of group behavior fall between these extremes. Also, many events are institutionalized in some ways and in other ways open to collective behavior—examples are public festivities

such as New Orleans' Mardi Gras or the Calgary Stampede. Even an orgy can be planned in advance. Nothing could be more institutionalized than a performance of the Metropolitan Opera in New York, yet after Joan Sutherland has sung a difficult aria the whole audience leaps to its feet, shouting "Brava!" Such a moment contains an element of collective behavior.

Actors speak of having "good" and "bad" audiences. By this they mean that one performance may win delighted laughter and applause while the next may win hardly a giggle. The difference is in the audience, not in the players. If you happen to go to a comedy on an evening when the audience is responsive, you will probably laugh louder and enjoy the play more than you would if the audience were more subdued. Some writers call this audience effect collective behavior, while others use the term only for collective outbursts that are wholly noninstitutionalized efforts by a group to cope with a stressful social situation.

In this chapter we will deal both with extreme, unmistakable cases of collective behavior (such as riots, crazes, and panics) and with certain other phenomena involving group communication. The latter include the development of public opinion as well as social movements such as the civil-rights, environmental-protection and antiabortion movements. We will try to explain the conditions in which these phenomena take place, the phases they go through, and some of their effects on society.

## Conditions in which collective behavior occurs

The most widely used sociological model of collective behavior was developed by Neil J. Smelser.[1] This model is limited to true cases of collective behavior in which people try to arrive at quick solutions to problems arising out of strain. It does not include institutionalized events governed by social norms (such as football rallies, patriotic mass assemblies, and shouting "Bravo" at the opera) or propaganda and individual acts of deviance.

In Chapter 2 I mentioned that sociologists predict behavior in terms of "if . . . then" statements. Smelser's approach is of this type, but his model has six "ifs," and they must all come true in a particular order before the model will predict that "then" a given form of collective behavior will occur. These six "ifs" are very general conditions. In each historical case the particular events that correspond to these conditions are unique; yet if all six conditions are met, they will determine the outcome. This will become clear to you as we discuss the six "ifs."

1 *Structural conduciveness* is the first "if." It is the most general condition for collective behavior. This simply means that certain situations must exist for collective behavior to be possible. For example, there can be no panic buying or selling on the stock market and no runs on banks in a society where there is no stock market and there are no banks. Similarly, race riots can happen only where there are two or more races in the same community. There would have been no My Lai massacre if the American troops had been engaged in a mock battle in the Arctic instead of stalking Viet Cong in an Asian village. All of these conditions are obvious. They refer to the kind of situation that makes collective behavior *possible* but by no means *necessary*.

2 *Structural strain* is the second condition for collective behavior. It refers to a problem in the social environment, such as a conflict, a lack, an ambiguity, or a gap between expectations and reality. Any kind of strain may lead to any kind of collective behavior. What kind of behavior, if any, occurs will depend on the subsequent conditions in this list. Thus unemployment is a structural strain that might produce a march on Washington, support for a religious revival, an attack on a minority group, or none of these behaviors, depending on other factors.

3 A *generalized belief* is the third basic condition that can lead to collective behavior. People must be able to identify the problem and diagnose their situation before they can take action to correct the source of structural strain. For example, if unemployed workers come to believe that their misfortune is due to the mistakes of politicians, they may march on Washington. If they come to believe that God is punishing them for their sins, they may join a religious revival. If they believe that their jobs are being taken away from them by an ethnic minority, they may start a race riot or demand that immigration be stopped. The generalized belief is a kind of shared ideology, a system of meaning that calls for certain kinds of responses. However, this condition and the first two are not enough to cause collective behavior. Other "ifs" also must be met before this outcome is predictable.

4 *Precipitating factors* are the fourth condition for collective behavior. These dramatic events may or may not happen, but if they do they may trigger a collective response. For example, a racial situation may be very tense for a long time without any open violence. However, when one fistfight or act of police harassment occurs, this event may spark a race riot. The precipitating factor is usually unpredictable, and it may be avoided. However, when it happens after the other three conditions have come into existence, collective behavior is far more likely than before.

5 *Mobilization for action* is the fifth condition that must be met. Once the precipitating factor has occurred, participants have to be persuaded to join in the action. This is the moment when leaders may come forth and start shouting suggestions or urging people to take part. If they are successful at this point, collective behavior actually begins.

6 *Social control* is the sixth and final factor determining the outcome of the event. Before or during the action of the crowd, the police, the news media, the governor, or other influential people may take action to prevent or stop the collective action. If the social control is not effective, the collective behavior will run its course.

Thus Smelser's model says that *if* structural conduciveness exists and *if* structural strain exists and *if* an appropriate general-

INFORMATION FOR
DISASTER VICTIMS

Nick Sapieha/Stock, Boston

*Disasters usually bring out, not the worst, but the best traits in people.*

## Crowds

A crowd is a large, temporary group of people who have some common goal or interest. A Santa Claus parade and a lynching mob are examples. Not all collective behavior happens in crowds (streaking, for example, was practiced by many individuals but rarely by large groups), but the crowd has always been of great interest to the student of collective behavior. There is something frightening about the intense involvement that is sometimes seen in a large crowd. If you have ever seen a film showing Hitler's mass audiences, you will understand what I mean. A sea of adoring faces were turned his way, and hundreds of thousands of people would lift their arms in unison and call out "Sieg Heil!" Imagine how hard it would be to be the only person in that crowd *not* shouting "Sieg Heil!" The power of a mob is overwhelming.

Scholars who have written about collective behavior have been especially concerned with the harmful aspects of crowds — their fickleness, their excitability, and their ability to make people do things that they would never do alone. To be sure, all of this is true, and we will discuss these aspects of crowds. However, it is important to realize that not all crowds are destructive mobs. Groups behave in different ways, depending on the situation. For example, the behavior of a crowd at the scene of a disaster is remarkably different from a panic.

### DISASTERS

Sudden disasters, such as floods, forest fires, explosions, earthquakes, and tornadoes, do not usually lead to disorganized and irresponsible behavior. In fact the opposite often happens. Before the event actually occurs it is often hard to persuade people that a disaster is likely and that they should be pre-

ized belief exists and *if* precipitating factors occur and *if* the participants can be mobilized for action and *if* social control fails to stop the event, *then* collective behavior will occur. In a sense these six "ifs" are a checklist that allows sociologists to look back at an event of collective behavior and see what made it happen — what generalized beliefs were involved, what situation of strain existed, and so on. However, such a list does not predict future events of collective behavior very well. The six conditions are not sure to occur; if any one of them is lacking, collective behavior may not develop.

pared. If the police drive through a neighborhood and warn residents to leave because a high dam may break, many people will shrug off the warning. They think the police are overly cautious. People rarely panic at such times. When the air-raid sirens accidentally went off across a wide section of the United States, supposedly signaling an atomic attack, nobody panicked. In fact hardly anyone even turned on the radio to find out whether the alarm was real or not. Many people looked out their windows, saw that no one else was panicking, and chose to ignore the warning. Only when they hear bombers overhead or see a wall of water rushing toward them will some people believe that the danger is real.

Ordinarily the behavior that occurs after a disaster is orderly. People pick themselves up, perhaps dazed, injured, and disorganized, and check on the safety of their loved ones. Then they start helping others. The usual social organization of the community may be destroyed by the disaster, and so people step outside their usual roles. They may direct traffic or join together to fight a fire. People who hold high-status jobs in everyday life may follow orders issued by a laundry worker who seems to know how to cope with the emergency. Neighbors who have not even nodded to each other for years suddenly come to each other's aid, sometimes taking big risks. There is often a strong sense of solidarity within the community for a time after the disaster.

### PANIC

Panic seems to arise only in very specific kinds of situations, and people behave far differently in those situations than they do after a disaster. When a person is in a dangerous situation (e.g., a burning building or a battlefield), a great deal of self-control is necessary to keep from running away. Often in such situations each person's chances for survival are better if others are willing to re-strain themselves. Thus it is bad enough to be under enemy fire, but if one's comrades run away the situation is even more hopeless. If anyone is going to run away, it is safer to be among the first then among the last. This being the case, if one person runs away all the others are likely to run too. The same is true in the case of a burning building, especially if there are not enough exits. More people will escape if people leave in an orderly fashion than if they stampede.

Panics take place when people believe that there are not enough escape routes. If no escape routes are open, there will be no panic because there is nothing to compete for. In the mine explosion reported in Chapter 2 the miners did not panic because there was no possibility of escape for anyone.

Other situations are similar to panics in certain ways. One is the stock market collapse or bank run. If a bank is believed to have plenty of money to cover all withdrawals, there will be no panic. However, if the money is limited it is far better to be among the first to sell stocks or withdraw savings. The race to reach the teller's window is similar to the race to reach the exit from a burning building. Both show the human character at its most selfish.

### THE ACTING CROWD

Herbert Blumer, a longtime student of collective behavior, uses the term **acting crowd** to refer to potentially violent mobs that choose a course of action on the spot, for example, rioters. He uses the term **expressive crowd** to describe groups that may simply show especially strong feelings, for example, by dancing in the streets on Bastille Day. It is only the acting crowd that Blumer, (as well as other writers on the subject) fears. The acting crowd can become an angry mob that can be persuaded to set fires, loot, overturn cars, or attack others.

There are at least four different ways of explaining the acting crowd: contagion theories, convergence theory, emergent-norm theory, and game theory.

### Contagion theories

LE BON: THE IRRATIONAL MOB  The French sociologist Gustave Le Bon was the author of *The Crowd*, perhaps the most influential book on collective behavior ever written.[2] Although Le Bon wrote during a fairly stable period at the turn of the twentieth century, the crowds he described were those of the French Revolution. These crowds had made some unsettling and fateful decisions. Le Bon was not alone in seeing the revolution-

ary mob as a frighteningly unpredictable, fickle, and even irrational phenomenon. His description makes for breathless reading whether it is accurate or not.

Le Bon believed that a certain process operates within a crowd that makes normal people lose their rational abilities and act at a primitive mental level. The reason for this loss of rationality is contagion. The members of a crowd are open to control by a leader, who "hypnotizes" them, and they are likely to imitate each other as well. As a result the crowd becomes unified. All its members perform similar kinds of actions, and all are under the influence of a single, unified group mind that is unstable and irrational. He called this phenomenon the "law of mental unity of crowds." The decisions made by such a mob are likely to be different from those that the average member would have arrived at alone. Le Bon believed that the influence of crowds on human history was almost always tragic rather than beneficial.

FREUD: THE ROLE OF THE LEADER  Later writers have expanded the theory of crowd contagion, mostly by trying to explain how it operates. By far the best known of these later theorists is Sigmund Freud, who emphasized the influence of the leader on a crowd of followers.[3] Freud was not satisfied with Le Bon's explanation of how crowd behavior becomes irrational. However he did accept Le Bon's claim that people in crowds do lose their rationality and self-control. As we will see shortly, this assumption is not shared by all sociologists today.

Freud believed that feelings left over from a person's early childhood were an important factor in his or her behavior as an adult. He believed that people could be caught up in a crowd because of two wishes of which they might not be aware.

The first wish was to go back to being taken care of by a parent. The leader in a crowd gives the impression that he or she is like a strong parent looking after children. Freud thought people wanted a hero to wor-

Drawing of Freud by David Levine. Reprinted with permission from *The New York Review of Books*. Copyright © 1975 NY Rev. Inc.

*Freud emphasized the influence of the leader on a crowd. He had to flee from Austria to escape the crowd that followed this leader.*

ship because this satisfied their desire to be childish and dependent.

The other wish in Freud's theory of collective behavior was the wish to *identify* with other people. Identification is a psychological way of sharing someone else's experience, almost as if one *were* that other person. By identifying with the leader, the person in a crowd imagines that he or she shares the leader's special power. By identifying with each other, the people in a crowd feel a stronger sense of togetherness and solidarity. This feeling is similar to the feeling brothers and sisters have for each other because they share the same parents.

The most serious weakness of Freud's theory is its emphasis on the influence of a leader. It is simply not true that all crowd phenomena take place under the direction of one or more leaders. Many, perhaps most, acting crowds don't have definite leaders.

BLUMER: EMOTIONAL REACTION  In contrast to Freud's explanation for crowd behavior, Herbert Blumer's theory is based on the symbolic interactionist viewpoint described in Chapter 6. He too accepted Le Bon's view that acting crowds are irrational, but he suggested his own explanation for the contagion that supposedly occurs in such crowds.

In normal situations a person generally interprets the communications of others before responding to them. However, in the crowd situation, according to Blumer, a sort of chain reaction sets in and rationality is no longer possible. He calls this process *circular reaction* and compares it to the excitement that sometimes builds up within a herd of cattle. That is, one animal may become excited and the others, seeing its rapid breathing, bellowing, and wild body movements, will become agitated themselves and behave in a similar way. This excitement eventually *circles* back to the animal that started the whole process. In this way an acute fear builds up and may result in a stampede. People, like animals, may become excited or frightened by the behavior of others. They may then respond to this excitement *directly*, without thinking about it, and their responses may build up into a general state of hysteria.

Such circular reactions take place when some precipitating event has drawn people together and stirred up their emotions. A "milling" process then begins, in which people are influenced by each other's strong feelings and build up a state of collective excitement. At this point they may set out to achieve a common goal such as racing for an exit, attacking their enemies, or overturning cars.[4]

Blumer's work on collective behavior has been criticized in recent years for several reasons. For one thing, it is clear that acting crowds are not nearly as unified as his theory suggests. If such a "circular reaction" were going on, all the participants in a crowd would act pretty much alike, but this is not the case. In a riot, for example, different people do different things. One may smash auto windshields; another may put up a barricade or collect trash to set fires; others may throw stones at enemies; and still others may concentrate on taking home stolen TV sets. Indeed, many people may just stand around watching; some may even try to persuade the rioters to stop. There is a kind of division of labor in a riot that is not necessarily irrational.

The whole concept of the "circular reaction" is open to question. Clearly, some emotional actions may excite other people. If you stand on a street corner and scream, you will at least give passers-by a few goose pimples; they may stop what they are doing, but they may not join you in screaming. However nervous you make them, it is doubtful that they will lose their reason and respond directly, like stampeding cattle. Therefore some modern writers on this subject hold that the thinking of crowd members is not very different from ordinary thinking. If this is so, then Blumer must have exaggerated the difference between ordinary behavior and collective behavior by treating the "circular reaction" as a crowd phenomenon different from ordinary communication.

The arguments against Blumer's theory are also criticisms of the other contagion theories. If the critics are right, crowds are not irrational groups with uncontrollable and homogeneous impulses.[5] The issue is not settled, however.

### Convergence theory

A basic assumption of contagion theories is that a person caught up in a crowd may be influenced to do things that are entirely out of character. Convergence theory rejects this assumption. Instead, it holds that a crowd may give people a chance to do what they have secretly wanted to do all along but have been kept from doing. According to this theory, a mob is a group of people with the same hidden impulses who suddenly let loose those impulses. Convergence theorists agree that "a crowd is a device for indulging ourselves in a kind of temporary insanity by all going crazy together."[6] In other words, crowd behavior is not something that is suddenly "caught" through contagion. If enough people with the same hidden wish gather together and one person begins to act out that wish, the others may do likewise. As Floyd Allport wrote, criticizing Le Bon's description of contagion in the French Revolution, "Nothing new or different was added by the crowd situation except an intensification of the feeling already present, and the possibility of concerted action. The individual in the crowd behaves just as he would behave alone, *only more so.*"[7]

There is some evidence for this point of view in studies of the ghetto riots of the 1960s. The behavior of rioters was not random, as the contagion theory would predict, but selective. Black-owned shops were not looted. The rioters did not forget who were their friends and who were their enemies.

It is possible to take a position somewhere between the contagion and convergence theories. That is, although it may be generally true that the participants in collective behavior act according to hidden wishes, contagion may influence people who lack such wishes. Furthermore, we each have within us not one but many hidden tendencies. What determines which one we will act out? Perhaps it is contagion that makes us choose one tendency rather than another in a particular situation.[8]

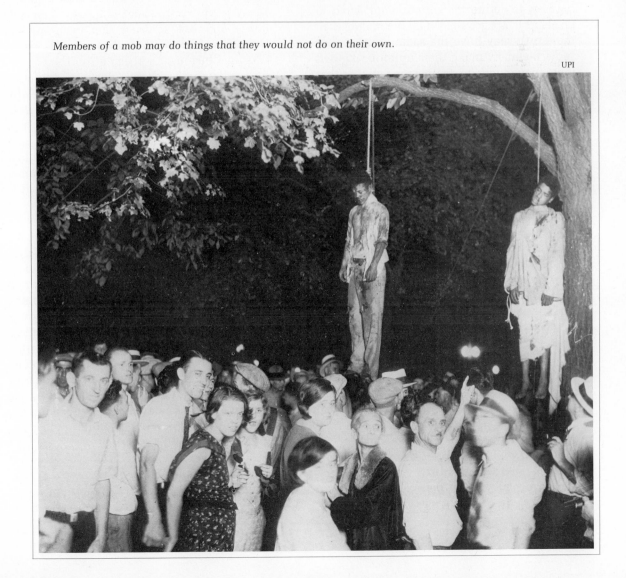

*Members of a mob may do things that they would not do on their own.*

UPI

### Emergent-norm theory

Collective behavior is often defined as group activity that is *not normatively regulated*. This definition does not entirely suit our purposes, however, because one theory holds that collective behavior *is* normatively regulated — but that the norm is a new one invented on the spot. This theory is called the emergent-norm theory.

According to this theory, collective behavior occurs in situations that are not covered by existing rules of conduct. Members of the crowd have to make the rules themselves. They usually begin by wondering how to define the situation and what to do about it as a group. Not all the members of the crowd may have the same opinion, but some members make their opinions known more than others do. If a person believes that his or her opinion is very much in the minority (whether this is actually so or not), he or she is likely to keep silent.

One sociologist illustrated this group experience to his class by walking out of the classroom in the middle of his lecture without any explanation. Half an hour later students were still milling around in the classroom and the hall, trying to arrive at some shared interpretation of the situation and some norm for reacting to it.[9]

The emergent-norm theory holds that most crowd reactions can be understood in terms of the tendency to conform. Just as a person gives up his or her own opinion about which of two lines is longer when faced with the unanimous opinion of a small group, people also tend to agree with what seems to be the shared opinion of a large crowd. Crowd phenomena thus illustrate the power of social control in creating and enforcing a new, emergent norm. Unlike contagion and convergence theories, which assume that the members of a crowd become uniform in their conduct, emergent-norm theory recognizes that many different opinions may exist, even though they may not be expressed openly. The silence of those who disagree looks like passive support and adds to the illusion of uniformity.[10]

Collective behavior often happens when ordinary procedures don't work. For example, thousands of people had to hike miles across dry hills to reach the site of the Altamont Rolling Stones concert. There they found that there were not enough toilets for such a large number of people. Strangers formed small groups to discuss the situation. The norms of "straight" society were rejected, as no longer applying. People began to relieve themselves in public. This deviance made other deviations more likely. Many people were shocked by the open sexuality and use of drugs that resulted, but they felt alone in their disapproval. There was an illusion of agreement on the emerging normative system. Besides, too few police officers were present to enforce the rules of "straight" society. A motorcycle gang undertook to "police" the crowd, and its methods resulted in injuries and one death. After the event many people looked back on their behavior with some shame, realizing how cowardly it had been to give in to social pressure.

### Game theory

The final approach we will discuss is the newest way of looking at collective behavior. It is not inconsistent with emergent-norm or convergence theory, but it is quite different from contagion theory. Instead of assuming that some sort of emotional contagion sweeps through a crowd, turning its members into irrational beings with no self-control, game theory assumes that the members make rational decisions. Game theorists simply say that there are some special characteristics of situations in which collective behavior occurs.[11]

Game theory begins with the assumption that every person makes his or her own decisions at all times, even in an acting crowd. There is no such thing as a "group mind." It is true that individuals may have goals that many others disapprove of (such as looting a store, storming the Bastille, lynching a suspected rapist, or wiping out all the inhabitants of the village of My Lai), but they decide whether to do these things the same way that they make other decisions. They weigh the probable rewards and the probable costs of various courses of action and then try to choose the act that maximizes the rewards and minimizes the costs. Looting a store may be a "reward" and getting arrested may be the "cost" that one may have to pay for looting. This is too high a cost for most people. Standing up in church and showing intense emotion may be a "reward," but getting laughed at may be the "cost" of such an action. The "payoff" is the net reward for a given course of action—the reward minus the cost. If it seems that the payoff will be high, a rational person will undertake the act; otherwise he or she will decide against it.

Every participant wants to maximize payoff, and each realizes that the other participants are doing the same thing. It often happens that the payoff for various possible acts depends on how other people will act. Thus a person may be unwilling to smash and loot a store alone because he or she is likely to have to pay the cost of being arrested. However, if the members of a large crowd decide to smash and loot together, the chance of any one member's being arrested may be much lower. Likewise, if several members of a congregation weep, clap, and shout for joy, the likelihood that anyone will have to pay the cost of being laughed at is lower. This is why people may be willing to do some things in a crowd that they would

*For some people, looting is a "reward" that is too costly unless other people join in. If they do, there's a riot.*

Wide World

not be willing to do alone. As Richard Berk has pointed out, they have not "lost their reason" but, rather, see that the chance of a good payoff has been improved by the responses of other crowd members.

Because most collective behavior involves violation of conventional norms, the person who starts the action takes a high risk. The others may not follow suit, and he or she may be punished. On the other hand, by taking the risk the leader may encourage others to act because they see that he or she is getting away with it. The person who acts first is usually someone who is especially likely to violate conventional norms—perhaps a child, a drunk, or a criminal. The leaders of collective behavior are usually of low status, while those of institutionalized groups are usually of high status.

In most forms of crowd behavior the action takes place because many members all want the same things and, by acting together, can increase the payoff for each member. This is a *collaborative* situation. However, panic is one form of collective behavior that takes place only when the situation is *competitive*. Suppose your "reward" is escape from a burning building with few exits in which there are many people who also want to escape. The "cost" may be to get trampled. If everyone pursues the same goal at once, the chances of a favorable payoff for each one are not increased but decreased. In any competitive situation each person who looks out for his or her own interests makes it harder for the others, who are looking out for theirs. That is, by acting together they increase the costs, not the payoff, for each other.

It is likely that further study will lead to a combination of game theory and emergent-norm theory, while convergence theory and contagion theories drop out of favor. Convergence theory simply does not explain everything that needs to be explained, such as rapid shifts within a crowd from one plan of action to another. Contagion theories seem to be downright misleading. They suggest that some psychological disease sweeps the members of a crowd into actions that they would oppose if they were in their right minds.

## Communication processes in large groups

All human activities involve communication, but not all group communication processes are alike. Here I will define several of them. These communication processes differ in the degree of control, manipulation, and planning involved. Rumor is the most unplanned, noninstitutionalized kind of communication, while propaganda is the opposite—the most purposeful and manipulative kind of communication.

### RUMOR

A **rumor** is a piece of information that is passed from one person to another throughout a group without being checked out, such as gossip about famous politicians or secret military weapons. Rumors can arise in any social setting, but they are most likely to arise in situations of social stress, for example, wartime. Rumors arise as a result of two factors: (1) the amount of *interest* people have in the subject matter and (2) the amount of *ambiguity* in the situation.[12] Ambiguity refers to the difficulty of checking the accuracy of a story because of incomplete information. For example, during World War II many Japanese living in Hawaii believed that Japan had won the war and that the U.S. government didn't want to tell the American people that they had lost. It is reasonable to suppose that this rumor was accepted because the Japanese wanted it to be so and because there was no way of proving that it was not so.

Not surprisingly, rumors are very common in situations in which collective behavior is taking shape. During the "milling" phase people trade stories and judge the validity of each one while deciding what they should do about the situation.

It is not possible to say whether in general a rumor tends to gain or lose in accuracy as it passes from one person to another. Most laboratory studies of rumor have been set up to pass a complex story from person A to person B to person C to person D to person E and so on, without allowing any discussion among the subjects. A real rumor does not usually spread in this way. Rather, it is passed along within a social *network*, so that each person may hear a version from several different sources and can judge which one, if any, to believe. People differ in their ability to judge the accuracy of a rumor. Critical discussion usually makes the rumor more accurate. If the rumor goes through many interactions, so that each person hears it several times from different sources, it will probably become more accurate if the hearers are critical but may become less so if they are not critical.[13]

### PUBLIC OPINION

Rumors are irregular and infrequent, but people exchange news, information, and opinions almost all the time. A **public** may be defined as a scattered group of people who are interested in, and have different opinions about, an issue and are involved in a discussion of the issue. The discussion is designed to produce a collective opinion that will influence the action of some group or individual.[14] Here we are talking not about *the* public but about a variety of publics, each concerned with a particular topic. For example, one public is concerned with the issue of abortion and includes both those in

UPI

The Chicago Tribune *mistakenly reported Dewey's election in 1948 because it went to press too early. Harry Truman kept this paper all his life.*

favor and those opposed. Another public is interested in the role of the military. It includes people who want more missiles, people who want to disband NATO, total pacifists, and others, including some who read a good deal on the subject but have no definite opinion. There are many publics in modern societies because of the large number of new issues and problems. We take it for granted that it is all right to be either for or against abortion or for or against the military. Differences of opinion are acceptable, and as information is exchanged and arguments take place public opinion may change. This is why polls "take the pulse" of the public; they want to see what shifts are taking place in the opinions of a population. On many issues people who belong to the same groups

*If too few doors are open in a burning theatre or too few windows open in a bank, the result can be a panic.*

and the same social class tend to hold similar opinions, though some groups have more influence on their members' opinions than others.

Not all the members of a public have an equal impact on the opinions of others. As one might expect, high-status people carry more weight than others. In fact their advice is often sought, especially if they are well known and responsible. These individuals, called *opinion leaders*, are usually better informed than other people. They read more, discuss more, and get more information before they form their own opinions. This process has been called the "two-step flow of communication." That is, the mass media influence opinion leaders in the first step, and in the second step those individuals pass on what they read and hear to other people for whom they are influential.[15]

## THE INFLUENCE OF THE MASS MEDIA

In a crowd situation large numbers of people are in face-to-face contact with each other. In a mass communication situation, on the other hand, thousands or millions of people, scattered over a large area, receive the same message from a distant source. These people have little opportunity to "talk back" to the information source or to discuss the message with one another. A million people read the same news at their individual breakfast tables. Twenty million people watch the same news on television. These media unquestionably affect public opinion and suggest certain kinds of actions to people in the audience. The effects of these media are very important, if only because they get so much attention from the average person in modern society. (Between the ages of 3 and 16 the average North American child spends one-sixth of his or her waking hours watching TV — more time than he or she spends on any other activity except sleep and play.[16]) What are the effects of the media on the public?

I have already mentioned that many people form opinions about issues through the two-step flow of communication. However, many other opinions seem to be formed through one-step processes. Some of these processes — including suggestion and propaganda — have a strong influence on collective behavior.

### Suggestion

The following example shows the power of suggestion. Several years ago the mass media reported that a peculiar thing was happening to car windshields in a particular area. For some unknown reason pitting marks seemed to appear on windshields and then to increase in size. Upon reading about this phenomenon hundreds of people phoned the police to report pitting in their windshields. Others covered their windshields with blankets or newspapers. There was much debate as to whether the epidemic of pitting was caused by vandalism, atomic fallout, or some other factor. Finally a team of scientists announced that there was no "epidemic" at all. The number of windshields that were pitted was no higher than usual. All that had happened was that people had heard the false report in the news and had looked *at* their windshields for once, instead of *through* them. As a result they had found pits that they would never have noticed otherwise.

This is an interesting example of suggestion but a harmless one. Far more serious are the effects of the mass media on patterns of violence. As mentioned in Chapter 3, studies suggest that many people who watch violence on television are more likely to behave

"But officer, I'm just streaking."

Jean-Claude Lejune/Stock, Boston

aggressively themselves afterwards than people who do not watch violence.[17] Moreover, a recent study of suicide has revealed the existence of a "Werther effect." Two hundred years ago, when the famous German writer Goethe published a novel about a young man named Werther who committed suicide, many people followed Werther's example and shot themselves. In several areas the book had to be banned to protect the public from its influence. Using American and British statistics, sociologists have shown that the number of suicides increases after a suicide has been widely reported in the newspapers.[18] For example, suicides increased in number just after the death of Marilyn Monroe. Some cities, such as Toronto, do not report in the newspapers suicides by people jumping in front of subway trains. This policy was adopted after reports showed that such stories tend to stimulate more suicides.

How many other, similar problems result from suggestions influencing the audiences of the mass media? We have no way of answering this question, but it is likely that the number is high. No airplane had ever been hijacked until a few years ago. The publicity given to the first hijacking seemed to stimulate more hijackings, and today every airport is constantly on guard to prevent them. Kidnappings and guerrilla activities such as those involving the Italian premier, Aldo Moro, are also similar in some ways to streaking, goldfish swallowing, and other fads that become commonplace after they have been given wide publicity. Lately it has become a routine event for protesters to slash art in museums and even blow up famous palaces like Versailles. It seems reasonable to assume that many protest demonstrations and even riots have been stimulated, at least in part, by reports of such events in the mass media. The effects of the media have not been studied enough, but they are probably a very important factor in modern life.

### Propaganda

**Propaganda** is the planned use of mass media to influence the beliefs and opinions of a population. Advertising is the most obvious example of propaganda, but governments have also used it in wartime to improve morale among their own troops and to lower it among the enemy. Thus during World War II the Germans broadcast radio messages from "Axis Sally" and the Japanese had a program by "Tokyo Rose," both with the goal of persuading American soldiers not to fight. The Allies, not to be outdone, dropped leaflets behind German lines. The most effective of these asked the reader to accept only a few points. The best one flattered the reader by claiming that German infantrymen were excellent soldiers who were not being outfought man for man but were being crushed by the superior weapons of the Allies. It did not use political arguments or make being captured sound attractive or even urge the reader to desert. It simply left the decision up to him and provided the basic facts about how to go about surrendering. Many German soldiers were carrying this leaflet when they turned themselves over to the Allies.[19] In contrast, most of the German leaflets dropped behind Allied lines attacked so many of the soldiers' beliefs that they seemed ridiculous and persuaded no one.

## Fads, fashions, and crazes

People who are exposed to the mass media become familiar with the same new things at the same time. As a result fads and fashions are more common in modern society than in earlier societies. A **fad** is a culture trait that suddenly becomes popular and then just as suddenly disappears. Goldfish-swallowing contests became a fad that swept college campuses some years ago, but today no one swallows gold-fish (I think!). More recently smiling faces on buttons, shirts, and many other objects were "in." In France the fad a couple of summers ago was sweat shirts with names of American universities on them. At first I was fooled and started a conversation with a young man wearing one from my alma mater, but I soon discovered that he spoke no English.

**Fashion** consists of culture traits that are popular for a short time and then are gradually replaced. Styles of household decoration and dress come in and out of fashion — skirt lengths are a familiar example. Fashions do not change quite as fast as fads, probably because most people cannot throw away their furniture or clothes and buy new ones every year. Fashions are usually started by high-status people and then copied by people of lower status. This is not always the case, however. Blue jeans, for example, were originally a working-class fashion, but they gradually became accepted by higher strata.

What is remarkable about fashions is the speed with which they catch on throughout the world as a result of the influence of the mass media. As I write this, lots of women are wearing cowboy boots. But shoes wear out quickly, so shoe fashions change almost as quickly as fads. Perhaps as you read this book you will be wearing Grecian sandals or glass slippers, your cowboy boots having long ago been dumped into the trash can. At one time your clothing style would have been determined by your social status, and you would not have been allowed to copy higher-status men or women. You might have worn the same type of shoes all your life.

Most fads and fashions require only a small amount of attention or emotional involvement. The blue-jeans wearer does not lie awake at night thinking about his or her jeans. But a craze is different. A **craze** is a fad

or fashion that becomes so important to people that they may spend a great deal of money and emotion on it. Land speculation booms have been a common type of craze. In the 1920s everyone wanted to buy land in Florida, and property values there became unrealistically high. During the seventeenth century the Dutch went through a tulip craze. People paid higher and higher prices for rare tulip bulbs until the majority of the Dutch people were buying and selling tulips. A rare bulb might sell for as much as a house. Then people realized that the craze would not continue forever and began to sell their bulbs; a panic and a financial crisis resulted.

## MASS HYSTERIA

One form of collective behavior that happens rarely is *mass hysteria*. This usually takes the form of a frightening misunderstanding that is shared by a large number of people and causes a lot of anxiety. For example, in the 1930s Orson Welles produced a radio program based on H. G. Wells' story *The War of the Worlds*. Its script sounded much like a regular newscast, reporting the invasion of the East Coast by Martians, and a great many listeners believed the story and became very frightened. Some got into their cars and fled.[20]

Another example was the "Phantom Gasser" reported in sensational stories by newspapers in Illinois. This person was supposed to have sprayed gas on sleeping women through their bedroom windows. After the first incident was reported, many other women claimed to have been gassed and to have been temporarily paralyzed by the fumes. One researcher interviewed everyone who knew anything about these incidents and concluded that the gasser was imaginary. The "Phantom" was a product of psychological anxiety made more intense by frightening newspaper reports.[21]

# Social movements

Not long ago the graduate students, secretaries, and faculty of my sociology department sent out for Chinese food and had a party. After everyone had finished eating, some of us began clearing away the plates and wine glasses while others made merry or got involved in conversations about ongoing research. Suddenly a lively, popular woman professor stopped and bellowed, "Just take a look around this room! Just look at what is going on!" We all laughed because we "saw" right away what she was pointing out: Every woman in the room was collecting and scraping dishes, while every man was sitting and talking.

Ten years ago our party might have been about the same, except that no one would have told us to look at what was going on. If anyone had done so, we would not have known what to "look for." No one would have laughed, because we would not have seen anything noteworthy. Moreover, any woman who called attention to the situation would have been considered hostile and "bitchy" and would have been disliked for complaining.

What has happened during the past decade that has made such a difference? The women's movement. What has it achieved? It has improved opportunities for women on the job and in other settings, but the change that this story illustrates is a change in the way people look at things. Modern Western societies—or at least most social strata within those societies—have been forced to accept a new value that was not part of the culture before: equality of the sexes. Today most men do not feel quite "right" about having their dishes cleared by female co-workers, even though it still happens now and then because of habit. A decade ago both sexes felt "right" about it, so much so

that only an especially aggressive woman would have complained that she was being treated unfairly.

A social movement is a collective effort to bring about a new order of life.[22] Examples include the civil-rights movement, the women's movement, the antiabortion movement, and the gay-rights movement. A social movement is different from a public in that it supports one point of view, while the public includes all the opposing views on a given issue. It is different from a crowd because it is a long-term collectivity rather than a quick, unplanned grouping. Crowds may appear in connection with a social movement, however, as in the case of the peace marches of the antiwar movement.

Practically every other chapter of this or any other sociology book will explain that social patterns are organized in terms of the shared values of a given society. We do not often ask where those values come from. Alain Touraine does ask this question, however, and his answer is that social movements are the source of new values.[23] I think he is correct. It seems to me that a new value was shared by everyone at the sociology department's party and that it clearly was a product of the women's movement, "a collective effort to bring about a new order of life." However, not all social movements favor new values. Some urge a return to the old order and to old values rather than the creation of a new order.

Social movements are familiar to us all. We are constantly being asked to demand a new order of life that would be more favorable to various groups. Anticolonialist movements around the world involve many millions of people. The civil-rights movement, the ecology movement, the American Indian movement, the Quebec Separatist movement, and the Gay Liberation movement are familiar to North Americans. Each of these movements makes some new moral claim on the conscience of the wider society in the name of a new value. This new value may be social equality and dignity for a previously stigmatized or degraded minority, political independence for a particular group, or conservation instead of wasteful consumption.

Primitive societies and ancient civilizations knew nothing of social movements. Peasant societies had them only occasionally, in the form of revolts. During the Middle Ages a variety of "millenarian" movements arose in Europe, usually in places where a class of uprooted poor people were living without any settled occupation or community ties.[24] These movements were often based on a belief in a messiah king with supernatural powers who was about to save the people from their misery. Often they expected this king to reign for 1000 years; hence the term *millenarian*.

Only in modern society have social movements been numerous. Industrial societies are far more complex than traditional societies; they include a great variety of competing groups, each demanding something for itself. Although all industrial societies give rise to social movements, totalitarian states try to suppress them. Totalitarian regimes often come to power as a result of such a movement and are therefore anxious to keep another movement from replacing them. The most common strategy used in such a case is to suppress dissenting movements. Sometimes this strategy is successful for a long time, as in Russia and Nazi Germany.

### FUNCTIONS OF SOCIAL MOVEMENTS

Touraine has suggested that social movements have three functions: mediation, pressure, and clarification of the collective consciousness.[25] By *mediation* he means that social movements are mechanisms for involving the individual with the larger society. They give each person a chance to participate, to make his or her ideas known, and to have some impact on the social order.

By *pressure* Touraine means that social movements almost always give rise to organized groups that try to get their policies put into operation. They lobby, hand out leaflets, organize demonstrations, and the like.

*Clarification of the collective consciousness* is the most important function of social movements. This is a matter of developing the ideas that are used in discussions throughout a society. Marx's term *class consciousness* refers to this process. He held that shortly before a revolutionary struggle begins, the members of a social class become more aware that they have common interests. They interpret social relationships more clearly and begin to notice facts that they would have overlooked before. The women's movement is another example. It has "raised the consciousness" of a great many people, including men. People are now more sensitive to matters such as referring to a mature woman as a "girl" or hiring women on the basis of beauty instead of their ability. All social movements perform a similar "consciousness-raising" function. Since the civil-rights movement black men have reacted with anger when they are called "boy."

Each social movement tries to make the whole society understand its own point of view, and this is what "raises" the consciousness of the society. To see how much progress has been made in our collective consciousness, look through any old pre-World War II magazine or novel. Many statements that seemed reasonable and even obvious at that time will seem outrageous today. They appear chauvinistic, racist, or snobbish. In most cases such statements embarrass us today because our collective consciousness has been clarified through the efforts of some social movement.

Thus we must recognize social movements as very important historical factors. They are a major source of social change.

The participants in a social movement are not living by old, established values but trying to introduce new values. Sometimes they succeed, sometimes not.

### THE LIFE CYCLE
### OF A SOCIAL MOVEMENT

Carl A. Dawson and Warner E. Gettys, writing in 1929 about collective behavior and social movements, outlined what they believed were the typical stages through which such movements pass.[26] The first stage is a period of social unrest. (This is somewhat like Blumer's "milling" stage.) Both leaders and followers become tense and excited.

If the tension is not resolved, the movement may pass into the second stage, "the popular stage of collective excitement and unrest." "Milling" continues, and the movement gains some focus, wider support, and the beginnings of a myth or ideal to guide it.

The third stage is the "formal stage of the formulation of publics." Policies and goals begin to emerge at this point through discussions within publics. Finally, if the movement is successful, it will enter stage four, the "institutional stage of legalization and societal organization." That is, the aims of the movement become accepted in the laws of the society. Thus the social movement changes from an out-group to the in-group. At this point one can no longer call it a social movement, for it has achieved its goals and no longer has to fight for them.

### TYPES OF SOCIAL
### MOVEMENTS

Social movements are always based on popular discontent. They can be classified by the types of goals they pursue.

Perhaps the most dramatic type is the *revolutionary movement* that seeks to overthrow the established authority, using violence if necessary. A revolutionary movement need not be large in order to have an impact. For example, at least at the beginning the Irish Republican Army was a fairly small group, but through terrorist activities it managed to cause a great deal of confusion.

Movements may differ greatly in the direction of their policies. A *reform movement* always looks toward new goals that its supporters think will correct existing problems. The civil-rights and women's movements are examples. A *reactionary movement*, on the other hand, wants to turn the clock back, so to speak, and bring back an old way of life that is considered better than the present order of things. The John Birch Society is a reactionary movement that tries to limit the extent of government involvement in social life. A *conservative movement* may simply try to keep some values the way they are. For example, one type of conservative movement tries to preserve old buildings and slow the rate of growth and change in big cities.

Some movements have far-reaching goals that would change the life of everyone in the society. Sometimes this type of movement is called a *utopian movement*, which means that it hopes to create a whole new type of society unlike any that now exists. Groups that form communes and organize a detailed life style for their members are utopian. The Oneida Community and the Shakers were nineteenth-century utopian communities. One group of this type had such strict rules that it even spelled out exactly how its members must get out of bed each morning—where to place each foot, and so on.

*Religious movements* have religious goals. Many people in Europe and North America have recently become interested in Eastern religious movements. A number of Indian mystics have large followings. Near my university I often encounter pale young men with shaven heads, wearing yellow monks' robes. They greet me with the chant "Hari Krishna!" and I reply politely, "Hari Hari!"

The most important type of movement

Peter Southwick/Stock, Boston

*There are few jobs available for unskilled workers, and this is the main reason for the great increase in the number of people on welfare.*

producing social change around the world today is the *ethnic* or *nationalistic movement*. The Chicano, Black Power, and American Indian movements are examples of this type. As suggested in the preceding chapter, our time is one in which ascribed communities are developing a strong awareness of themselves as "peoples."

## SOCIAL RESEARCH: *Sociologists at Work*

### THE WELFARE RIGHTS MOVEMENT

During the past twenty years welfare aid to poor American families has increased tremendously. In 1960, for example, there were only "745,000 families on the Aid to Families with Dependent Children (AFDC) rolls and they received payments amounting to less than $1 billion; in 1972 the rolls reached 3 million families and the payments reached $6 billion."[27] Some of this progress has resulted from the efforts of poor-people's movements. Frances Fox Piven and Richard A. Cloward, who were among the leaders of one of these movements, have written a book about poor-people's movements, a case study that will serve as the basis of our discussion. Their research is, of course, based on participant observation. Instead of being scientific and uninvolved, Piven and Cloward were among the most radical and active members of the movement.

The welfare rights movement developed out of the civil-rights movement. Most of the poor

327

urban population of the United States is black, and mobilizing them created the pressure that led to the great increase in welfare aid. The National Welfare Rights Organization (NWRO) was formed in the mid-1960s, at a time when the southern civil-rights movement had almost ended and its leaders were turning their attention to the northern urban areas, where they wanted to create "community organizations" to represent the urban poor in a lasting way.

Aid to Families with Dependent Children (AFDC) had begun in 1935, when the Roosevelt administration was trying to overcome the Great Depression. Although it was a worthy program, many of the poor could not benefit from it because it offered no help to able-bodied adults without children or to two-parent families. By 1960 the situation of the urban poor was very serious because of high rates of unemployment. In many cities there were areas in which over one-third of black men were jobless.[28] Still, little help was available. Of the few families who applied for relief, about half were turned away.[29] However, during his election campaign John F. Kennedy called for an effort to end poverty, and as President he did all he could to make the nation aware of the problems of the urban poor. He proposed laws to extend unemployment benefits, to help the children of unemployed workers, to increase social-security payments, and to raise the minimum wage. As the civil-rights movement became more and more successful in the South, boycotts and picket lines were organized in the North and demands were made to end housing and employment discrimination and the like.

President Johnson greatly expanded the antipoverty program begun during the Kennedy administration. He declared a "war on poverty," a policy that led to legislation such as the Juvenile Delinquency and Youth Offenses Control Act, the Community Mental Health Centers Act, and the Demonstration Cities and Metropolitan Development Act. All of these programs helped the black ghettos organize and demand further government aid. Community action agencies across the nation hired people to learn how welfare rules worked and how to help their clients fight for additional aid. Antipoverty lawyers also joined in this effort.[30] "Welfare Rights" leaflets were passed out to the ghetto poor to tell them how to get help. From about 1965 on the poor began to recognize their "right" to welfare and to demand it on a larger scale than before.

It was at about this time that riots took place in dozens of American cities. These events stimulated community leaders to become more militant in pushing for welfare rights. They brought lawsuits against local politicians and agency administrators. They led the poor in protests against the practices of local agencies. Between 1960 and 1963 the number of families applying for AFDC benefits increased by one-third. An increasing percentage of the applications were accepted—the figure rose from 55 percent in 1960 to 70 percent in 1968.[31]

Piven and Cloward's research showed that in 1965 for every family on AFDC at least one other family was eligible but was not receiving aid. Piven and Cloward proposed a radical strategy. They wanted social workers in the ghettos to persuade as many people as possible to apply for welfare. Their actual goal was to make welfare a federal responsibility instead of a local one. Why? Because then it would be possible to fight for a national income standard. Only that would benefit the poor in the long run. The movement, with its anger and agitation, could not last forever, they reasoned. While it was still hot, they would use the anger to create so much demand for relief that local governments would have to turn to federal sources of funding. Piven and Cloward frankly wanted to take advantage of the tense social environment created by the urban riots. Politicians were almost panicky just then. They would be more responsive to welfare pressure then than later in a less agitated period.

But this idea ran into opposition. Many leaders of the poor-people's movement felt that it would be more useful in the long run to organize the community than to push for all of their demands at once. These leaders thought that by organizing the poor they could continue to pressure the government long after the riot atmosphere had cooled. After all, other special-interest groups maintained permanent lobbies—homeowners' associations, trade unions, industrialists, and so on. Why not a welfare recipients' lobby? So they lost interest in the immediate situation and chose instead to plan for a long-term organization to represent the interests of the poor.

Piven and Cloward, on the other hand, argued that local politicians would increase welfare aid for a while—as long as the crisis lasted—and then pay more attention to the groups that demanded cutbacks in welfare spending. (The California-led tax revolt starting in 1978 proves that this prediction was right.) Thus they were for grabbing the chance to disrupt society and shake up local politicians so much that they would have to turn to the federal government for aid. Patient, long-term lobbying would never achieve the goal of federalizing welfare. But local politicians could achieve that goal if they found it necessary to demand it *themselves.* And they would demand it only in a severe crisis. Only a "welfare explosion" would force them to ask the federal government to take over their economic responsibility for welfare programs. So Piven and Cloward argued not for *organizing* the poor but for *mobilizing* them— sending them out in large numbers to demand their rights.

They lost the argument, and the leaders of the movement chose the "organizing" strategy instead of the "mobilizing" strategy. But they quickly ran into problems. How could they get poor people to remain involved in their organization? For a while they used their organization to demand special one-time grants for welfare recipients—an extra check to cover household furnishings, clothes, and the like. But as soon as a family had received its special grant it had no reason to remain in the organization. And soon the special grants were abolished. In 1969 the NWRO's membership reached a high of 22,000, but a year later it had fallen to almost zero.

Still, the movement's leaders kept hoping. They wanted to become part of a huge international poor-people's movement. Some of them were invited to social-welfare conferences in foreign countries. Going to these events became more important to them than the relief they might be able to get for the poor. According to Piven and Cloward, "As NWRO's integration with other groups progressed, the political beliefs of those in the leadership stratum became more conventional, the militancy of the tac-

tics they advocated weakened, and the professed goal of membership expansion receded."[32] Leaders became local celebrities in the welfare agencies and sometimes, glorying in their new prestige, they lost sight of their organizations' goals.

By the 1972 election the antiwelfare position had become a major issue, one that Nixon used to gain voter support. He told the poor not to ask what government could do for them but what they could do for themselves. Yet some of Nixon's welfare proposals had a liberal effect. The federal minimum income standard and wage supplements would reduce the welfare burden of state and local governments. But in other ways the plan was not liberal at all. It would force all "employable" welfare recipients to take jobs at less than the minimum wage, for example.[33] Moreover, the Nixon administration encouraged the belief that the poor were people whose lives were marked by "social pathologies" caused by overly generous welfare payments that allowed them to be idle and to neglect their families. (This belief ignored the serious lack of opportunity that deprived the poor of money and jobs.)

The Nixon plan tried to motivate the poor to find jobs, using both punishments and rewards. Over time it might have forced the poor to take work at very low wages. But by the end of 1970 the American economy was in a serious recession, and Nixon's welfare reform bill was defeated in 1972. The NWRO claimed to have been a major power causing the defeat of the Nixon plan, but Piven and Cloward claim that it had little influence on the outcome.[34]

Like many organizations, the NWRO became top-heavy. Money collected by poor members went to support the head office. Very little of it was used to serve the needs of the poor themselves. The people had not really been organized at the grassroots level and after the crisis of the 1960s had passed they could not be organized. Local black and poor leaders had to rely on electoral politics to press the economic claims of the poor. This strategy was a failure in the 1970s. Piven and Cloward still claim that their own plan would have succeeded: The welfare rights movement should have mobilized, not organized.

# SOCIAL POLICY:
## Issues and Viewpoints

Two questions of policy that have become important in recent years are (1) should the mass media be censored to prevent news of violent actions from leading to similar actions by those who read newspaper accounts of such events or see them on television newscasts? and (2) How should the police respond to riot situations?

### THE MEDIA AND COLLECTIVE BEHAVIOR

We have discussed the effects of the media in other chapters, but then we were concerned with their effects on culture and on individual violence. Here we will turn our attention to the relationship between the media and collective behavior.

It is not possible to find out how many riots, terrorist attacks, murders, hijackings, kidnappings, suicides, political assassinations, and so on are stimulated by reports in the mass media. One way to find out would be to ban any reports of such events in the media of, say, five or six states for a period of several years. Then we could compare the murder rate, the number of riots, and the like before and during the censorship period. Such an experiment could never be done, of course, so we may never know the answers. In the absence of good research, your guess is as good as mine. I would guess that much of the violence of modern life results directly from ideas picked up from the mass media. For example, when a group of boys threw gasoline on a girl and set her on fire they were imitating a scene they had watched on television that week. The media suggest possible actions. Emotionally unstable people and children may be especially likely to be influenced by those suggestions.

It is reasonable to suppose that simply reporting riots, hijackings, crime, bomb scares, and the like costs human lives by stimulating people to imitate such actions. It is also reason-able to suppose that films and television help maintain our culture's emphasis on violence. These are assumptions, not proved facts, but it is very likely that this is an accurate view of the situation.

On the other hand, citizens have a right to be kept informed. It is hard to downplay riots, kidnappings, and other acts of violence. As one newscaster has remarked, television can't "hide" a story by printing it on the back page. Should the media be forbidden to report certain facts? This could lead to other, equally serious problems. Freedom of the press is an important tool for preventing tyranny. I certainly don't want the government to control the content of television programs or newspaper articles. Government officials could protect their own interests by hiding certain facts. The Watergate scandal, for example, would never have come to the attention of the public if the media hadn't been allowed to publish the facts. Only dictators want to censor news.

But obviously we do have a certain amount of censorship. Diplomats have to negotiate in secret. Some military matters must be kept secret. Gruesome pictures of accident or murder victims are not shown on television; the body is decently covered with a blanket. Newscasters don't show pornography on their programs. Newspapers can't print stories about a person that they can't prove. So we have a free press, but not without limits. Other values have to be respected as well—the right to privacy, national security, the need to protect people from seeing brutality, obscenity, and the like. The problem is the conflict between these values. As mentioned earlier, it is easy to choose between a right and a wrong. What is hard is to choose between two conflicting rights. The conflict here is between the right to be informed and the right to be protected against violence that might result from the reporting of violent acts by the mass media.

### THE POLICE AND COLLECTIVE BEHAVIOR

The best cure for a riot is prevention. Solve the underlying problem; don't ignore it. For example, in the 1960s ghetto riots the underlying problem was the oppression of black slum dwellers by American society. If the problem had been taken seriously earlier, the riots might not have occurred.

But if a crowd does form and violence is threatened, what should the police do to minimize the danger? Some years ago a social scientist wrote a manual for the Chicago police listing five procedures for preventing collective violence.[35] These procedures, which unfortunately have rarely been followed, are the following:

1 Remove or isolate the individuals involved in the triggering event before the crowd has begun to unify.
2 Prevent communication during the milling process by dividing the crowd into small units.
3 Remove the crowd leaders, if this can be done without using force.
4 Distract the crowd by creating diversions.
5 Prevent the crowd from growing by isolating it.

Sometimes, however, the police themselves are the rioters. This has happened several times during the past 10 or 15 years. For example, during the 1968 Democratic National Convention in Chicago television viewers watched the police go on a rampage. Since police work is frustrating and feels dangerous, police officers sometimes lose their tempers. Better training of officers might make for more self-control in stressful situations.[36]

In general, however, it is not the police who start the fighting. What often happens is that the police create the opportunity for a riot simply by being present and ready for action. The riot is a self-fulfilling prophecy: the police think there will be a riot, they show up in force, and sure enough there's a riot. When they don't show up there's no riot.

Not too long ago in Barcelona, Spain, I watched young people marching around in groups, waving banners and raising their fists. Before long several carloads of riot police drove up, with helmets, gas masks, and tear gas guns. "What's up?" I asked a street vendor. He cheer-

One problem for the police is how to prevent riots when groups like the Nazis organize a public rally.

fully informed me that if I waited a couple of hours I could see a riot. "It happens every week or so lately. Whenever the police show up." Like other sensible people, I went indoors and watched from a balcony. Pretty soon there were rubber bullets whizzing around and people chasing each other and scuffling in the street.

I don't know what I would have done if I had been the police chief. Part of his job is to send the police to any place where people are disturbing the peace. What else are police for? But they *did* look threatening, and the demonstrators seemed sure to respond. A similar example is the situation in Northern Ireland, where English troops were sent to stop riots between the Protestant and Catholic political extremists. Their presence only caused further rioting. At other times, of course, peace-keeping forces serve their purpose and restore order where order would otherwise be impossible. On balance, I think I'd prefer to live in a society in which there *are* police.

## SUMMARY

1. *Collective behavior* consists of actions by a number of people that deviate from the institutionalized patterns of everyday life. According to Smelser, it will occur only if six conditions are met: (1) structural conduciveness, (2) structural strain, (3) a generalized belief, (4) precipitating factors, (5) mobilization for action, and (6) ineffective social control.

2. Behavior after disasters is rarely disorderly. Routine, institutionalized procedures usually don't work, but people invent new ways of doing things, usually in a spirit of mutual concern and solidarity. Panics, on the other hand, arise in competitive situations where people believe there are not enough escape routes. Panic behavior is a scramble to protect oneself without concern for others.

3. The *acting crowd* is the form of collective behavior that is most often troublesome. It chooses a course of action on the spot, and can become violent. There are several theories that try to explain crowd behavior: (1) contagion theories, (2) convergence theory, (3) emergent-norm theory, and (4) game theory.

4. Contagion theories (Le Bon, Freud, Blumer) assume that the crowd is irrational and that normal people caught up in it will become irrational. People follow the crowd as a result of some sort of emotional communication. Le Bon explained this process as imitation, hypnosis, and suggestion. Freud thought it was largely a matter of identifying with the leader. Blumer believed it was caused by a "circular reaction" that goes on during the "milling stage"—a direct, unthinking reaction of people to each other's emotions.

5. Convergence theory assumes that people who happen to have similar hidden wishes and happen to gather in a crowd may, if someone starts the action, ignore their usual inhibitions and take part in mob violence. Their behavior is not acquired through "contagion" but stems from impulses that each participant already has within himself or herself.

6. Emergent-norm theory holds that in unusual situations a crowd may find ordinary norms inadequate. There may be no uniform opinion as to how to behave, but some people express their opinions and others do not. If the expressed opinions *appear* to represent those of all the members of the crowd, they become a new norm that others will follow out of their desire to conform.

**7.** Game theory sees collective behavior not as irrational but as the outcome of special situations in which participation in a crowd changes the payoff for some courses of action. Acting within a crowd may become rational, while doing the same thing alone would be too risky.

**8.** *Rumors* often arise during periods of stress, because they depend on ambiguity and on the intensity of interest in the subject matter.

**9.** Different *publics* exist within society, each one concerned with a particular issue. Some individuals ("opinion leaders") have more influence than others on people's opinions.

**10.** The mass media affect ordinary people in a "two-step flow of communication." The media first influence the opinion leaders, and they, in turn, influence others. *Propaganda* is the planned use of media to influence the opinions of others.

**11.** A *social movement* is a collective effort to bring about a new order of life. It is often the source of a new value. It may clarify the collective consciousness by trying to get the whole society to understand its own point of view.

# KEY TERMS

**acting crowd** a potentially violent mob that chooses a course of action on the spot.

**collective behavior** spontaneous, transitory, noninstitutionalized group action.

**craze** a fad or fashion that becomes so important to people that they spend a great deal of money and emotion on it.

**crowd** a large, temporary group of people who have some common goal or interest.

**expressive crowd** a group that shows especially strong feelings.

**fad** a culture trait that suddenly becomes popular and then disappears.

**fashion** a culture trait that is popular for a short time and is gradually replaced.

**propaganda** the planned use of mass media to influence the beliefs and opinions of a population.

**public** a scattered group of people who have different opinions about an issue and are involved in a discussion of that issue.

**rumor** a piece of information that is passed from one person to another throughout a group without being checked for accuracy.

**social movement** a collective effort to bring about a new order of life.

# FOR FURTHER READING

ALLPORT, GORDON W., and LEO POSTMAN. *The Psychology of Rumor.* New York: Holt, Rinehart & Winston, 1947. A classic study which reveals how stories get transformed in the repeated telling.

BERK, RICHARD A. *Collective Behavior.* Dubuque, Iowa: William C. Brown, 1974. A small paperback that criticizes older theories about collective behavior and argues that the phenomenon can be understood as rational behavior. Highly readable.

ELLUL, JACQUES. *Propaganda: The Formation of Men's Attitudes.* Translated by Konrad Keller and Jean Lerner. New York: Knopf, 1965. A contemporary French theorist and social philosopher examines propaganda in terms of its constructive value for society.

GUSFIELD, JOSEPH R., ed. *Protest, Reform and Revolt: A Reader in Social Movements.* New York: Wiley, 1970. This collection of articles emphasizes the political side of social movements.

LANG, KURT, and GLADYS E. LANG. "Some Pertinent Questions on Collective Violence and the News Media." *Journal of Social Issues,* vol. 28, no. 1, 1972. This essay examines the question raised in this chapter concerning whether mass media coverage tends to encourage new acts of violence. The Langs conclude that it sometimes does, but that the media also sometimes have the opposite effect, dampening acts of violence.

NYE, ROBERT A. *The Origin of Crowd Psychology: Gustav LeBon and the Crisis of Mass Democracy in the Third Republic.* Beverly Hills: Sage, 1975. A biography and account of LeBon's ideas.

PINARD, MAURICE. *The Rise of a Third Party: A Study in Crisis Politics.* Englewood Cliffs, N.J.: Prentice-Hall, 1971. A study of the rise of the Social Credit Party in Quebec, as well as other third parties and political movements, such as McCarthyism, Goldwaterism, and the farmers' movements.

SMELSER, NEIL J. *The Theory of Collective Behavior.* New York: Free Press, 1962. The leading contemporary theorist explaining hostile outbursts, social movements, and other patterns of collective behavior. Smelser's model is used by many other scholars today.

# THREE

## social
## institutions

12

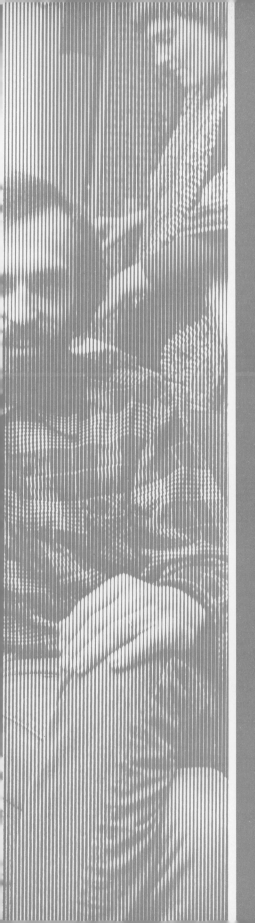

# THE FAMILY

Does a spirit live in your fireplace? In the days when Zeus and Apollo and the other gods lived on Mt. Olympus, every household had at least one live-in god that supposedly dwelled in the hearth and looked after the family's welfare. I imagine it chose the hearth because that was a cozy spot where the family gathered for intimacy. I don't even have a fireplace, but I think our household spirit lives in the coffee table instead.

Of course, household spirits were not awe-inspiring or majestic. If they had been, nobody could have endured having them around. Dignified spirits are for dignified places, but a home is the place for all the undignified activities that people don't like to perform in public. At home you can cut your toenails, belch out loud, and watch TV wearing only underwear.

The family is important because it comprises the people in whose company you feel free to do all of these graceless things and more. We often claim that the great thing about families is the love their members have for each other, but that is only part of the truth. The most beautiful, treasured moments of your life may be with your family but some of the worst moments will also be with them, and those times are just as important. Whoever has seen you at your worst and still cares is important to you.

In this chapter I want to discuss a little about sociologists' studies of family life. But first let me caution you not to expect too much. Because they care so much about family life, students often look to sociology for practical advice on how to live together happily. You may hope this chapter will do that for you. It won't. Sociologists who study families have no happier homes than anybody else. The deepest problems of human experience cannot be solved with pat formulas or sociological explanations. So, not expecting too much, let's consider what sociology does have to say about the family.

# Family organization and kinship patterns

Although all societies recognize special bonds between kin (people who are related either by birth or by marriage, such as husbands and wives, brothers and sisters, aunts and nieces), kinship patterns differ widely. The patterns that seem familiar and natural to North Americans would seem strange to members of most of the world's societies. Here I will simply mention some of the terms social scientists use in describing the most common patterns of kinship.

The core unit of kinship is a group that we all know well—the nuclear family (a husband, his wife, and their unmarried children). This unit is the "atom" from which larger kinship groupings are built. (It is sometimes called the *conjugal family* because it is based on marriage.) In about half of all societies, however, a new nuclear family is not usually independent. Instead, it becomes a new unit within the extended family, a household that is made up of the nuclear family plus various other relatives such as grandparents. (The extended family is sometimes called the *consanguine* family because the members are tied together by "blood"—that is, birth.)

The extended family usually consists of a husband, his wife, and their sons, plus the sons's wives and children. In some cases, however, the daughters bring husbands home and the husbands become part of the extended family. One type of extended family, called the joint family, is traditional in Hindu India, where brothers continue to share property even after their parents' death. The oldest male is the head of the family, but he cannot dispose of the family's property. Nowadays females are also entitled to a share of the property. The joint family does not always live together as a single household, however.

A composite family is formed when nuclear families live together in a single household. Besides the extended family, another important type of composite family exists in about one-fourth of the world's societies—the polygamous family, in which there are several wives or husbands. A polygamous family may be either polygynous or polyandrous. Polygyny means "several women" and refers to the marriage of a man to more than one wife. Often the various wives are sisters. Polygyny is widespread. Anthropologists have found that in 193 out of 234 societies the ideal is for a man to have two or

This polygymous family consists of a man, his 156 wives, and their children.

Marc & Evelyne Bernheim/Woodfin Camp

more wives.[1] Of course it is rarely possible for the majority of the men in a society to have more than one wife. This is because the ratio of males to females is nearly equal in all human populations and remains so unless it is changed by extreme events such as war or female infanticide (the killing of female babies). In order to give men an opportunity to have more than one wife, polygynous societies often match young women with older husbands. When the man dies, his young wife can marry into another polygynous household.[2]

Polyandry (which means "several men") refers to the marriage of a woman to more than one husband. This form of family is extremely rare. Its most common form is the sharing of a woman by two or more brothers. The Todas of southern India and the lowest class of Tibetans have practiced this fraternal type of polyandry, and the Marquesan islanders have practiced nonfraternal polyandry. However, other forms of marriage are also practiced in all three of these societies. Polyandry is usually permitted as the last resort in very poor societies in which female infanticide is institutionalized.

## RULES OF MARRIAGE

All societies have certain rules of endogamy and exogamy, which define for the individual the people who are eligible mates. Endogamy requires a person to marry someone within his or her own group. Pressure to marry "within the faith" is an endogamous rule found in many religious communities. Likewise, many ethnic groups require a person to marry a member of the same ethnic community. This rule may be so strictly enforced that anyone who breaks it will be shunned. (Quite apart from the rules of endogamy, people have a strong tendency to prefer mates who are similar to themselves in certain important ways. This is called homogamy, meaning the tendency for like to marry like. For example, you are likely to choose as your spouse someone from a similar social class to yours, with similar religious beliefs and similar intelligence, though there are no social norms that require you to do so.)

Exogamy requires a person to choose a mate from a different group. The taboo against incest is the most obvious example of an exogamous rule. It forbids one to mate with one's parents or siblings (and often aunts, cousins, and other kin). Many societies define marriage with any member of one's own lineage as incestuous.

### SYSTEMS OF DESCENT

Western societies reckon descent from both the mother's side and the father's side, a system called bilateral descent. It makes no difference whether an aunt or uncle, a cousin or a grandparent is related to us through our father or our mother. Both lines are equally important. We take our father's surname, but in all other respects we are tied by kinship to our mother's family as much as to our father's.

Our bilateral system is an uncommon form of kinship; only 30 percent of all known societies use it. Much more common are unilinear systems—systems that consider the male blood line or the female blood line, but not both, as kin. A unilinear system may be either matrilineal or patrilineal. In a patrilineal descent system each person, male or female, belongs to the father's line. This includes the father's father as well as his brothers and his brothers' children. Only the descendants of males are included, however, for daughters marry men of different line and give birth to children who belong to those other lines.

Matrilineal descent systems are the "mirror image" of patrilineal systems. In such a system a person belongs to the mother's line, which includes the mother, her sisters, and her sisters' children. When a man marries he remains part of his mother's line, but his children become part of his wife's line, not his own. The anthropologist Bronislaw Malinowski studied a number of matrilineal societies, including the Trobriand Islanders. He tells us that a male Trobriander usually has a warm relationship with his son, much like the relationship between uncles and nephews in our own society. However, a father does not have any real authority over his son. He does have authority over his sister's children and in fact is required to support them, for he belongs to their line and not to his own children's line. Some 15 percent of all the world's societies are matrilineal. The patterns of matrilineal and patrilineal descent are shown in Figure 12.1.

Matrilineal kinship systems should not be confused with *matriarchy*. The fact that the "family tree" is traced through the female line does not mean that women have authority over men. In fact, true matriarchy is unknown among all the societies in the world.

### SYSTEMS OF RESIDENCE

In Western society a bride and groom are usually expected to set up housekeeping on their own. This norm is called the rule of neolocal residence—the new conjugal family lives in a "new locale." Societies with extended families, on the other hand, require either patrilocal or matrilocal residence, depending on whether the newly married couple moves in with the husband's parents or the wife's. A few societies have *bilocal* rules that permit the couple to live with either the husband's family or the wife's. Systems of residence do not necessarily coincide with rules of descent; a patrilineal society, for example, does not always require patrilocal or even neolocal residence.[3]

**FIGURE 12.1**
*Unilineal descent*

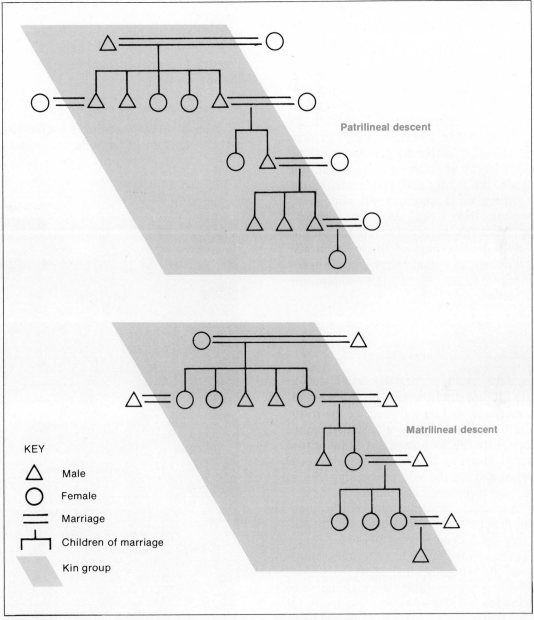

Patrilineal descent

Matrilineal descent

KEY

△ Male

○ Female

═ Marriage

⊓ Children of marriage

▨ Kin group

*Source:* David A. Schulz, The Changing Family (Englewood Cliffs, N.J.: Prentice-Hall, 1972), p. 45.

# Functions of the family

In primitive societies family and kinship ties are almost the only institutions that exist. All the functions of society—religious, political, economic, as well as emotional and protective—are carried out through these ties. In modern societies many of these functions have been taken over by specialized institutions such as schools, factories, churches, and government agencies. Still, the functions of the modern family are numerous and vital. For example, the family assigns a social status to children until they are old enough to determine their own. However, several other functions are even more important. We will discuss four of these functions: (1) regulation of sexual behavior and reproduction, (2) socialization, (3) protection, and (4) affection.

### REGULATION OF SEXUAL BEHAVIOR AND REPRODUCTION

A marriage ceremony formally establishes a family. It has traditionally been assumed that marriage will be followed by the birth of children. Within the family, stable sexual relationships can be maintained, both for the personal pleasure of the men and women involved and for the sake of society, which needs new members. The family's basic purpose is to create offspring who will become useful members of the society in adulthood, carrying the human species forward.

Few societies today have trouble maintaining their populations. Most have the opposite problem—their populations are growing too fast. Today we are less likely to believe that a couple has a duty to produce children. Yet most people prefer to marry rather than live alone, even if they do not plan to have children. Often these are people who feel dissatisfied with the instability of a series of temporary sexual relationships. Such a life style takes a good deal of emotional energy. Marriage offers a steady sexual relationship in the context of fairly secure interpersonal relationships. Even so, nonmarital and homosexual relationships are common in a large part of the population. We should consider them here before moving on.

### Nonmarital sexual behavior

Almost all other societies have more liberal attitudes toward nonmarital intercourse

Fredrik D. Bodin/Stock, Boston

than Western society. Most societies are concerned with preventing births outside of marriage but not necessarily with preventing sexual relations outside of marriage. In fact the majority of societies permit premarital sex. One study reported that less than one-third of all societies entirely disapproved of both premarital and extramarital relations. More often husbands are permitted more sexual freedom than wives.

There is, of course, a good deal of evidence that the rules of sexual behavior are becoming much more permissive in most Western societies. However, the most rapid increase in permissiveness occurred not in the present generation but in the years just following World War I. A study published in 1938, for example, showed that 14 percent of the women born before 1890 admitted to having premarital sexual intercourse, while 68 percent of those born after 1909 did so.[4] After the 1920s the frequency of sexual relations among unmarried youth seems to have remained fairly stable until the 1960s, when another large increase began.[5] This increase was greater for females than for males.

In the ten years from 1965 to 1975 there were marked changes in attitudes toward sex. One study of college women found that the view that premarital sex was immoral declined steadily from a high of 70 percent in 1965 to 34 percent in 1970 and 20 percent in 1975. Moreover, in the early 1970s there was a shift from the "double standard" to a single standard of behavior for males and females. Thus promiscuity is about equally disapproved for both males and females.[6]

What often seems to young people to be a conflict between the morals of their generation and that of their parents is in fact a conflict between their roles and their parents' roles. Any parent is likely to be more opposed to premarital sexual relations than he or she was before becoming a parent. Parents also tend to be less liberal in their attitudes toward sex than nonparents of the same age. This is because parents feel responsible for the consequences of their children's behavior, and this creates anxiety. One study illustrated this point by asking parents about their own premarital behavior and also asking them whether they approved of such behavior on the part of their children. Some 30 percent of the mothers had had sex before marriage, but only 3 percent would approve of it for their daughers and only 9 percent for their sons. Of the fathers, 51 percent had had premarital sexual relations but only 10 percent approved of it for their daughters and 18 percent for their sons.[7]

Parental disapproval does not necessarily stop children, however. Kinsey showed that the majority of boys have engaged in some sex play before adolescence and that about one-quarter of the girls have.[8] Most of this was homosexual in nature for both sexes. For white youths, but not black, religious devoutness strongly limits premarital sexual behavior.[9]

Some of the studies done during the past decade by feminists and sex-therapy researchers have uncovered some surprising facts about female sexuality. Shere Hite's study of American women reported that only a minority regularly experience orgasm during heterosexual intercourse, but almost all women are able to produce intense and multiple orgasms for themselves through masturbation. Obviously, the emotional experience of masturbation is very different from that of coitus, but Hite suggests that women might improve the sexual dimension of their own lives by overcoming the shame that so commonly accompanies masturbation.[10] Indeed, sex therapists nowadays often teach women to masturbate to orgasm as one phase in developing more satisfying sexual relationships with partners.

### Homosexual relationships

About 37 percent of adult American males and 13 percent of adult females have had at least one homosexual experience to the point of orgasm. About 4 percent of the males and 2 to 3 percent of the females are exclusively homosexual throughout their lives.[11] Yet homosexuality is still viewed with great disapproval by most people. Thus a 1977 survey of the Canadian population showed that 55 percent considered homosexual sex between people who are in love "absolutely wrong." (The same survey showed that only 15 percent of the sample felt that sex between single adults who are in love was absolutely wrong.)[12]

In the past few years the rise of the gay-liberation movement and its "backlash" have made these opinions political in nature. The gay movement has had some success in gaining acceptance for homosexuals, but it has not been very successful in gaining actual legal rights such as recognition of gay marriages as binding contracts.

Homosexuals are rarely able to maintain stable relationships with partners for long periods. Many homosexuals would like to have monogamous unions but few actually do. This is probably due in part to the lack of acceptance or recognition by "straight" society of unions of this sort.

There is no clear evidence that homosexuals are more likely to have psychological problems than other people. The psychologist Evelyn Hooker gave psychological tests to 30 male homosexuals and 30 otherwise similar heterosexual men. Her coworkers were unable to tell which of these tests had been given to homosexuals.[13] However, there is no doubt that the kind of life that many homosexuals are forced to live in order to keep their homosexuality secret is quite stressful. A study of male homosexuals in New York, San Francisco, the Netherlands, and Denmark concludes that a man's living arrangements have an important impact on his personal adjustment. This study compared homosexuals in four different living arrangements — living with a homosexual mate, living alone, living with parents, and living with a wife. Those who lived with

homosexual mates had the highest levels of self-acceptance and the lowest levels of depression, loneliness, and guilt. In addition, this group was less likely to want psychiatric treatment for homosexuality.[14] It seems that this arrangement protects the couple from the negative attitudes of heterosexuals and from much psychological stress.

## SOCIALIZATION

The main beneficiary of the family is the child. One can argue that the family might not exist if children did not have to be produced and raised. Many adults get along fairly well without permanent partners, but a child without a family is at a serious disadvantage. Children need to be in close, permanent contact with a few adults so that they can be prepared to play their roles in society when they themselves become adults. No fully satisfactory substitute for the family has yet been discovered.

Parents and siblings provide emotional support and act as role models. By performing the routine acts of daily living in the presence of young children, they teach them the roles of the group. Values are taught by example and discussion. This process — socialization — occurs in an unplanned, offhand way. For example, children overhear adult discussions while riding around in the back seat of the family car as their parents do grown-up errands. However pleasant it is for small children to spend time together in nursery schools, collective child rearing cannot take the place of family living. Socialization of children is one of the most important functions of the family.

## PROTECTION

The family performs another necessary service for children — protection. No other species has young that remain dependent on their parents as long as the human child does. Someone has to provide food, clothing, shelter, and other material benefits such as trips to the orthodontist, help in crossing busy streets, and money to buy subway tokens. The family performs these functions until the child is mature enough to perform them himself or herself. However, many studies show that grown-up children often continue to receive money and other kinds of help from their parents even after they have started their own households and are parents themselves.

### AFFECTION

In addition to money, presents, and other material forms of help, the family also provides emotional support for its members.

This is as important as any other function of the family. As a setting for warm, intimate relationships the family is unmatched by any other type of social group. Indeed, a person who does not have close ties with a family suffers a deprivation that can hardly be remedied. One of the great problems facing modern society is that of helping people find substitutes for the intimate family group when they lack such a satisfying relationship.

The importance of the family is not limited to emotional well-being. The family also affects health and life span. You have been told that cigarette smoking is a major cause of death. But you may not know that being divorced or separated is about as harmful to

The family might not exist if children did not have to be produced and raised.

DPI

your health as smoking. Loneliness kills. A recent book has revealed that heartbreak is a physical state as well as a psychological one. It shows, for example, that white adult males are about twice as likely to die of heart disease if they are single than if they are married. Among females, widows (both black and white) were much more likely to die of heart disease than married women. Many other diseases show similar patterns. Single, widowed, and divorced people usually die before they reach the age of 64—which is well below the average life expectancy of North American men and women.

The breakup of a family affects not only the adults' lives but the health of their children. A study of college students showed that they were more likely to die of coronary heart disease in later years if they were only children of if they had lost one or both parents before entering college.[15]

A Soviet study of life spans points to similar conclusions. It shows that people with long lives are generally those with warm family relationships, and that closeness to friends and members of the community also contributes to longevity.

Traditionally, women have found their greatest satisfaction in family relationships because they have been less involved in other matters than men. Studies have shown that women's marital satisfaction varies much more than that of males, usually declining during the first ten years of marriage. Contrary to widespread belief, having children does not contribute to marital happiness. On the contrary, the satisfaction of parents (especially mothers) in their marriage decreases during child rearing and rapidly recovers as the children grow up and leave home.[16] On the other hand, children may sometimes offer other satisfactions to the parents that compensate for unhappy marital relationships. Thus one study found that people who were dissatisfied with their marriage were more likely to say that their children were their only satisfaction.[17]

In later years parents find that good rela-

tionships with their children are a major source of satisfaction. Though most parents do not live with their children during this period, these relationships are usually close. In North America the extended family does not live under the same roof, but family members stay close enough together to make frequent visits possible. Only about 16 percent of all elderly Americans live more than an hour's ride away from their nearest child. A similar pattern is found in other Western societies.[18] Professional and managerial workers are more likely to move so far away from their kin as to weaken family relationships; among the working classes the generations keep in closer contact. One study of a British working-class neighborhood showed that the strongest tie is between the married daughter and her "mum."[19] This pattern is not found among all working classes everywhere, however. A study of workers' families in Hamilton, Ontario found that couples visited more often with the husband's parents than with the wife's.[20]

For a long time sociologists believed that the closeness of the kinship group had become weakened in industrial society. However, there is evidence that most families are *not* isolated from their relatives. In the United States, close ties between relatives are far more common than was thought only a few years ago,[21] and in the Canadian family these bonds are probably even closer.[22] A study of French Canadians in Montreal showed that a typical worker is able to recognize over 200 living relatives and that he meets an average of more than 40 relatives each month.[23]

# Variations in family structure

## ILLEGITIMATE CHILDREN

The anthropologist Bronislaw Malinowski discovered a universal norm that he called the *principle of legitimacy*: Every child born should be assigned to some male (whether or not he is the biological father), who will serve as the child's guardian, protector, and link to society. Malinowski claimed that in every known society a child who lacked such a "father" would be deprived of some respect. Research done since Malinowski's day has supported this generalization. All societies distinguish between legitimate and illegitimate children, and all societies in some way recognize illegitimacy, or the birth of a child to an unmarried woman.

In almost every society a child who is conceived before marriage but born after marriage is considered legitimate. In fact in many societies pregnancy is a prerequisite for marriage. Kingsley Davis has called attention to the fact that illegitimacy is a result of the very rule that legitimates families. Because all societies require parents to be responsible for their legitimate offspring, they need rules for defining which children are entitled to such protection and which ones are not. Whatever the ritual by which a father takes on the responsibilities of parenthood, it follows that children who are not covered by the ritual are not entitled to its benefits. If the claims of legitimate children are to be protected, the claims of illegitimate children cannot have the same weight. The illegitimate child cannot claim descent in the same way as the legitimate child, does not have the same inheritance rights, and generally receives little support from the father. The child has to be provided for in some way, but at the same time, providing for that child challenges the rights that society wants to reserve for legitimate children.

Notice that this functionalist explanation of illegitimacy does not suggest that illegitimacy is functionally necessary. It claims only that the rules defining *legitimacy* are necessary and that these rules logically imply the existence of illegitimacy. However, this theory is similar to other functionalist theories in that it holds that the present rules are necessary and should not be changed.

Although illegitimate children have low

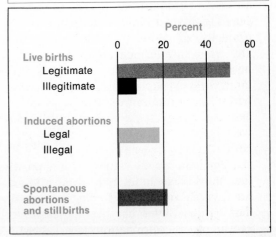

**FIGURE 12.2**
*The outcome of pregnancy in the United States, 1975*

*Source:* Data courtesy of the Population Reference Bureau, Inc., Washington, D.C., 1977.

esteem in all societies, illegitimacy continues to occur. The rates of illegitimacy vary greatly, however. This variation is usually thought to be due to varying degrees of social control. For example, the highest illegitimacy rates are found in the Caribbean.[24] To find out why, Judith Blake did a study of illegitimacy in Jamaica, where some 65 percent of all births are illegitimate.[25] She discovered that there are social sanctions against illegitimacy but that other values are sometimes more important than legitimacy. For this reason the sanctions against illegitimacy are rather weak. Mothers commonly put off the marriages of their daughters so as to lengthen the time during which the daughters can help their own families. This means that a young woman often enters a sexual relationship secretly, becomes pregnant, and has an illegitimate child. One result is that the woman's bargaining power in the marriage market is reduced and she has even less chance of marrying. Nevertheless in Jamaica most people eventually do marry.

North American illegitimacy rates are not exceptionally high compared to those of certain other societies. However, illegitimacy is increasing in the United States, while in most other societies it is either steady or declining. Among the American poor about 16 percent of all births are illegitimate, compared to about 2 percent among people who are better off. Why? Partly because the poor are often uninformed about contraception and unable to afford abortions. Also, a pregnant woman may choose not to marry her lover if he is unemployed.[26]

## DIVORCE

Although no society values divorce positively, almost all societies make some allowance for divorce, or at least for legal separation. The United States has the highest divorce rate among Western nations (see Table 12.1), but this is nowhere near the highest divorce rate in history. Many primitive societies have much higher divorce rates than any Western nation. Some 60 percent of all primitive societies seem to have higher divorce rates than the present U.S. rate.[27] For a long time the Japanese rate was very high. The Moslem divorce rate was also high, for in Arab countries divorce was traditionally a simple matter: A man could divorce his wife by saying three times, "I divorce thee."

At present about one-third of American marriages end in divorce, and this figure seems to be increasing. This does not mean, however, that people are rejecting the institution of marriage—they are simply fed up with the partner they chose the first time and want to start over again. Over half of all divorced women remarry within five years. Indeed, divorced people are more likely to remarry than widows.

Who gets divorced? The best predictor of divorce is age at first marriage. Teenage marriages are much more likely to end in divorce than marriages between older people.[28] Another factor is income. Financial difficulties—especially unexpected ones—increase the chance of a breakup.[29] But it's not just a

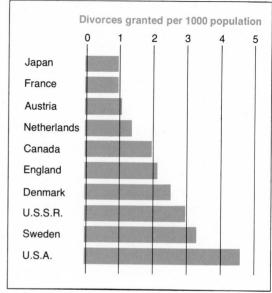

**FIGURE 12.3**

*Crude divorce rate for selected countries, 1974*

Divorces granted per 1000 population

*Source:* Data from U. N. Demographic Yearbook, 1975., Table 19.

matter of money: Couples in which the wife's earnings account for a large part of the family income are somewhat more likely to divorce than couples in which the husband is the sole breadwinner.[30] Differences in social class, religion, or educational achievement also seem to make for tension and therefore are likely to lead to divorce. Also, people who have been divorced before are more likely to divorce than people who are married for the first time.

Who remarries? We don't know much about this question, but we do know that people who are young when they are divorced or widowed are more likely to remarry than older people. Men who have a good income are also more likely to remarry. The same is not necessarily true of women, however. Well-to-do women seem to think twice before remarrying.[31]

The divorce rate is increasing in Canada

as well as in the United States—from 36 per 100,000 population in 1961 to 200 per 100,000 in 1974. Until 1968 divorces were very hard to obtain in Canada because the only reason that was accepted was adultery. Since then the laws have been liberalized, and this partly accounts for the increasing divorce rate.

William J. Goode studied the divorces of some 125 women from the Detroit area. Most of these women reported that divorce was a painful experience for them. The most traumatic period was when they separated from their husbands for the last time. The actual granting of the divorce decree was not a major crisis. Most of these women continued to see their old friends and felt fairly satisfied with their financial situation after the divorce.[32]

What about the children? A study of 300 university students from divorced families found that more than one-third were too young at the time of the divorce to remember any trauma involved. Only 22 percent of the students recalled any conflict between the parents. Over half of the children who came from openly unhappy homes thought that divorce was the best thing for everyone concerned.[33] Usually the children of divorced couples stay closer to their mothers than to their fathers, mostly because mothers usually win custody. The vast majority of Goode's sample of Detroit divorcees believed that their children were better off after the divorce. Of all the mothers who had remarried, only 6 percent thought that the children were worse off in the second marriage than in the first one.

To some extent, family breakup is linked to delinquency. However, it is not clear what causes those two factors to be connected. Both divorce and delinquency tend to occur in low-income families more than in higher-income families, so maybe it is really poverty that is responsible for the delinquency and not the divorce as such. Several studies have shown that divorce is no more harmful for children than unhappy families that stay together.[34]

## The universality of the family

The family may be the only institution that is found in all human societies. If it actually *is* universal, this would suggest that no society could survive without families. It seems clear that any society that lacked families would have trouble meeting certain important human needs. Who would look after the children and socialize them? These are the most obvious functions of the family, but there are other important functions besides caring for children—such as emotional support and regulation of sexual relations.

Is the family universal? G. P. Murdock studied 250 societies and found that each had small social units consisting of a husband, wife, and children, that is, a nuclear family. He defines the family as a social group with the following characteristics: (1) Sexual access is permitted; (2) reproduction occurs legitimately; (3) the group is responsible to society for the care and upbringing of children; and (4) the group is an economic unit—at least in terms of consumption.[35]

### SOCIETIES WITHOUT FAMILIES?

A few social scientists challenge Murdock's claim that the family is universal. They admit that reproduction, socialization, and consumption are always managed by a kinship unit of some sort. But they argue that this unit is not necessarily a nuclear family. In some cases the nuclear family's roles do not fit together to form a unit, separate from other units, that performs the four functions named by Murdock. For example, the Nayars of southern India and the present-day Israeli *kibbutzim* lack families of the sort described

*The Israeli kibbutz is like one large extended family.*

---

by Murdock, and the Russians practically abolished the family after the Revolution.

### The Nayars

Nayar households were once composed of a brother and a sister and the sister's children. Women did not ordinarily have husbands. Instead, they had a number of regular lovers. When a girl reached puberty her relatives chose a "husband" for her, whom she married in only a formal sense, and from whom she was divorced within a few days. After her divorce a woman was permitted to take lovers. The lovers might give her presents but were not expected to provide for her. If a child was born, one of the lovers paid a fee to legitimate the child. This lover was recognized as the *legal* father even though he may not have been the child's *biological* father. He lived not with his child but with his sister and her children. If he did not have a sister he might live with some other woman of the same lineage, have authority over her household, and be called her "brother." Thus the Nayar nuclear family did not live together, and the actual social unit was not the nuclear family but the brother–sister household.[36]

### Kibbutzim

On the Israeli *kibbutz* the basic economic unit is the entire community rather than the family. People do not own private property—even personal supplies are owned by the *kibbutz*. When a man and a woman marry they are assigned a room to share, and when a child is born it lives in the children's house under the care of a nurse. The children visit their parents for a few hours each day, but they spend most of their time with their nurse and the other children in their group. The entire community is a primary group, and it socializes the children. Marriage rarely occurs between people who grew up together in the same children's house, since they feel like brothers and sisters.[37]

There is some debate as to whether the *kibbutz* is an exception to the generalization that every society has nuclear families. The *kibbutz* is not a society but a segment of Israeli society. It is not clear that an entire society based on the *kibbutz* pattern could survive.

### The USSR after the revolution

Perhaps the largest experiment in changing family responsibilities ever done was carried out in the Soviet Union. After the revolution the Bolsheviks decided that the family was a counterrevolutionary institution. They made major changes in family law that had important effects on sexual, marital, and parental relationships. Marriage and divorce became simple matters of registration. The distinction between legitimate and illegitimate children was blurred in two ways. First, parents were no longer responsible for the behavior of their children; nor were they always expected to support their children, whether they were legitimate or not. Second, mature children, legitimate or illegitimate, were not responsible for their aging parents' financial welfare. It was official policy for children to be placed in child care centers so that their mothers could work. Ideally, children would be brought up in boarding schools away from the influence of their families. The Soviet Union remains officially committed to this program, but the boarding schools proved to be too expensive and there is still a shortage of child care centers.

Thus the Soviet ideal of collective child

socialization has never been achieved. A 1926 Soviet law held that any man and woman who lived together (whether or not they registered the fact) were legitimately married in terms of property rights and the rights of the spouse and children. A religious marriage had no legal effect in itself, but if it was followed by sexual relations it became a legal marriage. It was expected that as socialism progressed the family would disappear completely: "The family, creating a series of rights and duties between the spouses, the

*Despite wide-scale experimentation with state-controlled child rearing, family influence remains strong in the USSR.*

Constantine Manos/Magnum

parents and children, will certainly disappear in the course of time and will be replaced by governmental organization of public education and social security."[38]

The goals of these laws were liberal, but their effects were questionable. For example, bigamy became legal, and parents were unable to control their children. By 1935 Soviet law had shifted back toward the family, mostly because the society could not cope with the strain of raising children outside of family settings. Parents became responsible for the behavior of their children and could be fined by the authorities if their children misbehaved. By 1936 *Pravda* was saying that free love was "bourgeois" and contrary to socialist principles. Since 1944 only a registered marriage has been legal in the USSR, and divorces are more difficult to get than in many capitalist countries. Moreover, children born outside of the father's registered marriage cannot claim his property or his name. This policy has created a status of illegitimacy similar to that found in other societies. In the late 1960s Soviet family law was again becoming more liberal, though not as liberal as in 1926. Yet today family life is stronger in the USSR than in the United States. The main function—socializing children—is performed by the family whenever possible.

**CAN SOCIETIES SURVIVE
WITHOUT FAMILIES?**

Of the three cases discussed here, the Nayar society is the most convincing case of a workable and stable alternative to the nuclear family. It was successful in assigning the upbringing of children to adults in a household that included a responsible male, even though the sexual needs of adults were not fulfilled by members of their own household. This arrangement, however, is not among those suggested by people who object to the traditional roles of the Western conjugal family. Sociologists cannot agree

as to whether the nuclear family is a necessary part of every society; perhaps some new social experiment will fulfill the functions of the family more successfully. But for the present it is probably correct to consider the family universal. The kibbutzim do not constitute a whole society, nor did the Nayars. Each of these groups was only part of a larger society. One can find groups *within* almost every society that do not conform to Murdock's generalizations (communities of monks, for example), but these are not whole societies. It has yet to be shown that a society that lacks nuclear families can be a whole, independent, self-supporting system.

## Perspectives on social change and the family

If you are like most people, you have strong opinions about what families should be like. Here we will discuss the views of several important writers, past and present, on this question. For the sake of simplicity, we may call these views conservatism, radicalism, and liberalism.

**THE CONSERVATIVE VIEW**

Conservatism is a minority viewpoint among sociologists today. A true, old-fashioned conservative is hard to find. He or she would oppose individualism and rationalism as means of improving the human condition and would depend on tradition instead. The conservative views rapid social change as dangerous because it threatens tradition. Anything modern is dangerous.

Two conservative thinkers who wrote about the family were LePlay and Frazier.

### LePlay

Pierre Guillaume Frederick LePlay (1806–1882) wrote *The European Working Class* (1855) in an attempt to explain why family patterns varied from one society to another. He divided family life into three categories and discussed the situations in which these types were likely to occur. The first type was the *patriarchal* family—one in which the male head has complete authority. LePlay thought this system was suitable only for groups that didn't have enough social authority or an adequate political system outside the family—nomads, for instance.

LePlay's second type of family was the *unstable* family. This pattern is found in societies that are undergoing serious disorganization. According to LePlay, the late Roman empire, France after the revolution, and Athens after the war against Sparta were characterized by unstable families. The unstable family is individualistic. It is more like a private contract than an institutional duty. Property is not much passed down through the unstable family.

In the *stem* family, LePlay's third category, children leave home when they grow up and form "branch" families of their own. Those who remain at home inherit all of the family property, but they must be prepared to help the others when necessary. LePlay liked this system because it encourages the young to become independent but at the same time offers them some security. However, it works well only where land is plentiful. Where land is scarce, the branch families have trouble and the men have to become wage laborers instead of farmers. Private property and religion are necessary for the smooth maintenance of the stem family. This is why it is a conservative institution.

### Frazier

A well-known book by E. Franklin Frazier on the black American family also idealizes the past.[39] It was published in 1939, but its conclusions are similar to those of more recent writers, who have described the contemporary urban black family as unstable. Frazier saw the mother's role as central, partly for historical reasons and partly because

of the current situation. Historically, the black family had been held together by the authority of the slave master, if at all. After Emancipation the black male was often unable to provide as much for his family as his wife could, and this, together with the lack of a strong family tradition, led to a good deal of instability. Yet Frazier shows that many blacks did develop a strong family held together by the authority of the father. If blacks had not moved to the cities in such large numbers, they might have been able to maintain this pattern. Frazier believed that the pressures of urbanization were the most important cause of family breakdown. Moving to cities disorganizes families. Frazier called for a return to older patterns of family life.

## THE RADICAL VIEW

The radical does not look back to an ideal past when families were supposedly stable but looks to a future in which the family will no longer exist. This position was held both by Marx and his close associate, Friedrich Engels, who wrote more on the family than Marx did.[40]

### Marx and Engels

Radicals assume that the monogamous family has been held together by the institution of private property and that it is now a tool of capitalism. The family exploits humanity, especially women. Women have always been subordinate because of their dependence on the higher economic productivity of men. And women and children alike were forced to participate in an inhumane productive system when factories were first created.[41]

Engels believed communism would free people from exploitation, and he imagined the changes that would follow. He decided that when the two sexes were economically equal men would become even more monogamous than they are now. But then marriages could be ended without making people "wade through the useless mire of divorce proceedings."[42] Child labor would, of course, be abolished. Engels also expected more sexual freedom. He looked forward to a time when men would not "purchase a woman's surrender" with money or social power and when women would not have to give in to any man.

### THE LIBERAL VIEW: FUNCTIONALISM

We have already discussed functionalism. I mentioned that it leads one to think of a group as a whole system. Sociologists who specialize in the family have been especially interested in functionalism. Here we will look at two issues that concern functionalists: the relationship between modernity and the nuclear family and the functional explanation of sex role differences.

#### Industrialization and the nuclear family

What is a modern society? Among other things, it is a society with an *industrial* economy and a *neolocal* residence pattern. Is there a functional reason for these two characteristics to be connected? Is industrialization encouraged when nuclear families live separately from their kin? Does industrialization lead to neolocal residence? Functionalist writers such as Talcott Parsons, Neil Smelser, and William J. Goode have argued that there is a causal link between industrialization and the neolocal residence of nuclear families.

According to Parsons, social change always involves *differentiation*.[43] One example of differentiation is the separation of the family from the economic enterprise. Max Weber held that this separation was an essential condition for the rise of capitalism. Why? Because the success or failure of a business had to be distinguishable from the success or failure of a private household

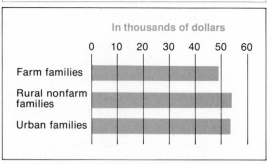

**FIGURE 12.4**

*Direct cost of raising a child to the age of 18 in the U.S. at 1977 prices. The birth rate is affected by the cost of child rearing, which increases with a shift from an agricultural way of life to an urban industrial way of life.*

*Source:* Population Bulletin "The Value and Cost of Children", Population Reference Bureau, Inc., Vol 32. No. 1, April 1977, p. 24.

budget. The keeping of separate checkbooks for office and home is one result of differentiation.

Smelser has examined how the family became differentiated from the economy. This took place during the Industrial Revolution, and Smelser paid special attention to the textile industry in England.[44] At first families wove textiles for their own use and sometimes for sale. But as the market for textiles increased, the question of efficiency came up. The businesses that succeeded assigned particular jobs to the most skillful workers, no matter what family they belonged to. Eventually the factory came to be separate from the family. As a result two separate institutions now carry out tasks that used to be performed by the family alone.

Parsons shows that as modernization continues, more and more functions that used to be performed by the family are taken over by new, specialized institutions. This, again, is differentiation. For example, the family used to educate children, but now the school performs this function.

Functionalists think the detached nuclear family is better for an industrial society because it opens up the labor market. Each family can move around and change jobs easily. The extended family made it harder for industrial workers to move around. William J. Goode explains the fast industrialization of Japan (as compared to China) as due to the fact that the kinship system was looser in Japan. Japanese youth were free to decide whether or not to move for the sake of a better career; Chinese youth were not.[45]

It's reasonable to believe that the detached nuclear family is especially compatible with industrialization. But several recent studies cast some doubt on this notion. For one thing, the modern nuclear family is not as isolated as Parsons and others believed. It is true that the extended kin don't live under the same roof, but they usually live nearby. To be fair to the functionalists, we might say that the Western family is more independent of its extended kin than lots of other societies; that is, it is *comparatively* isolated.

But there is an even more important point against the functionalist position.[46] Recent research has shown that the detached nuclear family is not *always* associated with industrialization and that it did not become the household pattern in Europe as a *result* of the Industrial Revolution. Most Europeans lived in detached nuclear families long before industrialization began. Nor does industry require the isolation of the family. In Yugoslavia, for example, an extended-family system has not prevented industrialization. Indeed, no country that has industrialized has developed a conjugal family pattern as a result of industrialization. We must conclude that industrialization and the nuclear family are sometimes found together but that the connection between them is not *necessary*.

### Sex role differentiation

We have called the functionalist model "liberal" because it demands neither a return to traditional family patterns nor an end to the family as an institution. In fact functionalists are not as interested in supporting any particular policy as they are explaining whatever patterns actually exist. Unfortunately, it is not always clear whether they are explaining the status quo or justifying it. For this reason they are sometimes viewed as reactionary — especially when they provide functional explanations of social phenomena that the critics want to change. Sex role differences within the family are an example of such an issue.

The leading functionalist theory regarding sex roles is that of Parsons and Robert Freed Bales.[47] They hold that kinship is becoming less important in modern society because we emphasize achieved status more than ascribed status. The more we emphasize the importance of, say, occupational achievement, the less we can emphasize the importance of extended-family relationships. And the status of the family is determined more and more by the achievements of the husband — father. Therefore the parents in the nuclear family specialize in different activities. This division of labor within the family leads to major differences between the roles of men and women. Dad is the instrumental leader of the family. Thus his job provides the income and determines the life style and prestige of the family. Mom is the expressive leader of the family. Thus she specializes in such matters as the children's emotional growth, their table manners, the color of the new sofa, the planning of outings, church attendance, and sending birthday cards. Expressive activities are done for their own sake, while instrumental activities are done for some practical reason.

Although the family no longer performs many of its former functions, it is still vital in certain areas — especially the socialization of children. Parsons thinks the detached nuclear family is especially good at socializing children — far better than any other type of family. This is because the small, isolated nuclear family is emotionally involved with the child. And because the family moves around so much it cannot have intense relations with other people. Hence, the spouses depend on each other for almost all their emotional support and for help with the children. This is why they specialize. Their roles become interdependent rather than similar. Maleness and femaleness become polarized. Romantic love and feminine attractiveness are emphasized. Also, the woman becomes almost professional in her mothering — learning everything she can from books and magazines so that she can become an expert on raising children. Males become more instrumental. That is, they specialize in managing the relationship of their families with the outside world. This

differentiation of roles makes the modern family well suited to the carrying out of its few remaining functions. What Parsons describes as a "modern" family is, in fact, very traditional.

I squirm a bit inside when I read Parsons' description of the modern family. It comes too close to romanticizing male dominance. But when Parsons and Bales published their book in 1955 no one squirmed. That was simply the way things were with families. Their description was accurate, since after World War II many women who had been working returned to their traditional roles as homemakers. Parsons and Bales viewed sex role differences as highly functional and very successful in meeting the

The couple entering this marriage may not hold to traditional views of the family. How can two people decide what claims and responsibilities are right for each of them?

Joel Gordon/DPI

needs of the family members—especially the children. Within ten years from the time their book was published, however, many women made it clear that they did not find their traditional roles satisfying at all. If Parsons and Bales were writing their book today, it would probably be quite different.

# SOCIAL RESEARCH:
## Sociologists at Work

In this section we will discuss two different topics. The first is the situation of old people in the stage of the life cycle in which "the nest is empty." The second is a review of the evidence on present-day trends and what they suggest about the future of the family in Western societies.

### OLD AGE AND THE FAMILY

Both the increasing life span of American parents and their tendency to bear children earlier mean that more and more married couples can expect to spend a good many years together after their youngest child has left home. What do we know about this phase of the life cycle?[48]

First, we have already mentioned the fact that such people are usually not as isolated as one might suppose. In the United States only about 3 percent of noninstitutionalized people over the age of 65 have no living relatives, and most have kin living nearby. However, all studies show that the majority of old people prefer to live in their own homes and not with their children, and in most cases they are able to do so. Only 8 percent of American households contain three generations, although one-third of old people do live with their adult offspring in two-generation households.

For the first decade or more after the youngest child leaves home, most couples continue to be helpful in supporting their children, who usually live nearby. In general, the parents are middle-aged, not old, and often the woman has a career when her first grandchildren are born. The parents thus can provide a constant flow of money, as well as services such as babysitting.

The marriages of middle-aged couples become more satisfying as the children leave, and this "upswing" seems to continue through the later years.[49] However, the nature of their relationship changes with time. Couples tend to value companionship more and romantic affection less, so that by the time they are over 65 their conversations are limited to conventional topics such as health, home repairs, and religion, and they rarely go away for an adventure together. After retirement their concerns as a couple become more expressive and less instrumental—the husband has given up his instrumental role. Sexual relations decline over the years, though this seems to result from boredom, not physical inability. The sex drive of normal women does not decline, and the decline among men seems to be a self-fulfilling prophecy. Upper-class couples keep up an interest in sex longer than working-class couples.[50]

Unfortunately, most women can expect to be widows. About 50 percent of all American women between the ages of 70 and 74 are widows; of those between 60 and 64, more than 25 percent are widows, but only 6 percent of the men are widowers. The first year or so after the loss of a spouse is a period of great loneliness; the death rate of surviving spouses increases, and so does the likelihood of suicide. In some ways, however, older widows are better off than younger ones. Young widows are left out of social life because their female friends are still occupied with their own husbands; older widows have the company of other old widows. Widows have less chance than widowers of remarriage, but when remarriage does occur among older people it is usually successful. The aging widow usually moves in with the family of a daughter. Of people over 80 years of age in the

United States, 25 percent of the men and 47 percent of the women live with their children. Thus widows are more likely to move in with their children than widowers are.[51]

Relationships with siblings (brothers and sisters) become more important in old age, for old people generally have more living siblings than any other relatives, including children. "Old people who have never married tend to maintain much closer relationships with their brothers and sisters than those who marry and have children. Persons without children tend to resume closer associations with siblings upon the death of a spouse, but interestingly, not as close as single persons."[52] Most relationships with grandchildren are not very close; the grandparents are "glad to see them come and glad to see them go." Small grandchildren are gratifying, but the older ones do not usually want to bother with their grandparents.

So it is that the life of older people is not a richly satisfying life, and it is often a lonely one.

The situation of the elderly ought to give rise to a "liberation movement," but so far it has not. People are forced into retirement at a fixed age, regardless of their wishes or ability, and are stripped of all roles that carry social power. Although few old people want to live with their offspring, about one-third have no choice. Other lifestyles would be possible if public attention were turned to improving the situation of the aging. For example, "retirement villages" are useful communities in which well-to-do aged people live together and generally enjoy life together.[53] Such villages could be provided on a wider scale for old people with average incomes. The problem of continuing involvement in public life for the elderly has not yet been given serious public attention, however.

## THE FUTURE OF THE FAMILY

Is the family a dying institution? Mary Jo Bane hints at her conclusions in the title of her book,

*Most old people don't want to live with their children. They need friendships with people of their own age, as well as with younger people.*

Patricia Hollander Gross/Stock, Boston

*Here to Stay.*[54] The evidence she presents supports the belief that the American family is alive and well—if not as sound as ever.

Bane begins with the relationship between parents and children. Of course the high and still rising divorce rate is upsetting. Family disruption cannot be, on the whole, a positive experience for children. But Bane points out that the percentage of children who lose a parent through death has gone down steadily over the years. Moreover, there has been a dramatic increase in the percentage of widowed and divorced women who continue to live with their children after their marriage ended. In 1940, by contrast, less than half of all women with children but without husbands took charge of their own families. The rest (we must suppose) sent their children either to orphanages or to other relatives. In 1975, even though divorces were more common, only about 3 percent of all children under 14 lived with neither of their parents. This is an encouraging fact, for it suggests that family disruption is not increasing, though the *pattern* of disruption has changed as a result of the fact that more family breakups are caused by divorce and fewer by death.[55]

But do people still want children? We know that the American birth rate has been lower during the past ten years than before. This does not mean that more people dislike children and are choosing to remain childless. On the contrary, fewer families remain childless and more couples choose to have small families. It seems that most people do want children—but they want fewer children than their parents and grandparents wanted.[56] This means that the children who

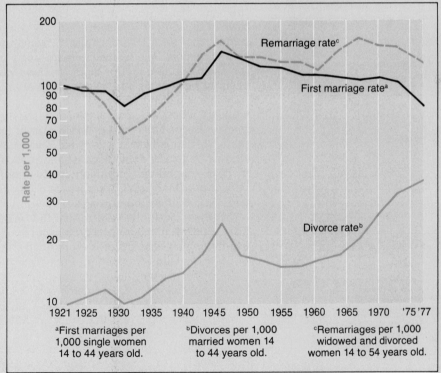

**FIGURE 12.5**

*Changes in the rates of first marriage, divorce, and remarriage for U.S. women, 1921–1977*

[a]First marriages per 1,000 single women 14 to 44 years old.

[b]Divorces per 1,000 married women 14 to 44 years old.

[c]Remarriages per 1,000 widowed and divorced women 14 to 54 years old.

*Source:* Courtesy of the Population Reference Bureau, Inc., Washington, D.C., 1977.

are born get more attention from their parents. And as we saw in the chapter on socialization, children who grow up in small families have many advantages over children who grow up in large families.

What about teenagers? Do they continue to have close relationships with their parents, or do we find more youths leaving home at an early age? In the mid-nineteenth century it was very common for young men, and to a lesser extent young women, to leave their families to live with other families as lodgers or as servants. Today this pattern has almost disappeared. More youths live at home and go to school. Teenagers are much more dependent on their parents for shelter and support than they were in earlier generations.[57]

**FIGURE 12.6**

*Likelihood of divorce for persons born 1945–1949 by educational level*

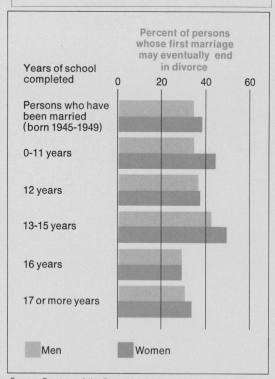

*Source:* Courtesy of the Population Reference Bureau, Inc., Washington, D.C., 1977.

Bane turns next to the relations between husbands and wives. She concludes that "marriage is far from withering away in contemporary America and is, in fact, enjoying unprecedented popularity."[58] Almost everyone gets married at some time or another. The percentage of people who marry is higher now than it was in the nineteenth century. Recently there has been a tendency for people under 30 to stay single. Whether this means that they are postponing marriage or that they reject marriage entirely is not yet clear. However, there is one advantage to this trend: It will probably mean more marital stability in the future. As we have seen, youthful marriages are most likely to end in divorce.

The high divorce rate is not the most extreme change in American marriage patterns in the twentieth century. The changes in family life cycle are more dramatic. Because women are having fewer children, they spend less time in the child rearing phase of their lives and more time doing other things. Increased life expectancy has brought an increase in the number of years a couple spends alone together after retirement. Marriages that don't end in divorce have to last longer—47 years will be the average during the next few decades.[59] Women are spending more time on their careers, and working seems to be good for them. Working wives seem to have somewhat better physical health than homemakers. However, the marriages of working wives are less stable and satisfying than those of homemakers.[60] This is at least partly due to financial problems. The women who work usually do so because they need the money. The burden of a job in addition to housework increases pressure and tension, and this may affect the marriage.

The conclusion remains, then, that marital disruption has not increased greatly but that the disruption that does occur is more often voluntary than involuntary, resulting from divorce instead of death. And this is not necessarily discouraging. Getting divorced can be like getting out of jail: a release from a wretched situation. What is happening now is that more couples are choosing to recognize a bad situation and look for a way out. Divorce is not a pleasant thing. But neither is old age—except in comparison to the alternative!

# SOCIAL POLICY:
## Issues and Viewpoints

There are two very different kinds of relatedness within the family—love and power. These are opposing tendencies. When love is full, the needs of each person are as central to each other family member as his or her own; when power comes into play, each person demands his own rights and pursues his own goals. To be sure, even lovers have their own needs. Often these are needs that can be met only through some sacrifice on the part of the other person, though that person may not see it as a sacrifice when love is present.

Several books about the role of power have appeared in recent years. *Sexual Politics*[61] and *The Politics of the Family*,[62] for example, are books that refer to the ways in which manipulation, exploitation, and power struggles operate in relationships where love is absent. Once an issue becomes defined as a power contest, someone must lose if anyone is to win. It is by unifying the purposes of family members that love prevents an issue from being a contest.

Though love is the greatest healer of social problems, it is a private experience, not a matter for public policy. It is useless to command parents to love their children or a man to love his wife. This aspect of the family is a private, not a public one. Society stands back, giving love a space in which to work without interference. While we make rules to govern all sorts of unimportant public affairs—stand behind the white line on the bus, do not feed the pigeons, do not fold, spindle, or mutilate—within the family there are few recognized guidelines for resolving conflict. If one partner wants to make love and the other does not, who should "win"? If one wants to have a child and the other does not, who should "win"? If a young woman wants her own apartment and her parents want her to live at home, who should "win"? These are not matters for public policy, for the answers to these questions come from the heart.

Yet duty exists also—in the family perhaps more than in any other institution. One has obligations to others that one must honor even if it stops being a pleasure to do so. One's love may disappear, but the children don't. Each person is dependent on the other members of his or her family to different degrees in different stages of the life cycle—sometimes completely, sometimes hardly at all. The claims of the dependent one are real, and when love is inadequate to support those claims social or even legal sanctions may be required. Most laws come into play only when standards are broken.

Technology has brought about two important changes in Western society that have affected all of us and led to demands for changes in the norms of family life. First, advances in medicine, agriculture, and sanitation have increased life expectancy by many years. Where more children survive than before, populations grow more quickly, and it is no longer necessary to give birth to large numbers of children in order to produce the next generation. Second, the development of contraceptives makes it possible to enjoy sex without reproduction. Contraceptives free people from responsibility for children but not from a responsible relationship with their sexual partners. Both of these changes raise ethical questions.

Other ethical situations are also changing. The extent of a woman's dependence on her husband changes when child rearing takes up less of her time. What are her legitimate claims in this new situation? Moreover, when one no longer has to produce large families to maintain the population, the attitudes toward homosexuality must be reconsidered.

I have called these questions "ethical" problems rather than "public policy" problems, but they have a "public" aspect. Many social movements are demanding changes in the norms that bear on these matters: the Sexual Freedom League, the women's movement, the gay liberation movement, and so forth. What their members are actually seeking is not freedom but a different set of obligations and claims in relation to other people. No one in society is ever "free" to act toward others as he or she pleases; we are all bound by norms that fit together as a system.

## CHALLENGES TO TRADITIONAL SEX ROLES

The traditional role obligations and claims of the sexes in the Western nuclear family centered on the function of bringing up children. Any movement that seeks to change these norms should first recognize why they have been maintained until now.

Male and female parents have traditionally played very different roles, and until recently, the obligations and rights of each were backed by social sanctions. The female was expected to look after the young, and society protected her claim for support in this task. The male was expected to support and defend his wife and children, and society protected his claim to a job that would permit him to meet these obligations. However, sanctions are used to enforce these norms only when the family cannot solve its problems on its own. Thus if a husband and wife agree that the husband will stay home while the wife supports the family, no one tries to stop them. However, if they cannot agree and both claim the right to stay home with the children, social sanctions will be imposed on the husband. He will have to show why he should not be required to support his family.

But suppose both the husband and the wife want to work and find themselves competing in the same limited job market. The husband would be hired. The wife would have to show why she should be given an equal chance.

Thus two different norms must be seen as part of the same system: (1) Men are expected to support their families if they can do so, and (2) they have first claim to a job that allows them to do so.

If a society changes one of these norms, the other will be affected as well. The women's movement has demanded that women and men be given equal employment opportunities. This new norm must be matched by a change in the first rule: Men and woman should have an equal obligation to support their families if they can do so.

If neither parent wants to work, one or the other must take a job whether he or she likes the idea or not. But if the opportunities and obligations of men and women are equal there is no way of deciding who must go to work. Society

needs a rule. It may be an arbitrary rule (such as whether to drive on the right or the left), but any rule that assigns responsibilities in a workable pattern will do. Perhaps there are reasons for thinking men that men are better suited for work outside the home; perhaps not. In earlier days the fact that the female could provide milk was a good reason for her to stay near the baby, but the use of baby bottles means that this may no longer be a major issue. Still, *some* rule is better than none. If society changes the norm so that the wife must work if the husband chooses not to, then society must change the other norm and give women priority in employment opportunities so that they can support their families.

Furthermore, if a woman is to meet her obligations she must have a good deal of authority over the family. For example, if she finds it necessary to move across the country to find a job her dependents must be willing to go with her. If she is to pay the bills, she must be able to determine the family budget. If she is to perform well on the job, her dependents must protect her mood, her rest, and her health by obeying her with good grace. These are the rights customarily enjoyed by men and now resented by many women.

In a word, the head of the household is the adult who is responsible for the economic welfare of the family. He or she must be given enough authority and privileges to carry out this obligation. If both parents find these tasks enjoyable, then the work, as well as the rights, can be shared equally. If both parents find them unpleasant, then one of them must do them anyway, and present norms define this as the obligation of the husband.

In childless families, on the other hand, there is no logical reason for either spouse to claim the right to be supported by the other. As the birth rate decreases, there are fewer children to be cared for by the average woman, and so the fairness of the traditional system may be called into question. Changes may be demanded either by men (who may feel that women are no longer making a full contribution to society) or by women (who may feel that they are denied the chance to find fulfilling alternatives to child-rearing). However, it should be recognized that (1) many women are still in an economically dependent situation while they care for children, and (2) they may be making a vital contribution to society in this role and have good reasons for preferring it to a career in the business world. Moreover, many mothers are working because they have to work. Any movement for true "liberation" will demand the right to choose among many alternatives, including both the opportunity to work and the opportunity to remain at home, depending on the situation.

## ALTERNATIVES TO THE PRESENT FAMILY

The family as an institution has survived for many thousands of years. However, during this century technological changes have affected group life beyond anything earlier generations could have imagined. The population explosion has brought our species to the limits of the earth's resources, and therefore humans *must* reduce their fertility. While previous generations were taught that they had a duty to produce many children, our children may pass laws requiring couples who want to have a baby to get a license showing that they are healthy, emotionally mature, and able to support a child.

There is plenty of evidence that not everyone is happy with present family norms. What was suitable and necessary in an agrarian economy with a high death rate may be unsuitable in the modern world. Thus the family is changing and probably will continue to change, though it seems that some form of family group will remain important for the foreseeable future.

Marriage involves two kinds of commitment: (1) that of the partners to each other, through loyalty, concern, shared responsibilities, and sexual relations, and (2) that of the partners to their children in a lifelong relationship. Besides these two basic commitments, marriage also leads to a set of relationships between each person and a wider network of people, including the mate's relatives, friends, and coworkers. A single, divorced, or widowed person misses out on relationships of this sort. For some this may mean freedom from unpleasant obligations, but for many others it results in a sad state of isolation. Therefore one of society's most pressing needs is to find ways of making up for these lacks.

The basic need for a partner is not always easily filled. Large numbers of people are de-

prived of committed, socially approved, stable relationships. Homosexual marriages, for example, are still not approved by society. Moreover, because women mature earlier than men and outlive men by several years, there are millions of women who must get along without mates. One change that would help solve this problem would be to encourage marriages in which the bride is somewhat older than the groom. Some writers have proposed a form of polygyny as a possible solution, but this has little chance of being accepted.

The anthropologist Margaret Mead has suggested that family formation be divided into two steps—marriage and parenthood. She proposes that couples by allowed to enter into partnership quite freely and to break up just as freely. However, only after a couple have been together for several years and known each other well should they be allowed to have children. It should be understood that their partnership *as parents* should be permanent whether their marriage is permanent or not. A couple's most serious commitment is to their children, not toward each other as marital partners. Adults may be better off without each other, but children are not better off without a parent. Hence, parenthood should be permitted only for couples who can guarantee lifelong commitment to their children as well as the children's network of grandparents, friends, aunts and uncles, half-siblings, and so on.

Not only do many people lack spouses, but millions of people lack family ties of any kind. Many have been deprived of such ties by divorce or by the death of a parent or spouse. Others live far away from their extended kin or are on bad terms with them. People living without the help and emotional support of the family need something to replace it, but there is no socially accepted institution that really substitutes for the family. Communes, for instance, are rarely successful. One worthwhile suggestion is for three or four families to meet regularly, share their work and their feelings, and not hesitate to influence one another's values and attitudes.[63]

Such experiments have not been widespread, and indeed the general opposition to them proves that most people are strongly committed to traditional family norms. Perhaps this in itself is the best sign that the family is in no real danger of disappearing.

# SUMMARY

**1.** The *nuclear* (or *conjugal*) *family* consists of a husband, his wife, and their unmarried children. The *extended family* is composed of the nuclear family plus the couple's siblings, parents, and other close relatives. *Composite families* are sets of nuclear families living in the same household. The *polygamous family* is a type of composite family. There are two basic types of polygamy: *polygyny* (several wives of the same husband) and *polyandry* (several husbands of the same wife).

**2.** *Endogamy* is a rule that one must marry someone within one's own group. *Exogamy* is a rule that one must choose a mate from a different group. The taboo against incest is an exogamous rule.

**3.** Western society reckons descent using a *bilateral system*, including the relatives of both mother and father. Most societies use *unilinear* systems of descent. These may be either *matrilineal* (descent through the mother's family) or *patrilineal* (descent through the father's family).

**4.** Western society is characterized by *neolocal residence.* That is, newlywed couples set up their own households. Other societies expect newlyweds to live either with the husband's parents (*patrilocal residence*) or with the wife's parents (*matrilocal residence*).

**5.** The main functions of the family are (1) providing for regular, stable sexual relations and reproduction; (2) socializing children; (3) protecting children; and (4) providing for affectionate interpersonal relationships. Despite the influence of the industrial way of life, most families are not isolated from their relatives.

**6.** Every society expects that every child born should be assigned to some male, whether he is the biological father or not. This male is to be the child's guardian, protector, and link to society. Children who have not been recognized by such protectors are considered illegitimate. *Illegitimacy* is a necessary result of rules that define legitimacy.

**7.** Almost all societies provide for divorce or legal separation. Childlessness is lined with divorce, not as a cause but because divorce tends to occur early in a marriage. Studies of the effect of divorce on children suggest that it is better for them than situations in which parents stay together even though they do not get along well.

**8.** Some scholars believe that the nuclear family is found in all societies. Others disagree, pointing to the Nayars of India, the *kibbutzim* of Israel, and the early years of the Soviet Union as cases of societies in which the nuclear family as a group has not performed all of the following functions: (1) permitting sexual relations, (2) legitimating reproduction, (3) caring for children, and (4) acting as an economic unit—at least in terms of consumption.

**9.** We have discussed three views of the family—conservative, radical, and liberal–functionalist. The conservative values the traditional family. This approach was taken by Frederick LePlay and E. Franklin Frazier.

**10.** The radical view is seen in the writings of Friedrich Engels. He believed that when the sexes became equal economically men would become more monogamous but marriages would be ended more easily. No couple would have to stay together for economic reasons.

**11.** Functionalists view the modern family as having been greatly influenced by industrialization. Many scholars see a connection between industrialization and the relative isolation of the nuclear family. However, there is evidence that the family is not as isolated from its kin as the functionalists have sometimes assumed.

**12.** Talcott Parsons suggests that sex role differences and the relative isolation of the nuclear family are beneficial to children and contribute to the emotional well-being of all family members. This view has been challenged by the women's movement.

# KEY TERMS

**bilateral descent**  a system that reckons descent from both the mother's side and the father's side.

**composite family**  a number of nuclear families living together in a single household.

**endogamy**  a rule requiring a person to marry someone within his or her own group.

**exogamy**  a rule requiring a person to choose a mate from a different group.

**extended family** (consanguine family)  a household made up of a nuclear family plus other relatives.

**homogamy**  the tendency to choose a spouse similar to oneself.

**illegitimacy**  the birth of a child to an unmarried woman.

**joint family**  a type of extended family in which brothers share property but do not always live in a single household.

**kin**  people who are related either by birth or by marriage.

**matrilineal descent system**  a descent system in which a person belongs to his or her mother's line of descent.

**matrilocal residence**  a rule requiring a newly married couple to live with the wife's family.

**neolocal residence**  a rule requiring a newly married couple to set up housekeeping on their own.

**nuclear family** (conjugal family)  a husband, his wife, and their unmarried children.

**patrilineal descent system**  a descent system in which a person belongs to his or her father's line of descent.

**patrilocal residence**  a rule requiring a newly married couple to live with the husband's family.

**polyandry**  the marriage of a woman to more than one husband.

**polygamous family**  a family in which there are several wives or husbands.

**polygyny**  the marriage of a man to more than one wife.

**unilinear descent**  a system that reckons descent from either the male blood line or the female blood line.

# FOR FURTHER READING

BUTLER, ROBERT N. *Why Survive? Being Old in America.* New York: Harper & Row, 1975. A Pulitzer prize winning attack on the misery and injustice of being old in a society that values youth. A shocker, done in a methodical way.

FRAZIER, E. FRANKLIN. *The Negro Family in the United States.* Chicago: The University of Chicago Press, 1966. First published 1939. A classic conservative study of family life during and after slavery.

GOODE, WILLIAM J. *World Revolution and Family Patterns.* New York: Free Press, 1963. Goode compares families around the world and concludes that a single family type—the conjugal family, approximately what we would call the detached nuclear family—is emerging.

LAING, R. D., and E. ESTERSON. *Sanity, Madness and the Family.* Middlesex, England: Pelican, 1964. Laing, a controversial writer holds that schizophrenia can be understood only by regarding the patient's whole family as an interacting social system which produces the bizarre responses resulting from abnormal patterns of communication.

LIBBY, ROGER W., and ROBERT N. WHITEHURST. *Marriage & Alternatives: Exploring Intimate Relationships.* Glenview, Ill.: Scott, Foresman & Co., 1977. The authors have collected essays and arguments that support the view that intimate relationships can flourish in nonfamily settings too, and enhance life greatly.

SCHLESINGER, BENJAMIN. *Family Life in Canada.* Toronto: McGraw-Hill Ryerson, 1976. Schlesinger is a social work professor who is interested in the changes—single-parent families, divorce and remarriage, among others—taking place in the contemporary family that set it apart from the traditional pattern.

SHORTER, EDWARD. *The Making of the Modern Family.* New York: Basic Books, 1977. A first-rate history of changes in family life in Western society. Shorter makes one glad we aren't living in the bad old days.

WEISS, ROBERT S. *Marital Separation.* New York: Basic Books, 1975. Weiss's research technique was to hold group discussions for people whose marriages were splitting. He listened to the tapes again and again, then described the most common sequence of adjustments.

13

# RELIGION

Every Sunday I spend a couple of hours with about fifty of my friends. We go through a routine of activities: We sing some songs, read some verses aloud together, and listen as one of us reads a passage from an old book. A few of my friends wear special robes and sing together. Usually there are some candles burning. People shake hands or hug and kiss, and it's not uncommon for someone who feels bad to weep quietly and be comforted by someone who is sitting nearby. Near the end of the session we gather around a table and solemnly eat small pieces of bread and sip port wine, reminding each other that we are eating the body and drinking the blood of a man who died 2000 years ago.

Does this seem weird? Of course not. My friends and I are ordinary, nice people. If we had been asked to write the script for a worship service, it is unlikely that we would have invented a mock-cannibalistic feast. Yet I feel all right about going through such a ceremony. In fact, it's one of the high points of my week. I am in touch with myself then. I feel sure that I belong on this earth—that indeed, I belong right there with those people, singing *Amazing Grace*, passing around a cup of wine, forgiving each other for our shortcomings, and looking forward to the future.

People sometimes do strange things in worship services. If you are an Orthodox Jew, you may wrap phylacteries around your arm and give thanks to God that you are not a woman. This doesn't mean that you hate women. It's just what your group has always said at a certain point in the prayer. If you lived in some other society, you might sacrifice an animal as an act of worship. The varieties of religious practices are endless. We can agree that many of these practices make no sense when looked at from a logical viewpoint. But religion is not logical. It is something else entirely.

Social scientists cannot show the validity of any particular faith, nor do they try to.

Religion is the relationship of humankind to some ultimate reality. Sociology deals with the relationships among human beings and can say nothing about ultimate reality, which, after all, cannot be studied empirically. Yet some of the greatest sociologists—especially Durkheim and Weber—were deeply interested in religion. They showed that faith and human social life are closely linked. Religion is at the root of the loyalty and involvement that draw human beings together. Viewing it in this light, both religious and nonreligious people may find that sociology has much to say on the subject of religion.

## Classification of religions

David Sopher has classified religions into three categories: ethnic, universalizing, and segmental.[1]

Ethnic religions are tied to a specific place and people. Most primitive or tribal religions are of this type, and so are some of the largest worldwide religions. Both Hinduism and Judaism must be considered ethnic religions because they are both closely tied to the land and people in which they originally developed. It is hard to say what the Chinese believe about ultimate reality today, since religion is discouraged by communism, but in the imperial period Chinese religion was clearly ethnic. It was a mixture of ancestor worship, Buddhism, and the worship of nature deities. Thus if we include the Chinese about one-third of the world's people are members of ethnic religions.

Universalizing religions are not tied to any particular region or ethnic group, although they may have been when they began. Members of universalizing religions consider their beliefs to be right for all humankind and feel that they have a duty to convert others to their religion, either personally or through organized missions. Each of the major universalizing religions—

**TABLE 13.1**

*Estimated membership of the principal religions of the world*

| RELIGIONS | ESTIMATED MEMBERSHIP |
|---|---|
| Total Christian | 983,620,900 |
|   Roman Catholic | 566,686,800 |
|   Eastern Orthodox | 72,815,000 |
|   Protestant[1] | 344,119,100 |
| Jewish | 15,032,378 |
| Muslim[2] | 576,160,200 |
| Zoroastrian | 233,550 |
| Shinto[3] | 55,156,000 |
| Taoist | 31,116,100 |
| Confucian | 174,189,200 |
| Buddhist[4] | 260,685,550 |
| Hindu[5] | 517,897,450 |
| | |
| Total world religious membership | 2,614,091,328 |
| Total world population[6] | 4,123,957,000 |

[1]Protestant statistics usually include "full members" (adults) rather than all baptized persons and are not comparable to those of ethnic religions or churches counting all constituents.
[2]The chief base of Islam is still ethnic, although some missionary work is now carried on in Europe and America (viz. "Black Muslims"). In countries where Islam is established, minority religions are frequently persecuted and their statistics are hard to come by.
[3]A Japanese ethnic religion, Shinto has declined markedly since the Japanese emperor gave up claim to divinity (1947).
[4]Buddhism has several modern renewal movements which have gained adherents in Europe and America and other areas not formerly ethnic-Buddhist. In Asia it has also made rapid gains in recent years and shown greater staying power under persecution than Taoism or Confucianism.
[5]Hinduism's strength in India has been enhanced by nationalism. Modern Hinduism has also developed renewal movements that have reached Europe and America for converts.
[6]United Nations, Department of Economic and Social Affairs; data refer to midyear 1977.

*Source:* Data from *Britannica Book of the Year 1978,* William Benton Publisher.

Buddhism, Christianity, and Islam—has at one time or another been the dominant religion in a particular region.

Christianity has been the most successful in gaining converts and has become by far the most widespread religion in the world. However, it has so many variations that it may be misleading to call it a single religion.

Segmental religions are offshoots of universalizing religions or new systems that integrate small groups into larger communities. These religions don't usually want to universalize. Often they develop in Third World countries exposed to European culture. They usually appeal to a particular social class and create a new sense of community among groups whose former religions were ethnic in character. The Native American (Peyote) Church, for example, unites groups of American Indians with different ethnic (tribal) backgrounds. Some new segmental religions claim to be part of a major universalizing system. Examples are the Neo-Buddhists among the lower classes of India, the Black Muslims, and the Happy, Healthy, Holy ("Sikh") organization in America. Although the segmental religions account for only a small portion of the world's population, they are important because they encourage social change. At least they tend to appear where major social changes are going on.

**FIGURE 13.1**

*Distribution of the world's religions*

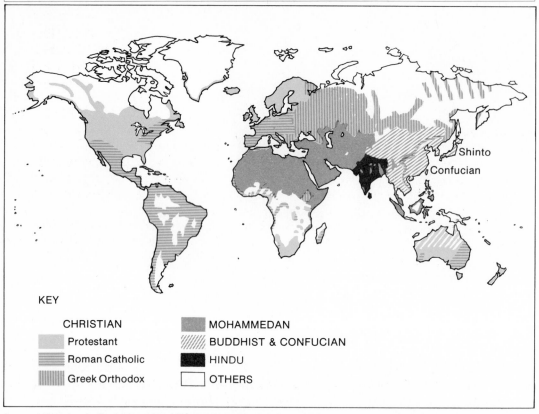

KEY

CHRISTIAN

Protestant

Roman Catholic

Greek Orthodox

MOHAMMEDAN

BUDDHIST & CONFUCIAN

HINDU

OTHERS

*Source:* J. Bartholomew, *The Advanced Atlas of Modern Geography* (New York: McGraw–Hill Book Company, Inc., 1962).

# The institutionalization of religion

Suppose you have your own beliefs about ultimate reality, your own religious practices, that are not shared by anybody else. Suppose you worship privately without telling anyone else about it, and suppose you are extremely devout in this personal way. Could we say that you are religious? Most sociologists would say not. This does not mean that we think such experiences are unimportant—they can be very important—but sociologists are concerned primarily with the practices and beliefs and experiences that people share as a group. Religion is a social institution. Any private, personal experience is religious, by this definition, only if it is linked to the *shared* orientation of a social group toward ultimate reality. Thus, the great sociological studies of religion have dealt with traditions that are passed down from one generation to another.

Much of what we know about the development of religions we owe to Max Weber. He found regular patterns in the way major world religions develop over time. Changes occur in the leadership, in the ritual, in the beliefs, and in the way the members organize. Let us look more closely at these types of changes.

### CHARISMATIC LEADERSHIP

Religions begin through the leadership of charismatic founders (such as Christ, Mohammed, or Buddha) and their followers. *Charisma* means "gift" in Greek, and Weber thought of a charismatic leader as gifted. Such a leader seems to have supernormal, possibly divine, powers.[2] Charisma is a source of social change, for it is opposed to the traditional institutions of society. Every charismatic leader says, in effect, "It is written . . . but I say unto you . . . !" Charisma is spontaneous, creative, and it stimulates new ways of thinking.

### THE ROUTINIZATION OF CHARISMA

But the charismatic phase of a religion is short and temporary. The religion can take hold only by becoming *routinized*—by becoming an institution in society. How does this happen? The crisis occurs when the founder dies. If the followers want to continue their religious experience, they have to decide how to replace the charismatic founder.[3] Generally they build up an authoritative institution to take the place of the founder. Weber called this process "the routinization of charisma." The movement is changed from an unusual, tradition-breaking experience into an organized, socially accepted institution.

This process has three different aspects: (1) The patterns of worship become ritualized; (2) the ideas and beliefs become more

rational; and (3) the religious community becomes organized, with well-defined roles and responsibilities.

### Ritual

Worship consists of ritual, liturgy and other forms of expression that become established patterns. Ritual grows up as a natural way by which human beings express their deepest experiences in a symbolic way.[4] But as time goes on, ritual becomes standardized. It then *elicits* attitudes instead of spontaneously *expressing* them. Thus one may enter church preoccupied and nervous, but by lighting a candle, kneeling, and murmuring a memorized phrase one may call up a feeling of reverence that lasts all day. Weber believed that as a charismatic religion becomes an institutionalized religion the ritual tends to become more complex.

### Belief

The second aspect of the institutionalization of religion is the development of beliefs. Every religion has a number of stories—such as the Biblical ones about Adam and Eve, Noah and his ark, the miracle of the loaves and fishes, and Lot's wife turning into a pillar of salt. They are myths. Myths are nonhistorical stories that are known by almost everyone in a group and symbolize great truths to the group's members. I don't mean that they are necessarily false when I call them nonhistorical. But whether they are historically true or not, people use myths to celebrate a fundamental reality in which both the narrator and the listener participate emotionally. Myth relates human beings to their environment, to their ancestors, to their descendants, and to the hereafter. Even the most primitive religions are rich in myths—stories that explain the world symbolically.

Besides myth, there is also theology, the organization of religious beliefs into a unified doctrine. Theology consists of philo-

*Religious rituals may allow people to release deep emotional feelings in symbolic ways. This New Guinea burial involves the entire community.*

sophical speculation about ultimate reality. Weber suggested that before a religion could develop a rational theology (one that people could discuss reasonably and logically) it had to have a professional priesthood.[5] Not all major religions develop a rational theology: Classical Chinese religion and ancient Buddhism were not rational. Nor did they have a professional priesthood. But both a professional priesthood and a rational theology developed in the early period of Christianity.

Weber pointed out the rational trend in all world religions—their tendency to make the intellectual aspects of their beliefs clear and consistent. There is a general shift from myth to theology—from story telling to reasoning and arguing. This shift is especially noticeable in Western culture.

### Religious organization

Weber held that the crisis of replacing the founder forces a religious movement to either adjust or fail. Usually, after the leader's death, the movement begins to organize and to create a system of roles. This creates problems of authority: The new roles have to be given certain responsibilities and powers. In the Christian Church this had been done by 100 A.D.

During the charismatic period there is an outpouring of new teachings. But after the

372

crisis caused by the founder's death the religion develops ways of determining which teachings will be considered authentic. In Christianity the clergy answered these questions. Thus the routinization of charisma actually amounts to a *limiting* of charisma. The teachings have to be acceptable to the authorities. It is the beginning of the establishment of orthodoxy. In time the religion that began as a dramatic break from tradition becomes orthodox and fits in smoothly with the other institutions of society. That's the way things generally go, Weber thought.

### ADJUSTING TO THE SOCIAL ORDER

As a religious movement adjusts to the loss of its founder, we have seen that it changes *internally*—by developing its rituals, its belief system, and its organization, and by becoming more and more rational and routine. It also changes *externally*—by coming to terms with the outside world. While the founder lived, the new religion was very different from other groups in society. Its members left their old lives, emphasized equality with other members, and considered their former status unimportant.[6]

But after the founder's death the group has to decide how to relate to the rest of society. It has three choices: (1) It can reject the old social order entirely. (2) It can accept the old order entirely. (3) It can accept the old ways in practice but reject them in spirit. If it chooses the third alternative, the group can encourage equality *within* its organization without attacking the status differences in the society around it. The early Christian Church took this position. For example, Saint Paul claimed that there was "neither bond nor free" in the Church yet also advised slaves to obey their masters (Epistle to Titus 2:9). This is the process of adjusting to the social order. Most religious movements have taken the same route, according to

Weber. This is the final phase in a religious movement. At this point it is no longer a new religion but an old, established one. Indeed, another new religious movement may begin at this point and shatter the routine of the old religion.

## The organization and functions of religion

The priesthood, or clergy, have two duties toward the members of their religion: to comfort them and to challenge them.[7] It's hard to do both. Much depends on the kind of religious organization in question. In general, comforting is the easier job. It involves soothing grievances and unifying the congregation. Challenging is more difficult. It involves speaking out on matters of social or moral evil and urging the congregation to live up to a higher moral standard, even if this requires some sacrifices. The priest or minister must be careful not to antagonize members in challenging them. Whether he or she can take an unpopular stand depends on the way the church is organized.

### TYPES OF CHURCH ORGANIZATION

There are three different types of church organization—though any particular church may not fit exactly into any of these types. Although their names are the same as those of three denominations of the Protestant Church, they are general types and should not be confused with those denominations.

A congregational religious organization hires and fires its own leader. Each local church is governed by lay members, and there is no church hierarchy with authority over the individual organizations. Baptists,

Disciples of Christ, and the Quakers are organizations of this type.

An episcopal religious organization is characterized by a well-defined hierarchy of authority. Clergy are assigned to their posts by officials higher in the hierarchy and are accountable to them for their performance. Both the Roman Catholic and the Anglican (or Episcopal) churches are of this type, though there are variations within both groups. In French Canada, for example, lay wardens control church funds.

In a presbyterian religious organization authority is in the hands of an elected regional board of ministers and lay members from a number of different congregations. This board, or *presbytery*, assigns clergy to their posts. However, a good deal of authority remains in the hands of a committee of laymen, or *elders*, in each church. The Presbyterian Church in the United States and the United Church in Canada are examples. This type of organization is a representative democracy.

The relationship of the minister to his or her "flock" differs according to the organizational structure of the church. Ministers in congregational churches change posts more frequently than those in churches of the episcopal type, often in order to avoid conflict with church members.[8] Whether a congregational or episcopal type of church is more likely to stimulate social change depends on whether the proposed change is supported mostly by the membership or by the clergy. For example, the Catholic Church was able to encourage the integration of parochial schools and other religious activities in the South more effectively than congregational Protestant churches because the Catholic hierarchy supported the policy of integration.

The clergy does not always take the lead in stimulating social change. In fact if the hierarchy of a church of the episcopal type is basically conservative, it may actually slow the process of change. For example, the hierarchy of the Roman Catholic Church has long opposed birth control, despite a growing popular movement supporting it. In this case a parish priest is required to speak out against a particular social change because he is accountable to the bishop, not to the parishioners. Some priests refuse to speak out, of course, just as many Catholics ignore church doctrine in this case, and so the hierarchy finds it hard to maintain its authority in this area. Still, the clergy in episcopal organizations generally have greater power over their parishioners than clergy in other systems.

## THE FUNCTIONS OF RELIGION

Does it really make any difference whether a group of people is religious or not? Does a group function any differently because of religion? One would have to answer these questions in different ways for different cases. At some historical times and places religion has had a great impact on group life, while at other times and places it has been only an empty form. Later in this chapter we will compare some of these cases and look for the differences in the effects of religion on group life. But is it possible to generalize about the effects of religion? If so, what are they? Let me suggest that religion—or the lack of it—usually does have an important influence but that any impact it has may be beneficial *(eufunctional)* at one time and harmful *(dysfunctional)* at another. I will list five functions of religion—and as you will see, each of them can have both positive and negative aspects.

1 Religion provides *support, consolation, and reconciliation.* In doing so it strengthens group morale. Human beings need emotional support when they are uncertain and disappointed, and they need reconciliation with their society when they are alienated from its goals. But this can be dysfunctional too: By

reconciling those who are alienated, religion can stand in the way of useful protest and thus contribute to a buildup of resentment. This may make reform more difficult in the long run, and revolution more necessary.

2 Religion provides authoritative teaching. This is its *priestly* function. It contributes to security and order. The dysfunctional aspect of the priestly function is that it may *sacralize* (make sacred) incorrect ideas and backward attitudes. This may have a harmful effect on a society's understanding of its environment and efforts to control nature. The trial of Galileo for the "crime" of suggesting that the earth revolved around the sun is an example of this kind of effect.

3 Religion sacralizes the norms and values of society, upholding the importance of the group's goals over the wishes of individuals. This is its *social control* function. Religion also provides ways of forgiving the wrongdoers and bringing them back into the social group. The dysfunction is that it can set back a society's adjustment to changing conditions. For example, the Christian Church long refused to allow its members to lend money at interest, despite the great need for this practice in a developing economy. The sacral freezing of norms is a source of many social conflicts, as is illustrated by the debate over birth control and abortion in the Catholic Church.

4 Religion provides standards for judging institutionalized norms. This is its *prophetic* function; an example is the Hebrew prophets, who were troublemakers in their own society. Prophets scold their followers and urge them to reform or repent. The dysfunction is that prophetic demands may be so extreme that they prevent the working out of practical solutions to social problems. By making demands on its members in the name of God, religion may make compromise impossible.

5 Religion performs important *identity* functions. It links the individual to the past and future. It gives his or her spirit a place in the universe and makes the universe meaningful.[9] However, there is a dysfunction too. By sacralizing the identity of the individual within his or her group it may increase intergroup conflict. Other ideological systems, such as communism and nationalism, have the same effect: They give people an identity but at the same time tend to increase intergroup conflict.

# Meaning, magic, and sorcery

## MEANING AND RELIGION

Why do human beings need religion? Possibly because it gives them a framework within which to deal with the limitations of life. We each have to face situations of *uncertainty, powerlessness,* and *scarcity.* By uncertainty I mean that we can never plan or control our affairs in such a way that they all work out well. Sometimes we fail. And yet, knowing that the outcomes of our plans are always subject to chance, we have to be able to function anyway; we have to cope with uncertainty. By powerlessness I mean that we have to live with the fact that some things are impossible. We cannot do everything we want to do, and yet we have to face our powerlessness with courage. By scarcity I mean that we have to face the fact that there may not be enough of everything to go around. What we have must be distributed in an orderly way. Thus social life may require that some people be deprived and frustrated.

We all have to deal with a crisis at some point, and it is then that religion helps us adjust. Why should a loved one die young? Why must we suffer illness? Why should a person go on living when his or her love is not returned? Such questions demand meaningful answers. If they are considered meaningless, support for society's norms is weakened. How can we maintain our morale when disappointment lurks at every step—and when we know that death awaits us in the end?

Religion makes life meaningful by fitting it into the context of an existence beyond the present. It supports our commitment to society's norms when we are at the breaking

Religion cannot be explained in practical, reasonable terms. What "practical" purpose is being served by the activities of these people?

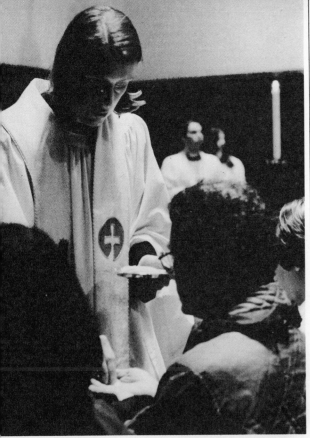

Ann Hagen Griffiths/DPI

Ian Berry/Magnum

point. It helps us adjust to the frustrations that are part of human life.

## RELIGION AS THE SACRED

When asked to define religion, most people say that all religions involve belief in, and worship of, a supreme being. This notion is mistaken. Some religions (including some forms of Buddhism) are entirely *agnostic*. That is, they hold no opinion about the possible existence of God.

Then what is religion? As Durkheim pointed out, the quality that seems to be shared by all religions is a sense of *sacredness*. The religious experience is the experience of the *holy* or the *sacred*—a quality that calls for great respect. Here is what Durkheim said about the sacred:[10]

1  It is recognized as a power or force.
2  It is ambiguous—both physical and moral, both human and cosmic, both positive and negative, both attractive and repulsive, both helpful and dangerous.
3  It is nonutilitarian. (You cannot control it for practical purposes.)
4  It is nonempirical. (You cannot study it by observation or experimentation.)
5  It does not involve knowledge. (It goes beyond logic or reasoning or proof.)
6  It strengthens and supports the worshiper.
7  It makes moral demands on the worshiper.

Sacredness is not something that objects have by nature; rather, it is assigned to them by religious thought and tradition. For example, a cross is not something that everyone would recognize as holy. It is a symbol that is meaningful to Christians and to others who have come, through cultural experience, to attach a sacred quality to it. Religion is very different from ordinary experience. It never helps people control nature—so it is useless in any practical sense. It is not based on ordinary forms of knowledge, judgment, or sensory evidence—it is separate from the everyday world.

## RELIGION AND MAGIC

I have just written that religion is not useful as a way of controlling nature. Yet most societies have traditional practices that seem in many ways to be religious practices but are directed toward the control of spirits or other forces beyond the reach of ordinary human powers. This is magic. Examples include rain dances, love potions, and curing warts with incantations. It is difficult to separate magic from religion because they may be mixed into the same ceremonies and institutions. Magic shares with religion the idea that people can make contact with forces beyond the world of the senses. But while religion offers a way of relating to supernatural forces, magic goes further. It offers techniques for *manipulating* those forces.

Bronislaw Malinowski distinguishes between religion and magic by pointing out that magic has an *end*. He contrasts a *magical* ritual (performed, say, to prevent death in childbirth) with a *religious* ritual (such as one performed to celebrate the birth of a child). While the magical rite has a practical purpose that is known to all who practice it, the religious rite has no practical purpose. Christening a child is not a means to an end but an end in itself. Its only purpose is to express the feelings of the participants[11] — to give thanks, perhaps, and to express the idea that they and the newborn are all children of God and that they care for one another.

Malinowski argues that people use magic when they lack practical ways of controlling the environment. For example, the Trobriand Islanders were skilled fishermen who sometimes practiced magic in the belief that it helped them catch fish. But they used these rites only in specific situations. When the Trobrianders used poison to kill fish in an inner lagoon, they made a huge catch with little risk or danger. In such cases they did not use magic. However, when they fished in the open sea, which was more dangerous and uncontrollable, they engaged in magical rituals.[12]

Both magic and religion relieve emotional stress. They help people cope with situations over which they have no practical control. Both involve mythology, taboos, and an atmosphere of wonder or awe. Magic

*Magic is the effort to gain control over supernatural forces and use them for human purposes.*

Maje Waldo/Stock, Boston

strengthens human confidence in the face of the unknown, while religion helps human beings face and adjust to misfortune. It is quite common for people to mix the two experiences.

### WITCHCRAFT AND SORCERY

A special form of magic is "black magic," or witchcraft and sorcery. These are used in calling on sacred forces to bring misfortune to others. But sorcery is not necessarily bad. I can think of several points in its favor. For one thing, it's a safe outlet for nasty emotions that might disrupt society if they were expressed directly. (Better to stick a pin into a voodoo doll than to run a sword through a real person.) Moreover, believing in witchcraft gives you the satisfaction of pinning the blame for your troubles on a witch. ("Sorry the cake fell, folks. It's that darn witch again!") Probably the main advantage of black magic, however, is that it is answered by "white" magic and religious ceremonies. Whenever people really believe that a loved one has been "hexed" or "possessed," they often call in their friends and spiritual advisers to ward off the expected evil. Thus by reinforcing social norms black magic actually performs a positive function.[13]

But sorcery certainly has bad aspects too. Obviously, the purpose of black magic is to harm others. Such rituals may release hostile feelings, but they also *create* hostile feelings. They probably do more harm than good. I have strangled many pillows in my time, imagining that they were the people I hated at the moment. I don't regret those imaginary murders at all. But I might be very frightened and guilty if I believed that by strangling a pillow or sticking a pin in a doll I could actually kill someone or that someone could kill me that way. Some people do believe such things.

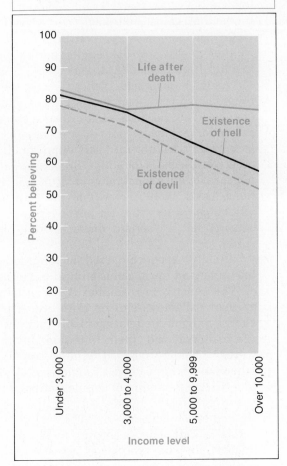

**FIGURE 13.2**

*Beliefs of U.S. Protestants by income level, 1968.*

Life after death

Existence of hell

Existence of devil

Percent believing

Under 3,000 · 3,000 to 4,000 · 5,000 to 9,999 · Over 10,000

Income level

*Source:* Data from Gallop Poll, American Institute of Public Opinion, 764, June 1968.

# Religion and social stratification

### WEBER ON THEOLOGIES AND SOCIAL STATUS

Weber is remembered mainly for studying how religion *causes* various effects. But here I want to talk about his view of religious beliefs as *effects* rather than causes.

Think of a religion as a package of beliefs, a set of assumptions about what is proper or improper, possible and impossible, and so on. It is reasonable to suppose that the religion shared by the members of a society will affect their ways of behaving. That is, religion is a *cause* of certain phenomena — an important independent variable. Weber believed this, and he showed how certain religions have been important independent variables. We'll come back to this point when we discuss the Protestant ethic.

But Weber realized that religion is also a dependent variable. He wanted to know why certain groups choose particular types of religions. He thought there were structural explanations for this. According to Weber, people choose their theologies according to how well they help them cope with the problems of daily living. Different social systems have different religious systems. What attracts particular groups to particular theologies?

Weber noted that *social classes and status groups differ in their religious preferences.* For example, groups such as craftsmen and small traders are less involved with nature than farmers and more involved in a way of life based on rational economic calculation. For them honesty is important and even profitable. So these groups (which are mostly lower middle class) tend to favor a religion that preaches that hard work and devotion to duty will bring a "just reward." Thus small traders and artisans generally support an "ethic of compensation."[14] That is, they tend to think that in the long run people get what is coming to them. No more, no less.

Peasants, on the other hand, are subject to the unpredictable processes of nature. Lacking a market economy (at least in traditional societies), they have no reason for believing in rational calculation. They don't hold to the idea of a "just reward." They are very concerned about the irrational forces of nature that affect their lives. Hail, for example, seems to fall on the just and the unjust

alike. So peasants usually are attracted not to a rational theology but, rather, to a system that offers magical ways of controlling nature.[15]

Weber found that rich business classes everywhere are oriented toward the here and now, not the hereafter. They are not attracted to prophetic or ethical religions. Indeed, the richer they are, the less likely they are to develop an otherworldly religion.[16]

What about militaristic societies? Weber pointed out that the warrior does not need an ethical system. He does not worry about ideas such as sin, salvation, and religious humility. He faces death, and unpredictable forces are part of his daily life. The things that are important to a warrior are honor and protection against evil magic. He prays for victory or happiness in a warrior's heaven. Neither an otherworldly religion nor a belief in ethical compensation attracts him.

As for bureaucrats, Weber thought their religious tendency was best seen in Confucianism. This Chinese religion had a strong aesthetic emphasis — yet it was practical, lacking any feeling for "salvation" or any otherworldly basis for ethics. Bureaucrats do not care for a personal religion with an emotional basis. Weber noted that the Chinese official performed rites for his ancestors but actually felt a "certain distance from the spirits."[17]

Finally, Weber compared the religions of the upper and lower status groups and classes. The upper groups emphasize honor rather than salvation, sin, or humility. They choose religious beliefs that justify their own life patterns and their situation in the world.[18] Underprivileged groups, on the other hand, tend to choose religions of salvation, to favor an ethic of compensation, and to support greater equality between men and women in religious affairs.[19] The reason salvation is important, according to Weber, is that people who experience stress and oppression in this world may look to the next world for relief. And Weber was aware that a different version of "salvation" was growing in popularity among the working classes of Europe. This was not the hope of salvation in heaven but a secular salvation—the revolution and the justice and equality that would follow it. This hope was not based on reli-

gion in the usual sense but on a secular ideology—Marxism. It is probably fair to think of Marxism—and indeed many other ideologies, such as nationalism—as having similar functions to those of religion. Ideologies often offer support, consolation, hope, and

**FIGURE 13.3**

*Beliefs of selected countries of the world, 1975*

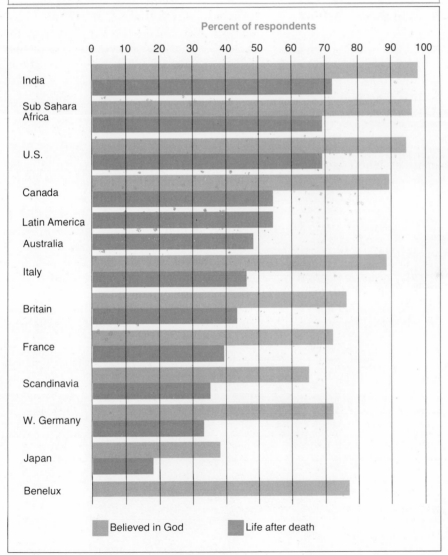

*Source:* Data from Lee Sigelman, "Multi-Nation Surveys of Religious Beliefs," *Journal for the Scientific Study of Religion* 1977, 16(3), pp. 290, 292.

**TABLE 13.2**

*Religious preferences, by color, United States (people aged 18 and older in 1972–1974 by percent)*

|  | WHITES | NONWHITES | TOTAL |
|---|---|---|---|
| Protestant | 60.3 | 83.8 | 63.6 |
| Baptist | (15.3) | (55.2) | (20.8) |
| Methodist | (13.1) | (15.6) | (13.5) |
| Other Protestant | (31.9) | (13.0) | (29.3) |
| Catholic | 28.3 | 8.9 | 25.6 |
| Jewish | 3.5 | 0.3 | 3.0 |
| No religion | 6.3 | 4.5 | 6.1 |
| Other | 1.4 | 2.3 | 1.5 |
| Religion not reported | 0.2 | 0.2 | 0.2 |
| Total | 100.00 | 100.00 | 100.0 |
| N | (3959) | (641) | (4600) |

*Source:* Norval D. Glenn and Erin Gotard, "The Religion of Blacks in the United States: Some Recent Trends and Current Characteristics," *American Journal of Sociology,* 83, 2 (September 1977), 444.

meaning to people in times when sacrifice and endurance are required of them.

## SOCIAL CLASS AND RELIGIOUS INVOLVEMENT: EMPIRICAL DATA

Modern polls and survey research support Weber's conclusion. There are, indeed, regular differences between the religious activities of different social classes. Lower-class people participate much less in church activities than middle-class people.[20] And they are more orthodox in their beliefs. For example, lower-class Americans are more likely to believe in hell, the devil, and life after death than middle-class Americans.

However, socially deprived people who *do* join churches are more intense in their participation than privileged people. It seems that religion gives them consolation for their unfortunate status. This is true of

**TABLE 13.3**

*People who reported attending religious services during the previous week, by color and religious preference (U.S. National Surveys, 1956, 1966, and 1973 by percent)*

| YEAR | WHITES | | | NONWHITES | |
|---|---|---|---|---|---|
|  | PROTESTANTS | CATHOLICS | TOTAL | PROTESTANTS | TOTAL* |
| 1956 | 40.0 | 70.0 | 46.9 | 46.6 | 47.5 |
| 1966 | 38.4 | 72.1 | 45.8 | 38.0 | 38.6 |
| 1973 | 37.0 | 56.7 | 39.7 | 43.6 | 41.9 |

Note: Catholic, Jewish, No religion, and Other included in Total
*Source:* Norval D. Glenn and Erin Gotard, "The Religion of Blacks in the United States: Some Recent Trends and Current Characteristics," *American Journal of Sociology,* 83, No. 2 (September 1977), 445.

people whose deprivation is based on income and also of those whose deprivation is based on other factors. Thus females participate more than males, the aged more than the young, and the poorly educated more than the well educated.[21] However, mentally handicapped people do not participate in church activities very much; instead, they turn to prayer and other private religious acts.[22]

## Religious groups in North America

### THE UNITED STATES

The thirteen American colonies were settled mostly by British Protestants—Anglicans in the South, Quakers in Pennsylvania, and Puritans and Congregationalists in Massachusetts and Connecticut. Maryland alone was a Catholic colony. There were hardly any Jews in America during the prerevolutionary period.

In the 1850s famine struck in Ireland and many Irish immigrants settled in the United States. The majority were Catholic, so that this was the first large group of Catholics in the United States. At about the same time, German Catholics began to settle in the Midwest. Both of these groups were seen as an economic threat by the local working class because they competed for jobs. Because the newcomers had to live in slums, Catholics became stereotyped as the dregs of urban society. In 1850 an immigrant was ten times more likely to be receiving public support than a native-born citizen.[23]

These factors contributed to the rise of anti-Catholic prejudice. Groups such as the Native Americans and the Know-Nothing American party—an anti-Catholic working-class party that used strongly bigoted language—were common.[24] Only in recent years has prejudice against Catholic Americans decreased much among Protestants. However, today young Catholic Americans have reached levels of education and income equal to those of the Protestant majority, and this is one reason why discrimination against Catholics has become much less common.

As I pointed out in Chapter 9, prejudice against Jews is largely a twentieth-century phenomenon. Anti-Semitism peaked in the 1930s and decreased greatly as a result of America's experience in World War II.

Thus today the United States is the home of many faiths, and members of different religions live together in reasonable tolerance and good will. The major religious group is still Protestant, with Baptists and Methodists the largest denominations. About 25 percent of all Americans are Catholic—and among blacks the percentage of Catholics is even lower. Only about 9 percent of all black Americans are Catholic. The great majority of Americans say that they believe in God—

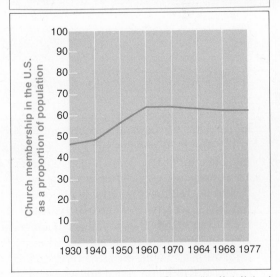

**FIGURE 13.4**

*Church membership in the U.S. as a proportion of the population, 1930–1977*

*Source:* Data from *Yearbook of American Churches* (New York: National Council Press, 1978).

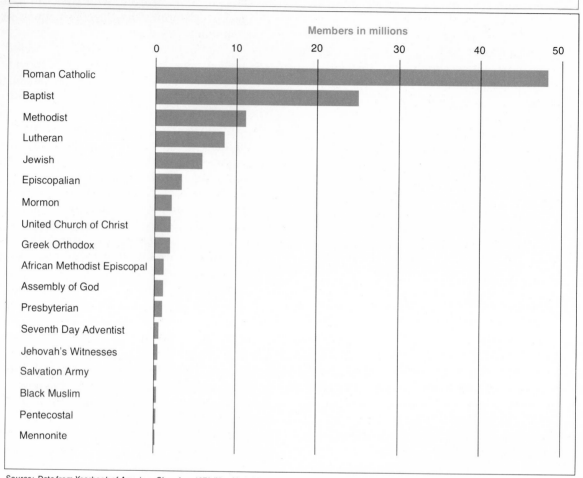

**FIGURE 13.5**

*Membership of major U.S. religious denominations*

Members in millions

0   10   20   30   40   50

Roman Catholic
Baptist
Methodist
Lutheran
Jewish
Episcopalian
Mormon
United Church of Christ
Greek Orthodox
African Methodist Episcopal
Assembly of God
Presbyterian
Seventh Day Adventist
Jehovah's Witnesses
Salvation Army
Black Muslim
Pentecostal
Mennonite

*Source:* Data from *Yearbook of American Churches,* 1972 (New York, National Council Press, 1972).

more than 95 percent, according to most polls. About 70 percent say that they believe in a life after death. And almost 40 percent of all Americans go to church every week—a higher percentage than in any other Western industrial society. It is clearly expected that the nation's leaders be members of some religion, though it doesn't seem to matter which religion it is. Sometimes the religious belief of a political leader becomes an issue in an

election campaign. This was especially true in 1960, when for the first time a Catholic candidate—John Kennedy—was favored by the voters. In 1976 Jimmy Carter's conservative Baptist beliefs troubled some voters, but not enough to prevent him from being elected. Fifty years ago, the religion of a political candidate was more likely to affect his or her chances of winning. Today, a candidate would lose votes by announcing that he or she is an atheist, but as far as specific religions are concerned the voters are fairly tolerant.

Canadians are almost equally divided between Catholicism and Protestantism; about 10 percent belong to neither group. About 75 percent of the Protestants belong either to the Anglican church or to the United Church of Canada, the result of the 1925 merger of the Methodist, Congregational, and most Presbyterian churches.

In Canada the hostility between Catholics and Protestants was related to the split between the French and English populations. The two groups had equal rights as founders of the society. But in the early period of Canadian history religious conflict was intense because conservative French Canadian bishops argued that the church should have authority over the state. This made it hard to reach the sort of compromise that had been reached in many other countries — the promise that church and state would be separate institutions and that neither would try to dominate the other. However, in recent decades French Canada has moved beyond this issue, so that separation of church and state is as secure there as it is anywhere else.

## Theoretical approaches to religion

At the beginning of this chapter I said that social scientists do not take positions on religious questions, for we cannot determine the truth or falsity of theological statements. And it is true that social scientists *as a group* don't take such positions. But lots of individual social scientists do. Here we will discuss the writings of four of them — Durkheim, Freud, Marx, and Weber — all of whom made strong statements about the part religion plays in social life. None of these scholars thought of himself as religious. Indeed, both Freud and Marx were highly critical of religion and actually hoped it would disappear.

### EMILE DURKHEIM RELIGION AS WORSHIP OF SOCIETY

In the years before World War I Durkheim wrote one of his most important contributions to functionalist sociology — *Elementary Forms of Religious Life*. In it he asked two questions: (1) What is religion? (2) What are the functions of religion for human society? It struck him that religion was very much a "social thing." He felt that to understand it at all one must focus on its collective basis.

Durkheim divided human experience into two very different areas, the *sacred* and the *profane*. The profane experience was everyday life, while the sacred experience was anything that stimulated awe and worship. Durkheim decided that the purpose of religion was to maintain the separation of the sacred from the profane through the practice of ritual. Today many people assume that the most important feature of religion is the private, inner experience of the individual and that the rituals performed in group meetings are unimportant outward displays that have little bearing on one's deep experience. But Durkheim thought that the ritual itself was of central importance.

People everywhere worship a sacred object, but what they consider sacred differs greatly from one place to another. Durkheim felt that people everywhere worship the same object but symbolize it in very different ways. What is this object of worship? It is society. To Durkheim, *God is society*. The group is made into a personalized, living entity. Religion sacralizes the traditions on which society is based. Society is the being that is greater than the individual. It is the source of the ideas and values that render a person's life meaningful. It makes him or her a social being. The purpose of religion, therefore, is to preserve society. It points out the value of society to humankind and makes it an object of reverence. In collective acts of worship society reaffirms and strengthens itself.

Although he was interested mainly in the group rather than in the individual, Durkheim recognized the supportive role of religion for the believer. Religion gives the believer a feeling of comfort and dependence. "The believer who has communicated with his god . . . is a man who is stronger. He feels within him more force, either to endure the trials of existence, or to conquer them."[25]

### SIGMUND FREUD: RELIGION AS ILLUSION

One of the most influential social theories of the twentieth century is Freudian psychoanalysis. While functionalists interpret religion as an invention designed to maintain the stability of *social groups*, Freud interprets it as an invention designed to maintain the stability of the *individual personality*. Both approaches stress the *usefulness* of the religion, though Freud goes beyond this idea, suggesting that it serves infantile needs that should be outgrown.

Nature, says Freud, often mocks our attempts to control it. The task of culture is to defend us from nature, and from this effort come all the achievements of civilization. On this point Freud agrees with the functionalists. However, he adds two new ideas: (1) that religion has done a poor job of defending us against nature, including our own nature, and (2) that religion is an illusion because "wish fulfillment is a prominent factor in its motivations." Religion disregards reality.[26]

Religion, Freud writes, "is born of the need to make tolerable the helplessness of man." Freudian analysis has shown not only that human behavior stems from hidden motives but also that it often reenacts behavior learned in earlier situations. These earlier responses, usually of an infantile nature, are repeated in adulthood in a disguised form. Religion, to Freud, is an example of this kind of repetition. It is a reenactment of infantile behavior in the face of human limitations. Maturity, however, means putting aside childish things. Freud claims that despite the consolations of religion humans remain helpless. He believes that religious ideas which "should solve for us the riddles of the universe and reconcile us to the troubles of life" have "the weakest possible claim to authenticity."[27] He believes people should give up such infantile responses. Each person will then "find himself in a difficult situation . . . that he is no longer the center of creation . . . but is it not the destiny of childishness to be overcome?"[28]

### KARL MARX: RELIGION AS IDEOLOGY

Not all social scientists (nor, indeed, all psychoanalysts) agree with Freud's view of religion. But his interpretation raises important questions. Many theologians have tried to develop a truly mature religious doctrine. Is the only mature response the claim that there is "nothing else" beyond one's own life? Freud thought so, and so did Marx, who believed that religion is a delusion imposed upon one class by another in order to dupe them into obedience.

Marx's views on religion are usually discussed in connection with a controversy between his followers and Weber's over the impact of religion on society. Marx's followers believe that the only basic forces in society are economic and technological; Weber's followers see religion as influencing social

Richard Kalvar/Magnum

*People who want to forcibly "deprogram" others justify their point of view with extreme, ideological attacks against the unusual religion.*

life also, causing changes that would not otherwise occur. Marx tended to see religion as an *effect* of other factors; Weber saw it more as a *cause* of other factors.

Marx held that groups of people tend to choose belief systems (or ideologies) that can be used to justify their own economic advantages. Some social groups have leisure and the chance to communicate with one another, and therefore develop convincing doctrines to support their dominance. Other groups (workers and especially peasants) may have neither the leisure nor the chance to discuss their situation, and they may not be fully aware of the fact that they are exploited. Indeed, the ruling group may be able to get the workers to believe that their rule is proper and any rebellion against it is a sin.

To Marx, religion was such a doctrine, an "opiate of the people" that prevents them from rebelling against their oppressors. Clearly Marx did not argue that religion has *no* effect. It has to have some effect if it is used by the ruling classes to dominate the workers. However, Marx did not expect religion to be a source of social change, and Marxist sociologists have generally ignored the study of religion.

### MAX WEBER: RELIGION AS A SOURCE OF SOCIAL CHANGE

Against the background of Marxism Weber's book *The Protestant Ethic and the Spirit of Capitalism*[29] stands out sharply. Weber, like

Marx, was curious about what caused industrial capitalism to develop. In other books he discussed the organizational, technological, and economic origins of capitalism.[30] In this study he focused on religion. He wanted to show that capitalism was a result of Protestantism, a result that early Protestants both expected and regretted.

Weber had noted that an unusually high number of European business leaders were Protestant. Remembering that the Industrial Revolution began shortly after the Protestant Reformation, Weber wondered whether the Reformation somehow caused the Industrial Revolution. He reasoned that the character traits that the Protestant value system encouraged were precisely the traits that a person would need to succeed in business. And yet the early Protestant leaders did not mean to encourage the acquisition of material goods; they were concerned with the salvation of souls. Protestantism did not *cause* acquisitiveness—this trait is as old as human nature—but it did create a system of *legitimate, rational* acquisitiveness. Several aspects of Protestantism contributed to this effect: (1) the legitimation of interest on loans, (2) the idea that secular work is a "calling" by which God may be served, and (3) the anxiety caused by the belief in *predestination*, the doctrine that each person is predestined to go either to heaven or to hell and cannot change that destiny.

The Catholic Church had forbidden Christians to lend money at interest, for this allowed a person to profit from the misfortunes and needs of others. This rule made capitalism impossible. Jews were allowed to accept interest, and during the Middle Ages their services were needed for business to be transacted on a regular basis. Some time after Calvin's day Protestantism began to allow

*Do religions tend to quiet protest against social injustice by telling people to pin their hopes on the next world?*

Bill Stanton/Magnum

**FIGURE 13.6**

*Organizational Chart of Heaven*

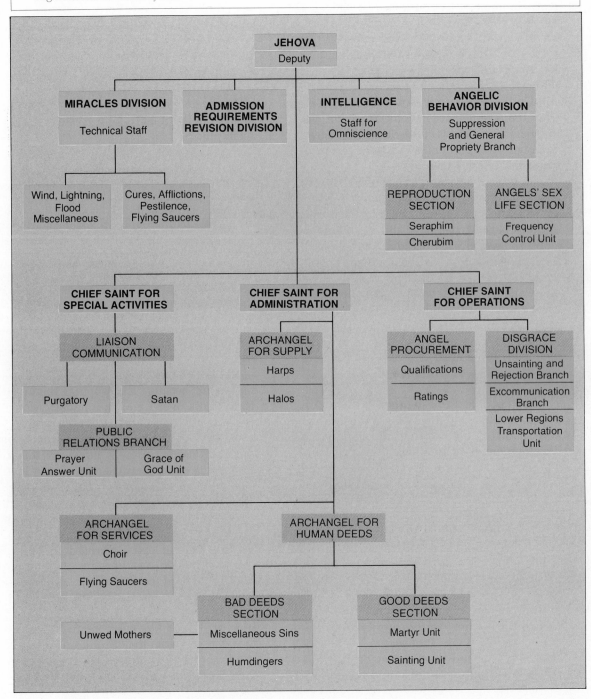

the taking of interest, and this freed devout Christians to invest their capital.

Protestantism also taught that one's work in the world could be viewed as a "calling" from God. One should devote one's life to worldly tasks with the same zeal that hermits or priests have for religious matters. No longer did one turn away from worldly things to serve God. The work of the world was God's work, and it required no less sacrifice than the work of a monk. A person was to forgo the pleasures of the flesh and instead work hard and prudently invest the profits of his or her labor, which are God's.

Finally, Protestantism (especially Calvinism) created a terrible sense of loneliness and anxiety by emphasizing that God was entirely beyond people's ability to understand and had already decided whether each individuals to be saved or damned. People could not earn salvation and should never allow themselves to believe that they were among the chosen. Indeed, in the minds of early Calvinists there could be no clue as to whether one belonged to the chosen or to the damned. People must live out their lives in anxiety, waiting to learn their eternal fate.

By the time Protestantism was in full swing, however, this chilling doctrine had been modified in a way that was vital for the development of capitalism. Although one still could not earn salvation, one could measure how well one was carrying out God's work on earth by how well it turned out. Thus a wealthy businessman who succeeded in his "calling" would seem to be acceptable to God. Money became a means of reducing people's anxiety about whether or not they were saved. Poverty, on the other hand, was evidence that people were not putting enough zeal into their work and probably were not worthy of salvation. Because hardworking Protestants were not supposed to spend their money on luxuries and because they were not supposed to inter-

fere with their poverty-stricken neighbors by helping them in their own "calling," they acquired wealth that they could neither spend nor give away. Fortunately, they were allowed to invest this money—and thus to become capitalist entrepreneurs. This ethic of worldly asceticism is the "Protestant ethic."

Early in the Protestant Reformation some of its leaders foresaw the effects that Weber was to spell out later. John Wesley wrote, for example,

I fear, wherever riches have increased, the essence of religion has decreased in the same proportion. Therefore I do not see how it is possible, in the nature of things, for any revival of true religion to continue long. For religion must necessarily produce both industry and frugality, and these cannot but produce riches. But as riches increase, so will pride, anger, and love of the world in all its branches. How then is it possible that Methodism, that is, a religion of the heart, though it flourishes now as a green bay tree, should continue in this state? For the Methodists in every place grow diligent and frugal; consequently they increase in goods.[31]

Wesley's fears were justified. The Protestant ethic became less popular among the Protestants over time, and modern Methodists are not noticeably different in this respect from members of other religious communities. Weber argues, however, that the Protestant ethic played a major role in the development of industrial capitalism.

The "Weber thesis" attracted much criticism. It was pointed out, for example, that capitalism was not unknown in the Catholic world. Several pre-Reformation Catholic groups "rivaled the Puritans in their hospitality toward capitalism in general and even usury in particular."[32] Perhaps the greatest weakness in Weber's thesis is that it is still possible even today to take the Marxist position that Protestantism didn't cause capitalism—capitalism caused Protestantism.[33]

Finally, we should note that if there ever was a distinctively Protestant ethic it no longer exists. In polls and surveys about values and ethics, Catholics and Protestants give similar answers. Indeed, if any single religious group has a "Protestant" ethic today, it is the Jews.

## The effects of religiosity

Since Marx and Weber developed the issue, sociologists have continued to argue about the relationship between religion and social change. Most sociologists think that religion is a factor that stands in the way of social change. It would be hard to accept that position totally. Still, it is probably true that *most* religions—regular, institutionalized, church-centered organizations—are conservative and back up established social institutions. For example, apart from a few remarkable men such as Martin Luther King, the ministers of American churches were slow to enter the civil-rights movement. Even black churches tended to take an otherworldly orientation, which tends to quiet protest. Gary Marx showed that within a nationwide sample of American blacks the greater their religious involvement, the less their militancy. This was not the case for the few respondents who held a commitment to the "social gospel" as opposed to a concern with the afterlife.[34]

Some sociologists have tried to determine whether deeply religious people behave differently than atheists or moderately religious people. That is, they try to measure religiosity and use this measure as an independent variable. The problem is in determining the validity of their variable. Mostly they ask respondents such questions as how often they go to worship services, how often they pray, whether they believe in heaven, and so on. They then construct a religiosity scale and compare the high scorers with the low scorers. In this way several regular findings have been made about people who score high on a religiosity scale. Those in the United States tend to be (1) intolerant,[35] (2) middle class rather than poor,[36] (3) unintellectual,[37] (4) conservative about social values, and (5) a decreasing portion of the population. Over the decades modern society is gradually abandoning the rites and beliefs of the great religious traditions.

But not all sociologists are convinced that religiosity is validly measured by this or any other empirical method. As David Riesman once noted, not everyone who is religious knows that he or she is. Although traditional beliefs are no longer believable to many people, their loss of belief has not brought about a loss of meaning and morale. Those who abandon beliefs usually continue to live bravely, and one cannot tell the believers from the unbelievers from their behavior. Somehow they maintain *faith* in the absence of *belief.* It may be a serious mistake to define such people as nonreligious, for, as Robert Bellah has noted, in the act of letting go of particular beliefs it is possible to discover the faith that lies beyond belief.[38] Modern society contains many such people. They are serious, committed to social ethics, and able to see meaning in life; they respond as fully as they can, without belief. I think it is misleading to call this orientation nonreligious.

If this objection is valid, however, it means that one cannot measure religiosity, for it may not be a true variable; rather, it may be a constant. Peel off one layer of religiosity and you find another layer underneath. If this is so, one cannot classify one person as deeply religious and another as less so— at least not on the basis of superficial statements about theological doctrines. The empirical comparison of religious and nonreligious people becomes impossible if this criticism is accepted.

# SOCIAL RESEARCH:
## Sociologists at Work

In this section we will look at a variety of religious movements, most of which are not familiar to middle-class North Americans. We will begin with a look at messianic movements and then discuss the current Western interest in Eastern religions.

Under what conditions do people become attracted to charismatic religious leaders? Fortunately, it is possible to compare many different cases of charismatic inspiration, for history is filled with movements that swept through societies like wildfire, igniting the hopes of the masses for the coming of salvation on earth. Many of these phenomena pointed not to a life after death but to a transformation of society on earth under the direction of a seemingly divine ruler. Examples of such movements include the Ghost Dance cult of the Plains Indians, the cargo cults of Melanesia, the flagellant movements of thirteenth-century Germany, and the anti-Christ fantasies of the Crusaders. Such social cults are called *millenarian* — in accordance the doctrine that Christ will return to rule for a millennium (1000 years) — or *messianic* — in accordance with the Jewish utopia, in which the Messiah is expected to rule. We will use the terms interchangeably.

Millenarian movements are very hard to explain. Why would a group of people wander around Europe in processions, beating themselves with leather scourges and iron spikes, as the flagellants did in the thirteenth century? Why would inhabitants of an idyllic South Sea island burn all their possessions and wait on the beach for ships to arrive, bringing them all the material objects of Western society, as the cargo cultists of Melanesia did? In recent years several scholars have addressed such questions and have described the conditions in which millenarian movements arise.

First, it is well established that such movements occur mainly among the oppressed and suffering. In some cases they represent the response of a society to foreign domination. In Europe the millenarian movements of the Middle Ages occurred especially among the peasants and those who were uprooted by being forced to become unskilled urban workers, beggars, or unemployed.[39] These movements often occurred after inflation, plagues, and famines had brought misery to the country.[40] In medieval Europe there was a large population living on the margin of society, without material or emotional support. They were not effectively organized in village communities, kinship groups or guilds. There were no regular methods of voicing their grievances or pressing their claims. Instead they waited for a prophet to lead them in a movement driven by a desperate enthusiasm.[41] There is evidence that the poor were emotionally alienated from the Church, perhaps because of the showy life style of the church officials, and that they suffered as a result. What they needed was consolation in the person of a genuinely holy person. Such a person they would accept — and even adore.

In some types of messianic movements the oppression comes from outside the society (as in the case of colonialism and when Moses led his people against the Egyptians).[42] Such a movement is often a violent struggle against the oppressor. The established political authorities may try to stifle it by force, as in the case of the Ghost Dance movement among the American Indians. Such movements arise mainly among people divided into narrow, isolated social units — villages, clans, tribes, and the like — in societies that have no overall unity or government. They have no way of acting together politically and are therefore unable to resist the oppressors. The millenarian cult is a way to overcome these divisions and to bring previously hostile and separate groups together into a new unity.[43]

Thus such religious cults are the forerunners of nationalistic movements, though they are led by religious rather than political leaders. This is because such societies are made up of fragmented parts, and any ordinary person would identify with the special interests of his or her own subgroup. Only someone with unusual charisma can unify the tribes, clans, villages, and other interest groups in his or her society. He tells them to love one another and to forget the petty loyalties of the past. In time, especially if the religious movement is successful, political parties and other institutions replace the millenarian cult. The protest becomes rational. Thus in Melanesia cargo cults have declined as political groups have become more effective.

On the other hand, in some movements the source of the suffering is not the oppression by outsiders but certain problems within the society—such as poverty and discrimination. Such movements always offer a hope of escape from the grimness of reality—usually through spiritual channels rather than through struggle against an enemy. Most of them offer a vision of material well-being on earth, though Christianity was unusual in that its hope of salvation was otherworldly.[44]

Modern Western society has seen few religious millenarian movements. However, other extremist movements have taken their place, for both nazism and communism are similar to millenarian movements. Both have appealed to the same social groups and have also offered the prospect of carrying out a mission of stupendous importance. This is the basis of the modern totalitarian party.[45]

### RELIGIOUS TRENDS IN THE WEST

During the 1950s church participation in America reached a peak. Over half the population attended weekly services, and church membership grew dramatically. Since then there has been a slow but steady decline, especially in the membership of liberal, yet conventional, churches. Fundamentalist and conservative churches have been slightly more successful in keeping up their membership. The Catholic Church seems to have lost more support than it gained by modernization.

So the basic trend of church participation is downward. At the same time, however, a huge variety of new religious organizations have sprung up in recent years, many of them with very unorthodox practices and beliefs. Some of these movements are within the Christian tradi-

tion and some are on its margins. Examples include the Pentecostal movement within the Catholic church—in which members "speak in tongues"—and such groups as those called informally by such undignified titles as "Jesus Freaks," "Moonies," and "Jews for Jesus." Even more remarkable are the non-Christian groups, many of which mix religion with either the occult or psychotherapy, or both. Yoga, Zen, transcendental meditation, Scientology, Synanon, est, Hare Krishna, and even Satanism may be included in this category.

What explains the large number of Westerners who have converted to these new religions? Are such groups likely to increase in number in the future? Three studies—one by Robert Wuthnow and his associates, one *(Turning East)* by the theologian Harvey Cox, and one by Max Heirich—try to answer these questions.

### Wuthnow's study

Wuthnow's 1973 study[46] was a large-scale survey of San Francisco Bay area residents. The researchers, all University of California sociologists, interviewed 1000 randomly selected respondents age 16 and up. One purpose of the study was to find out what percentage of the population knew about or expressed interest in the new movements just mentioned. Wuthnow divided these movements into three general types: (1) *countercultural groups* (Zen Buddhism, Transcendental Meditation, yoga, Hari Krishna, Satanism); (2) *personal-growth groups* (Erhard Seminars Training (est), Scientology, Synanon); and (3) *neo-Christian groups* (Christian World Liberation Front (CWLF), Children of God, groups that speak in tongues, Jews for Jesus, Campus Crusade for Christ). He reported that

the groups show a widespread impact . . . Nearly four out of every five persons claim to know a little about at least one of these movements, over half claim to know something about at least three of them, and about one person in every three claims to know something about five or more of them. More than half the population is currently attracted to at least one of them and about a third is attracted to at least two of them. Actual participation is much less common, of course; yet, one out of every five persons claims to have taken part in at least one of these groups. Eleven percent of the people interviewed also said they had taken part in other groups similar to these. Mentioned were groups such as Nichiren Shoshu, Aikido, Resurrection City, Meher Baba, and Divine Light.[47]

Table 13.4 summarizes the findings on the attractiveness of the various groups to people who have heard of them, as well as the extent to which they have participated in them. The largest number of people who have heard of these groups are attracted to est; the smallest number are attracted to Satanism.

What kinds of people are attracted to these

Jim Ritscher/Stock, Boston

*What is it about Eastern religions that is so appealing to Westerners today?*

**TABLE 13.4**

*Attraction to and participation in new religious and quasi-religious movements*
*(among those who have ever heard of such movements)*

| | COUNTERCULTURAL | | | | | PERSONAL GROWTH | | | NEO-CHRISTIAN | | | | |
|---|---|---|---|---|---|---|---|---|---|---|---|---|---|
| | TM | HARI KRISHNA | ZEN | YOGA | SATAN- ISM | SCIEN- TOLOGY | SYN- ANON | EST | CWLF | CAMPUS CRUSADE | JEWS FOR JESUS | CHILDREN OF GOD | TONGUES |
| Number | 323 | 388 | 303 | 483 | 368 | 233 | 523 | 60 | 113 | 195 | 215 | 149 | 262 |
| Percent attraction | | | | | | | | | | | | | |
| Strongly | 10 | 1 | 8 | 9 | 2 | 3 | 7 | 17 | 4 | 9 | 8 | 13 | 10 |
| Mildly | 29 | 12 | 32 | 34 | 8 | 22 | 40 | 37 | 31 | 30 | 21 | 24 | 15 |
| Turned off | 12 | 44 | 11 | 10 | 66 | 37 | 13 | 16 | 19 | 26 | 24 | 22 | 40 |
| Nothing either way | 49 | 43 | 49 | 47 | 24 | 38 | 40 | 30 | 46 | 35 | 47 | 42 | 34 |
| Ever taken part | 16 | 4 | 8 | 16 | 3 | 5 | 6 | 24 | 6 | 15 | 4 | 6 | 23 |

*Source:* Robert Wuthnow, "The New Religions in Social Context" in Charles Y. Glock and Robert Bellah, eds., *The New Religious Consciousness* (Berkeley: University of California Press, 1976), p. 270.

movements? As you might expect, the people who like the Neo-Christian movements are very different from those who are interested in the other types. Among other things, Wuthnow found that tolerance for radical political activity was highest among the countercultural and personal-growth supporters and lower among the Neo-Christian supporters.

The different types of groups attract people with different values and life styles. For example, Wuthnow asked respondents whether they approved of unmarried couples living together. He also asked whether they favored more freedom for homosexuals. He found that the countercultural and personal-growth movements appeal to people who accept unconventional life styles, while the Neo-Christian movement appeals to people whose attitudes toward such matters do not differ much from those of ordinary citizens.

In predicting the future of these movements, Wuthnow reasoned that if they appeal to categories of people who are likely to become more numerous in the future, they may be expected to increase greatly. But if they appeal to a part of the population that is decreasing in number, they may die out. So he looked at the relationship between support of these movements and a number of other variables, such as age and education. He found, first, that all three types of movement attract younger people more than older people. The countercultural movements tend to appeal to people in their teens, the personal-growth movements to somewhat older people—mostly in their twenties. (But est appeals to people between the ages of 30 and 50.) Thus we may conclude that these movements may be around for quite a while, since there is a continuous supply of young people being born and entering society. A movement that appealed only to old people might be expected to die out with them. But with youth continually being attracted to the groups, the movement could go on indefinitely if they stay involved for life once they join.

Another fact points to the same conclusion. The new movements appeal to better-educated members of society more than to less well-educated people. We know that the average level of education continues to increase. Hence, there will be a large population of well-educated individuals in the future. Any movement that appealed to poorly educated people would have a smaller base of support in the future.

But you may have thought of a different,

contradictory argument. Suppose these groups *do* appeal to young, well-educated people. People also stop being young. Maybe the movements appeal to youth while they are in the crisis of growing up, while they are at a troubled point in the life cycle. Perhaps they will eventually marry, establish careers, and generally make a place for themselves that feels more secure than their present situation. If so, maybe these movements will lose appeal to their members as they grow older. In that case we could expect their membership to peak in a few years and then level off or decrease as fewer young people enter the society. There is some basis for this argument. Wuthnow asked his respondents about the frustrations in their lives. He found that the countercultural groups (and to some extent the other two types as well) appeal most to people who are dissatisfied with their careers or their sex lives and are single and unemployed or working only part time. It may be that as people pass through these youth-related situations they will lose interest in the new movements. Wuthnow thus is unable to predict how much growth will occur. However, he points out that the people who do become involved with these groups develop a life style that differs greatly from the conventional American culture.

### Cox' study[48]

This cultural content was explored by the second researcher whom I want to mention. Harvey Cox teaches Christian religion at Harvard, which has become a center for the new Eastern (or neo-Oriental) religious groups. When the Hari Krishna devotees came to his door, shaven-headed, wearing saffron robes and thumping on drums, Cox invited them in and listened to their views. Why, he wondered, had these three young people—a Jew, an Irish Catholic, and a Protestant—become Hindus, clanking cymbals and chanting in the street? Why had thousands of other young people like them done the same thing? Within twenty blocks of the Harvard subway station, forty or fifty neo-Oriental religious movements thrive. Cox decided to send his students out to study these groups and to participate in a good many himself. He reports having had a marvelous time. He and his students fanned out through Cam-

bridge, armed with tape recorders and notebooks. They ate spicy vegetarian food at the "Golden Temple of Conscious Cookery." They twirled around with Sufi dancers (Muslims who used to be called "whirling dervishes") in the basement of an Episcopal church. They sat on black silk cushions facing the wall with other meditators at the Zen center. They stretched and breathed deeply in yoga classes. They went to sitar concerts, Tai Chi exhibitions, Zen swordplay demonstrations, and countless introductory lectures to this and that. And the more deeply Cox became involved, the more the practices he observed influenced his own life. His description seems much richer for being a report from personal experience instead of from outside observation. He describes with vividness and passion his trip to the Mexican desert, where he ate Peyote with the Indians and then relived his prenatal life and his birth, cradled by a crooning middle-aged woman named Maria, until the morning star rose and his spirit expanded throughout the cosmos in joy. He also describes "sitting" with Tibetan Buddhists at the Naropa Institute in Colorado for a summer. It was there that he became an "East turner" himself. He says that he will continue to practice meditation for the rest of his life, combining it with his Christian faith. For despite his attraction to Eastern religions he remains somewhat critical of Eastern mysticism as practiced by Americans. He believes that Christianity, with its emphasis on sacrifice, love, and interpersonal relations, continues to offer more to people who need to live and work in a meaningful world than Eastern religions do.

Cox estimates that several million Americans have been affected by some neo-Oriental practice or belief. He agrees that most of the converts are young—in their late teens, twenties, or early thirties. They are almost all white, educated, and middle class. Men and women are about equally involved, though males are the leaders. Few come from rural areas. An especially high number are Jews or liberal Protestants.

Cox suggests that not all East turners are attracted to these movements for the same reasons. He names six types of motives that seemed important to the people he met during his study of neo-Oriental groups:

1 Some seemed to be looking for simple human *friendship*. The communes and ashrams offered this.
2 Some were in search of *immediacy*. They were tired of looking for God through words and abstract ideas and wanted instead to have a direct personal experience of the Holy. One East turner described his previous religion as follows: "I'd sit or kneel or stand. I'd listen or read prayers. But it seemed lifeless. It was like reading the label instead of eating the contents. But here it happened to *me*. I experienced it myself."[49]
3 Some East turners were looking for *authority*—a swami or a guru with charismatic power. They needed a person who would offer them assurance and make their choices and decisions simpler.
4 Some turned East because it seemed more *"natural."* They were discouraged by the materialism and technology of the West and believed that the Asian tradition allowed more freshness, simplicity, and sensitivity to nature's rhythms.
5 A small number, mostly women, turned East *to avoid the male domination* of Western faiths. Cox notes that these people did not actually practice the neo-Oriental disciplines much—if they had done so they would have discovered that these groups have their own versions of male domination.
6 Finally, a handful of people had chosen the Oriental way because of a concern for *ecology* and *health*.

Cox says these motives are not uncommon. "When one examines this list of goals it quickly becomes evident that the East turners are not really very different from anybody else. They are looking for exactly what most people in America are looking for today. They have chosen a more visible and dramatic way of looking."[50]

If the turn toward the East cannot be explained by the motives of East turners, it has to be explained as a response to the problems and shortcomings of Western culture in general and Western religion in particular. In short, Christianity and Judaism may not be "working" as far as the East turners are concerned. Rightly or wrongly, they believe that Eastern approaches will work better for them and enable them to experience life in a fuller way.

If this is so, then researchers will have to explain religious conversions in a different way. Instead of searching for independent variables such as age, sex, marital status, income, or dissatisfaction with jobs or sex life, they will have to look (as Cox did) at the *content* of Christianity and of the faiths to which people are converting.

### Heirich's study[51]

The reason I want to mention Max Heirich's paper is because he reached the same conclusion.[52] In his study of conversion to Catholic Pentecostalism he began by studying the variables that sociologists usually list as sources of religious change. In this he was disappointed, for he found that conversion did not seem to result from psychological stress or from anything unique about the convert's socialization. What, then, causes a person to switch from one religion to another? Heirich's initial answer is *social networks.* Knowing someone who was a Pentecostal was an important precondition for becoming a Pentecostal. This is not a surprising finding. People presumably develop preferences for particular religions the same way they develop tastes for pizza or ping pong or collecting dolls—by being exposed to those activities.

True, but Heirich adds a qualifying remark. Social networks don't have any impact unless people are already on a religious quest of some kind. That is, a person who is searching for a religious solution to his or her problems is open to the influence of friends. He or she may be willing to attend a service at which Catholics speak in tongues, and may even join in. But a person who is not searching for a religion is unlikely to be affected by his or her friends. Our question then becomes, what leads large numbers of people to undertake a religious search? Heirich doesn't even try to answer this question conclusively—but he suggests that the answer hinges on "root realities." That is, the *content* of the present religion may no longer be adequate to cope with new ways of experiencing life. When something happens to shake up your world view, your idea of how the world functions and your proper place in it, only then will you undertake a religious search. Otherwise not. Thus when something happens to destroy one's clarity about "root reality"—one's basis for relating to the world—then the time is ripe for religious searching.

Several things may threaten a person's "root reality." Stress may play a part, in connection with other issues. (The people Wuthnow studied seemed to turn toward the new religions during the period of transition from adolescence to adulthood. This may be a stress-related source of religious conversion.) But other experiences may have a greater impact. If you have an experience that you cannot explain using the ideas you were taught as a child, it will affect your "root reality." Taking drugs might do it. Having an occult or ESP experience would do it. Going deep into your own personality in psychotherapy or an encounter group would do it. Seeing someone levitate would *definitely* do it.

This is how people change not only religious ideas but scientific ideas as well. The history of science shows that people develop a model that seems to work for most purposes — and then something happens that calls it into

question.[53] This is what happened when it was discovered that the sun doesn't revolve around the earth but vice versa.

It is possible that various fairly recent events (chiefly, I think, the spread of psychotherapy but also drug use and other odd findings such as acupuncture, the effects of yoga, and research on psychic phenomena) have called into question some of the "root realities" that we have always taken for granted. And if some of our basic ideas about reality need to be revised and Eastern religious movements can help us revise them, then religious change will tend in that direction. If this is so, the whole West may "turn East."

# SOCIAL POLICY:
## Issues and Viewpoints

### RELIGION AND THE STATE

Most modern Western societies share a common political policy toward religion: to have *no* policy. Unlike some communist countries, which use political means to oppose religion, or some other countries, which use political means to enforce religion, the liberal position is to define religion as a private area that should not be subject to political influence. In keeping with this general view, there is a tendency to use only secular symbols in public rituals. For example, the United States Supreme Court has banned collective prayers in public schools. This trend is part of the process of differentiation between the state and the culture. In earlier, undifferentiated times the political system and the religious system were virtually the same thing. Indeed, when a king converted to a different religion it was understood that his subjects were converted too.

Those days are past. The process of differentiation is going on everywhere as an aspect of modernization, and one can predict with some confidence that it will continue. However, a number of conflicts arise during this process, and governments are sometimes unable to avoid

making decisions that strongly affect religious groups.

The state must sometimes become involved in matters of religious practice or belief, especially in dealing with religious subcultures or with groups that hold deviant beliefs and norms. It is the proper business of the state to enforce social norms. As a result the courts have had to rule on such issues as the right of American Indians to use peyote in religious ceremonies, the right of Mormons to practice polygamy, and the right of Jehovah's Witnesses to refuse to salute the flag and to reject blood transfusions for their injured children. New charismatic religious movements will probably arise in the future, always challenging the established order by claiming that God requires the faithful to ignore "the laws of man."

In recent years another religious issue has come before the courts: "deprograming." Some parents are troubled by the conversion of their offspring (often as adults) to various sects and movements. They claim that their children have been "brainwashed" and that equally strong methods are necessary to undo the damage. In some cases they have arranged to have their children "deprogramed" — forced to give up their new religious practices. In other cases they have tried to win court orders giving them the rights to lock up their children for a specific time in order to keep them from practicing their devotions. The basis of their case is the right of parents to be given custody of their adult off-spring when those children become mentally ill. The assumption is that conversion to an unusual religion is evidence of mental illness, or that the conversion occurred only because the person had already become mentally ill.

Naturally, the courts are usually extremely reluctant to issue such orders. However, some have been issued, and members of groups such as the Krishna Consciousness community and the followers of Reverend Moon ("Moonies," as they are often called) have been removed against their will from their religious communi-ties. The most aggressive "deprogramers" are no longer in business, but other clever and forceful procedures are still being used to "undo" conversions to new religious move-ments.

This question clearly involves the individ-ual's civil liberties. People have every right to worship as they see fit, whether their parents approve or not. Of course if there is *other* evidence of mental illness besides conversion to an unpopular religion, the real question is how to look after the person when he or she is unable to organize his or her own life in a reasonable way. And if there is evidence that the religious group actually hypnotized or drugged the convert or forced the conversion in some other way, the courts should interfere—at least enough to make sure that the conversion was voluntary.

## RELIGIOUS MINORITIES AND VIOLENCE

We would like to believe that the era of religious wars ended several hundred years ago, but this seems not to be the case. The fights between Hindus and Moslems in India and Pakistan, be-tween Catholics and Protestants in Northern Ire-land, and between Jews and Moslems in the Middle East are evidence to the contrary. Some of the bloodiest wars in history were fought over theological points that seem trivial today. Each side usually kept up its morale by claiming that God favored its cause or even that it was fighting a Holy War in His name.

Actually, the fights between religious groups today are not over theological issues. Neither side is interested in converting the other to its own faith. In such conflicts the opposing sides are actually fighting because each side is an ascribed community (or ethnic group) that views itself as an in-group and the other side as an out-group. The fact that membership is based on religion is unimportant—it might just as well be based on skin color, language, caste, national origin, or any other ascribed character-istic. Hence, nonreligious Jews and nonreligious Arabs can be as hostile to each other as devout Jews and Arabs. Their hostility may actually be based on a rivalry for land or political power or prestige or some other valued object.

## SUMMARY

**1.** *Ethnic religions* are tied to a specific place and people. *Universalizing religions* are considered by their followers to be pro-per for all humankind and have been suc-cessful in converting others. *Segmental reli-gions* integrate small groups into larger communities.

**2.** A new religion begins with *charis-matic leadership.* When the leader dies, the

usual reaction is to change the movement into an organized institution, adjusting to the social order. This process has three as-pects: (1) Ritual becomes more formal and elaborate; (2) the ideas and beliefs become more rational; and (3) the religious commu-nity becomes more organized.

**3.** There are three different "ideal types" of church organization: (1) The *con-gregational* type hires and fires its own lead-ers; (2) the *episcopal* type has a well-defined hierarchy of authority within the whole faith; (3) the *presbyterian* type has an elected regional board of ministers and lay persons from different congregations with the authority to appoint clergy.

4. Religion has five functions, all of which have both positive and negative aspects: (1) It provides support, consolation, and reconciliation; (2) it offers authority and stability; (3) it sacralizes the norms and values of society; (4) it provides standards by which to judge institutionalized norms; and (5) it gives the individual a sense of identity with the past and the future.

5. Human beings seem to need religion because it enables them to cope with the limitations of contingency, powerlessness, and scarcity that are part of their existence. The religious experience is the experience of the sacred as opposed to the profane.

6. The main difference between magic and religion is that magic attempts to control forces beyond the world of the senses in order to achieve some personal goal. Witchcraft has some good effects but probably causes more harm than good.

7. Weber showed that different social classes prefer different kinds of religious systems. Traders hold a rational world view with an ethic of "just" compensation. Peas-

ants depend more on magic. Wealthy commercial classes prefer worldly religions; militaristic societies emphasize honor.

8. Members of the lower classes are less likely to join churches than members of the middle classes, but deprived individuals that do join tend to participate with great zeal.

9. Durkheim held that worshipers everywhere are actually worshiping society when they worship God. Ritual is the central aspect of religion.

10. Freud viewed religion as an illusion, and Marx saw it as a delusion imposed upon one class by another to lull them into submission.

11. Weber held that the rise of Protestantism enabled capitalism to develop. It encouraged an ethic of hard work and self-denial, allowed people to take interest on loans, and created a sense of anxiety about personal salvation.

12. Empirical studies of religiosity in the United States find that the most religious people tend to be intolerant, middle class, unintellectual, conservative in their social values, and a decreasing portion of the population.

## KEY TERMS

congregational organization   a religious organization that hires and fires its own leader and in which there is no church hierarchy.

episcopal organization   a religious organization in which there is a well-defined hierarchy of authority.

ethnic religion   a religion that is tied to a specific place and people.

magic   practices directed toward the control of spirits or other forces beyond the reach of ordinary human powers.

myth   a nonhistorical story known by almost

everyone in a group and symbolizing great truths to the group's members.

presbyterian organizations   a religious organization in which authority is in the hands of an elected regional board of ministers and lay members.

religion   the relationship of humankind to some ultimate reality.

segmental religion   a religion that is an offshoot of a universalizing religion or a new religious system that integrates small groups into larger communities.

theology   the organization of religious beliefs into a unified doctrine.

universalizing religion   a religion that is not tied to any particular region or ethnic group and whose members consider their beliefs to be right for all humankind.

# FOR FURTHER READING

BAUM, GREGORY. *Religion and Alienation: A Theological Reading of Sociology.* New York: Paulist Press, 1975. Mixing theology with sociology is a tricky business, easily botched. But Baum makes it work beautifully.

BELLAH, ROBERT. *Beyond Belief.* New York: Harper & Row, 1970. Bellah is one of the most sensitive writers now discussing religion in terms of its contemporary meaning. He goes beyond many other sociologists in his willingness to share his own depth experiences and personal quest for meaning with his readers.

CLARK, S. D. *Church and Sect in Canada.* Toronto: University of Toronto Press, 1948. One of the leading Canadian scholars in historical sociology, Clark here turns his attention to the social conditions underlying the development of various religious groups in Canadian society.

DURKHEIM, EMILE. *The Elementary Forms of Religious Life.* New York: Free Press, 1947. This is one of the major classics in the development of sociology. In it Durkheim searches for the common denominator that characterizes religion in its many forms, using primitive religion as a point of reference.

FREUD, SIGMUND. *The Future of an Illusion.* London: Hogarth, 1928. You will be able to find any number of other editions of this essay. It is Freud's statement of his own atheism. Do try reading one or two of Freud's works. You will be surprised at how simply he wrote.

GREELEY, ANDREW M. *Ethnicity, Denomination, and Inequality.* Beverly Hills: Sage, 1976. This is not a discussion of Catholics' faith, but of their position in American stratification. It's a success story.

*Journal for the Scientific Study of Religion.* This is the leading journal publishing articles on the sociology of religion.

O'DEA, THOMAS. *The Sociology of Religion.* Englewood Cliffs, N.J.: Prentice-Hall, 1966. A large part of this chapter has been drawn from O'Dea's book, but you will gain much by reading the original.

*Review of Religious Research.* This is another important journal to examine for papers on religion. Its orientation is more toward understanding theological meanings in social context than toward examining religious affiliation or other objective factors that lend themselves to quantification.

WUTHNOW, ROBERT. *The Consciousness Reformation.* Berkeley: University of California Press, 1976. An intelligent analysis of how the counterculture was encouraged by slight shifts in cultural patterns of meaning.

WEBER, MAX. *The Protestant Ethic and the Spirit of Capitalism.* Translated by Talcott Parsons. London: Allen & Unwin, 1930. Weber wrote so much on religion that it is hard to know which book to recommend most highly. Certainly, however, this has proved to be the influential one. In it he discusses his famous theory that Protestantism paved the way for capitalism.

YINGER, J. MILTON. *The Scientific Study of Religion.* New York: Macmillan, 1970. A leading textbook in the sociology of religion, this discusses the objective social factors connected with participation in particular religious groups. In addition, it also discusses problems of meaning, thus bringing together the objective and subjective approaches to the study of religion.

# EDUCATION

Did I read it or dream it? I don't know. But I have in mind an image of humanity as a bunch of individuals floating around in the ocean. We have a hammer, a few nails, and a lot of driftwood, and we are trying to build a raft for ourselves. The raft represents civilization. We have nothing solid to stand on while hammering, and most of us are clumsy carpenters, so we know we may not succeed. But as we work there is one overwhelming idea in our minds and we keep reminding each other, *"Don't drop the hammer!"*

Education is the hammer.

I'm not the only person who thinks education is so important. Around the world adults are telling young people, "Get as much education as you can. You'll depend on it later!" What they really mean is, "We'll all depend on it. Society needs you to gain knowledge and skills. Your education is for us all. Don't drop the hammer."

This, then, is a chapter about a vital institution. Education may be defined as a set of processes designed to transmit knowledge and skills and to develop mental abilities. It is crucial—in the developing societies as well as in our own, for it is through education that developing nations advance. The main difference between a modern society and a primitive one is in the levels of symbolic, mental activity of their members. Modern societies maintain a variety of institutions that produce and transmit knowledge—research institutes, universities, publishing houses, libraries, schools, scholarly societies, opera guilds, and clubs organized around purposes such as poetry reading, paper-airplane design, coin collecting, psychotherapy, the writing of local history, and countless other activities that require special skills.

## The functions of education

Education does different things for different people, but for society as a whole seven functions of education are especially important: (1) the transmission of civilization, (2) baby-sitting, (3) building national spirit, (4) establishing social relationships, (5) job training, (6) teaching values, and (7) certification.

### THE TRANSMISSION OF CIVILIZATION

The primary function of education is sometimes forgotten because of disputes over the less important functions. Civilization consists of complex ideas that can be transmitted from one generation to another only through years of interaction between students and teachers. In this activity students develop their knowledge and their skills of critical thinking and aesthetic appreciation. Some people would like to return to a simpler way of life. They would like to allow their children to grow up as wholesome little primitives, taught by Mother Nature alone and protected from the repression and complexity of modern society. This is not a new wish; it was suggested by Jean Jacques Rousseau more than two centuries ago.[1] However, it is clear by now that Mother Nature alone is a poor teacher and that culture is too valuable to give up without a struggle. It is easy to lose and hard to maintain. The transmission of civilization is therefore education's highest function.

### BABY-SITTING

The baby-sitting function of education is rarely recognized openly. Naturally, parents hope the schools do more than baby-sit, but even baby-sitting is of great value. Teachers care for such large groups of children that their services are quite cheap compared to the cost of private care for individual children. From this service parents gain the freedom to engage in personal and economic activities that they could not otherwise afford.

Christopher Morrow/Stock, Boston

*The baby-sitting function of education is rarely recognized openly.*

### BUILDING NATIONAL SPIRIT

A third function of the schools is not as important in the United States as it is in Canada, where many immigrant children are learning to be "New Canadians." The schools transmit nationalistic myths and symbols, teach history, and develop patriotic loyalty probably better than any other institution. The country where one has been educated remains one's "native land" throughout life.

### ESTABLISHING SOCIAL RELATIONSHIPS

Social relationships are established in educational institutions. Even if children could gain all the skills they need by reading books alone at home, they would miss some of the important benefits of schooling. A person develops social abilities through the give-and-take of peer group interactions; the playground is a school too.

Moreover, the friendships one makes in school can be an important resource for many years. For example, when a man needs a job he may telephone some of the "old boys" he knew in school 20 or 30 years before to ask if they know of any openings.

### JOB TRAINING

Job training is another function of educational institutions. This function is often emphasized by sociologists who study economic development. Some people see their schooling as an economic *investment* through which they add to their earning power by learning well-paid skills. Others consider their schooling as an end in itself, an item of *consumption* more than an investment. Both views are correct. It would be shortsighted to consider education only in terms of its effects on the economy, but it would be equally wrong to overlook those effects.

### TEACHING VALUES

Talcott Parsons has suggested that the classroom is especially important as a setting in which the child learns two values that are necessary to play adult roles in modern society: achievement and universalism.[2] He has pointed out that the family is based on the opposite values—ascription and particularism—and therefore cannot teach the child how to function in an impersonal social organization. Parents love their children because of who they are, not because of what they have done. Children do not have to earn their parents' admiration in a competitive market by outshining others. The relationship between parent and child is ascribed and particularistic.

Elementary school teachers are usually women who have a nurturant attitude toward children similar to the parent's. As children progress to higher grades they learn that teachers measure out approval according to the pupil's performance. All pupils are judged by the same standards. This is training for new values—achievement and universalism. In order to function in most adult roles a person must be motivated to perform well according to certain universal standards, and this is not a lesson that can be learned at mother's knee.

## CERTIFICATION

The certification function of educational institutions is a subject of much debate. Some say it is vital, while others argue that it is a social evil and must be eliminated.

In all the technologically advanced societies jobs are given to those who have certificates and diplomas; the better the job, the more prestigious the diploma has to be. But who gets the prestigious diplomas? There are two answers, both partly true. Answer number one is that the deserving people get the diplomas—the ones who are bright, steady, and hardworking. The others drop out or cannot keep up. Tests are given along the way to sort students into the "streams" they

Schools and universities that once admitted only white males now train women and minority students as well. These students are preparing for military careers.

belong in — a process not unlike grading eggs: Extra Large Grade As go on to college and a profession; Medium Grade Bs go to trade school and a menial job.

Answer number two is that the children from the upper and middle classes get the diplomas. Modern society has no hereditary aristocracy, but its upper classes pass along their privileges to their young in indirect ways. They provide them with good schooling, which is the ticket to high status.

Because both answers are partly true, they each have to be taken seriously, though they are incompatible. One answer emphasizes the importance of quality; the other emphasizes equality. It follows from the first answer that tests, "streams," and other competitive processes are defensible because they safeguard high-quality job performance. The most able people are given the most complex jobs. Every egg to its proper carton, every student to his or her proper occupation. It follows from answer number two that all students should be treated alike throughout their schooling; no departure should be permitted from the principle of equality of opportunity. However, it is not clear whether the principles of equality and quality can be reconciled, and if so, how.

## Trends in education

The "education explosion" is occurring at the same time as the "population explosion." As a result the number of students and teachers has multiplied at a fantastic rate. Meeting this demand will be one of the greatest challenges of our time. It must be recognized, however, that

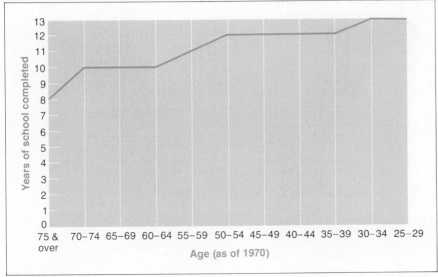

**FIGURE 14.1**

*One result of the U.S. emphasis on mass education is that people are staying in school for a longer period of time than they did in the past. Half the people aged 75 had completed 8 years of schooling or less, whereas half the people aged 25 had completed 13 years of schooling or more.*

Years of school completed

Age (as of 1970)

*Source:* Data from U.S. Bureau of Census, Census of Population 1970, Vol. I. Characteristics of the Population, Part I. U.S. Summary, sec. 2.

the educational problems facing the developed countries are different from those facing less developed countries. Here we will compare the situations of the United States, Canada, and the Third World.

### THE UNITED STATES

The American emphasis on popular education began very early. Within a few years after settlement all the New England colonies began putting up schoolhouses and hiring schoolmasters.[3] Today the United States provides a larger percentage of its citizens with higher education than any other nation. The quality of higher education in the United States is variable, of course. However, studies have shown that the average level of student performance is as high as or higher than it was a century or more ago.

The peak period of educational expansion for both the United States and Canada occurred when the postwar "baby boom" children passed through the school system, which had to expand to make room for them. Most of these students are now adults and the birth rate is declining, so some primary and secondary schoolrooms are empty. Universities also have declining enrollments. Yet a higher percentage of young people will enter colleges and universities in the years ahead than at any other time or in any other society in history.

#### Supplying the job market

Compared to the Soviet Union and much of Europe (especially Great Britain), the

**FIGURE 14.2**

*Median annual salaries of doctoral scientists, engineers, and humanists by field of employment, 1977*

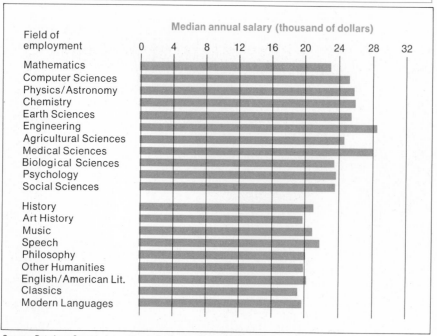

*Source:* Data from Commission on Human Resources, National Reaearch Council, Washington, D.C., 1977.

American educational system is remarkably unspecialized. The English boy or girl of 14 is already well along a specialized channel of studies that will get narrower and narrower as the years pass. However, the American boy or girl may be close to graduating from college before he or she must make a commitment to one particular subject, and even after that point it is not uncommon to change over into a new field. The broad education provided by the American school system gives a college graduate the basic skills needed for a wide range of occupational roles.

Postgraduate training, however, is quite specialized in the United States, and an M.A. or a Ph.D. program prepares a person for a very limited range of roles. With respect to these roles the problem of coordinating manpower needs with educational programs becomes severe. Universities increase or decrease their graduate admissions on the basis of social demand, political pressure, and availability of funds. Less attention is ordinarily paid to the question of whether the jobs for which students are being trained will be there when they receive their degrees.

The future availability of jobs can be predicted more accurately for some fields than for others, though economic factors make this task more difficult. For example, until the end of the 1960s the U.S. Office of Education predicted a huge need for scientists. Partly because the Vietnam War upset the U.S. economy and partly because the predictions were inaccurate, by the end of 1960s it became clear that the supply of newly trained scientists with Ph.D.'s was far greater than the demand. It is now estimated that the oversupply of scientists will continue until about 1985.[4]

When adults share in children's learning experiences, learning becomes easier and more pleasurable.

Mike Mazzaschi/Stock, Boston

### Variations in the quality of education

Schools aren't all equal. Consider, for example, the average amount spent per pupil in different states. In 1975 Mississippi spent $834 per pupil, or only 40 percent as much as New York, which spent $2005 per pupil.[5] Moreover, even within a given area there is great inequality. Suburban areas often spend twice as much per pupil as nearby city slums.[6]

Moreover, access to higher education is by no means equal for all Americans. Many high school graduates who decide not to go to college make that decision at least partly for financial reasons. High schools in some low-income areas do not offer the courses that students need for admission to their own state universities.

In reality, it is the children of well-to-do parents who most often go to college. The effect of this is that tax dollars support the education of middle- and upper-income families. To be sure, the whole society benefits from a well-educated population. But social scientists have been troubled by the possibility that the system perpetuates inequality. We'll come back to this issue later in the chapter.

### CANADA

It is hard to say much that is generally true about education in Canada because situations differ so widely from one province to another. Education is a provincial matter, not a federal one. In several provinces taxpayers specify whether their dollars will be used to pay for Catholic or Protestant schools, which may be run by entirely separate administrations. The Catholic–Protestant division usually coincides with the division between the French-speaking and English-speaking communities. Some of the most serious conflicts in Canadian history have developed out of this situation.

For a very long time—in fact until quite recently—Francophones have been less well educated than Anglophones. One reason was that the educational system in French-speaking areas was old-fashioned. It provided little practical or vocational training but emphasized a classical education. Naturally, many pupils who expected to become ordinary workers found this kind of education dull and difficult—so they dropped out early. However, in recent years the "classical colleges" have been completely reorganized. Quebec now has a number of popular institutions called CEGEPS (Collèges d'Enseignement Général et Professionnel), which fill a need for something between the high school and the university. Students attend for about two years and may take a variety of practical courses as well as college-preparatory courses. These institutions are succeeding in bringing the Québécois population into line with the English Canadian population in terms of job training.

Higher education has boomed in Canada in the past fifteen years or so. In the ten years between 1960 and 1970 the number of B.A.'s and similar degrees awarded in Canadian universities more than tripled. The number of advanced degrees increased even more. This expansion has made it necessary to invite foreign scholars to staff university faculties. One result is that many Canadians are afraid that certain subjects (e.g., literature and the social sciences) may be taught from a foreign point of view, using mainly American sources. This concern has stimulated renewed nationalism, in which more attention has been devoted to developing distinctively Canadian culture. At the same time, as so many Canadians are earning advanced degrees and are prepared to fill university teaching positions, an effort is being made to fill those posts with Canadians, not foreigners. This is simply one example of a difficulty that occurs in one form or another everywhere—the difficulty of coordinating the training of educated experts with changes in the labor market. It is very hard to plan many years ahead in order to produce people with the proper training to fill jobs that will become available in the future. This problem is even more serious in the developing nations.

## THE THIRD WORLD

The new nations are experiencing a major crisis. Their populations are increasing fast. At the same time, their citizens are demanding that all students be given more education than their parents received. It's an impossible situation. All the new nations give very high priority to educational spending, but it is never enough. Besides, there is another problem: In order to get qualified teachers, the government must pay salaries comparable to those offered by industry. But industry becomes more productive every year and can pay its workers larger salaries because their work is more profitable. Teachers' salaries have to be raised just to keep up. But teachers don't become more productive over time. That is, an average teacher cannot teach more children or teach them any better this year than last year. Therefore, just to teach the same number of children for the same length of time, the government has to keep paying more and more. And of course today there are more children, and each one wants more schooling.

The developing nations are having little success in meeting the demand for education. The number of illiterate people in the world is increasing, not decreasing. This trend, unfortunately, will probably continue for some time.

**FIGURE 14.3**

*The world's secondary education enroll-
ments 1950–1970. The absolute numbers of illiterates are increasing in the
world, despite the increasing percentage
of children in school. This is because of
the population explosion, which has
provided more pupils than any country
can afford to educate.*

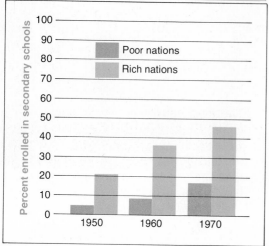

*Source:* Data from John W. Meyer, John Boli-Bennett, and Christopher
Chase-Dunn. "Convergence and Divergence in Development". *Annual
Review of Sociology,* I. Palo Alto, Calif.: Annual Reviews, 1975, p. 227.

## Liberalism and conservativism—the main issues

In previous chapters I
have asked you to decide what you think of a
given issue. As we go on defining issues, pay
attention to which side you are on each time.
This should help you see more clearly
whether you are mainly conservative or
mainly liberal on most issues. Of course you
can be liberal on one matter and conservative on another, but if you are like most people you will find that you are fairly consistent. Attitudes tend to cluster in a regular
way. After you get a feel for these patterns of

consistency, you will often find it possible to
guess how strangers view most issues after
you have heard their opinions on two or
three topics.

When people talk about education, two
issues distinguish *most* liberals from *most*
conservatives. The first has to do with the
relationship between education and social
change. The second issue is the link between
education and social status.

### EDUCATION FOR STABILITY OR REFORM?

Let's start with the first question: Does education mostly encourage social change or
does it tend to keep things the way they are?
The most obvious difference between liberals and conservatives is in the way they view
social change. Liberals welcome it; conservatives are wary of it. They have different ideas
about progress. A conservative thinks progress is a slow, evolutionary process. A liberal is much more likely to assume that
we can do something to create progress,
now, with a snap of the fingers, almost. And
the favorite liberal proposal for solving
social problems is usually this: Educate
people.

As conservatives go, Herbert Spencer
must have been one of the greatest champi-
ons of all time. He believed that human progress was slow and couldn't be rushed. Reform schemes of any kind were unrealistic
dreams that could only cause trouble. Progress could occur only through evolution—
the survival of the fittest and the *nonsurvival*
of the *unfit.* Reformers who want to help the
unfit survive only interfere with the process
of evolution. Trying to educate somebody
with low potential was useless, Spencer
thought. Thus it would be impossible to increase the potential of the working class by
providing free schooling. He wanted to educate only those children whose parents
could pay the fees. This view was social

Darwinism—the extreme in conservative social thought.

Lester Frank Ward was a wholly different sort of fellow. I imagine him as enthusiastic and optimistic. He was a midwesterner who had reached a high position in the American educational system through study. To him, knowledge was the major source of social change. Through education humankind could control its own evolution and progress beyond the law of the jungle, which Spencer believed was part of human nature.

Of course progressives followed Ward, not Spencer. Today liberals believe education can be used to fight all kinds of social evils. Teenagers are given driver education, antidrug education, sex education, and religious education, and are expected to become cautious, sober, chaste, and devout as a result. This doesn't always work, of course—but not for the reasons Spencer suggested. It is not because human nature is unchangeable but, rather, because driving, drug use, sexual behavior, and religious involvement are influenced by group pressure, not just by individual judgment. And it's not easy to change social norms by educating individuals. It's easy to present facts, but it's not easy to control group interaction. Education presents information. But you and I organize our lives on the basis of feelings, relationships, the desire to win approval, and the like, as well as information. These factors limit the ability of education to remake society.

There is another point of view besides the liberal and conservative approaches: the radical view. If Spencer was the champion of conservatives, Marx was the champion of radicals. But in this case Marx agreed in part with the conservative outlook. He would not encourage people to try to change society by reeducating people, not because he believed in the survival of the fittest but because the educational system is a conservative institution. It is part of the "superstructure," and as such it takes its orders from the ruling class.

Nicholas Sapiena/Stock, Boston

*Third world nations are struggling to educate their people in any way possible.*

Teachers will be fired if they try to bring about any important social change. Besides, they can teach only what they know, and what they know depends on what they have a chance to find out. The ruling class can control what workers find out. Who owns the newspapers? The ruling class. Who controls the spread of ideas? The ruling class. The rise and fall of various social classes depends on changes in technology, not on changes in the educational system.

Does education generally serve to maintain the status quo or to change society? On the whole, schools seem to be cautious in the teaching of ideas, at least at the elementary and secondary levels. Higher education is different, however. It rewards people for originality and daring—at least sometimes. Yet, conservative as they are, grade schools and high schools serve a vital function. They teach students skills that the society needs. In this sense even a conservative institution is necessary. Besides, schooling does make a person more open to new ideas, and to this extent it leads to social change in the long run.

### THE LINK BETWEEN EDUCATION AND STATUS

Now for the next question. You know that there is a strong relationship between education and social status. Well-educated people get better jobs and more prestige and authority, on the whole, than poorly educated people. Is this fair? If so, why? If not, why not?

This question is a strong test of a person's conservativism or liberalism. Most people, both conservatives and liberals, will say that this situation is fair. If you say it is unfair, you are either a very militant liberal or a radical. You object to the amount of inequality in modern society and would like to see major changes in our stratification system.

You will recall from Chapter 9 that the Davis–Moore theory of stratification[7] assumes that there are a fixed number of jobs in society and that the high rewards of some jobs are necessary in order to fill those jobs with qualified people. The skills required by these jobs are gained mostly through education. Therefore the competition for a high-quality education is intense.

*Education is used to instill the cultural values of a society.*

Ruiko/DPI

I've already described the educational process as similar to an egg-sorting process in which students are sorted into different cartons to be shipped to the appropriate jobs after graduation. Employers call employment agencies and order certain grades of eggs. They want college graduates for junior-executive jobs and high school graduates for jobs in the shop. They are prepared to pay more for the college eggs. Is this fair? And is it fair to ask for a college egg for the executive job? Is it reasonable to make a college degree a requirement for certain jobs and not others? Most people assume that it is. If you ask employers why they want college graduates for certain jobs, they will probably say that the job will be done better if they hire better-educated people. What other explanation could there be?

Randall Collins has suggested another reason, however. Employers have to work with junior executives every day. They have to train them to take over their own jobs when they retire. Maybe they just like to be around college graduates because college graduates understand the kinds of jokes they tell, know enough to serve the kind of Scotch they drink, read novels by Saul Bellow and Doris Lessing too, and so forth. They enjoy their company. Maybe they're only *telling* themselves that college graduates do the job better.

When we discussed Max Weber's theory of stratification we saw that Weber believed certain groups, called *status groups*, to have a very strong sense of group consciousness. Members of a social class may or may not identify with each other as a group — usually they don't. But members of a status group do. And money is not the key factor determining what status group you belong to. Many people have little money but have what my grandmother used to call "breeding" — taste, style, sophistication, polish.

In general, people are very aware of whether they belong to the same status group or not. It's a matter of life style; it's unmistak-

Cary Wolinsky/Stock, Boston

*Should teachers always reflect the values of the community that employs them?*

able. Weber noted that high-status groups hold onto their high prestige by emphasizing their special life style and "high" culture. What is the main basis of membership? Education.

Here is where Collins abandons the conservative point of view — the functionalist explanation.[8] He argues that there is no *functional need* to hire educated people for the high-status jobs. The job could probably be done well enough by a person with much less education. But Weber was right: Members of a high-status group prefer to hire as their coworkers and successors other members of their own group — people with similar

415

interests, values, background, and tastes. And the best way to be sure of hiring such people is to advertise for college graduates.

If Collins is right, then the relationship between education and social status is not fair. If it were functionally necessary, it would be fair. Do you agree with him? There is little evidence that conclusively supports either position. Both Collins and Ivar Berg[9] have done research that suggests that well-educated people are not necessarily more productive than less well-educated people—and they may even be less productive at

times. But their evidence is skimpy, and the issue is far from settled.

Moreover, it won't do to carry Collins' argument to extremes. Some jobs really do require special training. If you drop out of medical school, I won't let you take out my appendix. However, it may be true that educational requirements are often exaggerated beyond the level that is functionally necessary. When this happens hiring becomes unfair, for it discriminates against people who may be equally able to do the job.

# SOCIAL RESEARCH:
## Sociologists at Work

During the past decade or so researchers who specialize in the sociology of education have become public figures. It is their research that gets reported in *Time* magazine. They are the ones who hold press conferences to announce new findings. The reason for this stardom is that educational research is closely related to certain vital political issues. People care a great deal about the effects of various educational policies—such as whether racial integration is beneficial, whether busing is the way to achieve integration, whether women have been discriminated against in higher education, whether preschool education helps slum children catch up with rich kids, and so on. Millions of dollars are spent for research on such topics. And the findings are influential. Even the courts take them into account as evidence in some cases.

In this section we will deal with two very broad topics that have many different angles. The first one is the controversial issue of equality in education. The second is the question of how much education affects students and what kind of education affects students most powerfully.

### AN EQUAL EDUCATION FOR ALL?

We generally hold the view that all students—rich and poor, black and white, male and female—should have an equal chance to get the kind of education they want—the kind that will enable them to participate in society on an equal basis. But two important questions need to be answered: (1) How much difference does it make in the amount a child learns whether he or she goes to an excellent, rich school or a poorly equipped, overcrowded slum school? Is it because the schools are so different that students turn out so unequal in their abilities? (2) If we equalized the amount and quality of the education offered to all children, would this equalize their incomes later in life? Studies by James Coleman and Christopher Jencks were designed to answer these questions.

### THE COLEMAN REPORT

I have already mentioned the relationship between education and occupational status—income, prestige, and the like. Education pays. Moreover, as we have seen, the schooling of Americans differs greatly in quality. For a long time social scientists believed that the only hope of breaking the cycle of poverty was to bring the education of poor students (often black students) up to the same level as that received by more advantaged students. The educational system was one institution that could be changed. Not all institutions can be readily changed by public policy. So let's make the schools more equal, open up new opportunities for higher education, admit people who might not have been admitted before. This idea was accepted by almost all liberals during the 1960s as the most promising way to create more equality in American society.

Then James Coleman announced the results of a huge study that he had done for the U.S. government.[10] Pandemonium resulted. It showed that all of the assumptions of social scientists, and of liberal citizens and government leaders as well, had been mistaken. It was not unequal early schooling that created children's unequal levels of achievement in school but mainly factors beyond the control of the schools, such as the family. Students' family background determined their achievement much more than the schools they attended. Children from high-status families learned more than children from low-status families, regardless of whether their schools were modern and well equipped, with small classes and well-paid, well-trained teachers, or run-down, overcrowded, and understaffed. Social scientists suddenly realized that they didn't know what could be done to produce students whose levels of achievement would be more equal. Equalizing educational opportunities would not create a group of students with equal levels of ability.

## JENCKS ON INEQUALITY

But why was this goal so important? Why should we worry if some students can read and do math problems twice as well as other students? Why is it important to produce graduates with equal levels of ability? The answer is that we assume that their ability determines their life chances later, as they take jobs. And we are very disturbed to see how unequal life chances are. If people's abilities were more equal, we think they would earn similar salaries. That goal—equality of income and life chances—seems very desirable. Fairness and justice demand that the rich should not earn vastly more than the poor.

So it was assumed that if everyone had about the same education, then inequality would decrease. And in order to create equal results (e.g., equal income) the only hope was to create more equal education. We have already discussed the research of Randall Collins and Ivar Berg, among others, who pointed out that the average college graduate earns far more than the average grade-school dropout. Unequal education, then, seems to perpetuate stratification or so we all believed.

But in 1972, while liberals were still stunned by the Coleman Report, Christopher Jencks published his study, which shook them up even more.[11] It found that equal education would not do much to equalize income or any other life chances.

This seems to contradict everything I've told you up to this point. But it really doesn't. What I said was that the *average* person with, say, a B.A. degree earns a lot more than the *average* high school dropout. That's true. The more education one has, the higher one's income, on the average. You knew that before you ever read a sociology book.

But you also knew something else. As Jencks pointed out, while educational achievement affects your chances of earning money, it is not the only factor involved. There is still much more inequality than can be explained by differences in education. Suppose you know that a friend has had two years of college and is now working. Can you guess her salary on this basis? Of course not. There is a great deal of inequality among people with two years of college. Some are millionaires; others are living in poverty. Education is obviously not the only thing that determines how much one earns in a year. The average income of the person with a B.A. is more than the average income of the high school graduate, but not all B.A.'s earn exactly the same amount, nor do all high school graduates earn the same amount. So Jencks used statistics to show that if all the people in the United States had the same level of education, the amount of inequality of income would be reduced only very slightly.

What does determine income, then? Jencks says that luck plays a major role: whether you can hit a hockey puck well enough to play on a professional team, for example, or whether hail destroys your crops, or whether the Dow Jones average rises or falls, or whether the boss notices when you drink more than you should at the Christmas party. Many things besides education can affect income.

If this is the case, how can we equalize incomes? Jencks suggests that this must be done directly. If some citizens have too little money, give them more. There is no other way. Of course Jencks is aware that direct redistribution of income will meet tremendous political resistance. But he still says that there is no other realistic way to achieve greater equality.

As a matter of fact Jencks suggests that we can feel relieved about his findings, not discouraged by them. We had pinned too many hopes on the school. We had imagined that it could solve all of our problems. It can't. This means we can relax a bit. We don't have to have homogeneous schools, like peas in a pod. If equality of education were so important, the schools would have to be exactly alike to be fair. But we don't all agree on what they should be like. Parents have all sorts of contradictory opinions about how schools should function and what they should teach. Why not let people choose? Not all children are the same. Some flourish in a free school without competition. Others like to work on arts and crafts. Others want to play with computers all the time. Why not let them?

Jencks has suggested an "educational voucher" system. He proposes that the government pay each child's portion of the education budget to the school his or her parents choose. If the parents are disappointed by the school, they can "vote with their feet" by taking their tax money to a different school. This idea would encourage variety in education, not equality. But since we don't all agree on what is a good education and what is a poor one, we may as well allow for freedom of choice. I agree.

### EDUCATION'S IMPACT ON STUDENTS

How much does education affect people? Does it change their values? Does it affect their personalities, their politics? Can it stimulate students to continue growing intellectually? Can it offset unfortunate home situations? How much can education do?

A related question is this: What kind of educational institutions have the most impact on their students? Are some systems more effective in motivating students than others?

Obviously, these issues are far too broad to be answered fully here. I can touch on a few studies that treat these questions, but only briefly.

### Changing the student

How much you get from your schooling depends only partly on how good that schooling is—whether the classes are small, the teacher well trained, the laboratory well supplied, and so on. What you get depends even more on your own attitudes and motivations. If you want high achievement, have a deeper respect for scholarship than for fun and games, and feel self-confident enough to be critical of what you read and are taught, you will learn a lot and be able to use what you learn effectively.

But these personal factors—aspiration levels, self-esteem, value orientations, and the like—are developed outside the school, mainly in private social relationships—in the home, the play group, and the extended family. By the time a child reaches school, the likely outcome of his or her education is already partly established. What can the school do to change attitudes and motivations?

A number of studies have been done over the years to determine how much educational institutions can do to change the values and attitudes of students. I will mention some research based on very different levels of education—the preschool level and the college level.

Research on preschool education has been devoted largely to finding ways of stimulating culturally deprived children so that they will learn as quickly as children from high-status, well-educated families. These programs were influenced by the work of Martin Deutsch, who began providing enriched environments for Harlem preschoolers in 1962. By 1966 a much larger effort, called Project Head Start, was begun by the U.S. government. This project was designed to give poor children a short nursery school program before they started school. This "compensatory education" was supposed to create enthusiasm for school and teach poor children certain skills that would allow them to compete on a more equal basis with advantaged children. About half a million children go through such programs each year, and the effects at first are quite positive. Unfortunately, the advantages do not last beyond the third grade. Most of the children from poor families fall behind their middle-class schoolmates by this time, whether or not they participated in Head Start.[12] This research suggests that compensatory education must be

*By the time a child begins the first day of school, the likely outcome of his or her education is already partly established.*

Peter Vandermark/Stock, Boston

far-reaching and must be continued over a long period if it is to offset a deprived life style.

The findings of studies of the effects of college on social values are quite different from those of studies of preschool children. For one thing, their goal was not to find out whether intelligence or academic achievement could be raised but, rather, to find out how much college liberalized students' values, made them less authoritarian, more flexible, and so on.

Different studies have had different results, and one must conclude that some colleges have quite an impact on students while others do not. Small, elite, liberal-arts colleges seem to influence students quite strongly, and their influence lasts many years. For example, Theodore Newcomb's study of mainly upper-middle-class women students at Bennington College in Vermont found that these students became quite liberal, even radical, during their college years and were still liberal in outlook when the follow-up study was done twenty-five years later.[13]

The elite residential college has a strong student culture oriented toward intellectual inquiry and the exchange of ideas. Large, more varied universities, especially those whose students commute to school and do not live together in a close community, have far less impact on the values and attitudes of their students. It seems that it is not so much the influence of the faculty or the course content that changes students' values as the influence of the peer group, which maintains a stimulating and close-knit subculture.

### Competition in Education

When we consider what sort of schooling we prefer, many of us consider the degree of competitiveness as the most important factor. Some want free schools, where competition with other students is minimal, while others feel that competition stimulates good work and makes education challenging and exciting. What are the effects of competition? Is it harmful, as the supporters of free schools believe? Or is there a way of using competition to motivate students without threatening the self-esteem of those who do not perform well?

Studies have repeatedly shown that competition is a powerful stimulus to achievement. Many people benefit from this stimulation, and graduates of free schools are less motivated to achieve, possibly because they have been taught that competition is not a legitimate value. Coleman has proposed a system of education that would use competition but not individualism.[14] This idea occurred to him as he analyzed the results of a study of students in a number of different American high schools and discovered the resistance of their subcultures to intellectual life. Far from supporting learning, group norms in many high schools punished anyone who was so foolhardy as to be a good student. On the other hand, a boy who excelled in sports was usually admired, though both scholarship and athletics are competitive activities. Coleman pointed out that the two competitive systems

Peter Southwick/Stock, Boston

*Participation in athletic contests has been encouraged in the United States as a way of developing team spirit and aggression.*

Arthur Grace/Stock, Boston

were organized differently. In trying to get good grades students compete as individuals *against* all the other members of the group. When they excel, they make some of their friends seem dull in comparison. Groups have ways of showing their dislike of anyone who does too well in such a contest, and most bright students learn to channel their energies in some other direction simply for the sake of good social relationships.

Athletic contests, however, are team sports. When an athlete performs some great feat it helps his or her team win, and the other members share in his or her glory. It is not surprising that students prefer team sports to individual competitions. Coleman suggests that the same principle of competition be used to encourage intellectual activities. A few such events do take place—for example, debate contests and science fairs between schools—but many more could be organized. Indeed, the whole system of grading could be turned into an intramural competition between chemistry teams, history teams, and the like. The Soviet education system uses this kind of competition a great deal, and it works there. Maybe we should use it more too.

But could we? I am reminded of Marx's notion that the educational system always repre-

sents the social structure it is part of. Marx thought that education simply can never *lead* social change. If he was right, our educational system has to produce good capitalists. And what is a good capitalist? Someone who competes well as an *individual* against other *individuals.* Our economy works on the assumption that each individual struggles to outdo the others on his or her own merits. We don't get promoted as a team. We don't get rewarded for our team efforts. Schools have to prepare children for the economic roles they will fill as adults. If this is so, maybe we would make students unable to play these roles well if we used a system of group competition instead of giving out grades and prizes to individuals.

It is true that you are supposed to try to outshine your best friend in school. But there is role conflict involved. If you have close friends, do you want to make them look bad in comparison with you? No—you may feel a little guilty about doing so. I used to lie to my friends and tell them I got a B when I actually got an A. So there is a conflict between the two sides of your role as a student. The competitive side is successful only when you win. The noncompetitive, friendly side is successful only when you lose. No wonder most of us are undecided about doing well in school.

# SOCIAL POLICY:
## Issues and Viewpoints

### THE PRODUCTIVITY
### OF EDUCATIONAL SYSTEMS

Sociologists have pointed out a problem that educational planners will have to solve: how to get more education per dollar—or rupee, yen, or peso, as the case may be. It is a serious matter that, given present educational methods, every

nation must spend an increasing portion of its national budget just to keep its educational output at the current level—and that level is not good enough. Moreover, it is very hard to establish a rational system of priorities in spending on education, and it is even more difficult to introduce new educational methods. What policies seem promising as ways of meeting the increasing demand for useful schooling?

The most important goal for new countries is to achieve literacy for all, which, according to UNESCO estimates, requires four or more years of schooling. However, in many countries four years of schooling may not produce functional literacy, for not all educational systems are equally effective; many students repeat grades or drop out between grades. Besides the ability to write, simple arithmetic can be most useful; farmers can become more effective in their planning if they have the ability to add, subtract, multiply, and divide so they need more than four years.

Many community workers in developing countries have missed the point about what should be taught in the schoolroom; they give adults lessons in hygiene, agricultural technology, and the like when they should be concentrating on basic literacy.[15] After farmers can read, it will be easy to teach them other facts by passing out booklets. Literacy has a "multiplier" effect: Once a population is widely literate, additional levels of education can be reached much more efficiently.

On the other hand, modern technology may also be of great help to educators in developing countries and advanced countries alike. Some promising experiments have used television and radio for mass education. The "open university" in Britain depends heavily on correspondence and mass media instruction, and at least one Latin American country plans to use television for basic instruction throughout its elementary schools. These new ideas can greatly increase educational productivity, though of course they will not replace all of the functions of educational institutions. Considerable experience in university classrooms suggests that television is a fairly effective, but unpopular, method of learning. However, in a few years you may be able to check out a cassette-recorded television course from the library and play it at home whenever you want to—even while cooking breakfast or taking a bath. Such flexibility may make education via television far more popular than it is today.

There have been other proposals for improving educational productivity—some of them far more daring than the idea of television instruction. Consider Ivan Illich's ideas, for example.[16] Illich is a former priest who has a dramatic style of speaking and lots of offbeat ideas. He loves to challenge our assumptions about what is good about modern institutions. (For example, he argues that modern medicine does about as much harm as good.) Here I want to mention his recommendations for improving education in the developing countries.

Close the schools, says Illich. He claims that whenever schooling is set up as an official institution in a society, people get the idea that the only way to become educated is by attending classes. They come to believe that they don't know anything important unless they learned it in a class taught by a certified instructor. They believe they are unable to learn whatever they need to know by looking around and finding out for themselves. They become helpless, passive consumers of education, uncritical, unable to take charge of getting the knowledge they need or want. Unless it is organized for them and presented in a classroom, they think they can't learn.

This is nonsense, according to Illich. Just look at the things you know: how to speak English, how to knit, how to cook and keep house, how to write checks, how to drive a car, how to use a camera, how to swim, how to fix a flat tire or a broken zipper, how to play the guitar or tie a trout fly. You may know the names of the entire Dallas Cowboy football team or the reason why Libras should or shouldn't marry Scorpios or the names and present whereabouts of all the Watergate burglars or how Catherine the Great supposedly died when a horse was dropped on her. (If you don't know that one, I can't tell you here. But you can ask someone else, which is how you found out all those other things.)

See how much you learned outside of school? Then why go to classes at all? You really go to get the diploma. Illich suggests that we stop giving out diplomas. Then people will start finding out things just because they want to know them. Illich would like to see a number of substitutes for regular schools. One idea is to provide places full of the kinds of things people need to use, such as car engines, photographic darkrooms, and sewing machines. This would be a place to go to learn how to use equipment.

Another of Illich's ideas is the "skill exchange." This would allow all of us to list our skills and the conditions under which we would be willing to teach others what we know, along with our addresses. Then we could "earn" lessons by giving lessons, thereby contributing credits to our account. When I read Illich's book I decided to use this idea in a course I was teaching on the sociology of education. Once a week we would spend an hour exchanging lessons. On the blackboard I recorded what each student offered to teach and what each student wanted to learn. We set up contracts to last, we expected, several weeks or even months. Everyone thought it would be an interesting experiment.

It wasn't. First of all, the subjects people offered to teach were limited to trivial matters that required no preparation. No one offered to teach calculus or French or music theory or logic, though all of the students were at least in their third year at the university and they all had advanced knowledge in some area and a fair knowledge of many complex subjects. They offered to teach crocheting, ballroom dancing, kite making, and other activities with no intellectual content. I'm not against crocheting. My point is that the students all underrated how much they had to contribute to other people. And so, to please the teacher (me), they signed up to learn something silly that seemed like a waste of time, given the pressure of their other courses. And then, of course, they didn't show up. In a couple of weeks it was clear that everyone was fooling around or cutting class on skill exchange day. We gave up.

Then we talked about it. I concluded that we had proved Illich wrong. If college students couldn't organize and maintain a skill exchange, if they doubted their own ability to teach so much that they offered only frivolous courses, how could anybody expect people in developing countries to do better — people who had maybe 4 or 5 years of schooling, compared to the 16 or so years that the members of my class had? But the students concluded that the experiment had proved Illich right. That is, they had been part of the educational system all their lives. They had come to believe that only a certified teacher in a class situation could teach anything worth learning. If they had been paid for their work, they would have taken the job seriously — for then they would have been real teachers and would have been expected to offer good instruction. But this was impossible for them as students. Their sixteen years in school had reduced

their confidence in their ability to educate themselves or each other. Besides, they pointed out, they were enrolled in other courses that had requirements for which they would be graded. It was wise for them to put all their attention into studying for those courses. They wondered why they should learn calculus or French from each other. They would rather save the energy for the courses that counted.

I had believed that my class was the perfect group on which to experiment with Illich's scheme. They believed they were the worst possible group for such an experiment. They believed that Illich's own logic would show that they could not take responsibility for their own education — that their schooling had made them dependent and passive in learning. The only fair test of Illich's plan would have to be made on a group of people who had little or no education, people who were not also enrolled in any courses elsewhere

If my students are right, this is a discouraging conclusion. I never thought there was any hope of educating people by closing the schools. But I did think that the skill exchange idea might *add to* regular schooling. This seemed very promising. But it appears that regular schooling reduces the possibility of carrying out the skill exchange idea. In that case I don't think it could offer anything very useful to the people in developing countries who must find ways of increasing the productivity of their educational systems. Closing the schools is hardly the way to start improving education, despite Illich's persuasive arguments.

## EDUCATION AND THE LABOR MARKET

Earlier I mentioned the difficulty of coordinating specialized education with the changing labor market, especially in the case of graduate-level education, which is very expensive but often goes to waste when no suitable jobs are available for those who complete their training. There are two problems — one technical and the other organizational and political. The technical problem is the difficulty of predicting manpower requirements in various fields several years in advance. It is not possible to be very exact in predicting what kinds of jobs will be available in the future. Economists and demographers are working hard to solve this problem. The other problem is that the predictions that are made do not always influence educational planning. It is usually the *current*, not the predicted, labor market that determines enrollment in various advanced training programs, but this method is not very efficient. For example, one less developed region found itself short of doctors. This led to a great popular demand for increased admissions to medical schools, which had already expanded according to plan. Many university buildings were converted into medical schools at great cost. The first graduates filled the shortage, and later graduates couldn't find jobs. Soon the expensive new medical schools were half empty and the entering students were competing for admission to agronomy courses, the newest field to show a labor shortage.

In effect, then, educational expansion should be planned in response to manpower predictions, not popular demand. However, in a free society popular demand is backed by political pressure that is hard for a government to ignore. The public must understand this problem before it can be solved.

## QUALITY AND EQUALITY

Having considered the issue of equality, what policies seem most reasonable now, and why?

Unfortunately, we can't do away with stratification among adults by providing equal education for children and youths. But there is still good reason to provide higher-quality schooling for deprived youths. People should have as much schooling as they need and want—and the *kind* of schooling that they need and want. Moreover, segregated schooling is unjust, simply because being left out is a demoralizing experience, even if the segregated schools are attractive buildings with small classes, well-trained teachers, and so on. Moreover, there is plenty of evidence that black children who are excluded by being segregated experience many important handicaps that may have lasting effects.

### Busing

Not only have the courts acted to enforce integration in all American schools, but the American population, both black and white, generally believes that integration is a good thing for their children. Unfortunately, because of segregation in housing, especially in urban areas, the only way to achieve racial balance in the schools is busing. And most Americans disapprove of busing. They believe, on the whole, that it is better for children to go to local schools, where parents have a chance to know each other and to participate in school functions together. Hence, the issue of busing has become a bitter one in recent years. No one can see a solution that provides for widespread school integration without busing. And attempts to set up busing plans have been defeated in many areas. This is an issue, then, that needs further public attention.

### Variety or homogeneity?

When we plan to create equality in schooling, what we mean is to see to it that all schools have about the same degree of excellence. But how can we do this if we don't agree about what excellence is? My idea of a good school may be very different from yours. One of us might like free schools and the other schools that emphasize art or science or religion.

Lacking agreement, we generally solve the issue by simply making schools as much alike as possible. However, pupils probably benefit from different kinds of educational experiences. There are two approaches to providing equality. One is the "roast-beef-and-mashed-potatoes" approach. You serve everyone the same dish, choosing a menu that most people can tolerate but no one finds exciting. The other approach is the "smorgasbord" system: Give everyone the right to go back to the serving table for whatever strikes his or her fancy—even if it's five helpings of pickled herring. Since we don't know that children are any the worse for filling up in school on the equivalent of pickled herring, why not let them? This is the plan Jencks favors in his proposal for educational vouchers—different kinds of schools for people to choose among.

## EDUCATION AND SOCIAL CHANGE

We have already discussed the debate between Spencer and Ward over whether education is a conservative force, teaching values and getting students to accept the status quo, or whether it is (or may be) a force for social change. Now we will take another look at this issue and try to decide which position is more nearly correct.

Sometimes education is conservative; sometimes it produces social change. As mentioned earlier, different levels of education have different kinds of effects. In the developing countries primary school education is enabling whole populations to do things that they could never have done before. Literacy enables people to read labels on cans, find their way around a strange city by the street signs, look through the want ads for jobs or used bicycles, and read the birth control leaflets that are handed out at the village well. These events *are* social change. There can be no doubt that the lives of literate people differ greatly from the lives of illiterate people. Thus in the developing countries primary school education has the most important impact.

Yet primary school education is almost always conservative. Governments organize school systems, and the schools almost always teach views approved by the government. Schoolteachers are not revolutionary leaders.

Many studies make this point. For example, polls asking opinions on racial issues show that a high school education has no impact on tolerance but a college education does.[17]

In fact there is a rather dramatic difference between the political and social values of people with a high school education and those with a college education. It seems fair to conclude that basic literacy brings a society into the modern world but that only higher education really stimulates people to question the values they are exposed to in daily life. The high school teacher is not as free to criticize as the university professor. More important, high school students usually live at home and are not as free to support ideas that their parents dislike as college students are. Finally, the nature of the intellectual work done at the university level requires students to do more critical thinking than they might do at a lower level, where simple memorization often is all that is required.

Perhaps it is for these reasons that university student movements have so often been a major force demanding social change in many societies. Such movements are far less active in the late 1970s than in the 1960s, but college-educated people are still the most progressive group in society, whether they are quiet or outspoken in calling for social reform.

It is likely that more and more people in North America will receive a higher education—perhaps even the majority. When this happens society will have a "built-in" drive for social change.

## SUMMARY

**1.** The main functions of education are (1) the transmission of civilization, (2) babysitting, (3) building national spirit, (4) establishing social relationships, (5) job training, (6) teaching values, and (7) certification.

**2.** The United States offers greater access to higher education than any other nation—nearly one-third of American youth earn a B.A. degree today. Education at the primary and secondary levels is not very difficult or specialized in North America, but higher education here is equal in quality to higher education in Europe. North American postgraduate education is generally superior to that available in Europe.

**3.** It's hard to predict job opportunities

for educated people. It seems likely that jobs will be scarce during the next ten years, especially for scientists.

**4.** American education is quite unequal from one region or community to another—some spend twice as much per child as others.

**5.** Less developed countries face great problems in meeting the demand for education of rapidly expanding populations.

**6.** Education is partly a conservative force in that teachers must teach what the government wants them to teach. However,

higher education is an important force for social change.

**7.** Collins has argued that the relationship between education and high status is not based on any real need to fill high-status positions with highly educated people. Rather, he believes that upper-status groups use education as a standard for judging life styles. They prefer to fill good jobs with "their own kind"—people whose tastes and values are similar to their own. Education is thus used as a way of discriminating against members of other status groups.

## KEY TERMS

**education**   a set of processes designed to transmit knowledge and skills and to develop mental abilities.

## FOR FURTHER READING

BOOCOCK, SARANE S. *Introduction to the Sociology of Learning.* Boston: Houghton Mifflin, 1972. This is a comprehensive treatment of the sociology of education, not as specialized as any other book on this list.

BRETON, RAYMOND. *Social and Academic Factors in the Career Decisions of Canadian Youth.* Ottawa: Canadian Department of Manpower and Immigration, 1972. A skilled survey analysis of the educational and occupational aspirations of high school students.

COLEMAN, JAMES S., ET AL. *Equality of Educational Opportunity.* Washington, D.C.: Government Printing Office, 1966. This is the original document that is usually referred to as the "Coleman Report." It caused a great stir throughout the social sciences and even in government, for its findings did not turn out as expected. On the whole, subsequent studies have tended to confirm its original findings, however.

HYMAN, HERBERT H.; CHARLES R. WRIGHT; and

JOHN SHELDON REED. *The Enduring Effects of Education.* Chicago: University of Chicago Press, 1975. The authors collected evidence from a variety of sources that prove in a dramatic way that schooling makes a tremendous difference in people's lives. Every additional year of education has effects that can be measured and that last a lifetime.

JENCKS, CHRISTOPHER, ET AL. *Inequality: A Reassessment of the Effect of Family and Schooling in America.* New York: Basic Books, 1972. An important study of inequality in the United States, concluding that it is less a result of unequal education than previous research had led us to believe. You will have to work a fair amount to read this book, but it is a major piece of research.

METZ, MARY HAYWOOD. *Classrooms and Corridors: The Crisis of Authority in Desegregated Secondary Schools.* Berkeley: University of California Press, 1978. A readable account of the way authority is maintained in different school settings. Metz observed interaction in two desegregated urban junior high schools.

ROSENTHAL, ROBERT, and LENORE JACOBSON. *Pygmalion in the Classroom.* New York: Holt, Rinehart & Winston, 1968. This is the study that demonstrated for the first time the effect of a teacher's expectations upon the performance of children.

STEINBERG, STEPHEN. *The Academic Melting Pot: Catholics and Jews in American Higher Educa-* *tion.* New York: McGraw-Hill, 1974. Is there anything incompatible about being religiously committed and being productive as a scholar? That's one question Steinberg tries to answer in this historical and survey study.

15

# POLITICS AND SOCIETY

In the distance, near the city hall square, there is bedlam. People milling about, shouting insults at one another. The electoral campaign is in full swing. Vote for this, vote for that. Vote for this one because he personifies promise. No, vote for that one because *he* personifies promise. Orators harangue the crowds. Applause, whistles. Trust me: I who this, I who that. There is no end to candidates. And each says the same thing. Each sacrifices his interests for those of the people: it should consider itself fortunate, the people, to have such defenders, such devoted friends. But the friends of the people are not each other's friends. Provocations, fights, pandemonium. Accusations fly back and forth. Exhortations: let us change society, let us change man. In the name of mutations, one does away with systems. Down with the Establishment, long live the Revolution. Disorders, riots. Coups d'état. Down with government, long live imagination. Down with life, long live death. I have heard these slogans before, in another place. Barcelona, Berlin. Men change, their cry remains.

—Elie Wiesel, *The Oath*
Random House, 1973

Their cry remains because politics is an unavoidable part of social life. It will always be with us, because human beings cannot agree on their goals. When people have different goals, coordination becomes necessary. And the process of coordination is politics, which is a polite way of saying domination. When my goals conflict with yours, one of us will win and the other will lose, unless one or both of us change our minds. So politics is about how a group of people with different goals manages to arrive at a common plan of action.

The task of political sociology is to show how this process works. Sometimes it is orderly and polite. The opponents may flatter each other, and when one side realizes that it is losing, its leaders may bravely face the television cameras, admit defeat, and take off for Palm Springs to play golf.

But politics is not always polite. Sometimes the opponents are openly hostile. Some regimes are tyrannical, using police force to silence their critics. Sometimes the outcome of politics is outright warfare.

Hence the saying that war is simply "a continuation of politics by other means."

Political sociologists must therefore study a variety of processes. Those who focus on democracies, such as the United States, Canada, and most European nations, may ask questions such as: How do interest groups and coalitions form and break down? What influences the extent to which citizens participate in politics? When do voters tend to support left-wing parties and when are they likely to support right-wing parties? How do people learn to favor those parties?

Political sociologists who study other societies are likely to ask questions such as: What determines whether a society will become democratic or totalitarian? Can we predict the results of rebellions, or when and where they will occur? What political developments can be expected in the Third World in coming years, and why?

We'll discuss a few of these questions later in the chapter. First I want to define a few of the terms that we will be using.

## Power, politics, and the state

### WHAT IS POLITICS?

By **politics** I mean any action involving the collective pursuit of collective goals.[1] This definition can apply to the collective goals of any group—a family, a corporation, even a couple on a date. Thus we sometimes hear the phrase "politics of the family"[2] used to describe conflicts over issues such as where a family will spend its Christmas vacation. A seduction can be regarded as "sexual politics."[3] A factional fight within the board of directors of Stickum Glue, Incorporated can be regarded as "company politics." However, for the purposes of this chapter I will limit our discussion of politics to conflicts over the collective goals of some unit of *gov-*

*ernment*—such as a nation, a city, or a province. Some of the concepts that political sociologists use to analyze politics can also be used in describing the internal political processes of corporations and other private, nongovernmental collectivities. This is especially true of certain terms introduced by Max Weber: legitimacy, power, and authority. Let's discuss these terms more thoroughly.

### LEGITIMACY AND POWER

What is the **state?** That is, what characteristics define a government? What does it need in order to qualify as the real thing—*the* state, or *the* government of a particular area? Max Weber claimed that the state is the organization that has a monopoly on the legitimate use of violence in a given territory. Only the state has the right to use force when necessary to back up its policies. If you catch a thief crawling through your window, you may hang onto him until the police arrive, but you are not supposed to punish him yourself. Only the state has the right to sentence people to prison or put them to death.

The key term in this definition is **legitimacy.** The state has the *right* to use force. Individuals do not. But this legitimacy comes from the people. It depends on the people's believing that the state is necessary and that its actions are lawful and valuable to society. As long as its legitimacy is unquestioned, the state will rarely need to use force. But if the legitimacy of its use of power is widely questioned, the state is in a dangerous situation. A regime is in serious trouble if the people believe that its military is illegitimate, its police brutal, and its courts unfair. It may have **power**—the ability to get its orders obeyed despite widespread opposition—but it does not have **authority.**

Authority is power plus legitimacy. It is the ability to use power because the members of the society recognize such power as legitimate. Democratic governments that lose their legitimacy do not keep their power very long. (During the Watergate scandal, for example, top government officials were stripped of their power as soon as they lost their legitimacy.) On the other hand, dictatorial governments that lose their legitimacy may remain in power even though the people do not consider them legitimate. The government of South Africa, for example, has long been viewed as illegitimate by the great majority of the population (i.e., the blacks), but they are powerless to rid themselves of that government.

You can think of power as a naked sword and of authority as a sword in its scabbard. Power does not have to display itself as long as it is recognized as legitimate. Various "props" are displayed instead. Politicans appeal to the patriotic feelings of their audiences. Flags and military bands help make a political campaign exciting. Judges wear special robes or wigs and police officers wear special uniforms for the same reason— they are the props of legitimacy. As long as the wearer is believed to have authority, he or she actually has it. Legitimacy, like beauty, is mostly in the eye of the beholder.

### THREE BASES FOR LEGITIMACY

On what basis does a group back up its political leaders? Weber suggested that three different bases have been used in different times and places. Sometimes a leader is given legitimate power because custom dictates that he or she is "in line" for such status. This is **traditional authority.** Sometimes a leader gains power on the basis of his or her personality. This is **charismatic authority.** Sometimes a leader is given power because he or she has been elected or appointed under the rules of a constitution or some other legal system. This is **rational-legal authority.** All three forms of authority have

Shackman/Monkmeyer

*Democratic elections are our way of choosing
leaders, whose authority is rational-legal.*

Napoleon were supposed to have special qualities that ordinary people didn't have. Such leaders are followed because they are believed to have direct access to the truth. Their authority is based on the faith of their followers. Thus as long as Napoleon's soldiers worshiped him, disobedience would have been unthinkable and his army was almost unbeatable. However, a few errors on his part caused his downfall.

Rational–legal authority is far more common today than in the past. Our legislators, dogcatchers, health inspectors, and admirals have power that is based on a rational set of rules. In a bureaucracy each person is assigned to a particular office, each of which has a specific range of powers supported by rational–legal authority.

## THE ROLE OF INTEREST GROUPS

In a constitutional democracy of the kind familiar to North Americans, politics is based on the interplay of opposing interest groups, unified groups that want to influence the state in their favor. These groups may form on the basis of economic (class) interests (e.g., labor unions, the American Medical Association), though other concerns may be even more important to some people than their economic interests (e.g., gun control, gay rights). Cultural interests often lead to the formation of groups that struggle in the political arena. For example, the Quebec nationalists are more concerned with preserving their culture than with raising their standard of living. Religion is another cultural basis for interest group formation; in earlier days terrible religious wars swept through Europe because such groups demanded that everyone else accept their beliefs. Even today religious differences play an important role in political contests—for example, in fights over abortion law or state support of religious schools. Not all cultural differences are religious in nature, however.

been of great importance at one time or another.

Throughout history most rulers have depended on traditional authority. Pharoahs, tribal chieftains, and landowning nobles have all been obeyed because "it has always been that way." Even today some of the most stable governments in the world are headed by constitutional monarchs. Thus British prime ministers may rise and fall, but Queen Elizabeth's status is secure, and in her lies the security of her state.

Charismatic leadership occurs when a remarkable leader steps forward to call people to a new way of life. Mao, Gandhi, and legitimacy. When a large enough number of people question the legitimacy of the regime, a rebellion may occur. For example, in October 1970, when a terrorist group kidnaped a British official and a Canadian official and killed the Canadian, the government of Canada feared that a rebellion was about to occur in Quebec. It responded with drastic measures that were legally sanctioned by the War Measures Act. In reality, however, there was no crisis of legitimacy. The Quebec terrorists were a tiny minority and were not supported by the general population. But by overreacting and using unnecessary force the government increased the underlying mood of dissatisfaction. Six years later the voters chose a party that favored the separation of Quebec from Canada through nonviolent political means.[4]

## Pluralism

When I was a graduate student in Berkeley during the 1960s—the time of the civil-rights movement, the ghetto riots, the War on Poverty, the assassinations, the Vietnam War, and the sit-ins and campus riots—everyone argued about politics. But the political sociologists were way ahead of everyone else. They usually won the arguments. However, I finally discovered that once you understand three basic viewpoints—pluralism, elitism, and Marxism—you can predict how most political arguments will go. And if you can anticipate the next point and say it first, very casually, you can win.

Let's consider these three viewpoints and how they have changed over the years. We begin with pluralism, which is the view that the best way to preserve freedom in a society is to have within it a lot of powerful groups that represent various interests. Until the 1960s most political sociologists were pluralists because pluralism seemed to offer the best answers to some of the questions

Owen Franken/Stock, Boston

*Throughout history most rulers have depended on traditional authority. But the "stage-props" vary. Some rulers have crowns—some have umbrellas.*

Fights over marijuana laws, the fluoridation of water, or pornography are all based on different values, each led by an active cultural-interest group.

Whenever a major interest group fails to persuade a regime to meet its demands, its members may withdraw their loyalty from that regime. If the group is powerful enough, this could plunge the regime into a crisis of that sociologsts have been asking for generations.

In order to explain pluralism I should point out that it was developed at the same time that sociology was born, and for the same reason. They were both ways of answering the same question: What makes it possible for a society to hold together? People began to think about this question because their society barely *was* holding together at the time. Two hundred years ago Western society was going through dramatic changes resulting from two "revolutions"—one political and the other economic. The economic one was the Industrial Revolution. The political one has been called the "democratic revolution."[5] It was the shift away from rule by absolute monarchs to rule by a parliament or some other elected group. The democratic revolution included the Boston Tea Party, the storming of the Bastille, and other related events. And there were other issues to be settled at the same time because the economy was shifting from an agricultural one to an industrial one.

European society in particular was giving up old, traditional relationships and developing an entirely new social structure. Tradition was the "glue" that had held society together. When it began to break apart, it was not clear whether any basis for holding society together remained.

Before the Industrial Revolution the lives of ordinary people had been organized by their involvement in their families, their communities, and their church. Industrialization freed the serfs and turned many of them into factory workers. This "freedom" had certain negative aspects: People now worked among impersonal strangers for cash wages. They were supposed to become rational and efficient. Values that had been sacred became unimportant. Belonging to a group became less possible: People became isolated "atoms" instead of members of close-knit communities. Social life became

unsettled and insecure. The "government" was no longer the local artistocrat but a mass democracy organized as a centralized bureaucratic state. People's rights became unclear; how those rights were to be enforced became even less clear.

Social theorists therefore began to search for a new set of rules, a new system by which people's lives could be organized. This is what is meant by *social integration*. The main answers to the question of what makes social integration possible were proposed by Tocqueville and, later, Durkheim. Both emphasized the importance of secondary centers of power mediating between the individual and the state.

## DE TOCQUEVILLE

A Frenchman of aristocratic background, Alexis de Tocqueville, visited the United States in 1831 because he believed that its democratic government was an image of Europe's future, in which he was deeply interested. His classic book, *Democracy in America*,[6] combines ethnographic reporting with good political theorizing. Though he thought democracy was unavoidable, Tocqueville was not very enthusiastic about it. He expected its emphasis on equality to lead to cultural mediocrity by trimming everyone down to the same size.

Democracy was a great threat to liberty, according to Tocqueville, because the tyranny of the majority would be more oppressive than the tyranny of aristocrats had been. The minority would have to conform, and their freedom was in danger. Worse yet, Tocqueville thought that democracy was likely to lead to dictatorship. He wrote, "I believe that it is easier to establish an absolute and despotic government among a people in which the conditions of society are equal than among any other; and I think that if such a government were once established among such a people, it not only would oppress men, it would eventually strip each of them of several of the highest qualities of humanity."[7]

Tocqueville wanted to find ways in which a democratic society might be protected from tyranny, and he thought several features of American society might serve this function. In particular, he recognized the importance of a free press and of law and lawyers. Moreover, he was the first to emphasize the role of voluntary associations in protecting liberty. This has become a basic idea in pluralist theory.

Tocqueville argued that in a strongly centralized democratic state the elites that had power in predemocratic society no longer exist; each person must deal with the state as an isolated individual. In any real contest with the state a single person wouldn't stand a chance. Only by organizing themselves in groups can individuals gain enough power to stand up against the government. Indeed, Tocqueville found that Americans have a strong tendency to join voluntary associations—social clubs, professional associations, ladies' auxiliaries, and the like. These groups of like-minded individuals often turn into powerful interest groups. Thus Tocqueville recommended that a democratic society prevent tyranny by encouraging a plurality of free, independent organizations.

### DURKHEIM

Emile Durkheim shared many of Tocqueville's ideas and also contributed to pluralist theory. He saw that the rise of the nation-state had freed people from traditional ties and created a greater role for the individual. In earlier times people had been seen not as individuals but as members of families or of feudal estates; most people were under the authority of these traditional organizations. In modern society the state regulates matters that used to be regulated by the church, the guild, the commune, or the family. Thus legal centralization meant legal individualism. By freeing the individual from the control of traditional authorities the state itself gained control over him or her. At the same time, social controls were weakened. Social order was harder to maintain. Deviance and political crises became more common.

Durkheim's recommendation was the same as Tocqueville's: To stop would-be tyrants and to strengthen social order in a heterogeneous population, create new voluntary associations to replace the defunct traditional ones.[8] By organizing into groups, like-minded individuals can attain some degree of power in a checks-and-balances arrangement. Durkheim was especially hopeful that professional associations, trade unions, and other occupational organizations might serve this purpose. Freedom in a modern society depends upon the maintenance of a plurality of competing, countervailing centers of power.

### DEMOCRACY AND PATTERNS OF SOCIAL DIVISION

Since Tocqueville and Durkheim many sociologists have continued to try to identify the conditions under which democracy is possible. Contemporary political sociologists have added to pluralist theory by suggesting that if a democracy is to be stable, the divisions within it should not *coincide* but *crisscross.*[9] Let me illustrate this point with an example.

Consider the two great nations that dominate world affairs today—Oz and Atlantis. As every schoolchild knows, Oz and Atlantis have very similar language, religion, and drinking patterns. By an odd coincidence exactly half the population of each nation consists of teetotalers while all the others are enthusiastic tipplers. Half the population of each nation speaks Sanskrit; all the others speak Fortran. Half the population of each nation is Zen Buddhist; all the others are

Druid. The two societies are very similar indeed, except that in Oz the boundaries separating religious, linguistic, and drinking or nondrinking groups coincide, while in Atlantis they crisscross. (See Figure 15.1.) As you can see, in Oz any boundary that would separate the two religious communities would also divide the population in terms of language and drinking habits. This is not the case in Atlantis, where Druids are equally distributed among the Fortran and Sanskrit speakers and where drinking is equally common in both religious groups and in both linguistic groups.

Now you must answer this question: Which society is more likely to be torn apart by political conflicts and which is more like-

ly to be characterized by moderate, middle-of-the-road politics marked by compromise? Which is more likely to succeed as a stable democracy, Oz or Atlantis? Why?

If you guessed that Atlantis is more likely to succeed as a democracy, you get an A. Pluralist theory suggests that a large number of power centers can stop any would-be tyrant or even any group that becomes too powerful. This theory is correct if the lines separating the various interest groups *cut across* each other. However, in Oz it is clear that there are three bases for conflict—language, religion, and drinking habits. The three bases combine to create two opposite camps that disagree in every possible way. The chance of conflict is great, and there is

In a plural society, groups form to support or oppose particular points of view. Anita Bryant is the leader of one "bloc" that opposes homosexuality.

UPI

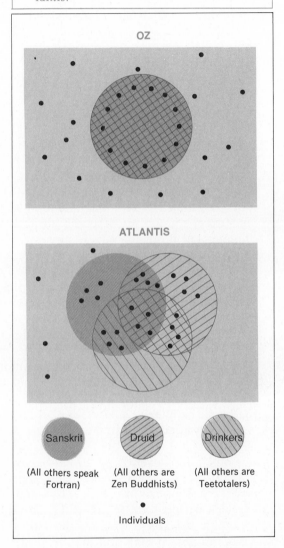

**FIGURE 15.1**

*Population characteristics, Oz and At-lantis.*

OZ

ATLANTIS

Sanskrit

Druid

Drinkers

(All others speak
Fortran)

(All others are
Zen Buddhists)

(All others are
Teetotalers)

Individuals

one disagreement are their allies in another. They thus have a reason for tolerating other groups. The social divisions between the plural interest groups crisscross, and this makes for political compromise.

### PLURALISM AND AMERICAN POLITICS

Pluralism is a normative theory; that is, it tries to show how a society *should be* organized if democracy is to succeed. Whether any given society is actually organized in this way is a question of *fact*, however. Not surprisingly, there has been much debate over the question of whether the United States is a true pluralist society or whether it is actually dominated by a ruling elite. Sometimes the term *pluralist* is used to refer to writers who believe that the United States not only *should be*, but actually *is*, characterized by a number of competing groups that each have a certain amount of power over some matters but not over a number of different issues. These writers argue that power is divided among a variety of groups and that every group must therefore take the interests of others into account.

Indeed, some writers go so far as to claim that power is *too* evenly distributed, that interest groups can rarely gain enough support to bring about even greatly needed changes. David Riesman said some years ago that America is in a social stalemate because there are so many veto groups, that is, interest groups that can "veto" government policies. Each group is able to block any action that conflicts with its values and interests, but no one group is able to make much of an impact with a program of its own.[10] This point of view is not widely accepted, however—although the American Medical Association has so far been able to block national health insurance. Far more people are worried about the opposite possibility—that a coalition of groups may have a lot of power behind the scenes. These people claim that

little basis for agreement between the two groups. Within each group agreement is very likely, but between the two groups it is unlikely. No matter which group manages to gain control of the government, it is not likely to be very concerned about the rights and wishes of the other. In Atlantis, on the other hand, most people find that their enemies in such coalitions control both the foreign and domestic policies of the U.S. government, as well as the policies of local governments.

This debate became especially important during the 1960s, when the "military – industrial complex" was seen as the force behind the Vietnam War. In order to gain a better understanding of this point of view, let us turn to the second great tradition of political thought — elitism.

## Elitism

The pluralist believes that democracy is possible; the elitist believes that it is a fraud. **Elitism** is the belief that some group or other (an *elite*) always gets the upper hand and rules the masses. A German sociologist, Robert Michels, reached this unhappy conclusion by studying the relationship between democracy and bureaucracy in politics.

Interest groups form in a plural society to take care of such problems as protecting the environment.

Wide World

In 1911 Michels published his book, *Political Parties*.[11] In it he described what he called "the iron law of oligarchy," which holds that any group that organizes itself will be taken over by an oligarchy. (*Oligarchy* is rule by a few people who can choose their own successors.) The group that Michels studied was a political party.

Michels found that the German Social Democratic party was, despite its name, an oligarchy. Although it began with the most democratic of ideals, the party was subject to the same conditions that are faced by any other organized group: The situation itself endangers a group's democratic ideals from the moment it organizes. It is impossible to make decisions efficiently when too many people are involved. The only solution is to organize — to elect officers and give them the authority to make some decisions on their own.

This is a fatal move, for once an ordinary member has tasted the joys of high office he or she will not want to give up that position. And the chances are that this will not be necessary because as an officer the member will gain knowledge and skills that are beyond the reach of ordinary members who might prefer a new leader. What is good for the officer, however, is not necessarily good for the group. The officer's main concern may be to stabilize the organization and his or her own position in it, while the other members may have a more idealistic program in mind. If they find that the officer is becoming too conservative and self-serving, they may turn him or her out of office, but even so the job will go to a successor that he or she has chosen. The real decisions in any organization are made behind the scenes by the elite, including those who have been voted out of office. This, said Michels, is an "iron" law: It never fails.

Elitists believe that democracy always

loses in the end, because the people who really govern any large social group are always a very select few. A true elitist does not call for revolution because it would only pass power from one elite to another. This would hardly be worth the effort. Elitists today do not claim that rule by elites is *preferable* to participatory democracy. They simply argue that it cannot be avoided.

### A PLURALIST REPLY

Elitists do not take seriously the pluralist argument that political freedom can be guaranteed by balancing power among a plurality of interest groups. Yet the pluralists have by no means lost the argument; in fact they may even be ahead by several points. One point for the pluralist side was scored by the book *Union Democracy*, which showed that the elitist argument did not always apply to American trade unions.[12]

Michels had argued that unions have to have bureaucratic leadership in order to be effective, but that whoever gets into a leadership role is likely to manage to stay there. The history of trade unions shows that Michels was basically correct. Few unions are led by workers. However, the authors of *Union Democracy* were able to show that Michels was not *always* correct and that when this was the case it was for pluralist reasons. They chose a union that did not have oligarchical leadership—the International Typographical Union. This organization not only had two different "parties" among its members but sometimes even replaced its officials at election time. How was it possible for the printers to maintain democratic control of their elected leaders? Within their union there are a number of different organizations run by members on a voluntary basis—clubs, leisure time associations, and the like—and these groups participate in political affairs within the union. Thus Tocqueville's argument defeated Michels' argument. To put it simply, a plurality of

Owen Franken/Stock, Boston

*In democratic societies trade unions and other organizations are independent. In totalitarian societies they are either forbidden to organize or are controlled by the state. Pluralist theory claims that independent associations help preserve freedom.*

voluntary organizations within a larger organization creates bases of power that enable members to defend their own interests against the elite in power.

However, even the trade unions and other associations that are oligarchies can still help maintain liberty in a democratic society. It is better to have a plurality of strong associations such as unions, churches, lodges, and cooperatives than for people to have to deal with the state as individuals. There is some protection in strong collectivities, even when those collectivities are not run according to democratic principles. But this is true only if they are independent of the state. As Tocqueville and Durkheim suggested, the associations that existed before the democratic revolution were autocratic, not democratic. Noble families and guilds, for example, did not give their members freedom, yet they were strong enough to protect their members.

It is when organizations are *not independent*—when their leaders are appointed by, and accountable to, the state—that totalitarianism is likely. In the Soviet Union, there are many organizations, but those organizations are controlled by the state and cannot protect their members against its influence. Instead of being part of a pluralist society, such associations are tools for governmental control.

### THE PLURALIST–ELITIST SYNTHESIS

New ideas arise out of conflicts between old ideas. If pluralists and elitists are indeed in conflict, the theory that results from that conflict will be different from either of the original theories. Let's look at how the two theories have combined.

Vilfredo Pareto is a good example of an elitist. He argued that the ruling elite of any society is always very small, but that within the society a counterelite usually develops and becomes strong enough to overthrow the ruling elite. Pareto called the ruling elite "foxes" because they are clever and corrupt. The counterelite is made up of confident, idealistic young people, whom Pareto called "lions." He believed that the fate of all foxes is to be overthrown in revolutions by lions, and that the fate of all lions is to become foxes. Thus he suggests that anyone who tries to reorganize society is wasting his or her time—the revolutionary leaders themselves will become corrupt after they have come to power.[13]

How can a pluralist react to such a challenge? One solution is to become a "plural-ist–elitist" like Karl Mannheim or Suzanne Keller. Pluralist–elitists accept the elitist argument but change its meaning. They agree that every society has leaders and that every group within a society has leaders. They ask, What's wrong with that? It is also true that when one set of leaders is overthrown another set takes over. But this only proves that leaders are necessary.

Mannheim suggested that there are two types of power: functional power and arbitrary power. Personal power is arbitrary and, therefore, undesirable; but elites usually have functional, institutional power. Indeed, Mannheim claimed that one of the main trends in modern times is toward the replacement of personal power with functional power.[14]

Keller even defines elites in a pleasant way. An elite, she says, is a minority of individuals who serve a collectivity in a socially useful way.[15] To Keller, there is nothing incompatible between saying that a society is pluralist and saying that it is elitist. A society may consist of a plurality of subgroups, each of which is led by its own elite. She suggests that as society becomes more complex and as roles within the society become more specialized, elites become more numerous and each area of social life is represented by a more or less separate elite. Thus we now have elites not only in government but in the movie industry, the arts, the clergy, and so forth.

Sometimes we admire our elites and sometimes we envy them. Social integration is easier when we admire our elites. When we envy them, social conflict is more likely—especially if the elites are snobbish and unresponsive to ordinary people.[16] Tocqueville said that the French Revolution happened mostly because the aristocracy lost its sense of duty to the ordinary peasant.[17]

Keller believes that elites have a duty to provide not only political leadership but moral leadership as well. She reminds us of a point made by Durkheim, who claimed

*As the division of labor increases, the jobs and life styles of members of a single society come to differ greatly. For example, how well do you understand the problems of these farm workers?*

that integration in traditional societies was very different from integration in modern societies. The way people got along in the old days was by being alike — having similar backgrounds, similar religious practices, similar ideas about how family members should treat one another, similar ideas about morality in every area of life. There were no "oddballs" in preindustrial society, no individuality or new ideas. Everybody had to agree on everything. This was the only way people could integrate their activities harmoniously. Durkheim called this pattern mechanical solidarity. (Yes, it is an odd term; I agree.)

On the other hand, the solidarity (i.e., friendly relatedness) that you and I have for each other as fellow members of modern society is organic solidarity. By this Durkheim meant that although we are very different, we are interdependent. As the division of labor increases, the jobs and life styles of members of a single society come to differ greatly. I may be unable to understand much about your experience, and so you and I will have different opinions and different habits. Modern society is heterogeneous. What makes integration possible is that we depend on each other. We *have* to find some way of making deals or agreements or contracts. Our interdependence forces us to bargain with each other and offer at least a moderate amount of respect to each other.

With organic solidarity, we are much less committed to sharing values. For example, we don't say prayers in school anymore. Prayer is supposed to be private. We have a right to have individual, unusual ideas of morality. What makes it possible for us to get along when we disagree about important matters? According to Keller, Durkheim did not realize the importance of new elites. As the leaders of the various subgroups within modern society, they must coordinate the relationships among those groups. Keller therefore calls them "strategic elites." The special duty of strategic elites is to make sure that the people in each section of society are

441

committed to the basic goals of the whole society. This is an important contribution. Moreover, Keller claims that it is less possible today than in the past for one strategic elite to dominate the others. This is because each represents a particular area (e.g., the arts, religion, industry) and that as a result they compete among themselves. As long as the elites are plural rather than unified, they are no threat to liberty or democracy. They cannot become too overbearing because their spheres of activity are limited and they have plenty of opposition.

Notice how we have twisted and turned and changed our minds since we began talking about elitism. At first elites were villains; now they are heroes. Mannheim and Keller have combined pluralism and elitism, showing that they are not opposites but that they both have valid statements to make about modern democratic societies. But in doing so they have changed the meaning of the term *elites*. To Pareto, the word meant clever foxes and domineering lions. To Mannheim and Keller, it refers to moral pace setters and influential experts.

Still, I think the synthesis holds up. Both elitism and pluralism are rather conservative points of view. Elitism suggests that it is useless to try to change the government. Pluralism suggests that the working classes in industrial societies don't *need* to rebel to get their interests protected. All they need is a variety of independent voluntary associations—lobbies, clubs, fraternal orders, trade unions, and so on. These enable each interest group to show its strength when necessary. And if each group is led by an "elite," why should this trouble anyone? All a democracy needs is to be sure that these groups are independent and that they are "plural"— that there are several elites representing many interests, not just one. This will do more to preserve the rights of ordinary people than anything else. Without it a revolution might be necessary.

You may be wondering whether North

American society is in *fact* led by a plurality of elites, or whether it is a single, united "power elite" representing *one* point of view, *one* social class, *one* set of interests, and so on. This is a factual question, not a normative one. You can hold to the elitist—pluralist theory and say that the United States *ought* to be led by a plurality of elites. This is a *normative* statement—a philosophical position that you would justify with the arguments that we have just discussed. You might go on to say that *in fact* the United States does not have a plurality of elites. To justify this point of view you would need evidence in the form of facts and figures, not just reasoning.

Some facts come to mind that relate to this question. Remember the Bohemian Grove and the Rancho Visitadores, mentioned in Chapter 9? I consider them powerful evidence that the top elite in the United States is a single, unified group of friends. Tentmates and riding partners, in fact. Real pals. And actually, most political sociologists who are in *favor* of a plurality of elites agree with Domhoff. The top elite seems to be more united than Americans have assumed in the past. How dangerous is this? Are Americans unknowingly ruled by a bunch of rich cowboys and Bohemians? I can't answer that. All I can say is that the pluralists I know are sometimes *listening* to the Marxists instead of simply arguing with them, as they used to do. So we will consider Marxism next.

## Marxism

Be careful about calling people "Marxists." You never can tell, until you check, whether a person claims that title or rejects it. As a matter of fact in his later years Karl Marx himself declared, "I am not a Marxist." Presumably we should take his word for it and extend the same courtesy to anyone else who claims or rejects the title, because the qualifications for it are so ambiguous. Therefore, although we are about to discuss certain views that are related to Marxism, we will be using the term here in its loosest possible sense. Marxism here simply means any doctrine that is supposedly derived from the teachings of Karl Marx.

Marx had one thing in common with elitists: He believed that every society, past and present, is dominated by a ruling group. However, he differed from elitists by claiming that a proletarian revolution would not simply bring a new elite to power. Instead it would put an end once and for all to social classes and to the domination of one class by another. Only then would liberty be possible.

On the issue of liberty Marx differed from pluralists by disagreeing that a variety of countervailing groups can protect individuals from a ruling elite. Freedom will come only after the revolution, and never in a capitalist democracy. Marx was not impressed with the claim that freedom and equality are guaranteed by law to citizens of democratic nations. He claimed that only *economic* equality really counts. What use is freedom of speech to someone who has nothing to eat? What use is the right to vote to someone who has no shoes? To Marx and his followers, political rights are empty, for they have never once in any country succeeded in abolishing private property and returning to the workers the profits of their own labor.

In the United States today the leftists (those who lean toward Marxism) hold that the nation—and in a sense the whole world—is governed by a ruling elite. And since Americans discovered that their government had deceived the public during the Vietnam War, in the Watergate scandal, and by participating in the overthrow of governments of other nations, the leftists have not been alone in this view. However, long before Watergate or Vietnam these critics were arguing that government secrecy allowed the "military–industrial complex" to influence national policy for private gain. They

claimed that the United States was ruled by an *irresponsible* elite that was unresponsive to the people.[18] The term *military–industrial complex* refers to an elite of high officials and managers with close ties to both the armed forces and big business who "scratch each others' backs." Business profits from the production of military equipment, so it supports politicians who believe in maintaining a big military establishment. These people are not elected, but they have great influence on government decisions. We'll come back to them later. First we will take a look at present-day Marxists' interpretations of certain developments that Marx himself did not predict.

## MARXIST EXPLANATIONS OF HISTORICAL DEVELOPMENTS

Over the years Marxists have found certain facts hard to explain. Things simply have not turned out the way Marx predicted. Among those developments are the following:

1 The communist revolutions have not happened where and when Marx predicted that they would.
2 Modern corporations are owned by large numbers of stockholders who do not have any say in the management of their "capitalist" enterprises.
3 The workers in capitalist societies have become richer rather than poorer.

### The communist revolutions in nonindustrial countries

There certainly have been communist revolutions. But they were not the ones Marx expected. He thought there would be uprisings of industrial workers in the most advanced capitalist societies. But the only real revolutions have taken place in countries like Vietnam, China, and Cuba—nations that are only beginning to industrialize. And instead of being led by urban workers they have been led by intellectuals with the support of peasants.[19] In fact such revolutions are more "nationalistic" than "communistic." The real target is not capitalists because there aren't any capitalists—or hardly any. In developing countries industrialization depends on capital controlled from abroad, and it is organized by the colonial power that dominates the society. The target, therefore, is the foreign colonial power, and the revolutionaries are people who want to modernize their society and make it independent.

Of course the colonial power from which the developing nation wants to free itself is usually a capitalist society. And not surprisingly, the capitalist society will try to stop the revolution. For example, in the 1960s the Chileans voted a leftist regime into power using legal democratic procedures. But the new regime, led by Salvador Allende, opposed a foreign corporation, ITT, which had strong allies in the U.S. government. Allende is no more. His regime has been replaced by a right-wing government that tortures political prisoners. The people who overthrew Allende were supported by the U.S. government at the urging of ITT, whose economic interests were threatened by Allende's policies. The U.S. government has interfered in similar ways with the rights of people around the world to choose their own form of government. This interference is strongly resented by the people of the Third World, and it is not surprising that they turn to communism.

Contrary to Marx's predictions, communism is not very attractive to workers in the advanced capitalist societies, who are actually quite well off. Most European societies have strong socialist labor parties but weak communist parties.[20] Nor have the successful communist revolutions always achieved what they set out to achieve. Elitist theory has been right more often than not. The Russian revolution produced some changes, but it also brought a new elite to power. The revolutionary leaders took over

the means of production and went on to exploit the workers themselves. They used totalitarian methods to rule the masses and forced rapid industrialization at a terrible price. They industrialized *after* the revolution, not before it. Their revolution was not the one Marx had expected, which would have produced human liberation, not labor camps and repression of artists and political dissidents. Many writers call the Soviet system not Communism but "state capitalism." It has the worst features of capitalism, but is run by the government instead of by business executives.

### Corporate ownership

Marx did not foresee how capitalism itself would change. Capitalism is no longer a system of family-owned firms but one of huge corporations owned by millions of people. You may own some shares yourself, but that doesn't make you a "capitalist." You don't exploit workers. You have nothing to say about the management of the company in which you own shares. You may not even know who is on the board of directors.

Then who are the "capitalists" whom Marx hated so bitterly? They might be the top executives in the corporation who actually manage the firm. But if so Marx's theory is still wrong, because executives are not owners but salaried employees. Marx considered ownership the only standard for determining who is a capitalist. He thought salaried managers would not be driven to exploit workers. After all, the profits don't go directly to *them*.[21]

If neither stockholders nor top executives are the capitalist ruling class, then who is? Remember Michels and his "iron law of oligarchy"? This gives us a clue. There are too many stockholders to run the corporation themselves, so they let a tiny group of stockholders—who own maybe 5 percent of the stock—decide policy for the whole corporation. This smaller group controls the executives. Moreover, by "pyramiding" stockholdings they gain control over many other firms. It goes like this: The "inner circle" of stockholders owns and controls, say, 30 percent of the stock of a company. Then their company buys 20 percent of another company, thereby controlling it. That company may control yet another company, and so on. The result is that the top elite controls three or four firms, though it owns only a small bloc of shares.[22] Think about the size of these corporations. Some of them, such as General Motors, Standard Oil, IBM, and ITT, are as powerful as many whole nations. The decision-making elite controls as many resources as most heads of state.

Thus Marx was mostly right. Rather than exploiting workers, the ordinary stockholder today does not control the corporation at all. The capitalist that Marx had in mind was the entrepreneur who set up a business and managed it himself—the typical "robber baron." In Marx's day that was a fair picture of a capitalist. But not today. The modern capitalist doesn't own the company, only a small part of it. And the workers, since they are doing very well themselves, have little reason to hate the owners.

### The increasingly affluent working class

Marx's third mistake was to predict that as industrialization progressed the situation of the working class would get worse and worse. Competition between firms would force capitalists to work their employees harder and harder. They would speed up production, lengthen the work day, force the workers' wives and children to work too, and so on. The business cycle of booms and depressions would fluctuate wildly until capitalism brought about its own downfall.

Since the Great Depression of the 1930s none of these predictions have proved correct. There have been only minor recessions, and capitalism is stronger than ever. Capital-

ist economies are producing the greatest wealth the world has ever known, and the workers are sharing in the wealth. To be sure, there is poverty in capitalist societies, but most of the poor are unemployable. The workers have done well. The current high rate of unemployment in North America has caused some hardship, it's true, but with unemployment insurance and other benefits it is by no means as severe as Marx predicted.

Present-day Marxists have argued that there are two reasons for the stability and success of capitalist economies since World War II. The first is the high level of spending for military goods; the second is the exploitation of underdeveloped nations. Marx did not expect capitalism to become an international system. But according to André Gunder Frank, the industrial countries have acquired their great wealth by exploiting other countries and thus preventing economic growth in those areas.[23] This view is widely accepted by neo-Marxists.

### NEO-MARXISM

In response to the three historical developments just described, and perhaps for other reasons as well, the Marxist view of capitalism has changed over the years and can now be labeled neo-Marxism. No longer is the revolution thought of as a struggle of workers against local capitalists. Instead, it is seen as a struggle of developing nations against capitalist nations—not a direct conflict between social classes but a conflict between nations that serve different social classes. This new interpretation recognizes that most communist revolutions today are struggles against foreign economic domination.

Neo-Marxists also recognize that modern capitalism is *corporate* capitalism. This means that the ruling elite is but a segment of all stockholders. Power is not held by every stockholder but by a small oligarchy of stockholders. This group controls economic interests in every part of the globe and has far greater power than any capitalist of Marx's day.

Finally, many leftists, recognizing that Marx's prediction of increasing instability and poverty in capitalist societies was incorrect, have concluded that the success of capitalist societies depends on economic imperialism and militarism.

All of these neo-Marxist views are subject to further debate and study. They are far too complex for us to cover completely here. But I do want to mention C. Wright Mills, who contributed to the discussion even before it became an issue to most other sociologists.

Mills published his book, *The Power Elite*,[24] in 1956 — long before the Vietnam War. President Eisenhower warned the nation in his farewell address that a small group of high-ranking military and industrial leaders was gaining too much power. It was this group that the New Left leaders later blamed for the Vietnam War. But Mills anticipated the notion "military–industrial complex" when he wrote about the "power

The military constantly buys and destroys equipment, either on the battlefield or as it becomes obsolete. Many people are employed in businesses connected to buying, selling, and creating these materials. This gives the military a sometimes not so obvious influence with legislators who are concerned about employment.

UPI

elite." He was strongly opposed by political sociologists at the time. Most of them were pluralists, and they believed that the United States was quite democratic because its leadership was divided among a number of different interest groups that balanced one another so that no one elite held too much power.

Mills disagreed. He admitted, of course, that there are many interest groups and that they do tend to limit one another. Still, he claimed that most Americans don't realize that certain elite groups form coalitions that have far too much power. This is what he meant by the "power elite." The people who control the major corporations also have close ties with the government. Retired generals get plush offices in corporations that compete for defense contracts. Executives shift back and forth between private companies and top government agencies. Members of the board of directors of one corporation are also on the boards of other corporations, so that there is an "interlocking directorate" at the top of the international corporate pyramid. This rich elite can influence domestic and foreign policies—policies that set prices, transfer money from one country to another, raise or lower the level of employment, prop up reactionary regimes around the world, and guide the national economy.

Mills argued that the pluralist model applies only to the middle sector of the American stratification system—such as Congress, where one pressure group does counteract another. This is "countervailing power." But within the power elite there is no countervailing power. The power elite is a small group of people, many of whom know each other, whose interests are the same.

When Mills' book first appeared, most political sociologists didn't believe him. But there is more and more evidence to support his ideas. We have already mentioned Domhoff's *Bohemian Grove*. In other writings Domhoff has described the network of ties linking the power elite. Members of the elite intermarry, send their children to the same boarding schools, contribute to the same cultural and charitable foundations, and so on. The elite is not totally unified, however; instead, it consists of a number of overlapping circles and cliques, some of which are hostile toward others.[25]

Most neo-Marxists claim that the power elite (the military–industrial complex) *must* use the armed forces to dominate underdeveloped countries. This is because advanced capitalist societies have to spend vast amounts on the military as well as control the world's markets. Spending money on weapons is a way of wasting profits that cannot be profitably invested in industry. Capitalism, say the neo-Marxists, creates a constant surplus that has to be drained off somehow, otherwise it would cause a depression. (When a surplus exists, demand drops off and industry has to slow down production.) The best way to keep demand for production high is to support an ever-growing military establishment. The military constantly buys and destroys equipment, either on the battlefield or as it becomes obsolete.[26] By buying and wasting material that comes off the assembly line, the military helps keep the machines humming and the profits pouring in. Besides, the military has to be ready to fight at all times because it is necessary to keep less developed countries from breaking away from the control of capitalist societies.

### PROBLEMS WITH THE NEO-MARXIST VIEW

Liberal economists agree that capitalism creates a surplus and that military spending has prevented serious depressions. However, they do not agree that military spending is the *only* way to prevent depressions. It is entirely possible, they say, to spend the money on projects that will improve the quality of life, not destroy it. And projects such as rapid-transit systems, urban renewal, and medical research could easily use up the surplus.[27]

Moreover, Stanley Lieberson has concluded from his research that the American economy does not depend on military spending.[28] If defense spending were cut in half, the economy would benefit, not lose, from the cut—though certain industries would lose a lot. Then why don't Americans cut defense spending? Lieberson says it is because most interest groups won't *gain* much from such cuts and a few groups stand to lose a great deal. In a pluralistic system interest groups fight hard only for the policies that are vital to them. He thinks the United States is basically a pluralistic system; as a result the majority cares so little that it allows a few interest groups to control government spending.[29]

## Conclusion

We began with three different viewpoints—pluralism, elitism, and Marxism. But each of these views has shifted somewhat, and in some ways they have merged. The chief debate that goes on today is between the pluralist and Marxist positions. Elitism has been absorbed by the other two viewpoints. Pluralists have accepted the elitist assumption that even in a free society that is made up of many independent, competing interest groups *each group is led by its own elite.* Marxists have accepted the elitist assumption that capitalist society is secretly controlled by a "ruling class" or "power elite" that skillfully manipulates a million puppets dressed in American uniforms.

## SOCIAL RESEARCH: Sociologists at Work

### ELECTORAL SYSTEMS AND PARTICIPATION

If you have lived in one Western society all your life and move to a different one that is also democratic, you will probably be surprised and confused at the way it works. Not all democracies have the same procedures for electing political leaders. And once elected, politicians in different countries may go about their work in quite different ways.

One difference is that American political parties are not run the way parties are in many other countries. If a Republican member of Congress disagrees with the official Republican stand on a particular issue, he or she can vote against his or her party, usually without regret-

ting it. Indeed, if his or her constituents do not go along with the general Republican view on the issue, it would be foolish *not* to vote against that position. In the United States, then, a great variety of political views may be found within a single party. There are many kinds of Democrats. Some Democrats are more like Republicans than most Republicans are. Thus it is common for voters to vote for a particular candidate on the basis of his or her record rather than on the basis of his or her party.

In most parliamentary democracies such a thing never happens. Parties are highly disciplined. A politician, once elected, almost always votes for the position that his or her party favors—otherwise he or she will be in trouble. And the parties are markedly different. The voters know what policies each party supports. They decide how to vote on that basis, and after the election they rarely try to influence an elected official to change his or her position on a given issue. Ordinarily the party that wins the election will "form a government," that is, put together a cabinet of ministers and other leaders who may propose legislation. Bills that are introduced to the legislature will usually pass, unless the opposition can get together a coalition that is strong enough to defeat a particular bill. Indeed, the defeat of a bill may cause the government to fall, for it is a sign that some members of the majority party have voted with the opposition. This casts doubt on the party that has won the election and formed the government. At this point the majority party will probably call for a vote of confidence to prove that it can continue to lead the government. Of course even if it manages to get all its bills through the legislature without any trouble the government will have to call an election every few years as required by the nation's constitution.

Another difference between democratic systems is that some European democracies work on the principle of "proportional representation." That is, when the votes are counted for the whole polity (i.e., the nation), each party will be given a number of seats (or voting members) in the legislature based on its percentage of the total vote. The North American system is quite different, of course. Each electoral district elects its own representative, and "the winner takes all." This means that small parties almost never win elections. Therefore voters usually will not waste their votes by supporting a small party but will choose between the two leading candidates. For this reason only a few candidates compete in any given election, and often the race is between two candidates. In polities that use proportional representation, on the other hand, it is not uncommon for 20 or 30 parties to divide up the vote. After the election they have to sort out their alliances and coalitions. The coalition that wins the greatest support is allowed to form the government—to choose the prime minister and the cabinet. When the coalition loses an election within the legislature, the whole arrangement has to be renegotiated.

The Canadian and American governments differ somewhat, even though neither system uses proportional representation. In Canada, but not in the United States, minor parties can gain power at the provincial level. However, at the federal level such parties are rarely important. A small party, such as the Social Credit party, might be popular in one or two provinces, but

it will not gain enough nationwide support to oust one of the major parties.[30] In recent years, however, the New Democratic Party (NDP) has gained enough support to count as a major party, rivaling the Liberal and Progressive-Conservative parties in popularity.

North Americans do not participate as actively in party politics as citizens of many other nations. Canadians vote slightly more regularly than Americans do. In U.S. presidential elections about 60 percent of those who are eligible actually vote, while in Canadian federal elections about 73 percent vote.[31] In contrast, the average voter turnout in some Western European countries is above 80 percent.[32]

Although in the United States voter turnout for off-year state elections is smaller than that for presidential elections, in Canada the turnout for provincial elections is as high as that for federal elections. Turnout seems to be related to the competitiveness of the election, with the highest turnouts occuring in elections that offer the most diverse choices.[33]

Whether people are active in an election—either as party workers or as ordinary voters—depends on three different factors: (1) the importance of the election to them; (2) the extent of their communication with others, either personally or through the media; and (3) their emotional and psychological characteristics.

When the voters see the choices facing them as relevant to their own lives, they are likely to vote; otherwise they are not. Those who are especially affected by government policies are especially likely to vote. Thus government employees show high turnout rates, as do all groups whose economic well-being is strongly influenced by government agencies. However, as suggested earlier, one's main interests need not be economic but may be social or moral. Abortion issues, for example, tend to bring out Catholic voters in large numbers.

In times of crisis dramatic new policies may be proposed and the parties may take extremely opposing positions with regard to those policies. This happened, for example, when the New Deal was proposed as a means of ending the Great Depression. In such times elections tend to bring out lots of voters who would ordinarily stay home and grumble about having to choose between Tweedledum and Tweedledee.

## THE LEFT AND THE RIGHT

Robert Alford has analyzed the election results of Great Britain, Australia, the United States, and Canada, focusing on the factors that influence support for parties of the right and of the left. It is clear that certain social groups lean in the same direction in all societies. Catholics, for example, tend to support left-of-center parties in all four countries.

The British are most likely to vote according to their social class, the Australians only slightly less so. American voters are much less likely to choose their parties on the basis of class, and the Canadians are least likely to do so.[34]

## RECENT TRENDS IN AMERICAN VOTING PATTERNS

Gerald Pomper has analyzed the recent voting patterns of Americans using data from the presidential elections of 1960 through 1972. He tells us that the voters have become less loyal to par-

ticular parties—many call themselves Independents and many are switching from the Democrats to the Republicans or (more often) vice versa. Even among loyal party followers, fewer than half have always voted for the candidates of one party.[35] Political analysts used to find that Independent voters were relatively poorly informed, on the whole, but this is no longer so. They know as much about issues and candidates as partisan voters do.

Pomper believes that social class is not very strongly related to party preference in presidential elections but that it continues to have *some* impact on voting choices. He has classified the voters into two groups—manual and nonmanual workers—and found the relationship between occupational level and party identification to be as shown in Figure 15.2.

Gender does not make much difference in voting. Most issues receive similar support from males and females. Except for southern women, who vote less, women participate in politics as much as men do. There is one important difference, however: Women are more likely to oppose the use of force than men. Because of their

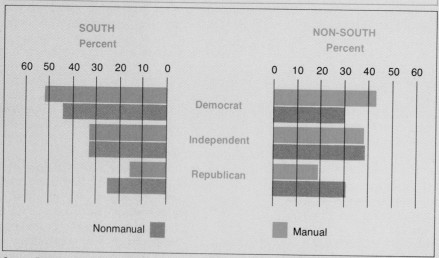

**FIGURE 15.2**
*Party identification by type of employment and region, 1972*

SOUTH
Percent

60  50  40  30  20  10  0

NON-SOUTH
Percent

0  10  20  30  40  50  60

Democrat

Independent

Republican

Nonmanual ▉        ▉ Manual

*Source:* Data from Gerald Pomper, *Voters' Choice: Varieties of American Electoral Behavior.* (New York: Harper & Row, 1975), p. 41.

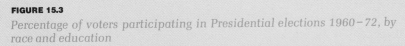

**FIGURE 15.3**

*Percentage of voters participating in Presidential elections 1960–72, by race and education*

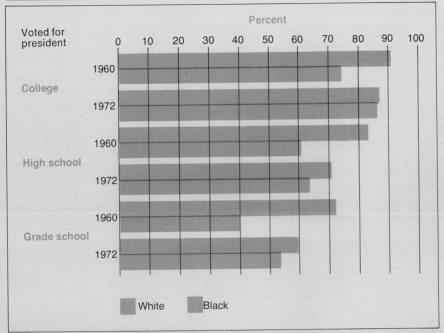

*Source:* Data from Gerald Pomper, *Voters' Choice: Varieties of American Electoral Behavior.* (New York: Harper & Row, 1975), p. 41

stronger opposition to the Vietnam War, women were more likely to support Democratic presidential candidates, who seemed to be "doves" compared to their Republican opponents.[36]

Most political analysts, including Pomper, noted a marked increase in cynicism toward the government during the 1960s and early 1970s. This trend was especially strong among well-educated young people, who generally take a more liberal position than older voters. They were particularly upset by the Vietnam War.

Pomper also studied the effect of race on party support. Before the 1960s black Americans participated relatively little in politics—often because they had been discouraged or prevented from registering. However, since the civil-rights movement made its great drive to register black voters blacks have come to vote almost as often as whites. And educated blacks have be-

come particularly active as political leaders. But increased participation does not mean increased trust. On the contrary, blacks are highly suspicious of the government.

Within the working class more than any other social class, white voters and black voters are far apart in their political views. In recent elections racial issues have had about as much impact on the outcome as class issues.[37]

## POLITICAL PARTICIPATION IN TOTALITARIAN REGIMES

We have mentioned political participation in connection with democracy because it is vital to a democratic system. Ironically, however, some of the highest rates of political participation are found in societies that are not liberal democracies but totalitarian regimes. (*Totalitarianism* is the doctrine that citizens should be under the total control of the state.) For example, in the Soviet Union almost 100 percent of the eligible voters actually vote, though the voting choices available to them are very limited. Voting is nearly compulsory. Refusing to vote is an act of political defiance. Thus, the rate of participation in itself is not a valid indicator of a population's acceptance of its government.

Totalitarianism requires the fullest possible participation of citizens in activities that are programed by the regime. Only a modern society can enforce such a high rate of participation under such close control as in the regimes of Hitler, Mussolini, and Stalin. Thus totalitarianism is impossible without industrialization. Tyranny is thousands of years old, to be sure, but preindustrial tyrannies lacked the technology that enables modern tyrants to communicate with even the most private and isolated parts of the society.

The purge trials of Stalin and the Gestapo's midnight knock on the door showed how a totalitarian regime can pursue and haunt its victims. Citizens must carry identity cards, and a detailed dossier follows them into every new role and enables their superiors to monitor their conduct.

Totalitarianism can arise out of either a leftist or a rightist political movement. Stalin and Hitler proved this. Such regimes have a great deal in common. They have a single ideology under the leadership of a single party. No opposing group is tolerated, and the whole population is expected to participate enthusiastically in any activities that the party proposes. The rights of private institutions are not respected. Youth groups or trade unions, for example, are not independent but must be sponsored by the

*Voter registration drives have brought out far more minority voters in recent American elections.*

Dan Miller/DPI

party, and anyone who is eligible is expected to participate. Almost all German children belonged to Hitler Youth, and almost all Russian children belonged to the Octobrists and the Pioneers. Even the privacy of the family is violated. Revolutionary propaganda, for example, praises children who inform the authorities of their parents' counterrevolutionary activities.

In the past all totalitarian regimes arose out of mass political movements in which popular enthusiasm for some ideology—communist or fascist—became so strong that it overwhelmed the organizations that might have provided a check against the centralized power of the state.[38] Once in power, the regime was safe from attack.

### MASS REBELLIONS

Up to this point our discussion of politics has focused on the normal workings of partisan contests within democratic societies. Of course this is not the only area of political activity. Sometimes people cannot achieve vital goals through democratic processes, and in such cases they may rebel. In much of the rest of this chapter we will consider rebellions.

Mass rebellions are political crises in which a large portion of a country's inhabitants try to overthrow the established government. They may or may not succeed in bringing about social change. Successful rebellions or social movements that result in real, lasting social change are commonly called social revolutions. The word *revolution* can be used in a variety of senses, even to describe peaceful movements such as the Industrial Revolution, the sexual revolution, and so on. However, here we restrict the term to violent political conflicts. Moreover, we will not discuss anticolonial rebellions (such as the Algerian revolt against the French) or secessionist civil wars (such as the Biafran struggle for separation from Nigeria), but only rebellions aimed at changing the regime of a whole society.

Scholars have asked two kinds of questions about these rebellions: (1) What social conditions cause them? (2) What factors determine whether they will succeed or fail? The first question has been researched more fully than the second, but we will discuss both.

### Brinton on the origins of mass rebellions

Crane Brinton's book *The Anatomy of Revolution* is the best-known study of political rebellions.[39] It compares four famous revolutions: the French (1789), the Russian (1917), the American (1776), and the English (1640). Brinton was able to make the following generalizations about the social conditions that led to these conflicts:

1 *Economic Upgrading.* In all four societies the economy had been improving before the revolution. The rebels were not starving, miserable, oppressed people but discontented people who felt cramped and annoyed. The revolutionists were driven by the hope of a better life.
2 *Strong Class Hostility.* Bitter resentment existed between the social classes in prerevolutionary society—not between widely separated classes but between the socially privileged aristocracy and the new well-to-do class only slightly below the aristocracy. Revolutions, according to Brinton, are more likely when social classes are fairly close together in status.
3 *Desertion of the Intellectuals.* In all four societies many intellectuals turned against the regime before and during the revolution.
4 *Inefficient Government.* The machinery of state became outmoded, unresponsive, and unable to cope with the economic growth, the new well-to-do classes, the new business methods, and the new technology that flourished in the period just before the rebellion.
5 *Self-Doubt in the Ruling Class.* Many members of the old ruling class came to distrust themselves and lost faith in the traditions of their class. Some of them became humanitarians and joined the attacking groups. An unusually large number seemed to lead immoral lives. The ruling class, losing confidence in its own legitimacy, became politically inept.
6 *A Financial Crisis.* In the case of the French, English, and American revolutions one of the main causes of revolution was financial breakdown. Brinton notes that the breakdown of administration in Russia was caused mainly by that country's involvement in World War I and was only partly financial. In all four countries the weakness of the governmental structure was clear very early in the revolution.
7 *Clumsy Use of Troops.* The government tried to use forces that it no longer controlled. At first it seemed as if the government might be able to keep itself in power through the use of force.

However, in all four cases the use of force failed to stop the revolution.

Brinton is careful about generalizing on the basis of these four rebellions. However, other research supports many of his conclusions about revolutions, which are indeed marked by a good deal of dissatisfaction on the part of the ruling class, especially the youth. Also, the intellectuals usually play an important part and the state also often makes mistakes in its use of force in trying to stop the revolution.[40]

### Davies on the origins of mass rebellions

James Davies also wanted to find out the source of rebellions, though his study was much more limited than Brinton's. Davies was concerned only with the economic conditions leading up to three rebellions—Dorr's Rebellion (1842), the Russian Revolution (1917), and the Egyptian Revolution (1952). To some extent his findings are inconsistent with Brinton's gener-

alization that the prerevolutionary economy is healthy and on the upswing.

Davies specifically wanted to test two conflicting theories, both based on Marxist thought. The first is the famous thesis that proletarians would unite when they became terribly poor because they would have "nothing to lose but their chains." Second, Marx stated that unrest among workers would come about not when they became poor but when their condition did not match the growing well-being of the capitalists. This suggests that social tension rises along with deprivation *relative to* the capitalist class and that this relative deprivation occurs while living conditions are actually improving. This second viewpoint was supported by Tocqueville's analysis of the French Revolution, as well as by Brinton.

Davies' findings suggest that both theories may be correct, for the three rebellions that he studied happened during long-term periods of steady improvement in general welfare that were interrupted by a sudden decline. Figure 15.4 is a simple model of such a reversal.[41]

Following Davies' suggestion, a number of scholars have worked with the idea that a psychological variable, relative deprivation, is the basic precondition for rebellion, and that the greater the deprivation among members of a population, the greater the amount of strife and violence that occurs.[42] The underlying explanation is that in a rapidly declining economy the achievements of the population fall short of their reasonable expectations based on past experience. It should be noted, however, that not all evidence supports the relative-deprivation explanation. In particular, it fails to account for the incidents of collective violence that occurred in France between 1830 and 1960.[43] This subject is now being studied by dozens of scholars.

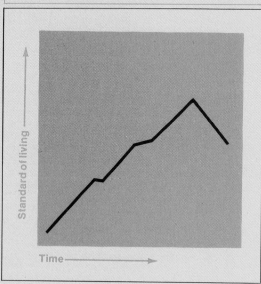

**FIGURE 15.4**

*Davies' model of revolutionary tendencies*

### Russell on the outcome of rebellions

D. E. H. Russell's book *Rebellion, Revolution, and Armed Force* is an attempt to specify the conditions that are necessary for the success of a rebellion.[44] Russell points out the popularity of two contradictory ideas: (1) Repressive force *will not* work, and (2) repressive force *will* work. Those who hold the first view claim that oppression cannot last forever. "The pot must boil over eventually." If the masses are in open rebellion, they can defeat any army and overthrow any regime. The more force the regime uses, the more likely it is to backfire by arousing the anger of the people. This view is often used to explain the Cuban rebellion of 1959, which was successful.[45] Those who hold the second view claim that an army that is loyal to the regime can put down a popular rebellion. "Who could win against such odds?" This view is used to explain the Hungarian rebellion of 1956, which was not successful.

The question of whether force does or does not work had never been systematically studied. Therefore Russell decided to randomly sample 14 mass rebellions, half of which were successful and half of which were unsuccessful, and then determine whether the loyalty of the army determined the outcome. "Disloyalty scores" were calculated for the armed forces of each nation based on the degree of their disloyalty, the amount of time they were disloyal, and the percentage who were disloyal at a given time. Russell found that in no successful rebellion did the regime retain the loyalty of the armed forces. This is true even of the Cuban revolution; Castro's small band of guerrillas won, but only because some of Batista's soldiers deserted or refused to fight.

Disloyalty of a regime's armed forces is a necessary but not sufficient condition for the successful outcome of a rebellion. In three cases the military was disloyal to the regime but the rebellion failed anyway.

One conclusion is that it is important to consider not only the conditions influencing the *rebels*, but also the conditions influencing the *regime*. If the army does not defect, oppression *can* last. The people will *not* triumph. Russell agrees with Frantz Neumann's view that twentieth-century governments have all the tools for physical, economic, and psychological force. As Neumann has put it, "Indeed, there exists in modern history no example of a successful revolution against a halfway strong state. . . . Every strong state can deal with its opposition; totalitarian polities have no difficulty whatever with this. . . . In the modern period of conscious precedence of politics, revolution can be successful only within the ruling class and only with the help of the political machinery itself."[46]

Moreover, there are no cases of successful rebellion in an industrial society. As Frank Tannenbaum has pointed out, "All of our social revolutions have been in agricultural countries where the population was predominantly rural."[47] From this evidence Russell regretfully concludes that there is very little hope for suc-

Whether a rebellion succeeds or fails depends partly on the support of the local people and partly on how effectively the regime is organized to keep its troops loyal.

Wide World

cessful revolution in oppressed societies like South Africa, which is industrialized and in which the armed forces are recruited entirely from the white ruling class. If justice is to come to South Africa, it must result from the use of sanctions by foreign powers.

# SOCIAL POLICY:
## Issues and Viewpoints

A person's diagnosis of society's political ills is based on his or her theoretical views. Not suprisingly, elitists and pluralists differ greatly from Marxists in their diagnoses and in the remedies they prescribe. I will first mention some of the issues currently debated by elitists and pluralists. Then we will look beyond these controversies to some of the political realities that governments are likely to face in the years ahead and the adjustments that they may have to make to those realities.

### THE CASE FOR DEMOCRATIC PARTICIPATION

As mentioned earlier, many pluralist and elitist theorists agree on certain points. Both groups have traditionally been concerned with the question of whether democracy can be maintained and, if so, under what conditions. It is generally agreed that not all members of a society can take part equally in the making of decisions that affect the whole group. Most political outcomes will be influenced by elites. At the same time, however, many pluralists and elitists agree that a great deal of protection against oligarchy and oppression may be provided by the existence of many independent centers of power—organized interest groups in particular. Although this means replacing participatory democracy with some form of representative government, it seems unavoidable. No one can imagine a modern society setting its policies through public discussion like a Greek city-state.

However, are we mistakenly calling our system of government "democratic" when we actually elect elites to rule us? Is a responsive representative system the most we can hope for? Peter Bachrach has argued that democratic participation is possible to a much greater extent than pluralists and elitists have been willing to settle for.[48] He believes that too many people are unable to influence the organizations and institutions of which they are members. Democracy should be valued not just as a *method* of making good decisions but as an experience that we all need in order to fulfill our humanity. It is vital that we participate in public affairs and share in decision making. Even if a wise leader could make all the right decisions for us, that would be a poor substitute for democracy.

Bachrach admits that we cannot all take part in top-level government decision making, but he suggests that we recognize the political aspects of many private organizations. For example, it is well known that corporations have great political power and that their executives are a political elite that answer to no one but themselves. Bachrach and other writers urge that the workings of many institutions be made more democratic. For example, why shouldn't customers and workers have some say in the policies of the stores and banks where they do business? They would not necessarily do a better job than the elites, but they would help achieve the democratic ideal of full participation. There is, then, a renewed demand on the part of political liberals for a greater commitment to democracy at all levels of social organization, both private and governmental. This is the spirit behind the welfare rights movement, the demand that students be included in the governing bodies of universities, and similar trends.

There is little quarrel with such movements in principle. No one wants to appear to be opposed to democracy. However, not everyone is convinced that commitment to democratic movements will do much to solve the society's basic problems. Democratic decision making is not a cure-all, and sometimes it is a clumsy process, as anyone who has served on many committees will agree. Sometimes it is absolutely impossible to be democratic. As Barrington Moore has noted, we do not want an airplane pilot to consult all the passengers about when and how to get the plane off the ground. Democracy has its uses, but so does technical know-how.

## THE CASE FOR REVOLUTION

Most radicals think liberals are living in a dream world. The ideal of democratic participation is fine, they say, but it will never come true because the ruling class will not let it. Besides, equalizing the political rights of citizens would be meaningless unless the economic rights of citizens were equalized as well. Nowhere has the ruling class given up its privileges willingly; liberation and equality are gained only through revolution.

*Terrorism, riots, and guerrilla wars have much in common. These tactics often aggravate standard military forces because they cannot be controlled by usual military actions.*

UPI

What are we to make of this argument? Like most other ideological statements, it is true in many ways. There can be little doubt that certain liberal societies, including the United States, have exploited weaker nations as often as they have helped them. Still, the results of revolutionary movements have been so mixed that one should think at least twice before proposing any new ones. It is not uncommon for the revolution to come first and *then* the decision on the form of government desired. One result is that rebel leaders often turn against the people who brought them to power and become as oppressive as the elite they overthrew. One may agree that revolution is justified in a given case yet doubt its value as a general policy.

## THE POLITICAL CHALLENGES OF THE FUTURE

People who think about what sort of political system would best meet the challenges of the future quickly pass beyond the terms *capitalism, socialism, democracy*, and *revolution*. For example, in *An Inquiry into the Human Prospect*[49] Robert L. Heilbroner argues that neither capitalism nor socialism as we know them can serve as blueprints for the future because both depend on continued industrial growth. For a number of good reasons, such as the increasing scarcity of natural resources, increasing pollution, and the overheating of the atmosphere, industrial technology will not be able to go on expanding at current rates. If it does so, the human population is doomed. However, the rapidly growing populations of the poor nations will require those countries to industrialize rather than cut back.

Expansion is necessary merely to keep standards of living at their present miserable levels, let alone to improve them.

Given the need to limit industrial growth, Heilbroner doesn't expect rich nations, either capitalist or socialist, to maintain their economic supremacy. People already understand the possibilities of blackmail and extortion, as is shown by the large number of hijackings and kidnapings that have occurred in recent years. There is good reason to expect a more serious form of blackmail—nuclear threats. Within a few years many poor nations will have nuclear weapons. When their people are starving, it will not be surprising if they turn to nuclear blackmail, threatening to destroy cities like Chicago, Tokyo, or Kiev unless large amounts of money are spent to support their people.

The alternatives to these grim prospects are hardly more desirable. What kind of government would be able to force birth control on an unwilling population or put down the protests of hungry mobs? Heilbroner suggests that it would be a strong government but probably not a democratic one. Though his own political philosophy is liberal, he thinks it is likely that the problems that lie ahead may be so serious that the only government able to solve them would be an oppressive regime.

This is an unhappy note on which to end a chapter. But politics is never a happy topic because it deals with the domination of some people by others. However, only by imagining disagreeable futures can we develop ways of responding to them or avoiding them. From this point of view the topics we have discussed may become your deepest concerns in the years ahead.

## SUMMARY

**1.** *Politics* is any action involving the collective pursuit of collective goals. The *state* has a monopoly on the legitimate use of force. Its effectiveness depends in part on its *legitimacy* (the recognition that its use of power is lawful and socially valuable). *Authority* is a combination of *power* (the ability to have one's way despite opposition) and *legitimacy*.

**2.** Legitimacy may be traditional, charismatic, or rational-legal. The last form is typical of modern bureaucratic states.

**3.** In constitutional democracies various interest groups form on the basis of shared economic or cultural interests and try to influence the policy of the government in favor of their interests.

**4.** Three major theoretical views of politics are *pluralism*, *elitism*, and *Marxism*. Tocqueville and Durkheim, both pluralists, held that minority rights depended on the existence of many competing groups within a society. Those groups must be independent and must be strong enough to limit the power of the centralized state. Later pluralists have added that the differences that separate those groups should not coincide but crisscross.

**5.** Robert Michels, an elitist, described the "iron law of oligarchy": Whenever a group organizes itself and chooses leaders, those leaders will gain enough power to remain in office and/or choose their successors. True elitists believe that democracy is a fraud and that revolution is useless because elites always rule in the end.

**6.** Some theorists are both pluralists and elitists. They recognize not only that many groups exist within society but that they always have leaders or "elites." Such writers hold that these elites are functionally necessary and are not necessarily oppressive.

**7.** Marx believed that all societies have been ruled by elites but that after the proletarian revolution there will no longer be social classes, and hence there will be no ruling elites.

**8.** Neo-Marxists have had to explain why three of Marx's major predictions were incorrect: (1) The communist revolutions have not occurred in industrial societies, as Marx predicted, but in societies that are just beginning to industrialize. Workers in capitalist societies are not fond of communism. (2) Marx did not expect a capitalist system in which a large number of stockholders own most of the assets yet do not manage them. Present-day Marxists claim that the ruling class is a tiny elite that owns only 5 or 6 percent of the assets but controls much more. (3) Marx predicted that the working class would become more miserable as capitalism progressed, but this has not proved to be the case. Neo-Marxists say that this is because whole nations have become capitalists, exploiting the underdeveloped nations and sharing the benefits with the workers. The rich countries prevent depressions by keeping demand for production high through military spending. But many scholars do not agree with the Marxist view that capitalist economies need such spending.

# KEY TERMS

**authority**   power plus legitimacy.

**charismatic authority**   power based on the personality of the leader.

**crisis of legitimacy**   the situation in which large numbers of people withdraw their support from a regime.

**elitism**   the belief that some group always gets the upper hand and rules the masses.

**interest group**   a unified group that tries to influence the state in its favor.

**legitimacy** the right to give orders.

**Marxism** any doctrine that is supposedly derived from the teachings of Karl Marx.

**mechanical solidarity** the pattern in which people get along by being alike in their backgrounds, religious practices, ideas about morality, and so forth.

**neo-Marxism** the Marxist view of capitalism, updated to correspond with developments since Marx's time.

**organic solidarity** the pattern in which people are interdependent even though they are very different in experience, opinions, habits, and so forth.

**pluralism** the view that the best way to preserve freedom in a society is to have within it a number of powerful groups that represent various interests.

**politics** any action involving the collective pursuit of collective goals.

**power** the ability to get one's orders obeyed despite opposition.

**rational-legal authority** power based on the rules of the constitution under which the leader has been elected or appointed.

**state** the organization that has a monopoly on the legitimate use of force in a given territory.

**traditional authority** power based on the customs under which a leader gains his or her position.

**veto group** an interest group that can prevent any action that conflicts with its values and interests.

# FOR FURTHER READING

BARNET, RICHARD J., and RONALD E. MULLER. *Global Reach: The Power of the Multinational Corporations.* New York: Simon & Schuster, 1974. Open this book at any page and you will learn something interesting, such as the fact that CBS owns Steinway Piano Company and RCA, NBC's parent, owns Hertz car rentals, plus millions of other facts about multinationals' power.

BLACK, DONALD. *The Behavior of Law.* New York: Academic Press, 1976. Law is part of the political process too, and this book has gained a lot of attention since its publication. It's a very serious book.

DAHL, ROBERT A. *Who Governs?* New Haven, Conn: Yale University Press, 1961. This is a study of city politics; its conclusions are pluralist. Who does govern? Dahl says it depends upon the issue. On one issue, one group will be decisively influential. On the next issue, another group will emerge and win. Nobody wins all the time. That is good news if we can believe it.

DAHRENDORF, RALF. *Class and Class Conflict in Industrial Society.* Stanford: Stanford University Press, 1959. Dahrendorf is one of those few academics who became influential in practical political administration. For a while I thought of him as West Germany's answer to Henry Kissinger, but he seems to have dropped all that now. This is a major study of class relationships, a useful corrective to some Marxist ideas.

FRIEDENBERG, EDGAR Z. *The Disposal of Liberty and Other Industrial Wastes.* New York: Anchor Books, 1976. Friedenberg does social commentary of an imaginative, off-beat sort. I think he is more interested in stirring up questions in readers' minds than in answering them.

MARCHAK, PATRICIA. *Ideological Perspectives on Canada.* Toronto; McGraw-Hill Ryerson, 1975. A comparison of several ideologies—liberal, old-left, and new-left—and their applications to explaining particular historical events. Marchak asserts that the liberal perspective failed to explain protest and that the new left is the only approach able to interpret and predict adequately.

MOORE, BARRINGTON, JR. *The Social Origins of Dictatorship and Democracy.* Boston: Beacon

Press, 1966. The year this was published, it won three prizes as the most outstanding book, chosen by historians, sociologists, and political scientists alike. And yet I never found a historian, a sociologist, or a political scientist who quite agreed with his theory. It is an effort to explain why some nations became fascist, other democratic, others revolutionary socialists. Plan to take your time with this book. It is long and full of historical details.

# ECONOMIC LIFE

You are an economic theorist. That is, you have certain beliefs and assumptions about the way the economy works. Unlike professional economic theorists, however, you may take your theories for granted without knowing that you do so. I suggest that we examine some of the beliefs that many people take for granted.

The best way to discover your own beliefs is to pay attention to your feelings. They will lead you straight to a belief every time. Most of us tend to ignore feelings that are too big to deal with. For example, when I see a picture of starving children I quickly turn the page. This time don't turn the page. Look at the picture and watch what you feel. Suppose I tell you that every minute about twenty-eight human beings die of hunger or its effects and that three-quarters of them are children. What do you feel now? I feel hopeless, and that is why I turn the page quickly. Underneath this hopelessness there is both resentment and guilt, which are feelings that I want to avoid.

My feelings of resentment and guilt are about scarcity and waste. We can't avoid such feelings in this chapter because economics is the social science that deals with the production, distribution, exchange, and consumption of scarce goods and services. The key term here is *distribution*. When distribution is unequal, some people are needy and others can afford to be wasteful. When we are needy, watching someone else waste things makes us resentful. When we are rich and spending freely, seeing someone else who is in need makes us feel guilty.

Politeness involves helping each other avoid feeling guilty or resentful. Polite rich people do not have a feast in front of hungry people. Polite poor people pretend they are not hungry (even if they are) so that rich people need not feel guilty about their wonderful meals. We won't be polite here. Let's look at our resentment and guilt. This

needn't lead to despair, for our feelings are a consequence of one of our economic beliefs: that *scarcity* is unavoidable.

So here is the first unexamined assumption: We can never produce enough to go around. This is certainly a common belief, but it is not necessarily true. I have no idea how to provide enough goods and services for all the world's needy people, but I believe it is possible. And if we start from the assumption that it is possible, we will look for ways of doing it. Nobody knows yet which solutions will work. But I suggest that we look for some. We are in this together. Those twenty-eight deaths a minute are a part of my world, and yours.

We're not going to get all the answers here. We'll only start. The difficulty is this: You never know what information you need to solve a problem until you have the answer. We don't really know what questions to ask. We know that it is very important to find out how economies work, but we can't predict which topics will be useful as we consider the problem in the years ahead. We can prepare by developing an inquiring mind, holding a problem and suspending judgment until we get some good answers.

In this chapter I will start with a quick sketch of economic history. Then we will discuss the attitudes toward the proper relationship between the free market and political regulation that have been popular at various times. After that we will devote the balance of the chapter to information about various aspects of economic life—food production, labor relations, automation, and the problems of the poor nations. Some of these findings may prove useful to you later. And I suggest that whenever you react with feeling to something you read, pay attention to those feelings and notice what beliefs they rest upon. This is how you will find out what your unexamined economic theories are. Then you can examine them.

# The historical development of economic systems

## PRIMITIVE ECONOMIES

Throughout most of human history the technology of production was, by modern standards, very limited—hunting animals, fishing, gathering nuts, grubs, or berries, and the like. Though such a life style may not appeal to many of us, it is not necessarily a life of hunger. In fact some primitive groups have more food than they need. They can afford, for example, to eat the tastiest pieces of fruit and throw away the rest. Other groups, however, are closer to the possibility of starvation. No primitive group is satisfied to limit its production to the bare minimum required for survival. Every group encourages its members to put aside something extra so that it can be offered to guests or to honored leaders or stored up for times of shortage.[1] Moreover, many primitive peoples devote a good deal of their energy to making objects that are not useful. Things like feathered headdresses are not economic investments but objects that can be worn or offered to others in a system of etiquette or ritual, enabling a person to sustain his or her pride and social status. We do much the same thing when we work at our hobbies, wear fashionable clothing or give one another bottles of cognac at Christmas time.

Indeed, it is hard for us to understand a primitive society as an "economic" system at all, since in such societies most objects are produced and distributed as gifts, to satisfy kinship obligations, to be used in rituals, and the like, not to be owned or sold for profit. The idea of *quid pro quo* (giving something in order to get something) is at the heart of a market economy, but most primitive economies do not involve markets. In such a society people do not necessarily exchange scarce goods or labor in order to get what they need. They may give the right hind quarter of a slaughtered pig to mother's mother and half of their yams to mother's sister as a matter of tradition and without

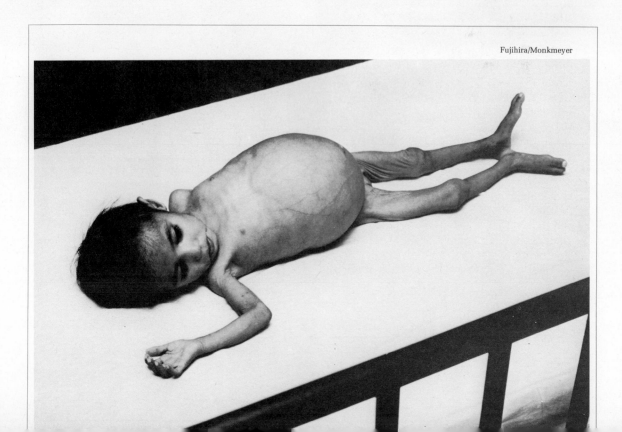

Fujihira/Monkmeyer

expecting to be repaid. But at the same time they may receive fish or fruit from some other relative, also as a matter of tradition, and may call upon their nephews for help in building a hut or canoe.

The French sociologist Marcel Mauss was interested in economic systems based on gift giving. He suggested that modern society is less gracious than primitive society. For us, exchanges are mostly "economic," while primitive people emphasize ceremonial exchanges. The giver is expected to give and the receiver is expected to give in return, but the timing and exact amount of the return gift are open to much variation. The gift

is a symbolic binding together of a kinship unit or tribe.[2]

In 1922 Bronislaw Malinowski wrote a classic description of the *Kula* system, the ceremonial gift exchange pattern of the inhabitants of a circle of islands located hundreds of miles apart in the South Seas.[3] In the *Kula* system red necklaces were sent as gifts in a clockwise direction from island to island, while white bracelets were sent in a counterclockwise direction. Thus each necklace giver would eventually receive back the very necklace that he had once given. Each item would make a complete circle about once in ten years. Obviously, supply-

In primitive economies, food is caught, trapped, or collected. Many societies still use some simple economic technologies, either as the sole or partial source of their livelihood, such as these Ecuadorian Indians do.

Jerry Frank/DPI

and-demand theory cannot account for such patterns of exchange.

Economic exchanges fall into three main patterns.[4] The first pattern, **reciprocity,** is a two-way exchange of goods or services, as illustrated by the ritualized gift giving of families, clans, and tribes. Farmers in many societies help each other at harvest time. Goods or services are given because it is traditional to do so. The only economic calculation involved is the loose principle that the goods or services received should "balance out" in the long run.

The second pattern of exchange is **redistribution.** This involves bringing economic goods and services to a central source — usually governmental — and then redistributing them throughout the population. This pattern was common in ancient Asian and African civilizations. Modern examples include charity and taxation. Like reciprocity, redistribution is characterized by the absence of self-serving calculations. In this case the basic principle of calculation seems to be "justice."

The third pattern of exchange, which is more familiar in Western civilization, is **market exchange.** In this case goods and services are exchanged in a market context. Prices are not set by tradition but result from bargaining for economic advantage. Formal economic analysis can be applied only to this type of exchange, and we will be concerned mainly with this type in the rest of the chapter.

### EXPLOITATION OF LABOR

The development of agriculture was one of the most important breakthroughs in human history, but it must have happened only under special conditions. Most hunters and gatherers are unwilling to take up farming because it involves more work than they are used to doing.[5] However, the most primitive methods of agriculture required less work than the methods to which people were driven later by the scarcity of land. In a few parts of the world this simple technology, sometimes called the "slash-and-burn" system, is still in use. The cultivator simply cuts and burns a plot of forest land, plants some seeds in the ash-fertilized soil, and waits for the harvest. The same area may be planted again the following year, but after that the soil becomes less fertile and the cultivator must burn a new area. After twenty years the first plot can be burned again more easily than a forest plot that has never been burned, so that ideally the cultivator should hold enough land so that only a small area has to be worked at any one time. This technology rarely yields a large crop per acre; on the other hand, it doesn't require much labor either. However, when land becomes scarce, cultivators have to burn a plot so often that trees cannot grow there again. As a result many large areas of the world that were covered with trees in prehistoric times are now grassland.[6]

As land grew scarce, it became necessary to increase output per acre. Agriculture began to require more labor, and, probably at about the same time, the concept of property arose. Human inequality had existed before, but now social *classes* were formed and land ownership became the basis for continuing and even increasing inequality. Those who own land can employ people who don't own land to cultivate it, paying them either with wages or with a share of the crop. Not only do the owners work less than the laborers, but they can also consume more.[7] The possibility of exploiting the labor of others occurred very early to some landowners, who used warfare to supply their manpower needs. They enslaved their captives and used the surplus created by them partly to live well and partly to maintain an army with which to capture a fresh supply of agricultural slaves. Some American Indians had slaves, and so did the Africans who were themselves caught by European and American slave dealers on the Gold Coast.[8]

The gentleman-warrior class never found it practical to keep all of the lower classes in slavery; they needed a class of freemen to keep the slaves from rebelling. The freemen were able to make a living by serving the needs of the rich. They became townspeople—artisans, traders, and the like—and sometimes built up foreign trade and a money economy. Where agriculture was very productive, quite a large class of townspeople could exist.

Still, in most parts of the world the idea of investing for the sake of profit did not develop far. Indeed, the idea of a self-regulated market economy was not accepted until about 200 years ago even in Europe.[9] Though foreign trade existed, it was held in check for a long time by the concept of a "just price," a rule that forbade taking advantage of another person's need. In other areas it was held back by rules based on status. Only in England, with its unusual historical conditions, did real capitalism develop.

### COMMERCIAL FARMING IN ENGLAND

In England, as in most of medieval Europe, agriculture was carried out through a feudal organization of labor in which serfs were attached to land owned by lords. However, certain developments in England changed the nature of agriculture there and opened up the possibility of industrialization. The lords found that serf labor was inefficient and began to employ full-time workers to cultivate the best part of their land; the rest of the land was rented out.[10] The Italians and the Dutch began to manufacture woolen textiles using English wool, and many English lords enlarged their flocks of sheep. Ordinary peasants were also able to keep a few

sheep, allowing them to graze on the "common," or public pasture.

By the thirteenth century the population of England had increased greatly. Suddenly the Black Death, encouraged by overcrowding, swept across Europe and reduced the population of some areas by one-third.[11] Where there had been an oversupply of labor there was now a shortage, and the peasants were put in a more favorable position. In Western (but not Eastern) Europe they gained their freedom. The population decrease also reduced the land shortage, making it possible for most families to keep sheep on open pastures and produce wool for cash.

This situation continued through the sixteenth century, when the landlords began to enclose the commons in order to prevent the peasants from pasturing their sheep there. By then farming had become a commercial activity geared to a money economy, and the enclosures made scientific agriculture even more feasible. By the eighteenth century, for example, crop rotation was widely practiced, so that land could be cultivated every year without decreasing in fertility. The enclosures were a serious loss for the peasants, however, who were freed from feudalism at the terrible price of losing their land and becoming wage laborers.[12] The development of the wool industry in England, along with the enclosure movement, led to the establishment of the cotton industry, and it was through the cotton industry that the Industrial Revolution took place.[13]

### THE INDUSTRIAL REVOLUTION

As the enclosure movement was taking away the peasants' land for commercial farming and driving the peasants away, there was a new increase in population. Thus a large supply of labor became available at the time when great innovations were being made in the production of cotton textiles. This new industry absorbed many of the workers in the world's first system of factory manufacture, which was organized by merchants who were no longer content to buy from artisans. The factories were so efficient that the artisans, unable to compete with the productivity of machines, were ruined and had to become factory workers themselves. Though there was a good supply of food for this rapidly growing worker population, their situation was miserable. They worked long, hard hours for very low wages. The factory owners were constantly looking for ways to increase output per head so as to make even more profit, which could then be plowed back into the business.

Cotton textiles led the way, but industrialization spread into other industries as well. New scientific discoveries were continually being put to use in industry. Gradually the whole world was drawn into this productive system as colonial empires were built up to provide raw materials for industries in the leading industrial countries. Mining, lumbering, and other extractive industries in the colonies required the labor of native workers, who were not used to a money economy and often were not attracted by wages. In some colonies, particularly in Africa, the native populations were required to pay taxes in cash. The colonial government did not want their tax money—it just wanted to force them into the labor market which they had not been willing to enter because they had no need for cash.[14]

At home, capital developed as a source of wealth. Fortunes could be made by trading in securities—paper that entitled the owner to returns on capital investments made by others long before. Thus people might get rich without contributing either labor or money to the productive process.[15]

# Modern economic systems

## CAPITALISM

As we have seen, Marx failed to foresee how capitalism would develop in the twentieth century. Modern capitalism is far different from the system Marx knew. It is no longer an economy dominated by individual entrepreneurs, or "robber barons," but one dominated by giant corporations in which ownership is divided among hundreds of thousands of shareholders who formally "own" the firm but who have no control over its management.[16] Control over decisions made within the corporation is in the hands of professional managers who may or may not own large amounts of stock themselves. In such companies the stockholders obey the management, not the other way around. Most stockholders are interested in their stocks only as investments.[17]

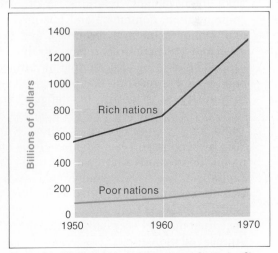

**FIGURE 16.1**

*World Economic Development, 1950–1970, in 1964 US dollars*

Source: John W. Meyer, John Boli-Bennett, and Christopher Chase-Dunn. "Convergence and Divergence in Development," *Annual Review of Sociology*, I. 1975. Palo Alto, Calif.: Annual Reviews, Table 1, p. 227.

In general, the holders of large blocks of stock favor the payment of low dividends so that most of the profits can be plowed back into the firm. Small investors (who far outnumber the large stockholders) prefer a high rate of dividends. Although the managers are closer in outlook to the large investors, they usually compromise between the two views.[18]

In former years capitalists were the masters of their own firms; today corporation executives are almost at the mercy of their employees, for no one person can know enough to challenge the wisdom of a group of specialists. Power is shared among committees of experts. John Kenneth Galbraith has called this new group of executives the "technostructure" and claims that they are the real ruling class in modern capitalism.[19]

Galbraith also points out that the modern corporation is strongly connected with government, which it both influences and is influenced by. Although a decreasing number of conservatives grumble about "government interference in the free-enterprise system," this influence is generally accepted as a fact of life by the corporation executives themselves. The government is involved in labor–management relations, workmen's compensation, commerce and business, the exploitation of natural resources, and even wage and price controls. It pays for the education and training of personnel for industry and for a lot of research that is of great value to industry. Most of all, its "defense" contracts for war matériel provide a steady demand for goods and services. Since World War II this demand has cushioned the economic depressions that characterized early capitalism. It is small wonder that modern executives are less committed to individualism and freedom from government interference than the early capitalists, given this reciprocal relationship.

Government power over business increased in response to the public demand for coordination as the economic and social structure grew more complex. This increase in government control was in response to the difficult problem of achieving justice and equality in the face of bigness. It may be true, however, that business influence over government has also increased.[20]

Corporation managers have become less hostile to government regulation partly because industry benefits so highly from a stable market. Some modern products are in the design stage 10 or 15 years before coming onto the market. Modern managers are as interested in accurate estimates of future costs and demand as they are in maximizing profits. They will do whatever they can to stabilize prices, demand for their product, and so forth, even if it means accepting government regulation or cooperating with their "competitors" in setting prices. Price-cutting competition is not characteristic of advanced capitalism.[21]

### Labor relations in advanced capitalism

The history of industrialization is marked by changes in the organization of labor as well as management. One of the typical forms of labor organization before the Industrial Revolution in England was the "friendly society." These clubs of workers were interested in using political influence to affect terms of apprenticeship, wages, and the quality of goods produced, but they served a number of other functions as well. They were social and drinking clubs. They took care of workers' savings and provided insurance against death, illness, and the like. Above all, however, they showed a tendency to unite with the masters on matters affecting the welfare of industry as a whole.

With the increasing separation of workers from their capital and from the products of their labor during the Industrial Revolution, the nature of trade unionism also began to change. During the first half of the nineteenth century more specialized unions began to develop in Britain. These unions made greater efforts to gain better wages and were definitely in conflict with the employer group. This was the type of union that fought so hard for workers' rights in both Britain and the United States.

During the nineteenth century labor agitation in the United States followed a roughly cyclical pattern.[22] In good times, when labor was scarce, workers could demand wage increases with more chance of success; furthermore, there was more money for union organizations and strikes. During depressions strikes were less effective and workers demanded protective legislation from the government or talked about cooperating with industry to build a new economic structure.[23]

The most recent stage of labor development is "business unionism". Unions have tended to organize strikes in more rational ways, to reduce violence, and to discipline the workers. Much of the heat and emotion has disappeared from strikes, and the revolutionary overtones that strikes frequently had have clearly decreased in the mid-twentieth century. Peaceful collective bargaining has become a more common method of conflict resolution. Violence seems to be limited to the "unofficial," or "wildcat" strike, in which groups of workers not only have grievances against management but also feel that they are "getting the runaround" from big unions or big government.[24]

Both labor and management recognize the need to maintain demand for the company's products because both employment and profits depend on sales. This problem has promoted the need for advertising, which stimulates demand for goods, often in advance of their existence. However, advertising alone could not have succeeded in keeping demand at the high levels necessary to keep modern factories humming. As mentioned earlier, the arms race has helped stabilize demand at a high level. American capitalism has yet to discover how to maintain a steady demand for products and services while planning for peace, not war. It must also find out how to overcome the increasing gap between the income levels of the rich nations and the poor.

## The welfare state

A number of capitalist societies have softened the edges of capitalism, giving their citizens the benefits of economic stability, social justice, and peaceful international relations. It is not always clear whether one should call countries like Sweden capitalist or socialist. The welfare state is somewhere between those two systems. Income is redistributed through progressive taxation and free education, including university training. Many other social benefits are available to all citizens. Medical-care costs are very low. Generous pensions are provided for the old, the handicapped, and anyone else who is unable to work. Pleasant housing is provided for the poor. Women are given paid maternity leave, and the costs of bearing a child are paid by the state.

To achieve these things the Swedish government has played a strong role in the management of industrial firms and trade unions, sometimes using nationalization, sometimes using economic incentives and political regulation. However, as Joan Robinson has pointed out, the welfare state is just as nationalistic as other societies, drawing a clear line between its own citizens and the other peoples of the world.

## SOCIALISM

Marx believed that capitalism contained "the seeds of its own destruction." The poverty of the masses would increase along with the gathering of wealth into fewer and fewer hands. The business cycle would produce wider swings between "booms" and "busts," so that in the most advanced states the means of production would at last be seized by the workers and the economy would be transformed into a centrally organized one.

We have seen that capitalism has not developed according to Marx's program, but for that matter, socialism has not followed his program either.

For one thing, Marx expected the revolution to produce, fairly soon, a new social system—true communism. Under communism the state would wither away because it would be unnecessary. Goods and services would become so abundant that nobody would want to hoard anything selfishly and the very concept of private property would disappear. People would take what they need without greed and contribute what they could, unselfishly, according to their abilities. No one would lord it over anyone else.

By now it is clear that no communist revolution has led to genuine communism. What has appeared instead are several *socialist* societies, each with its own brand of socialism. The system in the USSR differs from the Chinese approach, which differs from the Yugoslav system, and so on. But they all have one thing in common: The means of production are publicly owned, either by the nation-state or (in the case of Yugoslavia) by the workers who do the actual production in a factory. People do have private property—their own clothes, radios, jewelry, cars, and so on. But they are not supposed to own anything that earns income from the labor of anyone else. This means that no one lives on unearned income such as dividends on stocks and bonds. Making a private profit is called "profiteering" and is forbidden, though social classes still exist, with some people holding privileges that others lack.

In socialist countries the market system is not used to determine what goods should be produced or the prices at which they should be sold. Instead, the state uses detailed planning to decide how much of each item should be manufactured and where it should be allocated. It is not necessary for a firm to make a profit if the government decides that its products are needed for the public welfare. Thus *in socialist societies the economy is subordinate to the political system.*

Let's look at three socialist societies and compare the ways in which they function.

### The Soviet Union

The first communist revolution occurred in a nation only barely touched by industrialization, not in an advanced capitalist state. Therefore Marx's writings could not serve as a guide to the Bolsheviks who seized power in Russia. They had to bring about industrialization themselves. Their initial effort to make industrial decision making more democratic was unsuccessful, so they turned to political force. Their purpose was to force farmers to produce more for the urban population and, at the same time, to deprive the masses of consumer goods so that available resources could be used to build up heavy industry as quickly as possible. Production was organized according to a plan, not according to the demands for commodities, but such planning often led to a flow of materials that was less than efficient. In recent years the government has recognized this problem and has acted to make market forces more influential in regulating production than before. And besides the official plan there is an unofficial black market that plays a major role in the economy. However, the market is still far less important in the Soviet Union than in capitalist countries. Consumer preferences have little influence on the types of goods and services provided. Instead, Soviet planners now look to other countries to see what styles consumers prefer there, and then try to copy those designs. Thus a new car is likely to look like an out-of-date Ford, Volvo, or Plymouth.

The state owns almost all the means of production—mines, land, factories, and so forth. Workers earn wages and have some choice among occupations, but they are not allowed to look for work in any region or industry they please.[25] Although the Soviet

Robert W. Young/DPI

*Many developing countries gain greatly in agricultural productivity when they put land redistribution plans into effect.*

economy has made a lot of progress since the revolution, its gross national product (the total value of goods and services produced in a given year) in the 1970s is estimated at about half the U.S. gross national product.[26]

Still, the Soviet system has certain advantages over capitalism. There is no balance-of-payments problem because imports are held to the level that can be paid for by exports.[27] Government services are paid for out of profits from business, not income taxes, and without such taxes there are fewer "loopholes" to protect special interests. There is never a problem of unemployment, for those who cannot find the jobs they want are assigned to jobs that must be done. No class of persons lives on unearned income.

The most serious problems remaining in the Soviet Union are more political than economic. One of these is the government's lack of responsiveness to the people. This is a holdover from the period of rapid industrialization. Such unresponsiveness is not an inherent aspect of socialism, however, as the case of Yugoslavia shows.

### Yugoslavia

In 1950 the Yugoslavs were successful in a bold move to break away from Soviet control, though they remained committed to socialist principles. Since then they have developed a highly democratic version of socialism. Learning from the failure of early economic experiments in the Soviet Union, the Yugoslavs set up a system in which workers control industry. An industry is owned by a Workers' Council consisting of from 20 to 100 workers. The council chooses managers and decides what to produce and how profits should be used. The councils may borrow capital or import raw materials from other countries.

The Yugoslav political system is decentralized, with the greatest power held by communes at the local level. "In the final redistribution of 'public resources,' which serve to cover the general requirements of the community (budget, social, and public services), the commune has at its disposal greater resources than the federation or republic."[28] Because of the decentralization of power, problems of coordination sometimes arise—for example, a road was built in one area but never connected to any road in the next district. Many citizens do not even think of themselves as "Yugoslavs" but view

China is still an agricultural society with very little mechanization of work. The size of their population allows them to use people instead of machines in many cases. These workers are processing cotton.

Wide World

themselves as "Serbs," "Croats," and so forth. Still, the system is very effective in involving the workers in the affairs of their industry and society, and any changes made in Yugoslavia will have to conform to the democratic methods that are so highly valued there.

### China

Thirty years ago the situation of China was much like the situation of India or Bangladesh today—very poor. In Shanghai trucks drove along the streets every morning, loaded with corpses. Every block or two a truck would stop to pick up the body of another person who had died on the street during the night. But that was before the revolution.

Unlike the Russian revolution, the Chinese revolution started in the countryside and moved to the cities. Since the revolution, the social changes have been made with the cooperation of the peasants. The collectivization of land and the introduction of better agricultural methods raised productivity per person as well as per acre.[29] Each work team owns its land, equipment, and social-welfare fund. Income is distributed to individuals on the basis of earned work points. Consumer goods are available. Unlike the situation in the early years of the USSR, peasants are never forced to sell so much of what they produce that they don't have enough left to feed themselves.[30]

Planning is more efficient in China than in the Soviet Union because the needs of consumers determine what will be produced and in what quantities. The government simply arranges contracts between industries at various points of the production process.

The Chinese are determined to destroy class divisions. Government officials must periodically work on a commune so that they will remember to serve the people. Work is praised, and people are encouraged to criticize the party and the government. The economic system is based on appealing to people's sense of moral duty, not to the desire to get ahead. It works because people *do* seem to respond to moral appeals. The Chinese economy has not grown very fast, but it has achieved a great deal because of its commitment to equalizing the distribution of wealth in society. Unfortunately, not enough statistics are published to enable researchers to compare the effectiveness of the Chinese system with other economic systems. It is possible that our conclusions about China are mistaken because outsiders are not allowed to see the side of Chinese society that has developed more slowly.

## The development of economic thought

One of the purposes of this chapter is to make you aware of economic theories that you may have taken for granted. This is important because your theories guide your decisions and the policies you support. And these policies make life better or worse. Economic policies have a huge impact on you and me and on people on the other side of the world—and on all of our children and grandchildren.

Obviously, we cannot review the whole history of economic thought. Therefore I will use one issue—the relationship between market forces and political regulation—to show how theories have flip-flopped from one extreme to another in only 200 years.

If you have been properly socialized in a capitalist society, you probably assume (maybe with strong feelings) that the free-enterprise system is the only reasonable way of taking care of human needs. And you may also assume that any interference with the workings of the market system is unwise, to put it mildly. But markets are not a necessary ingredient of human society. Some societies distribute goods and services without using market exchange. Your parents may have given tomatoes to their neighbors without

*Markets have not been necessary in many preindustrial societies in the past. However, today most people in the world buy products and pay for them in cash. This is a general store in Morocco.*

expecting anything in return. The same neighbor—or perhaps another one—may have sent over a loaf of banana bread or offered to babysit, also without expecting to be paid. This is *reciprocity*, not exchange. We couldn't run a society as complex as ours using this kind of system alone, but many primitive societies get along quite well with simple reciprocity. On the other hand, even in our society we depend on generosity as well as exchange. Consider the system of

"grants" that provides for needy people and worthy causes. You may have a scholarship, for example. Maybe your professor's research is funded by a grant from the Ford Foundation, the Canada Council, or the National Science Foundation. Maybe you contributed to the local newspaper's fresh-air fund to send slum children to summer camp. Such grants are not given with the expectation that anything will be given in return.

However, for us the market is the primary mechanism of distribution. How does it work? Everyone is supposed to want to own things, and everyone has to sell something to earn a living. A person may sell either goods (products) or services (labor). These things are bought and sold in the market. Because so many people are buying and selling, no single individual or firm (presumably) can control the prices at which goods and services are exchanged. Price is determined by the relationship between supply and demand. When we do business, you and I, we each assume that the other is trying to get the best possible bargain and that all the other buyers and sellers are doing likewise. If I don't like your offer, I'll try to find someone who will make a better offer. You know this, so you keep the competition in mind when you make your offer.

You may take this situation for granted and feel all right about it, especially if you are used to doing business. But some people dislike the fact that in a capitalist system everyone is expected to seek the greatest possible profit instead of serving the public interest. A system of market exchange assumes that "I'm not in business for my health," that I will take advantage of every chance to make a profit. You are supposed to know this and watch out for your own interests instead of expecting me to protect your interests for you.

Of course we do set limits to competition. I'm not supposed to lie or cheat or make false claims in my advertising or run away with your rent deposit, for example. The government will punish me if I cheat you, steal from you, or break a contract that we have signed. So we depend on the government to support the conditions that make markets able to function. This leads us to the question, How much should the government be involved in economic transactions? How much government regulation is desirable and how much is a nuisance? For example, if I charge an unfair price for something you need and can't get elsewhere, should the government interfere and keep me from taking advantage of you? Points of view on such questions differ greatly. Most people would agree that government should at least force people to live up to their contracts, and perhaps that it must limit monopolies or even actively fight inflation, depression, unemployment, and other economic problems. Beyond that, the government has to be involved in economic relationships with other societies. Should the government try to make its own society richer at the expense of others? May it use political and military power to force other nations to make favorable economic agreements with important companies whose interests it wants to protect? These issues have to do with the proper relationship between the government and the "natural" functioning of markets in a situation of free competition.

Not only do individuals differ on many of these issues, but the general opinion of people today differs from that of the previous generation. Public opinion on matters of economic policy is always changing, as the following paragraphs will show.

### MERCANTILISM

We begin with mercantilism, the economic policies of the seventeenth and eighteenth centuries—the period when Europe was ruled by absolute monarchs. Mercantilists thought that the best way to increase na-

tional power was to increase national wealth—which meant to increase the nation's supply of gold and silver. The state encouraged this policy in every possible way. Mercantilism involved the regulation of industry and trade by centralized political power. The monarch granted monopoly power to industries that manufactured goods for export, and in return demanded a fee which was the principal source of government finance. It limited imports and set up colonies to provide gold, silver, and raw materials. Mercantilism was the dominant economic system in Europe until Adam Smith's views became popular.

### ADAM SMITH

Adam Smith (1723–1790) attacked mercantilism in *The Wealth of Nations.* He began by rejecting the assumption that wealth equals money or treasure. The wealth of a nation, he argued, is its power to produce goods. Money is simply a medium of exchange. The real source of wealth is specialized labor. Why? Because the more specialized labor is, the more productive it is. And the specialization of labor depends on the size of the market for its products and the availability of capital. Thus increasing trade by enlarging the market is the key to economic growth. Smith recommended free trade instead of the protectionist policies of mercantilism. He wanted to abolish tariffs and other restrictions on international trade. Storing up gold and silver seemed unimportant to him. Wealth was not *money* but *products* being traded to meet human needs.

Smith's approach was called laissez faire, which means, roughly, "let it be." It held that the state should not regulate the economy but should allow it to regulate itself. If they were given the chance, businesspeople would enlarge their markets and thus enrich the nation.

You may ask, what prevents a few individuals from gaining control of the market if the government doesn't regulate them? What keeps them from fixing prices and so on? Smith believed that *in a completely free economy* businesspeople would not pool their power to control prices and output. Instead, they would put their capital into the most productive enterprises. The economy would regulate itself. And he believed that if tariffs were abolished, each country would produce whatever was most profitable, given its resources. The best possible distribution of goods would result from free international trade.

Thus Smith was opposed to government support of particular businesses. The state should not grant favors to certain economic groups but let them all compete freely in the market. The market, unregulated, would reward those who produced needed goods at the lowest prices. Both the public and the nation would benefit from free competition. The state should guarantee that contracts are honored. It should provide a setting that encourages business in general. But it should not protect particular enterprises.

### KARL MARX

Although we have discussed Marx's theories at several points in this book, we haven't focused on his analysis of the relationships between economic and political forces. You will recall that Marx distinguished between the *economic structure* of a society and what he called the *superstructure*. The economic structure included both the technology of production and the social relationships that occur when people act together to produce goods. These economic structures are basic—they determine everything else, including the superstructure. Among the social relationships that are part of the economic structure are *social classes*. Marx was especially interested in two of those classes—the bourgeoisie (the capitalists) and the

Marx expected the workers in industrial society to have an increasingly difficult life, so they would eventually rebel. This unemployed worker is unhappy, but not likely to revolt.

Wide World

proletarians (the industrial workers). It is through social classes that the economic structure gives rise to the superstructure.

The superstructure includes institutions such as laws, schools, the government, the church, and the military. In early capitalism the superstructure serves the bourgeoisie. To put it more simply, the politicians and the armed forces help keep the workers in a subordinate position, and religious leaders feed them ideologies so that they won't rebel. Marx wasn't saying this is how the government, the church, the military, and other institutions *should* act. He was saying that this is how they *would* act. The capitalists ordinarily have more power than the workers. With that power they can influence the government to pass laws that are unfavorable to the workers and put down their riots, strikes, and demonstrations. Under such conditions *the political forces in society back up the economic forces.*

But this situation does not last forever. The capitalists have to drive the workers harder and harder simply to maintain their profits. The competition between capitalists also drives them to buy more efficient machines, and this also increases productivity. Eventually an hour of each worker's labor yields several times as many products as it did before.

Economic depressions get more severe. Workers may riot, but gradually they become more politically aware. They join unions and make demands. Finally they create a revolutionary party that destroys the capitalist system and brings in a socialist one. By then competition will have forced the capitalists to buy such efficient machinery that the workers can run it with little effort. Each person will work a few hours a day to satisfy basic needs and will be free to spend his or her spare time developing more important human qualities such as knowledge and creativity.

Thus Marx believed that as the workers become more and more threatening, the political forces will no longer support the economic system. In fact it is through political force (revolution) that the workers will destroy the economic system (capitalism). In other words, as an economic system weakens, *the economic and political forces come into conflict, and this conflict ultimately dooms the system.*

## THE MODERN MARKET SYSTEM AND GOVERNMENT REGULATION

In the preceding chapter we discussed Marx's historical predictions and noted that neo-Marxists have had to revise the theory to explain historical developments. No one knows what Marx would think if he were with us today—but no one knows what Adam Smith would believe either. He certainly would not believe everything he wrote in *The Wealth of Nations*. Few people believe in free enterprise any more—at least as Smith described it. Certainly business leaders don't want the government to leave the economy to its own devices. They don't want public ownership, of course, but they like the stabilizing influence that a strong government provides. What has happened to economic theory since Smith's day?

First, Smith assumed that, if left alone, the market would be quite competitive. No firm would gain the power to control prices or output. But the trouble is obvious: The market is *not* perfectly competitive. Price and output can be manipulated more easily than Smith supposed. Suppose, for example, that you and I are two sulfur producers who control the entire supply of sulfur. We can call the tune. Since buyers cannot go elsewhere for their sulfur, we control the price. Or suppose the government builds a dam that becomes the only source of electricity for an entire region. Where is the competition in this situation? Obviously, the government will set the price for the electricity produced by the dam. Much of what we use in today's economy is produced by systems that do not set prices on the basis of competition.

During the 1920s and 1930s economists began to realize that the model of perfect competition was unrealistic. They developed other models that assume *imperfect competition*. For example, modern economic theory recognizes that firms may set prices not on the basis of their costs but on the basis of political agreements with other firms. Businesses may behave uneconomically in the short run by cutting prices in order to drive their competitors out of business—and then raise prices as high as they please. In addition, politics may influence the price system quite directly: A firm may set its prices at a given level because the government has put pressure on it.

One of the leading economic theorists of the early twentieth century was John Maynard Keynes (1883–1946). In contrast to Smith, Keynes held that the government could and should stabilize the economy. He welcomed the partnership between business and the state because he realized that capitalist economies can develop serious imbalances that can be corrected only by government action. Not only *can* they develop imbalances—they can be *expected* to do so. Thus long periods of unemployment and depression are to be expected. In explaining depressions, Keynes suggested that the main assumption made by Adam Smith and his followers—that economic systems automatically use whatever resources are available, including capital—was wrong.

Keynes showed that you and I may save money in order to invest it in business but find that available investments are unattractive. Capital may not be needed. Businesses may not be able to obtain loans at rates that profits will cover, so there may arise both an excess of savings and a reluctance by business and consumers to spend. If enough people save their money instead of spending it or investing it, the factories lay off workers. In the days before unemployment insurance, such a depression may not correct itself through the market forces. Keynes and his followers argue that the best way out is for the government to take action to correct the instability. There are several ways of doing this. One is by buying or not buying goods. This is called fiscal policy. The government can spend like no one else. So if demand is low, the government should spend, spend, spend to bring it up. Spend on highways, hospitals, space exploration, and so on. The government can also change policies that affect the distribution of income—such as the income tax laws or the rules that determine who is eligible for welfare. These policies influence consumption, which, in turn, affects the market.

A second tool that the government can use to stabilize the economy is called monetary policy. This involves manipulating the prime lending rate or the total money supply; in the United States it is the main concern of the Federal Reserve Board.

Since Keynes' day we have all become increasingly aware of how political factors influence the economy. We are deeply interested in taxation policy, defense policy, and welfare policy. The only thing that is impossible is to do what Smith recommended—to have *no* economic policy, that is, to leave the economy alone. Whatever action the government takes, it will have some impact on the economy. So whenever you vote, you may be voting either for the policies of Adam Smith or for those of John Maynard Keynes, though neither name will be on the ballot. Nowadays Keynes is winning far more often than Smith.

# SOCIAL RESEARCH:
## Sociologists at Work

Imagine that your plane has been hijacked and has landed in some unknown airport. You are put into a bus that speeds through the countryside. How long will it take you to guess where you are? Unless you see a familiar flag you may not guess what country you are in, but you will know almost immediately whether you are in a developed or less developed nation. The gap between the rich nations and the poor ones is unmistakable. We live in two worlds on the same planet—our world and the Third World. Each has its own economic problems. In actuality, the problems are interrelated. But the experiences and way of life that are characteristic of our economic system are amazingly different from those of the less developed economies.

In discussing the trends and prospects of the Western industrial societies I want to pay particular attention to two broad topics (1) work and (2) the shift toward a postindustrial society.

## WORK

Who works? In what jobs? There are great differences in the area of employment. Age, sex, and ethnicity—to mention only three factors—affect participation in the work force. Just recently, for example, there has been a large group of youths entering the labor force—the babies of the baby boom, now maturing. Hence, there are more young people than are needed to fill the jobs that usually hire young adults. In ten years the situation will be different; unemployment patterns will be linked to age in a different way. The best jobs are now held mostly by middle-aged men. Old people have trouble finding or holding jobs, just as youths do. Even older people who have not yet reached retirement age are likely to be unemployed for a long time if they lose their jobs.

For several decades women have been entering the work force in large numbers. Between 1948 and 1967 alone, female participation increased by 70 percent in the United States. Nowadays almost half of the working women in the United States have school-aged children.[31] However, the structure of women's occupations has changed very little. Women have always been hired as nurses, teachers, secretaries, clerks, and so on. They still are. Jobs that were reserved for men in the early days of this century are still reserved for men, though this may soon change. What has happened is not that "male" jobs have opened up for women but, rather, that "female" jobs have increased in number.

Women do have trouble combining careers with motherhood. Often one of these roles has to be eased a bit to make room for the other. They are more likely to take up casual, temporary jobs than men. Many women leave their jobs when their babies arrive and return at about the age of 30. Those who continue to work often have fewer children.[32] Women who work while their children are young generally do so because they need the money—because their husbands are unemployed or not well paid.[33] Working wives gain some authority in the household and have greater influence on the family's financial affairs. They do somewhat fewer household tasks than full-time homemakers do.

Ethnicity is another factor that is strongly related to patterns of occupation. In North America immigrants have typically taken low-paying jobs and gradually moved up the social ladder as the next wave of immigrants arrived to fill the lower-status jobs. However, different ethnic groups have moved upward at different rates. Some groups, such as Jews and Armenians, came from a strong commercial background that worked to their advantage. Others, such as Polish, Irish, or Italian peasants, have found it hard to move upward into middle-class jobs. Black Americans are the most disadvantaged group, for they have very high rates of unemployment relative to whites and are often discriminated against. Employers either deny them jobs because they are black or discriminate indirectly by denying them jobs because they lack certain qualifications. Those who lack technical skills have often been discriminated against elsewhere in the social system—particularly in education.[34]

Jerry Frank/DPI

### ALIENATION

You will spend a major part of your life on the job. What will it be like? Exciting? Dull? Exhausting? Fulfilling? Easy? Challenging? Maddening? Fun? Jobs have all of these qualities in different proportions. I remember my worst job: dipping ashtrays in glaze all day. I couldn't even stop for a drink of water. Try that job for a few months and you will understand very well the experience that we are going to discuss next—alienation.

*Alienation* is loss of belief and interest in the goals toward which one's activities are directed. Alienation produces a loss of commitment to one's group and sense of powerlessness. This is particularly evident in the workplace, but also in political and other social contexts. Some signs

of alienation are the rise of crime, labor unrest, and social protest. Marx was among the first to state that there was a close relationship between alienation and the system of mass production that was developing at that time. Craftsmen usually feel proud of their products because they make each item from start to finish. But in industry workers have no autonomy. Industrial work is divided into a series of repetitive acts that are assigned to different people. The pace of work is determined by the rhythms of machines, not the needs of human beings. Your arm is just one more lever to be synchronized with all the others. And the product is not yours. It belongs to the factory owner, who sells it and pays you wages. Do you feel powerless, bored by meaningless tasks, dulled in spirit and fatigued in body? That's what we mean by alienation.

Some kinds of factory work are more alienating than others. Robert Blauner has classified industrial jobs into three categories: (1) crafts (2) assembly line work, and (3) continuous-process manufacture. (The third category consists of processing products, such as liquid chemicals or oil, that flow continuously through tubes and are manufactured by automatic procedures.) As you might guess, assembly line work is the most alienating. Blauner found that workers who oversee continuous-process manufacture have more responsibility and that the timing of their work is fairly flexible. For example, the workers he studied kept a hot plate in their control room and could heat up a can of soup if they wanted to. They could read their meters a little earlier or a little later than required by their schedule if they wanted to eat their soup while it was hot. There are no hot plates on the assembly line. Marx was the writer who first discussed alienation. He had observed the great increase in alienation in the early days of industrialization, when work was being broken into component jobs and assembly line techniques were increasing. He couldn't foresee automation.

Blauner suggests that the growth of alienation over time may be described as an inverted U—increasing during the early and middle stages of industrialization and declining again as automation is introduced in the advanced stage—our own time.[35] Several other scholars have followed up Blauner's research with similar

482

studies. Some of their findings support Blau-ners; others don't. A study of Canadian manual workers from three industries—printing, auto-mobile, and oil—produced results that largely agree with Blauner's. This study found work in-tegration highest in oil, next highest in printing (a craft), and lowest in automobile manufac-ture.[36] Similar patterns have been discovered in a study of Detroit automobile workers, many of whom had mental-health problems or difficulty adjusting to life. The more skilled, more varied, more responsible, and higher-paid workers showed fewer signs of such problems. Further-more, since prejob characteristics such as level of education did not seem to explain these dif-ferences, it seems that the job situation itself was the main cause of these personal prob-lems.[37] On the other hand, a British study of au-tomobile workers found that, although they were indeed alienated, many workers chose to work on the assembly line because of the high pay.[38]

So many studies of assembly line work have found that it alienates the worker that some in-dustries are moving away from it whenever pos-sible. Some automobile plants have changed to an assembly system that is quite similar to craft work in that the worker is responsible for a se-ries of tasks. In Swedish factories small teams of women can be seen putting together an entire engine. They find the work far more interesting and are more committed to it than assembly line workers. The savings resulting from higher morale partially offset the losses in productivity resulting from this shift toward handicraft assembly.

More common than team assembly work, however, is the widespread tendency of facto-ries to mechanize even further through automa-tion.

### AUTOMATION

Strictly speaking, almost all industrial advance has meant "automation" in that tasks that re-quire low-level skills have been taken over by automatic machines. The distinctive character of automation today, however, is that products are produced continuously and are not touched by human hands. Compared with the assembly line, automated production requires less physi-cal labor and less supervision of workers. How-ever, the work is usually removed even further from the control of the workers than in assembly line production. Moreover, modern automation requires higher-level skills than those needed in older factory systems. Unskilled positions are often eliminated. At the higher skill levels new jobs requiring more knowledge and training have emerged.

The economic effects of automation are not yet fully understood. The main issue is whether automation increases unemployment among the less skilled workers, whose jobs are eliminated and who sometimes may not be able to move into higher positions. This debate has not been settled.[39]

Nor are the social and psychological effects of automation completely clear. One line of re-search—consistent with Blauner's findings—suggests that workers in automated settings are more satisfied with their working conditions because they have more control over their work and have to pay less attention to detail.[40] How-ever, not all automation has these happy results. One study of automation in Pennsylvania con-cluded that the improved technology did not do much to reduce alienation besides raising the status of jobs.[41] Evidently the various studies produce somewhat different results because they measure alienation in different ways and focus on different aspects of the job that might affect workers' satisfaction. One study might look at the amount of physical effort required. Another might consider the degree of special-ization. Another might analyze worker supervi-sion. In any case most workers say that they are satisfied with their jobs. When the sociologist asks more detailed questions, however, it ap-pears that their satisfaction is relative. For ex-ample, the worker may remark that "it's as good a job as I could probably get anyplace else. It's boring, but the pay is okay." Does this statement reveal satisfaction or alienation? I'm not sure, myself.

### OCCUPATIONAL ROLES

Different types of jobs make different demands on the worker and therefore have different ef-fects on the people who do them. Let's compare the problems of some of the different occupational roles, classifying them into four general categories: (1) executives, (2) professionals, (3) foremen, and (4) low-skilled workers.

### The executive role

The executive is a coordinator of information. He or she makes decisions and communicates them to the departments and individuals that carry them out. The executive role is often a stressful one. People want quick decisions, yet a decision may be hard to arrive at in a situation of contradictory demands—no one can satisfy everyone. The executive must be prepared to issue unpleasant orders or to fire incompetent employees even if they are friends.[42]

The lower-level executive has problems too. Junior executives have a status that is some-where between the top level and lower levels and is often unclear. This situation may lead to concern with the symbols of status, such as number of telephones, location of office, or size of desk.[43]

### The professional role

The term *professional* implies "professing" or "believing." All professions involve commitment to standards of knowledge and excellence. Still, the professional must be paid, and therefore some tension may develop between the service and commercial aspects of the role. Freelance professionals normally charge a fee for their services. Other professionals (such as teachers and clergy) are removed from the market for their services—they do not charge their

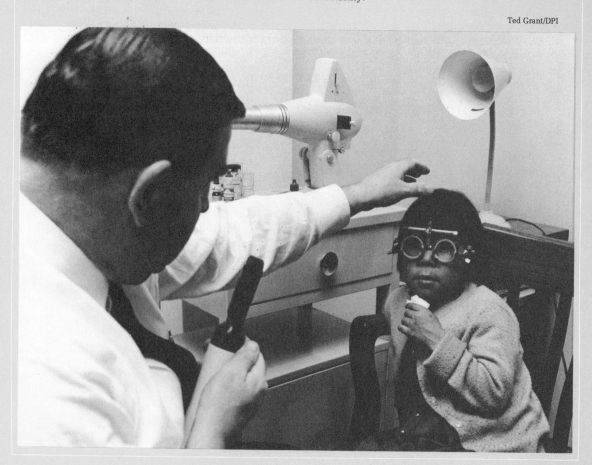

*Some professionals choose to work in areas that would otherwise be without their services rather than to earn as much money as possible. This man serves an Eskimo community.*

Ted Grant/DPI

clients (e.g., students or church members) directly but receive a salary from the organization that employs them.

Many professional roles have high status, but the status of semiprofessional occupations is unclear. Engineering technicians are a good example. They may be as skilled as engineers but are usually less well paid, have less prestige, and have fewer chances for advancement. One reaction to this situation is similar to that of junior executives—concern with symbols. The technician may do a lot of job hopping and claim a lot of office space, clerical help, and other symbols of the engineer's role. People in semiprofessional roles often make collective efforts to "professionalize" the role in the public eye.[44] Nurses and social workers, for example, have started movements to upgrade their status and stake out special responsibilities that only their certified members are allowed to perform.

### The foreman

The foreman or forewoman in a factory is caught between conflicting expectations. The managers assume that he is their agent, and the subordinates assume he is supposed to be protecting them and representing their interests. Not surprisingly, both groups feel ambivalent toward him and he tends to identify first with management, then with workers, and then only with other foremen.[45]

### The low-skilled worker

All of the occupations mentioned so far have *conflicting* role demands. Not so with the low-skilled worker. The strains in this role do not result from ambiguity. The worker knows exactly where he or she stands—at the bottom. The strains come from the facts that the pay is low, the worker may reach the end of the career line in his or her twenties, there are layoffs during recessions, and the job is unchallenging. Workers often react to these problems by trying to defend their failure or by focusing on outside goals such as fixing up the basement or helping their children achieve greater success. Their feelings of alienation and class-consciousness may be quite strong.[46]

Let's move beyond the subject of work and consider some of the trends and prospects of modern societies. What is the general shape of our immediate future as an economic system, and what will be the cultural consequences of current trends?

### POSTINDUSTRIAL SOCIETY

So many changes are taking place in the technology and life style of modern Western nations that it may be appropriate to name our era not industrial but *post* industrial.[47] One of the main changes that has been taking place is in the percentages of jobs in different sectors of the economy. We generally classify jobs into three categories: (1) The *extractive* sector consists of agriculture, lumbering, fishing, mining, and so on. (2) The *industrial* sector consists of manufacturing and construction. (3) The *service* sector consists of such occupations as nursing, television, piloting, sales, and other nonmanufacturing jobs.

Over time the relative size of these sectors has changed continuously. A few hundred years ago almost everyone in Western societies was involved in farming or other extractive jobs. Now only about 4 percent of the population of North America is actively engaged in agriculture. (In contrast, the percentage in most less developed nations is often about 70 percent.) In general, the extractive occupations have declined in number while the industrial sector has increased markedly over the past few generations and is now staying steady at about one-third of the labor force. The same changes have occurred in Canada and the United States, though Canada's extractive sector is slightly stronger and its manufacturing sector a bit weaker than those of most other advanced nations. This is because Canada has been supplying minerals, lumber, and other raw materials for industries based elsewhere—a pattern that alarms some Canadian economists, who would prefer that Canada export finished products instead of raw materials.

In all the advanced nations the service sector is enlarging rapidly. One effect is that a smaller percentage of all workers do manual jobs and a larger percentage do white-collar jobs. Moreover, education is becoming universal and very extensive. Most jobs require skills that are acquired in schools and universities. Thus the "knowledge industry" is itself a major part of the service sector. More people are devoting their careers to teaching or to generating and disseminating ideas and cultural products. There is a great market for books, television programs, records, magazines, films, as well as many personal experiences, such as foreign travel, group therapy, learning macrame and yoga, and so forth. Far more of your budget will go for such items than your grandparents spent for comparable products in their day. Our life style differs, therefore, as dramatically from the life style of the workers Marx observed in early factories as theirs differed from the life style of peasants and knights.

In many ways we are an incredibly materialistic society and a wasteful one. However, we may be moving into a period in which consumption will be less significant and other values will claim more of our attention. Many social scientists say that we must expect a leveling off of economic growth in postindustrial society.[48] For one thing, supplies of the world's nonrenewable resources will become much more limited during our own lifetimes, so we will have to stop our excessive consumption. But that may be just as well. Shopping has become a pastime, and much of it is unnecessary. (When I want to be good to myself I buy something I don't need.) But Vivian Rakoff has suggested that we are already entering a phase beyond wasteful consumerism. He argues that we will *do* more instead of *have* more. For example, the wearing of blue jeans by rich and poor alike may show that we are becoming less concerned with clothes.

Rakoff maintains that the current interest in therapy and encounter groups proves his point. We will become more concerned with human interaction and self-discovery as we give up our interest in buying and collecting belongings. For example, a generation ago psychotherapy was a luxury that only rich people could afford and only a few well-educated people found interesting anyway. Working-class people and most middle-class people were not interested in it. Now it is a part of popular culture. Rakoff expects members of all social classes to take up such concerns as we move into the postindustri-

al society. As we come to live more simply in material terms, we may develop our creativity and personal experience in cultural terms.[49]

## MULTINATIONAL CORPORATIONS

A final aspect of postindustrial society that we should discuss is the growth of multinational corporations. These affect not only the advanced nations but the less developed ones as well. However, most criticism of such corporations has come from people in well-to-do modern societies who are worried about the loss of political strength of their own states. I am thinking in particular of Canadian nationalism—the concern about economic threats to Canada's autonomy. However, the same situation exists in a number of countries.

Since World War II there has been a dramatic growth in the corporations that have operations in many different countries. These firms are so powerful that they sometimes control the economies of the nations in which they operate. Shell Oil is an example; so are General Motors, ITT, and Exxon. Such corporations are richer than most nation-states. They are commonly (though not always) owned and controlled by Americans. They make other nations into "branch plant economies." For example, if such a corporation owns a branch plant in Canada, Argentina, or Algeria, it may send top managers there but will probably hire local people to do lower-level work. Entire towns may become dependent on the jobs provided by that plant. But if its operations turn out to be unprofitable, the corporation executives can simply move the plant and leave the employees in the lurch. The nation's political influence may be too little to protect their interests.

Thus the nation-state is simply being bypassed by a world economic integration that is beyond any government's control. Nationalism assumes that people who live in a particular country should have the voting power to collectively control their own fates. Of course not all countries are independent. Under colonialism, for example, local people were ruled by administrators sent out from the colonizing country. Today political imperialism is dead. Almost all colonies now are formally independent and have the opportunity to elect their own governments. But those nations did not gain economic independence when they won their political freedom. On the contrary, the world's economic system is becoming more unified all the time.

Wallace Clement's studies[50] have documented the impact of the multinational ownership pattern on the Canadian economy. Clement has shown that the economic elites who actually run the most important firms in Canada are for the most part Americans, not Canadians. And he has shown that some regions of Canada—especially Ontario—are particularly subject to foreign ownership. For example, Ontario is the home of about 36 percent of the Canadian population, who earn their income largely from industrial jobs. In the manufacturing sector, 72 percent of Ontario's taxes are from foreign-controlled companies.[51] Many of these companies exist to provide products for the American urban population, using Canada's resources. In British Columbia, for example, wood, pulp and paper, and hydroelectric power are the resources. In other areas mining, gas, petroleum and potash, fish, and coal are the resources. The regions that receive these raw materials can live well on the income from manufacturing jobs, but the regions that are the sources of the materials may become relatively underdeveloped instead of using the raw materials to develop their own industries.[52] Unless there is some way of enabling local citizens to make their demands heard, resentment and economic problems may increase in certain areas, while the workers in the foreign-owned plants are content with things the way they are.

However, the advanced nations are not the only societies whose economic independence is in danger. The less developed nations face far more serious problems. These will be our concern in the final section of the chapter.

# SOCIAL POLICY:
## Issues and Viewpoints

The developing nations face a completely different and almost overwhelmingly difficult set of problems. Indeed, in many cases these nations are not developing at all but going downhill. We can't be sure that they *will* develop, but we can be sure that there will be trouble for all of us in a few years if they don't.

The economic decisions and actions of nations on one side of our planet have an impact on those on the other side, sometimes in ways that may not be obvious. We all have to share the same resources, adding to or subtracting from the world's supply of raw materials, buying and selling goods that may have been produced by people in distant lands. When you eat a banana or buy a new tire, you are affecting the economic well-being of someone in another part of the world whom you will never meet and whose name you might not be able to pronounce. And that person is affecting you.

The first item on our planet's agenda is to feed hungry people. After that a lot of problems will almost solve themselves. But how can we eliminate hunger? Experts agree that this problem can be solved. There is no single solution, though, because there is no single problem. Hunger is caused by a variety of problems.

Actually, enough calories are produced on earth to feed all the world's hungry people. Why, then, do people still starve? There are many reasons, but the main one is that the food isn't where it ought to be when it is needed. There are transportation problems and storage problems (lots of grain is eaten by mice, for example). There are serious financial problems—the hungry don't have the money to pay for their supper. There is waste: Much of the world's food goes to fatten cattle or feed chickens so that you and I can eat steak and eggs instead of corn or beans.

But the solution is not for us to give up steak and eggs, for there is no reason why production can't be increased so as to produce a varied and

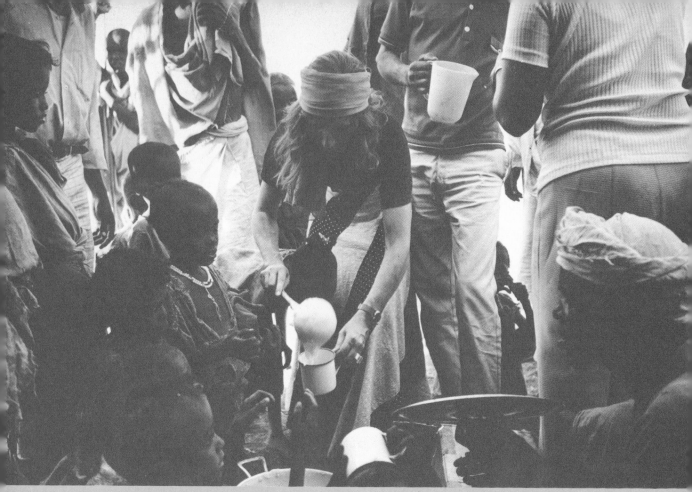

Thomas Hopker/Woodfin Camp

*Powdered milk supplied by international relief organizations can only be a stopgap measure in dealing with world hunger. Given a chance, these people can feed themselves.*

protein-rich diet, not just a subsistence diet, for everyone. Food production could double in the developing countries by the end of the century. But people have to know what to do and have to organize in new ways to get it done. This is partly a matter of planning, but other factors are important as well. For example, education will make the job easier, since literate people can read brochures explaining new farming methods or the advantages of birth control. Health care will help too, since healthy people can produce more.

Without doubt, the most important issue related to food shortage is land tenure. In many developing countries the land is cultivated by people who do not own their own farms. Agrarian reform is badly needed in such areas—in fact many of the "communist" revolutions of recent

years were actually agrarian rebellions by peasants trying to rid themselves of exploitive landlords. It is clear that agrarian reform could vastly increase agricultural productivity. There is no single "right" system of land tenure—several have been tried and have worked. Both collective farming and small family holdings can be effective. Several societies have increased their food production dramatically simply by redistributing farm land.

However, I don't want to suggest that land reform alone will solve the problem of hunger. Along with land reform must come various programs that enable the peasants to take advantage of their new situation. Credit must be made available so that the farmer can buy fertilizer, tools and so forth. The government should send agents into the countryside to show people how

488

to use new technologies both in the home and on the farm. In the case of collective farming systems, the government must organize and manage the plan, at least for a while.

## CAPITAL ACCUMULATION AND VICIOUS CIRCLES

A key problem in the developing countries is how to obtain capital to get the economy moving. Western societies have no problem obtaining capital. Most people have incomes that more than cover their basic living expenses, and if business offers them attractive profits they will invest their surplus; this money is used to pay for new factories and equipment. But economic growth is a problem in places like Malaysia, Tanzania, and Uruguay. There the shortage of capital makes modernization very hard to achieve. Capital is necessary to pay for the agricultural improvements that I have already mentioned—fertilizers, tools, irrigation, storage bins, transportation systems, and so on. It is also necessary for industrial growth and for social-service systems such as hospitals, schools, and family planning centers. Even if the poor nations never produce much for export, they will need *some* industries to provide for their own needs.

Capital is scarce in the Third World because the economies of those nations are caught between two vicious circles having to do with the supply and demand of goods. One vicious circle limits the supply of capital while the other limits the demand for capital.[53]

On the *supply* side, capital is scarce because people are unable to save. They can't save because their incomes are too low, and their incomes are too low because the economy is unproductive. The economy is unproductive because it is based on obsolete, unmechanized systems of production, so that an average worker can't turn out many products per hour of work. The capital that would pay for fast, efficient machinery is not available. That's the first vicious circle.

The other vicious circle is on the *demand* side. Capital is scarce because people won't invest their savings if they don't expect to make a good profit on their investment. But businesses can't offer them high profits because they can't be sure of selling their products. There is too little demand. People certainly *need* goods, but they have such low incomes that they can't afford to pay for what they need. Thus there is not enough income to stimulate demand and not enough demand to stimulate investment. That's the second vicious circle.

Economists and politicians who study developing societies realize that if they could somehow obtain enough capital and invest it in the right places these vicious circles would become beneficial—capital would generate income, which would generate investment. Western societies obtained their initial capital for industrialization by allowing a great deal of exploitation. That's what Marx was so furious about—the long hours of work that the workers put in with so little return. The capitalist factory owners took the profits earned by the workers and invested them in more industry. It was a terrible period. Every society that has ever industrialized has oppressed workers to some extent. The Soviet Union's industrialization was achieved by oppressing the peasants—taking their food away to feed the urban workers, even if the peasants themselves starved. Thus two different models both succeeded in squeezing a surplus out of the poor in order to pay the initial costs of industrializing. Capitalist countries (such as the United States and Britain) did it through an exploitive laissez-faire *economic* system. Communist countries did it through an exploitive *political* regime using totalitarian methods.

After the initial capital has been invested in industry, the profits can be reinvested. Industrialization can then continue fairly steadily, and in time the system can become less oppressive. Ordinary workers can begin to share in the profits that their labor has produced. But in the early stages of development it is very hard to obtain capital. If the profits were divided up and given to the workers, they would probably consume them instead of investing in machinery and fertilizers. They are poor; they can't afford to invest. Hence, societies that are committed to fast economic growth are unlikely to be very egalitarian.

## EQUITY VERSUS GROWTH

However, growth isn't everything. Equality is a value that must be recognized for its own sake. If it is incompatible with the goal of economic growth, then we must consider both sides carefully. The nations that are now developing give different weights to the values of growth and equity. A few societies have managed to accumulate a lot of capital without much coercion and are growing fast without oppressing their citizens. Yugoslavia is such a society. The Yugoslav self-management system has, remarkably, induced workers to reinvest an average of some 30 percent of their net income per year, without oppression.[54] China has stressed the value of equality over growth, and it is finding it very difficult to stimulate much saving for additional investment. China's economic growth rate was the lowest of any Asian nation during the period from 1957 to 1970.[55] However, it is clear that emphasis upon equity usually creates better living conditions and a healthier society. India, for example, has placed greater emphasis on growth than equity, but its growth rate is only slightly better than China's and most evidence suggests that its poor citizens are not nearly as well off as China's.

### THE RELATIONSHIP BETWEEN RICH NATIONS AND POOR NATIONS

All the people who live on this planet are interdependent, even though we live on different continents and in different political and economic systems. You may be wondering how you can affect the people of the Third World. There are several areas in which individual decisions in the West can influence the relationship between the rich nations and the poor ones.

Think about land reform. More than once, Western nations have supported reactionary regimes in the less developed countries, even giving them military aid to prevent land reform.

Yet nothing can do more to feed hungry people than land reform. Pay attention to the government's attitudes toward reactionary regimes in the Third World.

Another issue to consider is international trade. Rich nations can exploit poor nations; they have all the power and can set the terms of trade. Rich nations, for example, can set such high tariffs that poor nations cannot sell their products abroad. Such a policy protects the rich at the expense of the poor. On the other hand, when rich nations want certain goods their demand can upset the economies of the poor nations. For example, many Third World nations produce almost entirely for export—their economies depend on coffee, cocoa, or sugar. They might do more for their people by producing food for them instead of crops for export, since exports are usually controlled by giant foreign corporations rather than small family farms. Some developing nations have tried to protect themselves against the control of multinational corporations by nationalizing industries owned by outsiders. This is risky because it angers the owners of those industries and can lead to political or military pressure.

Finally, we have to prepare ourselves for some major changes. For a long time the rich countries have been able to grow richer because they have been able to buy oil from other countries at low prices. Our technology is based on oil. Among other things, it has enabled us to produce huge quantities of grain cheaply and to sell the grain to other countries. Those countries have become dependent on the U.S. grain supply.

But all this is changing. Oil won't be cheap again. The countries that buy American grain will have to start feeding their own populations, somehow. And they can—if we don't stop them.

## SUMMARY

**1.** Primitive economies use principles of reciprocity and redistribution rather than market exchange. Market exchange is the principle underlying modern economic systems.

**2.** The earliest form of agriculture was probably the "slash-and-burn" system, which required little labor but much land. As agriculture became labor intensive, people began to enslave others in order to exploit their labor. But a free class always existed too, and these people became townspeople.

**3.** In England capitalism stemmed from the development of commercial farming, which was made possible by the enclosure movement that displaced peasants from the land and made their labor available for factory work. Industrialization began with the cotton factories and spread to all areas of production. The colonial governments were established to extract raw materials for the industrial nations.

**4.** Modern capitalism, unlike the crudely exploitive system that Marx knew, is not dominated by individual business leaders. The modern corporation is owned by thousands of stockholders and managed by a "technostructure"—a corps of experts. Modern capitalism is also more interested in planning ahead with secure control than in maximizing profits. Hence, it does not resist, but rather welcomes, government control.

**5.** Labor relations are less violent today than they used to be. Workers, like management, encourage advertising, which stimulates demand for products.

**6.** Welfare states such as Sweden are partly capitalist and partly socialist. The government owns many businesses and is involved in the management of others. Social-security benefits are very well organized, and income is equalized to a great extent.

**7.** Socialism has not developed as Marx predicted. There are several different versions of socialism. All of these versions use economic planning rather than the market as a system for distributing goods and services.

The Soviet Union industrialized through extensive political coercion—particularly of farmers—and remains unresponsive to public opinion. The Yugoslav system depends chiefly on workers' control of industry and is highly decentralized. The Chinese system allows the consumers' requirements to determine the distribution of supplies; the government arranges contracts between industries. The Chinese system is egalitarian, but China's growth rate has not been remarkable.

**8.** Western views of the proper relations between the state and the market forces have undergone many changes. Under mercantilism, the system in use during the period of absolute monarchies, the government tried to regulate the economy and accumulate gold, silver, and raw materials. Adam Smith introduced the notion of *laissez faire* to economic thought, suggesting that governments should guarantee that contracts are honored but otherwise allow the market to regulate itself. Karl Marx maintained that the government, being part of the superstructure, is normally controlled by economic forces; that is, the ruling class always gives orders to the government. However, when class conflict leads to revolution the workers gain control of the political forces and overthrow the economic system.

**9.** Modern economists are aware that the market is not always perfectly competitive. Monopolies can interfere with competitive pricing. Keynes suggested that in a capitalist system government action is not only unavoidable but desirable to control the business cycle. The government can influence the market through fiscal and monetary policy.

## KEY TERMS

**economics**  the social science that deals with the production, distribution, exchange, and consumption of scarce goods and services.

**fiscal policy**  a governmental policy of spending or not spending on goods and services.

**laissez faire**  the belief that the state should not regulate the economy but should allow it to regulate itself.

**market exchange**  a system in which goods and services are exchanged in a market context.

**mercantilism**   the belief that the best way to increase national power is to increase national wealth (i.e., the nation's supply of gold and silver).

**monetary policy**   a governmental policy of manipulating the prime lending rate or the total money supply.

**reciprocity**   two-way exchange of goods or services.

**redistribution**   a system in which goods and services are brought to a central source and then redistributed throughout the population.

# FOR FURTHER READING

BECKER, GARY S. *The Economic Approach to Human Behavior.* Chicago: University of Chicago Press, 1977. Becker has been proposing plain, ordinary economic models to account for complex forms of social behavior, such as crime and leisure activities. Fascinating ideas.

FORM, WILLIAM H. *Blue Collar Stratification: Autoworkers in Four Countries.* Princeton: Princeton University Press, 1976. The picture Form draws is neither very alienated nor very exciting. These workers sound like plodders, not revolutionaries.

HEILBRONER, ROBERT. *"None of your Business." New York Review of Books.* vol. 22, no. 4, March 20,1975. If you want to read and fret about multinational corporations, this article will provide a review of several recent books dealing with the subject and you can take it from there.

HEILBRONER, ROBERT. *The Worldly Philosophers.* New York: Simon & Schuster, 1961. Another delightful book with style and grace. This one is about the history of several economic theorists, including biographical details that make them come alive. To learn more about Malthus, Ricardo, the utopian socialists, and other classical theorists, there is no better source than this one.

POLANYI, KARL. *The Great Transformation.* Boston: Beacon Press, 1957. Polanyi's position is that Western economic theorists tend to assume that the natural, customary way goods and services have been allocated throughout history is by the market mechanisms of exchange. He argues that this is a simple fallacy.

ROBINSON, JOAN. *Freedom and Necessity.* New York: Random House, 1970. A charming and informative little economic history of the world. It takes hardly any time to read but is worth rereading a number of times.

SHEPPARD, HAROLD L., and SARA E. RIX. *The Graying of Working America: The Coming Crisis in Retirement-Age Policy.* New York: Free Press, 1978. The authors point out a major social problem that will face us soon, when more people will retire than start work:

SMELSER, NEIL J. *Social Change in the Industrial Revolution.* Chicago: University of Chicago Press, 1959. Smelser sat a year in the British Museum in Karl Marx's chair (he thinks) reading some of the documents Marx used in his analysis of early capitalism. Then he wrote his own version of the history of the textile industry in that period, which differed from Marx's.

SMELSER, NEIL J. *The Sociology of Economic Life.* 2nd ed. Englewood Cliffs, N.J.: Prentice-Hall, 1976. Much of this chapter has been drawn from Smelser's book, which merits your additional attention.

TERKEL, STUDS. *Working.* New York: Pantheon, 1974. This is a popular book you can buy in lots of drugstores. It simply describes what people commonly experience in their many various modern jobs. Highly readable.

THOMPSON E. P. *The Making of the English Working Class.* London: Penguin, 1968. Several of my radical friends are extremely enthusiastic about this historical book. I include it because they would never forgive me for leaving it off.

# FOUR
## changing society

17

# POPULATION AND ECOLOGY

How many children do you expect to have? How many children did your parents have? Let me guess. I think you want two children and that your parents had three or four. I am no mind reader, but I have looked at surveys that asked large samples of respondents about desired family size. Big changes are taking place in this area. People in industrial societies are becoming highly aware of the problems facing humankind because of the population explosion.

In this chapter I want to introduce you to **demography,** the study of human populations. Sociologists have been interested in demography for a long time. They have been concerned with the description and explanation of the three processes that determine the size of any given population—*fertility, mortality,* and *migration,* or the rates at which people give birth, die, and move into or out of a given area. In addition, we will discuss **ecology**—the relationship between the physical environment and the human population that lives in that environment. Obviously, in the long run a population that uses its resources recklessly will create problems for itself and for future generations. For all of these reasons we want to take a long view in this chapter—a look at our own future as a species inhabiting a small planet. We will think about how this world can be preserved for generation after generation after generation so that our great-grandchildren can go on whirling through space, breathing our air and walking in the forests that we have planted and saved for them. We are the gardeners of Eden, you and I.

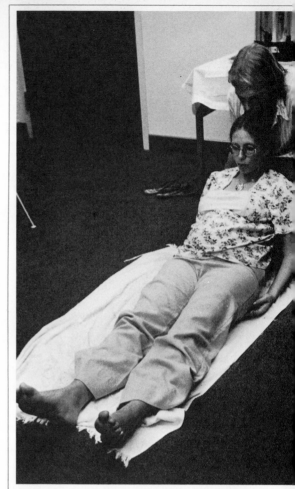

Al Kaplan/DPI

*Fertility has been declining in Western societies for several years. Raising children has become a matter of choice for both husband and wife; thus the babies that are born are usually planned for and wanted.*

## Basic demographic processes

### FERTILITY

**Fertility** refers to the rate at which a population gives birth. Don't confuse the terms *fertility* and *fecundity*, please. A woman's **fecundity** is her capacity to bear children.

Female fecundity extends from about age 14 to almost 50, though adolescents and women past the age of 40 have relatively low fecundity.[1] We know little about the reproductive span of males, apart from the fact that at about age 40 the production of active sperm apparently declines.

Fertility refers to the rates of *actual* childbearing in a population. The simplest measure of fertility in a population is the **crude birthrate,** the number of births per year per 1000 people. In general, the poorest nations have the highest fertility rates, for reasons that we will discuss later in the chapter.

Imagine a population in which women marry at the age of 20 and bear as many children as they can. How many children do you suppose the average woman would have in such a society? You have probably seen photographs of families with 16 or 17 children lined up, like stair steps, with a beaming Ma and Pa standing in the rear. Such families would be unusual in our imaginary population. The average woman (fortunately, I think!) does not have that degree of fecundity. The most fertile population I know of is the Hutterites of Canada and the western United States. Among married Hutterite women 45 to 54 years of age, the average number of children born was 10.6, as compared to about 2.6 for a similar group of American women in the general population.[2]

Populations differ greatly in fertility. What factors determine the number of babies that will be born in a society in a given year? Kingsley Davis and Judith Blake have listed eleven different variables that determine fertility. Any other factor that you can think of will have its effect through one or more of these mechanisms. They are as follows:

1 *Age of entry into sexual unions.* Societies differ markedly in the average are of marriage. In Western societies a couple is supposed to marry only when the husband is able to support a wife and family. In many parts of Asia, on the other hand, marriages take place very early, since matches are arranged by the family and couples do not have to be self-supporting.
2 *Permanent celibacy.* Societies with a late marriage age have a high percentage of permanent celibates (unmarried people). Ireland is an extreme case: about one-quarter of all the middle-aged people there have never married.
3 *Part of reproductive life spent after or between unions.* A certain percentage of widowed and divorced people never remarry. Periods of legal and informal separation between marital unions vary in length. In some societies they may be quite long, and this reduces the number of babies born.
4 *Voluntary abstinence.* Almost all societies discourage lovemaking during late pregnancy and just after a child is born. This norm doesn't affect fertility because almost all women have low fecundity for a while after childbearing. However, use of the "rhythm method"—that is, abstinence at the time of ovulation (generally around the midpoint of the menstrual cycle) will reduce fertility rates.
5 *Involuntary abstinence.* In some societies men's jobs require them to be away from their

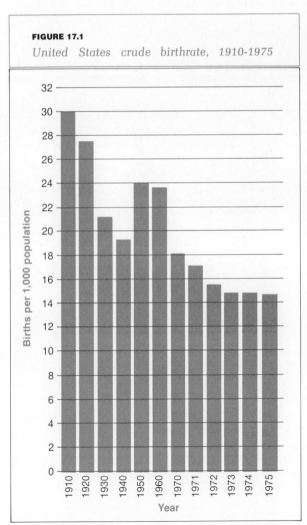

**FIGURE 17.1**

*United States crude birthrate, 1910-1975*

*Source:* Data from Statistical Abstract of the United States, 1977. Table 75, p. 55.

wives for long periods. This pattern can affect fertility rates.

6 *Frequency of intercourse.* It is possible that diet, temperature, humidity, and certain diseases may affect the average frequency of sexual intercourse in different populations. However, we don't know much about this topic.

7 *Involuntary causes of fecundity or infecundity.* Gonorrhea is an important source of infecundity throughout the world. High altitude and extreme hunger are other factors that limit fecundity.[3]

8 *Use or nonuse of contraception.* One of the most popular forms of contraception in the world is the latex condom. In North America, a pill taken orally is the most commonly used contraceptive. Contraception is the first factor that occurred to me when I thought about this list of factors. But obviously it is not the only variable affecting birthrates. Most preindustrial societies don't have the technology of contraception, yet it is unlikely that the average woman in any society reproduces to the limit of her fecundity. Various social norms have the effect of limiting births.

9 *Voluntary causes of fecundity or infecundity.* Simple operations such as salpingectomy for females and vasectomy for males provide permanent freedom from further parenthood without affecting sexual pleasure or changing personality. Vasectomy is the simpler of the two operations, and if a reliable method can be found to reverse its effects it may become the most widely used method of birth control.

Prolonged breast feeding also limits fertility. It is estimated that the period of sterility following the birth of a child averages 13 months in a population that engages in prolonged breast feeding but only 4 months in a population with no breast feeding.[4]

10 *Fetal mortality from involuntary causes.* On the average, about 20 percent of all known pregnancies abort themselves.[5]

11 *Fetal mortality from voluntary causes.* Induced abortion is one of the most important means of birth control. Primitive and hazardous methods of abortion have been practiced throughout human history. Modern surgical methods make induced abortion a very safe operation when it is done early. However, abortion is illegal in so many countries that many abortions are done using unsafe methods and thus are very dangerous to women.

## MORTALITY

**Mortality** refers to the rate at which a population dies. The **crude death rate** is the most commonly used measure of mortality. It may be defined as the number of deaths per year per 1000 people. The crude death rate for the United States from 1920 to 1970 is shown in Figure 17.2.

However, demographers usually prefer to use a more precise measure of mortality: the *age–sex-specific death rate* (the number of deaths per 1000 people in each age–sex group). This method is illustrated in Figure 17.3, which shows male age-specific death rates for the United States, Canada, Venezuela, and Mauritius in 1966.

There are still great differences in mortality among nations, though this is less true than before World War II. The life expectancy at birth of people in several African nations is only 35 years, while in Burma, Cambodia, and India it is about 45 years. On the other hand, in the developed nations the

**FIGURE 17.2**
*United States crude death rate, 1920-1975*

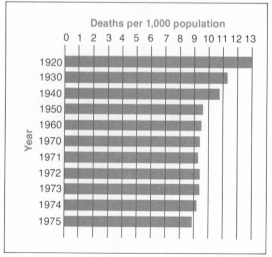

*Source:* Data from Statistical Abstract of the United States, 1977. Table 98, p. 67.

**FIGURE 17.3**

*Male age-specific death rate for United States, Canada, and Costa Rica*

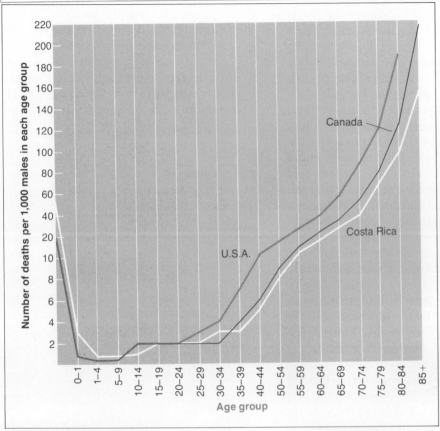

*Source:* Data from United Nations Demographic Yearbook, 1975. pp. 360-369; and Statistics Canada, Vital Statistics. 1972. vol. 3, Table 14, pp. 90-91.

mean life expectancy at birth for both sexes is around 70 years.

Mortality declined gradually in the industrialized nations between the late eighteenth and late nineteenth centuries. Within the past century the reduction in mortality in Europe and the other developed nations has been phenomenal. In 1900, for instance, the average life expectancy at birth in the United States was only 47.3 years, compared to 71 years in 1971. The decline of mortality among infants and youth has been much greater than among older people.

At present mortality from infectious diseases is quite low in the developed nations and has been greatly reduced in the poorer nations. In the developed countries most deaths result from degenerative diseases such as cancer and heart disease. Because these diseases are not (yet) curable, mortality rates in the developed countries have remained almost unchanged since around 1955. In the less developed nations malnutrition and inadequate medical services prevent further reductions in mortality.

Most of us are not familiar with death,

except among the very old. It is hard for us to imagine how precarious life must have seemed to people for whom high mortality was part of their ordinary experience. Have you ever gone through old family letters? If you have read letters that are over 100 years old, you may have noticed how often the comments are related to physical well-being. No wonder! Almost any family history, such as that of George Washington, will illustrate the high mortality rates of earlier days. When George was only 11 his father died. When Martha married George she was a 26-year-old widow who had already borne four children. Two of those children had died in infancy; one died at age 17; and the fourth died in early adulthood. Yet this was not a remarkable number of deaths for that time.

Perhaps because of our unfamiliarity with death, our mourning rituals have weakened. Early in this century people followed strict rules of etiquette in interacting with bereaved people. Today, however, neither the bereaved nor their friends know quite how to act toward one another. In fact a common reaction is to try to deny the very existence of the bereavement. The lack of mourning rituals and the attempt to act as if death had not occurred may combine to retard emotional healing and prolong the period of emotional upset.[6]

Another apparent result of the decline in mortality is a change in the nature of religion. There is a decline in emphasis on the next world and an increased emphasis on how religion can aid people in this world.[7] One important reason for wanting to believe in an afterlife may be that desire to be reunited with friends and relatives who have died. In a low-mortality society only the elderly have lost many loved ones. Thus reduced mortality also reduces society's concern with immortality. On the other hand, negative attitudes toward traditional religion may decline as mortality decreases. Why? Because it is easier to believe in a loving and all-powerful god when fewer loved ones die young.

## MIGRATION

In a low-mortality society the nuclear family can operate by itself with less outside support than in a high-mortality society. Possibly this is one reason why in industrial societies family ties are loosened and the family is economically and physically more mobile.

**FIGURE 17.4**

*Regional origins of U.S. immigrants, 1901-1930 and 1971-1976. The absolute numbers of immigrants were much higher in the earlier years shown in the top chart*

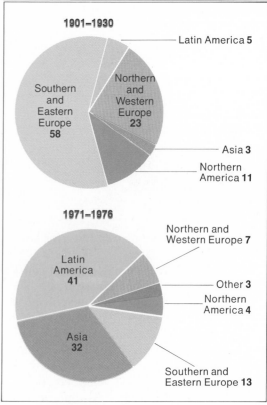

*Source:* Population Reference Bureau Chart Series I: and 1975 and 1976 data supplied by the Statistics Branch, U.S. Immigration and Naturalization Service.

In turn, this mobility helps maintain a society in which there is extreme division of labor. We need to move around easily if we are to function well in our economic system. Where mortality is high, therefore, economic development may be slow. People may feel too insecure about their health and safety to leave their kin and move across a continent for the sake of a job.

**Migration** is the movement of people into or out of an area. Migration trends vary from one nation to another and even from one year to another. Although mortality and fertility rates have generally declined, migration has not. Annual data on migration within the United States have been available only since 1947, and these figures show little change over time. Every year about 20 percent of the people in the United States have moved. Around 6 percent have changed their county of residence and about 3 percent have moved to a new state.[8]

What about migration from other areas to North America? The peak year for immigration to the United States was 1907, when about 1,300,000 immigrants entered the country. The peak for Canada was 1913, when more than 400,000 immigrants arrived. Lately the United States has been admitting nearly 400,000 immigrants per year and Canada over 100,000.

**Causes and results of migration**

Moving is often stressful. Not only is packing and unpacking hard work, but the replacement of relationships with new ones is painful. Therefore when people decide to move they are likely to choose a place where they know someone—or, preferably, many people. Once one person has moved to a new area it becomes easier for others to follow. Hence, the volume of migration from one specific place to another tends to rise once a small nucleus of people from the original place has established itself at the new location.

Migrants have a higher rate of mental disorder than nonmigrants in the place to which the migrants have moved, even when other differences between the two groups are controlled.[9] If you have moved far or often in your life, you will understand why. Moving disrupts your emotional and social life. One may flounder around miserably while forming new ties. In California, for example, three-fifths of the population was born outside the state. The rates of marital breakdown, most forms of crime, and suicide are higher in California than in the United States

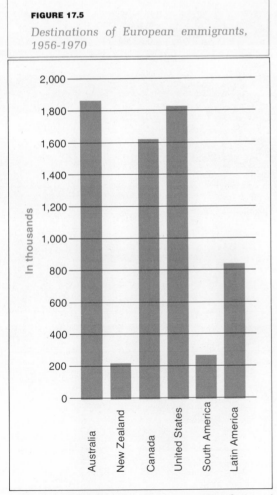

**FIGURE 17.5**

*Destinations of European emmigrants, 1956-1970*

*Source:* Data based on statistics of receiving countries. Courtesy of the Population Reference Bureau, Inc., Washington, D.C.

as a whole. On the other hand, California and other areas with high rates of in-migration often have a kind of vitality and excitement. The population is likely to be culturally diverse and tolerant of new ideas. Areas with high rates of out-migration (e.g., much of New England) tend to be conservative because the most rebellious and nonconformist members are likely to be the first to move away.

### Differences in migration patterns

Who moves, and why? There are differences in age and social class between movers and stayers. In addition, some regions have higher rates of migration than other regions. Let's look at these three factors.

Age is the most important factor in migration patterns. Migration rates are highest

*Moving disrupts emotional and social life, but it has become a way of life for many Americans.*

Tana Hoban/DPI

among young adults, but there is a secondary peak among very young children because often the migrating unit is a young married couple with small children. Among Americans in their early 20s almost half change their place of residence during a given year and about 15 percent move to a different county. Both sexes are about equally likely to migrate.

Social class is not a major factor in U.S. migration rates. College-educated people are a bit more likely to migrate than others. However, men with very low incomes are also likely to migrate. Self-employed people are unlikely to migrate because they would have to make new contacts in the new community. On the other hand, salaried corporation employees are often assigned to new locations and must either move or face losing their jobs.

As for geographic factors, migration in the United States has usually been from east to west. Another major pattern is the northward and westward movement of blacks. This shift began on a large scale during World War I, when northern industrial firms began to recruit labor for jobs that were formerly filled by newly arrived European immigrants. The movement of blacks out of the South is still going on, though about half the black population still lives in the southern states.

## Population composition

### THE SEX RATIO

The sex ratio of a population is defined as the number of males per 100 females. Thus a sex ratio of 100 represents a population in which there are equal numbers of males and females. A ratio of more than 100 means more males, under 100, more females. The North American sex ratio is about 95, which means that there are 95 men for every 100 women. This is because of the higher death rate of males, especially older males.

A nation's sex ratio may be very unbalanced after a war. Perhaps the most unbalanced sex ratio occurred in the Soviet Union after World War II, when about one-third of the males had been killed. This means that millions of Soviet women have never married.

### POPULATION PYRAMIDS

The age–sex composition of a population at a given time can be illustrated by a population pyramid, a diagram that shows the percentages of males in each age category of the population on the left side of a vertical line and the percentages of females in the same age categories on the right side of the line. Figure 17.6 shows the age–sex pyramids of Mexico, the United States, and Sweden in 1970. The shape of the pyramid is greatly affected by fertility trends. Mexico and most other developing countries have had high fertility rates during recent years, as the wide base of the pyramid shows. Children are a large part of the Mexican population. Sweden, on the other hand, has had a low fertility rate for many years. The sides of its pyramid are almost vertical up to the age of 60, when mortality begins to reduce the number of old people. The United States is in between these extreme types. It had a somewhat higher fertility rate than Sweden for several years until the late 1960s, but its fertility never approached the high levels found in Mexico today. Look at the bulge in the U.S. pyramid below the age of 25. This represents the "baby boom" of the 1940s and 1950s, which affected not only the United States, but also Canada, Australia, and New Zealand. The nations of Western Europe had a "mini-baby boom" compared to these four nations. As the baby boom citizens of the United States grow older, and if fertility levels remain as low as they are now, the pyramids of future years will show the bulge moving higher and higher in the pyramid.

Population pyramids can be used to

**FIGURE 17.6**
*Population pyramids of Mexico, United States, and Sweden, 1970*

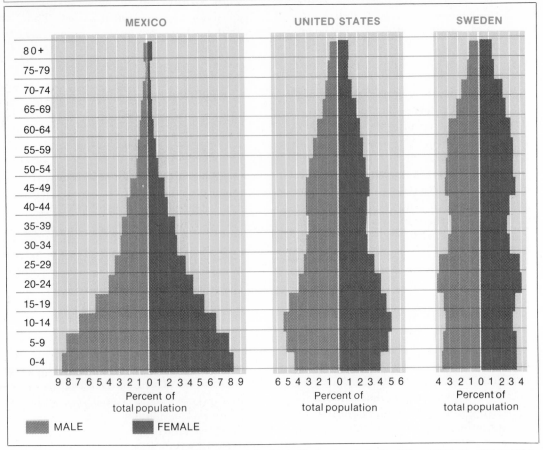

show how various groups differ from the general population. In Figure 17.7, for example, the wide base of the Hutterite pyramid, compared to the more vertical pyramid of the general Canadian population, shows that the Hutterites have a much higher fertility rate than the rest of the Canadian population.

## THE DEPENDENCY RATIO

The **dependency ratio** is the ratio of people in dependent age groups (both young and

old) to people in economically productive age groups. Obviously, children and very old people cannot work as hard as young and middle-aged adults—indeed, they must be supported almost entirely by others. Dependency may differ, of course, from one individual to another and from one social community to another. Farm children often contribute a good deal by looking after animals, gathering eggs, planting and weeding the garden, and so on. And in all societies some old people stay fit and active longer than others. I used to have my car repaired in

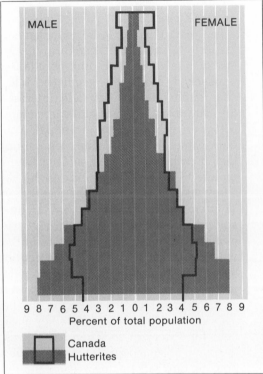

**FIGURE 17.7**

*Age and sex composition, Canadian Hutterites and Canadians in general, 1971*

MALE     FEMALE

9 8 7 6 5 4 3 2 1 0 1 2 3 4 5 6 7 8 9
Percent of total population

☐ Canada
■ Hutterites

*Source:* Statistics Canada, 1971. Census of Canada, Bulletin 14, Vol. 4.

many Mexicans to save surplus cash to invest in industry or agriculture.

## Population trends

### THE POPULATION EXPLOSION

A million years ago there may have been 125,000 human beings on earth.[10] Today there are nearly 4 billion. The rate of increase has grown steadily. By 8000 B.C. there were perhaps 5 million people on the earth; by 4000 B.C., maybe 85 million; by the time of Christ, perhaps 300 million;[11] by A.D. 1650, about 545 million. Then the growth rate really took off: By 1970 it was 19 per year per 1000 people. That is, if a group had 1000 members on January 1, it would have 1019 by the end of the year.

Scary? Absolutely terrifying. In 1973 the United Nations estimated that by the year 2000 the earth's population would be 6.4 billion if that growth rate continued. This means that at the 1973 rate the world's population would double in 35 years. In less than 700 years there would be one square foot of the earth's surface for every human being. In 1200 years the human population would outweigh the earth.[12]

But there's good news. It appears that 1970 was the peak growth year and that we may now be on the downhill side of the curve. In 1977, for the first time since data have been collected, the world's population growth rate began to decline—from 19 to 17 per 1000. But don't relax and sigh with relief yet. Compare that figure to the growth rate for the period just before the Industrial Revolution—.56 per 1000. The decline to 17 per 1000 means that, instead of doubling every 35 years, the world's population will take 41 years to double (which is a less frightening prospect but certainly nothing to celebrate).

The population explosion has not been the same everywhere. The tropical nations of Latin America have the highest rates of increase; Africa's growth has also been high.

a shop run by an 85-year-old woman in greasy overalls who poked the young mechanics with her cane if she wanted them to move faster.

The dependency ratio is affected by the **median age** of the population, which is that age that divides any population into equal groups, half older, half younger. In 1820 the median age of the U.S. population was 16. In 1970 it was 28. Obviously, the dependency ratio was higher in 1820 than it is now. Look at Figure 17.6 again. It is clear that Mexico's wage earners have more dependents to support than Sweden's. The Mexican dependency ratio is high because of the high fertility rate in that country. This makes it hard for

The growth rates of the United States, Canada, Japan, the Soviet Union, and Europe have all been below the world average for a number of years. The birthrates—not the growth rates—of the less developed countries averaged about 42 per 1000 in 1970. By 1977 they had dropped to 36 per 1000. The drop was greatest in South Korea, China, and Thailand. Less dramatic declines in birth rates occurred in Brazil, Egypt, India, the Philippines, and Turkey. However, some countries showed little or no decline in their birthrates, among them Mexico, Bangladesh, and Nigeria. So we may conclude that growth rates have probably peaked and are now declining because of widespread, but not universal, declines in fertility in the less developed areas.

But will the growth rate be reduced before it exceeds the rate of increase in the means of subsistence? If not, then the death rate will rise. Like the bumper sticker that reads "Cancer cures smoking," we could say, "Death cures surplus population." But we don't want to cure the population problem by starving the surplus. In fact there is a complex relationship between fertility rates and mortality rates, and we need to spend some time examining this connection. It was first discussed by Thomas R. Malthus.

### MALTHUSIAN THEORY

Malthus (1766–1834), an English economist and clergyman, published his first essay on population in 1798. He developed this theory further in six revisions of the essay—the last one published posthumously in 1872. Malthus was detested by theologians and later by Marxists, but his contributions were great. Both Darwin's theory of evolution and Keynes'. theory of economics were based on ideas derived from Malthus, and his influence on demography was enormous.

But people disliked the pessimistic conclusion of his first essay. In it he suggested that it would be impossible to avoid a rise in mortality. This is how he reasoned.

Malthus noted that the means of subsistence (e.g., wheat) grows only at an *arithmetic* rate. That is, at best it increases by a fixed amount each year. A wheat farmer might, for example, produce 100 extra bushels per year every year. This could be represented on a graph by a straight line angling upward—a steady rate of growth. But populations, if unchecked, grow at a *geometric* rate, like compound interest. You add interest back into your bank account and earn interest on it too, as well as on the principal. You add new babies back into the population and they become parents too, adding even more children. So a population might double every generation, as is happening today. This could be represented by an upward-sloping curve—an accelerating rate of growth. (An example is the story of the boy who is hired by a king on the following terms: On the first day he will be paid one grain of rice. Every day he will be paid twice as many grains of rice as on the day before. The king is pleased to hire such cheap labor—for a week or so. Then he realizes that the boy will soon own all the rice in the kingdom. So they talk business again and the boy gets the king's daughter instead. Moral: It pays to know about geometric growth rates.)

What Malthus was pointing out is that a geometric rate of growth will obviously tend to exceed an arithmetic rate of growth. There would always tend to be more babies produced each year than food to support them. But of course fertility can't outrun mortality for long. For a while the population may increase faster than the means of subsistence. What will happen then? There are three possibilities, all of which will raise the death rate: hunger, disease, and war. Malthus called these "positive checks." They operate to reduce the population to a level that can be supported by the available means of subsistence.

Malthus assumed that human beings are

driven by sexual needs and that they will always tend to reproduce almost to the limit of their fecundity. In the early versions of his theory he argued that human fertility would stay high under all conditions. Only an increase in mortality could check the growth of population. People couldn't be expected to stop having babies or even to slow down! If the food supply increased, the result would simply be more babies surviving, so that food would become scarce again. There's no way to get ahead. Populations will always increase right up to the limit of their resources. This is a gloomy conclusion.

Eventually Malthus changed his mind a little. In his later writings he expressed the hope that people could avoid hunger, disease, and war by limiting the birthrate instead. Instead of "positive checks" (factors that increase mortality) maybe populations could be limited by "preventive checks"—factors that decrease fertility. He considered birth control or any other way of limiting births within marriage to be immoral. However, he believed late marriage was the best way to reduce the birthrate.[13]

Since Malthus' day humankind has been luckier than he expected. The "positive checks" have not increased. On the contrary, death rates are lower throughout the world than they were in Malthus' time, chiefly because the means of subsistence increased far more than he could have foreseen. Agriculture has increased its efficiency many times over. A second factor, birth control, is also important. Contraception has become a common means of population control.

Then was Malthus wrong? So far, yes. But within our lifetimes he may be proved correct. The worldwide death rate will soon increase unless the means of subsistence can be increased at the same rate as the population. A rise in mortality can be avoided only through a sizable reduction in the birthrate, a large increase in the means of subsistence, or some combination of the two.

## THE DEMOGRAPHIC-TRANSITION MODEL

Malthus, who lived nearly 200 years ago, was not aware of the declines in fertility rate that were to come in this century. Modern demographers, who can look back upon these dramatic changes, have built a general model known as **demographic-transition.** This model is used to describe the process by which preindustrial societies with high rates of fertility and mortality are transformed into modern societies with low rates of fertility and mortality. Let's look at the historical developments on which the model is based.

Until about 300 years ago the world's birth and death rates were high and usually nearly equal. Of course this is not to say that in any given year the birth and death rates would be exactly equal; death rates in particular tended to vary greatly from year to year. In years when the food supply was adequate, population growth, at least in agricultural societies, was around 5 or 10 per 1000. Death rates tended to be very high in years of scarcity. Food shortages sometimes caused death by actual starvation, but they also caused malnutrition and undernourishment, which permitted the spread of disease. One of the most famous epidemics in human history was the Black Death, which occurred in Europe between 1347 and 1352 and killed nearly one-third of the population.

The Industrial Revolution caused a large reduction in peacetime mortality throughout the world. In Europe mortality rates decreased slowly in the eighteenth century as available food increased. During the nineteenth century mortality decreased much more rapidly, probably because of the following factors: (1) better nutrition; (2) improvements in sanitation, especially in cities, because of improved water supply and sewage systems; (3) prevention of disease through inoculation; and (4) advances in the cure of infectious diseases, especially later, after the discovery of antibiotics. Death rates remained high in the less developed countries, however, until the end of World War II, when they dropped rapidly and thus created the huge growth in world population.

Seeing the effects of the Industrial Revolution in the West, demographers believed that economic development would lead to lower mortality and fertility rates in *any* country. This, they said, would occur in four phases. In phase 1, the preindustrial stage, birth and death rates are both high. Because the birthrate is about equal to the death rate, there is little or no growth in population. In phase 2, as industrialization begins, the death rate begins to decline much faster than the birthrate, so that the population grows

rapidly. In phase 3 the birthrate declines more rapidly than the death rate and the population increases much more slowly than in the second stage. Finally, in phase 4 both birth and death rates stabilize at a low (and again about equal) level, so that population growth is small or even negative. (See Figure 17.8.)

The demographic-transition model explained why mortality declined in the West: Industrialization, economic development, and urbanization improved the standard of living. However, it did not account for the decline of fertility. Demographers more or less assumed that the birth rate would decline and that it would stay down, but they did not specify how industrializa-

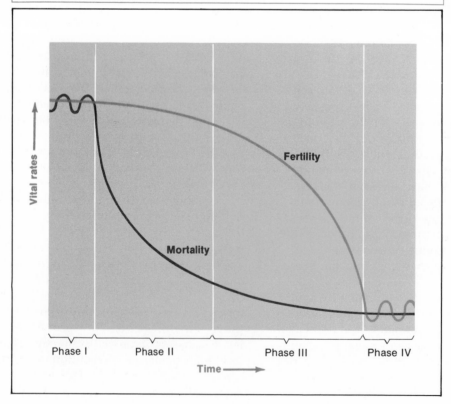

**FIGURE 17.8**
*Demographic-transition model*

tion, economic development, and urbanization would limit the birthrate.

Before World War II, when the mortality and the fertility rates of all industrialized nations had dropped and their populations were not growing at all, demographers assumed that these societies were in the fourth and final stage of demographic transition. After the war, however, demographers were astonished to find the birthrates in North America actually rising to levels that were higher than their prewar levels. Furthermore, new historical evidence from other societies has contradicted the model by showing a direct rather than an inverse relationship between economic development and fertility trends. Birthrates in England, for example, may well have increased during industrialization instead of decreasing. So the relationship between industrialization and fertility is more complex than the demographic-transition model would lead us to believe.

For one thing, we may need to distinguish between the immediate, direct effects of economic development and its long-run, indirect effects. They may run in opposite directions. Probably the immediate effect is to *increase* fertility. People can afford more babies, so they have them. Simple enough. But in the long run the effect of economic development has been to *decrease* fertility. Why? The demand for an educated labor force increases, so people have to spend more to educate each child. Hence, they can afford to educate fewer children than before. Along with economic development has come social-insurance systems (old-age pensions, unemployment and welfare payments, and so on), so people don't need to have children to look after them in their old age or if they become ill. There are many other indirect effects of economic development that tend to decrease fertility. We'll return to them later.

In a developed economy fertility may fluctuate widely, as the baby boom shows. Still, the demographic-transition model is probably a fairly accurate description of the long-term relationship between mortality and fertility. In the long run, after mortality declines fertility will also drop. Unfortunately, the decrease in fertility may be delayed so long that the population expands greatly in the meantime.

## ZERO POPULATION GROWTH

Throughout most of world history the population grew very slowly. Average fertility and mortality rates remained at about the same high level. Eventually the population will again stop growing, and we hope that this will happen because both fertility and mortality will be at about the same *low* level.

How could this goal be achieved? Each woman would replace herself and her husband if she produced an average of 2.1 children. However, in most populations young people are present in great numbers because of high fertility rates in recent years. If these young people produced only enough children to replace themselves, the population would continue to grow for many years. The bulge caused by the baby boom would move up the population pyramid, and the levels below would form a vertical column up to the age of about 60. Birthrates would equal death rates. At that point **zero population growth (ZPG)**—the point at which there is no natural increase in the population—would have been reached. (However, the population might still increase through immigration.)

A few countries, such as West Germany, have already reached ZPG. North America will not reach this goal for a while because of the baby boom. On the other hand, if fertility declines *below* replacement levels (as would happen if, say, the average woman produced only one child, not two), then we might reach ZPG sooner. This is unlikely to happen, though, so the populations of industrial nations will probably continue to grow for many years to come.

# The decision to have a child

As mentioned earlier, the demographic-transition model is still useful as a general guide. But it has been modified to include several other factors besides economic development. Here we'll take a brief look at those factors. What factors influence the decision to have a child? Many reasons might come up, but social scientists, having tidy minds, like to organize those reasons into categories. (I can imaging a couple of married sociologists taking a checklist to bed and interviewing each other about their desire to have a baby.) Joseph Spengler's checklist is a good one.[14] Spengler believes that the decision to have a baby is a function of three variables: (1) the couple's preference system, (2) its price system, and (3) its resources.

The couple's *preference system* consists of the value it places on having the child—relative to other goals. ("Which do you prefer, a new car or another baby, honey?") The *price system* is simply the cost of the additional child—not only financial costs but time and effort as well—relative to other goals. *Resources* consist of the money, time, and energy the couple has available for all of its goals.

Spengler's theory assumes that the probability of deciding to have another child will vary *directly* with the preference system. (The more you like children, compared to other things, the more likely you are to choose to have one.) It will vary *inversely* with the predicted price. (The more expensive children are to have and maintain, the fewer children people will choose to have.) Finally, the decision will vary *directly* with the amount of available resources. (The more money, time, and energy you have, the more likely you are to have a baby, if you're at all interested in having one.)

This simple theory is very helpful in clarifying the patterns of fertility in developed countries. The resources of developed nations in terms of both money and time have increased greatly over the past few centuries. According to the theory, this should have led to an increase in their birthrates. In fact, they have declined. Changes in the price and preference systems have counteracted the effects of increased resources. There was a period when birthrates *did* increase—the baby boom of the 1940s and 1950s. Income was rising fast then, so fast that it seems to have more than offset the effects of changes in the preference and price systems.

Let's look at a few major factors that have influenced the price system and the preference system over the past century. These have all tended to reduce the desired family size in Western societies during that period. Changes in the preference system include mortality rates, child labor laws, old-age support, rewards from society, and consumption patterns. Changes in the price system result from contraception, urbanization, the value of labor, and extended education.

### CHANGES IN THE PREFERENCE SYSTEM

#### Mortality

The most important reason for high birthrates is high mortality. People have extra babies only when they need them as insurance against the probable death of one or more of their other children. But mortality has declined in recent years, especially among infants and children. More children survive. Hence, fewer children need to be born for the parents to be reasonably sure that some will grow up.

#### Child labor

Farm children are economic assets—by the age of ten they can earn their own keep. During the nineteenth century the supply of land per person declined, so that each additional child was less of an asset than before. Also, child labor was never very effective in factories. As new laws limited the employment of children in industry, their economic value to their parents declined. At the same time, compulsory-education laws were introduced. Since schooling is an added expense to parents, children became costly. They were no longer economic assets to their parents.

### Support in old age

In Western societies, until a few years ago the only old-age support parents had derived from their own kin—mostly their sons. This is still true in the Third World. In most societies the poor consider children an absolute necessity. How else will they survive when they are too old or disabled to work? You and I have social security and retirement benefits. We don't need to depend on our children for support, so the value of a child is relatively lower for us than the values of other things that we may choose to spend our money on.

### Rewards from society

When mortality was high, a good citizen felt that it was his or her duty to produce a large family. Otherwise, the population might decline. Both the church and government encouraged high fertility rates. Today we have the opposite problem, so that most governments and religions now discourage couples from having large families.

### Conspicuous consumption

It is sometimes argued that we need status symbols more than our grandparents and great-grandparents did because our status is achieved and theirs was largely ascribed. If one's status is fixed, unchanging, limited by birth, one does not need to advertise it. It just *is*. But if our status is achieved, we are more likely to show it off. And to do this we have to buy things that we don't really need. If we want lots of status symbols (jewelry, fancy cars, and so on), we have to give up something else, namely, babies. So, at least according to this theory, fertility declines as

*Family-planning clinics around the world are offering the technology of contraception. No Third World nation's birthrates have dropped without such programs.*

Phiz Mezey/DPI
Marc & Evelyne Bernheim/Woodfin Camp

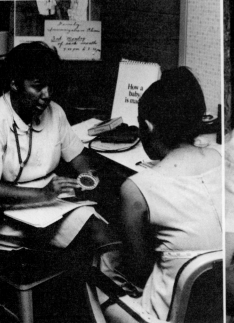

showy display of wealth increases. (Actually, I don't believe this theory.)

### Contraception

When birth control methods are crude, the decision *not* to have a child is a costly one. People have to pay a high price in terms of inconvenience, interference with sexual pleasure, and the dangers of primitive abortion methods. Thus to introduce cheap, effective, convenient methods of contraception is to change the price of having a child compared to the price of *not* having one. Everything else being equal, fertility will decline as a result.

### Urbanization

City space is expensive. Hence, it is more expensive to raise children in the city than to raise them in the country. Urbanization thus tends to cause a decline in fertility. On the other hand, the growth of American suburbs after World War II made living space cheaper. Freeways and subsidized mortgages made suburban living possible, and that, in turn, may have stimulated the baby boom.

### The value of labor

Increasing industrial productivity means that an average man or woman can produce more things in an hour of work than before and can therefore earn more money. On the other hand, child care is no more productive than before. (It still takes 2 minutes to change a diaper and 20 minutes to read a fairy tale aloud, for example.) In fact child care probably takes *more* time than it used to. This increased effort has to be weighed against the increase in income if the wife takes a job instead of having another child. As her pay increases, the cost of giving up the job to have a child also increases.

### Extended education

Children need more education today than they used to because they will have to perform more complex jobs. This is expensive. Whether the state pays or the family pays, it is always more costly for the parents if only because of the longer period of dependency. Hence, increasing levels of education help reduce family size.

# Ecological aspects of human survival

The world is a single ecological system. DDT or mercury dumped into the Great Lakes may eventually kill birds in the South Seas or the Mediterranean. Whales killed by the fishermen of one nation are an endangered species for all of us. If the temperature rises enough to melt the polar ice caps, the penguins won't be the only ones to notice. We may exploit one another in the short run, but in the long run nobody comes out ahead. It's our own nest we'll be fouling, our own resources we'll be depleting. What are those resources?

LAND

Figure 17.9 shows the distribution of the world's population. Obviously, this distribution is determined largely by the geographic characteristics of different areas—particularly the availability of land for farming. About 70 percent of the land on earth is unusable. Today crops are being produced on only 10 percent. That leaves 20 percent for further use—at most. Actually, using all of that land would create havoc because it would mean cutting down all the forests. But we could probably increase our total of farmland by about 50 percent without endangering the ecology. This would mean an increase from 1400 million hectares to about

**FIGURE 17.9**

*World population density*

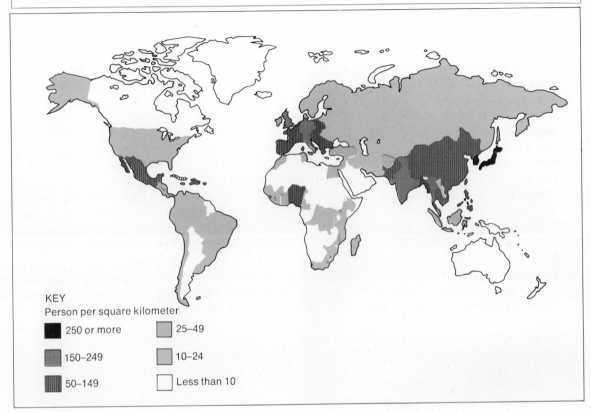

KEY
Person per square kilometer

- 250 or more
- 150–249
- 50–149
- 25–49
- 10–24
- Less than 10

2100 million hectares. (A hectare is about 2-1/2 acres.) The United Nations has stated that a reasonable goal is to open up 6 or 7 million hectares of land for farming by 1985. This would certainly solve the food crisis and could be done with a small fraction of the amount of money now spent on weapons. Much of this new land would be in Africa and Latin America, but some is available in southeast Asia as well.[15]

## WATER

Water is vital to the further development of agriculture. Many new, high-yielding varieties of wheat and rice require much more water than older varieties. In addition, an ample water supply would permit several crops a year in warm climates, rather than the single crop that is possible when the year is sharply divided into rainy and dry seasons.

Desalinization of water is done in several areas, but because the process is costly the water is used only for drinking. Industry competes with agriculture for the use of limited water supplies. However, if pollutants could be removed, much of the water used for industrial purposes could be reused for other purposes. The most promising source of additional water may be tubewells. Only about one-sixteenth of the farm land in poor nations is irrigated properly. With additional irrigation systems and improvement of existing ones, the crop yield of much existing farm land could *double*, even without any other input such as fertilizer. This alone might solve the food problem for many years. There's enough underground water in most places to make tubewell drilling and pumping a realistic goal—better than building enormous dams that can turn out to be failures.[16] On the other hand, large pumps may provide greater amounts of water in the short run but use up the groundwater in the long run. Providing water in dry areas will become more and more expensive as this happens.

### ENERGY AND MINERALS

The demand for energy and minerals will be increased not only by population growth but also by economic development. The world's population is now doubling about every 41 years. But the world's consumption of energy is doubling about every 12 years. Use of iron ore is doubling every 11 years.[17]

We know that the supply of energy from fossil fuels is going to be used up soon, but no one knows just how soon. Further development of water power will provide some energy when fossil fuels are gone. However, the major sources of energy will be atomic power and solar energy. If nuclear fission becomes the major source of the world's energy, the supply of high-grade uranium and thorium ores will eventually be used up. However, it is possible that other minerals could replace them. The United States is working to develop a safe and ecologically harmless breeder reactor that could use a common and cheap type of uranium. Unless it succeeds soon, the cost of atomic power will increase before the end of this century because of the shortage of uranium 235, the only kind of uranium that can be used by today's atomic-power plants.

The costs of metals will also be affected by the future costs of energy. High-grade iron ores are fast being used up. Getting metal from low-grade ore requires more energy. Thus as energy becomes more costly, so will metal.

## SOCIAL RESEARCH: Sociologists at Work

### WORLD FOOD SUPPLY

In this section we will look in more detail at the problem of hunger. Our discussion will be based largely on two important books: *How the Other Half Dies*, by Susan George,[18] and *Food First: Beyond the Myth of Scarcity*, by Frances Moore Lappe and Joseph Collins.[19] We will be especially concerned with the relationship between mortality and fertility. This is the relationship that Malthus sought to explain. Unfortunately, his theory led us astray. He believed that populations always reproduce almost up to capacity and only mortality keeps the population from expanding indefinitely. Not so. It is more nearly correct to say that *mortality determines fertility*. That is, people have extra babies when death rates from hunger are high.

This may not make sense to you. You might advise people to have *fewer* children instead so that there will be fewer mouths to feed and more chance for their existing children to survive. The little food they do have will go further if they have smaller families. Right?

Well, look at it from a different point of view. Suppose you are a mother in Bangladesh, serving rice to your hungry children. There is not enough to satisfy them. They are sick. You know most of them will die—maybe all of them. But you *must* have a son who will survive and contribute to the family income, especially as you grow old. What will you do?

Most poor people in this situation will have another baby. These kids are dying, they say, so let's keep trying and hope that eventually, some of them will survive. *This* is how the rate of mortality influences the rate of fertility. Malthus was wrong. It's not that fertility is naturally unavoidably high and that only mortality (from hunger, disease, or war) keeps the population from increasing to an unmanageable size. Rather, mortality varies and people adjust their fertility in response to it.

The mother in Bangladesh faces a vicious circle: The more children she has, the greater the odds against the survival of any one of them, and the greater the odds against survival, the more children are needed just to break even. But there's a good side to vicious circles: Whenever you manage to influence one variable, this indirectly affects the other variable as well. In this case we have two choices. We can try to reduce fertility so as to prevent starvation in the long run, or we can prevent people from starving, which will eventually reduce their fertility rates. Or, better still, we can work on both fronts at once, by increasing the means of subsistence and also promoting family planning programs. I vote for the dual approach.

The countries that are solving their growth problems are the ones that are eliminating hunger and, at the same time, emphasizing family planning and distributing contraceptives and birth control information as widely as possible. No country has slowed its growth rate without a birth control program. On the other hand, no birth control program has been successful unless the hunger problem was also being solved. It seems that you can't convince people to stop having babies until they see that there's plenty of food for the ones they already have. So let's focus on the hunger problem.

In estimating how well fed a population is, we might ask, What is the average amount of food eaten per capita? But per-capita figures can be misleading. In one society half the population may eat 1000 calories a day and the other half 3000 calories. In another society almost everyone may eat the same amount of food—2000

calories per day. The per-capita figures for the two societies would be the same, but the deprivation and misery suffered by their populations would differ dramatically. Hence, *equality of distribution* is more important than almost any other economic factor. We are talking not simply about the *amount* of food within a society but about how fairly it is *distributed*. Both factors together determine the amount of hunger and, thus, the likely rate of population growth.

The hunger problem is largely a distribution problem. The world produces about 3000 calories of grain per person per day, not to mention fruits, vegetables, and other foodstuffs. This means that there should be more than enough for everybody. Where does it all go?

Some of it is fed to livestock to produce meat that only the rich can afford to eat. Some of that meat is also fed to pets, not people. Meat eating is a wasteful form of consumption. Think of all the grain a steer ate in order to become a filet mignon for you and a piece of leftover hamburger for your dog.

Some of it is made into expensive, nonnutritious products such as soft drinks or chocolate-flavored breakfast cereals shaped like hearts and flowers but with about 5 cents' worth of grain in the gloriously decorated box. Or baby formula. God knows how many babies in less developed countries have died because saleswomen have talked their mothers into weaning them from the breast and feeding them with powdered formula that they couldn't afford and didn't have the sanitary facilities to mix up anyway. Their own breast milk was fine.[20]

Some of the food is simply stacked up in piles, to be eaten by mice or eventually dumped because it wasn't available where and when it was needed. Poor people usually can't afford food even if it is there. The warehouses may be bulging with rice, but the hungry people outside may not have the money to buy it.

Any country on earth could feed its own population if the proper political and economic arrangements were made. So why don't the less developed countries do what is necessary to feed their people? *They can't.* They don't have control over their own economies. For example, most nations depend on the production of cash crops for export. If held by local people, their

*Most of the food exported from North America goes, not to underdeveloped countries where populations are undernourished, but to rich countries.*

vast plantations could feed the population nicely. Instead, they produce coffee, cocoa, jute, sugar, rubber, cotton, bananas, and so forth for export. They are managed or indirectly controlled by giant multinational corporations with names that appear as famous brands on jars in your pantry.

Moreover, international food distribution is beyond the forces of supply and demand. The world's food supply is manipulated by a group of big corporations known as *agribusiness*. These giant firms can make deals to supply whole nations with grain or beef or coffee, and those deals affect the prices you pay a month later in the supermarket. If this bothers you, imagine how a Brazilian coffee picker might feel about it. In many countries the entire economy depends on a single export crop. The prices of that crop may be determined not merely by competition, the weather, and other such accidents of fate, but also by the policies of rich governments. The

U.S. government, for example, deliberately drove up the worldwide price of food during the Nixon administration in order to fix a balance-of-payments deficit. That involved creating an artificial scarcity for a time, which the Department of Agriculture can do without difficulty. I am not talking about anything unusual. What I am pointing out is obvious to anyone who listens to the farm report once in a while on the car radio: Farm commodities are produced and traded according to government plans and regulations. Political decisions thus are an important part of the economic system that determines the production and distribution of the world's food. Our governments and our corporations have enormous influence on what gets planted around the world and by whom it gets eaten.

Scarcity is not unavoidable. It is created by people, either on purpose or as an unintended result of other decisions. People could almost always create more of whatever is in short supply, given different structural arrangements. Agriculture is especially flexible. Canadian officials have said, for example, that it would be possible to increase food production by 50 percent in five years if necessary.[21] But it will not happen because it is not sufficiently profitable to agribusiness.

Often agribusiness doesn't directly own the land in other countries that produces these commodities. The land is usually held by local elites. In 1960 the United Nations Food and Agriculture organization found that a mere 2.5 percent of landowners with holdings of more than 100 hectares control nearly three-quarters of the earth's agricultural land. *And the top 0.23 percent control over half.* That was in 1960. We don't have up-to-date statistics, but we know that land ownership has become even *more* concentrated since then, not less.[22]

Until recently I imagined that North America was the world's breadbasket—that our expanding agricultural productivity was the margin of safety by which millions of lives could be saved each year. There is some truth to this picture, of course. Both Canada and the United States export large amounts of food, chiefly wheat, and indeed many nations have rescued their populations in bad years by buying that food. Some of the food has been shipped as part of the foreign-aid program. However, there is another side to the story. Although a lot of food is exported from North America, most of it goes to the industrial countries, not to Third World nations. For example, in 1974 the United States exported 114.5 pounds of wheat per person to Japan but only 7.5 pounds per person to India.[23] Only a small part of food exported was in the form of aid (which involves low-interest, long-term loans to the nations receiving the aid).

Moreover, although the United States and Canada are both major food exporters, they also import large amounts of food. In 1974 the United States ranked third in food imports, and over two-thirds of those imports come from less developed countries.[24] The United States does export beef—but it also imports beef. It buys over 40 percent of all the beef in world trade. This is a large amount of food to the people who are exporting it. More meat is sent from less developed countries to industrial nations than in

the other direction.[25] The United States is also the world's leading importer of seafood and is a net importer of milk products.[26]

Who, then, is sending food to whom? The hungriest people on earth may be the ones who are sending us our dinners.

I'm not suggesting that you skip dinner tonight or become a vegetarian or force your dog to become one. Individuals can't redistribute the world's food supply. We have to look for more effective answers.

What about increasing production? If there is a lot of food, then distribution may be less of a

*Underdeveloped countries often have to sell crops for cash to get foreign currency to pay for their equipment. This puts farm workers out of work, and they have even less chance of buying food than before.*

David Plank/DPI

problem because even the poor will have a decent meal if not a gourmet dinner. So how can food production be increased? Several major developments are taking place in this area—and unfortunately, many of them have negative as well as positive effects on the poor nations. The "Green Revolution" is an example.

In the past twenty years or so a number of new strains of grain—mostly wheat and rice—have been developed that can yield far larger crops than the strains used in the past—often several times as much food. Miracle seeds, you might call them. (They are actually called high-yielding varieties, or HYV). Naturally, the governments of the less developed countries have encouraged farmers to plant these new crops. This has made it possible for several crops to be grown in a single year where formerly only one could be produced. In many cases production has soared.

But there's a catch. These seeds don't automatically produce better crops. They also require more inputs than older strains—more water and more fertilizer. Without these added inputs, the yields may be no greater than before. And the ordinary peasant has limited water, fertilizer, not to mention modern farm machinery, pesticides, and so on. Moreover, little credit is available to peasants. So to pay for the new technology it is necessary to obtain foreign currency, and in order to do that, farmers have to sell cash crops instead of using the grain to feed their own families. Hence, the Green Revolution has stepped up the rate at which food produced in the Third World is pulled into the worldwide economic market. Instead of making the local people more self-sufficient, it has actually put them more than ever at the mercy of the international economy. Who benefits? Not the poor, but agribusiness. And in the long run the crop payoffs sometimes turn out to be disappointing anyway. For example, many HYVs start out with a spectacular production record but achieve this only by using heavy pesticides. Over a few years the pests become resistant to the chemicals. Then they can survive repeated sprayings with expensive pesticides that are injurious to other organisms. The farmer loses, and so does the human environment. The chemical manufacturers win, though.

Some less developed nations have borrowed heavily to invest in miracle seeds and in the technology that goes with them. Often this has been a serious mistake. Farm machinery increases the productivity of Western farms but is a very bad investment for most less developed nations. Tractors and combines are efficient in terms of human labor, but they don't make efficient use of land. They cost a fortune both to buy and to operate. Worst of all is the effect on the poor farm worker whose job is taken over by the machine.

Agriculture in the less developed countries must be labor intensive. That is, output must be improved through the profitable investment of labor, not labor-saving devices. People need jobs, and there aren't enough jobs in industry for those who are displaced by tractors. Moreover, the labor is available now; the capital for tractors isn't. The Chinese have proved that labor-intensive agriculture works: They have eliminated hunger, flooding, built backyard fertilizer plants, and equalized the distribution of food and other needs of daily life, all without importing expensive equipment. (Even the dams were built by hand.) There is work for everyone, and the population growth rate has declined by 20 percent.

What about foreign aid? The industrial nations have long contributed to Third World nations, both to increase their crop yields and to help them industrialize. How effective has this aid been and how much can it offer in the future?

Foreign aid is partly a myth and partly a failure. In the first place, most of the "aid" is not given outright but is in the form of low-interest loans to friendly governments.[27] The donations often consist of surplus wheat that is sent to poor nations in order to avoid a glut on the U.S. market. It has helped keep U.S. food prices high. The friendly governments then sell the food—they don't give it away. Hence, hungry people are not necessarily any better fed because of this aid. And there have been benefits for the American farmers. For example, sometimes wheat has been sent to areas where people had formerly eaten only rice as part of their ordinary diet. They became accustomed to wheat products, and this generated a market for wheat that has continued since that time. Only now they pay for it at commercial rates.

In the second place, despite their low interest rates, the loans made to poor nations under the aid program have become a major burden for their governments. The collective debt of 86 less developed countries doubled in five years.[28] These nations must keep on borrowing money just to meet their interest payments. By 1973 almost 40 percent of the aid money received by less developed countries was spent to repay the debt on past loans.[29] The U.S. government does not mean to be a loan shark, but its relationship with many of the countries that it wants to help may not be very helpful to them at all. To raise the money for loan payments, the countries of the Third World must export food instead of producing it for their own people. And we're back where we started from.

I'm also not looking for any villains; I don't know any. I do know a lot of well-meaning people who have limited knowledge and make mistakes even though they are doing the best they can. So let's look for new solutions, not villains.

# SOCIAL POLICY:
## Issues and Viewpoints

How should we respond to the population explosion? I think we should break this question into three areas: fertility, mortality, and migration.

### FERTILITY

Throughout history most laws that had to do with fertility were designed to increase fertility, not to reduce it. For example, during the reign of Augustus Caesar, fathers were given preference in public office according to the number of children in the family and mothers of large families had the right to wear special clothes and ornaments. More recent policies with similar goals include programs in which the government pays cash to help families support dependent children. Abortion and contraception have often been outlawed, and tax laws have been designed to encourage parenthood.

Laws that *restrict* fertility are much more recent. Japan was the first nation to pass such laws. After World War II its territory was greatly reduced and its living standards cut sharply. Abortion was legalized and the fertility rate fell dramatically.

One of the most successful contraceptive programs was carried out in Taiwan beginning in 1964. Private physicians were given IUDs and paid for each one they inserted, and other contraceptives were made widely available and encouraged through the mass media. In 1963 the total fertility rate in Taiwan was 5.4, but by 1971 it had declined to 3.7.[30]

During the 1960s the U.S. government changed its attitude toward family planning, gradually extending its financial and technical assistance to foreign nations in this area. By 1971 AID funding in this area was $95.9 million, or more than 5 percent of all AID obligations.[31] In addition, the Department of Health, Education and Welfare began to make funds available to state and local agencies for family planning programs. These programs have probably had their greatest impact on poorly educated people, who tend to be uninformed about birth control methods.

Many other policies affect fertility indirectly. For example, increasing the cost of child rearing (e.g., by increasing the number of years of schooling required) makes parenthood more expensive and thus lowers the birthrate. Even informing people about the high cost of child rearing may discourage them from giving birth: Most people underestimate how much it costs to provide for children. Making jobs available to women gives them other ways of spending their time besides caring for children. Increasing urban employment will also decrease fertility, because in the cities there are fewer jobs for children and more jobs for skilled workers.

Lower fertility, however, comes not from

family planning alone, nor from the policies just mentioned, but from the combination of these factors with a lower death rate and an improved standard of living.

### MORTALITY

Everyone is against mortality. In the past few centuries Western technology has found effective ways of translating those feelings into action: Death rates have lowered in every country that has industrialized, except during times of war. Since World War II, death rates have dropped remarkably in most Third World countries as well. There are many things that can be done to decrease mortality rates: Drain swamps. Purify drinking water. Install sewers. Innoculate children. Train midwives. And, more than anything else, improve the amount and quality of food available to poor people.

As mentioned earlier, land reform would go a long way toward solving the problem of hunger. People will feed themselves if they are allowed to do so. The main thing you and I can do is to make sure that our governments and business firms don't stop people from making needed changes. There have already been too many cases of Western interference in political struggles that might have produced real reforms in less developed countries. If you give to a charity that claims to help a poor country, try to make sure it is controlled by the people there.

Western nations should also give some thought to their own food supplies. The poor nations can't afford to export all their crops to us and still feed themselves. On the other hand, after their own basic food needs are met they may export a certain amount of food in return for cash payments. For example, Cuba stopped exporting sugar after Castro came to power. Once the Cuban population had enough to eat, it became possible to resume the production of sugar for export. Cuba can now afford to export part of its crop because its own basic needs have been met.

Looking to the future, algae and yeast may produce protein in large amounts. This type of protein can be produced sixty times as efficiently, in terms of energy, as beef protein.[32] Moreover, technology will certainly move in the direction of using crops more efficiently. Often leaves, stalks, hulls, and roots are thrown away. These could be used to produce fertilizers, animal feed, or even food for human beings. Meat production is too wasteful to be continued, at least using present methods. Experimental farms are feeding cattle diets of wood pulp, newspapers, and even their own processed manure, and the animals seem to be thriving.[33] There are many other ways of producing more food through new technology that have yet to be applied on a large scale. Mortality can be lowered still further around the world.

Finally, I want to mention the factors that affect mortality in the advanced societies. Our problems are quite different from those of the less developed nations. They involve changes in life style rather than medical or technological changes. Until a few years ago I assumed that lower mortality rates in the West were due to medical advances. But not so. Mortality had already decreased greatly before penicillin and other "wonder drugs" were discovered. Diseases such as typhoid fever, whooping cough, and tuberculosis became much less frequent after industrialization had taken place, because families became smaller and could therefore provide better living conditions for their children. Indeed, if all of the doctors and hospitals in North America were to disappear today but our levels of nutrition, hygiene, and other living conditions remained high, our mortality levels would not be affected very much.[34] Yet we continue to invest large amounts of money in medicine while overlooking other ways of cutting mortality rates. For example, we do nothing to improve the ambulance system, so that many people die before they can get to a hospital. When well-trained midwives deliver infants in the home the death rates among mothers and babies are lower than when hurried obstetricians deliver them in hospitals. Changes in habits would do far more to increase life spans than any known ways of improving medical treatment. For example, people could avoid heart attacks and lung cancer to a considerable degree by getting proper nutrition and exercise and not smoking. Cirrhosis, another major killer, strikes heavy drinkers far more than other people. Breathing air in a badly polluted city is estimated to decrease life spans by an average of three years. The number of deaths caused by traffic accidents would decline if drivers used seat belts, refrained from drinking, and bought only cars designed for safety.

Governments affect mortality through legislation. Every society has policies regarding suicide, infanticide, child abuse, and homicide, as well as traffic laws, safety codes, and hundreds of other laws that directly affect one's chances of dying or staying alive. The greatest impact of government on mortality, however, is in the area of foreign policy. The worst killer of all is war.

### MIGRATION

Governments also have policies that affect migration. They can control immigration, for example. However, they cannot entirely prevent illegal immigration or emigration. Some countries—especially communist countries such as the Soviet Union and the People's Republic of China—discourage emigration, but people still manage to leave those nations.

The USSR also controls migration within its borders. Even though its policies have become less severe since Stalin's death, the government, as the nation's main employer, can stimulate internal migration to certain areas (such as Siberia) through both positive inducements· and

coercion, and restrict internal migration to other areas by limiting the number of job openings there.

Governments are often as concerned with the type of migration as they are with the volume of migration. Many governments have tried to reduce ethnic diversity by allowing immigration only from nations that are similar in culture and racial composition. Many have also favored certain occupations. For example, the United States' 1965 immigration legislation gives preference to professional workers. As a result the United States has been accused of draining the best-educated people from the rest of the world.

Canada's new immigration laws, passed in 1977, allow the minister of manpower to set annual immigration levels with the approval of the provinces, and these levels can be changed to fit changing "demographic goals." An applicant's chances of being allowed to immigrate are affected by the goals of reuniting families, helping refugees, and economic growth. The law specifically bans discrimination.[35]

The political decisions surrounding the growth and migration of human populations are a major issue. In the years ahead, professional demographers will play an increasingly important role in judging actual and proposed population policies.

## SUMMARY

**1.** *Fecundity* is the capacity to give birth. *Fertility* is the rate of actual childbearing in a population.

**2.** Fertility is affected by eleven different variables: (1) age of entry into sexual unions, (2) permanent celibacy, (3) part of reproductive life spent after or between unions, (4) voluntary abstinence, (5) involuntary abstinence, (6) frequency of intercourse, (7) involuntary causes of fecundity

or infecundity, (8) use or nonuse of contraception, (9) voluntary causes of fecundity or infecundity, (10) fetal mortality from involuntary causes, and (11) fetal mortality from voluntary causes.

**3.** The crude death rate is the number of deaths per year per 1000 people. Mortality declined between the late eighteenth century and the late nineteenth century in the industrialized nations. It has declined more slowly since then. Since World War II it has declined greatly in the less developed nations.

**4.** Mourning rituals have almost vanished because of lower mortality rates. The emphasis of religion has shifted from the next life to this one, perhaps for the same reason. Mobility may be encouraged by lower mortality levels because people have more confidence in their future and can risk moving away from their kin.

**5.** About 20 percent of Americans move each year. Migration is stressful and causes behavioral problems in many people. Marital breakdown and deviance are affected by mobility. On the other hand, areas with high inmigration rates tend to be more tolerant and have more vitality than areas with low inmigration or net out-migration.

**6.** Young adults are most likely to move. Social class is not greatly related to mobility. Self-employed people are less likely to move than others. In the United States migration has been mostly westward and, to a lesser extent, northward as blacks have moved out of the South.

**7.** The sex ratio is the number of males per 100 females. The North American sex ratio is now about 95, and the ratio for the black population is even lower. After a war the sex ratio may be very unbalanced.

**8.** An age–sex population pyramid is a graph showing the composition of the population in terms of age and sex. A nation with a high fertility rate usually has a wide-based population pyramid. A nation in which fertility has been low for a long time has a pyramid with more vertical sides.

**9.** The dependency ratio is the ratio of people in dependent age groups (i.e., very young or old) to people in economically productive age groups. It is affected by the median age of the population, which is the age that divides any population into equal groups. The median age of the United States in 1970 was 28.

**10.** The peak growth year for the world's population may have been 1970, when the growth rate was 19 per 1000 people. In 1977 the rate had fallen to about 17. At that rate the world's population will double in 41 years.

**11.** Malthus pointed out that the means of subsistence grow at an arithmetic rate while the population tends to grow at a geometric rate. At first he believed that the only limits on such growth would be "positive checks"—mortality caused by hunger, disease, and war. Later he concluded that human beings might use "preventive checks"—such as lowering fertility through late marriage. He was opposed to birth control. Fortunately, the means of subsistence have increased much more than he expected, and death rates have decreased. Fertility has also decreased.

**12.** The demographic-transition model is based on the historical experience of Western societies. Birth and death rates were high and almost equal in preindustrial times. In the nineteenth century, as a result of improvements in nutrition, sanitation, and medicine, the death rates began to drop. After that fertility began to decline too. It was expected that the two rates would level off at a low level, but the postwar baby boom occurred instead. Now we know that economic development may increase fertility in the short run while decreasing it in the long run.

**13.** Spengler points out that a couple's decision to have a child is based on three factors. It varies directly with the preference system, inversely with the price system, and directly with available resources. The preference system is determined by several factors—mortality, the value of child labor, the need for support in old age and other social rewards for having children. The price system is affected by the availability and convenience of contraception as well as by urbanization, the value of labor, and the extent of education.

# KEY TERMS

**crude birthrate**   the number of births per year per 1000 people.

**crude death rate**   the number of deaths per year per 1000 people.

**demographic-transition model**   a model used to describe the process by which preindustrial societies with high rates of fertility and mortality are transformed into modern societies with low rates of fertility and mortality.

**demography**   the study of human populations.

**dependency ratio**   the ratio of people in dependent age groups to people in economically productive age groups.

**ecology**   the relationship between the physical environment and the human population that lives in that environment.

**fecundity**   a woman's capacity to bear children.

**fertility**   the rate at which a population gives birth.

**median age**   the age that divides any population into equal groups, half older and half younger.

**migration**   the movement of people into or out of an area.

**mortality**   the rate at which a population dies.

**population pyramid**   a diagram that shows the age–sex composition of a population at a given time.

**sex ratio**   the number of males per 100 females in a population.

**zero population growth (ZPG)**   the point at which there is no natural increase in a population.

# FOR FURTHER READING

*Demography*. This is an important journal.

FALK, RICHARD. *This Endangered Planet*. New York: Random House, 1971. One of a number of excellent and scary books about the ecological threat to various species on this planet, including our own.

HEER, DAVID. *Society and Population*, 2nd edition. Englewood Cliffs, N.J.: Prentice-Hall, 1975. Heer's book is the basis for much of this chapter. Because demographic realities are changing from one minute to another, I suggest you look at it right away.

KALBACH, WARREN, and WAYNE W. McVEY. *Demographic Bases of Canadian Society*. Toronto: McGraw-Hill Ryerson, 1971. An excellent medium-sized paperback on the Canadian population. Kalbach is an expert on migration, so the book provides a fine treatment of immigration, especially important for a nation with such a high rate of influx.

MALTHUS, THOMAS. *On Population*. Edited by Gertrude Himmelfarb. New York: Modern Library, 1960. The original essays that started the controversy are presented here.

MARSDEN, LORNA. *Population Probe: Canada*. Toronto: Copp, Clark, 1972. The first chapters are the most useful ones in this book, which is basically an argument for a Canadian population policy.

MITCHELL, DON. *The Politics of Food*. Toronto: Lorimer, 1975. Much of this book deals with the international food market and agribusiness, as it applies to the Canadian consumer.

*Population Index*. Another extremely useful journal for demographers.

SAUVY, ALFRED. *A General Theory of Population*. New York: George Weidenfeld, Nicolson, 1969. This is a big book, heavily theoretical.

18

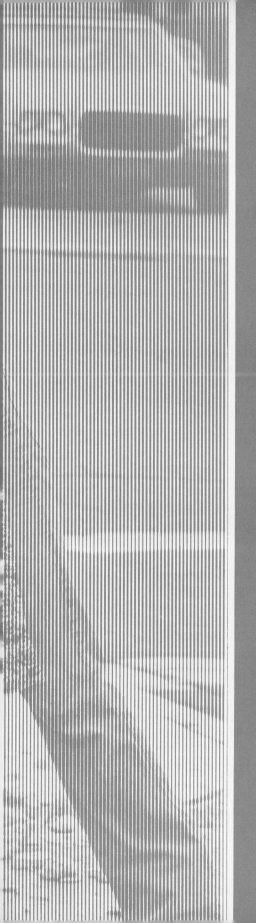

# URBAN LIVING

Pretend that you work for a large organization that must transfer you to a different place. It promises, however, that if you make a list of three places where you would be glad to live, it will transfer you to one of those places. Here's your chance. Of all the places in the world, which three would you choose?

I'd choose a house on Telegraph Hill in San Francisco or an apartment at Place des Vosges in Paris or a house on a side canal near the Rialto bridge in Venice. All of my choices are urban. My friends tend to choose places like a chateau in the Loire Valley or a mansion on the Hudson River an hour's drive from New York City. They want a more rural place where they can play loud music without worrying about bothering the neighbors. What about you? Would you like your home to be isolated and private or close to a variety of human activities?

A 1973 Gallup poll found that only 13 percent of Americans want to live in a city. Another quarter of the population would like to live on a farm, and the rest would prefer either the suburbs or a small town.[1] It seems that even most city dwellers would prefer a smaller place. Another survey, done in 1969, found that two-thirds of big-city residents hoped to be living elsewhere within ten years.[2] No doubt many of them got their wish. Yet people continue to move toward urban areas from the countryside, chiefly for economic reasons. Job opportunities are better in the city.

Whether you prefer big-city or rural living depends largely on what you like to do with your time — on your tastes and life style. If you have children, you might prefer to raise them in a quiet area where you can have a big back yard. But professionals, unemployed people, and those in white-collar jobs, especially if they are unmarried, usually prefer the city. It is easier to go out for an evening. High culture is more available. The city is stimulating, alive, exciting — it's where the action is. I'd rather have a seedy apartment in a lively city than a mansion in the suburbs.

In this chapter we will talk about urban living — past, present, and future. We'll begin with a discussion of the place of cities in the history of Western civilization. Then we'll note some changes in the patterns of urbanization in America. After that we'll turn to the old debate about the quality of life in urban and rural areas.

## The development of cities

A city is a large, permanent, densely populated settlement. Two important points about the development of cities should be kept in mind. The first is that cities always depend on the surrounding area to supply them with food and other materials. The second is that industrial cities are very different from preindustrial ones.

### THE ROLE OF AGRICULTURAL SURPLUSES

As agriculture improves, cities can grow. The two are connected. A society that is very low in economic productivity can support very few nonfarmers. But cities are large, densely populated areas in which people don't grow their own food. In a hunting and gathering society — that of the Plains Indians, say, or the Australian aboriginal tribes — one person can support only himself, occasionally his wife, and for a few years (until they can catch their own food), his children. City dwellers, who depend on food produced by others, can exist in large numbers only when technology is advanced enough to provide a large surplus. Technology makes its greatest steps forward when some new way of using energy is developed. When horses were harnessed and put to work, more people could survive on the surplus provided as a result. The invention of electrical generators ena-

Chris Reeberg/DPI

*No surplus, no cities. Urban residents depend on farmers' producing more than they need for their own families.*

bled even larger populations to live in cities. Atomic reactors will also increase productivity, so that populations can expand still further. The more productive the food producers can be, the larger the urban population can grow.

This much is clear: No surplus, no cities. But which came first, the surplus or the cities? Scholars used to assume that agricultural development happened first and that urban development followed. A few have argued that there was no surplus—that the growth of cities created famine in rural areas. This may have been true sometimes, but most of the time there must have been a surplus—otherwise the city dwellers would have "killed the goose that laid the golden egg" by starving the farmers who supported them.

A third point of view is that city dwellers themselves created the conditions that made their growth possible. They could have

done this by (1) forcing the farmers to work harder and produce more than they needed to produce and/or (2) providing technological innovations that increased productivity—for example, building large-scale irrigation projects that made agriculture more effective.[3] In other words, it is possible that cities "paid their own way" from the beginning by helping farmers increase productivity. In any case it is clear that city dwellers have always obtained their food from the farmers and that they have often used military or political power to do so. This requires us to look at the relationship between cities and empires.

## CITIES AND EMPIRES

Gideon Sjoberg has described the relationship between cities and the expansion and contraction of empires.[4] According to Sjoberg, elites have always been city people.

527

That is, the people who have "made history"—political, intellectual, or religious—have almost always lived in cities. And powerful empires have had many great cities. The cities of the Mesopotamian river valleys supported empires that were great for their time, such as the Babylonian kingdoms. But these empires were much smaller than the ones that came later in history as technology became more advanced—the Roman and, especially, British empires,

for example. What made cities so important in the political control of large regions? Why did empires depend on the existence of cities?

## Communication

The most obvious advantage cities offer is ease of communication. In the old days, cities had walls around them. Inside those walls commercial activities could flourish. Political, educational, and religious leaders

*Many inner cities are now improving instead of decaying. This area around Toronto's new city hall is being redeveloped with splendid architecture.*

could communicate with each other, thus reinforcing their social power. Bureaucratic officials work best in face-to-face contact, because only through personal interaction can they spot trouble in their organization. (This is why, even today, managers are found in large numbers in downtown New York City, which has more office space than all the other large American cities combined.) The preindustrial city depended even more on oral communication, so the leaders gathered in the center of the city, where they could contact each other whenever necessary.

The capital city of the empire was the site of the royal court, which attracted traveling entertainers and merchants. These travelers often brought news from outlying areas. The lesser ruling elites were often sent to administer smaller cities scattered through the empire. Those cities were usually located on communication routes so that the administrators could keep in touch with the capital city.

### Political coercion

Cities need a strong political system that can force farmers to give up their surplus to provide food for the city dwellers. The rulers usually controlled the farmers by owning the land that the farmers cultivated.

Political coercion is also necessary for commerce. Not only does it suppress bandits and pirates; it also coordinates the workers who build roads and other vital public works. All the important trading empires were great military or naval powers, and they used military force to provide the security in which trade could be carried on. Large empires often built up their cities by sending colonists to dominate outlying regions.

### The decline of empires

Imperial cities usually developed by diffusion—the spread of a cultural pattern from one people to another. Often new cities began as military bases—especially on frontiers. These frontier cities socialized the natives into the culture of the dominant group. As Sjoberg points out, this was usually a fatal mistake because it led to the decline of the empire itself.

Typically, this is what would happen: The ruling group would conquer the natives and then come to depend on them, especially if their languages differed. Thus the administrators would teach the natives how to run things, for example, in the military, in the bureaucracy, or in business. Naturally, the natives would pick up certain useful skills. Eventually, when the right time came, they would be able to attack the rulers, particularly in the frontier areas. In those regions new empires or nations might form by breaking away. Then the "mother country" would become less important and might even be invaded by its former subjects. This happened, for example, when the barbarians sacked Rome and destroyed urban civilization in the entire Roman empire. The Romans themselves had prepared the barbarians to carry out this attack. The same thing happened to the British Empire. The Indian elite who had been educated to serve as loyal bureaucrats for the British crown led the fight for independence—Mahatma Gandhi was an Indian lawyer who had been educated in England.

## THE CITIES OF
## MEDIEVAL EUROPE

Not all cities are imperial in origin. The cities of medieval Europe were quite different from those of the rest of the world.[5] Instead of being part of an empire, the medieval city was a free enclave within the harsh world of feudalism. Some of the greatest political traditions of the West developed within city walls. The medieval city helped transform European society by protecting the middle class—a free class of people in a society that otherwise lacked any freedom at all.[6] If the medieval city had not developed the basic

*Some of the great political traditions we cherish in the West developed in the medieval walled cities of Europe. Even the word "citizen," which implies one who may participate in one's own government, originally meant a resident of a city.*

rights that we enjoy today, we might still think of ourselves as "subjects" instead of as "citizens."

The Roman cities had disappeared by about A.D. 300. However, by about A.D. 1000 cities reappeared throughout Europe. These cities were entirely separate from the castles of the feudal lords, who didn't live in the cities and looked down upon those who did. The city was a true community—an association of people who swore to defend themselves as a group against any danger. Each city had a charter from the king that guaranteed several important rights—for example,

wars must be interrupted on market days so that people could buy and sell in peace.

The elites of the cities were not feudal lords but *patricians*. Below them were the craftsmen, who belonged to closed guilds. If an escaped serf managed to stay in the city for a year, he could keep his freedom, but this was not very easy to do. He might be unable to gain admission to the guilds and therefore might not find a job. A number of Jews also lived in the cities. They were vital to the economy because they were allowed to lend money at interest, something Christians were not supposed to do. Besides the commercial groups, there were religious and cultural leaders as well—the artists and priests connected with the cathedrals. Universities appeared in some medieval cities and attracted students from all over Europe.

But the peculiar thing about the European city was that it was free. It made its own laws. The imperial cities everywhere else were administered by an official appointed by the emperor. But the medieval cities elected their own mayors rather than having to accept an official appointed by the state. Election of mayors is common in North America, so you may not realize what an unusual political invention it was in world history.

But I'm not suggesting that the European city dwellers had no rulers. Far from it. The stratification system was as rigid there as anywhere else. The patrician elites and the guilds both had great authority. According to Max Weber, one of the main factors leading up to the Renaissance was the challenge to that authority by a powerful group of merchants and bankers—the free middle class. Beginning in Venice, this movement swept through all the cities of Europe. The new group did not *displace* the old elites, but it made social mobility possible, protested against tyranny, and made major cultural contributions. The medieval city gradually extended the status of citizenship to more and more people.

### THE PREINDUSTRIAL CITY TODAY

I began by describing imperial cities—cities in Asia and the Near East that were ruled by colonial administrators. What happened to them? They're still there, but they are not at all like the cities you and I live in. I'm not talking about the cities of Japan, say, which have become industrialized, but, rather, about cities like Bombay, Rangoon, Singapore, Djakarta, Manila, Hong Kong, and Bangkok. These were created to serve the empires of Europe, not the commercial needs of their own region. They were port cities in the trade network of the colonial powers. They have become much larger than they once were, but they have not yet become industrialized.

How do they differ from Western cities? For one thing, today's preindustrial city does not separate various social classes as clearly as they separate ethnic, caste, or occupational groups.[7] The rich and the poor do not live in distinct zones. They don't have suburbs or central business districts. Manufacturing is done either by independent craftsmen or by large, modern factories located at the edge of town.

Many preindustrial cities, such as those in Indonesia, are "ruralized." They look more like rural villages than cities. These cities, which may be found throughout Asia, Africa, and Latin America, have attracted migrants from the countryside in search of jobs. Since industrial jobs are still scarce, most of these immigrants take menial jobs—cleaning streets, delivering packages, putting up posters, and the like—if they are able to find any jobs at all. They live in shanty towns on the outskirts of the cities, many of them keeping pigs and chickens just as they did in their home villages.

When your country cousin moves to the city, she changes her way of life. She becomes more sophisticated; she experiments with new life styles. But the migrant to a preindustrial city lives pretty much the same sort of life as before. Hence, the preindustrial city does not play a modernizing role the way Western cities do. For such modernization to occur, the city must become part of a rapidly developing national economy.

## Urbanization

**Urbanization** can be defined as the movement of people from rural areas to cities and from small cities to larger

**FIGURE 18.1**

*Urbanization in the United States, 1800-1970*

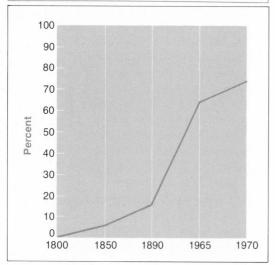

*Source:* Data for 1965 and 1970 from United Nations Demographic Yearbook, 1976. Table 7, p. 188. All other data from Adna L. Weber, *Growth of the Cities in the Nineteenth Century* (Ithaca, NY: Cornell Univ. Press, 1963), Table cxii.

some cities in India will have between 36 and 66 million inhabitants in the year 2000.[8] No city in any advanced society could even approach that size by the year 2000.

## WHY URBANIZATION?

What is going on? Why has the world's population tended to move into cities during the past 200 years? What is the reason behind urbanization?

There are two main reasons: (1) Urban living is more economical, and (2) food production has become a largely urban process.

As a nation becomes richer, its people spend less of their income on food and more on other goods and services. And those goods and services (except food) are produced more cheaply in cities than in the country. Cities have transportation and a large labor force. They are the best locations for many specialized services—wholesale trade, higher education, hospitals, banking, and insurance, for example.

The second reason for urbanization is the changing technology of food production. Before the Industrial Revolution, farmers were self-sufficient. In modern nations, they rely on artificial fertilizers, pesticides, machinery, electricity, gasoline, and a variety of other things that are produced in cities. In fact much "farm" work is done in cities. The food must be transported from the farm, processed, and distributed. These jobs are done by city people. Actually, for any typical food product—such as milk—the farmer today may receive less than half of the total selling price. The rest goes to city dwellers. Thus urbanization results from the economics of modern technology.

ones. Between 1800 and 1960 the percentage of the world's population living in cities with populations of 100,000 or more increased from about 2 percent to around 17 percent. In some countries the increase was even more dramatic. (See Figure 18.1.) Between 1950 and 1960 the rate of urbanization was double that of the preceding 50 years.

However, urbanization is finite—it has a beginning and an end. The advanced nations are probably nearing the end of the urbanization process, so that the portion of the population living in cities will not increase much and in fact may decrease.

Many developing nations have only begun to urbanize. For example, only a small percentage of all Asians live in cities. However, because the population of Asia is so huge, even that small percentage accounts for a large portion of the world's city dwellers. And this growth is only in its early stages. Kingsley Davis has estimated that

## CITY GROWTH IN NORTH AMERICA

At what size does a rural community become large enough to be considered a "town?" That depends on the standards set by census officials — and the officials of different countries have set different standards. A town of 1000 is "urban" in Canada, but not in the United States. A place has to have 2500 or more inhabitants to be "urban" in the United States. However, both Canada and the United States are over 70 percent urban.

Sometimes several towns expand until they run together and form a continuous urban area, though their governments are still separate. For some purposes they should be counted as a single city. U.S. census officials classify a metropolitan region consisting of a large central city surrounded by smaller, dependent cities (e.g., the San Francisco Bay area) as a standard metropolitan statistical area (SMSA). In Canada such a region is called a census metropolitan area (CMA).

In 1971 there were 23 Canadian cities with populations of over 100,000. Vancouver's population was over 1 million, and Montreal and Toronto each had more than 2.5 million inhabitants. In 1970 there were 153 American cities with populations of over 100,000, though many of these are actually parts of SMSAs. The 24 largest SMSAs have populations of over 1 million.

Two important trends have been taking place in North America in the past twenty years or so: (1) increasing suburbanization in both Canada and the United States and (2) the migration of blacks to inner cities in the United States.

### Suburbanization

Suburbanization may be defined as the movement of people from central cities to smaller communities in the surrounding area. Although suburbanization has taken place to some degree in many developed nations, it has been more extensive in North America than elsewhere. That is, there has been much more rapid growth in the areas just outside the central city or far from the downtown business district than within the inner city. New York City is an example.

Manhattan's population declined by about 400,000 between 1950 and 1970, but that of Staten Island, another borough of the city, increased from about 191,000 to 295,000 in the same period. Suburban Nassau County (on Long Island) more than doubled in population.

Why are people moving from the cities to the suburbs? Suburbanization has several causes:

1 *Residential use of land must compete with other land uses.* Increasingly, the land near central business districts is taken over by parking lots and commercial uses. As a result less is available for residential use.
2 *The population is richer.* There has been an increase in average income and number of leisure hours. Almost all families now can own a car, and the federally financed highway system has enabled more workers to afford commuting by car.
3 *Transportation is more flexible.* Most shipping used to be by rail and most commuters used to travel by public transportation. Nowadays trucks ship more than trains do, and factories have been able to move farther from the central business districts and railroad terminals. The spreading out of jobs reinforces the spreading out of residences.
4 *People want larger homes.* They can afford them now. As the average income of the people in the inner city increases, their urban homes feel more crowded. Houses that were built for two families are often converted into single-family houses. Many families are willing to commute to work in order to obtain more room in their housing.
5 *The government has helped people afford home ownership.* This is probably the most important factor of all. The federal government allows tax write-offs for interest payments. Moreover, both the U.S. and Canadian governments have made it possible for the average family to afford a mortgage. You can buy a suburban tract house with a very low down payment. But it is often much harder to get loans to buy or renovate houses or apartments in the central city. In effect, the government subsidized suburbanization after World War II by making suburban housing such a good bargain. S. D. Clark has argued that people didn't really move to the suburbs by choice. They didn't much care where they

*Urbanization and growth have taken many forms in North America.*

Jim Anderson/Woodfin Camp

Syd Greenberg/DPI

lived if the housing was a good bargain. The people who stayed in the city were the ones who *did* care about where they lived and about their life style. A different mortgage policy might have encouraged further urbanization instead of suburbanization.[9]

### The urbanization of blacks

In the United States the black population has been increasing faster than the white population, and it is estimated that by 1990 over 14 percent of the American population will be nonwhite.[10] Since World War II there has been an increase in the migration of blacks from rural areas in the South to cities in the North and West—so much so that blacks are now more urbanized than are whites. Many of these people are moving into the areas left behind by the whites who moved to the suburbs. It is estimated that by 1985, 75 percent of the urban blacks may live in central cities and only 25 percent in suburbs, while 70 percent of the whites will live in suburbs and only 30 percent in the central cities.[11] This trend amounts to *increased urban segregation.*

## Theoretical approaches to urbanization

I have a hunch that urban sociology has been largely shaped by the fact that the University of Chicago is located in Chicago. That's where urban sociology grew up—led by such scholars as Robert Ezra Park and Louis Wirth. Robert Redfield should be included in that group even though Redfield was not a sociologist but an anthropologist. They all had a very negative view of city life, and that view has stuck. We still have certain notions about the traits of city people that were picked up from these writers—either directly or, more likely, indirectly. And by all accounts Chicago was an ugly and unpleasant place in those days. My guess is that if the University of Chicago had been located in, say, Berkeley or Paris or Toronto these writers would have said

kinder things about urban life and urban sociology would have had different things to argue about.

As it is, I will begin by mentioning two aspects of urban sociology that came out of the Chicago school: (1) the question of how the way of life of city people differs from that of rural folk and (2) urban ecology.

### FOLK AND URBAN LIFE STYLES

People tend to think in terms of opposites. If I say "long," you may think "short." If I say "quick," you may think "slow." Sociologists do the same thing. Hence, our traditional way of theorizing is to set up categories of opposites to describe social groups. (Max Weber called these "ideal types"—meaning that they were set up as logical concepts, not just based on observation of reality.) No real society ever quite matches such a concept, but they can be used to compare societies—any society will seem closer to one extreme than to the other. Thus a typology (i.e., a set of ideal types) allows us to compare a variety of societies. One such typology is the distinction between *folk* life and *urban* life, as expressed in the writings of Redfield, who spent a lot of time doing field research in the Yucatan peninsula of Mexico and Wirth, who was concerned mainly with urbanism as a way of life.

### REDFIELD: THE FOLK—URBAN CONTINUUM

Redfield generalized from his observations of the Indian villages and towns of Yucatan.[12] As he described them, folk societies (that is, peasant societies) are small, isolated, and homogeneous, with no complex technology and no division of labor except according to sex and age. Men hunt and fish and women and children gather nuts, but there is little surplus food. Such societies are marked by solidarity and close relationships, by face-to-face communication between people who usually know each other well (there is no writing). Religion is very important, and social control is often carried out through religious institutions. Ritual is highly developed. Cultural patterns are based on feelings and tradition—not rational choices. Members of the group are uncritical and follow old folkways without questioning them. The family is the central social group. People help each other without expecting cash rewards, but only because they are bound by kinship ties in every aspect of their lives. Status is ascribed at birth.

**Urban society,** to Redfield, is the opposite of folk society. It is largescale, heterogeneous, and impersonal. It is too large to permit warm, close relationships. And it is too differentiated to allow any person to be so-

Mexican "urban" centers are still not very modern, despite Redfield's worry about how they would undermine folk culture.

Richard Davis/DPI

cialized thoroughly into all its norms. The result is diversity. People become nonreligious, individualistic, and tolerant. They make critical judgments about the various points of view they encounter. And work becomes a means to an end—cash or prestige—not simply part of relationships with kin.

It's easy to guess which way of life Redfield preferred. And he worried about what was happening to it. According to Redfield, modern communication is bringing folk communities into contact with urban people and undermining the culture of the folk group. People in those groups are beginning to question their traditions. Thus urban culture destroys folk culture. This is an evolutionary view; that is, Redfield believed that the transformation of the world is a result of the spread of urban culture into backward areas. (I imagine a vacuum cleaner salesman hacking his way through the jungle with a machete to spread the word.) He had nothing good to say about city life; in his opinion urbanization spoiled the charming rural communities that he loved.

Redfield probably exaggerated the impact of cities on the folk culture of Yucatan. Urban culture *does* tend to spread outward—but not as much in less developed countries as in industrial societies. And Mexico was—and mostly still is—underdeveloped. I have already told you how the preindustrial city differs from the industrial ones with which you are familiar. The cities of Yucatan are basically preindustrial. They are unable to create much social change. Migrants from the countryside continue to live a rural life style in shantytowns on the outskirts of the city. The city dwellers are greatly outnumbered. Instead of threatening the folk culture that surrounds it, the preindustrial city is lucky if it can preserve urban culture.

### WIRTH: URBANISM AS A WAY OF LIFE

While Redfield was developing his ideas about folk and urban societies, Wirth was also interested in the quality of city life. His description of urbanism as a way of life was consistent with Redfield's.[13] He defined the city as a "relatively large, permanent, dense settlement of socially heterogeneous individuals," and he was interested in showing the effects on social life of (1) large size, (2) density, and (3) heterogeneity. In general, he believed that it was nearly impossible to have rich interpersonal relationships in the city. Urban life destroyed the sense of community.

Density and size were the main causes of everything else that followed. Heterogeneity was really an effect of these two variables, for (as Redfield also suggested) the more people who interact in a community, the wider the possible range of ideas. Furthermore, the more people interact, the less intense their interactions can be. After all, how many people can you be really close to at one time? If you have to deal with hundreds or thousands of people each week, your relations with most of them will be impersonal.

That is why Wirth felt that city dwellers are generally superficial in their relationships. There's only so much attention and energy to go around. If you have to divide yourself up, if you have to keep moving through many temporary relationships, you won't be a very intense person and your life may lack intimacy and depth. Families become shallow. Kinship ties weaken. Groups that might preserve a strong feeling of community in a rural environment lose that richness in the city. Indeed, the moral fabric of society is weakened by the temporary, fragmented nature of urban social relationships. City people live by a "spirit of competition, aggrandizement, and mutual exploitation," Wirth wrote. They are rational and unsentimental, unlike rural or small-town people, who are more personal. City dwellers lack friendly relations with neighbors and maintain a self-protective aloofness. Such a lonely, emotionally empty life destroys all natural social groups and creates a number of social problems. Crime, delinquency, corruption, mental breakdown, and suicide are all more common in large cities than in small communities.

Wirth and his many followers seem to agree that because the city is so big, so busy, so nerve-wracking, so full of activity and change, it has harmful effects on people. No stable, enriching, cohesive social community can survive in such a setting. People's lives will be so pulled apart by the tension and loneliness of urban living that disorgani-

These French citizens in the heart of Paris are enjoying a street entertainer, just one type of action and variety that attracts people to the city.

Mark Antman/Monkmeyer

zation and mental illness will result. The health of the human personality can't escape damage in such a setting. Only a smaller, more personal social environment allows people to nourish and support each other or to maintain the order and tradition that make life worth living.

I don't think this picture is entirely accurate. The crime and delinquency part seems to be true. Urban areas have more crime per person than less densely populated areas. But the argument about impersonality doesn't hold up. I find rural people at least as aloof as city people. The city people I know do not all lack friends or warm relationships. So let me describe two somewhat different views of urban life. Following Claude S. Fischer, I will classify these views under these headings: (1) the determinist position (Wirth's), (2) the compositional theory, and (3) the subculture theory (Fischer's view).[14]

## THE COMPOSITIONAL THEORY

People who like city living naturally have risen to Wirth's bait with numerous arguments. Among other social scientists who defend cities are Herbert Gans and Oscar Lewis. One point on which they agree is that social groups are not necessarily destroyed by big-city life. Small, intimate, intense friendship groups, kinship ties, and other communities continue to exist in many cities. Indeed, Lewis goes so far as to claim that "in modern Western cities, there may be more give and take about one's private, intimate life at a single 'sophisticated' cocktail party than would occur in years in a peasant village."[15]

The compositional view sees differences between urban and rural living, of course. But it denies that the size and density of the city has any *direct* effect on the psychological traits and adjustment of its inhabitants. The people who live in the city *do* differ from those who live in the country. They usually differ in terms of occupation, education, age, sex ratio, marital status, social class, and ethnicity—to mention only a few factors. Such factors *do* have an effect on their experiences. Obviously, if you are a homemaker in the suburbs you will do many things that you might not do if you were a secretary in the city, and there are many things that you might do as a city dweller that you wouldn't do as a suburbanite. City and rural people differ because of the many opportunities and limitations that differ in their surroundings. But their personal qualities have nothing to do with the size or density of the city *as such*. A city environment does not affect a person's capacity for emotionally open and responsive relationships. No one is psychologically damaged by size or density. City dwellers can be as warm and generous and close to their friends as anyone else, other things being equal.

Hence, the compositional approach holds that the composition of a city's population differs from that of a small town in terms of factors such as age, social class, education, ethnicity, and marital status. But the size or density of a town does not directly influence the personal traits of its inhabitants.

Lewis, holding to the compositional approach, went to Yucatan to visit the villages and towns that Redfield had visited. He claims that Redfield was biased—that even in Yucatan the important differences were not between urban and folk cultures but between the different *social classes*. The conflict between social classes is a real conflict, whether it is in the city or the countryside, or so Lewis claims.

### THE SUBCULTURAL THEORY

Fischer has recently developed what he calls the subcultural theory, which combines elements of the determinist and compositional views. On the whole, it is closer to the compositional position. It agrees that most of the factors that create differences between city and small-town people are not *direct*, *necessary* results of the density or size of the city or town. However, important differences do occur, and they occur regularly. There is, indeed, greater diversity in the life styles that are found in the city than those found elsewhere.

And what variety! Radicals, hippies, artists, and experimenters of all kinds live in cities. They experiment with life styles, science, politics, handicraft design, and almost everything else. In the past two days, for example, I have had dealings of some sort with the following people: a "school without walls" that organizes outings to factories, city council meetings, and the like; a group that is encouraging people to have babies at home; a concert pianist who stuffs his piano with newspapers and silverware and calls it a "prepared piano"; a young man selling peanuts from door to door for the Unification Church; a club that shows German horror films; a cooperative funeral society that claims to have a cheaper way of disposing of bodies (if you don't mind being cremated); a hostel for women running away from brutal husbands (they wanted my old blankets); a sexual-information society that wants people to examine themselves and learn the proper name for each part; a group that will show you how to make wine from leftovers; another group that wants to sterilize all the dogs and cats in Toronto; a group that wants to convert the old Don Jail into an art gallery; and a club that promises to teach me to survive in the woods with only a length of rope, six matches, and a hunting knife.

Who says city people are lonely? Who says they are isolated or that they don't experience close relationships? How could anyone say such a thing! People who live in urban areas can belong to an incredible variety of different groups and can throw themselves into their activities with amazing passion and commitment. Political, religious,

Urban settings often attract immigrants who follow other members of their former culture. In large city parks one can see groups of people visiting together in many different languages.

Tim Eagan/Woodfin Camp

ethnic, and cultural groups of all kinds thrive in the city. They couldn't find members in small towns. It takes a *critical mass* to support a group. Suppose one person out of 5000 wants to learn about Japanese foot massage. In a small town that might total 4 or 5 people. In a large city, on the other hand, enough people might be interested to support a class with a paid instructor. Thus the city is *able to support a variety of subcultures*. In fact it is the density and size of the city that permits these subcultures to exist. These groups appeal to certain people and not to others. But in addition, they encourage their members to become even more different from members of other groups. In a small town people have *some* diverse tendencies and *some* varied opinions. When they become active in a particular subcul-

ture, as they can in the city, their differences become more marked. Creative, exciting subcultures can exist in the city and stimulate the intellectual growth of artists, writers, journalists, political reformers, and chess players. This is why such people often prefer to live in the city. But deviant subcultures such as criminal gangs, numbers rackets, pornography shops, and cocaine pushers can also exist more easily in cities.

Fischer argues that deviant subcultures exist more easily in the city for the same reason that other subcultures exist more easily in the city—because of the city's size and density. It follows, then, that the city encourages both deviance and creativity, and for the same reasons. If you have criminal tendencies, you'll find some friends in the city who will encourage you to commit crimes. If you have artistic tendencies, you'll find friends who will encourage you to be artistic.

As we learned in Chapter 7, anomie theory held that people become deviant because they become less involved in the social groups that provide social control and help people live up to agreed-upon standards of behavior. This theory assumes that deviants are mostly social isolates, nonbelongers. And Wirth and Redfield, among others, seemed to suggest that crime and delinquency and other forms of deviance occur more often in the city because the urban way of life fragments groups and leaves people isolated and uninvolved. Fischer disagrees. A greater percentage of deviants are found in cities than in towns, it's true, but not because of isolation. On the contrary, it is because deviant subcultures can form and can support their members' deviant tendencies. Diversity is partly a result of the size and density of the city, as the determinist approach suggests. City people *are* more heterogeneous than rural people. This is not because social groups are absent or weak, however, but because they are strong! Deviance and other forms of diversity are encouraged by subcultures. And a variety of subcultures can exist in urban environments because of the sheer number of people who live there.

Why do people often believe that urban dwellers are isolated, impersonal, and lacking in friends? Maybe it is because city people aren't very neighborly. Rural people, of course, *have* to depend on their neighbors for friendship and aid. They have no one else to turn to. But city people can, and do, choose their friends throughout the urban area, and hence are less likely to pay much attention to the people next door.[16] Not only Fischer's research but also that of other urban sociologists has shown that urban people tend to have their own "personal communities." That is, the network of personal ties will extend throughout and be-

yond the city. These ties may be maintained by daily telephone calls or frequent subway trips.

This does not mean that neighborhoods are unimportant, however. It is good to be able to borrow a cup of sugar from the woman next door or to offer her a geranium cutting or a ride to the drugstore. In different stages of the life cycle the neighborhood becomes more important than at other phases. For example, young childless couples do very little neighboring, while those who have children do a great deal. Older couples whose children are grown may or may not see much of their neighbors. It depends on where they live. Those who live in single-family homes are quite friendly with the people around them, but those who live in apartments see their neighbors rarely.[17] In any case it is clear that whether city dwellers are neighborly or not, they have as many social relationships as people from small towns.

## Urban ecology

*Urban ecology* is the study of the distribution of people and activities as it relates to the physical environment of a given city. I touched upon aspects of urban ecology when I mentioned that preindustrial cities differ from industrial cities in that they have undeveloped central business districts and poor residential areas located on the outskirts of the town. Urban ecologists often study the land use patterns of a region and observe the way those patterns change as population density increases. Ecological studies of this sort began in Chicago, chiefly under the influence of Robert E. Park and Ernest W. Burgess, in the 1920s. Burgess' description of the modern city as a series of concentric zones was a mental map shared by all urban ecologists for many years. Only gradually was the Burgess model modified

Anita Sabarese/DPI

*Not all of the city is overrun with people. Most cities have large parks where one can get away from day-to-day activities and have a quiet chat with a friend.*

by two other descriptions of the city, the sector model and the multiple-nuclei model.

## BURGESS: THE CONCENTRIC-ZONE MODEL

Burgess observed that North American cities, unlike many European cities, usually grow up in an unplanned, uncontrolled way. He was interested in finding out what factors determine the growth patterns and land use of the North American city. His answer was that the *value* of land determines a city's growth pattern. As a city grows, the value of

land increases, especially that of land close to the central business district, the area in which the big department stores and office buildings are found. As the value of land changes, the residential plan of the city changes too. The expensive land in the central business district is bought by commercial developers. Only a few rich families still live there, mostly in apartment buildings. Other well-to-do people move outside the city, where they can surround their big private houses with lawns, rose gardens, and swimming pools. The middle-income families of Burgess' day lived in apartments near the central business district or in detached houses with small yards farther from the center of town. (Since the 1950s this group has been moving into suburban tract developments, leaving the inner city to the poor.)

Burgess diagramed the city of Chicago according to this pattern of land use.[18] His diagram consisted of five major concentric zones, (see Figure 18.2), as follows:

*Zone I: The Central Business District.* This is the heart of the city and the most expensive land. At its center are found theatres, stores, elegant restaurants, investment banks, offices, and government buildings. A little farther out is the wholesale business district, with warehouses, the produce market, and the like.

*Zone II: The Transition Zone.* Beyond the business district is an area of seedy rooming houses, brothels, skid rows, and low-quality housing mixed with factories. In this zone the crime rates are the highest in the city, and this is where immigrants settle when they come to America.

*Zone III: The Working-Class Residential Zone.* In this zone are the homes of working people, often second-generation immigrants (at least in Chicago). As these families move up the social ladder they will move farther out.

**FIGURE 18.2**
*Burgess diagram of Chicago*

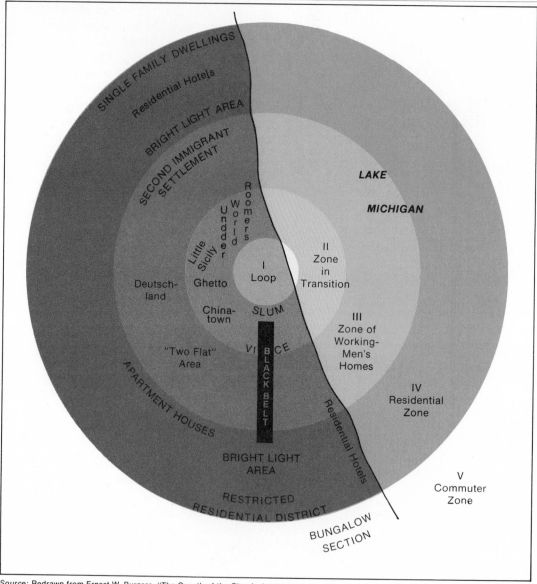

*Source:* Redrawn from Ernest W. Burgess, "The Growth of the City: An Introduction to a Research Project," in *Studies in Human Ecology*, ed. George A. Theodorson (Evanston, Ill.: Row, Peterson, 1961), p. 41.

*Zone IV: The Middle-Class Residential Zone.* Once these areas were composed of single-family houses, but in Burgess' day many Chicago neighborhoods in this zone were being built up with apartment buildings and local business districts.

*Zone V: The Commuters' Zone.* In this zone

are the small suburban cities. The men commute to jobs in the central business district each day, leaving this zone to the women and children. These areas are sometimes called "dormitory suburbs" or "bedroom communities."

Burgess' theory seems to fit Chicago and many other older *nucleated* cities, that is, cities that have a single center. However, many cities, like New York, Paris, and Los Angeles, do not have a single center that looks like a bull's-eye the way Chicago's Loop does. Burgess' drawing would not describe a nonnucleated city. Moreover, it does not apply to cities that hold to strict zoning plans and thus control their growth patterns. In addition, the construction of expressways has meant that cities that have undergone their fastest growth since the 1950s do not fit the Burgess model very well. Toronto, for example, still has luxurious upper-class mansions within a mile of its central business district. Nor does the Burgess model describe the growth pattern of preindustrial cities, where rich people more often live in the center of town than on the outskirts. Finally, a city's growth always depends in part on the terrain—hills, harbors, and the like. Therefore value is never the *only* factor determining land use patterns, as the Burgess model might suggest.

### HOYT: THE SECTOR MODEL

As sociologists became aware that the Burgess model did not explain all patterns of urban change, they searched for new models. Homer Hoyt's sector model seemed to explain the changes that took place in such cities as San Francisco and Minneapolis, which appeared to be shaped mostly by the transportation routes that cut through the city.[19] Hoyt suggested that the center of the original city has various districts, such as the industrial zone, the business district, and both affluent and modest residential areas. But each

**FIGURE 18.3**
*Sector model of urban expansion*

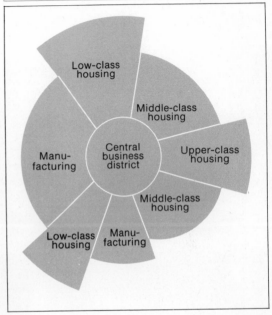

of these sectors expands like a slice of pie away from the center, usually following one of the transportation routes. (See Figure 18.3.)

### HARRIS AND ULLMAN: THE MULTIPLE-NUCLEI MODEL

Chauncey D. Harris and Edward L. Ullman proposed a third ecological description, the multiple-nuclei model.[20] This model suggests that a city's zones are formed early in its history and that each zone expands any way it can—not necessarily in concentric circles or in a pie slice pattern. Many separate business districts may grow up throughout the city, forming a patchwork of zones with separate nuclei. (See Figure 18.4.)

None of these three models fully explains the great variety of urban growth patterns shown by North American cities in the past few decades. "Urban sprawl" has been increasing so much that whole regions of the

**FIGURE 18.4**

*Multiple-nuclei model of urban expansion*

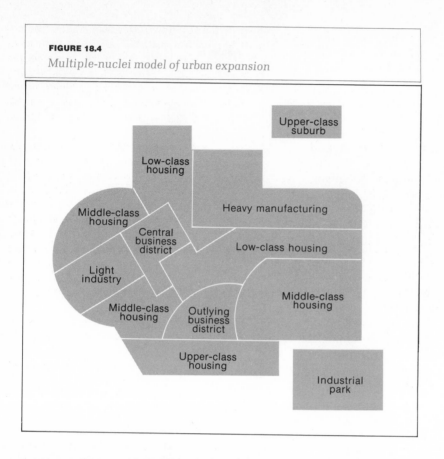

continent are becoming urbanized. We sometimes refer, not to particular cities, but to a giant **megalopolis**—a super city in which several cities merge together to make a whole urbanized region. One megalopolis is beginning to form between Boston and Washington. Another stretches from Los Angeles to San Francisco. It seems unavoidable that the countryside in such regions will fill in with suburbs and new towns so that the entire area will be urban before long.

# SOCIAL RESEARCH:
## *Sociologists at Work*

At the beginning of the chapter I asked you to think about the kind of place you would like to live in. Would it be urban or rural? Here we will discuss some research on the trade-offs people make in choosing a place to live. For many of us the choice is between an apartment in a city and a somewhat larger place for the same price in the suburbs. In making that choice we also make certain assumptions about what the environments are like and what we can expect from them. Some of those assumptions are correct. Some are not.

## CROWDING AND APARTMENT LIVING

One common belief is that housing conditions have a strong effect on one's personality. Not so. It is good, of course, to have pleasant, clean, comfortable housing rather than a slum dwelling. However, space itself does not seem to be a factor in psychological well-being.[21]

People who avoid living in high-rise apartments usually do so for one of three reasons: (1) It is hard to keep an eye on children in apartments, so they are likely to be either underfoot or too far away to be looked after properly. (2) Crime rates are thought to be higher in high-rise apartments than in single-family areas. (3) Apartment dwellers are assumed to be lonelier than other people. There is some truth to all of these points. It probably is generally true that children who live in the top floors of tall buildings can't run in and out of doors and play as freely as children who live in ground-floor housing, and this is why their parents often choose to

move to the suburbs. Crime rates may be somewhat higher in apartment buildings than elsewhere. However, this is not because the people living there mug each other. It is because such buildings contain areas such as elevators and stairwells. Criminals can usually get into such places quite easily unless there is a doorman on duty.[22]

I have already mentioned the argument over whether city dwellers are isolated and lack friends. It is true that apartment dwellers tend not to know their neighbors, but this does not mean that they are isolated. Most families that live in apartments probably wouldn't have much to do with their neighbors *wherever* they lived. For example, families in which the wife works are more likely to live in apartments than families in which the wife is at home all day. And working women do not "neighbor" much, on the whole.[23]

The general conclusion of all these studies is that although apartment dwellers might like more privacy, more space, and so forth, they are not psychologically damaged by living in an

*Some parts of the city are better equipped for children than others.*

Hugh Rogers/Monkmeyer

Art Irons, Jr./DPI

apartment. And as a matter of fact, urban residents are not as cramped for living space as rural people are. There are more people per room in rural areas than in urban areas.[24] But let's turn now to suburban living. What is it like?

### THE QUALITY OF SUBURBAN LIFE

Everybody knows what a North American suburb is like—right? It is green, open land filled with pastel-colored split-level houses complete with patios, barbecue grills, power lawn mowers, station wagons, and basketball hoops nailed above the automatic doors of two-car garages. The women drive the men to the train every day, then fill their time with kaffeeklatsches. Everyone is Republican, and everyone goes to church on Sundays. There is not much diversity; all suburbanites are WASPS, and their tastes are as standardized as their houses, their cars, and their minds. Anyone who moves to a suburb will quickly become like all the other suburbanites. Suburban life is an endless round of socializing marked by occasional wife swapping. We know these things because we have all read the same *Time* magazines and seen the same old Gregory Peck movie. And they aren't all so.

The fact is that many of us live in suburbs without even knowing it. There is no single model of suburbia; rather, there are many different kinds of suburban towns, some of which match the description I just gave but most of which do not. To census officials, a town is a suburb if it is close to a big city and has its own municipal government separate from that of the city.

In 1971 Louis Harris conducted a survey of suburban Americans. Most of them did not think of themselves as suburbanities but said that they lived in a small city, a town, or a rural area. Some of Harris' results were surprising. Most of the men, for example, were not commuters but worked in their own towns. Only one-third of the respondents were registered Republicans. Nearly half of the families had an annual income of less than $10,000. One-third of the families included a union member. Few of the families were transients—most had lived in the same community for more than ten years.[25] These results were not at all like the split-level American dream.

Bennett Berger studied a California suburb where most of the men worked in an automobile factory. He expected to see these men transformed into typical "suburbanites," but no such thing happened. They remained Democrats; they did not take up the churchgoing habit; their chief social interactions continued to be with their kin; they did not begin to dream of getting ahead in their jobs. In short, they maintained the same working-class life style that they had always had.[26]

Suburbs differ in all possible ways. Some are rich places that live up to our image of a bedroom community for executives. However, there are many low-income suburbs like the one Berger described. These working-class communities are often quite heterogeneous in terms of ethnicity and religion. Of those polled by Harris, some 12 percent were black, though in a few towns such as East Orange, New Jersey and Compton, California the majority of the residents are black. The residents of these poor suburbs are most likely to feel bored and dissatisfied. Still, only 10 percent of Harris's working-class respondents rated their community as below average.[27]

Most suburbanites are glad to be living where they live. Harris found, as expected, that they generally move to the suburbs in order to obtain a home of their own and to provide a better environment for their children. (Not all children like this environment, however. They are often bored and say that they hope to move away as soon as possible—but usually to areas that are even more rural!) Harris found suburbanites satisfied with the schools in their community and with the moral level of the community. Most said that they go to parties only once or twice a year. These people would not support low-income housing in the suburbs, but not because of racial prejudice. Blacks would be welcomed by a margin of three to one, but poor people of any color would not. The suburbanites also favored integrated schools but did not support busing to achieve integration.[28]

If anyone dislikes suburban living, it's the women.[29] Wives who move to the suburbs often complain that there is nothing much to do and that it is hard to get into town to do the things they would enjoy. So they spend a lot of time visiting with the neighbors, not necessarily enjoying this way of life but not knowing what else to do with themselves. Margaret Mead, an anthropologist who has opinions on a wide variety of subjects, believes suburban living has made American women far less vital and interesting than they might be. She notes that her mother's

and grandmother's generations included many women who were much more dynamic and involved in life than the generation of women who became adult after World War II. It was the nationwide trend of suburbanization that made so many women into feminine, but conventional, housewives and robbed them of creative involvement in social life.

# SOCIAL POLICY:
## Issues and Viewpoints

Why do Americans flee from the city as soon as they can afford to move? They are escaping from the "urban problem," a term that refers to a variety of situations that make city living dangerous, annoying, or disagreeable in the United States. But these situations are not unavoidable—they don't occur in cities everywhere, but chiefly in the American cities. Go to Paris or Stockholm or Amsterdam or Toronto or Montreal, for example, and then go to almost any American city. Then ask yourself why the major cities of the world's richest nation have become slums while so many cities elsewhere are lively, graceful, exciting places to live. This question has been answered in various ways by different city planners and urban sociologists.

### JACOBS: THE BLIGHT OF DULLNESS

Close your eyes and listen. Do you hear that jackhammer off in the distance? That's tomorrow's city under construction. One of the most far-reaching efforts to save the city is the huge *urban renewal* program financed by the government. Urban renewal—the demolition and rebuilding of run-down areas—is not a favorite solution just now, largely because of the criticism of Jane Jacobs, author of *The Death and Life of Great American Cities*.[30]

Jacobs wanted to know what made her own neighborhood, Greenwich Village, so lively. Why are areas like Greenwich Village such pleasant places to live while most areas in most American cities are dull, unpleasant, and unsafe? Her book accuses city planners and urban-renewal programs of *creating* dullness and destroying the social relationships that made life bearable in some of the seedy neighborhoods in American cities. Her proposals run counter to ideas that had been assumed by city planners. For one thing, she opposes zoning laws that keep different kinds of facilities separate.

Jacobs believes that diversity is the key to vitality. Every district should have a rich variety of uses and should bring many different types of people together—rich and poor, old and young, black and white. It should mix residential buildings with industries and businesses and new buildings with old ones. She insists that people want diversity and that it encourages them to participate in the community. The main reason for the development of slums is that anyone who can afford to will leave a dull, homogeneous area. Poor people, with nowhere else to go, move in and the area decays even more. Greater diversity would keep this from happening.

### Street life

Jacobs argues that vital, exciting neighborhoods have one thing in common: street life. People like to live where the streets and sidewalks are used and where there are lots of other people to watch. Moreover, street life reduces crime rates because the people in the street and in the windows overlooking it protect each other better than police cars can.

How can designers create street life? Jacobs argues that each street should contain a variety of structures serving several different functions so that the street will be used at all hours of the day and night. The liveliest areas are those in which buildings have stores and offices on the street and apartments above them. Even a tavern down the block enlivens the neighborhood by attracting patrons throughout the evening and giving the apartment dwellers a variety of passers-by to watch from their windows. Crowds attract watchers and participants. This is why even the parks should be small. Large open spaces let people spread out too far, and this creates dullness and attracts criminals.

Many ethnic sections of North American cities have the qualities Jacobs favors. Among them are Greenwich Village in New York, Old Montreal, Chicago's Back-of-the-Yards, and San Francisco's Telegraph Hill. In all of these areas short blocks, wide sidewalks, and narrow streets encourage shopping and social life rather than automobile traffic. High-rent apartments are scattered among low-rent buildings that artists and small businesses can afford. Diversity causes vitality.

**Planning dullness**

Jacobs holds that most city planners and architects create effects that are the exact opposites of those she admires. They build high-rise apartment buildings that separate the rich from the poor, the old from the young, the blacks from the whites. These buildings, which aren't very interesting, are located in residential zones. They are surrounded by large areas of useless open space where parents dare not let their children play. The residents rarely go out on the streets. Instead, they drive to distant shopping centers—there are no small local stores and, therefore, no friendly merchants to watch the street or provide a place for neighbors to meet. Some of these buildings—the luxurious ones—are protected by doormen, but they are still dull and impersonal. Other buildings are for the poor, and their isolation encourages crime. Jacobs blames these unattractive environments on both city planners and banks that refuse to make

loans for renovating old buildings in areas that are still vital. These areas are allowed to decay until they are taken over by slum-clearance programs that build new dullness to replace the dullness they tear down.

## GANS: THE SOCIAL CAUSES OF SLUMS

The most important attack on Jacobs' ideas is that of urban sociologist Herbert Gans, who has lived in, and written about, some of the neighborhoods Jacobs described.[31] His book, *The Urban Villagers*, is a delightful account of social life in a working-class Italian district in Boston, the West End, which was demolished by urban redevelopers even though its inhabitants had a rich communal life.[32] Gans shares Jacobs' view of the vital city and of the way people actually live in such places. However, he disagrees with many of her ideas about how to reform city planning. He calls her ideas "the physical fallacy," in which a neighborhood's social characteristics are attributed to architectural design rather than to social, cultural, and economic factors. His own explanation of the problems of cities is based on class relations, not physical layout. He says that ethnic districts like Boston's Italian North End are actually not diverse but homogeneous. They are working-class areas, and this is why so much of their social life takes place outdoors. Middle-class families prefer to entertain indoors and want to supervise their children's play indoors. Wherever they live, their social life will not be seen by passers-by; this is why middle-class areas look dull to the outsider. They are not dull to the people who live there.

Gans thinks Jacobs overestimates the power of planners when she suggests that they should stimulate street life. Middle-class people don't *want* to socialize in the street, nor do they want their children to play on the sidewalks. They want the privacy and quiet of low-density neighborhoods and elevator apartment buildings. Since their friends are scattered all over the metropolitan region, they want cars, expressways, and underground garages to make travel easy. They do not like neighborhoods where housing and businesses are mixed, even if they are more convenient than areas that are strictly residential. They prefer the supermarket, with its wide range of choices, to the small, ethnic grocery store. The places that Gans and Jacobs both enjoy actually are not holding their young people—when they have children of their own they move to the suburbs. Still, Gans agrees that charming working-class ethnic areas like the North End are reminders of our preautomobile past, well worth saving as low-rent districts that attract tourists and provide vital communities for people with low incomes.

### Real slums

Whatever is done to preserve ethnic neighborhoods, it won't solve the problem of the real slums. Most slums are inhabited by nonwhites who have no other place to go. They live in overcrowded old buildings that are similar to those found in other low-rent areas. Once an area becomes an overcrowded slum, however, renovating the buildings doesn't help. The solution is to reduce the crowding, but this is almost impossible for two reasons: (1) The absentee landlord makes huge profits from overcrowding; (2) most slum dwellers can't move away because they can't afford higher-priced housing and, because they are nonwhite, would not be accepted in better neighborhoods.

According to Gans, slums can be emptied only if there is low-cost housing elsewhere. But private enterprise cannot afford to build low-cost housing. Real-estate interests have forced public housing to be located in slums where they will not lower the value of neighbors' property, and any tenant whose income rises above a certain level must move out of such housing. This amounts to segregation of the poor in slums.

Jacobs believes the government should stop building public housing and instead subsidize private owners who make their buildings available to poor tenants. The problem with this idea is that most neighborhoods fight any attempt to provide low-income housing in middle-class areas. As long as the middle classes reject the nonwhite poor, the poor must remain in overcrowded slums. According to Gans, as long as there is discrimination against the poor the

government is probably going to have to build more low-income ghettos.

### Resolving the debate

What are we to make of the argument between Gans and Jacobs? My own view is that, as so often happens, there is merit in both positions. Jacobs' proposals would enrich the quality of urban living. The physical layout of the urban environment *does* affect the life styles of the inhabitants, and the kind of environment she prefers is one that middle-class families with children can enjoy as much as working-class people do. Anyone who has ever lived in a place like Paris will see her point. Practically everybody in Paris lives in six- or seven-story apartment buildings built over small shops and cafes. There are almost no single-family houses. Social classes are often mixed together, with rich people on the lower floors. A subway station is within two or three blocks of almost every apartment, and everyone spends a lot of time in the street socializing. The whole world loves Paris, for all the reasons Jacobs named. Parisians have no desire to move to the suburbs, though some have to do so for financial reasons.

Gans is correct in saying that Jacobs' proposals cannot correct the cities' worst problems. However, if, as her book's title suggests, great American cities are on their deathbeds, this is not the time to be choosy about medications, but the time to dose them with everything that seems promising. Any policy that will attract middle-class whites to the city and tend to integrate the suburbs should be tried.

### SUBSIDIZING CITIES

The American city's main problem is the American suburb. There is nothing wrong with a suburb as far as its inhabitants are concerned, but their departure from the city has robbed it of their money and their cultural contributions.[33] Suburbs waste valuable agricultural and park land by turning it into useless back yards and the like; moreover, they do not contribute taxes to support costly urban services. Schools, streets, parks, museums, and public-welfare services have to be kept up, but only working-class people remain in the city to pay those costs.

The move to the suburbs is due largely to subsidies provided by two legislative programs: (1) the nationwide system of expressways and (2) government loans for suburban houses. (The FHA and VA programs, by the way, apparently had another side effect too—stimulating the baby-boom. Many women who moved to the suburbs found it too hard to get out of the house, and so they filled up their time with extra babies. But that is another story.) Most European countries did not subsidize suburbs the way North American countries did. In Europe, families had to stay in the cities, so they kept up their apartments and public services.

However, the move to the suburbs is only part of the American urban problem. Suburbanization has occurred in other countries without such negative effects. The American cities filled up with the nonwhite poor who moved north from rural southern areas, a population that, quite correctly, felt that it would not be welcome anywhere else. This didn't happen in other advanced nations. Canadians moved to the suburbs in large numbers too, but the places they left in the cities were filled by European immigrants whose ethnic shops and restaurants increased the cities' vitality and made many well-to-do Canadians unwilling to move to suburbia. England built a number of "new towns"—well-planned, self-sufficient communities—for people who wanted to move away from the cities. At the same time, it accepted many immigrants from the Commonwealth, some of whom were nonwhite. The experience of these urban immigrants and that of the newly urbanized black Americans have been similar in some ways. There is tension between Pakistanis and many white Englishmen today, though the problem of racial conflict is not as great in Britain as in the United States.

### THE FUTURE

In addition to Jacobs' suggestions for diversifying urban neighborhoods, several other ideas are worth trying. One is to re-draw the boundaries of cities to include the suburbs in a single metropolitan government as Toronto has done. This would provide more tax dollars for urban services, though in some cases where this has been tried the suburbs have profited more from metropolitan government than the inner city.

Another possibility is halting the subsidization of expressways and mortages for single-family houses. This idea is almost certain to be opposed by the majority of the population, who by now live in suburbs. Still, if the suburbs have grown up on subsidies, it has been at the expense of the cities. Now is the time for a reversal in the flow of public subsidies in favor of cities. Expenditures on subways would benefit the inner city. Low-cost loans for building renovation and for the construction of new housing within the city could be made available.

Another new approach is "urban homesteading." Instead of tearing down condemned slum housing, city officials allow a family to renovate it and live in it. The family is then given title to the house as its homestead. This practice has helped revive decaying neighborhoods in several cities.

The most important task is to reverse the trend for inner cities to become black and suburbs to become white. This is not as impossible as Gans believes. Indeed, evidence from the 1970 census suggests that the crowding of blacks into the inner cities and their absence from the suburbs is caused by their lack of money. Albert I. Hermalin and Reynolds Farley, two University of Michigan sociologists, have calculated that if black families were represented in the suburbs to the same extent as whites *with similar incomes*, 55 percent of the black families would live in suburban areas, instead of the 17 percent that actually live there.[34] They show that "a low-income white family can obtain a suburban home or apartment more readily than a high-income black family."[35] Discrimination in real-estate practices, mortgage lending arrangements, and the like prevents blacks from obtaining better housing even when they can afford it.

Polls show that most blacks want to live in integrated neighborhoods and that most whites would welcome blacks *with similar incomes* as neighbors. There are many middle-class blacks who could afford such housing. This means that the percentage of blacks in the suburbs could be increased if the discriminatory practices mentioned by Hermalin and Farley were outlawed.

I have mentioned a few of the things that could be done to solve the urban problem. There are many others. To carry out any of these policies, however, political support is necessary. Thus the big question is, How much do people care about improving the quality of urban life?

# SUMMARY

**1.** A *city* may be defined as a large, permanent, densely populated settlement. The existence of cities depends on the production of surplus food by farmers. It may be that settlements have always existed and have "paid their own way" by providing the technology that made surpluses possible. Many scholars assume, however, that cities did not exist until a fairly advanced agricultural technology had been developed.

**2.** Imperial cities were places surrounded by walls where the elites lived with their servants and suppliers. Since face-to-face communication was vital, the rulers of the empire stayed in the capital city where they could meet together and sent out administrators to rule the lesser cities of the empire. When an empire gained enough power to provide safety for its trading groups it could expand over large areas. Gradually, however, the rulers came to rely on the people they had conquered, and in this way the subjects gained the skills they needed to overthrow their conquerors.

**3.** The cities of medieval Europe had more freedom than those of other societies. Today North American cities follow the medieval tradition by electing their own mayors. The idea of citizenship developed out of the participation of freemen in the European city.

**4.** Most non-European preindustrial cities are unlike modern Western cities. Their different social classes are not separated; they have few suburbs; and the central business district is not well developed. Poor migrants from the countryside tend to live in shanty towns on the edges of the cities, maintaining a rural life style if they can.

**5.** *Urbanization* involves the movement of people from rural areas to cities and from small cities to larger ones. In advanced societies this process is nearly complete. The cities of less developed societies, especially in Asia, will become enormous in the future. Urbanization takes place because most consumer goods are produced more cheaply in the city than in the countryside.

**6.** In North America more people are moving to the suburbs than to the cities. The people moving to the inner cities in the United States are largely blacks. The effect of these two trends is a highly segregated housing pattern—poor blacks in the city, well-to-do whites in the suburbs.

**7.** Robert Redfield and Louis Wirth took a "determinist" approach to the study of cities. They portrayed urban life as cold, large scale, heterogeneous, impersonal, and culturally diverse. Redfield believed that urban culture was destroying folk culture around the world.

**8.** The "compositional" approach holds that density and size *in themselves* do not affect the psychological traits of urban or rural residents. However, urban people differ from rural and small-town people because the populations of cities and towns are composed of people with different characteristics in terms of age, marital status, social class, occupation, ethnicity, and so on. These characteristics, and not the density or size of the settlement, determine the traits of the different populations.

**9.** The "subcultural" view leans toward the compositional approach but admits that the size and density of a settlement determine the variety of subcultures found within it. And those subcultures do have an effect on the people who belong to them. Thus city living supports more diversity—in both its deviant and its creative forms.

**10.** *Suburbanization* is the gradual movement of people from cities to the communities surrounding them. Suburban dwellers do not all have the same way of life. There are rich suburbs and poor ones, black ones and white ones, and so on. Many suburbanites would welcome well-to-do black neighbors but not poor neighbors of any color.

**11.** Researchers have shown that the belief that urban dwellers are lonely is a myth. They may not do much "neighboring," but they may have friends throughout the urban area.

## KEY TERMS

**census metropolitan area (CMA)** a metropolitan region consisting of a large central city surrounded by smaller, dependent cities (Canada).

**city** a large, permanent, densely populated settlement.

**folk society** a small, isolated, homogeneous society; a peasant society.

**megalopolis** a supercity in which several cities merge together to make a whole urbanized region.

**standard metropolitan statistical area (SMSA)** a metropolitan region consisting of a large central city surrounded by smaller, dependent cities (United States).

**suburbanization** the movement of people from central cities to smaller communities in the surrounding area.

**urbanization** the movement of people from rural areas to cities and from small cities to larger ones.

**urban society** a large-scale, heterogeneous, impersonal society.

## FOR FURTHER READING

CLARK, S. D. *The New Urban Poor*. Toronto: McGraw-Hill Ryerson, 1978. A study of poor rural people who moved to urban areas, where their existence is largely hidden.

DOWNS, ANTHONY. *Opening Up the Suburbs*. New Haven, Conn.: Yale University Press, 1974. Downs adds new data and political opinions to the controversy discussed in this chapter about racial integration in urban areas. Lively and important work.

GREER, SCOTT, *The Urbane View*. New York: Oxford University Press, 1972. Greer writes well on a comprehensive range of topics, including political aspects of urban development.

KORNBLUM, WILLIAM. *Blue Collar Community*. Chicago: University of Chicago Press, 1974. This is a contribution to the traditional field of urban ethnography that was begun by the Chicago school.

MICHELSON, WILLIAM. *Man and His Urban Environment: A Sociological Approach*. Reading, Mass.: Addison-Wesley, 1970. Michelson's elegant little book will introduce you to the urban research that examines the physical environment and its effects upon social interaction.

MUMFORD, LEWIS. *The City in History.* New York: Harcourt, Brace & Jovanovich, 1961. This is not a book you will read overnight, but is a major piece of historical scholarship and a vehicle for one of the leading modern social critics to reveal his appreciation of various kinds of urban environments. A classic in the field.

SEELEY, JOHN R.; R. A. SIM; and E. W. LOOSLEY. *Crestwood Heights.* New York; John Wiley, 1967. A description of the life style enjoyed by resi-

dents of an upper-class district of a large North American city.

SHILS, EDWARD. *Center and Periphery: Essays in Macrosociology.* Chicago: University of Chicago Press, 1975. These theoretical essays help clarify questions about cultural change moving from the urban to the folk culture.

*Urban Life and Culture.* A useful journal for urban sociologists and geographers.

19

# SOCIAL CHANGE

Sociology textbooks have to be revised about every three years because life is changing so fast. Today my newspaper tells me that a human baby may have been born through cloning, that a treatment for schizophrenia may have been found, that the Egyptians and the Israelis are preparing for peace talks, that economists are debating about what would happen to the economy of Quebec if it separated from Canada, and that President Carter has asked Congress to save New York City from bankruptcy.

By the time you read this chapter, these stories will be old news. You will know much more about schizophrenia, cloning, and Quebec's future than I do now. The Middle East may be at peace or at war by then, and New York's financial problems may be solved. But new issues will demand your attention—issues that I can't predict now.

The rapidity of social change makes socialization of children very chancy. Parents used to know, by and large, what attitudes and skills they should teach their children to prepare them for adult life. But today children are likely to know much more than their parents by the time they grow up. This fact changes our attitudes toward old people. In traditional societies old people are respected. They know more, and their wisdom is useful. But old people in our industrial society know better than to give advice to younger people; they are behind the times. In the past the older generation socialized the younger generation. Now the young may socialize the old. What is happening is that culture is being *created* from one day to the next. The new is arising out of the old, yet it is transforming the old at the same time.

Traditional society has given way to modern society. On balance, this is a good thing, I think. People are more open to new possibilities, but those possibilities demand flexibility. There is some strain involved. But before we talk about how modern society differs from traditional society, we need to know something about social change.

# Theoretical approaches to social change

Because sociologists are concerned with the changing patterns of social life over time, they often assume that social change may be following some orderly, regular trend over long periods. It is dangerous to make such assumptions, however. When we look closely we may find that other explanations are just as likely as the one we have taken for granted. This is why we will begin this chapter with a discussion of various theoretical approaches to social change.

History may be heading in any of several possible directions. A grouch will complain that "We're going to hell in a handbasket." An optimist will cheerfully argue that we are making all kinds of progress. Another person will look for cycles, saying that there are ups and downs in everything—you win a little, you lose a little. What goes up must come down, and vice versa. Obviously, all three positions are whopping generalizations. Yet various scholars have tried to defend each of these positions. I won't deal with pessimism here because it is a rather limited view. But I will mention the other two approaches—cycle theories and, more important, evolutionary theories.

## CYCLE THEORIES

In the days of the ancient Greeks the cycle theory was taken for granted, even by writers like Plato. It was assumed that every natural event was repeated endlessly. In our own century too, some social theorists have believed in historical cycles. Of these, perhaps the best known was Pitirim Sorokin, who fled from Russia after the Bolsheviks came to power and who taught at Harvard for many years. Sorokin believed that any society swings between two opposite types of culture, "sensate" and "ideational." The sensate periods are those in which a society emphasizes materialistic, pleasure-seeking values; the ideational periods are those in which it stresses ideals and spiritual concerns. While it is moving from the sensate to the ideational, or vice versa, the society is "idealistic"—a fortunate condition in which both sets of values are present.

According to Sorokin, the Gothic art of the medieval period shows that it was the most ideational period of Western history. The paintings of the time all portray Christ's suffering and the lives of the great religious figures of Christianity. By contrast, modern art shows that our time is the most sensate period of Western history. What art could be less spiritual than a giant Campbell soup can? Sorokin would have preferred to live in the Middle Ages.

Another theorist, the historian Oswald Spengler, has portrayed the life cycles of civilizations as similar to the life cycles of people. Civilizations are born, grow up, become senile, and finally die.[1] Today, however, few scholars hold to cycle theories. An opposing view has become increasingly popular—the assumption that the normal state of affairs is for societies to make progress, not to go downhill. The early sociologists took it for granted that progress was normal, and some believed it was inevitable. This view is hard to accept after the terrible wars of our century. Still, while progress is not *assumed* to be *normal,* most people think it is at least *possible.*

In many ways human beings *have* made progress over time. The theory that is used to explain this trend is called *evolutionism.*

### EVOLUTIONISM

#### Auguste Comte

Evolutionism is the belief that every society progresses toward perfection through stages of increasing complexity. None of the early sociologists questioned this belief. Auguste Comte and Herbert Spencer both tried to identify the various stages through which all societies must progress. Both believed that there was a single theme underlying all of human history: *It moves from the simple to the complex.* Therefore any development that comes early will always be simpler than any development that comes later—no matter what. For example, Comte noticed that the various branches of knowledge developed at different periods in history, and he argued that this was because the later sciences were more complex than the early ones. Thus sociology, the newest science, couldn't develop until biology was in existence. And biology developed after chemistry, which developed after physics, which developed after mathematics. Obviously, then, mathematics is the least complex science!

Comte believed that human thought had passed through three stages. In the first (or "theological") stage people think inanimate objects are alive. Thus a primitive person may believe that a tree is in pain while it is being cut down. (My next-door neighbor believes the same thing. She sings to her African violets.) Natural events are thought to be caused by spirits or gods with human emotions. In the second (or "metaphysical") stage events are explained in terms of abstract forces. The third (or "positive") stage is the scientific period, in which people explain events in terms of natural processes and do not expect total certainty.[2]

Comte suggested that not only societies but individuals and sciences pass through these three stages, though perhaps at different rates. (For example, a child might believe that a vacuum cleaner is a living monster and gradually give up this theory as he or she grows up.) Positivism is the scientific outlook—the assumption that natural causes can explain everything. Comte believed that human beings all tend to move toward this sophisticated outlook as we mature. This tendency is the underlying force that moves history in a forward direction, not ordinarily backward or in cycles. Everything moves

**TABLE 19.1**

*Time line showing important technological developments*

| | |
|---|---|
| 750,000 B.C. | Controlled use of fire |
| 10,000 | Domestication of the dog |
| 8000 | Emergence of food production |
| 7000 | Domestication of the ox |
| 4350 | Domestication of the horse |
| 3500 | Use of the wheel |
| 3500 | Metal-smelting |
| 3000 | Domestication of the camel |
| 2600 | Seagoing ships |
| 2500 | Domestication of water buffalo and yak |
| 1200 | Iron technology develops |
| 300 | Invention of pulleys, levers, screw, pump, and water wheel |
| A.D. 650 | Windmills first used in Moslem world |
| 850 | Gunpowder bombs (China) |
| 852 | Burning of coal for heating (England) |
| 900 | Widespread use of watermill for grinding grain (northern Europe) |
| 1250 | Watermill applied to making cloth, sawing wood, and extracting oil from vegetable seed |
| 1250 | Coal used by smiths as a source of energy |
| 1386 | Mechanical clock (installed in Salisbury Cathedral, England) |
| 1448 | Gutenburg Bible printed with movable metal type (Germany) |
| 1606 | Experimental steam engine (Italy) |
| 1709 | Use of coal in iron industry |
| 1712 | Commercially successful steam engine invented by Newcomen (England) |
| 1765 | Modern steam engine invented by Watt (England) |
| 1787 | Steamboat (USA) |
| 1790 | Sewing machine (England) |
| 1800 | Electric battery (Italy) |
| 1812 | Practical steam locomotive (England) |
| 1831 | Generation of electric current (England) |
| 1852 | Passenger elevator (USA) |
| 1859 | First oil well drilled (USA) |
| 1862 | Dynamite (Sweden) |
| 1874 | Chain-driven bicycle (England) |
| 1874 | Telephone (USA); four-cycle gasoline engine and carburetor (Germany) |
| 1880 | Patent of electric-light bulb (USA) |
| 1882 | Commercial use of hydroelectric power (USA) |
| 1887 | Gasoline-powered automobile (Germany) |
| 1892 | Diesel engine (Germany); gasoline-powered tractor (USA) |
| 1900 | Rigid airship (Germany) |
| 1903 | Flight of Wright brothers (USA) |
| 1923 | Bulldozer (USA) |
| 1926 | Rocket fired with liquid propellant (USA) |
| 1926 | Television (Scotland, USA) |
| 1937 | Jet engine (England) |
| 1945 | Nuclear explosion (USA) |
| 1946 | Electronic computer (USA) |
| 1951 | Hydrogen bomb (USA) |
| 1954 | Nuclear power plant put into operation (USSR) |
| 1957 | Artificial satellite (USSR) |
| 1958 | Laser (USA) |
| 1969 | Astronauts land on moon (USA) |
| 1975 | USA and USSR astronauts link in space |
| 1976 | Scheduled flights of supersonic aircraft (USSR, Britain–France) |

*Source:* "The Conquest of Energy," from *Humankind* by Peter Farb. Copyright © 1978 by Peter Farb. Reprinted by permission of Houghton Mifflin Company.

onward and upward in a single line of development. This view is called unilinear evolutionism. It assumes that there is a single set of stages through which every person, every branch of knowledge, and every society must proceed.

### Herbert Spencer

Spencer was Comte's best-known follower. In thinking about Comte's comparison of a society to an organism, he decided that societies that are at the same stage of growth must be similar in a number of ways.[3] And if this is so, then by comparing the accounts of travelers in foreign countries he should be able to classify societies in terms of their level of development. (You may have noticed a problem with Spencer's approach: If societies are like organisms, they will grow old and die instead of getting better all the time, but he was inconsistent because he didn't say that.)

Moreover, he was inconsistent on another issue as well. He seems never to have made up his mind whether he believed in unilinear evolution or not. In some places he wrote that all societies follow the same line of development. In other places he wrote that various societies follow different lines of development—a view that is called multilinear evolutionism. However, he leaned toward the unilinear theory and tried to fit the diversity of human societies into a single classification system. This effort made for bad history writing because it meant creating an imaginary series of developmental stages and then trying to make the histories of real societies fit that model. Of course you have to trim off a few awkward facts to make them fit—historians call that sort of trimming "cheating" or "fudging." Good historians "tell it like it happened," not like they imagine it was *supposed to happen*, according to some theory of development. Historians accused Spencer and other evolutionary writers of distorting historical evidence, and even sociologists became uncomfortable about the idea of unilinear evolution. And so, in the first part of this century, people began to drop evolutionism.

### Diffusionism

Evolutionism views different societies as if they were so many cabbage plants in a row, all planted at the same time and growing up under slightly different conditions. These conditions affect the rate of growth, so that some societies (or cabbages) are more mature than others. By looking at the mature organisms you can predict what the more backward ones will look like a little later. Little cabbages all grow up to be big cabbages, never turning into carrots or onions. Similarly, according to unilinear evolutionary theory, less developed societies will come to look like the advanced societies when they have matured further.

Of course this analogy breaks down when it is applied to human affairs. In a garden you don't have carrots imitating cabbages and growing big leaves. You don't have onions making war on parsnips and forcibly converting them into pseudo-onions. Eggplants never dominate tomatoes and rob them of their heritage through cultural imperialism. Organisms do follow a fixed line of development without changing their traits along the way. But human societies borrow cultural traits from each other. This means that they can skip whole stages of development. The Australian tribesmen, for example, are moving straight from the stone age into the industrial age as a result of European influence. This cultural borrowing is called *diffusion*. You can trace on a map the spread of a given trait. Ways of building canoes, the use of writing, the habit of smoking tobacco—examples of diffusion are countless. How many nations can build atomic bombs? Most of them learned how through diffusion.

Not all diffusion moves ideas from advanced societies to backward ones, though this happens quite often. Actually, the distinction between "backward" and "advanced" assumes a unilinear view of social change—otherwise we couldn't tell which society is ahead and which is behind. But "advanced" nations also borrow cultural ideas from "backward" ones—so which society is backward? Diffusion was a challenge to evolutionary theory, and partly for that reason sociologists gave up the whole idea of evolutionism and turned to other topics.

But that decision was awkward too. There were problems with evolutionism. But, on the other hand, there was *something* to it. Therefore, during the past fifteen years or so, sociologists have been developing a new version of evolutionism.

### Evolutionary theory today

What can be said for the idea of social evolution? Certainly, some things have to happen in a fixed order. For example, no hunting-and-gathering society could have discovered atomic energy. No preliterate society could have put together a large political empire. No society with a barter economy could have developed capitalism. *Some historical developments are necessary in order to make other developments possible.* This is why it makes sense to call some societies more "advanced" than others. Bows and arrows are less advanced than atomic bombs because they develop first. Certain innovations are crucial to further development. For example, only a society that grasps the con-

*Much of the technology used around the world has been transmitted by diffusion. People don't have to invent sewing machines and motor scooters for themselves—they can borrow the ideas.*

Rebecca Busselle/DPI

Fujihira/Monkmeyer

cept of zero can make further advances in mathematics, as well as the aspects of life that depend on mathematics.

This is what we mean by "progress." Humankind can develop ideas and institutions in later stages that would have been impossible in earlier stages. Thus modern theories of social evolution are attempts to explain the sequence in which such developments occur. However, it is also important to recognize what evolutionism does *not* imply. In order to make evolutionism stand up against criticism, theorists have had to make certain changes, which are as follows:

**1.** *Evolution is not inevitable.* Progress may take place—or it may not. A society that grasps a concept that *might* lead to further development may not see the implications of that concept. Thus the Mayan Indians understood the concept of the wheel (pottery toys with wheels have been found in their tombs), but they didn't recognize the usefulness of wheels for vehicles and machinery. Discovery of the wheel made further evolution possible, but obviously this didn't make it inevitable. Because it didn't happen.

**2.** *Evolution is not unilinear.* There is no single sequence of steps through which all societies must pass as they become more advanced. For that matter, some societies *don't* advance. They may stay about the same for thousands of years, or they may decline instead of progressing. Others borrow from other cultures and skip many stages of development. Cultural change does not follow a fixed order, as the growth of an organism does. We can predict that an acorn will become an oak tree, not a willow. But we can't predict what system of government India will have fifty years from now.

**3.** *Evolutionism is not social Darwinism.* Spencer thought human progress depended on raw competition between individuals or societies. We know better! Progress depends on cooperation more than competition. Through cooperation we can increase the total amount of resources available so that everyone benefits. We don't have to fight over the limited available food or water. By working together we can produce *more* food, build canals to bring in *more* water, and so on. One group does not have to wipe out other groups in order to survive.

**4.** *Evolutionism does not imply a final goal.* The word *progress* implies progress toward a goal, but we do not necessarily have to agree on all our goals to know whether we are getting ahead or going downhill. Your idea of progress may not be the same as mine, and therefore we won't always agree about whether a given change is an improvement or a step backward. Still, we often do agree. We all agree, for example, that the introduction of writing or voting is progress.

**5.** *Progress in one area may not be progress in another area.* For example, a technological advance may not be an aesthetic or moral advance. Our century has seen dramatic technological progress, but it has also seen as much cruelty as any previous century. Often an evolutionary breakthrough increases justice or raises living standards, but that is not always so. Thus an advance in social organization made it possible to build the pyramids, but the poor fellows who had to haul the blocks of stone probably didn't think they were getting a better deal. Likewise, landing on the moon was a fantastic technical achievement, but later generations may think of it as a huge waste of money. What society calls progress depends on what it values. We value rocket research, but whether it is necessary for further development is not yet known. An **evolutionary breakthrough** is an innovation that makes further advances possible. It may be an immediate blessing to all or it may cause suffering instead, just as the Industrial Revolution initially brought deprivation and disorder for many people. Thus, progress on one front is not necessarily progress on all fronts.

## FUNCTIONALISM

As mentioned earlier, sociologists dropped the idea of evolutionism because it was unable to account for the phenomenon of diffusion, and it has only recently been revived. Meanwhile scholars turned their attention to several other theories of social change. Among these was functionalism. Instead of asking what stages of development societies go through in developing their family patterns or their political systems or their economies, the functionalists focused on the part these arrangements play in the societies in which they are found.

Functionalism is the belief that a social pattern is best understood not in terms of its past historical development but in terms of its current consequences for the society in which it is operating. We have already looked at a number of functionalist theories. For example, we saw that stratification has certain effects (functions) in terms of getting well-qualified people to fill key occupational roles. We saw that religion has certain functions in terms of integrating a person into his or her group, and that the family has many functions—such as regulating sexual activity, socializing children, and providing emotional support. In all of these examples the institution in question is assumed to serve a *positive* function for the group. This is where functionalism is biased. It tends to be conservative, suggesting that whatever exists is good. I think the reasoning runs like this: "Whatever exists must exist because it serves some function. And if it serves a function, it shouldn't be changed." Naturally, nobody *says* such a thing. It sounds so obviously naive. Nevertheless, I think functionalist theories tend to run along those lines.

You may have noticed something else. Functionalist theories explain why things are the the way they are; they don't explain change. They are *static*, not *dynamic*. De-

spite this drawback, functional explanations are often interesting, and when functionalism is linked to evolutionism it becomes quite useful. We will discuss this combination in the next section. First it is necessary to describe how functionalism has been modified in recent years.

1. *Societies are not "integrated" systems in which every part is necessary for the whole to function.* This is obvious. Often we just limp along, surviving in spite of, not because of, certain social practices. We might be better off without them. And some customs are neither functional nor dysfunctional. Neither good nor bad. For them, no functional explanation is possible. For example, the buttons on men's coatsleeves serve no function at all. To explain their presence we must point out that they survive from the time when they were used to fasten on gauntlets. (Some of my students hold to a different, more interesting explanation—that they were sewn on by order of a general to keep soldiers from wiping their runny noses on their sleeves!)

2. *A custom may be helpful to part of the system and harmful to the system as a whole.* For example, the code of honor among thieves is helpful to professional criminals but does nothing for the society of which those criminals are a part.

3. *Elements that are suitable are not necessarily essential.* Substitutes are possible. For example, parliamentary democracy is suitable to an industrialized economy, but it is not essential. Some industrial societies have other forms of government.

4. *The components of a social system do not always fit together harmoniously.* Indeed, society can be viewed as a "tension management system."[4] There are strains, contradictions, and a never-ending series of problems in every society. When one problem has been solved, a new one pops up

to take its place. Some problems don't get solved. We simply cope, with varying success, sometimes for centuries.

After all this, what is left of functionalism? Well, the idea of **functional requisites** still seems useful. There are certain requirements that all societies must meet, at least at a minimum level. Socialization is an example. Child-rearing systems vary—but if a society fails to train its young for adult roles at all, that society will not survive.

Returning to the suggestion that evolutionism and functionalism can be combined, this is where the concept of functional requisities becomes useful. Societies that meet their functional requisites very well are more likely to survive than other social groups. And this is one basis for evolution. Let's see how well functionalism and evolution fit together.

## A functionalist theory of social evolution

Let's start with evolutionism. Our theory resembles Darwin's in that it accounts for change in terms of *variation* and *challenge*. In biology, mutation is a constant source of variation: Every so often a gene changes, for some mysterious reason, and a new trait crops up in a given organism. For example, variation in the length of horses' legs is due to mutation. Long ago horses were small—about the size of foxes. And there were challenges for them to face— meat-eating enemies such as, perhaps, tigers. Whenever tigers chased horses, they caught more of the short-legged ones. Hence, more long-legged than short-legged horses survived to reproduce. This explains why, over many generations, the whole species changed.

In human affairs, there are many other explanations besides mutation for the variation in the ways that different groups and individuals do things. The notion of *challenge* is important, however. In Darwinian theory, tigers challenge horses. In social theory, human relationships and natural events challenge human beings, and human beings adapt. Whenever a group finds a solution to a challenge to its survival, it probably prizes that solution and passes it along through its culture. Indeed, other groups, recognizing that it is a nifty trait, may borrow it. So a challenge fosters innovation, and an innovation (if it turns out to be useful) diffuses to other populations. (In biological evolution genes cannot be transmitted except through reproduction, so traits remain within a given population.)

(Of course, not *all* useful innovations are recognized. There is nothing inevitable about it. Some terrific ideas have been ignored or forgotten. But on the average, a good idea stands a fair chance of being adopted and kept—especially if it crops up just when people most need it.)

Good ideas do tend to arise when they are needed and not otherwise. This is why challenge is an important element in our theory. Challenge stimulates people to search for new ideas. No challenge, no innovation. People will stick to custom as long as it works even moderately well. As a result most human societies have remained primitive. Only twenty-one of them have progressed to becoming genuine civilizations, according to the historian Arnold Toynbee. When people are faced with a problem that demands adaptation, they may change—or they may not. If they do, the change may work—or it may not. If it doesn't, the group may vanish, just as short-legged horses vanished, thanks to the fast tigers. Institutions that survive may be those of the surviving groups. We forget the others that didn't survive.

But innovation poses new challenges too. Once a group starts changing it may be unable to stop for a long time. Society is not a stable, harmonious, well-integrated system—or at least *our* society is not. Some primitive societies may be. But contemporary societies are, at best, a "tension-management system." For example, if we cure malaria by eliminating mosquitoes, we can rejoice for a few years. Then we find out that the DDT we're using has problems of its own—problems that may be worse than mosquitoes. New problems arise as fast as old ones are solved. Modern society has an endless supply of new challenges.

The sources of change may be technology or unexpected ideas. In modern society technology changes rapidly. Whenever some new machine or medicine diffuses throughout the world, it affects other social institu-

*Human beings are very stimulated by challenges and one of the greatest challenges has been to travel and live in outer space. Shown here is a 10,000 inhabitant space colony proposed by the NASA—Ames/Stanford study. Scientists say such a colony might be built with existing technology by 1995.*

NASA

tions. In Chapter 3 I mentioned *cultural lag*,[5] the tendency of social institutions to fall behind technological change. Cultural lag produces a variety of social problems. Pollution is an example. Until recently our laws have allowed industry to exploit the environment almost unhindered. We have assumed that Mother Nature could heal her own wounds. Now she is gasping and moaning, but by the time we come to her aid with some new laws, she may be mortally wounded.

Ideas are another source of challenge. Many ideas come from confronting other people who think in different ways. The most stable, unchanging societies are almost always those that are isolated from contact with foreigners, whose strange beliefs and practices tend to unsettle one's habitual outlook and require re-thinking. When you have to deal with foreigners, especially face to face, you must either adopt their ways or at least try to reconcile them with your own. And doing this stimulates discovery and new solutions. For example, when the American journalist James Reston was in China he had appendicitis. His surgeons used acupuncture to anesthetize him. When he wrote about this in his column, thousands of Americans asked their own doctors about acupuncture. The American doctors were unable to ignore the challenge, so they began studying acupuncture. No one fully understands how acupuncture works—at least no one in the West. Hence, if we arrive at an explanation, it will have to be one that reconciles Chinese medical theory with Western science. Such a challenge would not have arisen without contact between the two societies.

When cultures meet, as, for example, during migrations, some people find themselves in an ambiguous position. They belong partly to one tradition and partly to another. These people are "marginal."[6] Their situation is both uncomfortable and stimulating. Because they have to reconcile two

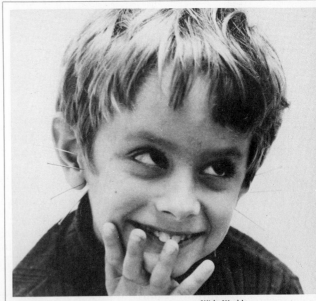

Wide World

*American doctors didn't believe in acupuncture until an American journalist described his own surgery in China. Now they are studying it too. This boy is being treated for deafness and his hearing has improved.*

ways of life, they often come up with creative innovations. For example, the Jews have been very creative—possibly because they have often been marginal.

Suppose you want to stimulate social change and innovation. How will you do it? One way might be to gather a lot of incompatible ideas and ask people to sort them out. Some of our most vital social institutions do just that. Universities do it. Libraries do it. Science does it. All of these institutions have built-in sources of social change. They challenge people simply by bringing dissimilar ideas together. Scientists, for example, are paid to conduct studies, publish their results, and read the findings that other scientists publish. Naturally, they criticize one another's work, and this criticism leads to scientific discovery.

Social evolution, thus, is mainly a response to challenge. Functionalists can contribute quite a bit to our understanding of this process by identifying evolutionary (or cultural) breakthroughs. That is, functionalism helps us analyze the effects of a given social pattern on other aspects of the social system.

Functionalists point out that all societies have certain functional requisites. They all have to meet certain basic problems, such as feeding and sheltering their populations, reproducing and socializing their children, giving emotional support to their members, settling disputes in an orderly way, and so on. Some societies solve some of these problems better than others do. Functionalism helps us understand how this is done in a given society. To understand whether an innovation is a terrific idea or a terrible one, we have to look at it along with other arrangements in the society and see whether they will fit together or not. This is functional analysis.

Successful innovations move societies forward and make them better able to cope with a wide range of problems. For example, a literate society can do many things that a preliterate society cannot do. So writing is an evolutionary breakthrough. By creating and diffusing these cultural breakthroughs human society has moved from one stage of evolution to the next. Talcott Parsons provides some examples of this process.

## Parsons: cultural breakthroughs and evaluation

Parsons is both an evolutionist and a functionalist. He has shown how certain civilizations solved problems better than other civilizations, thereby enabling further advances to take place. Two of the most important cultural breakthroughs described by Parsons are writing and the development of formally rational law.

Parsons classifies human societies into three main levels of development—primitive, intermediate, and modern. In his view,

it was writing that moved human society from the primitive level to the intermediate level and it was formally rational law (among other cultural breakthroughs) that moved society from the intermediate level to the modern level.

The invention of writing makes possible a great increase in cultural diffusion, both in space and in time. It enables one to "broadcast" messages to anyone who is literate and happens to come across the document. And a literate society can have a *history*. It can record events that are beyond the memories of living people. We discussed the importance of writing in Chapter 3. The point here is that it was one of human society's greatest breakthroughs. It led to major developments in many other areas. Written documents are *cumulative* in impact. This means that a literate society possesses enormously greater cultural capacity than a preliterate one. Accordingly, Parsons classifies literate societies as "intermediate" in their evolutionary development—a giant step ahead of primitive societies. Examples of such "intermediate" societies are the Egyptians; the Mesopotamians; the Incas; the Islamic, Chinese, Indian, and Roman empires; and the cultures of the Greeks and the Hebrews.

Parsons dates "modern" society from the Protestant Reformation of the seventeenth century. Several important evolutionary breakthroughs took place at that time. One of these was the development of formal law. Of course the Romans had a highly developed legal system, and in fact English common law was Roman law adapted to English life. However, a very special development took place in England in the seventeenth century: The law became independent of the crown. The legal profession began to protect private rights *in opposition to the crown*. The British government thus was put in the position of both defining and enforcing restrictions on its own power.

The development of formal law gave citizens a way of using the government to protect themselves *from* the government and using the law to protect themselves from the legal system. Parsons believes that the development of formally rational law was a cultural breakthrough because it provided for social order, for predictability, for security of private rights, and personal freedom, all at once. This social context encouraged additional cultural progress. It is one of the great achievements of Western civilization.

## Conflict theory and social change

I often have imaginary conversations with Karl Marx. In my fantasy he has a bushy white mane and beard and is almost handsome, but he is a fierce critic. I never win arguments with him, so I had hoped to tiptoe past in this chapter and not discuss social change with him at all. No such luck. He hailed me in his usual manner, by bellowing, "bourgeois idiologist!" I knew I was caught. I'd have to discuss the functionalist theory of evolution with him.

For a while the discussion didn't go too badly. Marx seemed to agree with the concept of evolution. His own theory, historical materialism, was in a way an evolutionary account of social change throughout history. Remember how he said that capitalism "contains the seeds of its own destruction"? This is clearly a theory of social change that points to a better future.

We also agreed on the importance of technological change in creating changes in social relationships. To be sure, Marx said that the productive system of a society would determine its social classes—the working class and the ruling class. And he said that clashes between those groups lead to social change. Moreover, he argued that competition between the bourgeois industrialists would force them to improve their technologies and that in the long run this would cause their own downfall. Thus

Marx believed that the future of human history was predictable, even inevitable.

When I mentioned the importance of challenges and contradictions as a source of innovation, he nodded. I mentioned how new ideas usually develop from the clash of opposing points of view. "Of course," he interrupted. "That's called the dialectic! But it isn't just *ideas* that clash. It's the interests of different social classes!"

I thought about this for a while and realized that what I had described as the challenge of being marginal was very similar to an idea that Marx had picked up from Hegel. Hegel had suggested that ideas always work themselves out by being challenged by opposing views. In time these pairs of opposites (which he called "thesis" and "antithesis") are reconciled in some new idea (or "synthesis") that uses whatever is valid in each of the opposing views but improves on both of them. This moves thought in a progressive direction. In time, the synthesis would itself become a thesis, would be opposed by a new antithesis, and finally would be replaced by another, more advanced synthesis. This whole process Hegel called "the dialectic."

Marx turned Hegel's dialectic into a theory of history, saying that instead of *ideas* fighting it was *social classes* that did so. Hence, Marx's theory of social change is called "historical materialism" or "dialectical materialism."

I was beginning to feel rather pleased by my success in winning Marx's approval as we discussed the concept of evolution. However, when I turned to functionalism and evolutionary breakthroughs my luck ran out. I said that societies probably tend to maintain the social practices that have been most useful in helping them meet their functional requisites. He frowned and called me a "lackey of the ruling class." Then he launched a major attack on functionalism, calling it a conservative ideology. The main point in his argument seemed to be this: It is not whether something is *useful*, not whether it is *functional*, that determines whether it will be kept by a society. What determines that is power, sheer *power*! The group that has enough power to get its way determines what institutions are maintained. Is capitalist exploitation of workers "functional"? Is it "useful?" Of course not! Exploitation continues because the capitalists still have power. When the workers have enough power to stop them, it will stop. You don't have to believe that everything that exists does so for a good reason.

He had won again. I had to agree with him on that point. Social practices that exist at any one time may indeed be harmful, not helpful. They may be maintained, not because they have proved valuable as solutions to the problems and challenges of the society, but simply because an oppressive group has the power to keep them going.

"So remember that! And tell your students to remember it too!" he growled.

"Yes, Karl, I will. I promise," I replied.

So you remember it too. This is your final lesson in conflict theory.

## SOCIAL RESEARCH:
*Sociologists at Work*

So far we have discussed social change at the societal level. We have seen how ancient literate empires differed from primitive hunting-and-gathering bands and how seventeenth-century England differed from other European societies of the time. We have talked about changes taking place across the centuries, changes involving all of humankind.

Now we're going to look at the social changes that are happening *within the individual* and *in our own time.* Throughout the world billions of human beings are changing their outlook, behavior, and expectations and adjusting to their fast-changing societies. What happens to the personalities of traditional people as they become modern people? This is the subject of a book by Alex Inkeles and David H. Smith entitled *Becoming Modern,*[7] a detailed survey of the attitudes and behavior of thousands of men working in six developing societies: Argentina, Chile, East Pakistan, India, Israel, and Nigeria in about 1964. (Women's work experiences couldn't be compared easily so they were not included.)

Inkeles and Smith were interested, first of all, in finding out whether there is any general set of attitudes or ways of behaving that can be considered *modern* as distinct from *traditional.* For example, our discussion of evolution assumes that humankind is moving in a certain direction, toward modernity—whatever that may be. But we may be mistaken. After all, traditional societies vary greatly. A traditional man herding sheep in North Africa is very different from a traditional man fishing on an outrigger canoe off Fuji or Samoa. And both of them are different from a traditional Siberian shaman curing a sick nomad with magical incantations.

If traditional people differ so much, may not modern people differ just as much? An office worker in Japan is obviously quite different from an office worker in Stockholm or Leningrad. Does it even make sense to call them all "modern," as if they all had some basic traits in common? Doesn't this amount to assuming unilinear evolution toward a single life style?

Inkeles didn't think so. While he recognized the great diversity that exists among industrial societies, he was also struck by certain similarities among the people of those societies. And he believed that modern people differ in regular ways from traditional people. So he set out to see whether certain experiences that occur in industrialized settings encourage the orientation that he calls "modern."

Inkeles and Smith organized a large team of researchers that included social scientists from all the nations that they planned to study. Then they developed a questionnaire containing nearly 500 items. (It took an interviewer several hours to question a single respondent.) The questions dealt with a variety of habits, beliefs, and opinions. The family was discussed, and such issues as women's rights and birth control were covered. Religion, politics, the position of the aged in society, the communications media, social stratification, and consumerism were all explored.

In each society respondents were chosen in such a way as to permit comparisons between people in three main job categories: (1) farmers, (2) factory workers, and (3) urban nonindustrial workers (barbers, cab drivers, street vendors, and so on). Inkeles firmly believed that working in a factory generally had a strong modernizing influence on people. He also wanted to consider the impact of other factors—urban living, edu-

cation, exposure to mass media, and so on. But the first task was to decide how to measure modernity.

## MEASURING MODERNITY

How would you arrive at a single "test" by which to classify men in terms of modernity or traditionalism? Inkeles and Smith did what psychologists often do when they are inventing an intelligence test: They looked at the correlations between the various items that they had included in their questionnaire. They started out with a set of items that had some bearing on modernity, and they refined their test by choosing items that were generally related. That is, a person who scored high on one item in this group might be expected to score high on others as well. Items that were not correlated with the others were tossed out.

*Modernity is coming to places like Kuwait. Except for the robed shopper, this market could be almost any place in the world.*

Omar Bessim/Monkmeyer

**TABLE 19.2**

*Simplified OM scale*

*Source:* Alex Inkeles and David H. Smith. *Becoming Modern.* Cambridge, Mass.: Harvard University Press, 1974.

*PURELY ATTITUDINAL ITEMS*[a]

1. Have you ever (thought over so much) gotten so highly concerned (involved) regarding some public issue (such as . . .) that you really wanted to do something about it?
   Frequently / Few times / Never

2. If schooling is freely available (if there were no kinds of obstacles) how much schooling (reading and writing) do you think children (the son) of people like yourself should have?

3. Two 12-year-old boys took time out from their work in the corn (rice) fields. They were trying to figure out a way to grow the same amount of corn (rice) with fewer hours of work.
   The father of one boy said: "That is a good thing to think about.
   Tell me your thoughts about how we should change our ways of growing corn (rice)."
   The father of the other boy said: "The way to grow corn (rice) is the way we have always done it. Talk about change will waste time but not help."
   Which father said the wiser words?

4. What should most qualify a man to hold high office?
   Coming from (right, distinguished, or high) family background
   Devotion to the old and (revered) time-honored ways
   Being the most popular among the people
   High education and special knowledge

5. Which is most important for the future of (this country)?
   The hard work of the people
   Good planning on the part of the government
   God's help
   Good luck

6. Learned men (scholars, scientists) in the universities are studying such things as what determines whether a baby is a boy or girl and how it is that a seed turns into a plant. Do you think that these investigations (studies) are:

   All very good (beneficial) / All somewhat good (beneficial)
   All somewhat harmful / All very harmful
   Some people say that it is necessary for a man and his wife to limit the number of children to be born so they can take better care of those they do have (already have).
   Others say that it is wrong for a man and wife purposely (voluntarily) to limit the number of children to be born.
   Which of these opinions do you agree with more?

7. Which one of these (following) kinds of news interests you most?
   World events (happenings in other countries)
   The nation
   Your home town (or village)
   Sports
   Religious (or tribal, cultural) events (ceremonies) or festivals

8. If you were to meet a person who lives in another country a long way off (thousands of kilometers / miles away), could you understand his way of thinking?
   Yes / No

9. Do you think a man could be truly good without having any religion at all?
   Yes / No

*BEHAVIOR-INFORMATION ITEMS*

10. Do you belong to any organization (associations, clubs), such as, for example, social clubs, unions, church organizations, political groups, or other groups? If "Yes," what are the names of all the organizations you belong to? (Scored for number of organizations.)

11. Would you tell me what are the biggest problems you see facing (your country)? (Scored for number of problems or words in answer.)

12. Where is (in what country is the city of) Washington / Moscow? (Scored correct or incorrect.)

13. How often do you (usually) get news and information from newspapers?
   Everyday / Few times a week
   Occasionally (rarely) / Never

[a]Words in parentheses are alternative phrasing for aid in translation. In every case the items should be adapted to make sense in the particular culture.

The advantage of the Inkeles–Smith scale is that it can be used cross-culturally. No matter what society you are visiting, it is probably correct to say that it measures modernity there as well as it does in the six nations where it was originally developed. Inkeles argues that it applies to people in socialist societies as well as to people in the Third World and in more modern countries. Using this scale (which has been simplified since Inkeles and Smith began) a researcher can give each respondent a score that indicates how modern or how traditional he is compared to people in other areas of the world.

### EXPLAINING HOW MEN BECOME MODERN

As soon as they had perfected their scale (called the OM scale, for "overall modernity"), Inkeles and Smith set to work comparing the average scores of workers in different categories. They looked at the effects of several variables, and on the whole, they were not surprised by the results. Education was by far the most important variable. Men who had been educated had higher OM scores for each year of schooling, and the differences were marked. In fact the impact of education on modernity was two or three times as great as that of any other variable.

Next in influence were a number of other variables. Job experience and exposure to the mass media were similar in degree of impact. Men who worked in factories had higher scores than urban nonindustrial workers, who in turn had higher scores than farmers. The differences between the factory workers and the urban non-industrial workers were not as great as the researchers had expected, however. It seems that people learn modern values and life styles by driving a cab or sweeping streets, though in general the factory is a somewhat better "school for modernity." The longer men had worked in these modern settings, the higher their scores tended to be.

However, it is not just the urban work situation that changes attitudes in a modern direction. The researchers found out an important fact by studying a cooperative in East Pakistan. Most of the farmers surveyed were peasants working in the situations in which peasants work throughout most of the Third World. Their modernity was quite limited. But one group of farmers in East Pakistan was part of a farm cooperative. These workers did not rely much on new machinery, but they had increased their production greatly, chiefly by reorganizing their methods of working. Inkeles and Smith found that their OM scores were markedly higher than those of other workers. Their experience in self-help and new interpersonal relationships had changed their attitudes.

Inkeles and Smith had expected to find that urban residence, as opposed to rural residence, influences modernity, but this is not the case. Living in a city does not, *in itself*, bring about more modern attitudes than living in a village or in a rural farm setting. To be sure, urban men do, on the average, differ from country people. But their greater modernity results not from living in a city but from other factors that often, but *not necessarily*, go with city life. City people are more often educated, are more likely to work in factories, and are exposed to the mass media more often than rural people. However, it is important to realize that *if* rural people had these advantages, they would probably shift toward modern views just as much as city people do. This fact may be an important consideration if, for example, it is desirable to locate more factories in the countryside in the future, to link them up with agriculture more effectively, as we proposed in Chapters 15 and 16.

### WHAT ARE MODERN PEOPLE LIKE?

By now we know something about how people become modern. But what are modern people like? How do they differ from traditional people in the same society?

**Modern man is well informed**

In all six countries studied by Inkeles and Smith, modern respondents were far more likely than others to be able to answer questions about geography, political affairs, consumer items, books, and the like.

Modern people also tend to have a high sense of *personal efficacy*. For example, they believe that a person's position in life depends more on his own efforts than on fate. They be-

*Of all the influences that modernize people, education is the most powerful. Schooling can go on in all kinds of settings.*

lieve that a job with more responsibility and more opportunity to exercise control is better than a job with little responsibility. They believe scientific research is beneficial. And at times they become so concerned about a public issue that they want to do something about it. (Traditional people, in contrast, are likely to take the opposite view on such matters. For example, they are likely to believe that fate or God's will is more important in solving a nation's problems than anything the people or the government can do.)

In a number of other areas modern people showed that they have greater hopes of being able to control their own situations. They tend to

have more ambition, for example. They believe that preventing accidents is more a matter of care than of luck. They believe that medicine is more effective in curing the sick than prayers. They want to make their own job and marital choices instead of allowing their family to decide these matters for them. They like to meet people and to make plans; they belong to more organizations; and so on.

The modern person is broader in identifying with a wider, more modern collectivity than is the traditional person. For example, modern men said they would take the advice of the government instead of the church. They would identify with the nation, not with the ethnic group, the religion, or the village. They believed in giving to charity, not because of fear of God, but because of generosity.

On the other hand, Inkeles and Smith had expected that modern men would be, in general, more trusting (e.g., when dealing with merchants or relatives) than traditional people. But this is not the case. Nor, on the other hand, are modern people more likely than traditional people to believe that kinship ties aren't very important. Inkeles and Smith had expected that as people modernize they think it is less important to support their kin and keep in touch with them. But this was not supported by the evidence. Another theory that did not hold up was that modern people are somehow more materialistic—that they are more likely to believe that money and goods bring happiness.

What does hold up, very clearly, is the image of modern people as *active, well-informed, participating citizens.* And their activism is oriented in a generally more liberal direction. They are more likely, for example, to support women's rights, birth control, scientific research, government planning, education, and so on. These traits occur among modern men all around the world, however they may differ otherwise.

Finally, though modernizing must involve some stress, the study did not find that modern people suffer more than traditional people from psychological problems. A number of items were designed to test this issue by asking whether the respondent had trouble sleeping at night, whether he often showed various symptoms of anxiety, and so on. It seems that people who modernize must cope with changes all around them, but that life in a rural village has its own problems. The two social environments do not result in markedly different degrees of psychological or emotional distress, at least as measured by the Inkeles–Smith questionnaire.

What conclusions can we reach? That the world is changing. That humankind is becoming modern. That modern people have different personalities than traditional people. And, so far as we can judge, that's fine. Just fine.

# SOCIAL POLICY:
## Issues and Viewpoints

In Chapter 1 I brought up a question that often troubles sociologists: whether research should (or can) be "value free." To what extent should sociologists keep their personal values from affecting their research? Is it possible to separate one's ethical, political, aesthetic, or emotional judgments from factual descriptions of society's institutions? By now you may have formed your own views on this question.

This book has not been oriented toward particular policies, nor has it tried very hard to be "value free." A policy-oriented book might discuss specific laws dealing with particular social problems. It might discuss how much various programs cost, how effective they have been, what lobbies are backing them, and so on. You may want to work along those lines, possibly by serving as an administrator or going into politics. But even if you do not become involved in practical social-action programs you will have to make judgments that somehow relate to issues that have been discussed, in a general way, in this book. It seems to me that the framework within which we interpret and understand the society around us strongly affects the particular policies we support. The purpose of this book has been to examine our assumptions and then to see how our values are affected by those assumptions. Let's go back and take another look at those assumptions.

In our discussion of culture we ran across the issue of cultural relativism. If you have to make policies that affect the life style of cultural groups other than your own, this issue is an important one. As an administrator, perhaps, or as a social worker, you may face the question of whether or not you should encourage people to give up their traditional customs in favor of a way of life that seems "natural" to you. How do you make judgments on such matters? Would you willingly work for a relief agency or family planning program that tries to get people to change their way of life? What standards would you use in deciding such matters?

What about the so-called culture of poverty? Can we assume that if we give people the opportunity to rise out of poverty they will change their life style and cope with their daily problems more effectively? Or, on the contrary, will poverty simply perpetuate itself? This issue is at the heart of many practical policies. It may arise for you as you confront some new legislative proposal in the future.

We have also discussed government control of the mass media. Should the government support excellence in the arts even if box office receipts are low? Should the government back popular culture or should it support a greater variety of cultural offerings—different shows for small ethnic communities, for people with offbeat artistic tastes, I don't have a firm opinion on this question, but I lean toward pluralism. Do you?

In the chapter on socialization we discussed some basic questions about the way children are socialized in our society as compared with the collective systems used in the Soviet Union and on the Israeli *kibbutz*. Do North American children receive enough guidance from adults, or are they forced to be too independent too early? Do they turn to peers for support when it would be better for them to turn to adults? I think so.

The issue of compliance with authority is enormously important. I am not sure that it could be affected by any political decision, but we should be aware of the strong tendency we all have to respond to the orders of anyone who seems to have authority and thus to avoid moral responsibility for our own action.

In touching on the subject of deviance we raised a number of issues. The question of what causes deviance *determines* policy in this area. For example, a commonly accepted explanation of delinquency is the "labeling" theory, which is based on role-self theory. If the labeling explanation is correct, then policy derived from it should be very effective. This is a policy of

"hands off"—the less one does to define a youth as delinquent, the more likely he is to think of himself as a lawful person and to live up to that self-image. According to this view, punishing criminals would be more harmful than helpful. I would feel uncomfortable with such a policy, however. If you would too, you may want to think about it in greater detail.

What about the more general question of allowing people to pursue their private vices if in doing so they do not hurt anyone else? Legalization of gambling, sexual deviance, drug use, and other forms of behavior that most people disapprove of would follow from this general policy.

When we turn to formal organizations, we come to a subject that affects everyone. But there is no particular public policy toward organizations. You will have to decide whether to take a job in a large organization or whether doing so would turn you into some sort of robot, unable to take responsibility or to respond with feeling to the people you know. Hence, your view of bureaucracy may determine your career. Not all writers view bureaucrats in the same way. Some see them as freer than, say, self-employed people. Others disagree. Is this an issue of "values" or a factual question?

The issue of racism and ethnic stratification affects the lives of millions of people. How can discrimination and racism be ended? What is the proper place of particularism in modern life? I don't know any general answers to such questions.

In our discussion of collective behavior and social movements we raised the issue of press coverage of behavior that is often imitated. Does such coverage give the idea of kidnapping or terrorism or hijacking or rioting to people who otherwise might not think of doing these things? If so, how can we overcome the problem without endangering freedom of the press?

Coming closer to home, you will have to make personal decisions about the proper roles and duties of family members. And you will also probably have to make decisions collectively, with other members of your church, your school board, or your government about matters related to family life. Should homosexuals be allowed to hold a dance in a public auditorium? Should welfare mothers not be supported if they live with their boyfriends? Should divorce be granted freely upon request, or should spouses have to prove that one partner is at fault before a divorce is granted? Issues like these arise on a regular basis. They have to be answered in the light of both factual information and informed, well-thought-out values based on some understanding of the functions of families.

Policies toward matters of religion come up from time to time. Even though we live in a political system that guarantees freedom of religion, sometimes that freedom contradicts certain other guaranteed rights. The courts then have to decide which set of rights takes precedence.

The field of education, perhaps more than

---

**TABLE 19.3**
*Predictions for the year 2000*

*VERY LIKELY POSSIBILITIES*

1. The application of lasers for sensing, measuring, communication, cutting, welding, power transmission, defense, and other purposes (already partially achieved)
2. Worldwide use of high-altitude cameras for mapping, prospecting, census, land use, and geological investigations (achieved)
3. Major reductions in hereditary and congenital defects (partially achieved)
4. Three-dimensional photography, films, and television (partially achieved through holography)
5. Use of nuclear explosions for excavation and mining, for the generation of power, and as a source of neutrons (partially achieved)
6. New techniques for inexpensive, convenient, and reliable birth control (achieved)
7. Control of weather and climate
8. General and substantial increase in life expectancy, postponement of aging, and limited rejuvenation
9. Chemical methods for improving memory and learning
10. Artificial moons for lighting large areas at night

*LESS LIKELY POSSIBILITIES*

1. Artificial intelligence (partially achieved with computers)
2. Artificial growth of new limbs and organs
3. Major use of rockets for commercial or private transportation
4. Effective chemical or biological treatment for most mental illnesses
5. Suspended animation for years or for centuries
6. Automated highways
7. Direct augmentation of human mental capacity by interconnection of the brain with a computer
8. Verification of some extrasensory phenomena
9. Practical laboratory conception and nurturing of human fetuses
10. Substantial manned lunar or planetary installations

*REMOTE POSSIBILITIES*

1. Life expectancy extended to substantially more than 150 years
2. Almost complete genetic control
3. Interstellar travel
4. Practical and routine use of extrasensory phenomena
5. Laboratory creation of living plants and animals

*Source:* Herman Kahn and Anthony Wiener. *The Year 2000.* New York: Macmillan, 1967.

any other area of sociological study, is linked to public policy. For one thing, education is controlled almost entirely by the state. Therefore it is impossible for the government to be completely separate from it and to allow schools and universities to set their own policies. The state pays the bills and decides what will be taught and what research will be funded. It responds to demands on the part of industry and the professions for people with certain skills. Almost everyone has ideas about what courses should be taught and what methods of instruction are most desirable. You probably do too.

In the chapters on economic life and population we considered some of the giant issues of our generation—the problems created by the rapid increase in the world's population and the need to feed it. I have suggested that the basic problem must be seen within the framework of the global economy—particularly the international market for food and agricultural products. How can we free people in the Third World to feed themselves? How can we help them achieve self-sufficiency as soon as possible? World hunger is the greatest policy issue of our lifetime. On it will depend the solution to the population explosion and all the misery and problems that it brings.

Finally, in the chapter on urban living we touched briefly on city planning and development. I suggested that policies aimed at correcting social problems in slums depend on the policy makers' ideas of what is and what is not a slum and their opinions on how slums come into existence. Such matters as the tax system, mortgage interest rates, freeway or subway construction, and zoning ordinances can affect the life of the city for years or even generations. By choosing between, say, urban apartment living and suburban split-level houses, we not only choose a way of life for ourselves but also affect the future of the community we live in.

Thus sociology can never be separate from values. We can be fair in representing various points of view without bias. We can be honest in considering evidence presented by people whose views differ from our own. We can respect one another and our right to hold opposing opinions. But we can never leave our values wholly to one side.

The world is an interdependent system. Your map may show nations in different colors with lines around them, but those lines and colors are misleading. Our deepest loyalty should be to humanity, not to our tribe, our nation, or to any other collectivity. I think the political goal of sociologists should be to create world government featuring justice and freedom. I do not expect to see it in my lifetime, but I hope you do in yours.

We have discussed a number of problems in this book, and you will face many others. May sociology be of service to you as you respond to those problems and search for solutions.

# SUMMARY

1. Some theorists have assumed that social change is cyclical, but the evolutionary view has been more common. Comte and Spencer were evolutionists in that they believed that social progress was normal.

2. Modern evolutionists hold that some developments are necessary in order to make other developments possible. However, progress from one stage to another is not inevitable, nor is there any single line of development through which all societies must pass. Diffusion allows some societies to skip certain stages. An *evolutionary breakthrough* is an innovation that makes further advances possible.

3. Functionalists look for the effects of social patterns instead of for their origins. Functionalism can be accepted today with modification, just as evolutionism requires modification. Societies are not integrated systems. They contain some elements that do not fit well with others. The solution to

one problem may cause a new one. However, some societies meet their functional requirements better than others do, and over time their social patterns tend to win out over those of less successful societies. This is one basis for social evolution.

**4.** Challenge leads to innovation. The challenge may be technological or may consist of confronting people with new ideas, as marginal people often do.

**5.** Parsons classifies human societies as primitive, intermediate, or modern. He believes that the invention of writing moved societies from the primitive level to the intermediate level and that the introduction of formal law, along with other cultural breakthroughs, enabled them to move into the modern period.

**6.** Conflict theories of social change are similar in some ways to evolutionary theories. Marx expected change to result from conflict between social classes. He based his theory of historical materialism on Hegel's "dialectic," which stressed the conflict of opposites and the resulting synthesis.

## KEY TERMS

**evolutionary (cultural) breakthrough**  an innovation that makes further advances possible.

**evolutionism**  the belief that every society progresses toward perfection through stages of increasing complexity.

**functionalism**  the belief that a social pattern is best understood not in terms of its past historical development but in terms of its current consequences for the society in which it is operating.

**functional requisites**  the requirements that all societies must meet, at least at a minimum level.

**multilinear evolutionism**  the belief that various societies follow different lines of development.

**unilinear evolutionism**  the belief that there is a single set of stages through which every society must proceed.

## FOR FURTHER READING

BELL, DANIEL. *The Coming of Post Industrial Society: A Venture in Social Forecasting.* New York: Basic Books, 1973. This is a weighty book in every sense of the word, and an important one.

DEWITT, ROBERT L. *Public Policy in Community Protest.* Toronto: University of Toronto Press, 1970. This deals with how an isolated group of Newfoundland fishermen adapt to indsutrialization and respond to political policies.

ETZIONI, AMITAI. *The Active Society.* New York: Free Press, 1968. Another heavy book. Etzioni is committed to applied research and in this work discusses the issues concerning how, when, and to what extent we can control social change through rational planning.

MALINOWSKI, BRONISLAW. *The Dynamics of Cultural Change.* New Haven, Conn.: Yale University Press, 1945. Malinowski was a functionalist anthropoligist who mostly studied South Sea Island societies. In this book he develops his theory of social change.

MOORE, BARRINGTON, JR. *Reflections on the Causes of Human Misery and Upon Certain Proposals to Eliminate Them.* Boston: Beacon Press, 1972. The title has an old-fashioned ring to it but the topics Moore discusses are altogether modern. It is a small book, covering a number of political issues. Although it is easy to read, it will not cheer you up.

MOORE, WILBERT. *Social Change.* Englewood Cliffs, N.J.: Prentice-Hall, 1963. I have drawn heavily from this book in the present chapter, but you should read the original, too, if you can. It is a small book, but very densely packed in writing style.

TOFFLER, ALVIN. *Future Shock.* New York: Bantam, 1971. This was a best-seller and deserved to be. It deals with the personal adjustments that are necessary for people living in fast-changing societies like ours. More exciting than fiction to read.

WHITE, LESLIE A. *The Evolution of Culture: The Development of Civilization to the Fall of Rome.* New York: McGraw-Hill, 1959. White is a leading anthropological theorist who was arguing in favor of an evolutionary model even while the idea was unpopular. Now it is quite popular.

# THE REFERENCE PAPER

## FINDING YOUR TOPIC

The secret of a successful term paper is the argument it develops. No matter how interesting your topic is, your paper will sound dull unless it generates a little suspense. So your first job is to find—or invent—a problem or puzzle to work on in your paper. Later you will have to think of how to "sell" the reader on your problem. A vacuum cleaner salesperson, for example, tries to make you believe that you *need* the machine, that you can hardly get along without it. It's the same with a term paper. Don't freely give your findings away to the reader. Convince us first that we *need* the information that you can provide. Show us how some problem exists that is absolutely crying out for a solution. Selling the problem is actually as important in a term paper as providing the answer. Set up an argument, show the confusion that exists because of the problem, and then if you can't solve it completely by yourself, that's all right. You can just modestly claim to have advanced sociology a tiny bit toward solving this important question.

For these reasons, I suggest that you pay a lot of attention to finding your topic. If your teacher hands out lists of suggested topics, don't just pick one passively; it may be too vague and broad for your purpose. You must narrow it down to a more specific question and build up suspense about its answer. Suppose your instructor suggests that you write on drug abuse or divorce. Fine! What *about* drugs or divorce? You have to make the question your own. Maybe you will want to show that rates of drug use or divorce are increasing or decreasing more than people generally realize, and that you know why this is going on. Or maybe you will want to evaluate the various treatment programs for drug addiction to discover which ones, if any, work successfully. Or maybe you will want to point out some effects of divorce on the emotional adjustment of the couple's

children. Try to show that your evidence corrects a widespread mistaken belief. Set up your argument before you try to settle it.

## GATHERING INFORMATION

The material you use in a paper can vary greatly. You can write a fine paper just defining a single word (such as "culture" or "power") that is widely used in the social sciences. But don't do this unless you can show that there is some confusion about the meaning of this particular word, and that your definition will straighten out problems that have confronted various writers. Of course, you will need to read a lot before tackling such a problem, if only to locate such problems in the writings of various scholars.

In general, however, you will write papers that deal with empirical, factual topics; for such papers you need evidence. Chapter Two suggests sources of evidence, such as historical documents, government statistics, public opinion polls, and the like. You may decide to do a survey of your own, possibly by telephoning a sample of respondents and interviewing them. Or you may decide to do field research—such as, say, sitting in a singles bar several nights to note what people say first when getting acquainted. In any case, you must be sure that your information will point toward a solution to a definite question.

## USING THE LIBRARY

Before writing your paper, spend time reading what other people have written on your chosen subject. The trick is to be able to find the most useful written material quickly and to keep track of what you learn from reading it. Fortunately, scholars will help you. They cite the sources of their information in footnotes and bibliographies, just as you will do when you write your own paper. Thus, all you may need is one good reference to start your research. After that, you can work your way backward by tracking down the sources that are mentioned by that author, and then sources that *they* mention in turn, and so on. Pretty soon you will have more references than you can read, and you will have to skim through them and select the best ones for your purposes.

However, this way of searching won't help you find recent articles. Suppose you start with a fairly old book. Any references in it will be even older. But you may need up-to-date publications, so you will have to look for additional sources in current journals and other recent sources of data. How should you proceed? I suggest that you take along a batch of index cards and record each of your references on a separate card, noting the author, title, place and date of publication, name of publisher, and pages. Below that, jot down whatever impressions you gain from reading the article or book that you may want to recall later.

### The card catalog

First go to the card catalog, which is probably located in a big wooden filing case near the middle of the room. However, many libraries are switching over to a microfilm system instead. In any case, the catalog has two separate file systems, one that is organized alphabetically by the authors' surnames, followed by their book titles, and the other organized by subject category. If you know the author's name, you should refer to the author/title catalog. The card will show the call number assigned to that particular book. Most libraries use the Library of Congress numbering system, in which sociology books have call numbers beginning with HM. Books are assigned to the shelves according to these numbers, so once you know its number, you can probably trot right over and pull your chosen book off the shelf.

Your library will probably have special shelves for reserve books—ones that are in high demand and therefore loaned for shorter periods. Some of your library's holdings may also be in special libraries around the campus. Reference books are always kept in a particular section, usually on the main floor. The catalog will show how to find the book you need.

If you don't yet have a reference to a particular book, you may start with the subject card catalog. Material on sociology will include such headings as *social surveys, deviant behavior,* and *demography.* Various books and journals are listed under each heading.

Suppose you decide to look for a general overview of the topic that you want to study. You may then begin with an article in the *International Encyclopedia of the Social Sciences.* Your card catalog may list it as REF H 40 A215; the REF indicates that it is filed in the reference section of the library. In this encylopedia are articles with bibliographies at the end. You should also become familiar with other reference books filed near it; these include *A Modern Dictionary of Sociology* and a more recent book, the *Encyclopedia of Sociology.*

### Journals and Abstracts

Suppose you want to find some up-to-date research on a topic. You may want to go straight to the journals. Your library probably subscribes to several sociology journals. The most widely used are the *American Sociological Review,* the *American Journal of Sociology, Social Forces,* the *British Journal of Sociology,* and the *Canadian Review of Sociology and Anthropology.*

There are so many journals that it is inefficient for you to just leaf through them, hoping to stumble across what you need. You should look first at a periodical index, the most useful one being *Sociological Abstracts.* These are big bound volumes, usually kept in the reference department, that summarize articles from many different journals. You may need some help in learning to use "Soc Abstracts," as they are called. Near the end of the final volume for each year, you will find a subject index. Abstracts on "immigration," for example, may be found in Section 20 (Sociology of the Occupations), Section 37 (Demography), and Section 21 (Industrial Sociology). The subject index will list all the abstract numbers for articles on these various aspects of immigration.

EXAMPLE: ABSTRACTS

> Immigration
>> Aspects of immigration. 74G6984
>> Attitudes of white South Africans toward South Africa's immigration policy. 74G6982.

This last number indicates that you should turn to G6982 in the volumes for 1974 to find the abstract of the article on white South Africans.[1]

Suppose, on the other hand, that you want to find abstracts on a wide subject area, not a narrow topic like immigration. You may then begin by looking at the table of contents at the front of each issue of *Soc Abstracts*. In either case, when you have found the abstract number, turn to the main body of the issue or volume to find the abstract. Then, if an abstract seems particularly important to your research, go find the original article in the journal elsewhere in the library.

Most libraries stock recent journals in little cubbyholes along a wall, but older copies will be bound and shelved with the other books in the stacks. For those older issues, you need to use the card catalog in the ordinary way to find the call number. Journal titles are listed in the author/title catalog.

If you are doing research on a general topic, before narrowing your topic down you may want to read a few book reviews to find some good leads to recent books. The last half of each issue of the *American Journal of*

Sociology and *Canadian Review of Sociology and Anthropology* are devoted to book reviews. Another source is *Contemporary Sociology*, published by the professional organization of sociologists, the American Sociological Association, entirely for reviewing books. The tables of contents classify reviews according to subject matter.

A final suggestion: Feel free to ask your librarians for help. That's what they are there for.

### WRITING YOUR REPORT

By the time you have finished reading, you will have found references to more articles and books than you can handle. Research can never be "complete," because everything you read leads you to something else. But you must eventually put a stop to your reading and spend time by yourself, letting everything jell until you know what you want to tell people about your investigation. (During this period I wander around the house moaning and drinking tea.) Then you must seat yourself firmly in front of your typewriter and stay there for a long time, no matter what exciting or distracting things you have a chance to do instead.

This is the time to "sell" your problem to the reader, so make a strong case for its importance. Then go on to tell your findings. Eventually you can wrap it up with a conclusion, reviewing the whole argument again briefly and pointing out what you think are unfinished pieces of the puzzle that somebody else should work on next.

I can't tell you *what* to say in your paper, but I have six suggestions about *how* to say it:

1 *Don't be wordy.* Cut excess phrases out, so every word counts.
2 *Don't be roundabout.* It is fine to say, "I think that . . ." instead of " It is the opinion of this writer that . . ."
3 *Nail down your claims.* If you say something that might be questioned, say how you know it is so. Where did you read it? Who told you?
4 *Respect your reader's point of view.* If you

---

1. I am indebted to Mary Pickles and Margaret Currie for examples on library research.

want to make a case for a particular church, or political party, or value (for example, the right to have free abortions, or the "immorality" of homosexual behavior), be aware that your reader may have a different opinion. Don't assume that all reasonable human beings *must* see things your way. I'm not saying that you must never let your own values show (though your instructor may say that, so check it out with him or her before you start), but I am saying that you don't want to seem insulting or naive or preachy. Do your soapbox act someplace else, not in your term paper. If you do show your personal biases, it is a good idea to label them as such, so the reader sees that you *know* you are going beyond the facts and expressing an opinion or judgment.

5 *Cite your sources.* It is fine to borrow other people's ideas, but say that you are doing so in a footnote. This is an easy place to slip up badly, and it can cost you a terrible price to do so. Plagiarism is regarded as a serious crime by scholars. If you are using somebody else's words, put them in quotation marks and use a footnote to say where the words were originally published. If you are using ideas suggested verbally, you can say in the text, " As Susan Jones has pointed out . . .," or you can say in a footnote, "Susan Jones, personal communication." Or you can have a special section thanking people for their criticism of your paper, and include Susan's name on that list.

6 *Try your paper out on a reader.* Before you type your final draft, it is a good idea to have a friend read what you have written and suggest ways of improving it. Though your draft will be messy at this point, you want your reader to look for spelling or punctuation errors, awkward style, and errors of fact. Every book that is published is read by a copy editor. You will do yourself a favor by finding a free copy editor in your family or dormitory. You want someone who will be super-critical, not someone who adores every word you say. However, in the long run it is your own paper, and if your reader offers suggestions that you don't like, you are certainly free to disregard them.

## Footnoting

For the most part, you will be citing publications, and you can choose between two different forms of footnoting.

The first system is the one used in this book. You insert a number at the point in your paper that is drawn from a particular reference. Then, either at the bottom of the page or at the end of your paper, you list those numbers in order and give the particular publication that each one refers to. Examples are shown below. Notice the order of the items and punctuation of these examples so you can follow the pattern in your own paper. Other variations are sometimes used, but the one below will work quite well. Whatever style you adopt, be consistent in using it.

EXAMPLE: FOOTNOTES

1. Herbert Marcuse, *Eros and Civilization* (Boston: Beacon Press, 1965), p. 97.
2. Marcuse, p. 202.
3. R. Stephen Warner, "Toward a Redefinition of Action Theory," *American Journal of Sociology*, 83(6), May, 1978, pp. 1317–1347.
4. R. Stephen Warner, "Sociological Theory in Historical Context," in *Sociological Theory: Historical and Formal*, by Neil J. Smelser and R. Stephen Warner (Morristown, N.J.: General Learning Press, 1976), pp. 1–133.
5. Warner, "Toward a Redefinition . . . ," p. 1322.
6. Not all cases are presented here because too few interviews were completed by Japanese respondents to give a reliable estimate about the opinions of the Japanese community in Salem.
7. Mary Haywood Metz, *Classrooms and Corridors* (Berkeley: University of California Press, 1978), pp. 99–101.

Let me draw attention to a few features of this footnoting system. First, notice that the authors' first names appear first, followed by their last names. Some students mistakenly put the surnames first, which is proper for bibliographies, but not for footnotes of this kind. Notice too that the book or journal title is underlined. If your paper is published, underlined material will be set in italics, but when you type, underlining is used in place of italics. The title of an article or chapter within a book or journal is not underlined but enclosed in quotation marks.

In footnote 2, since I repeated a reference to the Marcuse book that had previously been cited, I didn't repeat the whole story, but just the author's surname and the page. In footnote 5 I was also referring to a source previously cited, but I gave a little more information than in footnote 2. This is because there were two Warner articles footnoted previously, and I must make it clear which one I am referring to in this note. Finally, in footnote 6 I was not citing any publication but was explaining some small point about my research. Side remarks such as this one should be inserted in footnotes to avoid disrupting the flow of the discussion in the paper itself.

Let's consider the second system of footnoting. It has become more popular recently in journal articles than the first system. It does not use numbered footnotes at all, but refers to the items in the bibliography with a short parenthetical notation. Thus, at the end of a sentence you may simply put: (Warner, 1978). This informs the reader that you are referring to a 1978 article by Warner that is to be referenced in the bibliography. Suppose Warner has written two articles in 1978, and you refer to both of them. You label one "a" and the other "b", both in the parentheses and in the bibliography. Thus, you might insert: (Warner, 1978b).

### Bibliography

Whichever system of footnoting you use, you always supply a bibliography on a separate sheet at the end of your paper. It should list all the articles and books to which you have referred. This bibliography organizes the references in alphabetical order, according to the first letter in the authors' *surnames*, which are placed *before* the given names in this case. If a particular author's work is listed more than once, the early publications come first and subsequent ones follow in chronological order. You need not repeat the author's name each time, but draw a line in its place after it has appeared once. Page numbers are shown in the bibliography only to indicate where whole articles are located in a given book or journal. The particular pages that you cite for your own reference should be shown in the footnotes, not in the bibliography.

EXAMPLE: BIBLIOGRAPHY

MARCUSE, HERBERT. 1965. *Eros and Civilization.* (Boston: Beacon Press)

METZ, MARY HAYWOOD. 1978. *Classrooms and Corridors.* (Berkeley: University of California Press)

WARNER, R. STEPHEN. 1976. "Sociological Theory in Historical Context," in Neil J. Smelser and R. Stephen Warner, *Sociological Theory: Historical and Formal.* (Morristown, N.J.: General Learning Press)

————. 1978. "Toward a Redefinition of Action Theory," *American Journal of Sociology,* 83(6), 1317–1347.

This summary on citations may not be adequate to answer all the problems about details that arise while you are writing your paper. For further advice, consult a handbook of style, such as Kate L. Turabian's *The Student Guide for Writing College Papers,* University of Chicago Press, 1976.

# NOTES

# Chapter 1
## What is sociology

1. Seymour Martin Lipset, "Political Sociology," in Robert K. Merton, Leonard Broom, and Leonard S. Cottrell, Jr., eds., *Sociology Today: Problems and Prospects* (New York: Basic Books, 1959), p. 83.
2. Solomon Asch, *Social Psychology* (Englewood Cliffs, N.J.: Prentice-Hall, 1952), pp. 450–501.
3. Morris Janowitz and Dwaine Marvick, "Authoritarianism and Political Behavior," *Public Opinion Quarterly*, 17 (1953), 185–201.
4. Emile Durkheim, *The Rules of Sociological Method*, 8th ed., ed. G. Catlin and trans. S. Solovay and J. Mueller (Chicago: University of Chicago Press, 1938), p. 139.
5. Some contributions from the Chicago school of sociologists are: Robert Park, Edward W. Burgess, and R. D. McKenzie, *The City* (Chicago: University of Chicago Press, 1925); Nels Anderson, *The Hobo: The Sociology of the Homeless Man* (Chicago: University of Chicago Press, 1929); Harvey Zorbaugh, *The Gold Coast and the Slum* (Chicago: University of Chicago Press, 1929); William I. Thomas, *The Unadjusted Girl* (Boston: Little, Brown, 1931); Clifford Shaw, *The Jack-Roller* (Chicago: University of Chicago Press, 1930); Frederic Thrasher, *The Gang* (Chicago: University of Chicago Press, 1927).
6. Emile Durkheim, *The Division of Labor in Society*, trans. G. Simpson (Glencoe, Ill.: Free Press, 1933).
7. Leslie White, *The Science of Culture* (New York: Farrar, Strauss, 1949).
8. David F. Aberle et al., "The Functional Prerequisites of a Society," *Ethics*, 60 (1950), 100–111.
9. Morris Cohen, *Reason and Nature: An Essay on the Meaning of Scientific Method* (New York: Macmillan, 1931), p. 350.

# Chapter 2
## Methods of social research

1. Rex A. Lucas, *Men in Crisis: A Study of a Mine Disaster* (New York: Basic Books, 1969).
2. See Andrew F. Henry and James F. Short, Jr., *Suicide and Homicide* (New York: Free Press, 1954).
3. W. I. Thomas and Florian Znaniecki, *The Polish Peasant in Europe and America* (New York: Octagon Books, 1971), first published in 1919.
4. David McClelland, *The Achieving Society* (New York: Van Nostrand, 1961).
5. Philippe Ariès, *Centuries of Childhood* (New York: Knopf, 1962).
6. J. Mabley, "Mabley's Report," *Chicago American*, January 22, 1963, pp. 62–63.
7. J. Durand, "Mortality Estimates from Roman Tombstone Inscriptions," *American Journal of Sociology*, 65 (1960), 365–373.
8. W. Lloyd Warner, *The Living and the Dead* (New Haven, Conn.: Yale University Press, 1959).
9. Claire Selltiz, Marie Jahoda, Morton Deutsch, and Stuart W. Cook, *Research Methods in Social Relations*, rev. ed. (New York: Holt, Rinehart and Winston, 1959), p. 241.
10. Arlie Russell Hochschild, *The Unexpected Community* (Englewood Cliffs, N.J.: Prentice-Hall, 1973), p. 3.
11. Ibid., p. 6.
12. T. W. Adorno, Else Frenkel-Brunswik, Daniel Levinson, and R. Nevitt Sanford, *The Authoritarian Personality* (New York: Harper, 1950). For a critique of this study see R. Christie and Marie Jahoda, eds., *Studies in the Scope and Methods of the Authoritarian Personality* (New York: Free Press, 1954).
13. Else Frenkel-Brunswik, "Intolerance of Ambiguity as an Emotional and Perceptual Personality Variable," *Journal of Personality*, 18 (1949), 108–143.
14. Lenore J. Weitzman, Deborah Eifler, Elizabeth Hokada, and Catherine Ross, "Sex-Role Socialization in Picture Books for Preschool Children," *American Journal of Sociology*, 77 (May 1972), 1125–1150.
15. I am indebted to William F. Nicholls, who once used the Shaw remark in a lecture explaining spuriousness.
16. Selltiz et al., p. 443.

# Chapter 3
## Culture

1. E. B. Tylor, *Primitive Culture*, 7th ed. (New York: Brentano's, 1924), p. 1.
2. William Graham Sumner, *Folkways* (Boston: Ginn, 1940).
3. For a good discussion of the cow slaughter issue, see Marvin Harris, *Cows, Pigs, Wars and Witches* (New York: Random House, 1974)
4. William F. Ogburn, *Social Change* (New York: Viking, 1950), pp. 200–213.
5. R. L. Sharp, "Steel Axes for Stone Age Australians," *Human Organization*, 11 (1952), 17–22.
6. Ellsworth Huntington, *Mainsprings of Civilization* (New York: Wiley, 1945).
7. See Karl Marx, *Selected Writings in Sociology and Social Philosophy*, ed. T. B. Bottomore (New York: McGraw-Hill, 1956).
8. Harold Innis, *The Bias of Communication* (Toronto: University of Toronto Press, 1971).
9. Marshall McLuhan, *The Gutenberg Galaxy* (Toronto: University of Toronto Press, 1962).
10. Marshall McLuhan, *Understanding Media* (New York: McGraw-Hill, 1964).
11. Oscar Lewis, *La Vida* (New York: Random House, 1965).
12. Oscar Lewis, "The Culture of Poverty," in George Ritzer, ed., *Issues, Debates, and Controversies* (Boston: Allyn and Bacon, 1972), pp. 470–479.
13. Lola M. Irelan, Oliver C. Moles, and Robert M. O'Shea, "Ethnicity, Poverty, and Selected Atti-

tudes: A Test of the 'Cultural Poverty' Hypothesis," *Social Forces*, 47, no. 4 (June 1969), 405–413.

14. Anthony Leeds, "The Concept of the 'Culture of Poverty':Conceptual, Logical, and Empirical Problems, with Perspectives from Brazil and Peru," in Eleanor Burke Leacock, ed., *The Culture of Poverty: A Critique* (New York: Simon and Schuster, 1971), p. 250.

15. Herbert Gans, *Popular Culture and High Culture* (New York: Basic Books, 1974), p. 37.

16. Maxwell McCombs and Donald Shaw, "The Agenda-Setting Function of Mass Media," *Public Opinion Quarterly*, 36 (Summer 1972), 176–187.

17. *Report of the Commission on Obscenity and Pornography* (New York: Bantam Books, 1970), esp. pp. 169–309.

18. Surgeon General's Advisory Committee, *Television and Growing Up: The Impact of Televised Violence* (Washington: Government Printing Office, 1972), 5 vols.

19. Daniel Bell, "The Myth of Crime Waves," in *The End of Ideology* (Glencoe, Ill: Free Press, 1960), chap. 8, and Theodore N. Ferdinand, "The Criminal Patterns of Boston Since 1849," *American Journal of Sociology*, 73 (July 1967), 84–99.

## Chapter 4
## Socialization

1. S. K. Escalona, "Feeding Disturbances in Very Young Children," *American Journal of Orthopsychiatry*, 15 (1945), 78–80.

2. Bruce Eckland "Genetics and Sociology: A Reconsideration," *American Sociological Review*, 32, No. 2 (April 1967), 173–193.

3. J. W. B. Douglas, *The Home and the School: A Study of Ability and Attainment in the Primary School* (London: MacGibbon and Kee, 1964).

4. John Clausen, "Family Structure, Socialization, Personality," in Lois Hoffman and Martin L. Hoffman, eds., *Review of Child Development Research* (New York: Russell Sage, 1966), p. 14.

5. Glen H. Elder, Jr., and C. E. Bowerman, "Family Structure and Child-Rearing Patterns: The Effect of Family Size and Sex Composition," *American Sociological Review*, 28 (1963), 891–905.

6. J. K. Bossard and E. S. Boll, "Personality Roles in the Large Family," *Child Development*, 26 (1955), 71–78.

7. Clausen, p. 18.

8. Douglas, op. cit.

9. Susan Ervin-Tripp, "Language Development," in Lois Hoffman and Martin Hoffman, eds., *Review of Child Development Research*, (New York: Russell Sage, 1966) II, 92.

10. H. Hartshorne and M. A. May, *Studies in the Nature of Character* (New York: Macmillan, 1928–1930), 3 vols.

11. Urie Bronfenbrenner, *Two Worlds of Childhood* (New York: Russell Sage, 1970).

12. Howard S. Becker, *Boys in White* (Chicago: University of Chicago Press, 1963).

13. Erving Goffman, *Asylums: Essays on the Social Situation of Mental Patients and other Inmates* (Garden City, N.Y.: Doubleday, 1961).

14. Emile Durkheim, *Education and Sociology* (New York: Free Press, 1956), p. 87.

15. Ibid. pp. 85–86.

16. Ibid., p. 88.

17. Jean Piaget, *The Moral Judgment of the Child* (New York: Free Press, 1965).

18. Sigmund Freud, *Civilization and Its Discontents* (New York: Norton, 1961).

19. Ibid. p. 42.

20. Ibid. pp. 26–27.

21. Herbert Marcuse, *Eros and Civilization* (New York: Vintage, 1962). For a good, short introduction to Marcuse's analysis, see Theodore Roszak, *The Making of a Counterculture* (Garden City, N.Y.: Doubleday, 1969), chap. 3.

22. H. A. Moss, "Sex, Age, and Status Determinants of Mother–Child Interaction," *Merrill Pamer Quarterly*, 13(1967), 19–36.

23. J. W. Atkinson and D. C. McClelland, "The Projective Expression of Needs," *Journal of Experimental Psychology*, 38(1948), 405.

24. Matina S. Horner, "Toward an Understanding of Achievement Related Conflicts in Women," *Journal of Social Issues*, 28, no. 2 (1962), 157–176.

25. Ibid., pp. 162–163.

26. Ibid., p. 171.

27. Ibid., p. 172.

28. Adelina Levine and Janice Crumrine, "Women and Fear of Success: A Problem in Replication," *American Journal of Sociology*, 80 (January 1975), 964–74.

29. John Bowlby, *Attachment and Loss*, vol. I, *Attachment* (New York: Basic Books, 1969), p. 209.

30. Especially Jerome Kagan. See his *Understanding Children*. (New York: Harcourt Brace Jovanovich, 1971).

31. Greta Fein and Alison Clarke-Stewart, *Day Care in Context* (New York: Wiley, 1973).

32. Laura C. Johnson, and Eric Leightman, *Child Care Patterns in Metropolitan Toronto*, (Toronto: Social Planning Council, 1978). Findings from this source did not entirely agree with findings of other researchers on the subject.

## Chapter 5
## Sex roles

1. John Money and Anke A. Ehrhardt, *Man and Woman, Boy and Girl* (Baltimore: Johns Hopkins Press, 1972), p. 293.

2. Margaret Mead, *Sex and Temperament in Three Primitive Societies* (New York: Dell, 1935).

3. Randall Collins, *Conflict Sociology: Toward an Explanatory Science* (New York: Academic Press, 1975), pp. 228–249.

4. Eleanor E. Maccoby and Carol Nagy Jacklin, *The

*Psychology of Sex Differences* (Palo Alto, Calif.: Stanford University Press, 1974).

5. Alice Rossi, "A Biosocial Theory of Parenting," *Daedalus*, Spring 1977. My discussion follows Rossi's closely.

6. Jerome Kagan, "The Child in the Family," *Daedalus*, Spring 1977, 36.

7. Jean Lipman-Blumen and Ann R. Tickamyer, "Sex Roles in Transition," in Alex Inkeles, James Coleman, and Neil Smelser, eds., *Annual Review of Sociology* (Palo Alto, Calif.: Annual Reviews, 1975), I, 298.

8. Martin Meissner, Elizabeth W. Humphreys, Scott M. Meis, and William J. Scheu, "No Exit for Wives: Sexual Division of Labour," *Canadian Review of Sociology and Anthropology*, 12, no. 4 (November 1975), 432.

9. Hugh Armstrong and Pat Armstrong, "Women in the Canadian Labour Force, 1941–1971," *Canadian Review of Sociology and Anthropology*, 12, no. 4 (November 1975), 370.

10. Lorna Marsden, Edward Harvey, and Ivan Charner, "Female Graduates: Their Occupational Mobility and Attainments," *Canadian Review of Sociology and Anthropology*, 12, no. 4 (November 1975), 385–403.

11. Saul D. Feldman, *Escape from the Doll's House: Women in Graduate and Professional School Education* (San Francisco: Jossey-Bass, 1974).

12. This section draws heavily on Jo Freeman, "The Origins of the Women's Liberation Movement," *American Journal of Sociology*, 78, no. 4 (January 1973), 792–811. See also Freeman, *The Politics of Women's Liberation* (New York: MacKay, 1975).

13. Freeman, *The Politics of Women's Liberation*, p. 20.

14. Alice Rossi, "Equality Between the Sexes: An Immodest Proposal," in Robert J. Lifton, ed., *The Woman in America* (Boston: Beacon Press, 1964), p. 106.

15. Freeman, "Origins of Women's Liberation," p. 799.

16. Freeman, *Politics of Women's Liberation*, p. 145.

17. Based on *Men and Women of the Corporation*, by Rosabeth Moss Kanter, © 1977 by Rosabeth Moss Kanter, Basic Books, Inc., Publishers, New York.

18. Amitai Etzioni, *A Comparative Analysis of Complex Organizations* (New York: Free Press, 1966), p. 93.

**Chapter 6**
**Social groups**

1. Kingsley Davis, "Extreme Isolation of a Child," *American Journal of Sociology*, 45 (1940), 554–565, and "Final Note on a Case of Extreme Isolation," *American Journal of Sociology*, 52 (1947), 432–437.

2. Jean Marc Itard, *The Wild Boy of Aveyron* (New York: Appleton-Century-Crofts, 1962). See also J. A. L. Singh and R. M. Zingg, *Wolf Children and Feral Man* (New York: Harper, 1942).

3. Bruno Bettelheim, "Feral Children and Autistic Children," *American Journal of Sociology*, 54 (March 1959), 458.

4. René Spitz, "Hospitalism, An Inquiry Into the Genesis of Psychiatric Conditions in Early Childhood," in A. Freud et al., eds., *Psychoanalytic Study of the Child*, 3rd ed. (New York: International Universities Press, 1958), vol. 1.

5. Harry F. Harlow, "The Nature of Love," *American Psychologist*, 13, no. 12 (December 1958), 673–685, and "The Affectional Systems," in Allen M. Schrier, Harry F. Harlow, and Fred Stollnitz, eds., *Behavior of Nonhuman Primates*, (New York: Academic Press, 1965).

6. W. N. Kellogg and L. A. Kellogg, *The Ape and the Child* (New York: McGraw-Hill, 1933).

7. R. A. Gardner and B. T. Gardner, "Teaching Sign Language to a Chimpanzee," *Science*, August 15, 1969, pp. 664–666.

8. David Premack, "Language in Chimpanzee?" *Science*, May 21, 1971, pp. 808–821.

9. Boyce Rensberger, "Talking Chimpanzee Asks for Names of Things Now," *The New York Times*, December 4, 1974.

10. Desmond Morris, *The Naked Ape* (New York: McGraw-Hill, 1969).

11. Lionel Tiger, *Men in Groups* (New York: Random House, 1969).

12. See, for example, Erving Goffman, *Relations in Public* (New York: Basic Books, 1971).

13. Ibid., p. 7.

14. Robert Sommer, *Personal Space* (Englewood Cliffs, N.J.: Prentice-Hall, 1969), p. 50.

15. Ibid., p. 53.

16. See Marvin Scott and Stanford Lyman, "Territoriality, A Neglected Sociological Dimension," *Social Problems*, 15 (Fall 1967), 243–244. See also C. R. Carpenter, "Territoriality: A Review of Concepts and Problems," in A. Roe and G. G. Simpson, eds., *Behavior and Evolution* (New Haven, Conn.: Yale University Press, 1958).

17. Jane van Lawick-Goodall, *My Friends, the Wild Chimpanzees* (Washington, D.C: National Geographic Society, 1967), p. 140.

18. Goffman, *Relations in Public*, p. 84.

19. See Ray Birdwhistell, *Kinesics and Context* (Philadelphia: University of Pennsylvania Press, 1970).

20. Paul Ekman and Wallace V. Friesen, "The Repertoire of Nonverbal Behavior: Categories, Origins, Usage, and Coding," *Semiotica*, 1 (1969), 49–98.

21. Paul Ekman and Wallace V. Friesen, "Nonverbal Leakage and Clues to Deception," *Psychiatry*, 32 (1969), 88–108.

22. Charles Horton Cooley's best-known books are *Human Nature and the Social Order* (Glencoe, Ill.: Free Press, 1956), first published in 1909, and *Social Organization* (New York: Scribner's, 1909).

23. Cooley, *Social Organization*, p. 357.

24. Ibid., p. 359.
25. For a glimpse at John Dewey's ideas on education, see *Experience and Education* (New York: Collier, 1972), first published in 1938.
26. George Herbert Mead, *Mind, Self, and Society*, ed. Charles W. Morris (Chicago: University of Chicago Press, 1934).
27. Herbert Blumer's influence has been, like Mead's, transmitted primarily through his role as teacher. However, his book *Symbolic Interactionism* (Englewood Cliffs, N.J.: Prentice-Hall, 1969) contains a few of his important essays. This chapter was deeply influenced by Blumer's lectures, as no doubt his many former students will recognize.
28. Sheldon Glueck and Eleanor Glueck, *Unraveling Juvenile Delinquency* (Cambridge, Mass.: Harvard University Press, 1955).
29. Gresham M. Sykes and David Matza, "Techniques of Neutralization: A Theory of Delinquency," *American Sociological Review*, 22 (December 1957), 664–670.
30. Mark Granovetter, "The Strength of Weak Ties," *American Journal of Sociology*, 78 (May 1973), 1360–1380.
31. Stanley Milgram, "Behavioral Study of Obedience," *Journal of Abnormal and Social Psychology*, 67 (1963), 371–378.
32. Solomon Asch, "Effects of Group Pressure Upon the Modification and Distortion of Judgments," in Harold S. Guetzkow, ed., *Groups, Leadership, and Men*, (Pittsburgh: Carnegie Press, 1951).
33. Jonathan L. Freedman, J. Merrill Carlsmith, and David O. Sears, *Social Psychology*, 2nd ed. (Englewood Cliffs, N.J.: Prentice-Hall, 1970), pp. 217–220.
34. Hannah Arendt, *Eichmann in Jerusalem* (New York: Viking Press, 1963).
35. William Shakespeare, *Henry V*, act 4, scene 1.

## Chapter 7
## Deviance and control

1. Emile Durkheim, *Sociology and Philosophy* (Glencoe, Ill.: Free Press, 1963), p. 45.
2. Gwynn Nettler, *Explaining Crime* (New York: McGraw-Hill, 1974), p. 66. Other estimates place the discrepancy at between one out of three and one out of ten crimes.
3. John Hagan, "The Labelling Perspective, the Delinquent, and the Police: A Review of the Literature," *Canadian Journal of Criminology and Corrections*, vol. 14(April 1972), 150–165.
4. See Edwin M. Schur, *Crimes without Victims* (Englewood Cliffs, N.J.: Prentice-Hall, 1965).
5. James S. Wallerstein and Clement J. Wyle, "Our Law-Abiding Law-Breakers," *Probation*, 25 (Mar.–April 1947), 107–112, 118.
6. Edmund W. Vaz, "Delinquency among Middle-class Boys," *Canadian Review of Sociology and Anthropology*, 2 (1965).
7. James F. Short, Jr., "The Study of Juvenile Delinquency by Reported Behavior: An Experiment in Method and Preliminary Findings," mimeographed (Paper read at Annual Meetings of the American Sociological Society, 1955); Austin L. Porterfield, *Youth in Trouble* (Fort Worth: Leo Potishman Foundation, 1946); Edward E. Schwarz, "A Community Experiment in Measurement of Delinquency," *National Probation and Parole Association Yearbook* (1945), pp. 157–181; Fred J. Murphy, Mary M. Shirley, and Helen L. Witmer, "The Incidence of Hidden Delinquency," *American Journal of Orthopsychiatry*, 16 (1946), 686–696; Maynard L. Erickson and LaMar T. Empey, "Court Records, Undetected Delinquency, and Decision Making," *Journal of Criminal Law, Criminology and Police Science*, 54 (1963), 456–469.
8. Short, "The Study of Juvenile Delinquency by Reported Behavior."
9. The President's Commission on Law Enforcement and the Administration of Justice, *The Challenge of Crime in a Free Society*. (New York: E. P. Dutton, 1969), pp. 437–486.
10. Kingsley Davis, "Sexual Behavior," in Robert K. Merton and Robert Nisbet, eds., *Contemporary Social Problems*, 3rd ed. (New York: Harcourt Brace & Jovanovich, 1971), p. 342, n. 53.
11. Alfred C. Kinsey et al., *Sexual Behavior in the Human Male* (Philadelphia: Saunders, 1948), p. 597.
12. Kinsey, *Sexual Behavior in the Human Male*, pp. 650–651; Alfred C. Kinsey et al., *Sexual Behavior in the Human Female* (Philadelphia: Saunders, 1953), pp. 474–475.
13. Emile Durkheim, *Suicide: A Study in Sociology*, trans. John A. Spaulding and George Simpson (New York: Free Press, 1951).
14. Erich Goode, *Drugs in American Society* (New York: Knopf, 1972), p. 145.
15. Joel Fort, *Alcohol: Our Biggest Drug Problem* (New York: McGraw-Hill, 1973), pp. 114–115.
16. Goode, *Drugs in American Society*, p. 143.
17. Don Cahalan, *Problem Drinkers* (San Francisco: Jossey-Bass, 1970) p. 142.
18. G. Lolli, quoted in Israel Zwerling and Milton Rosenbaum, "Alcoholic Addiction and Personality," in Silvano Arieti, ed., *American Handbook of Psychiatry*, (New York: Basic Books, 1959) p. 627.
19. David McClelland, William N. Davis, Rudolf Kalin, Eric Wanner, *The Drinking Man*, (N.Y.: The Free Press, 1972) p. 334.
20. L. Kaiij, *Alcoholism in Twins: Studies on the Etiology and Sequels of Abuse of Alcohol* (Stockholm: Alcuquist and Wiksell, 1960).
21. D. A. Rodgers and G. E. McClearn, "Mouse Strain Differences in Preference for Various Concentrations of Alcohol," *Quarterly Journal of Studies on Alcohol*, 23 (1962) 26–33.

22. John Clausen, "Mental Disorders," in Merton and Nisbet, eds., *Contemporary Social Problems*, p. 29.

23. See Thomas Scheff, *Being Mentally Ill: A Sociological Theory* (Chicago: Aldine, 1966), and Thomas S. Szasz, *The Myth of Mental Illness* (New York: Harper, 1961).

24. Kenneth Westhues, *Society's Shadow: Studies in the Sociology of Countercultures* (Toronto: McGraw-Hill Ryerson, 1972), pp. 15–17.

25. Howard Becker, *Outsiders: Studies in the Sociology of Deviance* (New York: Free Press of Glencoe, 1963), pp. 19–22.

26. See Aaron V. Cicourel, *Social Organization of Juvenile Justice* (New York: Wiley, 1968).

27. Gary T. Marx, "Civil Disorder and the Agents of Social Control," *Journal of Social Issues*, 26 (Winter 1970), 19–58.

28. Edwin H. Sutherland, *White Collar Crime* (New York: Dryden, 1949).

29. Erving Goffman, *Stigma: Notes on the Management of Spoiled Identity* (Englewood Cliffs, N.J.: Prentice-Hall, 1963).

30. On this point see Barbara Wooton, "Sickness or Sin," *The Twentieth Century*, 159 (1959), 432–442.

31. Travis Hirschi, *Causes of Delinquency* (Berkeley and Los Angeles: University of California Press, 1969).

32. See David Rosenthal and Seymour Kety, eds., *The Transmission of Schizophrenia* (London: Pergamon, 1969), pp. 175–266.

33. See James S. Coleman, *The Adolescent Society: The Social Life of the Teenager and Its Impact on Education* (New York: The Free Press of Glencoe, 1961).

34. See Robert Martinson, "What Works? Questions and Answers about Prison Reform," *The Public Interest*, 35 (Spring 1974), 22–54.

35. See Norman Jaspan, with Hillel Black, *The Thief in the White Collar* (Philadelphia: Lippincott, 1960), pp. 233–234.

36. U.S. Congress, Senate, Committee on Government Operations, *Gambling and Organized Crime: Report of the Permanent Subcommittee on Investigations*, 87th Cong. 2d sess., 1962, S. Rept. 1310, pp. 13–16.

37. See Kingsley Davis, "The Sociology of Prostitution," *American Sociological Review*, vol. 2 (October 1937), 744–755, and "Prostitution," in Robert K. Merton and Robert Nisbet, eds., *Contemporary Social Problems*, (New York: Harcourt, Brace, 1952), pp. 262–288.

38. Compare Kai T. Erikson, "Notes on the Sociology of Deviance," *Social Problems*, 9 (Spring 1962), 307–314.

39. See George Herbert Mead, "The Psychology of Punitive Justice," in Lewis A. Coser and Bernard Rosenberg, eds., *Sociological Theory: A Book of Readings*, 2nd ed., (New York: Macmillan, 1964), p. 596.

40. See Robert A. Dentler and Kai T. Erikson, "The Functions of Deviance in Groups," *Social Problems*, 7 (Fall 1959), 98–107.

41. See Lewis A. Coser, "Some Functions of Deviant Behavior and Normative Flexibility," *American Journal of Sociology*, 68 (September 1962), 174.

42. Albert K. Cohen, "The Sociology of the Deviant Act: Anomie Theory and Beyond," *American Sociological Review*, 30 (February 1965), 10. Based on William J. Chambliss, "The Deterrent Influence of Punishment: A Study of the Violation of Parking Regulations" (M.A. diss., Indiana University, 1960).

43. Emile Durkheim, *The Rules of Sociological Method*, 8th ed., trans. Sarah Solovnay and John H. Mueller, ed. George E. H. Catlin (New York: Free Press, 1950), pp. 68–69.

44. Kai T. Erikson, *Wayward Puritans* (New York: Wiley, 1966), p. 6.

45. See Samuel A. Stouffer's classical study, "An Analysis of Conflicting Social Norms," *American Sociological Review*, 18 (December 1949), 707–717.

46. Cesare Lombroso, *Crime: Its Causes and Remedies* (Boston: Little, Brown, 1918, translated from French edition of 1899), p. 376.

47. Charles Goring, *The English Convict* (London: His Majesty's Stationery Office, 1913).

48. William H. Sheldon, in collaboration with Emil H. Hartl and Eugene McDermott, *Varieties of Delinquent Youth* (New York: Harper, 1956).

49. Sheldon Glueck and Eleanor Glueck, *Physique and Delinquency* (New York: Harper, 1956).

50. Kennedy McWhirter, "XYY Chromosomes and Criminal Acts," *Science*, June 6, 1969. See also Amir J. Berman, "Chromosomal Deviation and Crime," *Federal Probation*, June 1970, pp. 55–62.

51. One of the most careful and systematic studies in this vein is Albert Bandura and Richard H. Walters, *Adolescent Aggression* (New York: Ronald Press, 1959), especially Chap. 6.

52. John Dollard, Leonard W. Doob, Neal E. Miller, O. H. Mowrer, and Robert R. Sears, *Frustration and Aggression* (New Haven, Conn.: Yale University Press, 1939). See also Elton B. McNeil, "Psychology and Aggression," *The Journal of Conflict Resolution*, 3 (September 1959), 195–294; O. H. Mowrer, "Frustration and Aggression," in *Encyclopedia of Criminology* (New York: Philosophical Library, 1949), pp. 176–186.

53. Andrew F. Henry and James F. Short, Jr., *Suicide and Homicide* (Glencoe, Ill.: Free Press, 1954); "The Sociology of Suicide," in Edwin S. Schneidman and Norman L. Farberow, eds., *Clues to Suicide*, (New York: McGraw-Hill, 1957), pp. 58–69.

54. For an alternative interpretation of the causes of suicide, see Jack P. Gibbs and Walter T. Martin, *Status Integration and Suicide* (Eugene: University of Oregon Books, 1964).

55. Albert K. Cohen, *Delinquent Boys: The Culture of the Gang* (Glencoe, Ill.: Free Press, 1955).

56. Emile Durkheim, *The Division of Labor in Society* (New York: Free Press of Glencoe, 1964), Book 3, pp. 353–373.

57. Robert K. Merton, "Social Structure and Anomie," *American Sociological Review,* 3 (October 1938), 672–682. Revised and enlarged in R. K. Merton, *Social Theory and Social Structure* (Glencoe, Ill.: Free Press, 1957), pp. 131–194.

58. Clifford R. Shaw, *The Jack-Roller* (Chicago: University of Chicago Press, 1930), *The Natural History of a Delinquent Career* (Chicago: University of Chicago Press, 1931), and *Brothers in Crime* (Chicago: University of Chicago Press, 1938); Clifford R. Shaw and Henry D. McKay, *Social Factors in Juvenile Delinquency,* vol. 2 of National Committee on Law Observance and Law Enforcement, *Report on the Causes of Crime* (Washington, D.C.: Government Printing Office, 1931), and *Juvenile Delinquency and Urban Areas* (Chicago: University of Chicago Press, 1942).

59. Shaw and McKay, *Social Factors in Juvenile Delinquency,* p. 387.

60. See Edwin H. Sutherland and Donald R. Cressey, *Principles of Criminology,* 6th ed. (Philadelphia: Lippincott, 1960), chap. 4; Alfred Cohen, Alfred Lindesmith, and Karl Schuessler, eds., *The Sutherland Papers* (Bloomington: Indiana University Press, 1956), pp. 5–43; and Donald Cressey, *Delinquency, Crime and Differential Association,* (The Hague: Martinus Nijhoff, 1964). See also the commentaries by Daniel Glaser: "Differential Association and Criminological Prediction," *Social Problems,* 7 (Summer 1960), 2–6, "The Sociological Approach to Crime and Correction," *Law and Contemporary Problems,* 23 (Autumn 1958), 683–702, and "The Differential Association Theory of Crime," in Arnold M. Rose, ed., *Human Behavior and Social Processes: An Interactionist Approach* (Boston: Houghton Mifflin, 1962), pp. 425–442.

61. See Erving Goffman, *Stigma* (Englewood Cliffs, N.J.: Prentice-Hall, 1963).

62. George Grosser, "Juvenile Delinquency and Contemporary American Sex Roles" (Ph. D. diss., Harvard University, 1952).

63. Cohen, "The Sociology of the Deviant Act," p. 13.

64. One important effort to integrate cultural-transmission and anomie theory is the work of Richard A. Cloward and Lloyd B. Ohlin, *Delinquency and Opportunity: A Theory of Delinquent Gangs* (Glencoe, Ill.: Free Press, 1960).

65. For a discussion of moral responsibility and mental illness, see Helmut Schoeck and James Wiggins eds., *Psychiatry and Responsibility* (New York: Van Nostrand, 1962).

66. M. R. Yarrow, "The Psychological Meaning of Mental Illness in the Family," *Journal of Social Issues,* 11 (Dec. 1955) 12–24.

67. Benjamin Malzberg, *Migration in Relation to Mental Disease* (Albany, New York: Research Foundation for Mental Hygeine, Inc., 1968).

68. There are complex methodological difficulties involved in comparing rates of mental illness for males and females. For a discussion see Walter R. Gove and Jeannette Tudor, "Sex Differences in Mental Illness," *American Journal of Sociology* 82 (6) May, 1977, pp. 1327–36.

69. See especially Jerome K. Myers and Lee L. Bean, *A Decade Later: A Follow-Up of Social Class and Mental Illness* (New York: Wiley, 1968).

70. M. Harvey Brenner, *Mental Illness and The Economy,* (Cambridge, Mass: Harvard University Press, 1973).

71. Peter E. Nathan and Sandra L. Harris, *Psychopathology and Society* (New York: McGraw-Hill, 1975) p. 338.

## Chapter 8

### Organizations

1. See Robert Presthus, *The Organizational Society* (New York: Knopf, 1962).

2. Talcott Parsons, *Structure and Process in Modern Societies* (Glencoe, Ill.: Free Press, 1960), p. 17.

3. For a thorough discussion of who does and does not join and for the information on which this paragraph is based, see Nicholas Babchuk and Alan Booth, "Voluntary Association Membership: A Longitudinal Analysis," *American Sociological Review,* 34 (February 1969), and James Curtis, "Voluntary Association Joining: A Cross-National Comparative Note," *American Sociological Review,* 36 (October 1971).

4. Curtis, op. cit.

5. Presthus, p. 74.

6. Max Weber, *The Theory of Social and Economic Organization,* trans. by A. M. Henderson and Talcott Parsons (New York: Macmillan Publishing Company, Inc., 1947). © 1947, 1975 by Talcott Parsons.

7. This discussion draws upon Amitai Etzioni, *A Comparative Analysis of Complex Organizations* (New York: Free Press, 1961).

8. K. J. Scudder, "The Open Institution," *Annals of the American Academy of Political and Social Science,* 293 (1954), 80–82.

9. See H. A. Simon, *Administrative Behavior* (New York: Macmillan, 1945), for a full discussion of socialization as a means of control.

10. Frederick W. Taylor, *Scientific Management* (New York: Harper, 1911).

11. See, for example, Luther Gulick and L. Urwin, eds., *Papers on the Science of Administration* (New York: Columbia University, Institute of Public Administration, 1937).

12. For a summary of the Hawthorne studies see F. J. Roethlisberger and W. J. Dickson, *Management and The Worker* (Cambridge, Mass.: Harvard University Press, 1939).

13. Alex Carey, "The Hawthorne Studies: A Radical Criticism," *American Sociological Review*, 32 (June 1967), 403–416.

14. Reinhard Bendix and Lloyd Fisher, "Perspective of Elton Mayo," in Amitai Etzioni, ed., *Complex Organizations* (New York: Holt, Rinehart and Winston, 1961).

15. Robert Dubin, "Industrial Workers' Worlds: A Study of the Central Life Interests of Industrial Workers," *Social Problems*, 4 (1956), 136.

16. D. R. Walker and R. H. Guest, *The Man on the Assembly Line* (Cambridge, Mass.: Harvard University Press, 1952).

17. Ibid., p. 91.

18. Edward Harvey, "Technology and the Structure of Organizations," *American Sociological Review*, 33 (April 1968), 255.

19. Charles Perrow, *Organizational Analysis: A Sociological View* (Belmont, Calif.: Wadsworth, 1970).

20. Martin King Whyte, "Bureaucaracy and Modernization in China: The Maoist Critique," *American Sociological Review*, 38 (April 1973), 149–163.

21. See G. William Skinner and Edwin A. Winckler, "Compliance Succession in Rural Communist China: A Cyclical Theory," in Amitai Etzioni, ed., *A Sociological Reader on Complex Organizations*, 2nd ed. (New York: Holt, Rinehart and Winston, 1969).

22. Theodore Roszak, *The Making of a Counterculture* (New York: Doubleday, 1969).

23. Charles A. Reich, *The Greening of America* (New York: Random House, 1970).

24. William H. Whyte, Jr., *The Organization Man* (New York: Simon & Schuster, 1956).

25. Robert Merton, *Social Theory and Social Structure*, rev. ed. (Glencoe, Ill.: Free Press, 1957), chap. 6.

26. Melvin Kohn, "Bureaucratic Man: A Portrait and an Interpretation," *American Sociological Review*, 36 (June 1971), 461–474.

## Chapter 9
## Social stratification

1. For details see J. Richard Udry, "The Importance of Being Beautiful: A Reexamination and Racial Comparison," *American Journal of Sociology*, 83, no. 1 (July 1977), 154–60.

2. Saul Feldman, "The Presentation of Shortness in Everyday Life: Height and Heightism in American Society: Toward a Sociology of Stature," Paper presented at the American Sociological Association Convention in Denver, 1971.

3. Gerald Berreman, "Caste in India and the United States," *American Journal of Sociology*, 64 (September 1960), 120–127.

4. Gerhard Lenski, *Power and Privilege* (New York: McGraw-Hill, 1966).

5. See, e.g., Marvin E. Olsen and Judy Corder Tully, "Socioeconomic-Ethnic Status Inconsistency and Preference for Political Change," *American Sociological Review*, 37 (October 1972), 560–574.

6. Thorstein Veblen, *The Theory of the Leisure Class* (New York: New American Library, 1954).

7. See Gunnar Myrdal, *Asian Drama* (New York: Twentieth Century Fund, 1968).

8. Christopher Jencks, Marshall Smith, Henry Acland, Mary Jo Bane, David Cohen, Herbert Gintis, Barbara Heyns, and Stephan Michelson, *Inequality: A Reassessment of the Effect of Family and Schooling in America* (New York: Basic Books, 1972) p. 209.

9. Ibid., p. 210.

10. Ibid., p. 211.

11. U.S. Department of Commerce, *Statistical Abstract of the United States* (Washington, D.C., 1976), p. 415.

12. National Council on Welfare, *The Working Poor* (Ottawa, Ontario, June 1977), p. 1.

13. *The Working Poor*, p. 12.

14. *The Working Poor*, p. 29.

15. U.S. Department of Labor, Bureau of Labor Statistics, Bulletin 1875: *Occupational Outlook Handbook*, 1976–77 ed. (Washington, D.C., 1976), p. 19, Table 10.

16. *Statistical Abstract*, p. 413.

17. Ibid., p. 411.

18. Ibid., p. 415.

19. David Caplovitz, *The Poor Pay More: Consumer Practices of Low-Income Families* (New York: Free Press, 1963).

20. National Council of Welfare, *The Hidden Welfare System* (Ottawa, Ontario: National Council of Welfare, November 1976).

21. Larry L. Bumpass and James A. Sweet, "Differentials in Marital Instability," *American Sociological Review*, 37 (December 1972), 754–66.

22. Dennis Wrong, "Trends in Class Fertility in Western Nations," in Reinhard Bendix and S. M. Lipset, eds., *Class, Status, and Power* (New York: Free Press, 1963), pp. 353–354.

23. Urie Bronfenbrenner, "Socialization and Social Class Through Time and Space," in Eleanor Maccoby, T. M. Newcomb, and E. L. Hartley, eds., *Readings in Social Psychology* (New York: Holt, 1958), pp. 400–426.

24. William J. Goode, *After Divorce* (Glencoe, Ill.: Free Press, 1956), p. 46.

25. *Statistical Abstract*, p. 61.

26. Melvin Tumin and W. Arnold Feldman, *Social Class and Social Change in Puerto Rico* (Princeton, N.J.: Princeton University Press, 1961).

27. James Curtis, "Voluntary Associations Joining: A Cross-National Comparative Note," *American Sociological Review*, 36 (October 1971), 875.

28. Liston Pope, "Religion and the Class Structure," *Annals of the American Academy of Political and Social Science*, March 1948, pp. 84–91.

29. S. M. Lipset, *Political Man: The Social Bases of*

*Politics* (Garden City, N.Y.: Doubleday, 1959), esp. chap. 4.

30. H. Edward Ransford, "Blue Collar Anger: Reactions to Student and Black Protest," *American Sociological Review*, 37 (June 1972), 333–46.

31. Dale Fitzgeralds, "Social Participation and Its Effects on Personality," unpublished manuscript.

32. Robert M. Hauser and David L. Featherman, "Trends in the Occupational Mobility of United States Men, 1962–70," *American Sociological Review*, 38 (June 1973), 302–310.

33. On this point see Natalie Rogoff, *Recent Trends in Occupational Mobility* (Glencoe, Ill: Free Press, 1953).

34. S. M. Lipset and Reinhard Bendix, *Social Mobility in Industrial Society* (Berkeley: University of California Press, 1960).

35. Peter M. Blau and Otis Dudley Duncan, *The American Occupational Structure*, (New York: Wiley, 1967).

36. Lipset and Bendix, p. 73.

37. Blau and Duncan, p. 79.

38. Ibid., p. 262.

39. Ibid., pp. 300–301.

40. Ibid, pp. 355–359.

41. Jonathan Kelley, "Causal Chain Models for the Socioeconomic Career," *American Sociological Review*, 38 (August 1973), 493.

42. Harold Wilensky and Hugh Edmonds, "The Skidder: Ideological Adjustments of Downwardly Mobile Workers," *American Sociological Review*, 24 (April 1949), 215–231.

43. Bruno Bettelheim and Morris Janowitz, *Dynamics of Prejudice* (New York: Harper, 1950).

44. Andrew Hopkins, "Political Overconformity by Upwardly Mobile American Men," *American Sociological Review*, 38 (February 1973), 143–147.

45. August Hollingshead, R. Ellis, and E. Kirby, "Social Mobility and Mental Illness," *American Sociological Review*, 19 (October 1954), 577–583.

46. Peter M. Blau, "Occupational Bias and Mobility," *American Sociological Review*, 22 (August 1957), 393–399.

47. Hans Gerth and C. W. Mills, *From Max Weber* (New York: Oxford University Press, 1958), p. 194.

48. Ibid., p. 94.

49. W. Lloyd Warner, *The Social Life of a Modern Community* (New Haven, Conn.: Yale University Press, 1955).

50. Kingsley Davis and Wilbert E. Moore, "Some Principles of Stratification," *American Sociological Review*, 10 (April 1945), 242–249.

51. Ibid., p 244.

52. Wlodzimierz Wesolowski, "Some Notes on the Functional Theory of Stratification," in Lipset and Bendix, op. cit.

53. G. William Domhoff, *The Bohemian Grove and Other Retreats: A Study in Ruling-Class Cohesiveness* (New York: Harper & Row, 1974).

54. Ibid., pp. 31–2.

## Chapter 10
### Racial and ethnic groups

1. This definition is drawn largely from Frederick Barth, "Introduction," in Frederick Barth, ed., *Ethnic Groups and Boundaries* (Boston: Little, Brown, 1969), pp. 10–11.

2. See Harald Eidheim, "When Ethnic Identity Is a Social Stigma," in Barth, pp. 39–57.

3. Kathleen O'Brien Jackson, "Introduction to the American Indians," in Rudolph Gomez, Clement Cottingham, Jr., Russell Endo, and Kathleen Jackson, eds., *The Social Reality of Ethnic America* (Lexington, Mass.: Heath, 1974), p. 126.

4. For a thorough discussion of the past plight and future prospects of the American Indians, see Murray L. Wax, *Indian Americans* (Englewood Cliffs, N.J.: Prentice-Hall, 1971).

5. Fred Gross, "Indian Island: a Micmac Reserve," in Jean L. Elliott, ed., *Native Peoples* (Scarborough, Ontario: Prentice-Hall of Canada, 1971), p. 92.

6. See Frank G. Vallee, "Eskimos of Canada as a Minority Group," in Elliott, op. cit.

7. Stanford Lyman, "Red Guard on Grant Avenue," *Trans-Action*, 7 (April 1970), 21–34.

8. Charles F. Marden and Gladys Meyer, *Minorities in American Society*, 3rd ed. (New York: Van Nostrand Reinhold, 1968), p. 213.

9. William Peterson, "Success Story: Japanese American Style," *New York Times Magazine*, January 9, 1966, p. 36.

10. Marden and Meyer, p. 131.

11. Rudolph Gomez, "Mexican Americans: From Internal Colonialism to the Chicano Movement," in Gomez et al., p. 323.

12. See Joan W. Moore, *Mexican Americans* (Englewood Cliffs, N.J.: Prentice-Hall, 1970).

13. See Stanley Lieberson, *Language and Ethnic Relations in Canada* (New York: Wiley, 1970).

14. Robin W. Winks, *The Blacks in Canada* (New Haven, Conn.: Yale University Press, 1971), p. 1.

15. E. Franklin Frazier, *The Negro in the United States* (New York: Macmillan, 1959), p. 34.

16. Winks, p. 11.

17. Ibid., p. 29.

18. Robert Fogel and Stanley Engermann, *Time on the Cross* (Boston: Little, Brown, 1974).

19. See Marden and Meyer, p. 225.

20. Reynolds Farley, "Trends in Racial Inequalities: Have the Gains of the 1960s Disappeared in the 1970s?" *American Sociological Review*, 42, no. 2 (April 1977), 189–207.

21. Farley, p. 190.

22. Ibid.

23. Ibid., p. 206.

24. Ibid.

25. E. Digby Baltzell, *The Protestant Establishment: Aristocracy and Caste in America* (New York: Random House, 1964), pp. 110–114.

26. Charles Y. Glock and Rodney Stark, *Christian Be-*

*liefs and Anti-Semitism* (New York: Harper & Row, 1966).

27. Charles Y. Glock, Robert Wuthnow, Jane Piliavin, and Metta Spencer, *Adolescent Prejudice* (New York: Harper & Row, 1975).

28. M. Sklare, *America's Jews* (New York: Random House, 1971), pp. 182–191.

29. Herbert Blumer, "Race Prejudice as a Sense of Group Position," in J. Masuoka and P. Valien, eds., *Race Relations: Problems and Theory* (Chapel Hill: University of North Carolina Press, 1961), pp. 217–227.

30. Gertrude J. Selznick and Stephen Steinberg, *The Tenacity of Prejudice* (New York: Harper & Row, 1969).

31. See, e.g., Madison Grant, *The Passing of the Great Race* (New York: Scribner's, 1916).

32. M. F. Ashley Montagu, *Man's Most Dangerous Myth: The Fallacy of Race*, 4th ed. (Cleveland: World, 1964).

33. Karl Deutsch, *Nationalism and Its Alternatives* (New York: Knopf, 1969).

34. Robert Blauner, "Internal Colonialism and Ghetto Revolt," *Social Problems*, 16 (Spring 1969), 393–408.

35. Wolfram Eberhard, *Conquerors and Rulers: Social Forces in Medieval China* (Leiden: Brill, 1965), pp. 1–11.

36. Ruby Jo Reeves Kennedy, "Single or Triple Melting Pot? Intermarriage Trends in New Haven, 1870–1940," *American Journal of Sociology*, 49 (January 1944); see also Will Herberg, *Protestant, Catholic, Jew* (New York: Doubleday, 1960).

37. Andrew Greeley, *Ethnicity in the United States* (New York: Wiley, 1974).

38. Arthur R. Jensen, "How Much Can We Boost IQ and Scholastic Achievement?" *Harvard Educational Review*, 28 (Winter 1969), 1–123.

39. Muzafer Sherif, *In Common Predicament* (Boston: Houghton Mifflin, 1966), pp. 71–93.

40. Ibid., p. 84.

41. Harold Garfinkel, *Studies in Ethnomethodology* (Englewood Cliffs, N.J.: Prentice-Hall, 1967), chap. 2.

**Chapter 11**
## Collective behavior and social movements

1. Neil J. Smelser, *The Theory of Collective Behavior* (New York: Free Press, 1962).

2. Gustave Le Bon, *The Crowd* (New York: Viking, 1960), first published in 1895.

3. Sigmund Freud, *Group Psychology and the Analysis of the Ego* (New York: Liveright, 1951).

4. See Herbert Blumer's articles in Robert R. Evans, ed., *Readings on Collective Behavior* (Chicago: Rand McNally, 1969).

5. For a more ample critique of these theories, see Richard A. Berk, *Collective Behavior* (Chicago: William Brown, 1974).

6. E. D. Martin, *The Behavior of Crowds* (New York: Harper, 1920), p. 37.

7. Floyd H. Allport, *Social Psychology* (Boston: Houghton Mifflin, 1924), p. 295.

8. For a fuller discussion of convergence theory, see Ralph H. Turner, "Collective Behavior," in Robert E. L. Faris, ed., *Handbook of Modern Sociology* (Chicago: Rand McNally, 1964).

9. Ibid., p. 395.

10. Ralph H. Turner and Lewis M. Killian, *Collective Behavior*, 2nd ed. (Englewood Cliffs, N.J.: Prentice-Hall, 1972), p. 23.

11. Roger Brown, *Social Psychology* (New York: Free Press, 1965). See also Berk, pp. 67–74.

12. Gordon Allport and L. Postman, *The Psychology of Rumor* (New York: Holt, 1947).

13. H. Taylor Buckner, "A Theory of Rumor Transmission," in Evans, pp. 120–134.

14. Turner and Killian, p. 179.

15. Elihu Katz, "The Two-Step Flow of Communication: An Up-to-Date Report on an Hypothesis," *Public Opinion Quarterly*, 21 (Spring 1957), 61.

16. W. Schramm, J. Lyle, and E. B. Parker, *Television in the Lives of Our Children* (Palo Alto, Calif.: Stanford University Press, 1961).

17. Walter Weiss, "Effects of the Mass Media of Communication," in Gardner Lindzey and Elliot Aronson, eds., *The Handbook of Social Psychology*, 2nd ed. (Reading, Mass.: Addison-Wesley, 1969), p. 133.

18. David P. Phillips, "The Influence of Suggestion on Suicide: Substantive and Theoretical Implications of the Werther Effect," *American Sociological Review*, 39 (June 1974), 340–354.

19. Martin F. Herz, "Some Psychological Lessons from Leaflet Propaganda in World War II," *Public Opinion Quarterly*, 13 (Fall 1949), 471–486.

20. Hadley Cantril, Hazel Gaudet, and H. Herzog, *Invasion from Mars* (Princeton, N.J.: Princeton University Press, 1940).

21. Donald M. Johnson, "The Phantom Anesthetist of Mattoon: A Field Study of Mass Hysteria," *Journal of Abnormal and Social Psychology*, 40 (April 1945), 175–186.

22. This is Herbert Blumer's definition in A. M. Lee, ed., *Principles of Sociology*, 2nd ed. (New York: Barnes and Noble, 1964), p. 199.

23. Alain Touraine, *Sociologie de l'action* (Paris: Editions du Seuil, 1965). For a brief summary of Touraine's position in English, see Guy Rocher, *A General Introduction to Sociology: A Theoretical Perspective* (Toronto: Macmillan, 1972).

24. Norman Cohn, *The Pursuit of the Millennium* (New York: Oxford University Press, 1970).

25. Touraine, op. cit.

26. Carl A. Dawson and Warner E. Gettys, *Introduction*

to *Sociology*, rev. ed. (New York: Ronald Press, 1934), pp. 708–709.

27. Frances Fox Piven and Richard A. Cloward, *Poor People's Movements* (New York: Pantheon, 1977), p. 264.

28. Ibid., p. 267.

29. Ibid., p. 268.

30. Ibid., p. 271.

31. Ibid., p. 274.

32. Ibid., p. 324.

33. Ibid., p. 336.

34. Ibid., p. 346.

35. Joseph D. Lohman, *The Police and Minority Groups* (Chicago: Chicago Park District, 1947).

36. See Rodney Stark, *Police Riots* (Belmont, Calif: Wadsworth, 1972).

## Chapter 12
## The family

1. George P. Murdock, *Social Structure* (New York: Macmillan, 1949), pp. 213–214.

2. William J. Goode, *The Family* (Englewood Cliffs, N.J.: Prentice-Hall, 1964), p. 218.

3. David A. Schulz, *The Changing Family* (Englewood Cliffs, N.J.: Prentice-Hall, 1972), pp. 54–55.

4. Louis M. Terman, *Psychological Factors in Marital Happiness* (New York: McGraw-Hill, 1938).

5. See Kenneth L. Cannon and Richard Long, "Premarital Sexual Behavior in the Sixties," in Carlfred B. Broderick, ed., *A Decade of Family Research and Action* (Washington, D.C.: National Council on Family Relations, n.d.).

6. Ibid.

7. R. R. Wake, "Attitudes of Parents Toward the Premarital Sex Behavior of Their Children and Themselves," *Journal of Sex Research*, 5 (1969), 170–171.

8. See Alfred Kinsey, Wardell B. Pomeroy, and Clyde E. Martin, *Sexual Behavior in the Human Male* (Philadelphia: Saunders, 1948).

9. Mary E. Heltsley and Carlfred B. Broderick, "Religiosity and Premarital Sexual Permissiveness," *Journal of Marriage and the Family*, 31 (1969), 441–443.

10. Shere Hite, *The Hite Report: A Nationwide Study on Female Sexuality* (New York: Macmillan, 1976).

11. Wardell B. Pomeroy, "Homosexuality," in Ralph W. Weltge, ed., *The Same Sex: An Appraisal of Homosexuality* (Philadelphia: Pilgrim Press, 1969), p. 8.

12. "The Weekend Poll," *Weekend* Magazine, December 3, 1977, p. 3.

13. Evelyn Hooker, "The Adjustment of the Male Overt Homosexual," *Journal of Projective Techniques*, 21 (February, 1957), 18–31.

14. Martin S. Weinberg and Colin J. Williams, *Male Homosexuals: Their Problems and Adaptations* (New York: Oxford University Press, 1974), pp. 235–240.

15. James J. Lynch, *The Broken Heart* (New York: Basic Books, 1977).

16. Schulz, *Family* pp. 227, 228.

17. Eleanor B. Luckey, "Perceptual Congruence of Self and Family Concepts as Related to Marital Interaction," *Sociometry*, 24 (September 1966), 234–250. See also Eleanor Braun Luckey and Joyce Koym Bain, "Children: A Factor in Marital Satisfaction," *Journal of Marriage and the Family*, 32 (1970), 43–44.

18. Matilda White Riley and Anne Foner, *Aging and Society* (New York: Russell Sage, 1968), I, 169.

19. Michael Young and Peter Wilmott, *Family and Kinship in East London* (Glencoe, Ill.: Free Press, 1957).

20. Peter C. Pineo, "The Extended Family in a Working-Class Area of Hamilton," in Bernard Blishen et al., eds., *Canadian Society* (Toronto: Macmillan of Canada, 1971), pp. 115–125.

21. These data are summarized by Bert N. Adams, "Isolation, Function and Beyond: American Kinship in the 1960's," in Broderick, op. cit. See also Bert N. Adams, *Kinship in an Urban Setting* (Chicago: Markham, 1968).

22. K. Ishwaren, *The Canadian Family* (Toronto: Holt, Rinehard and Winston, 1971).

23. Philippe Garigue, "French Canadian Kinship and Urban Life," *American Anthropologist*, 58 (1956) 1090–1101.

24. William J. Goode, "Illegitimacy, Anomie, and Cultural Pentration," *American Sociological Review*, 26 (December 1961), 910–925.

25. Judith Blake, *Family Structure in Jamaica* (Glencoe, Ill.: Free Press, 1961).

26. Arthur A. Campbell, "The Role of Family Planning in the Reduction of Poverty," *Journal of Marriage and the Family*, 30 (May 1968), 238.

27. William J. Goode, "Family Disorganization," in Robert K. Merton and Robert Nisbet, eds., *Contemporary Social Problems* (New York: Harcourt, Brace and World, 1961), p. 404.

28. Based on *Here to Stay: American Families in the Twentieth Century*, by Mary Jo Bane, © 1976 by Mary Jo Bane, Basic Books, Inc., Publishers, New York.

29. Ibid.

30. Ibid.

31. Ibid., p. 34.

32. William J. Goode, *After Divorce* (Glencoe, Ill.: Free Press, 1956).

33. See Judson T. Landis, "A Comparison of Children from Divorced and Nondivorced Unhappy Marriages," *Family Life Coordinator*, 11 (July 1962), 61–65.

34. Gerald R. Leslie, *The Family in Social Context* (New York: Oxford University Press, 1967), p. 619.

35. Murdock, chap. 1.

36. E. Kathleen Gough, "The Nayars and the Definition

of Marriage," *Journal of the Royal Anthropological Institute*, 89 (1954), 23–24.

37. M. E. Spiro, "Is the Family Universal?" *American Anthropologist*, 56 (1954), 839–846.

38. Professor Brandenburgsky, as cited by Vladimir Gsovski, "Family and Inheritance in Soviet Law," in Alex Inkeles and Kent Geiger, eds., *Soviet Society* (Boston: Houghton Mifflin, 1961), p. 533.

39. E. Franklin Frazier, *The Negro Family in the United States* (Chicago: University of Chicago Press, 1939.)

40. Friedrich Engels, *Origin of the Family, Private Property, and the State*, ed. Eleanor B. Leacock (New York: International Publishers, 1971).

41. Karl Marx, *Capital* (New York: Modern Library), pp. 432–439.

42. Engels, p. 145.

43. See Talcott Parsons, *The System of Modern Societies* (Englewood Cliffs, N.J.: Prentice-Hall, 1971), esp. p. 26.

44. Neil J. Smelser, *Social Change in the Industrial Revolution* (Chicago: University of Chicago Press, 1959).

45. William J. Goode, *World Revolution and Family Patterns* (New York: Free Press, 1971).

46. Peter Laslett, *Family and Household in Past Time* (Cambridge: University of Cambridge Press, 1973).

47. Talcott Parsons and Robert Freed Bales, *Family: Socialization and Interaction Process* (Glencoe, Ill.: Free Press, 1955).

48. For an excellent survey of this topic see Lillian E. Troll, "The Family in Later Life," in Broderick, op. cit.

49. See Harold Fedman, "Development of the Husband-Wife Relationship," Preliminary Report, Cornell Studies in Marital Development, 1964.

50. See Elliott Feigenbaum, Marjorie F. Lowenthal, and Mella L. Trier, "Sexual Attitudes in the Elderly," paper presented at Gerontological Society meeting, New York, 1966.

51. Troll, p. 202.

52. Ethel Shanas et al., *Older People in Three Industrial Societies* (New York: Atherton, 1968), p. 166.

53. For a good discussion of a retirement village for welfare recipients, see Arlie R. Hochschild, *The Unexpected Community* (Englewood Cliffs, N.J.: Prentice-Hall, 1973).

54. Bane, op cit.

55. Ibid., p. 19.

56. Ibid., p. 9.

57. Ibid., p. 19.

58. Ibid., p. 22.

59. Ibid., p. 25.

60. Ibid., p. 60.

61. Kate Millett, *Sexual Politics* (New York: Doubleday, 1970).

62. R. D. Laing, *The Politics of the Family* (New York: Pantheon, 1971).

63. Frederick H. Stroller, "The Intimate Network of Families as a New Structure," in Herbert A. Otto,

ed., *The Family in Search of a Future: Alternate Models for Moderns* (Englewood Cliffs, N.J.: Prentice-Hall, 1970).

## Chapter 13
## Religion

1. David E. Sopher, *Geography of Religions* (Englewood Cliffs, N.J.: Prentice-Hall, 1967), p. 7.

2. Max Weber, *Theory of Social and Economic Organization*, trans. A. M. Henderson and Talcott Parsons, ed. Talcott Parsons (New York: Oxford University Press, 1947) pp. 358–359.

3. Ibid., p. 364.

4. Susanne K. Langer, *Philosophy in a New Key* (Cambridge, Mass: Harvard University Press, 1957), p. 40.

5. See Max Weber, *The Sociology of Religion*, trans. E. Fischoffs, (Boston: Beacon Press, 1964.)

6. Joaquim Wach, *The Sociology of Religion* (Chicago: University of Chicago Press, 1944), p. 111.

7. This conflict is spelled out in a book by Charles Y. Glock, Benjamin Ringer, and Earl R. Babbie, *To Comfort and to Challenge* (Berkeley and Los Angeles: University of California Press, 1967).

8. Luke M. Smith, "The Clergy: Authority, Structure, Ideology, Migration," *American Sociological Review*, 28 (June 1953), 242–248.

9. Kingsley Davis, *Human Society* (New York: Macmillan, 1948), p. 531.

10. Emile Durkheim, *The Elementary Forms of Religious Life*, trans. Joseph Ward Swain (Glencoe, Ill.: Free Press, 1954).

11. Bronislaw Malinowski, *Magic, Science, and Religion* (Glencoe, Ill.: Free Press, 1954), pp. 39–40.

12. Ibid., pp. 28–29.

13. This discussion of witchcraft and sorcery owes much to an unpublished paper by Dward E. Walker, Jr.

14. Weber, p. 97.

15. Ibid., pp. 80,97.

16. Ibid., p. 91.

17. Ibid., p. 90.

18. Ibid., p. 107.

19. Ibid., pp. 97, 104.

20. See Charles Y. Glock and Rodney Stark, *Religion and Society in Tension* (Chicago: Rand McNally, 1965); also Michael Argyle, *Religious Behavior* (London: Routledge and Kegan Paul, 1958), pp. 130–131.

21. Stefan Christopher, John Fearon, John McCorg, and Charles Noble, "Social Deprivation and Religiosity," *Journal for the Scientific Study of Religion*, 40 (Winter 1971), 385–395.

22. Jacob J. Lindenthal, Jerome K. Myers, Max P. Pepper, and Maxine S. Stern, "Mental Status and Religious Behavior," *Journal for the Scientific Study of*

*Religion,* 9 (Summer 1970), 143–149.

23. Ray Allen Billington, *The Protestant Crusade, 1800–1860* (New York: Rinehart, 1938), p. 24.
24. See Seymour Martin Lipset and Earl Raab, *The Politics of Unreason* (New York: Harper & Row, 1970), pp. 47–59.
25. Durkheim, p. 416.
26. Sigmund Freud, *The Future of an Illusion,* trans. W. D. Robson-Scott (Garden City, N.Y.: Doubleday, 1957), p. 3.
27. Ibid, p. 45.
28. Ibid., p. 88.
29. Max Weber. *The Protestant Ethic and the Spirit of Capitalism,* trans. Talcott Parsons (New York: Scribner's, 1930).
30. Max Weber, *General Economic History* (New York: Free Press, 1961).
31. Quoted by Weber in *The Protestant Ethic,* p. 175.
32. N. J. Demerath III and Phillip E. Hammond, *Religion in Social Context* (New York: Random House, 1969), p. 90.
33. Ibid., p. 98.
34. Gary T. Marx, "Religion: Opiate or Inspiration of Civil Rights Militancy Among Negroes?" *American Sociological Review,* 32 (February 1967), 64–73.
35. Charles Y. Glock and Rodney Stark, *Christian Beliefs and Anti-Semitism* (New York: Harper & Row, 1966).
36. N. J. Demerath III, *Social Class in American Protestantism* (Chicago: Rand McNally, 1965).
37. Ibid.
38. Robert Bellah, *Beyond Belief* (New York: Harper & Row, 1970).
39. Peter Worsley, *The Trumpet Shall Sound* (London: MacGibbon, 1967), p. 224.
40. See Norman Cohn, *The Pursuit of the Millennium* (New York: Harper & Row, 1961).
41. Ibid., p. 315.
42. See Vittorio Lanternari, *The Religions of the Oppressed* (New York: Knopf, 1963).
43. Worsley, pp. 227–228.
44. Lanternari, p. 312.
45. Cohn, p. 310.
46. Robert Wuthnow, "The New Religions in Social Context," in Charles Y. Glock and Robert Bellah, eds., *The New Religious Consciousness* (Berkeley: University of California Press, 1976), pp. 267–294.
47. Ibid., p. 274.
48. Harvey Cox, *Turning East: The Promise and Peril of the New Orientalism* (New York: Simon and Schuster, 1977).
49. Ibid., p. 96.
50. Ibid., pp. 100–101.
51. Max Heirich, "Change of Heart: A Test of Some Widely Held Theories about Religious Conversion," *American Journal of Sociology,* 83, no. 3 (November 1977), 653–677.
52. See Thomas Kuhn, *The Structure of Scientific Revolutions* (Chicago: University of Chicago Press, 1970).

## Chapter 14
## Education

1. Jean Jacques Rousseau, *Emile,* trans. and ed. William Boyd (New York: Columbia University Press, 1956).
2. Talcott Parsons, "The School Class as a Social System," in A. H. Halsey, Jean Floud, and C. Arnold Anderson, eds., *Education, Economy, and Society,* (New York: Free Press, 1961).
3. See Bernard Bailyn, *Education in the Forming of American Society* (Chapel Hill: University of North Carolina Press, 1960).
4. Allan M. Cartter, "Scientific Manpower for 1970–1985," *Science,* April 9, 1971, pp. 132–136.
5. U.S. Bureau of the Census, *Statistical Abstract, 1975* (Washington, D.C., 1976), p. 133.
6. James Bryant Conant, *Slums and Suburbs* (New York: McGraw-Hill, 1961).
7. Kingsley Davis and Wilbert E. Moore, "Some Principles of Stratification," *American Sociological Review,* 10 (1945), 242–249.
8. Randall Collins, "Functional and Conflict Theories of Educational Stratification," *American Sociological Review,* 36 (December 1971), 1002–1018.
9. Ivar Berg, *Education and Jobs: The Great Training Robbery* (New York: Praeger, 1970).
10. James S. Coleman et al., *Equality of Educational Opportunity,* (Washington, D.C.: Government Printing Office, 1966).
11. Christopher Jencks et al., *Inequality* (New York: Basic Books, 1972).
12. Marion S. Stearns, *Report on Preschool Programs: The Effectiveness of Preschool Programs on Disadvantaged Children and Their Families,* (Washington, D.C.: Government Printing Office, 1971).
13. T. M. Newcomb, *Personality and Social Change* (New York: Dryden, 1943), and T. M. Newcomb, K. E. Koenig, R. Flacks, and D. P. Warwick, *Persistence and Change: Bennington College and Its Students After Twenty-five Years* (New York: Wiley, 1967).
14. James S. Coleman, "Academic Achievement and the Structure of Competition," in Halsey, Floud, and Anderson, pp. 367–387.
15. See Gunnar Myrdal, *Asian Drama* (New York: Pantheon, 1968), esp. chap. 32.
16. Ivan Illich, *Deschooling Society* (New York: Harper & Row, 1971).
17. H. Zeigler and W. Peak, "The Political Functions of the Educational System," *Sociology of Education,* 43 (1970).

## Chapter 15
## Politics and society

1. Talcott Parsons, "The Political Aspect of Social Structure and Process," in David Easton, ed., *Vari-*

*eties of Political Theory* (Englewood Cliffs, N.J.: Prentice-Hall, 1966), p. 72.

2. See R. D. Laing, *The Politics of the Family and Other Essays* (New York: Pantheon, 1971).

3. Kate Millett, *Sexual Politics* (Garden City, N.Y.: Doubleday, 1970).

4. For a review of this crisis see Abraham Rotstein, *Power Corrupted* (Toronto: New Press, 1971).

5. Robert Nisbet, *The Sociological Tradition* (New York: Basic Books, 1966).

6. Alexis de Tocqueville, *Democracy in America* (New York: Vintage Books, 1945).

7. Ibid., vol. 2, chap. 7.

8. Emile Durkheim, *Professional Ethics and Civic Morals*, trans. Cornelia Brookfield (Glencoe, Ill.: Free Press, 1960).

9. Joseph R. Gusfield uses the phrase "linked pluralism" to refer to what we call "crisscrossing divisions." See Gusfield, "Mass Society and Extremist Politics," *American Sociological Review*, 27 (February 1962), 19–30.

10. David Riesman, *The Lonely Crowd* (New York: Doubleday, 1953). See also William Kornhauser, "Power Elite or Veto Groups," in S. M. Lipset and Leo Lowenthal, eds., *Culture and Social Character* (Glencoe, Ill.: Free Press, 1961).

11. Robert Michels, *Political Parties* (New York: Crowell and Collier, 1962).

12. S. M. Lipset, Martin Trow, and James Coleman, *Union Democracy* (New York: Free Press, 1956).

13. Vilfredo Pareto, *The Mind and Society*, trans. Arthur Livingston (New York: Dover, 1935).

14. Karl Mannheim, *Man and Society in an Age of Reconstruction* (New York: Harcourt Brace, 1940).

15. Suzanne Keller, *Beyond the Ruling Class* (New York: Random House, 1963).

16. E. Digby Baltzell, *The Philadelphia Gentlemen: The Making of a National Upper Class* (New York: Free Press, 1958).

17. Alexis de Tocqueville, *The Old Regime and the French Revolution* (New York: Doubleday, 1955), originally published in 1856.

18. Marc Pilisuk and Thomas Hayden, "Is There a Military–Industrial Complex Which Prevents Peace? Consensus and Countervailing Power in Pluralistic Systems," *Journal of Social Issues*, 21, no. 3 (1965), 67–117.

19. John H. Kautsky, "An Essay in the Politics of Development," in John Kautsky, ed., *Political Change in Underdeveloped Countries* (New York: Wiley, 1965).

20. John Kautsky and Roger Benjamin, "Communism and Economic Development," in John Kautsky, ed., *Communism and the Politics of Development*, (New York: Wiley, 1968), pp. 184–206.

21. See Ralf Dahrendorf, *Class and Class Conflict in Industrial Society* (Palo Alto, Calif.: Stanford University Press, 1959).

22. See John Child, *The Business Enterprise in Modern Society* (London: Collier-Macmillan, 1970).

23. Andre Gunder Frank, "The Development of Underdevelopment," in Robert I. Rhodes, ed., *Imperialism and Underdevelopment: A Reader* (New York: Monthly Review Press, 1970).

24. C. Wright Mills, *The Power Elite* (New York: Oxford University Press, 1956).

25. G. William Domhoff, *Who Rules America?* (Englewood Cliffs, N.J.: Prentice-Hall, 1967).

26. This argument was proposed by Paul A. Baran and Paul M. Sweezy, *Monopoly Capital* (New York: Monthly Review Press, 1966).

27. Barrington Moore, Jr., *Reflections on the Causes of Human Misery: And upon Certain Proposals to Eliminate Them* (Boston: Beacon, 1972), especially chap. 5. For a contrary view see Harry Magdoff, *The Age of Imperialism* (New York: Monthly Review Press, 1969), chap. 5.

28. Stanley Lieberson, "An Empirical Study of Military-Industrial Linkages," *American Journal of Sociology*, 76 (January 1971), 562–583.

29. Moore, p. 141. See also Robert W. Tucker, *The Radical Left and American Foreign Policy* (Baltimore: Johns Hopkins University Press, 1971).

30. S. M. Lipset, "Party Systems and the Representation of Social Groups," in Roy Macridis, ed., *Political Parties* (New York: Harper & Row, 1967), pp. 59–60.

31. John Courtney, *Voting in Canada* (Englewood Cliffs, N.J.: Prentice-Hall, 1967), pp. 200–201.

32. Herbert McCloskey, "Political Participation," in *International Encyclopedia of the Social Sciences* (New York: Macmillan, 1968), p. 253.

33. Mildred Schwartz, *Politics and Territory* (Montreal: McGill-Queens University Press, 1973), chap. 6.

34. Robert R. Alford, *Party and Society: The Anglo-American Democracies* (Chicago: Rand McNally, 1963).

35. Gerald Pomper, *Voters' Choice: Varieties of American Electoral Behavior.* (New York: Harper & Row, 1975), p. 41.

36. Ibid., p. 89.

37. Ibid., p. 140–141.

38. William Kornhauser, *The Politics of Mass Society* (New York: Free Press, 1959).

39. Crane Brinton, *The Anatomy of Revolution* (Englewood Cliffs, N.J.: Prentice-Hall, 1952).

40. Guy Rocher, *A General Introduction to Sociology* (Toronto: Macmillan, 1972), p. 536.

41. James C. Davies, "Toward a Theory of Revolution," *American Sociological Review*, 27 (February 1962), 5–19.

42. Ted Robert Gurr, "A Causal Model of Civil Strife: A Comparative Analysis Using New Indices," *American Political Science Review*, 62 (1968), 1104. See also Gurr, *Why Men Rebel* (Princeton, N.J.: Princeton University Press, 1969).

43. David Snyder and Charles Tilly, "Hardship and Collective Violence in France, 1830 to 1960,"

*American Sociological Review*, 37 (October 1972), 520–532.

44. D. E. H. Russell, *Rebellion, Revolution, and Armed Force* (New York: Academic Press, 1974).

45. See, for example, Theodore Draper, *Castro's Revolution: Myths and Realities* (New York: Praeger, 1962), p. 42.

46. Frantz Neumann, *The Democratic and the Authoritarian State: Essays in Political and Legal Theory*, ed. Herbert Marcuse (New York: Free Press, 1957), p. 267.

47. Quoted in Russell, op. cit.

48. Peter Bachrach, *The Theory of Democratic Elitism* (Boston: Little, Brown, 1967).

49. Robert L. Heilbroner, *An Inquiry into the Human Prospect* (New York: Norton, 1974).

## Chapter 16
## Economic life

1. Roger Revelle, "Food and Population," *Scientific American*, September 1974, p. 166.

2. Marcel Mauss, *The Gift* (Glencoe, Ill.: Free Press, 1954), p. 66. Originally published in 1925.

3. Bronislaw Malinowski, *Argonauts of the Western Pacific* (London: Routledge, 1922).

4. Karl Polanyi, *Primitive, Archaic, and Modern Economies*, ed. George Dalton (Garden City, N.Y.: Doubleday, 1968), p. 9.

5. Richard Lee and I. DeVore, *Kalahari Hunter-Gatherers* (Cambridge, Mass.: Harvard University Press, 1975).

6. Ester Boserup, *The Conditions of Agricultural Growth* (Chicago: Aldine, 1965).

7. Joan Robinson, *Freedom and Necessity* (New York: Random House, 1970), p. 43.

8. N. S. B. Gras, *An Introduction to Economic History* (New York: Kelley, 1969), p. 82.

9. See Polanyi, chap. 2.

10. Robinson, p. 54.

11. Gras, p. 163.

12. Robinson, p. 57.

13. Karl Polanyi, *The Great Transformation* (Boston: Beacon Press, 1957), p. 37.

14. Robinson, p. 64.

15. Ibid., p. 67.

16. A. A. Berle and Gardiner Means, *The Modern Corporation and Private Property* (New York: Macmillan, 1934).

17. Eugene V. Rostow, "To Whom and for What Ends Is Corporate Management Responsible?" in Edward S. Mason, ed., *The Corporation in Modern Society*, (Cambridge, Mass.: Harvard University Press 1959), pp. 53–56.

18. Paul A. Baran and Paul Sweezy, *Monopoly Capital* (New York: Monthly Review Press, 1966), p. 36.

19. John K. Galbraith, *The New Industrial State* (Boston: Houghton Mifflin, 1967).

20. See C. Wright Mills, *The Power Elite* (New York: Oxford University Press, 1956).

21. Baran and Sweezy, p. 63.

22. Clark Kerr, John T. Dunlap, Fredrick H. Harbison, and Charles A. Myers, *Industrialism and Industrial Man* (Cambridge, Mass.: Harvard University Press, 1960), pp. 209–210.

23. Selig Perlman, *A History of Trade Unionism in the United States* (New York: Macmillan, 1937), pp. 141–142.

24. Arthus M. Ross, "The Natural History of the Strike," in Arthur Kornhauser, Robert Dubin, and Arthur M. Ross, eds., *Industrial Conflict* (New York: McGraw-Hill, 1954), pp. 30–36; Alvin Gouldner, *Wildcat Strike* (London: Routledge and Kegan Paul, 1955), p. 95.

25. Paul A. Samuelson, *Economics*, 9th ed. (New York: McGraw-Hill, 1973), p. 877.

26. Ibid., p. 881.

27. Robinson, p. 98.

28. Majdan Pasic, "Self-Management as an Integral Political System," in M. J. Brookmeyer, ed., *Yugoslav Workers' Self-Management*, (Dordrecht, Holland: D. Reidel, 1970).

29. Robinson, p. 107.

30. Ibid. pp. 100–101.

31. Gertrude Bancroft McNally, "Patterns of Female Labor Force Activity," *Industrial Relations*, 7, no. 3 (May 1968), 204–205.

32. Andrée Michel, "Working Wives and Family Interaction in French and American Families," *International Journal of Comparative Sociology*, 11, no. 2 (June 1970), 157–165.

33. McNally, pp. 205–206.

34. See Peter Blau and Otis Dudley Duncan, with the collaboration of Andrea Tyree, *The American Occupational Structure* (New York: Wiley, 1967), pp. 238–240.

35. Robert Blauner, *Alienation and Freedom*, (Chicago: University of Chicago Press, 1964).

36. Michael Fullan, "Industrial Technology and Worker Integration in the Organization," *American Sociological Review*, 35, no. 6 (December 1970), 1028–1029.

37. Arthur Kornhauser, with the collaboration of Otto M. Reid, *Mental Health of the Industrial Worker: A Detroit Study* (New York: Wiley, 1965), pp 260–262.

38. John K. Goldthorpe, "Attitudes and Behavior of Car Assembly Workers: A Deviant Case and a Theoretical Critique," *British Journal of Sociology*, 17, no. 3 (September 1966), 228–230.

39. See Arthur M. Ross, "Introduction: The Problem of Unemployment," in Arthur M. Ross, ed., *Unemployment in the American Economy* (New York: Wiley, 1964).

40. See Jon M. Shepard, *Automation and Alienation: A Study of Office and Factory Workers* (Cambridge, Mass.: MIT Press, 1971).

41. Gerald I. Susman, "Process Design, Automation,

and Worker Alienation," *Industrial Relations*, 11, no. 1 (February 1971), 34–35.

42. See Eugene V. Schneider, *Industrial Sociology*, 2nd ed. (New York: McGraw-Hill, 1969), pp 146–150.

43. See Robert L. Kahn et al., *Occupational Stress* (New York: Wiley, 1964); Delbert C. Miller and William H. Form, *Industrial Sociology*, 2nd ed. (New York: Harper & Row, 1964), pp 480–486.

44. Harold L. Wilensky, "The Professionalization of Everyone?" *American Journal of Sociology*, 70, no. 2 (September 1964), 137–158.

45. See Richard H. Hall, *Occupations and the Social Structure* (Englewood Cliffs, N.J.: Prentice-Hall, 1969), pp 218–219.

46. Ely Chinoy, "Manning the Machines: The Assembly Line Worker," in *The Human Shape of Labor* (New York: Oxford University Press, 1968).

47. Daniel Bell, *The Coming of Post-Industrial Society* (New York: Basic Books, 1973).

48. Abraham Rotstein, ed., *Beyond Industrial Growth: The Massey College Lectures, 1974–75* (Toronto: University of Toronto Press, 1976).

49. Vivian Rakoff, "Perennial Man and the Slowed Machine," in Rotstein, pp. 99–116.

50. Wallace Clement, *The Canadian Corporate Elite* (Toronto: McClelland and Stewart, 1975), and *Continental Corporate Power: Economic Linkages Between Canada and the United States* (Toronto: McClelland and Stewart, 1977).

51. Clement, *Continental Corporate Power*, pp. 296–297.

52. Ibid.

53. Ragnar Nurkse, *Problems of Capital Formation in Underdeveloped Areas* (New York: Oxford University Press, 1962), esp. chap. 1.

54. Jan Tinbergen, "Self-Management and the Optimum Order," in Brookmeyer, p. 119.

55. Ta-Chung Liv and Kung-Chia Yeh, "Chinese and other Asian Economies: A Quantitative Evaluation," *American Economic Review*, 63 (May 1973), 215–223.

## Chapter 17
### Population and Ecology

1. See Moni Nag, *Factors Affecting Human Fertility in Nonindustrial Societies: A Cross-cultural study* (New Haven, Conn.: Yale University Press, 1962).

2. See Joseph Eaton and Albert J. Mayer, "The Social Biology of Very High Fertility Among the Hutterites: The Demography of a Unique Population," *Human Biology*, 25 (1953), 206–265.

3. See W. James, "The Effect of Altitude on Fertility in Andean Countries," *Population Studies*, 20 (July 1966), 97–101, and Ancel Keys et al., *The Biology of Human Starvation: I* (Minneapolis: University of Minnesota Press, 1950), pp. 749–763.

4. Robert G. Potter, Jr., "Birth Intervals: Structure and

Change," *Population Studies*, 17 (November 1963), 155–156, and Robert G. Potter, Jr., et al., "A Case Study of Birth Interval Dynamics," *Population Studies*, 19 (July 1965), 81–96.

5. Ibid., pp. 155–166.

6. Geoffrey Gorer, *Death, Grief, and Mourning* (Garden City, N.Y.: Doubleday, 1965).

7. Louis Schneider and Sanford M. Dornbusch, *Popular Religion: Inspirational Books in America* (Chicago: University of Chicago Press, 1958).

8. U.S. Bureau of the Census, *Current Population Reports*, Series P-20, no. 156, (Washington, D.C., December 9, 1966).

9. Everett S. Lee, "Socio-Economic and Migration Differentials in Mental Disease: State Pattern in First Admissions to Mental Hospitals for All Disorders and for Schizophrenia," *Milbank Memorial Fund Quarterly*, 61 (January 1963), 25–42.

10. Edward S. Deevey, Jr., "The Human Population," *Scientific American*, 203 (September 1960), 195–204.

11. United Nations Population Division, *The Determinants and Consequences of Population Trends* (New York: United Nations, 1953), p. 8.

12. Ansley Coale, "The History of the Human Population," *Scientific American*, 231 (September 1974), 51.

13. See Thomas Malthus, "A Summary View of the Principle of Population," in Thomas Malthus et al., *Three Essays on Population* (New York: Mentor, 1960), pp. 13–59.

14. Joseph J. Spengler, "Values and Fertility Analysis," *Demography*, 3 (1966), 109–130.

15. Susan George, *How the Other Half Dies: The Real Reasons for World Hunger* (Baltimore: Penguin Books, 1976), p. 299–300.

16. Ibid., p. 300.

17. Sir Harold Hartley, "World Energy Prospects," in Nigel Calder, ed., *The World in 1984*, I (Baltimore: Penguin Books, 1965), 71.

18. George, op. cit.

19. Frances Moore Lappe and Joseph Collins, *Food First: Beyond the Myth of Scarcity* (Boston: Houghton Mifflin, 1977).

20. Ibid., pp. 310–319.

21. George, p. 29.

22. Ibid., p. 58.

23. Lappe and Collins, p. 214.

24. Ibid.

25. Ibid., p. 215.

26. Ibid.

27. Ibid., p. 324.

28. Ibid.

29. Ibid.

30. S. M. Keeny, ed., "East Asia Review, 1972," *Studies in Family Planning*, vol. 4, no. 5, p. 119.

31. Phyllis Tilson Piotrow, *World Population Crisis: The United States Response* (New York: Praeger, 1973), p. 178.

32. George, p. 273.

33. Ibid.

34. Andrew Malleson, *The Medical Run-around* (New York: Hart, 1973).
35. Population Bulletin, *International Migration*, 32, no. 4 (September 1977), 19–21.

## Chapter 18
## Urban living

1. Gallup Opinion Index, 1973, no. 94:31.
2. Harris poll, 1970.
3. Norton Ginsburg, "The City and Modernization," in Myron Weiner, ed., *Modernization* (New York: Basic Books, 1966), p. 126.
4. Gideon Sjoberg, "The Rise and Fall of Cities: A Theoretical Perspective," *International Journal of Comparative Sociology*, 4 (1963), 107–120.
5. For a fuller discussion of the differences, see O. C. Cox, "The Preindustrial City Reconsidered," in Paul Meadows and Ephraim Mizruchi, eds., *Urbanism, Urbanization, and Change: Some Perspectives on Urban Life* (Reading, Mass.: Addison-Wesley, 1969).
6. Max Weber, *The City* (New York: Free Press, 1958).
7. Ginsburg, op. cit.
8. Kingsley Davis, "The Urbanization of the Human Population," in Sylvia Fleis Fava, ed., *Urbanism in World Perspective: a Reader* (New York: Crowell, 1968), p. 44.
9. S. D. Clark, *The Suburban Society* (Toronto: University of Toronto Press, 1966), p. 223.
10. Philip M. Hauser, "The Chaotic Society: Product of the Social Morphological Revolution," *American Sociological Review*, 34 (February 1969), 6.
11. Ibid., p. 7.
12. Robert Redfield, *The Folk Culture of Yucatan* (Chicago: University of Chicago Press, 1941).
13. Louis Wirth, "Urbanism as a Way of Life," *American Journal of Sociology*, 44 (July 1938), 3–24.
14. Claude S. Fischer, *The Urban Experience* (New York: Harcourt Brace Jovanovich, 1976), pp. 29–39.
15. Quoted by Harvey Molotch, "Urban Society," in Jack D. Douglas, ed., *Introduction to Sociology* (New York: Free Press, 1973), p. 508.
16. Claude S. Fischer, "On Urban Alienation and Anomie: Powerlessness and Social Isolation," *American Sociological Review*, 38 (June 1973), 323.
17. Jack Wayne, "The Case of the Friendless Urbanite," in Alan Powell, ed., *The City: Attacking Modern Myths* (Toronto: McClelland and Stewart, 1972), pp. 90–92. See also Barry Wellman, "Who Needs Neighborhoods?" in Powell, pp. 94–100.
18. Ernest W. Burgess, "The Growth of the City: An Introduction to a Research Project," in George A. Theodorson, ed., *Studies in Human Ecology* (Evanston, Ill.: Row, Peterson, 1961).
19. Homer Hoyt, *The Structure and Growth of Residential Neighborhoods in American Cities* (Washington, D.C.: Federal Housing Administration, 1939).
20. Chauncy D. Harris and Edward L. Ullman, "The Nature of Cities," *Annals of the American Academy of Political and Social Science*, 242 (November 1945), 7–17.
21. William Michelson, *Man and His Urban Environment* (Reading, Mass.: Addison-Wesley, 1970).
22. Oscar Newman, *Defensible Space* (New York: Collier, 1973). See also A. R. Gillis, "Population Density and Social Pathology," *Social Forces*, 53 (December 1974), 304–314.
23. William Michelson, "The Reconciliation of 'Subjective' and 'Objective' Data on Physical Environment in the Community," *Sociological Inquiry*, 43 (1973), 147–173.
24. Fischer, p. 48.
25. "Suburbia: The New American Plurality," *Time*, March 15, 1971.
26. Bennett Berger, *Working-Class Suburb* (Berkeley: University of California Press, 1960).
27. "Suburbia: The New American Plurality."
28. Ibid.
29. Fischer, p. 227.
30. Jane Jacobs, *The Death and Life of Great American Cities* (New York: Random House, 1961).
31. Herbert Gans, *People, Planning, and Politics* (New York: Basic Books, 1968).
32. Herbert Gans, *The Urban Villagers* (New York: Free Press, 1965).
33. Bernard Weissbourd, "Segregation, Subsidies, and Megalopolis," in Fava, pp. 540–556. This article has several useful economic policies to suggest beyond the ones we mention herein.
34. Albert I. Hermalin and Reynolds Farley, "The Potential for Residential Integration in the Cities and Suburbs: Implications for the Busing Controversy," *American Sociological Review*, 38 (October 1973), 595–610.
35. Ibid., p. 605.

## Chapter 19
## Social change

1. Oswald Spengler, *The Decline of the West*, trans. Charles F. Atkinson (London: Allen and Unwin, 1926–1929), 2 vols.
2. Auguste Comte, *Cours de Philosophie Positive* (Paris: Rouen, 1830–1842).
3. Herbert Spencer, *First Principles* (New York: Appleton, 1890); also *Principles of Sociology*, (New York: Appleton, 1898–1899), 3 vols.
4. See Wilbert E. Moore and Arnold S. Feldman, "Society as a Tension-Management System," in George Baker and Leonard S. Cottrell, Jr., eds, *Behavioral Science and Civil Defense Disaster Research Group* (Washington, D.C.: National Academy of Sciences, National Research Council, 1962), pp. 93–105.
5. William F. Ogburn, *Social Change* (New York: Viking, 1922), pp. 200–213.

6. Robert E. Park, *Race and Culture*, (Glencoe, Ill.: Free Press, 1950).

7. Alex Inkeles and David H. Smith, *Becoming Modern: Individual Change in Six Developing Countries* (Cambridge, Mass.: Harvard University Press, 1974).

# GLOSSARY

**achieved status**   status assigned on the basis of standards over which a person has some control.

**act**   the basic unit of human conduct.

**acting crowd**   a potentially violent mob that chooses a course of action on the spot.

**alienation**   the frustration and unhappiness of workers who have no control over how their labor is used.

**amalgamation**   the blending of racial types through long interbreeding.

**annihilation**   destruction of the entire population of one ethnic community by another.

**anomie**   normlessness or deregulation.

**anticipatory socialization**   trying out a role in one's imagination because one may play that role at some time in the future.

**ascribed status**   status assigned on the basis of standards over which a person has no control.

**assimilation**   the process by which a group integrates itself into the culture around it.

**authority**   power that is regarded as legitimate by the members of the group.

**bilateral descent**   a system that reckons descent from both the mother's side and the father's side.

**boundaries**   the codes and customs that define a person as a member or nonmember of a particular group.

**bureaucracy**   an organization with a hierarchy of offices set up to do work.

**bureaucratic authority**   authority that is seen as legitimate if its rulings are consistent with a set of abstract rules with which the members of the group agree.

**case study**   an in-depth investigation of a single case of a given phenomenon.

**caste system**   a closed stratification system.

**census metropolitan area (CMA)**   a metropolitan region consisting of a large central city surrounded by smaller, dependent cities (Canada).

**charismatic authority**   authority that is seen as legitimate because of the leader's magnetic personality.

**city**   a large, permanent, densely populated settlement.

**code**   a grammar or set of rules that may be passed along from one generation to the next.

**coding**   the process by which raw answers are sorted into categories that can be tallied and counted.

**coercive power**   power based on physical means of control.

**collective behavior**   spontaneous, transitory, noninstitutionalized group action.

**composite family**   a number of nuclear families living together in a single household.

**conflict model**   the belief that societies are usually in a state of conflict and that the basic condition of life is competition for power and status.

**congregational organization**   a religious organization that hires and fires its own leader and in which there is no church hierarchy.

**content analysis**   the study of representative samples of writing from a given period or by particular individuals in order to discover common or repeated themes.

**control**   a variable that is held constant in order to check the apparent cause-and-effect relationship between two other variables.

**counterculture**   the subculture of hippies and dropouts of the late 1960s and early 1970s.

**covert phase**   the phase during which one is preparing to act but has not yet begun to do so.

**craze**   a fad or fashion that becomes so important to people that they spend a great deal of money and emotion on it.

**crisis of legitimacy**   the situation in which large numbers of people withdraw their support from a regime.

**crowd**   a large, temporary group of people who have some common goal or interest.

**crude birthrate**   the number of births per year per 1000 people.

**crude death rate**   the number of deaths per year per 1000 people.

**cultural lag**   a term used to explain social problems that arise because there is a time lag between a technological change and the social and cultural changes required by that change.

**cultural relativism**   the assumption that all cultures are equally valid and that any culture deserves respect.

**culture**   a system of ideas, values, beliefs, knowledge, and customs transmitted from generation to generation within a social group.

**culture goals** the wants and ambitions that people are taught by their society.

**culture trait** the smallest unit of culture.

**demographic-transition model** a model used to describe the process by which preindustrial societies with high rates of fertility and mortality are transformed into modern societies with low rates of fertility and mortality.

**demography** the study of human populations.

**dependency ratio** the ratio of people in dependent age groups to people in economically productive age groups.

**dependent variable** a variable that is assumed to be the effect of an independent variable.

**detached observation** observation in which the researcher watches what is going on without getting involved.

**deviance** any form of behavior that violates the norms of a social group.

**discrimination** the process by which a dominant group informally deprives a minority group of equal access to privileges and opportunities.

**ecology** the relationship between the physical environment and the human population that lives in that environment.

**economics** the social science that deals with the production, distribution, exchange, and consumption of scarce goods and services.

**education** a set of processes designed to transmit knowledge and skills and to develop mental abilities.

**elitism** the belief that some group always gets the upper hand and rules the masses.

**endogamy** a rule requiring a person to marry someone within his or her own group.

**episcopal organization** a religious organization in which there is a well-defined hierarchy of authority.

**esteem** appreciation of a person regardless of his or her rank.

**ethnic group** a large collectivity in which membership is generally inherited and whose members share a feeling of identification with the group.

**ethnic pluralism** the situation in which ethnic groups are equal and live together on good terms.

**ethnic religion** a religion that is tied to a specific place and people.

**ethnic stratification** the situation in which ethnic groups form a hierarchy of dominance.

**ethnocentrism** the tendency to judge other ways of life by the standards of one's own group.

**evolutionary (cultural) breakthrough** an innovation that makes further advances possible.

**evolutionism** the belief in a law of historical progress; in sociology, that all societies go through stages of increasing complexity.

**exogamy** a rule requiring a person to choose a mate from a different group.

**experiment** a study of groups or individuals carried out in an environment controlled by the researcher.

**expressive crowd** a group that shows especially strong feelings.

**expulsion** the sending of minority group members to another country.

**extended family** (consanguine family) a household made up of a nuclear family plus other relatives.

**fad** a culture trait that suddenly becomes popular and then disappears.

**fashion** a culture trait that is popular for a short time and is gradually replaced.

**fecundity** a woman's capacity to bear children.

**fertility** the rate at which a population gives birth.

**fiscal policy** a governmental policy of spending or not spending on goods and services.

**folklore** a society's collection of jokes, superstitions, lullabies, old wives' tales, slang words, ghost stories, etc.

**folk society** a small, isolated, homogeneous society; a peasant society.

**folkway** the trivial norms or conventions shared by members of a society.

**frequency** a number that shows the total of items in a given category.

**functionalism** the belief that a social pattern is best understood in terms of its functions in a given society.

**functional requisites** the requirements that all societies must meet, at least at a minimum level.

**game stage** the stage at which a child can understand a set of roles as a system.

**gemeinschaft** a society held together by a set of stable, secure bonds; a community.

**gender** the awareness of being a member of one sex or the other.

**gender identity** (sexual identity) the sex of which one considers oneself to be a member.

**gender role** (sex role) the culturally defined set of behaviors that are considered sex-appropriate within a given society.

**generalization** a statement that applies to a whole class of similar events.

**generalized other** an abstract role that stands for a set of particular roles.

**gesellschaft** a society in which relationships are impersonal or associational.

**hierarchy** a chain of command in which each person has authority over several other people.

**homogamy** the tendency to choose a spouse similar to oneself.

**horizontal mobility** social mobility that does not involve a gain or loss of status.

**hypothesis** a specific prediction that may be verified by empirical findings.

**ideology** a doctrine used to justify a group's actions in pursuing its own interests.

**illegitimacy** the birth of a child to an unmarried woman.

**independent variable** a variable that is assumed to be the cause of a dependent variable.

**indicator** a concrete representation of an abstract variable.

**institution** a complex structure of roles organized around a central activity or social need.

**institutionalization** the process through which culture influences the social system.

**institutionalized means** the resources available to the individual to pursue his or her goals.

**institutional racism** indirect discrimination against minority races caused by established policies of institutions.

**integration** the situation in which equality is achieved by reducing the separation between ethnic groups and encouraging them to participate in the same activities.

**interest group** a unified group that tries to influence the state in its favor.

**internalization** the process by which one makes the society's values part of one's personality.

**joint family** a type of extended family in which brothers share property but do not always live in a single household.

**kin** people who are related either by birth or by marriage.

**labeling** the social definition of a person as deviant.

**laissez faire** the belief that the state should not regulate the economy but should allow it to regulate itself.

**legitimacy** the right to use force.

**legitimation** acceptance of the use of power by the leaders of a group because it is in line with the values of the members of the group.

**life chances** patterns of infant mortality, physical and mental illness, childlessness, marital conflict, separation, divorce, etc.

**life style** patterns of eating and dressing, cultural and recreational activities, relationships between parents and children, etc.

**looking-glass self** the self-image that a person acquires from the opinions of others.

**magic** practices directed toward the control of spirits or other forces beyond the reach of ordinary human powers.

**marginal person** a person who belongs to two or more groups that are supposedly mutually exclusive.

**market exchange** a system in which goods and services are exchanged in a market context.

**Marxism** any doctrine that is supposedly derived from the teachings of Karl Marx.

**matriarchy** a society in which women are dominant over men.

**matrilineal descent system** a descent system in which a person belongs to his or her mother's line of descent.

**matrilocal residence** a rule requiring a newly married couple to live with the wife's family.

**mechanical solidarity** the pattern in which people get along by being alike in their backgrounds, religious practices, ideas about morality, and so forth.

**median age** the age that divides any population into equal groups, half older and half younger.

**megalopolis** a supercity in which several cities merge together to make a whole urbanized region.

**mercantilism** the belief that the best way to increase national power is to increase national wealth (i.e., the nation's supply of gold and silver).

**migration** the movement of people into or out of an area.

**minority group** an ethnic group that is subordinate to another group.

**model** a mental map of a subject that may be incomplete or misleading but cannot be proved wrong.

**monetary policy** a governmental policy of manipulating the prime lending rate or the total money supply.

**morality of cooperation** the view that rules and obligations are rational agreements rather than fixed principles.

**moral realism** the view that rules have existed forever or were laid down by God or some other authority figure.

**mores** a society's important ethical rules.

**mortality** the rate at which a population dies.

**multilinear evolutionism** the belief that various societies follow different lines of development.

**myth** a nonhistorical story known by almost everyone in a group and symbolizing great truths to the group's members.

**nationalism** ethnic-group chauvinism.

**neolocal residence** a rule requiring a newly married couple to set up housekeeping on their own.

**neo-Marxism** the Marxist view of capitalism, updated to correspond with developments since Marx's time.

**norm** a rule that tells members of a society how to behave in particular situations; a rule that prescribes legitimate means of pursuing one's goals.

**normative power** power based on symbolic means of control.

**nuclear family** (conjugal family) a husband, his wife, and their unmarried children.

**organic solidarity** the pattern in which people are interdependent even though they are very different in experience, opinions, habits, and so forth.

**organization** a social unit deliberately constructed and reconstructed to pursue specific goals.

**overt phase** the phase during which an action is actually performed.

**participant observation** observation in which the researcher takes some role within the group being observed.

**particularism** bending rules or making special ones to fit special persons or groups.

**patriarchy** a society in which men are dominant over women.

**patrilineal descent system** a descent system in which a person belongs to his or her father's line of descent.

**patrilocal residence** a rule requiring a newly married couple to live with the husband's family.

**peer group** a group of people of similar status.

**play stage** the stage at which a child does not coordinate his or her activities with those of others.

**pluralism** the view that the best way to preserve freedom in a society is to have within it a number of powerful groups that represent various interests.

**politics** any action involving the collective pursuit of collective goals.

**polyandry** the marriage of a woman to more than one husband.

**polygamous family** a family in which there are several wives or husbands.

**polygyny** the marriage of a man to more than one wife.

**population** the whole number of units from which a sample is drawn.

**population pyramid** a diagram that shows the age–sex composition of a population at a given time.

**power** the ability to get one's orders obeyed despite opposition; the ability to achieve one's goals even in the face of opposition.

**prejudice** prejudging against individuals on the basis of characteristics believed to be shared by all members of their ethnic group.

**presbyterian organization** a religious organization in which authority is in the hands of an elected regional board of ministers and lay members.

**prestige** social honor attached to particular roles.

**primary group** a group whose members interact in a personal, intimate, and emotional way.

**propaganda** the planned use of mass media to influence the beliefs and opinions of a population.

**property** rights or control over goods and services.

**public** a group of people who share a particular code; a scattered group of people who have different opinions about an issue and are involved in a discussion of that issue.

**questionnaire** a printed list of questions given to respondents to answer themselves.

**quota sampling** sampling in which the percentage of people with a given characteristic is equal to the percentage of such people in the whole population.

**racial group** an ethnic group to which members are assigned on the basis of inherited biological traits.

**racism** the belief that ethnic and racial groups are based on genetic similarities rather than on social agreements.

**random sampling** sampling in which every member of the population has an equal chance of being chosen as part of the sample.

**rational-legal authority** power based on the rules of the constitution under which the leader has been elected or appointed.

**reaction formation** a mechanism for denying an unacceptable element of the personality.

**reciprocity** two-way exchange of goods or services.

**redistribution** a system in which goods and services are brought to a central source and then redistributed throughout the population.

**reference group** the group to which one compares oneself when judging one's own status.

**religion** the relationship of humankind to some ultimate reality.

**repression** the effort to restrain certain impulses within the personality.

**resocialization** the process by which an adult whose previous socialization was inadequate is made to behave in ways that the society approves of.

**role** the part each person must play to create a collective activity.

**role conflict** the situation in which a person occupies two roles that are regulated by incompatible norms.

**role taking** the ability of a person to imagine the role of another person with whom he or she interacts.

**rumor** a piece of information that is passed from one person to another throughout a group without being checked for accuracy.

**sanction** a reward for desirable behavior or a punishment for undesirable behavior.

**secondary group** a group whose members interact in an impersonal, unsentimental, and businesslike way.

**segmental religion** a religion that is an offshoot of a universalizing religion or a new religious system that integrates small groups into larger communities.

**segregation** forcing minority group members to work or live in separate areas whenever possible and to use facilities separate from those used by the dominant group.

**self-reflexive behavior** interaction with the self.

**sex** the biological fact of being male or female.

**sex ratio** the number of males per 100 females in a population.

**significant other** a person whose opinions are important to one; usually a family member.

**social class** a set of people with similar socioeconomic status.

**social control** the process by which members of a group support desired forms of behavior and discourage undesired forms.

**socialization** the process of learning the rules of behavior for a given social group.

**social mobility** movement from one status or occupation to another.

**social movement** a collective effort to bring about a new order of life.

**social stratification** a hierarchy of layers or strata that are unequal in terms of property, power, and prestige.

**social system** the interactions among two or more people; the roles and actual practices that exist among members of a social group.

**society** a large, permanent, self-sufficient, self-perpetuating group of interacting people.

**sociology** the study of human group life.

**standard metropolitan statistical area (SMSA)** a metropolitan region consisting of a large central city surrounded by smaller, dependent cities (United States).

**state** the organization that has a monopoly on the legitimate use of force in a given territory.

**status** a person's rank based on income, prestige, educaton, or power.

**status inconsistency** the situation in which a person ranks higher by one standard than by another.

**stereotype** a mental cartoon that exaggerates the traits of the typical member of a particular group.

**stigma** the mark of disgrace that is attached to people in disvalued roles.

**structured interview** an interview that uses a standard list of questions.

**subculture** a group whose members share values and ideas that differ from those of the wider society.

**sublimation** the process by which energy is channeled away from sexual concerns and into more refined concerns.

**suburbanization** the movement of people from central cities to smaller communities in the surrounding area.

**surplus repression** repression in excess of what is necessary for people to live together in a civilized way.

**symbol** anything that represents something else, i.e., anything that has meaning.

**symbolic interactionism** the belief that social relationships are built up through social interactions on a symbolic level.

**technology** the institutionalized application of knowledge to control nature for human uses.

**territoriality** the establishment of a certain zone or space that may not be occupied by any other person or animal.

**theology** the organization of religious beliefs into a unified doctrine.

**theory** a statement based on observed facts that explains what is supposed to be a causal relationship between those facts.

**traditional authority** authority that is seen as legitimate because it has existed for a long time; power based on the customs under which a leader gains his or her position.

**transsexual** a person whose sex has been changed through surgery and hormone treatment.

**transvestite** a person whose gender identity differs from his or her sex.

**unilinear descent** a system that reckons descent from either the male blood line or the female blood line.

**unilinear evolutionism** the belief that there is a single set of stages through which every society must proceed.

**Universalism** adhering to the same rules in dealing with all people.

**universalizing religion** a religion that is not tied to any particular region or ethnic group and whose members consider their beliefs to be right for all humankind.

**unstructured interview** an interview in which the respondent is asked questions that lead to an open discussion of the topic.

**urbanization** the movement of people from rural areas to cities and from small cities to larger ones.

**urban society** a large-scale, heterogeneous, impersonal society.

**utilitarian power** power based on material means of control.

**validity** the ability of an indicator to genuinely and accurately represent the variable that it is meant to represent.

**value** a standard used by members of a society to judge behavior and to choose among various possible goals.

**variable** a characteristic that changes among situations, individuals, or groups and can be measured.

**vertical mobility** social mobility that involves movement toward higher or lower status.

**veto group** an interest group that can prevent any action that conflicts with its values and interests.

**voluntary association** a group that people join because they support its goals and values.

**zero population growth (ZPG)** the point at which there is no natural increase in population.

# NAME INDEX

# SUBJECT INDEX

Abortion, 203, 324, 519
Abstinence, 497–98
Abstracts, 583–84
Access rituals, 145
Achieved status, 238–41, 266, 606
Achievement, 101–104, 405, 406, 419–20
Achievement motivation, 100–102, 103
Act, 161, 170, 606
Acting crowd, 311–18, 333, 606
Activism, 575
Acupuncture, 567
Advertising, 74–75, 471
AFDC, 328
Age:
  as basis for social discrimination, 239–40
  as factor in migration patterns, 502–503
  median, of population, 505
Age-sex population pyramids, 503–504
Age-sex-specific death rate, 498, 499
Agression (see Frustration-agression)
Aggressiveness, sex differences in, 120, 121
Agrarian reform, 488, 489, 520
Agribusiness, 516–17, 518
Agricultural technology, 518–19
Agriculture, 467, 468, 526–27
Aid to Families with Dependent Children
  (AFDC), 327, 328
AIM, 277
Alcoholism, 179–81, 183
Algeria, 298
Alienation, 219, 220, 227, 233, 482–83, 485,
  606
Amalgamation, 296, 304, 606
American Economic Association, 10
American Indian Movement (AIM), 277
*American Journal of Sociology*, 583, 584
*American Occupational Structure, The*
  (Duncan), 256
American Psychiatric Association, 184
American Revolution, 275, 280, 282, 453–54
American Sociological Association, 10, 584
*American Sociological Review*, 583
*Anatomy of Revolution, The* (Brinton),
  453–54
Anglophones, 280–82
Annihilation, 304, 606
Anomic suicide, 194
Anomie, 193, 198, 199, 202–203, 205, 542,
  606
Anthropologists, physical, 274
Anthropology, 8
Anticipatory socialization, 94, 106, 151, 606
Anti-Semitism, 285–87
Anxiety, 192
Apartheid, 292
Arbitrary power, 440
Arms race, 471
Artistic expression, 59–61
Ascribed community, 271 (see also Ethnic
  groups)
Ascribed status, 238–41, 266, 606
*Ashkenazim*, 285
Assembly line work, 482
Assimilation, 277, 296, 304, 606
Associations, memberships in, 251
Attenuation rule, 145
Authoritarianism, 39
*Authoritarian Personality, The*, 39
Authority, 96, 166–67, 214–15, 229, 233, 265,
  431, 432, 459, 460, 576, 606
Automation, 482

"Baby boom," 503, 509, 510, 512

Baby-sitters, schools as, 404
Bangladesh, 514–15
*Becoming Modern* (Inkeles and Smith), 570
Battered women, 131
Beatlemania research project, 24–30, 31, 32,
  33, 34–35
Behavior:
  and biological factors, 87–89
  collective (see Collective behavior)
  criminal, 196–97
  deviant, 174–76, 178, 179
  expressive, 141–46
  group, 308
  learned, 141–42
  role expressive, 198, 199
  role supportive, 198
  self-reflexive, 158, 170, 610
  sexual, 178, 184, 203, 342–44
  and socialization, 87–89
Bibliographies, 582, 585, 586
Bilateral descent, 340, 365, 606
Bilocal residence, 340
Birthrate, 250
  crude, 496–97, 606
Black Death, 468, 507
Black magic, 378, 379
Black Muslims, 369
Blacks, 274–75, 276, 282–85, 292, 298–99,
  451, 503, 536, 552–53
Blueprint, organizational, 217
Bohemian Club, 262–63
Bohemian Grove, 442
*Bohemian Grove and Other Retreats, The*
  (Domhoff), 262, 447
Bolsheviks, 472
Book reviews, 584
Boundaries, 271–72, 273, 287, 288–89, 293,
  302, 304, 606
Bourgeoisie, 236, 238, 478
Branch family, 353
*British Journal of Sociology*, 583
Buddhism, 368, 372, 377
Bureaucracy, 213–17, 230, 231, 233, 380, 576,
  606
Bureaucratic authority, 214, 233, 606
Bureaucratic relationship, 231–32
Busing, 424

Calvinism, 390
Canada, 212–13, 277–78, 280–82, 294, 385,
  410–11, 432, 433, 449, 450, 486, 487,
  499, 501, 504, 505, 517, 521, 533
*Canadian Review of Sociology and
  Anthropology*, 583, 584
Capitalism, 101, 354–55, 390, 444, 445–47,
  468, 472, 479, 480, 489
Card catalogs, library, 583
Case, 41, 42, 44
Case study, 29–30, 49, 606
Cash crop economies, 515–16
Caste system, 240–41, 263, 266, 606
Catholic Church, 286, 302
Catholics, 383, 384, 385, 390, 393, 397,
  410–11
Causal relationships, 161–62
Causal theory, 25
Celibacy, 497
Cell, 44
Census metropolitan area (CMA), 533, 554
Challenge, and innovation, 565–68
Charisma, in religion, 371–73, 392, 393
Charismatic authority, 214–15, 233, 431, 432,
  459, 606
Charismatic leadership, 217, 371–73, 392, 393,
  432
Chicago, land use, 543–45
"Chicago school" of social psychology, 12, 195
"Chicanos," 280
Child care institutions, 104–5
Child development, and family structure, 90
Child labor, 510
Childrearing, 92–93, 250
Children, decision to have, 510–12
Chile, Allende regime, 444

Chimpanzees, 144–45
China, 228–29, 294, 295, 443, 475, 490
Christianity, 369, 372, 373
Chromosomes, 112, 115, 191–92
Church (see Religion)
Circular reaction, 314
Cities, 526, 554, 606 (see also Urbanization)
  and agricultural surpluses, 526–27
  apartment living, 547–48
  central business district, 543
  communication, 526–27
  compositional theory, 539–40
  concentric-zone model, 543–45
  development of, 526–31
  dullness, 549–50
  ethnic neighborhoods, 550
  future of, 552–53
  growth of, in North America, 532–36
  imperial, 528, 529, 531
  medieval Europe, 529–31
  multiple-nuclei model, 545–46
  nucleated, 545
  planning, 549–50, 578
  politics, 529
  population in, 532
  preindustrial, 531
  sector model, 545
  slums, causes of, 550–51
  street life, 549–50
  subcultural theory, 540–42
  subsidizing, 551–52
Civilization, transmission of, 404
*Civilization and Its Discontents* (Freud), 99
Civil Liberties, 399
Civil Rights Act (1964), 129, 283–84
Civil Rights Bill (1968), 277
Civil-rights movement, 283–84, 324, 325, 326,
  327–28, 451
Clans, 152
Class, social (see Social class)
Class conflict, 270
Class consciousness, 237, 258, 260, 325
Classical approach, 221–23, 225, 226, 227 (see
  also Scientific management approach)
Clientele, 223
Close-knit network, 164–65
Code, 80, 606
  artistic expression as, 59–61
Coding, 41–43, 49, 606
Coding sheets, 41
Coercive power, 219, 220, 221, 233, 606
Collective bargaining, 471
Collective behavior, 308, 333, 606
  acting crowd, 311–18, 333, 606
  circular reaction, 314
  communication (see Communication)
  conditions for, 308–309
  contagion theories, 312–14, 315, 316, 318
  convergence theory, 314–15, 316, 318
  crazes, 322–23, 333, 606
  crowds (see Crowds)
  disasters, 310–11
  emergent-norm theory, 316, 318
  expressive crowd, 311, 333, 607
  fads, 322–23, 333, 607
  fashions, 322–23, 333, 606
  game theory, 316–18
  mass hysteria, 323
  mass media, 320–22, 330
  panics, 311, 318
  and police, 330–31
  press coverage, 576
  social movements, 324–27
Collective living, 16
Collectivity, 147–48 (see also Groups)
Collegial relationship, 231–32
Colonialism, 288, 291–93, 297
Commission on Obscenity and Pornography,
  75
Commitment, 219
Communes, 150
Communication, 69–71, 155–61, 210,
  318–22, 330, 333, 528–29
Communism, 228–29, 353–54, 393, 398, 472,
  489
*Communist Manifesto* (Marx), 258

Power of suggestion, 321–22
Prediction, 34–35
Prejudice, 287–88, 305, 609
Preliterate societies, 69–71
Prenatal factors, 112
Presbyterian religious organization, 374, 400, 609
President's Commission on the Status of Women, 129
Prestige, 242, 243, 244, 258, 259, 260, 261, 265, 267, 610
Primary groups, 148–50, 151, 152, 153–54, 168, 170, 610
Primates, 141, 142, 144
Primitive societies, economies, 465–67
*Principles of Sociology* (Spencer), 9
Probability, 34–35
Productivity, and education, 421–23
Professionals, 484–85
Progress, human, 563
Prohibition, 203, 204
Proletarians, 479
Proletariat, 236
Propaganda, 322, 333, 609
Proportional representation, 449
Property, 242, 258, 259, 260, 267, 610
Proportions, 27
Prostitution, 178, 188
Protestant ethic, 101, 102, 390–91
*Protestant Ethic and the Spirit of Capitalism* (Weber), 387
Protestant Reformation, 568
Protestants, 383, 384, 385, 390–91, 410–11
Psychoanalysis, 192, 193, 386
Psychologists, 6–8
Psychopathic personality, 192
Psychosis, 201
Psychotherapy, 168, 201–202
Public assistance, 72–73
Public housing, 551
Public Law 280, 277
Public opinion, 33, 319–20
Publics, 60–61, 74, 78–79, 80, 319–20, 324, 326, 333, 610
Punched cards, 41–43
Puritans, 190

Qualitative research, 41
Quantitative research, 41
Quebec, 280–82, 293, 432, 433
Questionnaire, 25, 27–28, 37, 41–43, 49, 162, 610
Quota sampling, 33–34, 49, 610

Race, 66–68, 248, 274, 288, 298–99
Racial group, 274–75, 305, 610
Racism, 288–89, 305, 576, 610
Radicalism, 352, 353–54, 457
Radio, and education, 422
Rancheros Visitadores, 263, 442
Random sampling, 34, 49, 610
Rape, 131
Rational-legal authority, 215, 431, 432, 460, 610
Reaction formation, 193, 205, 610
Reactionary movement, 326
*Rebellion, Revolution, and Armed Force* (Russell), 454
Rebellions, 453–56
Rebels, 195
Reciprocity, 467, 476, 492, 610
Records, bureaucratic, 216–17
Red tape, 187–88, 217
Redistribution, 467, 492, 610
Reference groups, 151–52, 170, 610
Reference paper, 582–86
Reform movement, 326
Reformers, 412–14
Reinforcement theory, 121
Relative deprivation, 128
Religion, 368, 391, 400, 500, 577, 610
 belief, 371–72
 Catholics (see Catholics)
 charismatic leadership, 371, 372, 392

charismatic phase, 371, 372-73
classification of, 368–69
conversion, 392–98
ethnic, 368, 400
functions of, 374–75, 385, 586
institutionalization of, 370–73
and magic, 378–79, 400, 608
meaning of, 375–77
myths, 371, 400, 609
need for, 375–77
organization, 372–74
Protestants, 390–91, 410–11
ritual, 371, 378, 385
as sacred, 377, 385
segmental, 369, 400, 610
and social change, 387–91
and social stratification 251, 379–83
and the state, 398–99
theology, 371–72, 400
theoretical approaches to, 385–91
trends, 393–98
universalizing, 368–69, 400
as worship of society, 385–86
Religious groups, 383–85
Religious movements, 326, 392–98
Religious wars, 399
Renaissance, 531
Report writing (see Reference paper)
Representativeness, 33–34
Repression, 98–100, 103, 107, 610
Research, 19, 41, 47–48, 575
Research report, 47, 582–86
Resocialization, 95–96, 107, 610
Resources, world, estimates of, 512–14
Respect, 97, 98
Retreatists, 194–95
Revolutionary movement, 326
Revolutions, 213–14, 457–58 (see also Rebellions)
Riots, 314, 315, 322, 328, 330–32
Rites of passage, 94–95
Rituals, religious, 371, 378, 385
Ritualists, 194, 195
Role conflict, 85, 107, 190, 205, 610
Role expressive behavior, 198, 199
Role models, 94, 121
Roles, 61–62, 85, 107, 190, 238–39, 240, 242, 483–85, 610 (see also Gender role; Sex role)
Role-self theory, 193, 197–98, 203–204, 576
Role supportive behavior, 198
Role taking, 157–58, 170, 610
Role theory, 198–99
Roman Empire, 529
"Root reality," 397–98
Roper poll, 33
Roundup Riders of the Rockies, 263
Rules (see Laws)
Ruling class, 262–63 (see also Elitism)
Rumors, 318–19, 333, 610
Rural life style, 539–40, 541, 542, 548
Russia (see Soviet Union)
Russian Revolution, 444, 453–54

Sacredness, 377, 385
Salpingectomy, 498
Sampling, 33–34
Sanctions, 58, 80, 185–86, 205, 610
Scapegoating, 200
Science, 4
Scientific management, 221–23
Schizophrenia, 89
Secondary groups, 148–50, 152, 170, 610
Secretaries, bosses and, 131–33
Segmental religion, 369, 400, 610
Segregation, 292, 305, 424, 536, 551, 552, 610
Self, the, 155–61, 170, 197–98
Self-control, 185
Self-image, 184
Self-reflexive behavior, 158, 170, 610
Self-regard, 153
Sensate culture, 558–59
Sex, 111, 112–14, 115, 136, 239–40, 247–48, 610
Sexism, 126, 136

Sex ratio, 503, 523, 610
Sex role, 104, 111, 118–23, 133–34, 136, 201, 355–57, 362–63 (see also Gender role)
Sexual behavior, 178, 184, 203, 342–44
Sexual Freedom League, 361
Sexual identity, 111, 136 (see also Gender identity)
Sheldon's constitutional typology, 191
Significant other, 153, 170, 610
Situational theories, 191, 193–99, 202–204
Skill exchange, 422–23
Slavery, 276, 282
Slums, causes of, 550–51
SMSA, 533, 554
SNCC, 130
Social capacity, 223
Social change, 412–14, 425, 558–65, 567, 569–70 (see also Social evolution)
Social class, 89, 201–202, 236–38, 241–43, 250–54, 258, 267, 280–82, 445, 450, 451, 467–68, 472, 475, 478–79, 503, 540, 610
Social control, 58, 80, 184–85, 205, 610
Social Darwinism, 13, 56, 412–13, 563, 565
Social divisions, patterns of, 435–37
Social evolution, 559–63, 564, 565–68 (see also Social change)
*Social Forces*, 583
Social groups, 152–62
Social history, 6
Social innovation, 567
Social integration, 434
Socialism, 471–75, 490
Socialization, 87–102, 103, 107, 151, 152, 185, 220, 221, 344, 558, 576, 610
"Social laws," 8–9
Social mobility, 255–58, 267, 531, 610
*Social Mobility in Industrial Society* (Lipset), 255
Social movements, 324–29, 333, 361, 576, 610
Social networks, 397
Social psychology, 39–40
Social sanctions, 185–86
Social science, 4–8
Social self, 152–62 (see also Self, the)
Social stratification, 241–42, 244–48, 250–62, 267, 379–83, 531, 610
Social structure, 62–63, 68–69, 74
Social system, 4, 16, 18, 20, 61–62, 80, 84, 86, 147, 610
Social work, 8
Society, 4, 20, 148, 564, 566, 568, 611
Sociobiology, 87
Socioeconomic status, 236
*Sociological Abstracts*, 583–84
Sociologists, 4, 8–12, 19, 144, 433
Sociology, 4, 10–19, 20, 29–35, 164–65, 430, 558, 611
Sociology journals, 583–84
Sorcery, 378–79
South Africa, 272, 292, 431, 456
Soviet Union, 92, 116–17, 265, 350, 351–52, 421, 440, 444, 452, 472–74, 475, 503, 521
Specialization, 223, 228
Spurious relationship, 45, 47
Standard metropolitan statistic area (SMSA), 533, 554, 611
State, the, 431, 460, 611
State capitalism, 444
*Statistical Abstract of the United States*, 37
Statistics, 36–37
Status, 123, 236, 238–43, 255–58, 259–60, 266, 267, 380, 414–16, 611
Status inconsistency, 241, 267, 611
Stem family, 353
Stereotypes, 121, 287, 288, 305, 611
Stigma, 183–84, 203, 205, 611
"Stigmata of degeneracy," 191
Stockholders, 469–70
Stratification, social (see Social stratification)
Stress, and modernity, 575
Strikes, 471
Structural functionalism, 12, 13, 15–17, 18, 19
Structured interview, 37, 50, 611